IMPORTANT:

HERE IS YOUR REGISTRATION CODE TO ACCESS
YOUR PREMIUM McGRAW-HILL ONLINE RESOURCES.

For key premium online resources you need THIS CODE to gain access. Once the code is entered, you will be able to use the Web resources for the length of your course.

If your course is using **WebCT** or **Blackboard**, you'll be able to use this code to access the McGraw-Hill content within your instructor's online course.

Access is provided if you have purchased a new book. If the registration code is missing from this book, the registration screen on our Website, and within your WebCT or Blackboard course, will tell you how to obtain your new code.

Registering for McGraw-Hill Online Resources

TO gain access to your McGraw-Hill web resources simply follow the steps below:

1. USE YOUR WEB BROWSER TO GO TO: **www.mhhe.com/molloy3e**
2. CLICK ON **FIRST TIME USER**.
3. ENTER THE REGISTRATION CODE* PRINTED ON THE TEAR-OFF BOOKMARK ON THE RIGHT.
4. AFTER YOU HAVE ENTERED YOUR REGISTRATION CODE, CLICK **REGISTER**.
5. FOLLOW THE INSTRUCTIONS TO SET-UP YOUR PERSONAL UserID AND PASSWORD.
6. WRITE YOUR UserID AND PASSWORD DOWN FOR FUTURE REFERENCE.
   KEEP IT IN A SAFE PLACE.

W9-AVI-618

TO GAIN ACCESS to the McGraw-Hill content in your instructor's **WebCT** or **Blackboard** course simply log in to the course with the UserID and Password provided by your instructor. Enter the registration code exactly as it appears in the box to the right when prompted by the system. You will only need to use the code the first time you click on McGraw-Hill content.

Thank you, and welcome to your McGraw-Hill online Resources!

*YOUR REGISTRATION CODE CAN BE USED ONLY ONCE TO ESTABLISH ACCESS. IT IS NOT TRANSFERABLE.

0-07-297830-9 T/A MOLLOY: EXPERIENCING THE WORLD'S RELIGIONS,3/E

REGISTRATION CODE

N0AG-9ZM3-AZ5Q-5BVD-U69L

EXPERIENCING THE WORLD'S RELIGIONS

Tradition, Challenge, and Change
Third Edition

MICHAEL MOLLOY

T.L. Hilgers,

principal photographer

 **Higher Education**

Boston   Burr Ridge, IL   Dubuque, IA   Madison, WI   New York   San Francisco   St. Louis
Bangkok   Bogotá   Caracas   Kuala Lumpur   Lisbon   London   Madrid   Mexico City
Milan   Montreal   New Delhi   Santiago   Seoul   Singapore   Sydney   Taipei   Toronto

 **Higher Education**

For Kathy, Peggy, and Tom,
Robert, Katie, and John,
merry companions
on the same journey.

Experiencing the World's Religions: Tradition, Challenge, and Change

Published by McGraw-Hill, an operating unit of The McGraw-Hill Companies, Inc., 1221 Avenue of the Americas, New York, NY, 10020. Copyright © 2005, 2002, 1999 by Michael Vincent Molloy. No part of this publication may be reproduced or distributed in any form or by any means, or stored in a database or retrieval system, without the prior written consent of The McGraw-Hill Companies, Inc., including, but not limited to, in any network or other electronic storage or transmission, or broadcast for distance learning. Some ancillaries, including electronic and print components, may not be available to customers outside the United States.

This book is printed on acid-free paper.

2 3 4 5 6 7 8 9 0 VNH / VNH 0 9 8 7 6 5 4

ISBN: 0-07-283506-0

Cover Photo: © *Alan Kearney/Getty Images/The Image Bank*

Publisher: *Lyn Uhl*
Sponsoring editor: *Jon-David Hague*
Senior marketing manager: *Zina Craft*
Art director: *Jeanne M. Schreiber*
Project manager: *David Sutton*
Production supervisor: *Tandra Jorgensen*

Senior designer: *Cassandra Chu*
Cover designer: *Bill Stanton*
Photo research manager: *Brian Pecko*
Art manager: *Robin Mouat*
Compositor: *GTS Companies*
Printer: *Von Hoffman Press, Inc.*

Library of Congress Cataloging-in-Publication Data

Molloy, Michael, 1942-
    Experiencing the world's religions : tradition, challenge, and change / Michael Molloy.—
3rd ed.
        p. cm.
    Includes bibliographical references and index.
    ISBN 0-07-283506-0 (alk. paper)
    1. Religions—Textbooks. I. Title.
BL80.3.M65 2004
200—dc22

2004042646

www.mhhe.com

Contents

2 Oral Religions   29

3 Hinduism   71

4 Buddhism   **119**

5 Jainism and Sikhism   **185**

6 Taoism and Confucianism   **207**

7 Shinto   255

8 Judaism   **283**

9 Christianity   **341**

10 Islam   *431*

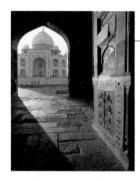

11 Alternative Paths   **489**

12 The Modern Search   **523**

Preface

Religions are ways of looking at reality, and they strongly shape both individuals and cultures. Religions are also value systems that shape decisions. We therefore cannot understand the turbulent modern world without taking its religions into account. Our contemporary world seems constantly on the verge of catastrophe. Yet—through the internet, television, immigration, and travel—it also offers new potential for people to grow close. For both reasons we need to understand each other's values and points of view—we need to study one another's religions.

There is also a reward for readers of this book beyond becoming good citizens of the world. It is quite wonderful for students to learn about world religions, because the religions lead to so many unexpected places and interesting people.

This book encourages readers to experience the religions of the world directly, even in their own communities. Luckily, even small communities have places of worship and meditation, which invariably welcome students who are interested in experiencing them. Every city has festivals, services, dances, or concerts sponsored by a variety of religions, and museums display religious art. Through the experience of various religions, students will discover not only the fascination of religion, but the beauty, as well, of poetry, art, music, architecture, and dance.

This edition owes a big debt of gratitude to students and teachers who have given me their recommendations. I made hundreds of changes to make the material more readable and to make connections with modern life. I have added material on indigenous religions, on Sunni Islam, and on Vajrayana Buddhism. Although the focus of this book is on major, living religions, I have also added material, as requested, on Greco-Roman religions, as background to Christianity, and on contemporary Zoroastrianism. I thank all of you who gave me your time and helpful advice.

Because I wrote this book for beginners in the study of religion, five aims guided me:

1. *Offering the essentials.* What would a person seeking to be an informed world citizen want to know about the major religions? This book tries to present that essential content, then point to places, texts, and people through whom more can be discovered.

2. *Clarity.* I often think of the ironic axiom, "When you see the spark of ambition, water it." Students almost always come to a course in world religions with eagerness to learn. But their initial enthusiasm can be drowned in waves of details, presented in academic language. I try to give the essentials in the clearest language that I can. Maps, photos, definitions, and timelines are added for additional clarity.

3. *Showing the multidisciplinary nature of religions.* A religion is not just a system of beliefs. It is also a combination of ways in which beliefs are expressed in ceremony, food, clothing, art, architecture, pilgrimage, scripture, and music. This book tries to make the multifaceted expressions of religion clear. The photographs have been chosen to help achieve this goal.

4. *Experience.* Religions are better understood through firsthand experience. I hope here to encourage students to imagine and seek out direct experience of religions both at home and abroad. Each chapter begins with a possible First Encounter and then includes a personal experience later in the chapter; these two sections have similar goals.

5. *Blend of scholarship and respect.* This book necessarily presents religions from an academic point of view. At the same time it tries to show its empathy for the thoughts and emotions of people who live within each religious tradition.

Supplemental materials are available to help students and teachers. They include:

- Print *Study Guide* by Richard Curran Trussell. This study guide contains chapter Learning Objectives; summaries; fill-in-the-blank, multiple-choice, and short-answer questions; possible paper topics; interreligious comparisons; and reflection exercises. It may be ordered separately or packaged at a discount with *Experiencing the World's Religions.*

- Online Learning Center (OLC) available at www.mhhe.com/molloy3. For each chapter, the OLC contains multiple-choice, fill-in-the-blank, and true/false questions (all different from the Study Guide for even more opportunities to master chapter content); electronic flash cards of key terms; fun crossword puzzles that further help students learn key terms; and internet links to sites that provide even more material for study.

- Using the registration codes provided with *Experiencing the World's Religions,* teachers and students have access, through the OLC, to *PowerWeb: World Religions. PowerWeb: World Religions* provides more than sixty supplementary readings on the religions presented in *Experiencing the World's Religions*. These readings are meant to provide a glimpse of current events and changes that take place in contemporary religion and the broader world.

- Instructor's Resource CD-ROM. This CD-ROM contains Concepts and Strategies for Teaching World Religions; for each chapter, it also contains Lecture Supplements, Video Resources, Internet Resources, a test bank of Multiple-Choice Questions and Essay Topics, a Computerized Test Bank that allows teachers to create exams easily and store grades in a gradebook, and PowerPoint slides, organized by chapter and section.

- Teachers have free access to McGraw-Hill's *PageOut* course management system at www.pageout.net. *PageOut* is a powerful way to build online course materials. Tests can be created and administered online using all the items from the test bank. Teachers can include links to the OLC and its many study tools. And teachers can add their own material for a truly customized web site.

Many teachers have shared their insights with me—I am simply passing on the torch. I am particularly grateful to Lucy Molloy, Walter Daspit, Sobharani Basu, Abe Masao, Winfield Nagley, and David Kidd. It is a joy to recall the influence of their unique personalities. Thanks to Thomas Hilgers for many fine photographs. I am grateful to the East-West Center for a grant that early on assisted my studies in Asia. Several monasteries were kind in allowing me to share in their life: Songgwang-sa in South Korea, Engaku-zan in Japan, St. John's Abbey in Minnesota, and St. Andrew's Abbey in California. I remain indebted to the late Alden Paine, whose encouragement at Mayfield was a model of kindness. Thanks to Jon-David Hague, my editor at McGraw-Hill, for his availability and help; to Brian Pecko for his photographic research; to Robin Mouat for her fine illustrations; and to Marie Deer, my copy editor.

Thanks also go to these teachers and scholars who offered their ideas for the first and second editions: Robert Platzner, CSU Sacramento; Brannon M. Wheeler, University of Washington; Thomas F. MacMillan, Mendocino College; George Alfred James, University of North Texas; Dr. D. Kerry Edwards, Red Rocks Community College; R. F. Lumpp, Regis University; Ramdas Lamb, University of Hawaii; R. C. Trussell, Pikes Peak Community College; G. David Panisnick, Honolulu Community College; Prof. Madhav M. Deshpande, University of Michigan; Robert J. Miller, Midway College; Mark MacWilliams, Saint Lawrence University; David D. Waara, Western Michigan University; John G. Spiro, Illinois Wesleyan University; Gerald Michael Schnabel, Bemidji State University; Rita M. Gross, University of Wisconsin—Eau Claire; Wendell Charles Beane, University of Wisconsin—Oshkosh; Dr. Ann Berliner, CSU Fresno; and Dr. Dan Breslauer, University of Kansas; Lee W. Bailey, Ithaca College; Charlene Embrey Burns, Loyola University, New Orleans; Philip Jenkins, Penn State; Kenneth Rose, Christopher Newport University; Lori Rowlett, University of Wisconsin, Eau Claire; and

Jared Ludlow, Brigham Young University—Hawai`i. To the reviewers of the third edition, I am also indebted:

- Richard A. Layton—University of Illinois, Urbana-Champaign
- Stephen Sapp—University of Miami
- Daniel Wolne—University of New Mexico
- Ralph Wedeking—Iowa Central Community College
- Robert Baum—Iowa State University
- Nikki Bado-Fralick—Iowa State University
- Brett Greider—University of Wisconsin, Eau Claire

The book is far better as a result of their reviews. Although it is a truism, this book has also been influenced by hundreds of other people who are also owed my sincere thanks. They planted in me seeds that I hope have come to flower.

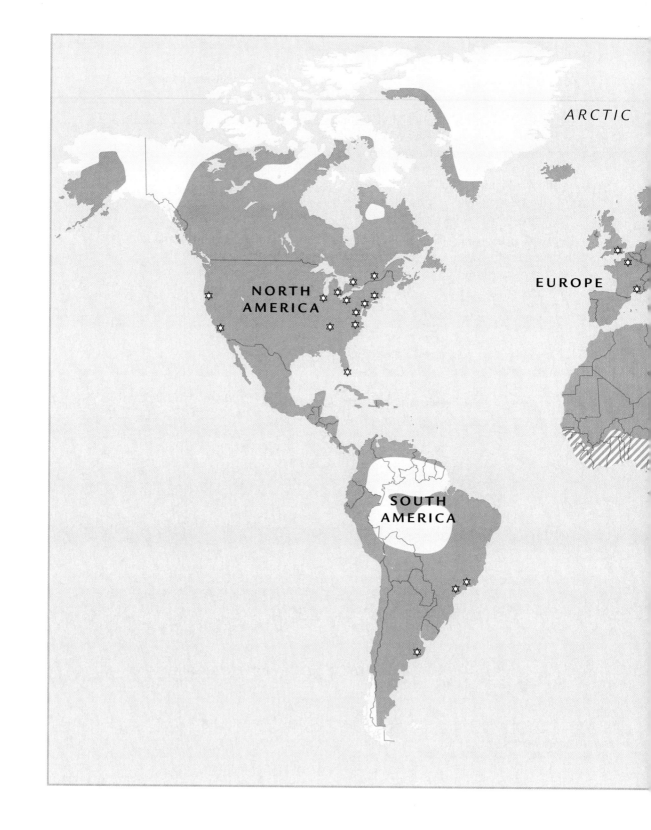

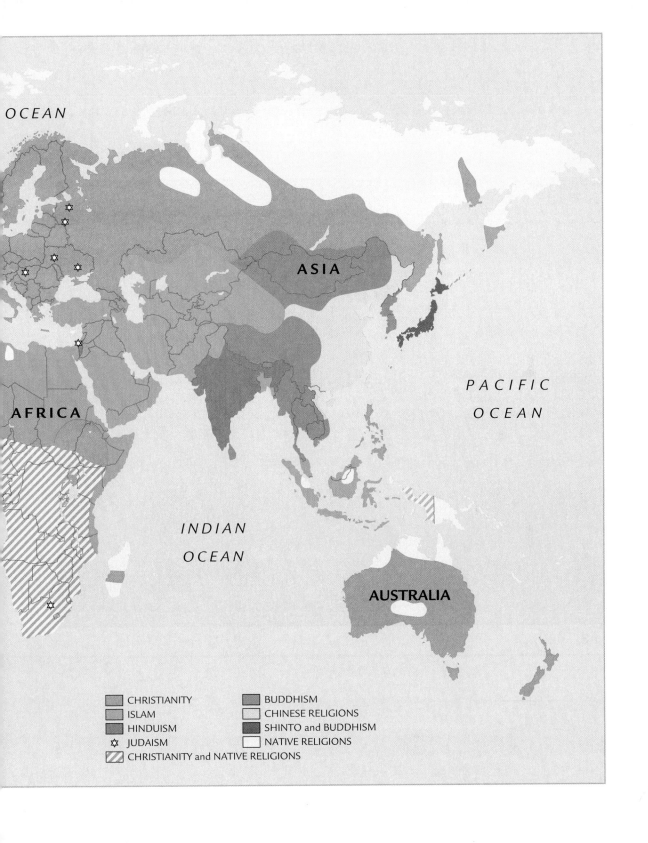

OCEAN

ASIA

PACIFIC
OCEAN

AFRICA

INDIAN

OCEAN

AUSTRALIA

CHRISTIANITY   BUDDHISM
ISLAM   CHINESE RELIGIONS
HINDUISM   SHINTO and BUDDHISM
✡ JUDAISM   NATIVE RELIGIONS
CHRISTIANITY and NATIVE RELIGIONS

CHAPTER 1

Understanding Religion

 FIRST ENCOUNTER

For months you have wanted to take a break from work and everyday life, and recently some friends invited you to vacation with them at their mountain cabin. At first you hesitate. This is not the kind of trip you had in mind. After reconsidering, you realize that a remote getaway with friends is just the change of pace you need.

Now, three weeks later, you have been traveling all day and have just arrived at the cabin. It is late afternoon, and the air is so cold you can see your breath. Your friends welcome you warmly, and there's a nice fire in the living room. Your hosts show you to your room and give you a short tour. Soon you are all fixing supper together—pasta, mushrooms, salad. During the meal you discuss your work, your zany relatives, and your mutual friends. Everyone is laughing and having a good time. It's confirmed: coming here was a great idea.

After supper, your friends won't let you help with the dishes. "I think I'll go out for a walk," you say, putting on your heavy, hooded jacket. As the front door closes behind you, you step into a world transformed by twilight.

What strikes you first is the smell in the air. There is nothing quite like the scent of burning wood—almost like incense. It fits perfectly with the chill. You walk farther, beyond the clearing that surrounds the house, and suddenly you are on a path beneath tall pine trees. As a strong breeze rises, the trees make an eerie, whispering sound. It is not exactly a rustle; it is more like a rush. You recall reading once that the sound of wind in pines is "the sound of eternity."

Moving on, you find yourself walking along the mountain's ridge. To your left you see the evening star against the blue-black sky. To your right, it's still light and you see why you are cold: you are literally above the clouds. You sit down on a flat rock, pull up your hood, and watch the pine tree silhouettes disappear as darkness spreads its thickening veil.

It's difficult to pull yourself away. All around you stars begin to pop out, and soon they are blooming thick as wildflowers. Overhead, the mass of stars resembles a river—it must be the Milky Way. You get up and slowly turn full circle to take it all in.

You had almost forgotten about stars. You don't see them much back home, let alone think of them. Where you live, stars appear in movies. Here, though, stars are mysterious points of light. You remember what you once learned: stars are so distant that their light can take millions of years to reach earth. You realize that some of the stars you see may no longer exist. Only their light remains.

At last you begin to walk back to the cabin. A cluster of clouds emerges on the horizon, lit from behind by the rising moon. You see your friends' wooden cabin in the distance. From here it looks so small. The stars seem like the permanent, real world, while the house appears little and temporary—more like a question mark in the great book of the universe. Questions flood your mind. Who are we human beings? Do we make any difference to the universe? Are we part of any cosmic plan? Is there any point to the universe at all? What is it all about?

WHY IS THERE RELIGION?

One of the world's most mysterious paintings, by French artist Paul Gauguin (1848–1903), depicts a group of people who stand or sit in a kind of timeless primeval world, arms lifted up to the sky.[1] Gauguin painted the work toward the end of his life and considered it to be his masterpiece. The title of the painting is an odd one: *Where Do We Come From? What Are We? Where Are We Going?* Like us when we look out at the night sky with wonder, Gauguin's figures appear as strangers in the cosmos. Gauguin's vision expresses amazement at how great we human beings are, yet also how small we are within the galaxy and how short our lives are.

Why do we sometimes feel disjointed, unconnected, alone? Where do we fit? Religion is among the greatest of human efforts to answer these questions. It helps unite us in communities that bring meaning to our lives; it

In his painting *Where Do We Come From? What Are We? Where Are We Going?* Paul Gauguin uses the images of a religious statue and people in postures of prayer to express the deepest human questions.

offers answers to our deepest questions; and it helps give us a sense of our place in the universe.

Speculations on the Sources of Religion

Why does religion exist? The most evident answer is that it serves many human needs. One of our primary needs is having a means to deal with our mortality. Because we and our loved ones must die, we have to face the pain of death and the inevitable questions it brings about whether there is any soul, afterlife, or rebirth. People often look to religion for the answers. Religion can help us cope with death, and religious rituals can offer us comfort. Human beings also desire good health, a regular supply of food, and the conditions (such as suitable weather) necessary to ensure these things. Before the development of modern science, human beings looked to religion to bring about these practical benefits, and they often still do.

Human beings are also social by nature, and religion offers companionship and the fulfillment that can come from belonging to a group. Moreover, religion often provides a structure for caring for the needy.

Human beings have a need to seek out and create artistic forms of expression. Religion stimulates art, music, and dance, and it has been the inspirational source of some of the most imaginative buildings in the world. Religion not only makes use of multiple arts but also integrates them into a living, often beautiful whole.

Perhaps the most basic function of religion is to respond to our natural wonder about ourselves and the cosmos—our musings on a starry night. Religion helps us relate to the unknown universe around us by answering the basic questions of who we are, where we come from, and where we are going.

Issues relating to the origins of religion have engaged thinkers with new urgency ever since the dawn of the age of science. Many have suggested that

Death is inevitable. In different ways, religion helps people understand and deal with that certainty.

religion is a human attempt to feel more secure in an unfeeling universe. The English anthropologist E. B. Tylor (1832–1917), for example, believed religion was rooted in spirit worship. He noted how frequently religions see "spirits" as having some control over natural forces and how commonly religions see those who die—the ancestors—as passing into the spirit world. Fear of the power of all these spirits, he thought, made it necessary for people to find ways to please their ancestors. Religion offered such ways, thus allowing the living to avoid the spirits' dangerous power and to convert that power into a force that worked for the good of human beings. Similarly, the Scottish anthropologist James Frazer (1854–1941), author of *The Golden Bough,* saw the origins of religion in early attempts by human beings to influence nature, and he identified religion as an intermediate stage between magic and science.

Sigmund Freud (1856–1939) theorized that belief in a God or gods arises from the long-lasting impressions made on adults by their childhood experiences, in which their parents play a major part; these adults then project their sense of their parents into their image of their God or gods. According to Freud, these experiences, of fear as well as of security, are the basis for the adult's attempts to deal with the anxieties of a complicated present and an unknown future. Freud argued that since a major function of religion is to help human beings feel secure in an unsafe universe, religion becomes less necessary as human beings gain greater physical and mental security. Freud's major works on religion include *Totem and Taboo, The Future of an Illusion,* and *Moses and Monotheism.*

Another psychologist, William James (1842–1910), came to his ideas on religion via an unusual course of study. Although he began his higher education as a student of art, he made a radical switch to the study of medicine. Finally, when he recognized the influence of the mind on the body, he was led to the study of psychology and then of religion, which he saw as growing out of psychological needs. James viewed religion as a positive way of fulfilling these needs and praised its positive influence on the lives of individuals. He wrote that religion brings "a new zest" to living, provides "an assurance of safety," and leads to a "harmonious relation with the universe."[2]

The German theologian Rudolf Otto (1869–1937) argued in his book *The Idea of the Holy* that religions emerge when people experience that aspect of reality which is essentially mysterious. He called it the "mystery that causes trembling and fascination" (*mysterium tremendum et fascinans*). In general, we take our existence for granted and live with little wonder; but occasionally something disturbs our ordinary view of reality. For example, a strong manifestation of nature—such as a violent thunderstorm—may startle us. It is an aspect of reality that is frightening, forcing us to tremble (*tremendum*) but also to feel fascination (*fascinans*). The emotional result is what Otto called *numinous awe.*[3] He pointed out how often religious art depicts that which is terrifying, such as the bloodthirsty Hindu goddess Durga.[4]

Carl Gustav Jung (1875–1961), an early disciple of Freud, broke with his mentor because of fundamental differences of interpretation, particularly about religion. In his books *Modern Man in Search of a Soul, Psychology and Alchemy,* and *Memories, Dreams, Reflections,* Jung described religion as something that grew out of the individual's need to arrive at personal fulfillment, which he called *individuation.* According to Jung, many religious insignia can be seen as symbols of personal integration and human wholeness: the circle, the cross (which is made of lines that join at the center), and the sacred diagram of the mandala (often a circle within or enclosing a square), which he called "the path to the center, to individuation."[5] He pointed out that as people age they can make a healthy use of religion to understand their place in the universe and to prepare for death. For Jung, religion was a noble human response to the depth of reality and to its complexity.

Various scholars have attempted to identify "stages" in the development of religions. Austrian ethnographer and philologist Wilhelm Schmidt (1868–1954) argued that all humankind once believed in a single High God and that to this simple **monotheism** (a belief in one God) later beliefs in lesser gods and spirits were added. The reverse has also been suggested, namely, that **polytheism** (a belief in many gods) led to monotheism. Influenced by the notion of evolution, some have speculated that religions "evolve" naturally from **animism** (a worldview that sees all elements of nature as being filled with spirit or spirits) to polytheism and then to monotheism. Critics of this view feel it is biased in favor of monotheism, in part because it is a view originally suggested by Christian scholars, who presented their belief system as the most advanced.

Scholars today hesitate to speak of any "evolution" from one form of religion to another. To apply the biological notion of evolution to human belief systems seems biased, oversimple, and speculative. Even more important, such a point of view leads to subjective judgments that one religion is more "highly evolved" than another—a shortsightedness that has kept many people from appreciating the unique insights and contributions of every religion. Consequently, the focus of religious studies has moved from the study of religion to the study of religions, a field that assumes that all religions are equally worthy of study.

Key Characteristics of Religion

When people begin their study of religions, they bring ideas from the religion in which they were raised or from the predominant religion of their society. They may assume, for example, that every religion has a sacred book or that it worships a divine being or that it has a set of commandments.

Note: Words shown in boldface type are key words that reappear with definitions in the "Key Terms" section at the end of each chapter.

Indeed, many religions do share all these characteristics, but some do not. Shinto, for example, does not have a set of commandments, nor does it preach a moral code; Zen Buddhism does not worship a divine being; and many tribal religions have no written sacred scripture. Nevertheless, we call them all religions. What, then—if not a common set of elements—must be present for something to be called a religion?

An obvious starting point for many scholars is to examine linguistic clues: What are the linguistic roots of the term *religion*? Intriguingly, the most common derivation of the word *religion* is "to join again," "to reconnect." The Latin roots of the word *religion* are thought to be *re-*, meaning "again," and *lig-*, meaning "join," or "connect" (as in "ligament").[6] If this derivation is correct, then the word *religion* suggests the joining of our natural, human world to the sacred world. In classical Latin, the term *religio* meant awe for the gods and concern for proper ritual.[7] We must recognize, though, that the term *religion* arose in Western culture and may not be entirely appropriate when applied across cultures; *spiritual path*, for example, might be a more fitting designation to refer to other religious systems. We will keep these things in mind when we use the long-established term *religion*.

Traditional dictionary definitions of *religion* read something like this: A system of belief that involves worship of a God or gods, prayer, ritual, and a moral code. But there are so many exceptions to that definition that it is neither comprehensive nor accurate. So instead of saying that a religion *must* have certain characteristics, it is now thought more useful to list a series of characteristics that are found in what are commonly accepted as religions. We may accept as a religion whatever manifests a reasonable number of these characteristics. Scholars do note, however, that what we ordinarily call religions manifest to some degree the following eight elements:[8]

> Religion [is] a way of life founded upon the apprehension of sacredness in existence.
>
> —Julian Huxley, biologist[9]

Belief system Several beliefs fit together into a fairly complete and systematic interpretation of the universe and the human being's place in it; this is also called a *worldview*.

Community The belief system is shared, and its ideals are practiced by a group.

Central myths Stories that express the religious beliefs of a group are retold and often reenacted. Examples of central myths include the major events in the life of the Hindu god Krishna, the enlightenment experience of the Buddha, the exodus of the Israelites from oppression in Egypt, the death and resurrection of Jesus, or Muhammad's escape from Mecca to Medina. Scholars call such central stories *myths*. We should note that the term *myth*, as scholars use it, is a specialized term. It does not in itself mean that the stories are historically untrue (as in popular usage) but only that the stories are central to the religion.

Ritual Beliefs are enacted and made real through ceremonies.

Ethics Rules about human behavior are established. These are often viewed as having been revealed from a supernatural realm, but they can also be viewed as socially generated guidelines.

Religious rituals are often symbolic reenactments of a religion's key stories. Here, monks in Bhutan perform Shacham. The dance shows Guru Rimpoche, who brought Buddhism to Bhutan, in a battle with the native God of the Wind, who rode on stags. Annual performances pass such stories across generations.

Characteristic emotional experiences Among the emotional experiences typically associated with religions are dread, guilt, awe, mystery, devotion, conversion, "rebirth," liberation, ecstasy, bliss, and inner peace.

Material expression Religions make use of an astonishing variety of physical elements—statues, paintings, musical compositions (including chants), musical instruments, ritual objects, flowers, incense, clothing, architecture, and specific locations.

Sacredness A distinction is made between the sacred and the ordinary; ceremonies often emphasize the differentiation between the sacred and the ordinary through the deliberate use of different language, clothing, and architecture. Certain objects, actions, people, and places may share in the sacredness or express it.

The Sacred

All religions are concerned with the deepest level of reality, and for most religions the core or origin of everything is sacred and mysterious. This sense of a mysterious, originating holiness is called by many names: Brahman, Tao, Great Mother, Divine Parent, Great Spirit, Ground of Being, Great Mysterious, the Ultimate, the Absolute, the Divine, the Holy. People, however, experience and explain sacred reality in different ways, as we shall see in the chapters that follow.

One familiar term for the sacred reality, particularly in the Western world, is *God,* and, as mentioned earlier, *monotheism* is the term that means a belief in one God. In some systems, the term *God* often carries with it the notion of a Cosmic Person—a divine being with will and intelligence who is just and compassionate and infinite in virtues. God is also called *omnipotent* ("having total power over the universe"). Although God may be said to have personal aspects, all monotheistic religions agree that the reality of God is beyond all categories: God is said to be pure spirit, not fully definable in words. This notion of a powerful God, distinct from the universe, describes a sacredness that is active in the world but also distinct from it. That is, God is **transcendent**—unlimited by the world and all ordinary reality.

In some religions, however, the sacred reality is not viewed as having personal attributes but is more like an energy or mysterious power. Frequently, the sacred is then spoken of as something **immanent** within the universe. In some religions, there is a tendency to speak of the universe not just as having been created but also as a manifestation of the sacred nature itself, in which nothing is separate from the sacred. This view, called **pantheism** (Greek: "all divine"), sees the sacred as being discoverable within the physical world and its processes. In other words, nature itself is holy.

Some religions worship the sacred reality in the form of many coexisting gods, a view (mentioned earlier) called *polytheism*. The multiple gods may be fairly separate entities, each in charge of an aspect of reality (such as nature gods), or they may be multiple manifestations of the same basic sacred reality.

In recent centuries, we find a tendency to deny the existence of any God or gods (**atheism**), to argue that the existence of God cannot be proven (**agnosticism**), or simply to take no position (**nontheism**). (Such tendencies are not strictly modern; they can also be found in some ancient systems, such as Jainism; see chapter 5.) However, if one sees religion broadly, as a "spiritual path," then even systems based on these three views—particularly if they show other typical characteristics of a religion—can also be called religions.

The mandala, according to Jung, illustrates "the path to the center, to individuation."

Religious Symbolism

Religions present views of reality, and most speak of the sacred. Nevertheless, because religions are so varied in their teachings and because the teachings of some religions, when taken at face value, conflict with those of others, it is common to assert that religions express truth *symbolically*. A symbol is something fairly concrete, ordinary, and universal that can represent—and help human beings intensely experience—something of greater complexity. For example, water can represent spiritual cleansing; the sun, health; a mountain, strength; and a circle, eternity. We frequently find symbolism, both deliberate and unconscious, in religious art and ritual.

Washing with water is a universal symbol of inner purification.

Symbols and their interpretation have long played an important part in analyzing dreams. It was once common to think of dreams as messages from a supernatural realm that provided a key to the future. Although this type of interpretation is less common nowadays, most people still think that dreams are significant. Sigmund Freud introduced his view of the dream as a door into subconscious levels of the mind; he argued that by understanding dreams symbolically we can understand our hidden needs and fears. For example, a dream of being lost in a forest might be interpreted as distress over losing one's sense of direction in life, or a dream of flying could be interpreted as a need to seek freedom.

Carl Gustav Jung extended the symbol-focused method of dream interpretation to the interpretation of religion. Some religious leaders have been cautious about this approach—popularized by the mythologist Joseph Campbell—lest everything be turned into a symbol and all literal meaning be lost. And specialists in religion oppose the view that two religions are basically the same simply because similar symbols appear in both.

Nevertheless, there are many scholars and religious leaders who recognize the importance of symbolic interpretation, because the use of religious

To ascend one of the pyramids in Teotihuacán was to seek a place where one could encounter the sacred.

symbols may point to some structure that underlies all religions. There is no doubt that many of the same symbolic images and actions appear repeatedly in religions throughout the world. Water, for instance, is used in all sorts of religious rituals: Hindus bathe in the Ganges River; Christians use water for baptisms; Jews use water for ritual purification; and Muslims and followers of Shinto wash before prayer. Ashes also have widespread use among religious traditions to suggest death and the spirit world: ashes are used by tribal religions in dance ceremonies, by Hindu holy men to represent asceticism and detachment, and by some Christians, whose foreheads are marked by ashes in observance of Ash Wednesday. Likewise, religious buildings are placed on hills or are raised on mounds and reached by stairs—all suggesting the symbol of the holy mountain, where the sacred can be encountered.

We also see in various religions the recurrence of a symbolic story of transformation: a state of original purity degenerates into pollution or disorder; a battle to fight disorder culminates in a sacrificial death; and the result is a renewed sense of purity and order. Scholars point out, too, that religions frequently use words in a symbolic way; for example, the divine is often described as existing "up above," insight can be "awakened," a person can feel "reborn," and so on.

When viewed this way, religious symbols, myths, and terminology at times suggest a universal symbolic "language" that all religions speak. Those interested in religious symbolism hope that understanding the "language" of symbols will help uncover what is universally important in all religions.

PATTERNS AMONG RELIGIONS

When we study religions in a comparative and historical sense, we are not looking to validate them or to disprove them or to enhance our own belief or practice—as we might if we were studying our personal religious tradition. Instead, we want to comprehend the particular religions as thoroughly as possible and to understand the experience of people within each religion. Part of that process of understanding leads us to see patterns of similarity and difference among religions.

Although we do look for patterns, we must recognize that these patterns are not conceptual straitjackets. Religions, especially those with long histories and extensive followings, are usually quite complex. Furthermore, religions are not permanent theoretical constructs but are constantly in a process of change—influenced by governments, thinkers, historical events, changing technology, and the shifting values of the cultures in which they exist.

> Religion is the substance of culture, and culture the form of religion.
> —Paul Tillich, theologian[10]

First Pattern: Focus of Beliefs and Practices

Realizing the limitations of all generalizations, we nonetheless might look for orientations shown by individual religions as a way of gaining some perspective on them. When we look at the world's dominant religions, we see three basic orientations in their conception and location of the sacred.[11]

Sacramental orientation The sacramental orientation emphasizes carrying out rituals and ceremonies regularly and correctly as the path to salvation; in some religions, correct ritual is believed to influence the processes of nature. All religions have some degree of ritual, but the ceremonial tendency is predominant, for example, in most tribal religions, in Roman Catholic and Eastern Orthodox Christianity, in Vedic Hinduism, and in Tibetan Buddhism. Making the Catholic sign of the cross, for example, is done in a certain way: only with the right hand, beginning with a touch on the forehead, then on one's chest, and finally on each shoulder, left to right.[12]

Prophetic orientation The prophetic orientation stresses that contact with the sacred is ensured by proper belief and by adherence to moral rules. This orientation also implies that a human being may be an important intermediary between the believer and the sacred; for example, a prophet may speak to believers on behalf of the sacred. Prophetic orientation is a prominent aspect of Judaism, Protestant Christianity, and Islam, which all see the sacred as being transcendent but personal. The television crusades of Evangelistic ministers are good examples of the prophetic orientation in action.

Mystical orientation The mystical orientation seeks union with a reality greater than oneself, such as with God, the process of nature, the universe, or reality as a whole. There are often techniques (such as seated meditation) for lessening the sense of one's individual identity to help the individual experience a greater unity. The mystical orientation is a prominent aspect of Upanishadic Hinduism, Taoism, and some schools of Buddhism. (Master Kusan [1901–1983], a Korean teacher of Zen Buddhism, described the disappearance of self in the enlightenment experience of unity with this memorable question, "Could a snowflake survive inside a burning flame?"[13]) Although the mystical orientation is more common in religions that stress the immanence of the sacred or that are nontheistic, it is an important but less prominent tendency in Judaism, Christianity, and Islam as well.

Any one of these three orientations may be dominant in a religion, yet the other two orientations might also be found in the same religion to a lesser extent and possibly be subsumed into a different purpose. For example, ceremony can be utilized to help induce mystical experience, as in Catholic and Orthodox Christianity, Japanese Shingon Buddhism, Tibetan Buddhism, Taoism, and even Zen Buddhism, which has a strongly ritualistic aspect of its own.

Second Pattern: Religious Views of the World and Life

Religions must provide answers to the great questions that people ask. How did the universe come into existence, does it have a purpose, and will it end? What is time, and how should we make use of it? What should be our relationship to the world of nature? Why do human beings exist? How do we reach fulfillment, transformation, or salvation? Why is there suffering in the world, and how should we deal with it? What happens when we die? What should we hold as sacred? The questions do not vary, but the answers do.

Given the great variety in their worldviews, it is not surprising that each religion defines differently the nature of sacred reality, the universe, the natural world, time, and human purpose. Religions also differ in their attitudes toward the role of words in expressing the sacred and in their relations to other religious traditions. By examining different views on these concepts, we will have further bases for comparison that will lead us to a more complete understanding of the world's religions.

The nature of sacred reality Some religions, as we have seen, speak of the sacred as transcendent, existing primarily in a realm beyond the everyday world. In other religions, though, sacred reality is spoken of as being immanent; that is, it is within nature and human beings and can be experienced as energy or holiness. Sometimes the sacred is viewed as having personal attributes, while elsewhere it is seen as an impersonal entity.

The nature of the universe Some religions see the universe as having been begun by an intelligent, personal Creator who continues to guide the universe according to a cosmic plan. Other religions view the universe as being eternal, that is, having no beginning or end. The implications of these two positions are quite important to what is central in a religion and to how the human being acts in regard to this central

Young nuns in central Myanmar study Buddhist scriptures, which they memorize, read, and write daily.

belief. If the universe is created, especially by a transcendent deity, the center of sacredness is the Creator rather than the universe, but human beings imitate the Creator by changing and perfecting the world. If, however, the universe is eternal, the material universe itself is sacred and perfect and requires no change.

The human attitude toward nature At one end of the spectrum of attitudes on this topic are religions or religious schools that see nature as the realm of evil forces that must be overcome. Nature is gross and contaminating, existing in opposition to the nonmaterial world of the spirit—a view, known as **dualism,** held by some forms of Christianity, Jainism, and Hinduism. At the other end of the spectrum, as in Taoism and Shinto, nature is considered to be sacred and needs no alteration. Other religions, such as Judaism and Islam, take a middle ground, holding that the natural world originated from a divine action but that human beings are called upon to continue to shape it.

Time Religions that emphasize a creation, such as Judaism, Christianity, and Islam, tend to see time as being linear, moving in a straight line from the beginning of the universe to its end. Being limited and unrepeatable, time is important. In some other religions, such as Buddhism, however, time is cyclical. The universe simply moves through endless changes, which repeat themselves over grand periods of time. In such a religion, time is not as crucial or "real," because, ultimately, the universe is not moving to some final point; consequently, appreciating the present may be more important than being oriented to the future.

Human purpose In some religions, human beings are part of a great divine plan, and although each person is unique, individual meaning comes also from the cosmic plan. The cosmic plan may be viewed as a struggle between forces of good and evil, with human beings at the center of the stage and the forces of good and evil at work within them. Because human actions are so important, they must be guided by a prescribed moral code that is meant to be internalized by the individual. This view is significant in Judaism, Christianity, and Islam. In contrast, other religions do not see human life in similarly dramatic terms, and the individual is only part of much larger realities. In Taoism and Shinto, a human being is a small part of the natural universe, and in Confucianism, an individual is part of the family and of society. Such religions place less emphasis on individual rights and more emphasis on how the individual can maintain harmony with the whole. Actions are not guided by an internalized moral system but by society, tradition, and a sense of mutual obligation.

Words and scriptures In some religions, the sacred is to be found in written and spoken words, and for those religions that use writing and create scriptures, reading, copying, and using sacred words in music or art are important. We see the importance of words in indigenous religions (which primarily pass on their traditions orally), in Judaism, in Christianity, in Islam, and in Hinduism. Other religions—such as Taoism and Zen Buddhism, which show a certain mistrust of words—value silence and wordless meditation. Although Zen and Taoism utilize language in their practices and have produced significant literature, each of these religions finds language limited in expressing the richness or totality of reality.

Exclusiveness and inclusiveness Some religions emphasize that the sacred is distinct from the world and that order must be imposed by separating good from bad, true from false. In that view, to share in sacredness means separation—for example, withdrawal from certain foods, places, people, practices, or beliefs. Hinduism, Judaism, Christianity, and Islam are among the religions that have been generally exclusive, making it impossible to belong to more than one religion at the same time. In contrast, other religions have stressed inclusiveness. Frequently, such religions also have emphasized social harmony, the inadequacy of language, or the relativity of truth, and they have accepted belief in many deities. Their inclusiveness has led them to admit many types of beliefs and practices into their religions, to the point that it is possible for an individual to belong to several religions—such as Buddhism, Taoism, and Confucianism—simultaneously. Such inclusiveness has led to misunderstanding at times, as in the case of a Christian missionary having "converted" a Japanese follower only to find the new convert still visiting a Shinto shrine.

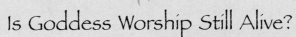

Is Goddess Worship Still Alive?

Although male imagery is dominant in contemporary religions, traces—and current practices—of Goddess worship are abundant.

- In India, the divine is worshiped in its female aspects as the Great Mother (also known as Kali and Durga) or as other female deities.
- In Catholic and Orthodox Christianity, Mary, the mother of Jesus, receives special veneration; she is held to possess suprahuman powers and is a strong role model for women's behavior.
- In the Mahayana Buddhist pantheon, Guanyin (Kannon) is worshiped as a female ideal of mercy.
- In Japan, the premier Shinto divinity is the goddess Amaterasu, patroness of the imperial family. In contrast to many other religious systems, the goddess Amaterasu is associated with the sun, and a male god is associated with the moon.
- In Korea and Japan, shamans are frequently female.
- In Africa, India, and elsewhere, some tribal cultures remain matriarchal.
- In Wicca, a contemporary restoration of ancient, nature-based religion, devotees worship a female deity they refer to as the Goddess.
- Symbolic forms of the female divine are still prominent in the rites of several religions. Common symbols include the moon, the snake, spirals and labyrinths, the egg, *yoni* (symbolic vagina), water, and earth. These symbolic representations of the female suggest generation, growth, nurturance, intuition, and wisdom.

The egg is often used to symbolize the female divine. Here an "Easter egg" hangs in the square fronting Our Lady of Tyn church in Prague, reminding us that at its root Easter is a celebration of fertility.

Third Pattern: Religious Views of Male and Female

Because gender is such an intrinsic and important part of being human, religions have had much to say about the roles of men and women, both on earth and in the divine spheres. Thus, views of what is male and what is female provide another basis for comparing religions.

In many influential religions of today, male imagery and control seem to dominate; the sacred is considered male and the full-time religious specialists are frequently male. But this may not always have been the case. Tantalizing evidence suggests that female divinities once played an important role in many cultures and religions. The most significant female deity was particularly associated with fertility and motherhood and has

Bishop Barbara Harris, shown here at her consecration in 1989, became the first female bishop of the Episcopal Church.

been known by many names, such as Astarte, Asherah, Aphrodite, and Freia (the origin of the word *Friday*). Statues of a Mother-Goddess—sometimes with many breasts to suggest the spiritual power of the nurturing female—have been found throughout Europe, as well as in Turkey, Israel, and the Middle East.

Why has patriarchal religion, at least for now, so overcome matriarchal elements? It is possible that matriarchy and Goddess worship were frequent in early societies but that matriarchal cultures were suppressed by male-led nomadic cultures, by the development of the tools and strategies of war, and by the growth of populous city-states that needed defense.

It appears that male domination spread significantly after 2000 B.C.E. In India, the Aryans who entered the subcontinent were led by males on horseback who worshiped gods that were almost exclusively male. In Israel, worship of a female deity was stamped out by prophets who preached exclusive worship of the male god Yahweh and by kings who wanted loyalty paid to them and their offspring. We read passages like this in the Hebrew Scriptures: "They abandoned the Lord and worshipped Baal and the Astartes. So the anger of the Lord was kindled against Israel" (Judg. 2:13–14).[14] The Christian New Testament forbids women to preach: "I do not allow them to teach or to have authority over men; they must keep quiet. For Adam was created first, and then Eve. And it was not Adam who was deceived; it was the woman who was deceived and broke God's law" (1 Tim. 2:12–14).[15] In Asia, Confucianism has been distrustful of women in general and has ordinarily refused them leadership roles. In Buddhism, despite recognition in scripture that women can be enlightened, in practice the great majority of leaders have been men.[16] This patriarchal tendency has shaped religious life, for good or bad, for the past three to four thousand years.

Nevertheless, changes—inevitable in religion, as in everything else—are occurring. As women take leadership roles in business and civic life, they are assuming similar leadership roles in religion in some societies. The study of comparative religion has helped this process by opening people's eyes to those religions of the past in which goddesses were worshiped and women played leading roles. Students of art, literature, and the history of religion

Note: This text uses the time designations B.C.E. ("before the common era") and C.E. ("of the common era") in place of the Christianity-centered abbreviations B.C. ("before Christ") and A.D. (*anno Domini*, "in the year of the Lord").

are finding abundant evidence of female mystics, poets, shamans, and prophets. It is possible that religion in general is turning away from exclusively patriarchal patterns and beginning to include once again matriarchal values and practices.

MULTIDISCIPLINARY APPROACHES TO THE STUDY OF RELIGION

One of the most fascinating things about religion is that it has influenced so many areas of human life. Consequently, religion can be studied from the point of view of several disciplines. History and literary study have provided two traditional ways of approaching religion, and more recently the fields of anthropology, psychology, and sociology have offered a new look at religion from the perspective of human behavior.

There are other approaches, too. We can focus our study on a single religion or look at several religions at the same time. Believers may opt to explore their own religion "from the inside," while nonbelievers may want to concentrate on the answers that several religions have given to a single question, such as the purpose of human life. Following is a list of some common approaches to religion.

Psychology Psychology (Greek: "soul study") deals with human mental states, emotions, and behaviors. Despite being a fairly young discipline, psychology has taken a close look at religion because it offers such rich human "material" to explore. A few areas of study include religious influences on child rearing, human behavior, and self-identity; group dynamics in religion; trance states; and comparative mystical experiences.

Mythology The study of religious tales, texts, and art has uncovered some universal patterns. Mythology is full of the recurrent images and themes found in religions, such as the tree of knowledge, the ladder to heaven, the fountain of life, the labyrinth, the secret garden, the holy mountain, the newborn child, the suffering hero, initiation, rebirth, the cosmic battle, the female spirit guide, and the aged teacher of wisdom.

Philosophy Philosophy (Greek: "love of wisdom") in some ways originated from a struggle with religion; although both arenas pose many of the same questions, philosophy does not automatically accept the answers given by any religion to the great questions. Instead, philosophy seeks answers independently, following reason rather than religious authority, and it tries to fit its answers into a rational, systematic whole. Some questions philosophy asks are, Does human life have any purpose? Is there an afterlife? and How should we live? Philosophy is essentially the work of individuals, while religion is a community experience; philosophy tries to avoid emotion, while religion often nurtures it; and philosophy is carried on without ritual, while religion naturally expresses itself in ceremony.

Theology Theology (Greek: "study of the divine") is the study of topics as they relate to one particular religious tradition. A theologian is an individual who usually studies his or her own belief system. For example, a person who is in training to become a Christian minister might study Christian theology.

The arts Comparing patterns in religious art makes an intriguing study. For example, religious architecture often uses symmetry, height, and archaic styles to suggest the sacred; religious music frequently employs a slow pace and repeated rhythms to induce tranquillity; and religious art often incorporates gold, haloes, equilateral designs, and circles to suggest otherworldliness and perfection.

Anthropology Anthropology (Greek: "study of human beings") has been interested in how religions influence the ways a culture deals with issues such as family interaction, individual roles, property rights, marriage, child rearing, social hierarchies, and division of labor.

Archeology Archeology (Greek: "study of origins") explores the remains of earlier civilizations, often uncovering the artifacts and ruins of religious buildings from ancient cultures. When possible, archeologists translate writings left by these people, much of which can be religious in origin. Archeology occasionally sheds light on how one religion has influenced another. For example, the excavation of a cuneiform library at Nineveh 150 years ago revealed a story (in the *Epic of Gilgamesh*) that is similar to—and may have influenced—the biblical story of Noah and the flood. Archeology can also reveal religious material that enables scholars to decipher an entire writing system. For example, the discovery in the early nineteenth century of the Rosetta Stone (which contained the same inscription in three different scripts) led researchers to unlock the meaning of Egyptian hieroglyphics.

Comparative religion The academic study of religion has intensified as a result of the increasing interaction between different cultures, as well as the translation of religious documents from around the world. Scholars attempt to examine objectively all elements of specific religions, and departments of religious studies have been set up by universities to analyze and teach the growing body of knowledge.

Comparative religion is the approach we are going to follow in this book. Let us now take a closer look at the history of this field and its way of approaching its subject matter.

KEY CRITICAL QUESTIONS

Comparative religion as a field of study is now more than two hundred years old, and scholars have become increasingly aware of the complexity of their task. Among the questions they ask are these: What should we study in order to properly understand religions? What attitudes should we have when we study the religions of others? How can researchers be objective?

It may seem to many that studying religions is a fairly straightforward, though time-consuming, endeavor: scholars read the scriptures of the various religions, talk with practitioners, visit or research the sacred sites, and experience the major ceremonies. We must keep in mind, though, that in the first century of comparative religious scholarship, scholars had little ability to travel. Their studies were often limited to what they could read. Scholars would read the scriptures of specific religions, read accounts by others who had experienced some of the sacred sites and rituals, make comparisons based on what they had read, and publish their conclusions. Moreover, archeology and anthropology, because they were only in their earliest stages, could not be utilized to enhance scholars' studies and conclusions. Among scholars who had to rely on such an approach— sometimes called "armchair scholarship"—were James Frazer and E. B. Tylor, mentioned earlier. But the limitations of that style of work soon became apparent.

Studying the scriptures of religions, early scholars encountered many problems. Sometimes the texts of the scriptures were incomplete, or the translations that scholars might need to depend on were not accurate. Also, scriptures of many religions often contain *hagiography* (Greek: "holy writing" or "saint writing"). Hagiography is not objective history, written to present dry facts, but rather it is storytelling whose aim is to inspire devotion; some or all of the details might be pious elaboration. Again, outside help (from archeology and other sciences) was unavailable to check scriptural stories for historical accuracy.

Another large area of concern involved the study of religions that did not have written scriptures but had only oral traditions. Scholars of religion asked numerous questions: How should the oral traditions be studied properly? In the case of oral religions, are religious artifacts and ritual words the equivalent of scriptures? And how can we understand the meaning of religious rituals and artifacts for the people who actually use them?

In more recent times, scholarship in religions has increasingly been carried out by people trained in the behavioral sciences. This scientific tendency began seriously with the work of the French sociologist Émile Durkheim (1858–1917). Before Durkheim, it was commonly thought that each major religion was the creation of a "great founder." But Durkheim insisted on studying religions as group phenomena that were subject to social laws. He pointed out that religious behavior is relative to the society in which it is found, and that a society will often use a religion to reinforce its own values. Durkheim argued that societies, rather than great founders, create religions. Durkheim based his conclusions on research, and he urged thinkers to base their conclusions on evidence rather than mere speculation.[17]

The scientific orientation that Durkheim helped establish has greatly influenced contemporary scholarship in comparative religion. Modern work in religions depends heavily on anthropological investigation in the field, done by specialists who have learned the necessary languages and have lived among the people they study. One anthropologist who became highly regarded for this type of research was E. E. Evans-Pritchard (1902–1973),

The student of religions will recognize that this informal neighborhood shrine in downtown Bangkok includes elements from several religions. Old trees are held sacred in many indigenous religions. The offerings reflect Hindu and Buddhist traditions.

who lived among the Azande and Nuer peoples in the Sudan. Another esteemed researcher is the American anthropologist Clifford Geertz (b. 1926), who lived in Bali, Java, and Morocco and has written about the specific religious practices there. Geertz has championed what he calls "thick description"—a description not only of rituals and religious artifacts but also of their exact meaning for practitioners.

This research-based approach would seem to be the proper way to study religions. But it raises its own problems and questions: Are we listening only to the opinions of the researcher, or are the voices of the people who are studied truly being heard? Can an outsider, no matter how sensitive, be truly objective? Doesn't a researcher automatically contaminate the research? And is it possible that informants might give deliberately false answers to questions that they consider inappropriate? (They do.)

There are also moral questions: Does the research arise from respect, or is the researcher's curiosity just another example of cultural domination—a new form of colonialism? (A *New Yorker* cartoon expressed this well. Two friends in a forest village are talking about a sad-looking foreigner nearby. The foreigner, dressed in a safari suit and sun helmet, is tied up and awaiting his fate. One villager asks, "Another missionary?" "No," says the friend. "It's another anthropologist.") A second moral question relates specifically to the study of native religions. Any researcher inevitably introduces new ideas and new objects (clothing, flashlight, camera, video recorder). But is it ethical to bring significant changes to a culture that may have been unchanged for thousands of years? (Of course, this problem is becoming less pressing, as modern life—brought by radio and airplane—enters even the remotest areas around the globe.)

Researchers have turned their attention not only to indigenous religions but also to unique variants within major world religions. Just below the surface of some major religions are often older religions, still alive, sometimes in blended forms. These syncretic forms are common, for example, among Catholic Christians in Latin America, Muslims in Indonesia, and Theravada Buddhists in Southeast Asia. But greater awareness of the enormous variety among practitioners of major religions has raised new questions: Can we really talk anymore about a single "Christianity" or "Buddhism" or "Islam"? Do the so-called world religions really exist, or are they just useful fictions?

The scholar Wilfred Cantwell Smith has argued in his book *The Meaning and End of Religion* that the notion of monolithic world religions is a fiction that should be abandoned. He even argues that ultimately the only religion is that of each individual. Other scholars have enlarged his critical approach. Some have pointed out that the religious experience of women within a religious tradition may be quite different from that of men. (In Islam, for example, women's religious experience takes place at shrines and in the home, whereas men's religious experience is more centered on the mosque.) We should also recognize that within a single world religion the personal religious experience of an individual will be quite different for a child, a teenager, or an adult. And the meaning of being a "Buddhist" or "Christian" or "Hindu" will differ, depending on the culture or historical period that the individual inhabits. (Think of the difference between being a Christian in the Roman Empire of the first century and being a Christian in North America in the twenty-first century.) Lastly, there is the fact that individuals in some societies, such as in China and Japan, practice forms of religion that effortlessly blend elements from several major religions.

Although this book obviously has not abandoned the category of world religions, it tries to show that religions are not separate, homogeneous, or unchanging. It sees world religions as grand patterns but recognizes that we are true to these religions only when we acknowledge the great diversity within them.

WHY STUDY THE MAJOR RELIGIONS OF THE WORLD?

Science investigates; religion interprets. Science gives man knowledge which is power; religion gives man wisdom which is control.

—Martin Luther King, Jr.[18]

Because religions are so wide-ranging and influential, their study helps round out a person's education, as well as enrich one's experience of many other related subjects. Let's now consider some additional pleasures and rewards of studying religions.

Insight into religious traditions Each religion is interesting in its own right, as a complex system of values, relationships, personalities, and human creativity.

Insight into what religions share The study of religions requires sympathy and objectivity. While it is true that being a believer of a particular religion brings a special insight that an outsider cannot have, it is also true that an outsider can appreciate things that are not always obvious to the insider. This is particularly true of shared patterns of imagery, belief, and practice.

Insight into people Understanding a person's religious background tells us more about that person's attitudes and values. Such understanding is valuable for successful human relations—in both public life and private life.

Tolerance Because human beings are emotional creatures, their religions can sometimes allow inflamed feelings to override common decency. As history shows, religious communities have occasionally relied on censorship and authoritarianism to impose their will. Examining the major religions of the world helps us develop objectivity and tolerance toward people of varying religious traditions.

Appreciation of differences In a multicultural world, tolerance of differences is valuable, but enjoyment of differences is even better. Variety is a fact of nature, and the person who can enjoy variety—in religion and elsewhere—is a person who will never be tired of life.

Insight into everyday life Religious influences can be found everywhere in modern culture, not just within religious buildings. Politicians make use of religious images, for example, when they speak of a "new covenant" with voters. Specific religions and religious denominations take public positions on moral issues, such as abortion and war. Our weekly routines are regulated by the originally Jewish practice of a six-day work week followed by a day of rest, and the European-American school calendar is divided in two by the originally Christian Christmas holidays. Even comic strips use religious imagery: animals crowded onto a wooden boat, a man holding two tablets, angels on clouds, a person

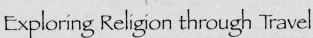

Exploring Religion through Travel

Travel, which at one time was affordable for only the very rich, is now an option for a broad spectrum of the population—and something wonderful for people interested in religion. Studying religions from books is somewhat limited, as compared to a first-hand experience of the great religious art, architecture, music, and ceremony to be found across the globe. It is especially wonderful to visit other countries during their major religious festivals, such as Easter in Italy or the Buddha's birthday in Korea. The difference between studying books about religion and actually experiencing the living expressions of religion throughout the world can be likened to the transforming experience in the film *The Wizard of Oz:* when the main character Dorothy (Greek: "gift of God") begins her mythic journey, accompanied only by her dog Toto (Latin: "whole"), her black-and-white world suddenly turns to color. (This book encourages such firsthand experience; sections titled "Religion beyond the Classroom" that appear at the end of each chapter will offer suggestions for specific places to visit.)

There are innumerable programs designed specifically for young travelers. Many colleges offer study-abroad programs, including summer courses that incorporate travel, as well as semester and year-long study programs abroad. Scholarships and other financial aid may be available for these programs. Large travel companies also offer summer tours for students, particularly to Europe and Asia; these companies are able to offer affordable tours by scheduling charter flights and inexpensive hotel accommodations. Programs such as these often make an excellent first trip abroad for students. Young travelers touring on their own can also join the Youth Hostel Association of their country and make use of a worldwide network of inexpensive youth hostels, which is quite extensive in Europe but also exists in

the United States and many other countries around the world.

Senior citizens (people 55 years and above) can take advantage of Elderhostel programs. Elderhostel offers a wide variety of activities—educational courses, excursions, and service projects—all around the world, usually lasting from one to several weeks.

Travelers who have limited time should look into travel packages that include the costs of airfare, hotel, and car or tour bus. Many countries also sell railroad passes. The Eurailpass and Britrail Pass are the best known and can be purchased through any travel agent. Retirees, often with more time and open schedules, might consider cruises that include sightseeing opportunities on land. Moreover, there are agencies and clubs through which home owners can exchange the use of their house or apartment with people from another region or country.

Information on travel, youth hostels, and home exchanges can be found in the travel sections of libraries and bookstores. There are also many fine guidebooks for travelers, some for the general traveler and others for quite specialized audiences. Good guidebooks should be read in preparation for travel, and at least one should be carried along on the trip. Intellectual preparation and practical planning before travel make the journey an even richer experience. Recommended guidebooks for students are the *Lonely Planet* series and the *Let's Go* series from the Harvard Student Agencies. Specialized travel books relating to religion are also available, such as guides to English cathedrals, Japanese temples, and pilgrimage sites around the world. The Internet is a good source of travel information, including the dates of religious festivals in other countries. And, of course, travel agents can help in planning and making reservations.

meditating on a mountaintop. The value of the study of religions is that it helps us recognize and appreciate the religious influences that are everywhere.

Appreciation for the arts Anyone attracted to painting, sculpture, music, or architecture will be drawn to the study of religions, because various religious traditions have possibly been the most significant patron of these arts. The study of religions is a gateway to these forms of art and many others.

Enjoyment of travel One of the great pleasures of our age is travel. Climbing up the temple of Angkor Wat in Cambodia or a Mayan pyramid in Mexico is quite different from just reading about them. The study of world religions gives travelers the background necessary to fully enjoy the many wonderful places they can now experience directly.

Insight into family traditions Religions have influenced most earlier cultures so strongly that their effects are readily identifiable in the values of our parents and grandparents—even if they are not actively religious individuals. These values include attitudes toward education, individual rights, gender roles, sex, time, money, food, and leisure.

Help in one's own religious quest Not everyone is destined to become an artist or a musician or a poet, yet each one of us has some ability to appreciate visual arts, music, and poetry. In the same way, although some people may not be explicitly religious, they may have a sense of the sacred and a desire to seek ways to feel at home in the universe. Those who belong to a religion will have their beliefs and practices enriched by the study of the world's religions, because they will learn about their religion's history, major figures, scriptures, and influences from different points of view. Others may have little interest in traditional religions yet nonetheless insist that they have a strong interest in spirituality and may describe their lives as a spiritual quest. For any person involved in a spiritual search, it is extremely helpful to study a variety of religions. Stories of others' spiritual quests provide insights that we may draw on for our own spiritual journey.

THE PILGRIMAGE

With open minds, eager for the many benefits of studying religions, we now begin an intellectual pilgrimage to many of the world's important living religions. We will first look at a sample of religions often associated with native peoples across the globe. We will then go on to study religions that emerged on the Indian subcontinent and then to the religions that arose in China and Japan. Next we will travel to the area east of the Mediterranean Sea—a generally arid region that nonetheless has been a fertile ground for new religious ideas. Finally, we will encounter some of the newest religious movements and will consider the modern religious search.

Our journey, though academic and intellectual, may prompt strong emotions in some readers. For some it will be a prelude to an actual physical pilgrimage. For others it will be an intellectual pilgrimage that will provoke both doubt and insight.

We begin with the knowledge that at the end of every journey we are not quite the same as we were when we started. Ours is a journey of discovery, and through discovery, we hope to become more appreciative of the experience of being human in the universe.

The journey begins.

RELIGION BEYOND THE CLASSROOM

You can learn a great deal about religious practice and the artistic manifestations of religion without having to travel far from home. For example, you only have to look under "Churches" in the yellow pages of a telephone book to find listings that will probably extend for pages. In addition, Saturday newspapers often have religious news and announcements of upcoming events.

What were once considered "minority" religions are becoming widespread, and any city will have meeting places for a variety of religions. North America, in particular, has many Chinese and

Tibetan Buddhist temples, Catholic monasteries and retreat houses, Zen meditation centers, Muslim mosques, Greek and Russian Orthodox churches, Hindu temples, and Hindu or Buddhist vegetarian restaurants. Cities and counties with a diversity of ethnic minorities are particularly rich in religious places of worship and meditation. Call up and ask about making a visit. People in religious centers almost invariably welcome outsiders, and they will direct you to other people and places within their tradition. Find out when there are services, concerts, and meetings; and if you are seriously interested, ask to be put on their mailing list.

Although travel abroad requires more planning, effort, and money, it provides unforgettable experiences. It can be done more easily than most people think and at virtually any age. Most religions encourage travel for religious reasons—this is the meaning of a pilgrimage, an ancient custom that is still very much alive. The goal of a pilgrimage is not only to visit a particular place but to grow spiritually. Even if your reason for travel is not conventionally religious, the experience will surely result in personal growth.

FOR FULLER UNDERSTANDING

1. Explore the insights of Freud or Jung about religion, and use those insights to examine the religious tradition with which you are most familiar. How would Freud or Jung understand that religion?
2. Early in this chapter we examined some human needs that religion sometimes fulfills. Can you add any needs to that list?
3. Karl Marx argued that religions arise as an escape from poverty and social oppression. Consequently, he thought that when social problems were eliminated, religions would die away. What arguments and examples would you give for and against this position?
4. In this book we will focus on architecture and travel as two aspects of studying religions. Make a list of interesting religious buildings and travel destinations in your area.
5. Keep a notebook or journal of references to religion that you see in newspapers and on television. What patterns do you see? What issues recur?

RELATED READINGS

Campbell, Joseph, and Bill Moyers. *The Power of Myth.* New York: Doubleday, 1991. An investigation of myths, fairy tales, and religious symbols in readable style. See also Campbell's more difficult *The Hero with a Thousand Faces* (Princeton, NJ: Princeton University Press/Bollingen, 1968), which focuses on the journey of the mythic hero in several religions and cultures.

Ellwood, Robert S. *Introducing Religion.* 3d ed. Englewood Cliffs, NJ: Prentice-Hall, 1993. A good summary of the major elements of religion, such as personal growth, ritual, ethics, and art.

Gibson, Clare. *Goddess Symbols.* New York: Barnes & Noble, 1998. A popular, well-illustrated introduction to goddesses and female figures in religions of the past and present.

Housden, Roger. *Sacred Journeys in a Modern World.* New York: Simon & Schuster, 1998. Reflections on travel as a religious metaphor, with journal entries and fine photos of visits to sacred sites.

Kraemer, Ross Shepard. *Her Share of the Blessings.* New York: Oxford University Press, 1992. A scholarly focus on the little-known religious roles of women in religions of the Greco-Roman period.

Lyden, John, ed. *Enduring Issues in Religion.* Farmington Hills, MI: Greenhaven, 1995. Responses by representatives of major religions to the great religious questions, among which are these: "What is religion?" and "What is the sacred?"

Olsen, W. Scott, and Scott Cairns, eds. *The Sacred Place: Witnessing the Holy in the Physical World.* Salt Lake City: University of Utah Press, 1996. A sensitive collection of prose and poetry about discovering the sacred in nature, by writers such as Annie Dillard, Denise Levertov, Richard Wilbur, and John McPhee.

Pals, Daniel L. *Seven Theories of Religion*. New York: Oxford University Press, 1996. A very readable survey of major theories of the origin and purpose of religion, including theories of Freud, Marx, Eliade, and Evans-Pritchard, with good biographical sketches of the thinkers.

Panikkar, Raimundo. *The Intrareligious Dialogue*. Rev. ed. Mahwah, NJ: Paulist Press, 1999. Proposals for dialogue between religions, drafted by a Christian priest active in India; with many quotations from Christian, Hindu, and Buddhist scriptures.

Streng, Frederick J. *Understanding Religious Life*. 3d ed. Belmont, CA: Wadsworth, 1985. A discussion of the transforming power of religion in the lives of individuals and of society, ending with thoughts about how religions can be studied objectively.

KEY TERMS

agnosticism: Literally meaning "not know"; the position that holds that the existence of God cannot be proven.

animism: From the Latin *anima*, meaning "spirit," "soul," "life force"; a worldview common among oral religions (religions with no written scriptures) that sees all elements of nature as being filled with spirit or spirits.

atheism: Literally meaning "not God"; the position that holds that there is no God or gods.

dualism: The belief that reality is made of two different principles (spirit and matter); the belief in two gods (good and evil) in conflict.

immanent: Existing and operating within nature.

monotheism: The belief in one God.

nontheism: A position that is unconcerned with the supernatural, not asserting or denying the existence of any deity.

pantheism: The belief that everything in the universe is divine.

polytheism: The belief in many gods.

transcendent: Not limited by the physical world.

CHAPTER 2

Oral Religions

 FIRST ENCOUNTER

As it is for most visitors, your first stop in Hawai`i is crowded Waikiki, on the island of O`ahu.* After four days of swimming, sightseeing, and viewing the sunsets, you fly to Maui for a few days, and then on to the much less populated island of Hawai`i—called the Big Island by local residents. From the airport in Hilo, you begin to drive upcountry, toward the little town of Volcano. The area around Hilo, on the rainy side of the island, resembles the tropical paradise of fantasy: the leaves of the trees are bright lime-colored flames, and the yards of the houses are planted with vanda orchids and fragrant white-flowered plumeria trees.

As you drive inland and upward, lawns and homes yield to fields of beige grass and clusters of dark brown rock. Banyan trees give way to small silver-leaved `ohi`a lehua, as delicate as their red flowers. Now you are closer to the volcanoes that are still producing the island. The land here is raw

---

Note: The `okina (glottal stop mark) is used throughout this book in the spelling of certain Hawaiian words. It is indicated by a backward apostrophe.

and relatively new. You check into the old lava-rock hotel near the volcanic crater and look forward to settling in for the night. After supper you listen to ukulele music in front of the big fireplace in the lobby and watch a man and two women perform a slow hula for the guests.

The next morning, after a good sleep, you walk out to the rim of the crater. You are a bit startled by the steam rising through cracks and holes in the rock. You hike down a trail that leads to a bed of old lava, passing yellow ginger and tiny wild purple orchids on the way. The lava in the crater at this spot is dry; it crunches underfoot. Here and there you see stones wrapped in the broad leaves of the *ti* plant and wonder why they're there.

On the way back up the trail, you fall in step with a woman who explains that she was raised on the Big Island but now lives on another island. She is here just for a few days, to visit the volcano area and to see old friends. She tells you about Pele, the goddess of fire, whose place of veneration is the volcano.

"When I was young I learned that Pele came from the island of Kaua`i to Maui, where she lived in Haleakala Crater before she moved to this island. Nowadays, people here are mostly Buddhist or Christian, but they still respect Pele. I know a man who says Pele once appeared to him. He told me she had long hair and was surrounded by fire. Other people have seen her on the road. Pele gets a lot of offerings—mostly *ti* leaves and food. But when the lava is flowing toward Hilo, people also bring out pork and gin," the woman says with a little grin, "and my friends tell me that the offerings work."

The lava, she explains, is active now at the other end of a series of craters, closer to the ocean. She suggests that you drive to the lava flow before dark and adds, "Be sure to have good walking shoes, as well as a flashlight in case it gets dark before you go back to your car. Be sure not to take any lava rock away with you. They say it brings bad luck, you know."

In midafternoon, you drive down the curving black asphalt road, past old lava flows, to the highway near the ocean. You stop and park near the cars of other lava watchers, then begin hiking with a few people across the fresh lava, toward the ocean. About half a mile in, you encounter yellow caution strips and overhear an officer warning one man to stop. "Further on it's just too dangerous. It looks solid on top, but you can slip through the crust." You and the others crowd up next to the barriers and see steam rising on the right up ahead. Through the rising steam you glimpse a bright orange band of molten lava underneath the dry crust as it falls into the ocean.

Sunset comes quickly, and even more people arrive, some with blankets around their shoulders. As darkness falls, the flowing lava becomes more visible, and the steam takes on a reddish glow. "Look over there," someone says. In the distance a bright stream of orange lava slides down a hill, a slow-motion waterfall of fire. You watch at least an hour as the sky becomes completely dark. Now the only light comes from the flowing lava and a few flashlights. It is, you think, like being present at the time of creation: this land is being born.

The next morning in the lobby you see the Hawaiian woman again. "Well, did you see Pele last night?" she asks, smiling. You smile back. For the rest of your stay you wonder about Pele, about what else might remain of native Hawaiian religion. Isn't hula, you ask as you think back over what you've read, an expression of Hawaiian beliefs? Why do people make offerings of *ti* leaves? How much of the ancient religion lives on?

DISCOVERING ORAL RELIGIONS

All around the world, native peoples follow their spiritual traditions. Among the Ainu in far northern Japan, the Inuit (Eskimo) in Canada, the aboriginal peoples of Australia, the Maori of New Zealand, and the many indigenous peoples of Africa and the Americas, religious teachings have been passed on primarily by word of mouth rather than through written texts. In some areas, the ancient religious ways of traditional peoples may not be easily apparent, but certain characteristics may live on in local stories and customs.

There is as yet no agreement on how to speak of these ancient religious ways. Various terms include *traditional, aboriginal, indigenous, tribal, nonliterate, primal, native, oral,* and *basic.* Each term is inadequate. For example, although the word *native* is used frequently in the Americas, that term in Africa—with its memories of Offices of Native Affairs—can be offensive. The words *oral* and *nonliterate* describe correctly the fact that most indigenous religions were spread without written texts. But there have been exceptions: the Mayans and Aztecs, for example, had writing systems, and even many traditional religions without writing systems have had their sacred stories and beliefs written down by scholars at some point. The distinction between oral religions and others is also blurred by the fact that religions that have written texts are also, to a large degree, transmitted orally—for example, through preaching, teaching, and chanting. The term *traditional* would be suitable, except that all religions but the very newest have many traditional elements. Some terms, such as *primal* and *basic,* may be viewed as derogatory (like the older term "primitive religions"). The word *indigenous* has the advantage of being neutral in tone. (It means the same thing as *native,* except that it comes from Greek rather than Latin.) Unfortunately, it is a word that is not commonly found in regular spoken vocabulary, and one hesitates to use it if a more everyday word can be found. There is no easy solution. In this text, the word *oral* is used in the title of the chapter, in order to emphasize the importance of the non-written expressions of these religions, such as dance, costume, masks, and memorized chants. However, we will use several of these terms rather interchangeably throughout the text, always with the understanding that no term is perfect.

Oral religions are found in every climate, from the tropical rain forest to the arctic tundra, and some are far older than today's dominant religions. Because most of them developed in isolation from each other, there are major differences in their stories of creation and origin, in their beliefs about the afterlife, in their marriage and funeral customs, and so on. In fact, there is as much variation among oral religions as there is, for example, between

Buddhism and Christianity. In North America, for instance, there are several hundred Native American nations and more than fifty Native American language groups. The variety among oral religious traditions is stunning, and each religion deserves in-depth study. But because of the limitations of space, this book must focus on shared elements; regrettably, we can barely touch on the many differences.

(You can complement your study of basic patterns by making your own study of a native religion. One that is especially worthy of study is the religion practiced now, or in the past, by the indigenous peoples of the area in which you currently live. The Internet and library are good places to start your search. Look under general words and phrases such as "native religions," "tribal religions," and "indigenous religions." After investigating the native religion of your area, develop some questions you might ask of native residents, and perhaps look for an opportunity to actually have experience of a native religion near your home.)

Past Obstacles to the Appreciation of Oral Religions

Up until the early part of the twentieth century, scholars focused more on religions that had produced written texts than on those that expressed themselves through orally transmitted stories, histories, and rituals. This lack of attention may have been due in part to the fact that religions with written records are easier to study because they don't necessarily require travel or physically arduous research; moreover, when scholars master their particular languages, they can study, translate, and teach the original writings either at home or to students anywhere.

There has also been a bias toward text-based religions because of an assumption that they are complex and that oral religions are simple. Greater research into oral religions, however, has dispelled such notions of simplicity. Consider, for example, the sandpaintings of the Navajo people and the ceremonies of which the paintings are a part. "In these ceremonies, which are very complicated and intricate, sandpaintings are made and prayers recited. Sandpaintings are impermanent paintings made of dried pulverized materials that depict the Holy People [gods] and serve as a temporary altar. Over 800 forms of sandpaintings exist, each connected to a specific chant and ceremony."[1]

Indigenous religions have, of course, created much that is permanent, and sometimes even monumental. We have only to think of the Mayan pyramids in Yucatán and the great city of Teotihuacán, near Mexico City. But native religions often express themselves in ways that have less permanence: dance, masks, wood sculpture, paintings that utilize mineral and plant dyes, tattoo, body painting, and memorized story and chant. Perhaps we have to begin to see these transitory expressions of religious art as being equal in stature to more permanent sacred writings and artistic creations. Geoffrey Parrinder, for example, writes that "African art provides a kind of scripture of African religion." He calls African art the "indigenous language of African belief and thought."[2]

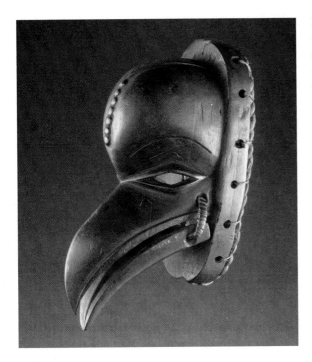

In Angola's Chokwe culture birds of prey are considered protective because of their keen vision. This Chokwe bird mask dates from the early twentieth century.

The Modern Recovery of Oral Religions

We know about native religious traditions through the efforts of scholars from a number of disciplines, particularly anthropology. One pioneer was Franz Boas (1858–1942), a professor at Columbia University and curator at the American Museum of Natural History in New York. Others of note who have contributed to this field have been Bronislaw Malinowski (1884–1942), Raymond Firth (1901–2002), Mary Douglas (b. 1921), and E. E. Evans-Pritchard, mentioned in chapter 1.

The ecological movement has also made our study of oral religions more pressing. Environmentalist David Suzuki argues that we must look to native peoples and religions for insightful lessons in the relationship between human beings and nature. In his introduction to the book *Wisdom of the Elders,* he writes that the earth is rapidly moving toward what he calls "ecocrisis." He quotes the ecologist Paul Ehrlich in saying that solutions will have to be "quasi-religious." Suzuki argues that "our problem is inherent in the way we perceive our relationship with the rest of Nature and our role in the grand scheme of things. Harvard biologist E. O. Wilson proposes that we foster *biophilia,* a love of life. He once told me, 'We must rediscover our *kin,* the other animals and plants with whom we share this planet.'"[3]

Some of this interest derives, of course, from a sometimes romanticized view of native peoples and their relationship with nature. We should recognize that some native peoples, such as the Kwakiutl (Kwakwaka`wakw) of the Pacific Northwest, have viewed nature as dangerously violent, and others have seriously damaged their natural environment. Despite such cases, one finds in many indigenous religions extraordinary sensitivity to the natural elements.

The development of recording technology (especially photography and sound recording) has helped the recovery of native religious traditions. Photography captures native styles of life and allows them to be seen with a certain immediacy. Ethnomusicology involves the recording of chants and the sounds of musical instruments that might otherwise be lost. Gladys Reichard, a specialist in Navajo ceremony, has written that chanters in the Navajo religion need to memorize an "incalculable" number—that is, thousands—of songs.[4] The fact that listeners can replay such recordings has no doubt added to the appreciation of this music.

> All our histories, traditions, codes were passed from one generation to another by word of mouth. Our memories must be kept clear and accurate, our observation must be keen, our self-control absolute.
>
> —Thomas Wildcat Alford, Shawnee[5]

Artists around the world have begun in the past century to find inspiration in native wood sculpture, masks, drums, and textile design. Pablo Picasso (1881–1973), for example, often spoke of the strong influence that African religious masks had on his work. By the early 1900s, West African masks had found their way to Paris and the artists there. A scholar describes the effect of one African work on several artists who were close friends. "One piece . . . is a mask that had been given to Maurice Vlaminck in 1905. He records that [André] Derain was 'speechless' and 'stunned' when he saw it, bought it from Vlaminck and in turn showed it to Picasso and Matisse, who were also greatly affected by it."[6] French artist Paul Gauguin moved to Tahiti and the Marquesas to find and paint what he hoped was a fundamental form of religion there, and some of his paintings allude to native Tahitian religious belief.[7] The work of such artists as Picasso and Gauguin helped to open eyes to the beauty produced by indigenous religions.

The religious art of native peoples of course needs no authentication from outsiders. And outsiders present a problem: they tend to treat native religious objects as purely secular works of art, while people within an oral religious tradition do not make such a distinction. Oral religions exist generally within **holistic** cultures, in which every object and act may have religious meaning. Art, music, religion, and social behavior within such cultures can be so inseparable that it is hard to say what is distinctly religious and what is not. Although we can find a similar attitude among very pious practitioners of the dominant world religions, for whom every act is religious, people in modern, industrial cultures commonly see the secular and religious realms as separate.

Fortunately, the bias that once judged native religions to be "primitive" manifestations of the religious spirit—as opposed to the literate, so-called higher religions—is disappearing. It is an inescapable fact that the span of written religions is relatively brief—barely five thousand years—yet scientists now hold that human beings have lived on earth for at least a million (and possibly two or three million) years. Although we do not know how long human beings have been manifesting religious behavior, we believe it goes back as long as human beings have been capable of abstract thought.

STUDYING ORAL RELIGIONS: LEARNING FROM PATTERNS

The study of oral religious traditions presents its own specific challenges. Our understanding of oral religions comes primarily from the various methods described in chapter 1, yet some of these approaches have proven less effective in the study of oral religions than they have in the examination of large-scale literate religions. Hence, we depend on more recent tools to learn about oral religions. Studies by anthropologists, sociologists, and cultural historians are presently changing the way we make sense of many of the phenomena associated with oral religions, and new studies will continue to reshape our understanding of these traditions over the next decades.

It would be ideal if we could study and experience each native religion separately; barring that, however, one workable approach is to consider them collectively as "sacred paths" that share common elements. Thus, in this chapter we will concentrate on finding patterns in native religions—while keeping in mind that beyond the patterns there is enormous variety. The patterns we identify in oral religions will also enrich our encounter with other religions in later chapters. Three key patterns we will consider are the human relationship with nature, the framing of sacred time and space, and the respect for origins, gods, and ancestors.

Human Relationships with the Natural World

Most oral religions have sprung from tribal and small-scale cultures where survival requires a cautious and respectful relationship with nature. In the worldview of oral religions, human beings are very much a part of nature. People look to nature itself (sometimes interpreted through traditional lore) for guidance and meaning.

Some native religions see everything in the universe as being alive, a concept known as *animism* (which we discussed briefly in chapter 1). The life force (Latin: *anima*) is present in everything and is especially apparent in living things—trees, plants, birds, animals, and human beings—and in the motion of water, the sun, the moon, clouds, and wind. But life force can also be present in apparently static mountains, rocks, and soil. Other native religions, while more theistic, see powerful spirits in nature, which temporarily inhabit natural objects and manifest themselves there.

In an animistic worldview, everything can be seen as part of the same reality. There may be no clear boundaries between the natural and supernatural and between the human and nonhuman. Everything has both its visible ordinary reality and a deeper, invisible sacred reality. Four Oglala Sioux shamans, when asked about what was *wakan* (holy, mysterious), said, "Every object in the world has a spirit and that spirit is *wakan*. Thus the spirit[s] of the tree or things of that kind, while not like the spirit of man, are also *wakan*."[8] To say that nature is full of spirits can be a way of affirming the presence of both a universal life force and an essential, underlying sacredness.

Among many peoples, certain objects in particular—a specific rock, tree, or river—are thought of as being animated by an individual spirit that lives within. And in some native traditions, we find deities that care about and influence a whole category of reality, such as the earth, water, or air. Among the Yoruba of Africa, storms are the work of the deity Shangó, a legendary king with great powers who climbed to heaven (see chapter 11). The Igbo (Ibo) pray to Ala, an earth-mother deity, for fertility of the earth. Women also pray to her for children, and men pray to her to increase their crops. In the Ashanti religion, Ta Yao is the god of metal. The work of blacksmiths and mechanics is under his charge.[9]

In a world that is animated by spirits, human beings must treat all things with care. If a spirit is injured or insulted, it can retaliate. Human beings must therefore show that they respect nature, especially the animals and plants they kill to eat. Human beings must understand the existence and ways of the spirit world so that they can avoid harm and incur blessings. (We will revisit this spirit world later, when we discuss trance states and the spiritual specialist, the shaman.)

Native American religions are noted for their reverential attitude toward the natural world; human beings and animals are often pictured as coming into existence together, and the sun, moon, trees, and animals are all considered kin. Hehaka Sapa, or Black Elk, an Oglala Sioux, although he had become a Christian, explained the sense of relationship to nature that he had experienced when he was growing up among his people in South Dakota. In his autobiography, which he dictated in 1930, he points out that his community, which traditionally lived in *tipis* (circular tents made of animal skins and poles), arranges itself in a circle—as does all nature, which is constantly making circles, just like the sun, the moon, and the whirlwind.

Native American religions often express the kinship bond between human beings and animals in ritual. (To a lesser extent, some other religions do this, as well). Åke Hultkrantz, a Swedish scholar, clarifies with an example the meaning of many dances that imitate animals. "Plains Indian dances in which men imitate the movements of buffaloes . . . are not, as earlier research took for granted, magic rituals to multiply the animals. They are rather acts of supplication in which Indians, by imitating the wild, express their desires and expectations. Such a ritual tells us the Indian's veneration for the active powers of the universe: it is a prayer."[10]

> Birds make their nests in circles, for theirs is the same religion as ours.
>
> —Black Elk, Oglala Sioux[11]

For many Native Americans there is no strong distinction between the human and animal worlds, but rather a sense of kinship. To exploit nature mindlessly is as sacrilegious as harming one's own mother. As Smohalla of the Nez Perce people said, "You ask me to plow the ground. Shall I take a knife and tear my mother's breast? Then when I die she will not take me to her bosom to rest."[12]

Native religions also frequently embrace an ethic of restraint and of conservation concerning nature's resources. One is expected to take only what one needs and to use all the parts of an animal or plant. In traditional Hawai`i, for example, fishing in certain areas would be temporarily forbidden (*kapu*, or taboo) in order to allow the fish population to be replenished.

Of course, the ideal was not universally maintained, and even native peoples have sometimes been unaware of the destructive effects of their actions. We think, for example, of how the native people of Easter Island virtually deforested their entire island. Given an example like this, it is clear that native peoples who did not live in harmony with nature could not long survive.

It is difficult, perhaps, for urban human beings today to experience fully the intimate connection with the rest of nature that has been a common aspect of oral religions. The predominant contemporary view sees human beings as fundamentally different from other animals. Perhaps this tendency is a result of our modern culture, which emphasizes the skills of writing and reading. We also have little connection with the origins of our food, and we live and work indoors. Electric light diminishes our awareness of day and night and obstructs the light of the moon and stars. Except for insects, rodents, and the most common birds, we seldom see wildlife firsthand. Traffic noise drowns out the sounds of wind, rain, and birdsong.

In contrast, consider the sense of kinship with animals found, for example, among the Haida people of the Pacific Northwest: "the Haida refer to whales and ravens as their 'brothers' and 'sisters' and to fish and trees as the finned and tree *people.*"[13]

Another example of contrast is apparent in the way the BaMbuti, forest dwellers of central Africa, perceive their forest. Outsiders might find the darkness and thick foliage frightening. But, as Colin Turnbull has written, for the people who live within it and love it, the forest "is their world. . . . They know how to distinguish the innocent-looking *itaba* vine from the many others it resembles so closely, and they know how to follow it until it leads them to a cache of nutritious, sweet-tasting roots. They know the tiny sounds that tell where the bees have hidden their honey; they recognize the kind of weather that brings a multitude of different kinds of mushrooms springing to the surface. . . . They know the secret language that is denied all outsiders and without which life in the forest is an impossibility."[14]

Sacred Time and Sacred Space

Our everyday lives go on in ordinary time, which we see as moving forward into the future. Sacred time, however, is "the time of eternity." Among the Koyukon people of the Arctic it is called "distant time," and it is the holy ancient past in which the gods lived and worked.[15] Among Australian aborigines it is often called the "dream time," and it is the subject of much of their highly esteemed art.

Sacred time is cyclical, returning to its origins for renewal. By recalling and ritually reliving the deeds of the gods and ancestors (as Christians do through the yearly celebration of Christmas and Easter), we enter into the sacred time in which they live. Oral religions even tend to structure daily lives in ways that make them conform to mythic events in sacred time; this creates a sense of holiness in everyday life.

Like ordinary time, ordinary space exists in the everyday. Sacred space, however, is the doorway through which the "other world" of gods and

Art of the aboriginal Australians typically portrays mystical beings and the distant past. This painting portrays Wallunqua, a mystical serpent.

ancestors can contact us and we can contact them. Sacred space is associated with the center of the entire universe, where power and holiness are strongest and where we can go to renew our own strength.

In native religions, sacred space may encompass a great mountain, a volcano, a valley, a lake, a forest, a single large tree, or some other striking natural site. For Black Elk and his people, after the Lakota had moved west, it was Harney Peak in South Dakota. In Australian aboriginal religion, Uluru (Ayers Rock) has served as this sacred center. In Africa, Mount Kilimanjaro and other high mountains have been considered sacred spaces.

Sacred space can also be constructed, often in a symbolic shape such as a circle or square, and defined by a special building or by a boundary made of rope or of rocks, such as Stonehenge in England. It can even be an open area among trees or buildings, such as the great open space between the temples of Teotihuacán, near Mexico City.

Respect for Origins, Gods, and Ancestors

Origins   Most oral religions have cosmic tales of their origins that are regularly recited or enacted through ritual and dance. Some tell how the world originated from a supernatural realm. According to other emergence stories, the earth rose out of previous earths or from earlier, more chaotic material forms. Often the land and creatures emerged from watery depths. In a Hopi creation story the earth, before it took shape, was mist.

Stories of the origin of a tribe may be connected with its story of the earth's creation. Among the Acoma Pueblo there is a story of two sisters who lived entirely underground. Eventually they climbed up the roots of a tree and into the sunlight through a hole in the ground, to become the first human beings on earth. One became mother of the Pueblo.[16]

Gods   Native religions frequently speak of a High God who is superior to all other deities and is considered to be wise, ancient, and benevolent. The Inuit speak of a Great Spirit living in the sky who is female and to whom all human spirits eventually return. In a few African religions, too, the High God is female, neuter, or androgynous; and in some religions there are two complementary High Gods, characterized as male/female, brother/sister, or bad/good. The BaKuta of central Africa speak of the twins Nzambi-above and Nzambi-below, although in their myths the lower twin disappears and Nzambi-above becomes the High God.[17]

In some African religions, stories of the High God, who is almost always the creator of the world, offer some explanation for the ills of the world or the distance between human beings and the divine. Many African religions tell how the High God created the world and then left it—sometimes out of dismay at human beings or simply for lack of interest. "Many people of central and southern Africa say that God (Mulungu) lived on earth at first, but men began to kill his servants and set fire to the bush, and so God retired to heaven on one of those giant spiders' webs that seem to hang from the sky in morning mists. In Burundi, however, it is said that having made good children God created a cripple, and its parents were so angry that they tried to kill God and he went away."[18]

Although oral religions often revere a High God, altars and imagery dedicated to a High God are not common. Instead, native religions tend to focus on lesser deities, especially those associated with forces of nature, in their prayer, ritual, and art.

In a few cultures, such as in Mexico and western Africa, large temples have been built, temple rituals have been held, and priesthoods have been created to carry out religious ceremonies, but such developments are relatively rare. More commonly, ceremonies in oral religions are performed at small shrines, either in the home or outdoors—at a river bank, a large tree, or a rock formation.

The large and mysterious stone carvings on Easter Island are thought to be ancestral images.

Religion of the Pueblo Peoples

One of the great sights of the world is the group of multistoried buildings hidden high up in the cliffs at Mesa Verde, Colorado. Inhabited for more than 700 years, the now-empty buildings give an unparalleled view into the life of the Ancestral Pueblo peoples (also called Hisatsinom and Anasazi). Visitors can walk down from the top of the cliff, via narrow stone paths and stairs, to visit some of the houses and to experience the plazas that were once used for ceremonial dance. Visitors can then climb down a wooden ladder to enter a *kiva,* a dark and womb-like ritual chamber beneath the surface. There they can see the *sipapu,* the hole in the floor that is a symbol of the emergence of human beings into this world. The kiva and sipapu show how thoroughly oriented to the earth was the religion that was practiced here.

The cliff dwellings at Mesa Verde are only one site in what was—and still is—a wide-ranging culture. The territory of this culture includes large parts of what are now Arizona, New Mexico, Utah, and Colorado. Similar cliff dwellings may be seen at the Canyon de Chelly in Arizona and at Bandelier National Monument in New Mexico. In New Mexico one may also visit the great spiritual center of Chaco Canyon, once a flourishing city. Tens of thousands of pilgrims would come here regularly, and as many as forty thousand would be present at the time of the twice-yearly solstices. This site is sacred to the Pueblo peoples even today.

The builders of these cliff dwellings and cities moved away in the late thirteenth century, most probably because of a prolonged drought. But they traveled east, west, and south to create and join other communities, many of which continue to exist. Although the people who once lived at Mesa Verde and Chaco Canyon are gone, their descendants—the Pueblo peoples—continue to thrive. They still inhabit multistoried homes, still use the kiva for their ceremonial religion, and still dance the dances of their ancestors. Their earth-based religion—despite centuries of opposition—is very much alive.

The development of the Pueblo peoples can be studied in four phases: the long period before European contact; the early colonial period, which was extremely repressive; the later colonial period, marked by resurgence, conflict, and syncretism; and the modern period, characterized by revitalization of the traditional religion.

During the earliest period, which lasted for several thousand years, the people at first survived by hunting and gathering. They gradually developed agriculture, and after about 300 C.E. the cultivation of squash, maize, and beans made a settled culture possible. At this time the Ancestral Pueblo people began to create villages and to build multistoried buildings of earth and stone, some with hundreds of rooms. Arts also developed, particularly pottery, weaving, and painting. The religious life of the Ancestral Pueblo peoples is not fully known, but some evidence comes from traces of ancient roads and from archeology, petroglyphs, and paintings. Some of their buildings were oriented to coincide with the solstices and equinoxes. The presence of kivas suggests that ceremony took place there, and in some of the kivas the remains of wall paintings have been found. Remaining petroglyphs show elements from nature, including stars and moon, and in the period from about 1200–1250 C.E. there was a profuse growth of the cult and imagery of *kachinas*—benevolent guardian spirits who are believed to appear among the people on ceremonial occasions (and who will be discussed in a moment).

When the large settlements, such as the one at Mesa Verde, were abandoned, their people moved to villages—primarily in modern-day northeastern Arizona and northwestern New Mexico—but they took with them their religious beliefs, images, and ritual, especially the cult of the kachinas. The traditional style of multistoried buildings continued, as well, suggesting to the Spanish colonizers the name by which the peoples are still commonly known: *pueblo* in Spanish means "village." (The Pueblo peoples who live in New Mexico are sometimes called the Eastern Pueblos; those in Arizona are called the Western Pueblos.)

Despite the fact that many villages were built high atop mesas and in other isolated locations, the next periods were marked by conflict with outsiders. Conflicts initially arose when Spanish soldiers and missionaries began to arrive from Mexico in 1529. Taking control of the area and calling it Nueva España (New Spain), the Spanish attempted to force the native peoples to swear loyalty to Spain and to accept Christianity. This was a period of rigid subjugation, as the Spanish tried to destroy the traditional religion.

This Corn Dance is part of celebrations at Santa Clara Pueblo in New Mexico.

The traditional religion, however, did not die out, but continued "underground"—both literally and figuratively. It reasserted itself strongly 150 years after the first contact. A revolt, largely for the sake of religious freedom, began in 1680, led by a native religious leader named Popay (Popé). More than twenty Franciscan friars were killed, churches were destroyed, and the Spanish governor fled to El Paso. Spain reestablished control in 1692, but now it was, wisely, less insistent on conversion, and Pueblo peoples were allowed to continue their traditional religious practices. Both indigenous and Christian religious practices continued side by side, sometimes blending. (One example of this mixture can be seen in the fact that indigenous religious dance and ritual often occur on the feast day of a pueblo's Christian patron saint.)

Conflict arose again when American settlers and government officials took control of the region in 1848, after Mexico had ceded the land to the United States. Government policies generally attempted to destroy Native American religions and to force Native American cultures into assimilation.

A new era began in 1934 (under John Collier, sympathetic head of the Bureau of Indian Affairs), and then developed further as Native Americans began to gain political autonomy in the 1960s. A major advance was the government's return, in 1970, of Blue Lake, a site sacred to the Pueblos, along with 48,000 acres of land, including the sacred mountain of Taos. It was the first example of the return of native land for religious reasons.

Many mountains, lakes, and rivers in the region are sacred to the Pueblo peoples. Kachinas are believed to live there, and the souls of the dead are sometimes believed to travel there. Rio Grande Pueblos, for example, see a sacred pattern in their mountains: Taos is in the north, Truchas in the east, Sandia in the south, and Jemez in the west; and at the center, at San Ildefonso, is Black Mesa. The Taos Pueblos believe that Blue Lake is the home of their ancestors, and it is a place of pilgrimage.

The Pueblo villages in New Mexico are located in a long band that stretches northward from the Albuquerque region to Taos. Of the many pueblos, the Laguna, Isleta, and Acoma are farthest south; the Santo Domingo, San Ildefonso, and Tesuque pueblos are in the middle (close to Santa Fe); and the Picurís and Taos pueblos are farthest north. Two Zuñi territories are to the west, one on each side of the border between New Mexico and Arizona. The Hopis live even farther west, in villages on three high mesas in Arizona (northeast of Flagstaff). (Visitors are allowed in most villages, although they are asked to be sensitive about the inhabitants' privacy—a growing concern. Some religious ceremonies are open to the public, but photography and note-taking are generally not allowed, in order to ensure respect.)

The Pueblo peoples share many features of their architecture, governance, and religious practice, but there are also great differences among them in all these areas. Each of the more than two dozen pueblos governs itself independently, and there are multiple languages spoken: Keresan, Zunian, three Tanoan dialects (Tiwa, Tewa, Towa), and Hopi. The independence of each pueblo may have actually been to its advantage, helping each unique culture to survive. Despite the pressures to change, the Pueblo peoples have kept their identities intact—particularly through fidelity to their religious beliefs and practices.

Each pueblo has its own religious traditions. Here we will touch on just a few. The stories of human origins differ among the peoples and clans, but many tell of human emergence from a lower world, of assistance from supernatural beings in learning to live, of help from animals, and of wanderings before final settlement. Among the seven Keresan-speaking pueblos, for example, the story of origins tells of how people moved upward through four different-colored worlds. Standing in an eagle's nest on top of a tree, with the help of a woodpecker and a badger, they made a hole large enough to climb up into this world.

Religious traditions are passed on through initiation ceremonies, male and female secret societies, and special rites conducted by priests. We get a sense of the complexity possible simply by considering the religious societies of the Zuñis. The Zuñis have six religious societies (dedicated to the sun, rainmakers, animal deities, war gods, guardian spirits, and priests of the guardian spirits); and each society has its own calendar, ceremonies, and ritual objects. Religious symbolism is equally complex. Among the Zia, for example, four is a sacred number. It symbolizes the four seasons, four directions, and four stages of life (infancy, youth, adulthood, old age). It is used in many designs found in Zia art. (The state flag of New Mexico, which shows a cross-like symbol made of four lines in each of the four directions, is based on a Zia design).

Some of the Pueblo peoples, influenced by Christianity, are monotheists; but many retain belief in the traditional deities, and they sense no disharmony. The Great Spirit, they believe, can take many forms. Among the Hopis, for example, more than thirty gods are recognized. Perhaps the most important are Tawa, the sun god, prayed to each morning; Mu-yao, the

Ancestors Many indigenous religions make little distinction between a god and an ancestor. Both are important, because living people must work with both for success in life. Spirits of ancestors must be treated well out of love for them, but also out of respect for their power. Some native religions, such as the Navajo, have not wished closeness with the spirits of the dead, fearing them. But more commonly the dead are venerated. In African religions ancestor spirits are commonly thought to bring health, wealth, and children if they are pleased, and disease and childlessness if moon god, imagined as an old man; Sotuqnangu, god of the sky, who sends clouds and lightning; and Kokyang Wuuti, called Spider Woman in English, who is thought of as a loving grandmother.

Among all the Pueblo peoples there is a belief in guardian spirits, who play a role something like angels and patron saints. These are the kachinas. They are not gods, but are the spirits of ancestors, birds, animals, plants, and other beings. They are believed to have once lived among the people, then to have retreated to their own world; but they return yearly. They are represented by human beings when the human beings are dressed in specific masks and costumes.

One of the most complex systems of belief in guardian spirits is found among the Hopis, where traditional religion has been least affected by other cultures. From February through the summer, dancers represent the spirits, and more than two hundred different masked figures appear in the dances. In the Hopi language they are called *katsinam* (singular: *katsina*). Bird and animal spirits are based on many birds and animals, including the deer, badger, sheep, cow, horse, hummingbird, and eagle; and nature spirits express the rain cloud, rainbow, moon, and fertile earth. Some figures show human characteristics, such as warriors, corn-grinding maidens, guards, clowns, and children. There is also a wide variety of ogre-like figures. Each has a name, special costume, and specific mask. The Zuñi recognize similar guardian spirits, whom they called *koko*.

The Hopi and the Zuñi are also well known for their painted representations of these spirits, called *tithu*. (Outsiders know the figurines as "kachina dolls.") They are re-creations in miniature of the masked kachina figures that dance in the villages. The tithu were originally created to be given as gifts from the masked dancers to girls in the villages—a form of religious teaching through images. But they have become collector's items, cherished by outsiders. Those that are old and authentic have a simple beauty that comes from natural colors, made from plants and crushed rock. Newer tithu, often made for the tourist trade, use bright colors made from acrylic and synthetic dyes, and they have costumes and painting sometimes done in elaborate detail.

Dances are an especially significant part of the life of all the pueblos. They retell the stories of creation, emergence, and migration, and they are performed throughout the year under the sponsorship of the religious societies. Dances also include practical purposes—to ensure rainfall, fertility of the earth, and good harvest, or to achieve a bountiful hunt and protection from danger. We get an idea of their purposes from some of their names, such as Corn Dance, Snake Dance, and Elk Dance.

Because of their association with agriculture and hunting, many dances occur from the beginning of spring through harvest time. The major dances of the Zuñi, however, come in midwinter. It is believed that the gods and the spirits of the dead return to earth at that time and eat with the people. Eight special houses are prepared to receive the special messengers of the rain gods, who are called *shalakos*. The figures are ten feet high and bear their masks on poles. They look like giant birds. The dances include visits by the shalakos to the houses, chants that retell the mythic stories, rituals of blessing, and races. Visitors who have the privilege of observing these and other Pueblo ceremonies come away with a renewed appreciation for the variety of religious paths and a sense of amazement at the persistence through the centuries of such beautiful, ancient ways.

they are not. The way to appease angry ancestors is through ritual, sometimes including sacrifice. The ancestors often are thought to live in an afterlife that is a state of existence much like earthly life. Belief in reincarnation is found sometimes, as in native Tahitian religion and in many African religions, from the Diola of Senegal to the BaKongo of the Congo region. In traditional Hawaiian religion, it was believed that the spirits of the dead went to an underworld, while the spirits of cultural heroes ascended into the sky.

Some indigenous peoples of western Canada erect a totem pole to honor an ancestor. Images on the totem pole are related to the ancestor's life story.

SACRED PRACTICES IN ORAL RELIGIONS

Read myths. They teach you that you can turn inward, and you begin to get the message of the symbols. Read other people's myths, not those of your own religion, because you tend to interpret your own religion in terms of facts—but if you read the other ones, you begin to get the message.

—Joseph Campbell[19]

In oral societies, everyday religious activity and practice are significant because their primary purpose is often to place individuals, families, and groups in "right relationships" with gods, ancestors, other human beings, and nature. Rituals are the basic way in which human beings ensure they are living in harmony with each other and with nature. Rituals are frequently devoted to major aspects of human life: key events in the life cycle, rules concerning certain kinds of behavior, sacrifice, and access to the spirit world. In addition, artifacts such as masks and statues are an essential part of specific rituals.

Life-Cycle Ceremonies

In oral societies, the human journey through life is aided and marked by rites of passage. In addition to being important to the individual, these rites also help hold the society together by renewing bonds and admitting new members to the community.

Rites of passage mark an important life event, such as the birth of a child. In some native religions, a woman about to give birth goes off by herself to bear her child at a sacred site or in a house built for that purpose. Birth is considered a powerful time for the mother and child, and the blood associated with it is believed to have dangerous power.

After the birth, the newborn is often celebrated with a public event that may occur immediately or anytime from a week to a year after the actual birth. In some parts of Africa, babies do not become members of the community until they receive their names in a special public ceremony that is accompanied by song, dance, and a meal. A name is chosen carefully because of the influence it is thought to have on the child's future.

Special rituals also mark a person's entry into adulthood. They may include a period of instruction in sex, adult responsibilities, and tribal history and belief. They often involve an initiation ritual that may be experienced in seclusion or in the company of other initiates. Rites can include a symbolic death—painful and frightening—meant to turn a boy into a man. Across Africa, circumcision for boys in their early teens is a common rite for entering adulthood.

In western Africa, initiation societies oversee coming-of-age rituals. "The Poro [a secret initiation society] is for boys, controlled by a hierarchy of elders, different in each village, which meets in a sacred grove where the clan founder was buried. The purpose of the initiation is the rebirth of the youths, who are said to be swallowed by the Poro spirit at the beginning and returned to their parents as reborn at the end of the initiation."[20] A parallel initiation society exists for girls, who receive sexual instruction and training in the skills necessary for marriage.

A girl's first menstrual period may also be marked publicly. For example, among the Apache, a four-day ceremony marks a girl's *menarche* (first menstruation). During the ceremony, which is elaborate, the girl performs a dance, receives a massage from her female sponsor, kneels to receive the rays of the sun, and circles repeatedly around a ceremonial cane.

In Native American religions, a common ritual of early maturity is the "vision quest," or "dream quest," which may involve prolonged fasting and some kind of preliminary cleansing, such as washing or undergoing a sweat bath. Details of the construction of the sweat lodge and the attendant ritual can include cutting willow branches, during which tobacco might be offered; gathering sticks, rocks, moss, and sweet grass; making an altar and heating a stone; rubbing smoke over the body; marking the ground; and saying appropriate prayers at each stage.

For years before the vision quest the young person may receive training to prepare for the experience. Commonly, a tribal religious specialist will create a sacred space by ritually marking the four directions of the compass and the center. The sacred space, set apart from the community, should be a place of natural beauty.

The seeker remains in the sacred space until a vision, or dream, comes. Although the vision quest is often a part of the coming-of-age ceremonies for males, among some peoples it is also employed for females. The vision

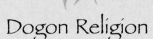

Dogon Religion

As many as 300,000 Dogon people live in Mali and Burkina Faso, in western Africa. Their approximately seven hundred villages stretch about 125 miles along the Bandiagara Cliffs, about 200 miles south of Tomboctou (Timbuktu). The Dogon people moved to this mountainous area after 1400 C.E. They wanted to avoid pressure to convert to Islam and being taken away in slavery by the empire of Mali. Their villages, created for safety, are frequently built into the rocks.

The origins of the Dogon are uncertain, but their traditions speak of several migrations, apparently from the east. For at least the past five hundred years they have been settled permanently where they live today. Their region was once inhabited by another people, the Tellem; but these people disappeared for unknown reasons, leaving behind villages and artifacts. (The Tellem people are associated with the modern-day Kouroumba, who live in southern Burkina Faso and northern Togo.) Tellem culture, nonetheless, may have influenced the Dogon. Today the Dogon live by agriculture, carefully growing squash, millet, papaya, eggplant, and onions in a very dry region.

The details of the Dogon stories of creation and human origin are not entirely clear, but they tell of Amma, an original deity, who created serpent-like creatures called Nommo, who are associated with water and fertility. The stories go on to tell of the creation of eight additional fishlike Nommo. These eight Nommo were the ancestors of the Dogon and taught them the arts of civilization. The fishlike characteristics of the eight ancestral Nommo are thought by some to indicate that the Dogon came from the region of the Niger River.

Traditional Dogon religion (*Omolobulo*) focuses less on cosmology than on practice. Dogon religious practice is especially concerned with bringing rain and fertility, securing reverence for ancestors, and assisting the dead to reach the world of the spirits.

There are three religious associations devoted to the three purposes just mentioned—the Lebe, Binu, and Awa societies. Lebe is the god of the earth and fertility, and each village has a shrine dedicated to him. The shrine priest (*hogon*) and the members of the Lebe society work to maintain the purity of the earth and hope to encourage its fruitfulness. The Binu society establishes contact with totemic ancestors who are enshrined in Binu temples; it invokes their help at planting time and in other cases of special need. The Awa society, which plays an important role in male initiation, is responsible for funeral ceremonies. Constituted by men who have been initiated through circumcision, the Awa society performs funeral ceremonies (*bago bundo*), and is also responsible for the performance of later memorial services (*dama*).

The most spectacular and best-known rites are those performed for the dead. The ceremony that is held for a recently deceased person is not exactly a funeral, because it may occur some time after the death. Its purpose is to assist the spirit to move from the world of the living to the world of the dead. The multi-day ceremony includes complex dances, with masked dancers. They are clothed with white shells strung across their chests, and skirts of black and red. Their masks are extraordinary. Many of them are surmounted by an abstract human design that looks like a petroglyph figure. The most unusual mask (*sirige* mask) is made from a single wooden pole whose height is nearly 20 feet (6 meters). The dancer keeps it on and upright by holding its strap in his teeth. Other dancers, representing waterbirds, dance on stilts. Later, another dance ceremony ends the period of mourning, and the bones of the deceased are placed in caves in the cliffs. Every sixty years a ceremony (called *sigui*) is performed to pass on the power of deceased initiates to young initiates.

Dogon wood sculpture is also highly valued. Wooden figures with arms extended straight up are particularly memorable: they represent the divine first Nommo created by Amma, and they are associated with rain. Other figural sculptures of the Dogon people represent deceased family members and distant ancestors.

Dogon architecture is equally memorable because of its blend of simplicity and power. Temples are made of dried mud with multiple windows, openings, and spires that sometimes are crowned with ostrich eggs, symbols of fertility. Grain is stored in circular buildings that have tall conical roofs; the

Dogon memorial rituals are intended to help spirits move from this world to the world of the dead. Here, a group of masked Dogon performs a funeral dance.

wooden doors of the buildings are decorated with carved patterns derived from religious tales. Men's discussion halls (*togu na*) have thick thatched roofs that are supported by complicated human-shaped carved posts, which show both male and female characteristics. Set in cliffs and mountains, the villages—most of which shelter no more than a few hundred people—astonish with their inventiveness and beauty.

Animals play an important role in Dogon culture. The fox, a trickster figure, is particularly important. In Dogon creation stories the fox, impatient to find his wife (who is also his sister), disrupts Amma's orderly creation. Because the fox cannot speak clearly in human language, he communicates at night through cryptic messages. These are the basis for examining the future. A diviner creates an outdoor grid pattern of squares in sand, adding upright sticks, mounds of earth, and various designs. Food to attract a fox is left out overnight, and paw prints found the next day are read to tell the future. Other animals are also significant: crocodiles are kept as symbols of strength and tortoises are kept as symbols of long life.

Despite their relative isolation, the Dogon people face the cultural challenges that all indigenous peoples and religions face today. To provide just one example, reruns of American television programs—dubbed in French—are broadcast throughout Mali (televisions are often powered by electrical generators). Also, tourism (particularly from France and Germany) has increased contact with outsiders. Islam has been successful among the Dogon in recent years, and more than a third of the people are now Muslim. Unfortunately, the Islamic prohibition of religious images has meant that old family heirlooms are being sold off; conversion has also brought a decline in the carving of masks and statues for religious purposes. One can only hope valiantly that the complex practices and wisdom of traditional Dogon culture will continue to exist, in order to offer guidance to the centuries ahead.

The Vision Quest

Among the Ojibwa, who live in the northern plains and Great Lakes area of North America, fasting was often expected of children as preparation for a great fast upon reaching puberty. Girls were expected to make a special fast at menarche, but boys were expected, in addition, to undertake a vision quest. "The Ojibwa boy was led deep into the forest, where a lofty red pine tree was selected. In this tree, a platform of woven sticks covered with moss was placed upon a high branch as a bed upon which the youth was to conduct the fast. Perhaps a canopy of branches would be prepared to shelter him from the wind and rain. Left alone in this place, the youth was strictly warned not to take any kind of nourishment or drink. He was to lie quietly day and night on this platform in a patient vigil for his vision." He might be checked secretly by elders and would be allowed to go home if he could not continue, but he would have to return the following year. "When visions rewarded the fast, they commonly took the form of a journey into the world of the spirits, a spiritual journey on a cosmic scale. During this journey the visionary was shown the path upon which his life should proceed. He was associated with one or more spirit beings who would serve as his guardians and protectors throughout his life."[21] The boy would also gather, or later be given, physical symbols of his guardian spirits, which he would keep for the rest of his life to remind him of his quest and the spirits' protection.

quest may be used at other times, too—particularly when the individual or the group must make an important life decision.

In oral societies, as in almost all other cultures, marriage is a ritual that not only publicly affirms and stabilizes a union but also cements economic arrangements and, through the ceremony, ensures fertility. In both Africa and North America, however, marriage in tribal cultures has been primarily a practical arrangement. Among Native American peoples, marriage has usually been celebrated simply as a social contract that is worked out by the families. Monogamy has been the norm, but divorce is acceptable when a marriage is not successful. In indigenous African religions, marriage is sometimes marked by rituals to unite the two lineages and transfer the power of fertility; but its religious aspect in many religions "is not distinctive. It is regarded as the normal sequel to rites of adolescence, whose purpose was to prepare for this state."[23]

As the final passing from this life, death is accompanied by rituals that serve to comfort close relatives, assist the spirit of the dead person in moving on, and protect the living from bad influences that could come from an unhappy spirit. Because the spirit of the dead person may be sad to leave the family circle, it must be helped to make its trip to the spirit world by placing clothing, food, money, and favorite objects with the body. In the case of a chief or other notable person, the body may be embalmed or mummified for public display until a large funeral can be arranged. In the past, great African chiefs have had wives, children, and servants buried alongside them. Among Native American tribes, the sacrifice of relatives and attendants to accompany a dead leader has also occurred. For example, after the death of the Natchez leader Tattooed Serpent in 1725, two of his wives and six others, after preparation by fasting, were strangled as a part of the funeral ritual.[24] In Native American religions, bodies of the dead are usually buried, but sometimes they are placed on platforms or in trees.

Taboo and Sacrifice

A **taboo** is a rule that forbids specific behavior with regard to certain objects, people, animals, days, or phases of life. Taboos represent a codification of the social and religious order. In our language, *taboo* means, often negatively, something that is prohibited. This is essentially the viewpoint of an outsider. From inside native religions, a taboo is often better seen as a way of protecting the individual and of safeguarding the natural order of things.

Taboos frequently relate to sex and birth. Blood, too, is always an element of mysterious power—both helpful and dangerous. For example, in some but not all groups, menstruating women are expected to remain separate from everyone else because menstrual blood is considered powerful and dangerous. In contrast, a few cultures (such as the Apache) hail a girl's menarche as a time when she has power to heal illness.

Probably because of the blood involved during childbirth, a woman in some native cultures must remain alone or in the company of women only during the birth—not even the woman's husband may be present. In traditional Hawai`i, for example, women of high rank gave birth in isolation, at the site of special large stones used only for this purpose. Oral societies also frequently forbid a husband from resuming sexual relations with his wife for some time after childbirth—this period can even last until the child is weaned.

Like birth, death is also surrounded by taboos concerning the spirit of the dead person, who may seek to reward or take revenge on the living because of the way he or she was treated in life. The afterlife can be a shadowy, uncertain realm that the departing spirit is reluctant to enter, especially if the spirit is leaving a happy family circle. Proper rituals must be performed, accompanied by public mourning, to avoid angering the dead person's spirit.

A number of taboos regulate other social behavior. One common taboo relates to rank: people of high position, such as chiefs, nobility, priests, and shamans, must be treated with extraordinary care because of their special powers; taboos protect them from insult or inappropriate action. In traditional Hawaiian culture, for example, the shadow of a commoner could not fall on a member of the nobility. In a strongly hierarchical native culture, such as in many African groups, the health of the people and the fertility of the land are believed to depend on the health of the sacred king. To maintain his health, the king is protected by taboos—particularly regarding the people with whom he may associate. Because of these taboos and the fear his role inspires, the sacred king may live a life quite separate from his subjects.

Foods and food sources in many cultures are governed by taboos. Among some African peoples, commoners have been forbidden to touch or eat the food of a king. In traditional Hawai`i, women were forbidden to eat certain foods.

Do not kill or injure your neighbor, for it is not him that you injure. Do not wrong or hate your neighbor, for it is not him that you wrong, you wrong yourself. Moneto, the Grandmother, the Supreme Being, loves him also as she loves you.

—Shawnee rules[25]

Traditional Hawaiian Religion

The essentials of traditional Polynesian culture and religion were brought to Hawai`i by settlers who came over the sea from islands in the southern Pacific Ocean. It is widely thought that the distant ancestors of the Polynesians of Hawai`i were Melanesians from Papua New Guinea and the Solomon Islands, who journeyed eastward, about 1500 B.C.E. As these peoples immigrated to Samoa, to Tahiti and the other Society Islands, and to the Marquesas, what we now call Polynesian culture evolved. Then, after 200 C.E., at least two major waves of immigration—apparently from the Marquesas and, slightly later, from Tahiti—came to the previously uninhabited islands of Hawai`i.

Because of the great navigational skills of the Polynesians, their culture spread through much of the Pacific Ocean. Ultimately Polynesian culture established itself within an immense triangle of islands. At the far north was Hawai`i; at the western tip was Aotearoa (New Zealand); and at the eastern tip, about two thousand miles west of what is now Chile, was Rapa Nui (Easter Island). Although each island group developed its own characteristics, we find significant similarities among the indigenous cultures of all these Polynesian islands.

Before contact with westerners, the Polynesian people of Hawai`i had a well-developed belief system, made of many strands. Their belief system spoke of a primeval darkness (po), in the midst of which a separation had occurred, forming the sky and the earth. In the space between the two, all the varied forms of life emerged. (This emergence is beautifully detailed in the *Kumulipo,* the most elaborate of the Hawaiian chants of creation.) The primal deities of sky and earth were Wakea and his female consort Papa. But the Hawaiian religion also spoke of thousands of other deities (*akua*) who were descendants of the earliest gods. Some of these deities may have arisen from the memory of divinized ancestors, and others may have been the personification of specific aspects of nature. Their worship seems to have arisen at different times on different island groups, and systematization took place only slowly, never being static but growing in layers.

Of the thousands of deities that eventually were said to exist, several dozen were commonly invoked, and the greatest deities had priesthoods dedicated to their worship. Among the most important were Ku and Lono, gods who were in many ways complementary. Ku, with several manifestations, was a god of vigorous action. He was the patron, for example, of digging, bird catching, and fishing. In a darker aspect he was also patron of war.

The second god, Lono, was a god of peace, associated with rain, fertility, love, and the arts. Although a large part of the year was dedicated to Ku, the winter period was a different matter. It was a time of truce, under the protection of Lono, and during this time the temples dedicated to Ku were temporarily closed. The four-month period dedicated to Lono began when the Pleiades first appeared above the horizon in the night sky—something that happened between late October and late November. This period was called *Makahiki* (literally, "eye movement"), a term which referred to the appearance and movement of the stars. The time was given over to religious services, dance, sports contests, and leisure. During Makahiki, priests of Lono collected offerings in his name. To announce the presence of Lono, his priests bore around each island a white banner made of *kapa* (bark cloth). It was attached to a long pole that had at its top the face of Lono or his bird-like symbol. (The people of Hawai`i thought of Captain James Cook as Lono because the explorer's ship arrived in January during Makahiki, and also because his ship, with its white sails, had a startling resemblance to the banner of Lono.)

Two other gods of importance were Kane and Kanaloa, traveling companions or brothers who came together from their homeland of Kahiki to the Hawaiian islands. The two were said to have introduced and planted all bananas in Hawai`i.[27] Kane was protector of the water, but was seen in many other aspects of nature—particularly in thunder and the rainbow. Houses often had a shrine to Kane, the heart of which was a phallic stone, and at it Kane received daily prayer. Kanaloa was associated with the sky and the ocean—particularly with ocean fishponds, marine life, the tides, and sailing.

These major gods (with the possible exception of Kanaloa) had their own temples. In the lunar calendar followed by the Hawaiians, ten days in each

This empty offering platform stands before Pu`ukohola, generally regarded as the most important of the Hawaiian religious sites. Ceremonies at Pu`ukohola are infrequent, but when they occur, they attract Hawaiians from all islands.

active. Pele was so important that she also had her own priests and, later, priestesses. Other popular goddesses included Pele's younger sister Hi`iaka, of whom Pele was sometimes jealous; Hina, goddess associated with the moon; and Laka, the patron of hula.

Some gods and demi-gods were especially popular because they were known for their mischief, and their exploits inspired storytellers and chanters. Kamapua`a—sometimes considered a form of Lono—was a fierce and capricious god, whose primary appearance was as a wild pig. He pursued Pele and was repeatedly rebuffed, but finally gained success. The demi-god Maui, born of the goddess Hina and a human father, was a powerful trickster. A kind of Prometheus figure, he is said to have stolen the secrets of fire for human use, pulled the Hawaiian islands out of the water with his special fishhook, and roped the sun to make it travel more slowly in the sky. His exploits were recounted throughout Polynesia.

Just as deities had many aspects, they could also manifest themselves in varied shapes (*kinolau,* "multiple selves"). Pele, for example, might show herself as a girl, a white dog, a volcano, fire, or an old woman with long hair. (The ethnobotanist Isabella Abbott recounts a characteristic tale told her by her father. He said that once he gave an old lady a ride in his truck and offered her a cigarette. Before he had a chance to light her cigarette, however, it had lit by itself and the old lady was smoking it. Then suddenly she disappeared.)

Deceased ancestors were, and are, also thought of as having elements of divinity. Known as `aumakua, they act as powerful family guardians. Like the gods, they might appear in varied forms—the best-known shapes being those of animals such as sharks, dogs, owls, turtles, and giant lizards (*mo`o*).

Worship of the deities and ancestors was of many kinds. It could include formal offerings by priests at temples, private offerings by individuals at outdoor shrines, and family prayers at home. Offerings were fruits, flowers, kava (`*awa*), black pigs, and certain red fish. (Human sacrifice was introduced about 1200 C.E. at temples dedicated to Ku, particularly in preparation for war, but this practice was not a part of earlier Hawaiian religion.)

lunar month were sacred to one of these four gods and most work was forbidden on those days.[28] Fishing and the planting and harvesting of food plants were regulated by this calendar.

The goddess Pele was also a major subject of devotion. She was worshiped as a goddess of fire, active in volcanoes. Tales about her describe her arrival in Hawai`i at the small island of Ni`ihau, east of Kaua`i; her volcanic activity on Kaua`i, O`ahu, and Maui; and the final movement of her irascible spirit to the Big Island of Hawai`i, where volcanoes are still

Places of worship varied in size—from enormous stone temples to small wayside shrines, temporary altars, and the site of sacred objects in the home. Many temples and shrines were used for specific purposes, such as treating the sick or requesting good fishing, rain, or an increase of crops. The design of temples, called *heiau,* was derived from that of temples in Tahiti and the Marquesas, and seems to have become more elaborate over time. The heiau generally were outdoor stone platforms, often enclosed by walls. In the heiau, images of the deities (*ki`i*) were set up, food offerings were placed on wooden platforms, and priests performed carefully memorized chants. Large heiau could also include thatched houses for priests, kitchens for the preparing of offerings, and storage rooms for drums, gourds, and other ritual objects. Women normally did not enter the heiau, but upper-class women prayed at their own houses of worship (*hale-o-papa*). We know that at some point, however, there were women in the priesthood of Pele, and it is possible that women had other religious roles that are not known. (Because the Hawaiians had no written records until Western contact, scholars must rely on a limited amount of evidence: archeological remains, historical artifacts, parallels with other Polynesian religions, oral traditions, and written descriptions and drawings made at the time of early contact.)

The priests, usually males from the nobility, were considered one type of *kahuna* (specialist). Priests, called *kahuna pule* ("prayer experts") were the highest in rank among the kahuna. But there were other types of specialists, who were divided and named according to their skills—and some were female. Among the most important specializations were herbal medicine and healing, massage, midwifery, architecture, agriculture, astronomy, navigation, canoe building, sorcery, prophecy, and dance.

A complex system of classification came to exist in all traditional Hawaiian society, and religion provided the taboos (*kapu*). The social divisions seem to have grown stricter and more complex over the centuries, and stern sanctions—often death—reinforced the prohibitions. Society was strongly hierarchical—made of nobles (*ali`i*) of descending grades, common people (*maka`ainana*), and slaves (*kauwa*). Men and women had quite different social roles and ate separately. Women lived apart during their menstrual period. Possibly because of fears about the dangerous power of menstrual blood, prohibitions were imposed on what women could eat, what they could touch, and the kind of work they could perform. They could not eat pork, coconuts, or most kinds of bananas, and they were not allowed to raise or prepare *kalo* (taro), the primary food.

Underpinning the entire social system was a notion of spiritual power, called *mana.* Nobles, who were considered to be representatives of the gods, were believed to have the greatest mana; but their mana had to be protected. Commoners, for example, had to crouch or prostrate themselves when close to nobles. (When Captain Cook set foot on

Antisocial actions may also be subject to taboo. In Native American religions, taboos and rules encourage a sense of harmony with other members of one's people. Strong taboos against adultery and stealing within the tribal unit, for example, are enforced by shame, warnings, shunning, and expulsion, often administered by a tribal council. Nevertheless, although harmony is important, warfare against another people has at times been considered justified.

When a taboo has been broken or a spirit must be placated, the person or group must atone for the lapse, often through sacrifice. The usual offering is food and drink. A **libation** (the act of pouring a bit of drink on the ground as an offering) may be made or a portion of a meal set aside for a spirit. An animal may be sacrificed and its blood poured out on the ground or on an shore in Hawai`i in 1778, most people who had been watching him disappeared; the few who remained visible fully prostrated themselves.) Mana could be transferred, as from teacher to student, and it could be absorbed by clothing and other personal effects. It was believed to exist in human remains (bones, hair, fingernails)—a fact that demanded care for these elements and careful burial. Powerful and striking features of nature—specially shaped rocks, great trees, waterfalls—were also believed to manifest mana.

In 1819, King Kamehameha the Great, who had unified the islands, died. In the same year, his son King Kamehameha II ate with women, an act that represented a clear and public rejection of the old system of prohibitions. (This act was influenced by several decades of Western contact.) Many heiau were destroyed and allowed to fall into ruin, most images of the gods were burned, and the religious priesthoods officially ended. The following year, Protestant Christian missionaries arrived from Boston, and Christianity stepped into the vacuum.

Traditional religion, however, did not entirely die out. Elements of it remain alive even today. Among the clearest are widespread reverence for Pele, veneration of ancestors, and belief in guardian spirits. Descendants of Hawaiian nobility are shown respect. Blessings and dedications, although performed by modern ministers, are often done in traditional style with sea water and ti leaves (ki), and hula and traditional musical instruments are occasionally used during Christian services. Prayerful chants in Hawaiian are performed at the beginning of hula; the goddesses Laka and Hi`iaka are often invoked; and the dances frequently retell the stories of the goddesses and gods. (Research is ongoing about how correct religious protocol is arrived at and about the proper use of chants for specific deities and `aumakua.) Public prayer at dedications is expected, and one frequently hears the prayer leader address both God (Akua) and "our `aumakua." There have also been theoretical attempts at integrating the traditional native polytheism with monotheism, by saying that the many traditional deities are angels or are just aspects of the one God.[29]

The revival in recent decades of hula, Hawaiian language, and traditional arts has brought about a new interest in ceremonies of the traditional religion. Since the unpopulated island of Kaho`olawe was returned by the U.S. Navy to native Hawaiian groups, some trained associations have performed traditional religious practice there, including carrying the banner of Lono during Makahiki. Hula groups that visit the island often build an altar to Laka and recite chants to her when they first arrive on the island. A good number of heiau have been repaired and even rebuilt, including several large ones on Maui and the Big Island of Hawai`i. Some traditional religious services have been conducted at the reconstructed heiau and there may be further attempts to restore traditional religious practices.[30]

altar as an offering of the life force to the deity. Sacrificial animals ordinarily are food animals, such as chickens, pigs, and goats.[26] After the sacrifice, all the participants (including ancestral and nature spirits) may eat the cooked animal—thus pleasing the spirits by feeding them and including them in the meal.

Although it has been rare, human sacrifice (and sometimes cannibalism) has occurred in some native cultures. The sacrifice of human beings was practiced (at least for a time) for specific purposes in Aztec religion, Hawaiian religion, and among tribal peoples of New Guinea; it was much less common among native peoples of North America and Africa.

Before leaving the topic of taboos, it might be good to note that taboos exist plentifully in every society, including our own. Many are associated with sex, marriage, and parenthood. In modern societies, for example, taboos exist against polygamy, incest, and marriage between close relations. Such taboos may seem "natural" to the society that enforces them but "unusual" to outsiders. Taboos are not inherently valid across groups and societies but are culturally determined.

Shamanism, Trance, and Spiritual Powers

As we have seen, native religions take for granted that a powerful and influential but invisible spirit world exists and that human beings can have access to it. A **shaman** acts as an intermediary between the visible, ordinary world and the spirit world. The shaman can contact this realm, receive visions of it, and transmit messages from it, often to help or heal others. As one commentator remarks, "The shaman lies at the very heart of some cultures, while living in the shadowy fringes of others. Nevertheless, a common thread seems to connect all shamans across the planet. An awakening to other orders of reality, the experience of ecstasy, and an opening up of visionary realms form the essence of the shamanic mission."[31] Sometimes the spirits speak through the shaman, who knows entry points to their world, which may be reached in dreams or trances by climbing a sacred tree, descending through a cave into the underworld, flying through the air, or following a sacred map.

The shaman understands the primordial unity of things and experiences a shared identity with animals and the rest of nature. Thus the shaman can interpret the language of animals, charm them, and draw on their powers. The shaman gains the powers of animals and the rest of nature by wearing items taken from important animals, such as deer antlers, lion skins, and eagle feathers.

Part of becoming a shaman involves having one or more encounters with the spirit realm in the form of a psychological death and rebirth. A person may have experienced some great loss—of sight, of a child, or of something equally precious. He or she may have had a mental breakdown, been terribly sick, or suffered a serious accident and come close to dying. Upon recovering from such an extreme experience, this person can have new powers of insight and healing, which can lead to becoming a shaman. Those who have experienced vivid dreams and visions that are thought to be manifestations of the spirit world are also sometimes trained as shamans.

The shaman often blends the roles of priest, oracle, psychologist, and doctor. A common English term for the shaman is *medicine man,* yet it stresses only the therapeutic role and obscures the fact that shamans are both female and male. In Korean and Japanese native religious paths, in fact, shamans are frequently female.

The shamanic trance state that brings visions, both to the shaman and to others, can be induced in several ways: weakening the visual boundaries (for example, by sitting in the darkness of a cave or hut for prolonged periods), fasting, experiencing sensory deprivation, making regular rhythmic

I enter the earth. I go in at a place like a place where people drink water. I travel a long way, very far. When I emerge, I am already climbing threads [up into the sky]. I climb one and leave it, then I climb another one. . . . You come in small to God's place. You do what you have to do there. . . . [Then] you enter, enter the earth, and you return to enter the skin of your body.

—Bushman trance dancer[33]

Isaac Tens Becomes a Shaman

Isaac Tens, a shaman of the Gitskan people of northwest Canada, spoke to an interviewer in 1920 about how he had become a shaman. On a snowy day at dusk, when he was gathering firewood, he heard a loud noise, and an owl appeared to him. "The owl took hold of me, caught my face, and tried to lift me up. I lost consciousness. As soon as I came back to my senses I realized that I had fallen into the snow. My head was coated with ice, and some blood was running out of my mouth." Isaac went home, but he fell into a trance. He woke up to find medicine men working to heal him. One told him that it was now time for him, too, to become a *halaait* (medicine man). Isaac refused. Later, at a fishing hole, he had another fainting spell and fell into a trance again. He was carried home. When he woke up, he was trembling. "My body was quivering. While I remained in this state, I began to sing. A chant was coming out of me without my being able to do anything to stop it. Many things appeared to me presently: huge birds and other animals. They were calling me."[32] Eventually he began to treat others.

sounds (such as drumming, rattling, bell ringing, and chanting), and dancing in a repetitive way, especially in circles. The ingestion of natural substances is also common; peyote cactus, datura, cannabis (marijuana), coca, opium, and the mushroom *Amanita muscaria* have all been used to induce trance states, both by the shaman alone and sometimes by participants in a ceremony.

Some Native American peoples have used a **calumet**—a long sacred pipe—for smoking a special kind of tobacco that is far stronger than commercial cigarette tobacco; it is so strong, in fact, that it can have a hallucinatory effect. The bowl of the pipe is usually made of clay but sometimes of bone, ivory, wood, or metal, and the stem is made of wood. Many pipes are also made of stone. (A red stone, popular among Plains Indians and Eastern Woodlands Indians for this purpose, was quarried in Pipestone, Minnesota.) The calumet is an object that gives protection to the person who carries it. The pipe is smoked as part of a shared ceremony that establishes strong bonds among all the participants, and oaths sworn at these ceremonies have the greatest solemnity.

Rituals involving the use of peyote have developed primarily within the past two centuries in some native North American tribes.[34] The practice seems to have moved north from Mexico, where peyote grows easily and has long been used for religious purposes. When the fruit of the peyote cactus is eaten, it elicits a psychedelic experience that lasts six or more hours and produces a forgetfulness of the self and a sense of oneness with all of nature. Ceremonies commonly begin in the early evening and last until dawn.

Among North American tribes, the rituals involving peyote are often mixed with Christian elements. For example, a member of the Native American Church described his preparation for the ceremony: "First we set up an altar—a Mexican rug and on it a Lakota Bible in our own language. We use only the revelations of St. John in our meetings. It's . . . full of visions, nature, earth, stars. . . . Across the Bible we put an eagle feather—it stands for the Great Spirit. . . . On the left is a rawhide bag with cedar dust to sprinkle on

A shaman wearing animal pelts uses a spoon to place a food offering into a ritual fire during the midsummer Ysyakh festival in Siberia.

the fire. That's our incense."[35] The blending of elements, he says, is intentional, because it illustrates that, at their core, all religions are the same. It is interesting to note that, although the use of peyote is illegal, its religious use by the Native American Church has been legally upheld.

In native African religions and their Caribbean offshoots, powerful, invisible, ever-present spiritual forces that can do either tremendous good or tremendous evil are directed and diffused by diviners, healers, and others through incantations, potions, and figurines used for what is sometimes called **sympathetic magic.** Magic in the hands of certain individuals can be used, as one commentator remarks, "for harmful ends, and then people experience it as bad or evil magic. Or they may use it for ends which are helpful to society, and then it is considered as good magic or 'medicine.' These mystical forces of the universe are neither evil nor good in themselves, they are just like other natural things at [our] disposal."[36]

Spiritual powers and trance states are believed to make it possible to look into the past and future, a process called **divination** (from the Latin *divus,* "god," and *divinare,* "to foretell"). Looking into the past helps determine the

This is a men's northern traditional dance at the Council Tree Powwow, held yearly in Delta, Colorado, and hosted by the Ute nation.

causes of illness and other misfortune, while looking into the future guides an individual to act wisely. It is a common belief in African religions that an individual has a predetermined future that can be discovered through divination.

The general worldview common to native religions allows for a number of specialized religious roles. A diviner looks for causes of sickness, depression, death, and other difficulties. A healer works with a person afflicted with physical or mental illness to find a cure. A rainmaker ends drought. Malevolent sorcerers manipulate objects to cause damage; they take fingernails, hair, clothes, or other possessions of the victim, then burn or damage them, or bury an object in the victim's path, in order to cause harm. Witches need only use their spiritual powers. "Another belief is that the spirit of the witches leaves them at night and goes to eat away the victim, thus causing him to weaken and eventually die. It is believed, too, that a witch can cause harm by looking at a person, wishing him harm or speaking to him words intended to inflict harm on him."[37] The powers of these sorcerers and witches are also employed of course, for good ends, as well.

The Navajo people use sandpaintings as part of their healing rituals. After each ritual, the sandpainting is destroyed.

Artifacts and Artistic Expression in Oral Religions

The masks, drums, statues, rattles, and other objects that are important in oral religions were once seen as curiosities to be collected and housed in anthropological museums. Today, however, we view them differently; we realize that we must respect both their importance to the cultures that produced them and their inherent artistic value. The arts of oral religions are not created by "artists" as "art" but as functional objects to be used in particular settings and special ways. Navajo sandpaintings, for example, are often ph tographed and reproduced in books as though they were permanent works of art. In fact, when used by a healer, they are temporary creations that are made and then destroyed as a part of the ritual. And unlike art in most Western cultures, sacred objects and images in native religions are not separate endeavors but an essential part of the religious expression itself. Although modern secular culture does not usually think of dance or tattoo or body painting as religious expression, in many native religions these art forms all fulfill that role.

In religions that do not rely on the written word, artistic expressions take on unique significance because they are filled with meaning and remind practitioners of the specifics of the oral tradition. Statues and paintings, of course, are common in a great many religions, both oral and written. Dance, which takes on particular importance in oral religion, incorporates religious objects such as carved and painted masks, headdresses, costumes, ornaments, and musical instruments. In native Hawaiian religion, *hula kahiko* (ancient hula) is danced in conjunction with chanting to honor the gods. Instruments for marking rhythm and *lei* (wreaths of flowers or other plants worn around the head, wrists, and ankles), when used in hula, are considered religious objects.

Chants, too, are essential, because they capture many of the stories and words of the tradition so they can be memorized and used properly in sacred ceremonies. Chanters must not only have prodigious memories and be able to recall thousands of chants, they must also be able to create special variations on traditional chants and oral texts for individual occasions.

Masks play a significant role in oral religions, especially when used in dance. When a dancer is wearing a mask and any accompanying

Although hula is still a form of entertainment that travelers can enjoy at tourist hotels, it is also a key element of Hawaiian religious and cultural celebrations.

costume, the spirit is not merely represented by the masked dancer. The dancer actually becomes the spirit, embodied on earth, with the spirit's powers. Among the BaPunu in Africa, for example, dancers not only wear masks but walk on stilts—the overall effect must be intense. Particularly complex masks have been produced in the Pacific Northwest by such tribes as the Haida, Tsimshian, and Kwakiutl (Kwakwaka`wakw).[38] Some of their masks, especially those depicting animal spirits, have moveable parts that make them even more powerful for those who wear and see them.

Besides masks and statues, other forms of wood carving can manifest religious inspiration. Perhaps the most famous of all wood carvings is the carved pole, commonly called a *totem pole*, found in the Pacific Northwest. The totem pole usually depicts a group of **totems** (animal figures that are revered for their symbolic meaning, such as the bear, beaver, thunderbird, owl, raven, and eagle) stacked one on top of another. The animals may memorialize ancestors or represent badges of kinship groups, with specialized meaning for the individual or the family responsible for the totem pole.[39] Some totem poles are a part of the structure of a traditional wooden house or lodge. Others—apparently a later development—are raised to stand alone, frequently to mark an important event.

Sacred images are reinterpreted on this contemporary blanket from the Pacific Northwest coast. The white borders, which originally would have been made of shells, are today made of buttons.

Other important art forms that can have religious meaning are weaving, clothing decoration (such as beading), and basketry. These creations may seem to have less obvious religious significance, but the imagery used is frequently of religious derivation, particularly figures from tribal myths, nature deities, and guardian birds and animals.

Feathers and featherwork also feature prominently in many oral religions because of their powerful association with flight and contact with the world above and beyond our own. Richard W. Hill, in an essay on the religious meaning of feathers, remarks that "some cultures associate certain birds with spiritual or protective powers. Birds are believed to have delivered songs, dances, rituals, and sacred messages to humankind. Feathers worn in the hair blow in the wind and evoke birds in flight. For followers of the Ghost Dance religion of the late nineteenth century, birds became important symbols of rebirth."[40] Feathers are worn in the hair, made into headdresses, and attached to clothing. In Native American cultures, they are also attached to horse harnesses, dolls, pipes, and baskets.

The symbols that appear in myths and in dreams are the basic vocabulary of oral religious art. Common symbols include a great mountain located at the center of the universe, the tree of life (also called the world tree),

Halloween: "Just Good Fun" or Folk Religion?

Although many of us may think of oral religions as having no connection to our modern, everyday life, elements from them persist, particularly in our celebrations of traditional folk holidays.

- *Halloween* means the evening before All Hallows' (All Saints') Day, which falls on November 1. Although Halloween gets its name from Christianity, the celebration is, in fact, a continuation of *Samhain* (pronounced *sá-win*), the new year festival celebrated in pre-Christian England and Ireland. There is a strong theme of death and rebirth, as winter comes on and the old year disappears. It was believed that spirits of ancestors roamed free at this time and needed to be fed and placated. We see this underlying the practices of children going door to door, receiving food. We also see it in the many Halloween costumes that suggest death (skeletons) and communication with the spirit world (angels, devils, and religious figures).

- Although Christmas has a Christian name and purpose, the origins of this festival, too, are pre-Christian. It began as a festival of the winter solstice, when the days are the coldest and shortest in the northern hemisphere. People compensated by celebrating a holiday of extra light, warmth, and abundance. The lighted Christmas tree and the evergreen wreaths and decorations have nothing to do with the story of Jesus' birth; rather, they are clear symbols of fertility and life, which the celebrants hope will persist through a cold winter. The giving of presents is related to this idea of abundance, and the Christian Saint Nicholas has been transformed over the past two hundred years into the grandfatherly Santa Claus. Like a wizard, Santa Claus flies through the air, carried by his

Awe of the spirit world is prominent in folk religions. In the United States, this awe comes alive at Halloween.

magical reindeer, dispensing presents from his overflowing bag to children all around the earth.

- Easter's Christian meaning is mixed with elements that derive from the Jewish Passover, but underlying this tradition are symbols of fertility and new life—eggs, flowers, and rabbits. (The name *Easter* comes from an Old English term for a spring festival in honor of Eastre, goddess of the dawn.) Easter has maintained a close tie to nature in that it is always celebrated at the time of a full moon.

We can see in these examples of contemporary folk religion the "universal language" of religious symbols. It is the same language, whether found in folk religion, native religions, or the other religions that we will take up in the chapters ahead.

the sun and moon, fire, rain, lightning, a bird or wings, death's head and skeleton, a cross, and a circle. These images, however, often appear in unusual forms; for example, lightning may be represented by a zigzag, and the sun may look like a swastika or the tree of life like a ladder. Colors are universally used with symbolic meaning, although the exact meaning differs from culture to culture.

PERSONAL EXPERIENCE: GODS IN HAWAI`I

On the southernmost island of the Hawaiian Islands lies Pu`uhonua `o Honaunau ("place of refuge"), once a sanctuary for Hawaiians who had done something that was *kapu* ("taboo," "forbidden"). They could escape punishment and be purified if they could reach Pu`uhonua `o Honaunau, or one of its sister sanctuaries, by water or land.

Seeking refuge from the frenzy of life in Honolulu, I fly to the Kona airport and drive my rental car down the Big Island's southwest coast to Pu`uhonua `o Honaunau, now run by the United States National Park Service. After a short walk toward the shore, I see the tall, long stone wall of the sanctuary. Closer to the ocean are its heiau (temples), made of large, nearly black lava rock, around which grow ti plants to demarcate a sacred space and to ward off evil spirits. Most dramatic to my outsider's eyes are the tall carved wooden images (in Hawaiian, called ki`i, and in English, commonly called tikis) that once no doubt beckoned to the refugee who sought out this place at the ocean's edge. The offering platform and thatched houses near the ki`i have been restored so that I can see what it might have been like when this was a sacred site within traditional Hawaiian religion. Because the official kapu system was dissolved in 1819 by King Kamehameha II, it is no longer a place for seeking sanctuary—at least officially.

Even on this sunny day, the stone wall, the tall images, and the stark landscape speak not of the "peace and comfort" we may typically associate with a refuge but rather of power, law, and awesome majesty. The ground is hard, black lava rock and white coral, and except for the coconut trees here and there amid the few structures, there is little green vegetation. Ocean waves lap at the shore, but an almost eerie quiet reigns.

Late afternoon: I'm the only person here. It is not hard for me to imagine being a native who has fled from home and now awaits a priestly blessing in order to be made safe for returning home. I sense that the Hawaiian religion drew its power from the land, from this very place. The rocks that make up the heiau are petrifications of fire, water, air, and earth. This is not the tour director's tropical fantasyland. Nor, I realize, is it a place of living religious practice. But that doesn't matter to me today. What I sense in the land is alive, even in this religious museum.

As I drive back up the hill toward the main road, I see a small directional sign that says "Painted Church." Ready for an experience of contrast, I follow its arrow and soon arrive at Saint Benedict's Catholic Church—a tiny, white wooden structure that has elements of Gothic style. A sign near the door says that its interior was painted a century ago by a Belgian missionary priest. The church sits on a grassy hillside, with a small cemetery spreading out below. I ascend the wooden stairs of the church and walk in.

The interior is "tropical Gothic." Ten small windows have pointed Gothic arches. The wooden pillars look like candy canes, painted with red and white swirls; their tops turn into palm trees, with fronds like

The *kiʻi* at Puʻuhonua ʻo Honaunau may have been intended to ward off unwanted visitors, from this or the spirit world.

painted feathers on the pastel sky of the ceiling. Behind the altar is a mural of Gothic arches, stretching back into an imaginary distance, creating the pretense of a European cathedral. On one side wall, Saint Francis experiences a vision of Jesus on the cross. In another painting, Jesus is being tempted by Satan. The other wall shows a man on his deathbed, his face bathed in heavenly light. A cross of execution, the pains of death—these are not pleasant experiences, but they are softened by the way they are depicted here.

Back outside, from the top of the stairs, I see the shining ocean below and can even make out the Hawaiian place of refuge at its edge. This little church, charming as it appears, presents old familiar themes: a High God, a sacrificial victim, an offering of blood, a restoration of justice. The themes may not be obvious, but they are there. This, I reflect, is the religion that replaced the native Hawaiian religion; the cycle of replacement evident here is typical, I think, of what has happened to so many other native religious traditions. Does it make all that much difference how religions die and rise? I am deep in thought as I pass a stone grotto enclosing a statue of Mary and then walk past the resident priest's small house. From inside come the sounds of a roaring crowd and of a radio announcer. "Strike two!" the voice shouts. I get in my car and drive away, still seeking refuge.

In a painting at Saint
Benedict's Church on the
Big Island of Hawai`i,
Jesus wards off tempta-
tions offered by Satan.

ORAL RELIGIONS TODAY

Native religions show many signs of vitality. Some indigenous religions are
spreading and even adapting themselves to urban life. For example, religions
of the Yoruba tradition are practiced not only in western Africa, their place
of origin, but also in Brazil and the Caribbean, and they are growing in
cities of North America (see chapter 11). Awareness of indigenous religions
is also becoming widespread, and respect for them is taking many shapes.
In some countries (such as Mexico, Ecuador, and Peru) we can see a growth
in governmental protection of the rights of indigenous peoples. Native peoples themselves are often taking political action to preserve their cultures. In
many places (such as Hawai`i, New Zealand, and North America) a renais-
sance of native cultures is taking place. Sometimes this involves primarily
cultural elements, but where the indigenous religions are still practiced those
religions are increasingly cherished and protected.

   In some places, however, indigenous religions appear fragile. There are
four principal threats to their existence: the global spread of popular culture,

loss of natural environments, loss of traditional languages, and conversion to other religions.

Radio, television, films, and airplanes are carrying modern, urban popular culture everywhere. (American television reruns that are broadcast in Mali are an example of this.) One realm in which the change has been very evident is the realm of clothing. Traditional local clothing began to disappear widely in the twentieth century, as business wear became the standard for more formal occasions in much of the world; even informal clothing is now becoming standardized (baseball caps, for instance, are everywhere). Some cultures are trying to hold on to their traditional clothing, but that usage is regularly challenged. Traditional clothing will increasingly be worn as a statement of cultural difference, or to mark special occasions, as it now is in Japan and Korea. (The situation is similar in the world of architecture, as "international style," with its concrete and plate glass, displaces traditional styles.) As modern urban culture spreads across the earth, it tends to dominate everyone's worldview. It would be hard to convince today's young people to undergo deprivation in preparation for a vision quest when all they need to visit other worlds painlessly are a videotape and a television set. Everywhere we go, we find blue jeans, T-shirts, rock music, pizza, and Coca-Cola. (Some even believe that popular culture is becoming a religion of its own, displacing all others.)

Another great threat to indigenous religions is their loss of traditional lands and natural environment. Because so much personal and group meaning comes from the natural environment, its degradation or loss can be devastating to a native people's identity. Logging interests are a problem almost universally, but especially in Southeast Asia, Indonesia, Brazil, Alaska, and the western part of Canada. Much of northern Thailand, where many native peoples live, has already been badly deforested, and the logging companies are now beginning the same process in Myanmar, another home of indigenous peoples. Fights are intense over conservation, land ownership, and governmental protection. Luckily, there have been gains (such as in New Zealand and Australia), where aboriginal rights to land have been recognized.

A third threat is the loss of native languages. It has been estimated that of the approximately six thousand languages that are spoken in the world today, only three thousand will remain in a hundred years. It is instructive to look at charts of Native American languages; one gets a good sense of how many languages and dialects have already been lost. In the United States and Canada, only about five hundred thousand indigenous people still speak their native languages. A single example of this phenomenon is the Kwakiutl (Kwakwaka`wakw) of British Columbia. Although their population has been rising, and is now as high as five thousand, only about 250 people speak the native language. Clearly, loss of a native language will endanger the continued transmission of the religion that expresses itself in that language.

A fourth threat is the spread of proselytizing religions, particularly Christianity and Islam. In the Pacific, native cultures are undergoing a revival, but few elements of the native religions of those cultures remain unchanged from their earlier forms. Christianity, brought since the nineteenth century by missionaries (particularly Methodist, Catholic, and, more recently, Mormon), has replaced some beliefs and reshaped others. Christianity has spread widely in sub-Saharan Africa in the past hundred years, creating both mainstream Western denominations and independent African Churches. As a result, there are now more black members of the Anglican Church than there are white members. Islam has also gained many converts in Africa. (One example we have already seen is the Dogon of western Africa, many of whom are now Muslim.)

Despite the threats to their existence, indigenous religions continue to exist in several forms throughout the world. In their purest form, they live on in those pockets where modern influence has penetrated the least, such as in Borneo and the Amazon River Basin. They may also coexist, sometimes in diluted form, alongside other religions. In Taiwan, Korea, and Japan, for example, shamanism exists side by side with Buddhism, Christianity, and other religions. (Because the shamans are often female, their native religious practices allow them roles that are not open to them in the adopted religions.) Indigenous religions have also intermixed with mainstream religions. In the Caribbean, the gods of African religions have sometimes been combined with forms of French and Spanish Catholicism in the religions of Voodoo and Santería (see chapter 11). In Central America, people who are otherwise practicing Catholics also worship deities of earlier native religions. We see similar types of synthesis in Mexico and the southwestern United States.

In North America, in the Pacific, and in Africa, people have continued or are attempting to restore the practices of their ancestral ways. In New Zealand, for example, Maori culture is experiencing a revival in canoe building, tattooing, dance, and wood sculpture. This attempt at revival is complicated by debates over such issues as landownership and the introduction of Maori language into schools and public life. In Hawai`i, a renaissance of Hawaiian culture, language, and hula necessarily means retelling the stories of the gods and goddesses of Hawaiian mythology. Some schools now teach all their lessons in Hawaiian, and hula schools are flourishing. Citizens of many native nations in North America are instructing their young in traditional dance and other religious practices. Nevertheless, how to deal with a traditional belief in deities in the face of some dominant monotheistic religions presents intriguing questions. One result, as in the Native American Church, is that beliefs and practices now often incorporate both oral and text-based traditions.

Interest in oral religions is a potential restorative for cultures that have moved quickly from their traditional rural homes to concrete high-rise apartments in the city. In oral traditions, we see religion before it was compartmentalized. These holistic traditions help us to see the religious dimensions that can be found in our own everyday life and to expand our sensitivity to nature. Their remembrance of the sacred past makes holy the present and the future.

RELIGION BEYOND THE CLASSROOM

Places of interest for those who want to explore oral religions include sacred natural sites, locations where native religious life persists, the remains of native religious buildings, and museums that display the arts of oral religions. Some native religious events in North America are open to outsiders. (Schedules and policies about visitors are available on official websites of indigenous groups, as well as from state and province offices. Photography is generally not allowed at these religious events, and behavior and clothing must be respectful.) Although powwows are usually not religious, they allow viewers to experience native dance and costume, which manifest elements derived from religions. Many powwows are held in the southwestern United States, particularly during the summer (check official websites). Religion and anthropology departments of local colleges are a good source for finding regional places of interest and ceremonies open to nonnatives. The following list is a small sample of sights in North America available to the general traveler.

United States

California—Los Angeles: Southwest Museum
Colorado—Mesa Verde National Park (contains native dwellings and kivas); Dolores: Anasazi Heritage Center
Hawai`i—Big Island: Pu`uhonua `o Honaunau (a place of refuge with several reconstructed temples); O`ahu: Kane`aki Heiau in Makaha Valley (a reconstructed temple)
Illinois—Collinsville (slightly east of St. Louis, Missouri): Cahokia Mounds (remains of the largest and most complex indigenous urban center north of Mexico; a UNESCO World Heritage site)
Minnesota—sites at Red Lake, Leech Lake, and White Earth

New Mexico—Bandelier National Monument contains remnants of native cliff dwellings (Canyon de Chelly in Arizona has similar native cliff dwellings); Taos: Taos Pueblo
New York—New York City: Museum of Natural History, Museum of African Art, Museum of the American Indian
Ohio—Peebles (20 miles from Bainbridge): Great Serpent Mound (a serpent-shaped mound, possibly inspired by a constellation or aligned with the summer solstice, attributed either to the Fort Ancient people or the earlier Adena culture).
Texas—Fort Worth: Kimball Art Museum (has Mesoamerican and African collections)
Washington, D.C.—National Museum of African Art

Canada

'Ksan, British Columbia: Gitskan village (includes seven tribal houses, a longhouse, and many totem poles)
Ottawa: Canadian Museum of Civilization
Vancouver: Museum of Anthropology at the University of British Columbia (houses a large collection of totem poles, masks, and other artifacts)
Victoria: Royal British Columbia Museum (features a fine collection of masks); Thunderbird Park (displays totem poles outdoors)

Mexico

Chichén Itzá: Mayan pyramids
Davisadero: Tarahumara native community
Mexico City: National Anthropological Museum and recently uncovered sites next to the cathedral
Oaxaca and Monte Albán (sites of Zapotec and Mixtec ruins)
Teotihuacán (near Mexico City): Temple of Quetzalcoatl and the pyramids of the sun and moon

FOR FULLER UNDERSTANDING

1. Where you live is now or once was home to native peoples. Make up a list of their traditional religious sites, beliefs, and practices. Visit the sites with friends or classmates, and make a report to your class. What lessons about living can be learned from the native culture of your region?

2. Visit a museum or gallery in your area that houses special examples of oral religious objects. Make a drawing of a single object. Explain in writing its background, use, and maker.

3. Investigate the relatively new festival of Kwanzaa. Who created it and why? What are its rituals? How would you compare it to a long-standing folk celebration such as Thanksgiving, Christmas, or New Year?

4. Why do you think there has been a resurgence of interest in native religions in recent times? What reasons make you think that the interest will last? What reasons suggest that the interest may be short-lived?

5. Some have said that urban people in the modern world romanticize the attitudes toward nature held by indigenous peoples. What is your assessment of this opinion? See if you can find published texts or articles that illustrate your assessment.

6. Investigate the history of Easter Island. (As a part of this, you might like to see the film *Rapa Nui*.) Where did its people originate? What kind of culture did it have? How are its statues explained? What caused its decline? What religious practices are carried on there now?

RELATED READINGS

Abbott, Isabella Aiona. *La`au Hawai`i: Traditional Hawaiian Uses of Plants*. Honolulu: Bishop Museum Press, 1992. A demonstration by a Hawaiian botanist of the holistic nature of traditional religion. Abbott specifically discusses the religious dimensions of Hawaiian agriculture and the use of plants in religious ceremony and hula.

Becket, Jan, and Joseph Singer. *Pana O`ahu: Sacred Stones, Sacred Land*. Honolulu: University of Hawai`i Press, 1999. Description and evocative photographs of ancient sacred sites on the island of O`ahu.

Charlot, John. *Chanting the Universe: Hawaiian Religious Culture*. Hong Kong: Emphasis International, 1983. A well-illustrated presentation of the values and ideas of traditional Hawaiian religion and culture.

Deloria, Vine, Jr. *God is Red*. Golden, CO: Fulcrum, 1994. An updated version of the classic manifesto of Native American religious rights.

Fitzhugh, William, and Chisato Dubreuil, eds. *Ainu: Spirit of a Northern People*. Seattle: University of Washington Press, 2001. A well-illustrated collection of essays on Ainu history, religion, and culture.

Hill, Tom, and Richard W. Hill, Sr., eds. *Creation's Journey: Native American Identity and Belief*. Washington, DC: Smithsonian Press, 1994. A collection of large photographs of native art from both North America and South America, with sensitive descriptions of the art objects.

Hollyman, Stephanie, and W. E. A. Van Beek. *Dogon: People of the Cliffs*. New York: Abrams, 2001. A portrait of the Dogon in both words and fine photographs.

Johnston, Basil. *Ojibway Ceremonies*. Lincoln: University of Nebraska Press, 1990. An insider's description of the important traditional ceremonies of his people, including the naming ceremony, marriage ceremony, and funeral ritual.

Knudtson, Peter, and David Suzuki. *Wisdom of the Elders*. Toronto: Stoddart, 1993. A collection of ecological worldviews and wisdom from native cultures around the world, divided into topics such as plants, animals, sacred space, and the kinship of all living things.

Medicine Crow, Joseph, et al. *All Roads Are Good: Native Voices on Life and Culture*. Washington, DC: Smithsonian, 1994. An excellent collection of essays and photographs that give insight into contemporary indigenous thought about religion, ceremonial life, and culture in North America.

Reid, Janice. *Sorcerers and Healing Spirits*. Rushcutters Bay, NSW: Australian National University Press/ Pergamon Press, 1989. An engaging study of healing among aboriginal peoples in northern Australia.

Willett, Frank. *African Art*. Rev. ed. London: Thames & Hudson, 1993. A scholarly but readable discussion of African art, with good illustrations, particularly of masks and statues.

KEY TERMS

calumet: A long-stemmed sacred pipe used primarily by many native peoples of North America; it is smoked as a token of peace.

divination: A foretelling of the future or a look into the past; a discovery of the unknown by magical means.

holistic: Organic, integrated; indicating a complete system, greater than the sum of its parts; here, refers to a culture whose various elements (art, music, social behavior) may all have religious meaning.

libation: The act of pouring a liquid as an offering to a god.

shaman: A human being who contacts and attempts to manipulate the power of spirits for the tribe or group.

sympathetic magic: An attempt to influence the outcome of an event through an action that has an apparent similarity to the desired result—for example, throwing water into the air to produce rain, or burning an enemy's fingernail clippings to bring sickness to that enemy.

taboo: A strong social prohibition (Tongan: *tabu*; Hawaiian: *kapu*).

totem: An animal (or image of an animal) that is considered to be related by blood to a family or clan and is its guardian or symbol.

CHAPTER 3

Hinduism

 FIRST ENCOUNTER

The plane that you have taken into India from Nepal circles in preparation for landing at the Varanasi airport, near Benares. Looking down from your window seat, you can see the blue-white Ganges River, quite wide here. Everything else is a thousand shades of brown. Beyond the coffee-colored city, the beige fields spread out, seemingly forever.

At the small airport, a dignified customs inspector with a turban and a white beard asks, "Why have you come to India?" Before you can think of an appropriate response, he answers his own question. "I know," he says with a smile and a wave of the hand. "You westerners are all the same." He shakes his head from side to side. "You have come for *spirituality.*" After pausing briefly, he adds, "Haven't you!"—which sounds more like a statement than a question. It takes you a second to understand his quick pronunciation of that unexpected word—*spirituality.* In a way, he is right. You *have* come for that. You nod in agreement. He smiles again, writes something down on his form, and lets you through.

As you take the small black taxi to your hotel, you realize that you have just accepted—willingly or not—the ancient role that the customs inspector has bestowed upon you. You are now just one more pilgrim who has come to Mother India for her most famous product: religious insight. You are now a Seeker.

After unpacking at your hotel, you walk out into the streets. It is dusk. Pedicab drivers ring their bells to ask if you want a ride, but you want to walk, to see the life of the streets. Little shops sell tea, and others sell vegetarian foods made of potatoes, wheat, beans, and curried vegetables. Children play in front of their parents' stores. Down the street you see a "gent's tailor" shop, as a thin cow wanders past, chewing on what looks like a paper bag. Another shop sells books and notepaper, and others sell saris and bolts of cloth. From somewhere comes a smell like jasmine. As night falls, the stores are lit by dim bulbs and fluorescent lights, and vendors illuminate their stalls with bright Coleman lanterns. Because you will be rising long before dawn the next day to go down to the Ganges, you return early to your hotel and go to sleep.

The following morning the telephone rings, waking you out of a dream. The man at the front desk notifies you that it is four A.M. Being somewhat groggy, you have to remind yourself that you are in Benares. You get up and dress quickly.

At the front of the hotel you wake a driver sleeping in his pedicab. You negotiate the fare, climb onto the seat, and head off to the main crossing of town, near the river, as the sky begins to lighten. The pedicab drops you near the *ghats* (the stairs that descend to the river), which are already full of people, many going down to the river to bathe at dawn. Some are having sandalwood paste applied to their foreheads as a sign of devotion, and others are carrying brass jugs to collect Ganges water.

As you descend to the river, boat owners call to you. You decide to join the passengers in the boat of a man who has a white handlebar mustache and looks like a Victorian patriarch. Off you go, moving slowly upstream. Laughing children jump up and down in the water as men and women wade waist-deep and face the rising sun to pray. Upstream, professional launderers beat clothes on the rocks and lay them out on the stones of the riverbank to dry.

The boat turns back downstream, passing the stairs where you first descended to the river. In the bright morning light you see large umbrellas, under which teachers sit cross-legged, some with disciples around them. Who, you wonder, are these teachers? The area near the shore is crammed with people and boats. On a nearby boat, people shout, *Ganga Ma ki Jai*—"Victory to Mother Ganges!"

The boat continues downstream. On the shore, smoke rises from small pyres, where bodies wrapped in red and white cloth are being cremated. The boatman warns, "No photos here, please." The boat pulls in to shore downstream of the pyres, and everyone gets off. Walking up the stairs, you see small groups of people quietly watching the cremations. At the pyres, a man tends the fires with a bamboo pole, and a dog wanders nearby.

Later, as you make your way back to the center of town, you notice a pedicab with a covered body tied on the back. It cycles past women sitting beside the road selling plastic bracelets and colored powders. The pedicab

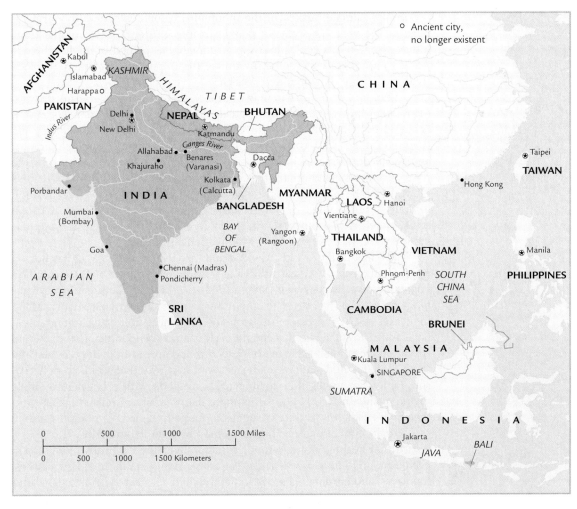

FIGURE 3.1
India and the area
of Hindu influence

must be on its way to the pyres, you think. The blend of opposites fills your
mind: on the banks of the very same river, laundry is washed and bodies
are burned; in the streets, life and death are side-by-side—yet no one seems
to notice the contrasts. Here, the two are one.

THE ORIGINS OF HINDUISM

Looking at a map of India (Figure 3.1) you can see that this subcontinent,
shaped like a diamond, is isolated. Two sides face the sea, while the north is
bounded by the steep Himalaya Mountains. There are few mountain passes,
and the only easy land entry is via the narrow corridor in the northwest, in
the vicinity of the Indus River, where Pakistan now lies. It is the relative
isolation of India that has helped create a culture that is rare and fascinating.

India's climate, except in the mountain regions, is generally warm for most of the year. This allows people to live outdoors much of the time. Indeed, some may even claim that the climate has helped promote religious values that, at least for some, minimize the importance of material goods such as clothing, housing, and wealth.

Although hot and dry in many parts, India has many rivers and streams. Most important is the Ganges, which flows out of the Himalayas and is enlarged by tributaries as it moves east toward the Bay of Bengal. By the time the Ganges has reached the town of Benares (also known as Varanasi and Kashi), the river is enormous; in fact, after the summer monsoons the river becomes so wide that often one cannot see to the other side. Because the water of the Ganges is regular and dependable, it has enabled civilization to flourish across much of northern India. It has also given Indian culture a sense of security, protection, and even care, which has led to the popular name for the river, *Ganga Ma* ("Mother Ganges").

The religious life of India is something like the river Ganges. It has flowed along for thousands of years, swirling from its own power but also from the power of new streams that have added to its force. Hinduism, the major religion of India, has been an important part of this flowing energy. Many influences—early indigenous religion and influences from later immigrants—have added to its inherent momentum. It has no one identifiable founder, no strong organizational structure to defend it and spread its influence, nor any creed to define and stabilize its beliefs; and in a way that seems to defy reason, Hinduism unites the worship of many gods with a belief in a single divine reality. In fact, Hinduism is more like a family of related beliefs, and the name *Hinduism,* if used to suggest a unified religion, can be misleading.

But the limitations of Hinduism may also be its strengths. It is like a palace that began as a two-room cottage. Over the centuries, wings have been built on to it, and now it has countless rooms, stairs, corridors, statues, fountains, and gardens. There is something here to please and astonish—and dismay—almost everyone. In fact, its beliefs are so rich and profound that Hinduism has greatly influenced the larger world, and its influence is growing still. In this chapter we will explore the various elements of this religion's foundation and the stages in which additions were made to the sprawling house of Hinduism.

The Earliest Stage of Indian Religion

In the early twentieth century, engineers who were building a railroad discovered the ruins of an ancient culture in the Indus River valley. Today, most of the Indus River lies in Pakistan, but it traditionally formed the natural border of northwestern India—in fact, the words *India* and *Hindu* derive from *Indus.* The culture that archeological workers uncovered there flourished before 2000 B.C.E. and is named the Harappa culture, after one of its ancient cities (Timeline 3.1).

Archeologists were amazed by the type of civilization they had found. The cities contained regular streets and solid brick houses. Pots and coins

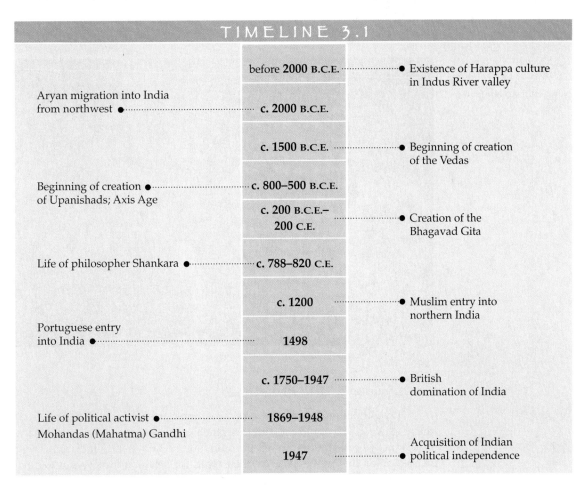

	before **2000** B.C.E.	● Existence of Harappa culture in Indus River valley
Aryan migration into India from northwest ●	**c. 2000** B.C.E.	
	c. 1500 B.C.E.	● Beginning of creation of the Vedas
Beginning of creation ● of Upanishads; Axis Age	**c. 800–500** B.C.E.	
	c. 200 B.C.E.–**200** C.E.	● Creation of the Bhagavad Gita
Life of philosopher Shankara ●	**c. 788–820** C.E.	
	c. 1200	● Muslim entry into northern India
Portuguese entry into India ●	**1498**	
	c. 1750–1947	● British domination of India
Life of political activist ● Mohandas (Mahatma) Gandhi	**1869–1948**	
	1947	● Acquisition of Indian political independence

Timeline of significant events in the history of Hinduism.

were found, as well as evidence that running water was used for toilets and baths. As historian Arthur Basham remarks, "no other ancient civilization until that of the Romans had so efficient a system of drains"[1]—a genuine sign of technical development. This complex culture had also invented a writing system, which scholars are still working to decipher.

Property owners marked their belongings with seals bearing the images of animals, such as the bull, tiger, and rhinoceros, as well as images of men and women. Three seals show a male, sitting in a yogic meditation posture, with horns on his head.[2] Small pillars that suggest male sexuality were also found. Because many of these same symbols still appear in contemporary Indian culture, we can assume that some current religious practices have survived from the distant past. For example, the male with the horns on his head may be a deity and an early form of the god Shiva, and the pillars resemble the low columns that some contemporary Indians worship in honor of Shiva (see page 97). It is also quite possible that the present-day worship of the divine Great Mother and of tree spirits goes back to this early time.

The ancient Vedic fire ceremony is a part of this New Delhi wedding.

The Aryans and Their Religion

It is widely thought that around 2000 B.C.E. another people entered India from the northwest. They brought with them their own religion, which would make its distinctive contribution to what would later be known as Hinduism. These people called themselves Aryans, their word for *noble,* and they seem to have spread in several directions from their place of origin—probably southeastern Europe. Some settled in Iran (whose name derives from *Aryan*), and others went to western Europe, becoming the ancestors of the Greeks, Romans, and Germans. The "Indo-European" language they spoke, which scholars have reconstructed, is distantly related to the family of languages that includes Sanskrit, Hindi, Greek, Latin, French, Spanish, German, and English.

The Aryans who came to India spread throughout the region of the earlier Harappa culture, which may have already disintegrated by the time the Aryans came. They were an active, warrior-dominated, patriarchal society that herded animals and loved horses. Whether their entry into India was rapid or gradual is not certain. It may have extended over many centuries between approximately 2500 and 1500 B.C.E. Their advance was certainly helped by their technology, particularly horsedrawn chariots. The Aryans had a social system of three classes—priests, warriors, and commoners. When the Aryans took over the Harappa culture, they generally placed the conquered people, whom they called *dasas* (servants), below their own classes—although some evidence suggests that there was assimilation into higher ranks as well.

Aryan religion consisted of the worship of mostly male gods who were believed to control the forces of nature. The father of the gods was Dyaüs Pitr, whose name means "shining father." (He is clearly the same god as the Roman god Jupiter and the Greek god Zeus Pater.) The god Indra, god of storm and war, received great attention because of the strength his worshipers hoped to receive from him. He was possibly the memory of a military ancestor, deified by later generations. The god of fire, Agni (whose name is related to the English word *ignite* and to the Latin word for fire, *ignis*), carried sacrifices up to the world of the gods. Dawn and renewal were the charge of the goddess Ushas, one of the few female deities. The god Rudra brought winds. Varuna was the god of the sky and justice; Vishnu was a god of cosmic order; and Surya was the major sun god. The god Soma was thought to cause altered states of mind and to expand consciousness. He worked through a ritual drink, possibly made from a psychedelic mushroom that had the same name (*soma*) and allowed contact with the realm of the gods. The god Yama ruled the afterlife.

Worship of the gods took place at outdoor fire altars. Priestly specialists set apart a square or rectangular space, purified it with water, and constructed one to three low altars inside the space for sacrifice. The usual offerings were milk, clarified butter (called *ghee*), grains, and sometimes animals. A special horse sacrifice, believed to confer great power on a king, occurred on rare occasions.

Sacred chants, which the priests knew from memory, were an essential part of the ceremonies; and because they believed that the chants had power of their own, the priestly class protected them and handed them down orally from father to son. It is these chants, in written form, that make up the core of the Aryans' earliest sacred literature, called the **Vedas.** Although many of the Aryan gods are no longer worshiped, elements of the Aryan religion—such as the use of fire and some of the ancient chants by a priestly class—continue to be of great importance to Hindus today.

The Vedas

The Vedas, which originally were preserved only in oral form but eventually were written down, are the earliest sacred books of Hinduism. The name means "knowledge" or "sacred lore," and related words in English are *vision* and *wisdom*. Although scholars date the earliest versions of the Vedas to about 1500 B.C.E., pious Hindus consider them to be far more ancient. They say that the Vedas were revealed to *rishis* (holy men of the distant past), who did not create the Vedas but heard them and transmitted them to later generations. It is also possible that some of the Vedic material may reflect assimilation of pre- and non-Aryan traditions.

There are four basic sacred text collections that constitute the Vedas. The Rig Veda[3] ("hymn knowledge") is a collection of more than a thousand chants to the Aryan gods; the Yajur Veda ("ceremonial knowledge") contains matter for recitation during sacrifice; the Sama Veda ("chant knowledge") is a handbook of musical elaborations of Vedic chants; and the Atharva Veda ("knowledge from [the teacher] Atharva") consists of practical prayers and charms, such as prayers to protect against snakes and sickness.

The Rig Veda, the most important of the Vedas, has an account of the origin of the universe. The universe is said to have emerged from a division and cosmic sacrifice of a primeval superperson, Purusha. But the account includes an admission of uncertainty: "Who knows it for certain; who can proclaim it here; namely, out of what it was born and wherefrom his creations issued? The gods appeared only later—after the creation of the world. Who knows, then, out of what it has evolved?"[4]

The term *Vedas* sometimes indicates only these four collections. In its more common use, it also refers to some later material as well. Detailed ceremonial rules, called Brahmanas and Aranyakas, were added by later generations to each of the four Vedic collections. The Brahmanas, named for the priests who would use them, give details about the proper time and place for ceremonies, the preparation of the ground, ritual objects, and purification rites. The Aranyakas ("forest books") allowed the rituals to be understood and practiced in nonliteral, symbolic ways by men who had left society and become ascetics in the forests. The four Vedas end with even later works, called the **Upanishads,** which express philosophical and religious ideas that arose in introspective and meditative traditions.

THE UPANISHADS AND THE AXIS AGE

Around 500 B.C.E., the Indo-Aryan civilization experienced such widespread and important changes that the period is known as the Axis Age, meaning that everything turned in a new direction at this time. Interestingly, great changes were also taking place in other religions and cultures as well: it was the time of the Buddha, Confucius, major Hebrew prophets, and early Greek philosophers.

After many centuries, the Indo-Aryans had become so firmly settled in the Indus and Ganges river valleys that the environment and their own indigenization began to influence their traditional religious practices. The older Aryan religion had been active, optimistic, patriarchal, and polytheistic. Questioning of religious beliefs and practices—perhaps prompted by the settled agricultural lifestyle—began to emerge with strength. It is possible that pre-Aryan religious disciplines reasserted themselves, and there may have been resentment against the Aryan priestly class. Some critics questioned the value of the Vedic sacrifices, and we know from the Aranyakas that certain people abandoned social life to live alone in the forests, giving themselves much time for thought and religious experimentation. Thinkers questioned the ancient belief in many gods, seeking instead a single divine reality that might be the source of everything.[5] Some went even further and saw all things as being mystically united. And a few rejected religious ritual altogether.

During this period there seems to have been interest in all sorts of techniques for altering consciousness, such as sitting for long periods in meditation, breathing deeply, fasting, avoiding sexual activity, practicing long periods of silence, going without sleep, experimenting with psychedelic plants, and living in the darkness of caves. All of these things could be done by people of any social class—not just by priests. Evidence of this intellectual ferment and the practice of spiritual disciplines is recorded in the Upanishads.

The Origin of the Upanishads

The Upanishads are a collection of about a hundred written works that record insights into external and internal reality. Although several interpretations of

An ascetic carries water from the Ganges as a cow pursues its own path.

the origin of the name *Upanishads* have been proposed, the name is commonly thought to be derived from words that mean "sitting near."[6] If the term's derivation is correct, it would suggest disciples sitting near a master, learning techniques for achieving religious experience. In any case, primary to the Upanishads is the notion that with spiritual discipline and meditation both priests and nonpriests can experience the spiritual reality that underlies all seemingly separate realities. Unlike much of the earlier Vedic material, which dictates that only hereditary priests can be religious masters, the Upanishads tell us that a person who has the necessary experience can be a spiritual master. The Upanishads thus possibly continue the religious interest of the forest dwellers of the Aranyakas.

The Upanishads are written primarily in dialogue form, appearing both as prose and as poetry. Because they were produced over many hundreds of years, dating them is not easy. It is generally thought that those in prose form (such as the Chandogya, Brihadaranyaka, Taittiriya, and Kena Upanishads) may be earlier works than those in poetic form (such as the Katha and Mandukya Upanishads). About a dozen Upanishads are especially popular.

Important Concepts of the Upanishads

The most important notions in the Upanishads are *Brahman, Atman, maya, karma, samsara,* and *moksha.*[7] These primary concepts, which would become

A brahmin and his associates perform a sundown ceremony that opens an all-night temple festival in Bali.

essential notions in much later Hindu spirituality, continue to be taught today.

Brahman and Atman   The term **Brahman** originally stood for the cosmic power present in the Vedic sacrifice and chants, over which the priest had control. (The Sanskrit word *Brahman* is neuter and comes from a stem meaning "to be great.") In the Upanishads the word *Brahman* was expanded to mean a divine reality at the heart of things. One of the most famous dialogues appears in the Chandogya Upanishad. It involves a priestly father and his son in discussion. The young man, Shvetaketu, has been away studying and memorizing priestly lore—chants and rituals—with a specialist for many years. The young man's father questions him about what he has learned, and his son proudly recites the many formulas he knows. The father then asks him what he knows about Brahman, the Supreme Spirit; but the young man knows nothing. Trying to assist the son's understanding, the father asks his son to fill a glass with water, put salt in it, and leave it overnight. The next day he asks his son to find the salt:

> "Bring me the salt you put into the water last night."
> Shvetaketu looked into the water, but could not find it, for it had dissolved.
> His father then said: "Taste the water from this side. How is it?"

"It is salt [salty]."

"Taste it from the middle. How is it?"

"It is salt."

"Taste it from that side. How is it?"

"It is salt."

"Look for the salt again and come again to me."

The son did so, saying: "I cannot see the salt. I only see water."

The father then said: "In the same way, O my son, you cannot see the Spirit.
But in truth he is here.

"An invisible and subtle essence is the Spirit of the whole universe. That is
Reality. That is Truth. Thou art That."[8]

The Upanishads insist that Brahman is something that can be known—
not simply believed in. The Shvetasvatara Upanishad, for example, says "I
know that Spirit whose infinity is in all, who is ever one beyond time."[9]
Brahman, the Divine Spirit, is so real that it may be known directly, and, as
the boy Shvetaketu learned, knowledge of it can be as immediate as tasting
a flavor.

What is it to know Brahman? The Upanishads insist that it cannot be put
fully into words, but they give hints. Brahman is the lived experience that all
things are in some way holy because they come from the same sacred source.
It is also the experience that all things are in some way ultimately one, a concept that seems to defy common sense—since the world appears to be divided
into many objects and types of reality. Nevertheless, when we consider reality
more deeply, we recognize many unities: a piece of wood can become a boat
or a house or fire or ash; water can turn into a cloud or a plant. So, on closer
inspection, all apparent separations and divisions blur. To experience Brahman
is to know, firsthand, that every apparently individual reality in the world is
actually a wave of the same sacred ocean of energy. Brahman, according to the
Upanishads, "is the sun, the moon, and the stars. He is the fire, the waters, and
the wind."[10] Brahman is "the God who appears in forms infinite."[11]

Brahman is also referred to by three words that help describe its nature
as perceived by the knower: Brahman is *sat,* reality itself; *chit,* pure consciousness; and *ananda,* bliss. And although Brahman can be experienced
within our everyday world of time and space, those who speak of their
experience say that Brahman is ultimately beyond time and beyond space.
Thus the Upanishads often add that experiencing the timelessness of Brahman
can bring an end to everyday suffering and to the fear of death.

The notion of **Atman** is related to Brahman and is an equally important
term in the Upanishads. Although Atman is sometimes translated as *self* or
soul, the notion of Atman in the Upanishads is different from the notion of
an individual soul. Perhaps the term Atman would be better translated as
deepest self. (Sometimes it is translated as *subtle self.*) In Hindu belief, each
person has an individual soul (*jiva*), and the individual soul confers uniqueness and personality. But Hinduism asks this question: At the very deepest
level, what really am I? I am clearly not just my body—my height and
weight and hair color, all of which are subject to alteration. But am I then

my tastes, thoughts, and memories? Or is there more? Is there not in me a reality more fundamental than those changing individual characteristics? According to the Upanishads, at the deepest level of what I am is a divine reality, a divine spirit, that everything shares. The Upanishads teach that it is true to say that I am God, because, for the person who understands reality at the deepest level, everything is God. Atman, when experienced fully, is identical with Brahman. Atman, like Brahman, is divine, holy, and time-less. Often the term *Brahman* refers to the experience of the sacred and divine reality within nature and the external universe, while *Atman* refers to the experience of the sacred within oneself. However, the same divine nature simply has two names, and both terms may be used interchangeably.

Maya   The Upanishads speak of the everyday world as **maya,** which is usually translated as "illusion."[12] This translation, though, needs explana-tion. Its root suggests illusion and mystery (as in "magic"), but it also has a more positive, objective connotation that suggests the original stuff of which something is made (as in "material"). The word *maya* thus contains both meanings: "magic" and "matter." To say that all reality is "maya" is not to say that the world does not exist or that the world is a totally false percep-tion. The world is real but not in quite the way most people assume. For one thing, human beings view the world as consisting of individual things and people, all separate. In reality, the world is one basic holy reality that takes on many different forms. The Shvetasvatara Upanishad advises us to "know therefore that nature is Maya, but that God is the ruler of Maya; and that all beings in our universe are parts of his infinite splendour."[13]

People also assume that the world is solid and permanent. In reality, the outside world is more like the inner world of thoughts and dreams—it shifts and changes, just as thoughts and dreams do. People assume that time is real, that it advances at a regular rate, and that past, present, and future are distinct divisions. In reality, time is relative.

The model of reality set forth by the Upanishads is less like a machine made of individual moving parts; it is more like a great consciousness. This view also produces a sense of amazement at the forms and shifts the universe takes—it is all, ultimately, unexplainable magic.

In the Upanishads, death is not a tragedy. However, as I look out at real-ity from my own individual standpoint, I may see the end of my life as the end of everything. The Upanishads see things differently. First, individuals are not as individual as they suppose but rather are all the manifestation of the Divine Spirit, which does not end when the individual dies. They are also the continuation of earlier forms of life that have simply taken new forms. Hinduism, from about 500 B.C.E., generally adopted the belief that everything living has its own life force and that every life force, when it loses one form, is reborn into another. This process is known as reincarnation.

Karma   The general Hindu notion of rebirth assumes that human beings have at one or another time existed as a "lower" form, such as animal, insect, and possibly even plant. Hinduism also recognizes grades of human life, from limited and painful to exceptionally pleasant and free. Human beings are also capable of achieving "higher" forms of life, such as superhuman beings and demigods. Rebirth can move in either direction, and the human stage is a dangerous one because each human being must make dramatic choices about how to live. If a human being does not live properly, he or she may be reborn into a very poor or cruel human family—or possibly in the form of life that may be even more limited and difficult, such as a dog, a pig, or an ant. A human being can also make a spectacular leap upward beyond the human level to a superhuman existence or even beyond, to complete freedom.

What determines the direction of one's rebirth is **karma.** The word comes from a root that means "to do" and implies the notion of moral consequences that are carried along with every act. Karma is the moral law of cause and effect, and belief in karma is a belief that every action has an automatic moral consequence.

Some teachers say that karma is intrinsically neither good nor bad but only seems so to the person who experiences it. In this conception, karma is like gravity—it works like a force of nature. It is like rain, which can cause a plant to grow just as it can bring a picnic to its end. Karma helps explain why some people are born with great gifts while others are born with no advantages at all.

Samsara   The term **samsara** refers to the wheel of life, the circle of constant rebirth, and it suggests strongly that the everyday world is full of change as well as struggle and suffering. The Hindu view of human life, because of its belief in reincarnation, is rather different from that commonly held in the West. Think of the times you've heard someone say, "You only live once." This view of life is not shared by Hindus, who believe an individual is constantly being reborn, having come from different earlier forms and going on to emerge in new forms in the future. Because our present human life is so short, we may think that we would like several lives in the future as well. But how many would each of us really like? Ten might sound reasonable, but a hundred? a thousand? ten thousand? a million? It's tiring to just think about all those lifetimes! And many of those forms would inevitably be unhappy ones. Sooner or later most of us would want to jump off the merry-go-round of life. We would want escape, release, liberation. This leads us to the next important concept of the Upanishads.

Moksha   The term **moksha** means "freedom" or "liberation" and comes from a root that means "to be released." In the Upanishads, moksha is the ultimate human goal. It has various connotations. Moksha certainly includes the notion of getting beyond egotistic responses, such as resentment and anger, which limit the individual. Furthermore, unlike the modern ideal of seeking complete freedom to satisfy one's individual desires, moksha implies liberation even from the limitations of being an individual—from being born a particular person at a specific time to a unique pair of parents—a person with distinct physical characteristics, emotions, desires, and memories. One can take action to overcome these restrictions (for example, by leaving home), which is sometimes a means of attaining moksha, but one can also accept the limitations even while living with them, thereby gaining inner peace and mental freedom.

As one becomes freer, one looks at life less from a selfish and egotistic point of view and more from a perspective that embraces the whole. The unity and sacredness that everything shares become a part of everyday experience. Kindness to all—to animals as well as to people—is one natural result of this new insight, and kind actions also generate helpful karma. Detaching oneself from pleasure or pain is another practice that leads to freedom from egotism.

Ultimately, with enough insight and ascetic practice, the individual can go entirely beyond the limited self to know the sacred reality that everything shares. When insight and kindness are perfect, at last the pain of rebirth ends; the limitations of individuality are gone, and only Brahman remains. The Brihadaranyaka Upanishad explains complete freedom: "when all has become Spirit, one's own Self, how and whom could one see?"[14]

The Upanishads, though sometimes obscure, are devoted to promoting an insight into ultimate oneness. But the Upanishads do not give detailed instructions for achieving that kind of insight or for living spiritually in the everyday world. Such guidance would have to be developed by later Hindu commentators and practitioners.

LIVING SPIRITUALLY IN THE EVERYDAY WORLD

The Hinduism that guides people's lives today is a practical mixture of elements, some of which came from the early stages of religious practice, which we've already discussed, and others that developed later. For the ordinary layperson, Hindu practice usually involves devotion to at least one deity. It recommends finding one's proper work and then doing it unselfishly. Hindu practice may also include the study of religious texts, meditation, and other specifically religious disciplines. The following section will deal with the elements of this practical synthesis, much of which can be found in the short classic, the Bhagavad Gita.

The Bhagavad Gita

The **Bhagavad Gita** ("divine song" or "song of the Divine One") is part of a very long epic poem called the Mahabharata. The Mahabharata, written some time between 400 B.C.E. and 400 C.E., tells how the sons of Pandu (Pandavas) conquered their cousins, the Kauravas, with the help of the god Krishna. The Bhagavad Gita was inserted at some time into this poem but has its own identity and is often printed separately from the Mahabharata. The Bhagavad Gita, shaped by the priestly class between 200 B.C.E. and 200 C.E., has become a spiritual classic. It recalls themes from the Upanishads, but it also tries to strike a balance between mysticism and the practical needs of everyday life. Action and adherence to duty are approved and can even be thought of as a spiritual path. As the Bhagavad Gita says, "the wise see knowledge and action as one."[15]

Portrayals of Krishna are popular among his devotees and frequently show him as a boy or young man. In this vivid water-color garden, Krishna and his consort Radha are venerated by cows.

The Bhagavad Gita, like the Upanishads, is written in dialogue form. It occurs almost entirely between two figures: a prince, Arjuna, and his charioteer and advisor, Krishna. Arjuna's royal power is threatened by his hundred cousins, called Kauravas, and he must decide whether to fight with his brothers against them to restore his throne or to accept their rule. He is torn. On the one hand, he knows that his rule is correct, but on the other, he wants to avoid violence. That his enemies are close family members makes the matter even harder. Depressed, Arjuna "[throws] aside his arrows and his bow in the midst of the battlefield. He [sits] down on the seat of the chariot, and his heart [is] overcome with sorrow."[16] In response, Krishna, who later reveals that he is a form of the god Vishnu, explains the need for action. "Now you shall hear how a man may become perfect, if he devotes himself to the work which is natural to him. A man shall reach perfection if he does his duty as an act of worship to the Lord."[17]

Contrary to the teaching of nonviolence, which was at the time of this epic's creation growing strong in India in such religious traditions as Buddhism and Jainism, Krishna advises Arjuna to fight to protect his throne and the structure of society—to fight is his duty. At a moment of great revelation, Krishna shows Arjuna that a divine reality is at work within everything in the universe—in living and also in dying. Krishna even says that for the warrior "there is nothing nobler than a righteous war."[18]

The recommendation that Arjuna should fight has posed a moral problem for some followers of Hinduism. Mohandas Gandhi (1869–1948) is typical of those who have solved this problem by saying that the Bhagavad Gita is religious allegory. Gandhi held that the call to arms is not about real war but rather a call to fight against dangerous moral and psychological forces, such as ignorance, selfishness, and anger. This interpretation, though it seems to go against the literal intent of the text, has been influential.

We should note here the nobility of the personality of Krishna in the Bhagavad Gita. His dignity is a subject that has inspired much art and literature and has been portrayed frequently in film and on television.

The Caste System

When Krishna urges Arjuna to do what his position as a warrior demands, he is reinforcing the **caste** system (a division of society into social classes that are created by birth or occupation). The caste system, the prevalent social system of the Aryans, had already been mentioned in the Rig Veda: "When they divided Purusha [the first person, a superbeing], in how many different portions did they arrange him? What became of his mouth, what of his two arms? What were his two thighs and his two feet called? His mouth became the brahman [priest]; his two arms were made into the rajanya [warrior-noble]; his two thighs the vaishyas [merchants]; from his two feet the shudra [peasant] was born."[19]

The caste system receives further religious approval in the Bhagavad Gita, which recognizes that there are different types of people and that their ways to perfection will differ, depending on their personality type and role in society.[20] For example, active people will perfect themselves through the unselfishness of their work, and intellectual people will perfect themselves through teaching and study.

Traditionally, the caste system was based on more than one's type of work, and in modern times it does not always indicate the type of work a person does. Castes (as the term is commonly used) are really social classes (*varna*), which are subdivided into hundreds of subcastes.[21] The caste system dissuades members of different castes, and often subcastes, from intermarrying. It remains strongest in the countryside and in more conservative southern India, but it is weakening in the cities, where people regularly eat together in restaurants and travel together in buses and trains. Members of society are divided into five main social classes:

1. The priest (*brahmin*)[22] traditionally performs Vedic rituals and acts as a counselor. In modern times, members of this caste are also in demand as cooks, which is seen as a natural extension of the priestly relationship with fire and sacrifice. This function is practical because **brahmins**, being of the highest caste, may prepare food for people in all other castes as well as their own.

2. The warrior-noble (*kshatriya*) has the role of protecting society. This is the traditional caste of the aristocracy.

3. The merchant (*vaishya*) class includes landowners, moneylenders, and sometimes artisans. Males of the three upper castes (brahmin, kshatriya, and vaishya) receive a sacred cord during a ceremony in their youth and afterward are called "twice-born."

4. The peasant (*shudra*) does manual labor and is expected to serve the higher castes. The origin of this caste probably goes back to the Aryan subjection of native people, who were forced to do the work of servants. The peasant is called "once-born."

5. The untouchable (*dalit*) traditionally does the dirtiest work—cleaning toilets, sweeping streets, collecting animal carcasses, and tanning animal hides. What was probably an early concern for hygiene led to the separation of untouchables from the rest of society. Untouchables have routinely been denied the use of wells used by other social classes and have even been forbidden from entering many temples. They have often been forced to live in ghettos and sometimes have been horribly mistreated. Their low status prompted the Indian reformer Mohandas Gandhi to promote another name for the class—*Harijan* ("children of God")—and he urged their inclusion in regular society.[23]

The Stages of Life

Just as the individual's path to "correct action" is suggested by caste and subcaste, traditional Hinduism holds that each stage of life also has its proper way of being lived. Every culture recognizes specific life stages through which each individual passes. In modern secular life the stages seem to be childhood, adolescence, the career years, and retirement (these stages are strongly colored by employment—or the lack of it); but in India the notion of life stages is more religious. The conception was shaped by the ancient ideal of the development of the upper-caste male, particularly of the priestly caste:

1. Student (*brahmacharin*): This first stage is spent laying a religious foundation for life. The young person, between the ages of 8 and 20, studies religious works. Celibacy is a necessary part of the training.
2. Householder (*grihastha*): Marriage (traditionally, arranged by the parents) occurs at about age 20, and the person fulfills the demands of society by raising children.
3. Retiree (*vanaprastha*): When grandchildren arrive, the individual may retire somewhat from ordinary life to spend time once again on religious matters. The ancient ideal was to go into the forest to live, possibly with one's wife, away from society. In reality, retirees often continue to live with their children and with other relatives in an extended-family setting, but they may eat separately from the rest of the family and spend time on religious pursuits with friends.
4. Renunciate (*sannyasin*): To enter this last stage is considered to be appropriate only after retirement. It is not expected of everyone but is simply an option. If one wishes to live entirely free from society, one is permitted to leave home. For such a person, the entire world is now his home. A man may leave his wife, although he must ensure that she will be supported. Celibacy is expected, and the sign of this devout, celibate state is an orange robe. The **sannyasin,** considered to be outside the caste system, is free to wander, begging his food along the way, and many temples have endowments to feed such pilgrims. The sannyasin may remain a constant traveler, making pilgrimage to the sacred sites of India, or he may settle in an **ashram** (religious community) or even live in a cave. The purpose of this kind of life is to hasten mystical insight, to free oneself of all attachments, to end rebirth, and to attain moksha.

The Goals of Life

Although the Hindu spiritual ideal—such as the lifestyle of the sannyasin—is generally world-denying, Hinduism also exhibits a respect for more worldly goals. In order of increasing value these goals are pleasure (*kama*), economic security and power (*artha*), and social and religious duty (*dharma*). These life goals, which may be pursued simultaneously, are acceptable and even virtuous, as long as they are tempered by moderation and social regulation. Considered highest of the goals, however, is moksha—complete freedom.

The Yogas

Although the Bhagavad Gita endorses quiet contemplation, it also recommends active spiritual paths. It endorses not only meditation but also the work demanded by one's caste and individual place in society. The various types of **yoga** are methods that can be used to help people live spiritually.

The word *yoga* means "union" and is related to the English words *join* and *yoke*. A yoga is a way for people to perfect their union with the divine, and because the yogas suggest roads to perfection, they are also called *margas* ("paths"). There is a tolerant recognition in Hinduism that different sorts of people need different spiritual paths, and an individual's caste and personality type will help determine the appropriate yoga to practice.

Jnana Yoga ("Knowledge Yoga")   This type of yoga brings insight into one's divine nature by studying the Upanishads and the Bhagavad Gita and their commentaries and by learning from gurus who have attained insight. **Jnana yoga** is particularly appropriate for priests and intellectuals.

This yoga was highly refined by a school of philosophy that is still quite vital, the school of Vedanta ("Veda end").[24] The term refers to the Upanishads—which come at the end of the Vedas—and to the fact that the Vedanta school has used the ideas of the Upanishads as its primary inspiration.

The greatest teacher of Vedanta, Shankara (c. 788–820), argued that everything is ultimately one—all is Brahman.[25] According to Shankara, although our ordinary experience leads us to see things as being separate and different, this perception is mistaken. To show that sense perception can be wrong, Shankara used the example of a person who at dusk is frightened by a coil of rope—the observer mistakenly perceives the rope to be a snake. In the same way, Shankara would say, a person who perceives things as being ultimately separate and different from Brahman is mistaken. In his *Crest-Jewel of Discrimination,* the author likened Brahman to gold, which can take many shapes. Brahman "is that one Reality which appears to our ignorance as a manifold universe of names and forms and changes. Like the gold of which many ornaments are made, it remains in itself unchanged. Such is Brahman, and 'That art Thou.' Meditate upon this truth."[26] Similarly, the waves of the ocean and the drops of water in the waves may be considered separate entities; but the larger truth is that they are all just the same ocean in varied, changing forms.

Shankara thought that spiritual liberation was achieved when the individual personally came to understand the unity of all things. Shankara so emphasized *monism*—the oneness of everything—that his branch of the Vedanta school is called *Advaita,* which, literally translated, means "not-two-ness" (*a-dvai-ta*). The significance of the term is very subtle. If I say that all reality is "one," some "other" reality could also exist—something in contrast to the one. But the term *not-two* makes clear that ultimately there is no other reality.

For Shankara, therefore, any devotion to a god or goddess who is thought to be different from the worshiper is also mistaken. This rejection of devotion, however, posed a great problem for those types of Hinduism that emphasized it. As a result, later thinkers of the Vedanta school, such as Ramanuja (c. 1040–1137) and Madhva (fl. 1240), qualified or denied ultimate monism. They emphasized passages in the Upanishads that seem to speak of Brahman as being separate in some way from the world. They could thereby create systems that made room for religious devotion.

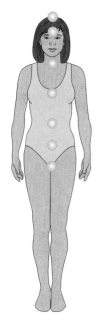

Karma Yoga ("Action Yoga") This type of yoga proposes that all useful work, if done unselfishly, can be a way to perfection. (The word *karma* here is used in its basic sense of "activity.") Much of what we ordinarily do is motivated by money or pleasure or praise, but deeds performed without a desire for reward are the heart of **karma yoga**. As the Bhagavad Gita says, "Desire for the fruits of work must never be your motive in working."[27]

Bhakti Yoga ("Devotion Yoga") Most of us have at one time or another fallen in love, and we know that there is something purifying about the experience, because it forces us to look outward, beyond ourselves, to another object of affection. Religions utilize this purifying power when they promote devotion to a god or saint—who is often made visible in a painting or statue. Hinduism, because of its belief in multiple gods, offers rich possibilities for devotion. In the Bhagavad Gita, Krishna tells Arjuna, "Regard me as your dearest loved one. Know me to be your only refuge."[28]

Bhakti yoga can involve various expressions of devotion—most commonly chants, songs, food offerings, and the anointing of statues. Bhakti yoga can extend also to acts of devotion shown to one's **guru** (spiritual teacher), to one's parents, and to one's spouse. The gods worshiped in bhakti yoga will be described later.

The chakras are centers through which energy rises from the base of the spine to the crown of the head.

Raja Yoga ("Royal Yoga") This type of yoga promotes meditation. The term **raja yoga** does not appear in the Bhagavad Gita but was introduced later to refer to the steps of meditation described in the box "Hindu Meditation: More Than Emptying the Mind." Nonetheless, Chapter 6 of the Bhagavad Gita describes basic meditation—sitting quietly, turning inward, and calming the mind. Done for short periods of time on a regular basis, meditation lowers stress and brings a sense of peace; done for longer periods of time, it can induce new states of consciousness.

There are many types of meditation. Some involve emptying the mind of thought; others involve focusing on some physical or mental object. Meditation can be done with one's eyes closed or open or focused on a point a short distance in front of the face. A word or brief phrase, called a **mantra,** is often recited with each breath to help clear the mind of thought. (The short mantra *Om*—which is sometimes called the sound of creation—is frequently used.) Meditation can be done in silence or to gentle music; it can also be done while gazing at a candle, at the moon, or at moving water. Some advanced types of meditation involve techniques taken from additional yogas. They may have the meditator create symbolic mental images (frequently of a deity), contemplate a sacred diagram (called a *yantra*), or repeat complicated sacred phrases.

Hatha yoga has spread beyond Hinduism because of its benefit to health and relaxation.

The many techniques of meditation are called *sadhanas* ("practices"), and **kundalini yoga**—one form of raja yoga—offers additional help toward the goal of meditation yoga. It emerged from a tradition called Tantrism, which focused on use of the body and all its energies to reach higher consciousness. Kundalini yoga teaches that there are seven psychic centers, called *chakras* ("wheels"), that exist one above the other along the spinal column. Meditation and physical exercises (as described below) help the meditator lift spiritual energy—called *kundalini* and envisioned as a coiled serpent—from one center to the next. Each chakra is like a gateway through which the kundalini passes, bringing increased insight and joy. When the kundalini reaches the topmost and seventh center of energy at the crown of the head, the practitioner experiences profound bliss. The topmost center of energy (*sahasrara*) appears in imagery as a lotus flower, and reaching it is compared to the opening of a lotus.

Hatha Yoga ("Force Yoga")   When most of us in the West think of yoga, we think of the physical exercises of **hatha yoga.** These exercises, which were originally developed to help make long periods of meditation easier, mostly involve stretching and balancing. Breathing exercises are sometimes considered a part of hatha yoga.

In addition to these five yogas are others. In fact, any set of techniques that leads to greater spirituality can be considered a yoga.

A priest prepares
to worship Shiva.

DEVOTIONAL HINDUISM

Indians have been primarily a rural, agricultural people, and even today only about fifteen percent of the population lives in cities. The rest live, as they have for centuries, in more than half a million villages. Men in the villages spend most of their waking hours working as merchants, craftsmen, and farmers, while women marry when young and spend most of their time preparing food, running their households, and caring for their children. The duties of everyday life leave little time to pursue more philosophical paths.

For the majority of Hindus, then, some of the spiritual disciplines just mentioned—study, meditation, and special physical exercises—have had limited appeal. Instead, the great majority of Hindus have followed the path of devotion (**bhakti**) to a god or gods. Hindus worship their gods in village temples and at home altars. Most worship daily, and there are special days dedicated to individual gods. **Puja,** devotional ritual commonly performed at an altar, involves the offering of flowers, food, fire, and incense to images of a god or gods, as well as the singing of hymns.

The earliest layer of devotional Hinduism, probably traceable to the pre-Aryan Harappa culture, seems to have involved the anointing of phallic stones, devotion to female divinities of fertility, and the worship of nature spirits. This type of religious devotion continues in India today.

The Aryan religion introduced the Vedic gods as additional objects of worship. Some of these, such as Indra and Agni, were once highly popular, while others, such as Dyaüs Pitr, lost devotees and moved to the background quite early. In this devotional pattern we can see that a certain fluctuation of interest is natural: throughout history, in all religious devotion, the stock of some gods rises while the stock of others falls.

Certain gods and goddesses seem to have emerged separately, not as a part of the Vedic pantheon—of these Krishna is one of the best known. Some animal forms became deified, and all deities were eventually incorporated loosely into what is today a fairly large pantheon.

Although Hinduism is often described as a religion that promotes a belief in many gods, in reality individuals often focus their devotion on only one of the gods. Sometimes that god is considered to be the greatest of all divine manifestations. There is also an underlying monotheistic tendency in Hinduism because all gods are frequently considered expressions of a single divine reality. Devotion to an individual god or goddess is often justified by saying that although the divine is ultimately formless, human beings must worship the divine through physical manifestations, giving rise to much painting, sculpture, music, and ceremony in honor of the gods described in the following sections.

The Trimurti: Brahma, Vishnu, and Shiva

Three gods have been particularly important in the devotional and artistic life of Hinduism. Although of differing origins, they have sometimes been linked together, particularly in art and philosophy, to represent the three forces of creation, preservation, and destruction. The three gods are Brahma, Vishnu, and Shiva. When linked together, they are often called the **Trimurti,** which means "triple form."

Brahma represents the creative force that made the universe. He is considered the personal aspect of Brahman and has been thought of as the special patron of the priestly class, the brahmins. Brahma is commonly depicted as an ancient, thoughtful king sitting on a throne. He has four faces, each looking in one of the four directions, and eight arms, each holding symbols of power. His companion animal is a white goose.

In India, worship of Brahma as a separate deity has declined over the past two hundred years, although he is still frequently represented in art, where he is pictured beside Vishnu or Shiva. Perhaps this decline in interest resulted from the popular view of Brahma in India as grandfatherly, distant, and less powerful than either Vishnu or Shiva. (Ironically, however, devotion to Brahma remains quite alive in Thailand, where local Buddhist practice shows many influences from Hinduism. Statues of Brahma appear frequently in outdoor "spirit houses," where food and flowers—and sometimes dance—are offered to him for good luck and protection.)

Vishnu represents the force of preservation in the universe. In the Vedas he is a god associated with the sun, although his role there appears to be small. Thought of as light and warmth that destroys darkness, Vishnu grew in stature until finally becoming a major god of Hinduism. Today Vishnu (in various forms) is the most important object of devotion in India, and about three quarters of all Hindus in India worship him or his manifestations. His followers are called Vaishnavites (or Vaishnavas).

In painting and sculpture, Vishnu is shown in many forms, though usually with a tall crown and a regal manner. Almost always he has four arms, which hold symbols of power. His companion animal is a great eaglelike bird, Garuda, on whom he flies through the universe.

Because Vishnu is associated with loving-kindness, it is believed that he can appear on earth at different times and in various physical forms to help those in need. Ten major incarnations (or **avatars**) of Vishnu are commonly listed, of which one is still to appear. Some previous incarnations were in animal form: a fish, a boar, and a tortoise. Another was Siddhartha Gautama, the Buddha—an intriguing inclusion, which helped Hinduism partially re-absorb Indian Buddhism (see chapter 4). The incarnation yet to come will be a savior figure on horseback who will judge the human race. Two incarnations of Vishnu are wildly popular—Rama and Krishna.

Rama may have been a historical figure who later took on mythic proportions. He appears in the great epic the Ramayana, whose stories of Rama have inspired dance as well as art. One of the most commonly told stories concerns the abduction of Rama's wife, Sita, by Ravan (or Ravana), the demon king of Sri Lanka. Rama, a king, gains the help of Hanuman, leader of the monkeys. Hanuman helps Rama in killing Ravan and in locating and returning Sita. Perhaps because of his image as a helper, Hanuman is today an immensely popular god in his own right.

In addition to the Ramayana, a later work called the Ramcharitmanas, written in Hindi in the sixteenth century by Tulsidas, has spread devotion to Rama and become a popular sacred text. In northern India, Rama is so revered that the term *Rama* is really a synonym for "God."

Krishna, another incarnation of Vishnu, may have begun as an object of fertility worship. He is depicted in several forms, which might indicate that he is a coalescence of traditions. In the long epic the Mahabharata, Krishna appears as a mature and solemn god. In later devotional works, the Puranas ("legends"), he is younger; there he is friends with *gopis* (milkmaids who look after herds of cows), and he steals butter and plays the flute, expressing the playful aspect of the divine. In depictions of Krishna, his face and skin are often blue, the color of the sky and of heaven, indicating his true otherworldly nature. His closest milkmaid companion is Radha, with whom he is romantically linked in the Hindu mind.

Shiva, the third of the Trimurti and the god linked with destruction, is the most complicated of the gods, both in origin and in conception. The horned figure, sitting in yogic meditation posture, that is found on seals from

Surrounded by the flames of destruction, Shiva as Nataraja (Ruler of the Dance) is the power at work in all death and regeneration. ▶

नटेश

Morning rituals in the Ganges may include the veneration of the lingam.

the Harappa period may be an early form of Shiva, meaning that some aspects of the present-day god may extend back to pre-Aryan India. Another early form is apparently the Vedic god Rudra, a dangerous god of mountains and winds, whom worshipers probably began to call *shiva* ("lucky") in order to neutralize the fear he inspired. In later times, however, his link with destructiveness is often shown in pictures of Shiva appearing at cremation grounds above a human body that is dissolving in flames.

Shiva's connection with destruction may be hard for many non-Hindus to appreciate. In Western religions, creation is associated with a good God, and destruction comes from what is not God—from sin or evil or Satan. In Hinduism, however, destruction is considered to be simply another part of the divine energy at work in the world. Destruction is a type of recycling, the necessary loss of form, which occurs so that new forms may appear; and death is always thought of as leading to new life. We know that the seed disappears when the tree grows, and the flower must die to make the fruit. Thus Shiva is also associated with re-creation.

The destructive side of Shiva is portrayed in the bronze statues called *Shiva Nataraja* ("ruler of the dance"). As he dances, Shiva is surrounded by a ring of fire (symbolic of destructive and transformative power), and his long yogi's hair flies in the air. He has four arms. In his upper right arm

is a drum, symbolizing creation and the beginning of time; and in the upper left arm is a flame, symbolizing destruction. His lower left arm is pointing to his upraised foot, suggesting that everyone should join him in his dance. His lower right arm is extended in blessing, which in a symbolic way says "Don't be afraid." He dances on a dwarf-demon, representing the ignorance of all those who do not understand that death is part of the divine process. The art historian Heinrich Zimmer explains that "conquest of this demon lies in the attainment of true wisdom. Therein is release from the bondages of the world."[31]

The aspect of Shiva that brings re-creation is represented by sexually suggestive forms. (We should note here that in nonindustrial societies the bearing of children is crucial—both for the economic survival of the family and for the care of the parents in their old age. Parents pray to have many healthy children.) A frequent representation of Shiva is a columnar *lingam*—often black, which adds to its mystery. It usually rests on a *yoni*— a circular base that is the female complement to the lingam. The lingam may be a large, natural stone worshiped outdoors; a metal object small enough to be worn around the neck; or a wooden piece of an appropriate size for worship in the home. Shaivites (devotees of Shiva) may pour various liquids, such as milk and rosewater, over the lingam in an act of devotion.

Fertility is further emphasized by Shiva's companion animal Nandi, the bull, and by Ganesha, the elephant-headed son of Shiva, who has become a symbol of strength and abundance. Both are frequently found in temples dedicated to Shiva. Worship of Shiva is most common in Kashmir and southern India. We should note, too, that Shiva is closely linked with destruction only when he is viewed as part of the Trimurti. Among Shaivites, he is the sole God and is not exclusively related to destruction.

The elephant-headed god Ganesha *(left)*, the son of Shiva, is believed to help devotees overcome obstacles. Pictures and statues of him are often found in shops in India, where he is prayed to daily for success. Hanuman, the monkey-headed god *(right)*, is revered for his help to the god Rama. He is extremely popular in northern India.

Those who have riches build temples for Thee; what shall I build? I am poor. My legs are the pillars; this body of mine is the temple.

—Basavaraja, in praise of Shiva[32]

Worship of the Divine Feminine: Devi

The three gods of the Trimurti are usually portrayed as masculine. But of all the great world religions, Hinduism perhaps most strongly recognizes the female aspects of divinity. This may come from a practical interest in fertility. Worship of female divinities, too, seems to have been a part of pre-Aryan religion, and elements of that early worship have lived on.

The Great Mother, also called **Devi** ("goddess"), is worshiped throughout India but particularly in the northeast. She is portrayed in many forms and can be both loving and cruel. She is especially harsh to those who show themselves unworthy of her love. Devi is frequently worshiped with extreme human feeling. The worshiper may take on the emotions and even the clothing of a child or spouse of the Great Mother. The mystic Ramakrishna (1836–1886), priest at a temple near Calcutta, spoke of his special devotion to her. "I practised austerities for a long time. I could no longer eat or sleep. My longing for the Divine Mother was so great that I would not eat or sleep. I would lie on the bare ground, placing my head on a lump of earth, and cry out loudly: 'Mother, Mother, why dost thou not come to me?' I did not know how the days and nights passed away. . . . When I reached the state of continuous ecstasy, I gave up all external forms of worship; I could no longer perform them. Then I prayed to my Divine Mother: 'Mother, who will now take care of me? I have no power to take care of myself.'"[33]

The Divine Feminine appears as several goddesses, of which the most popular are Durga and Kali. The goddess **Durga** ("awe-inspiring," "distant") is frequently represented with ten arms, full of implements used to destroy evil. Her face is serene, surrounded by a halo, and she wears a crown. She rides a tiger, which helps her conquer all dangerous obstacles.

Kali ("dark") is more fearsome still. She is often shown wearing a necklace of human skulls, and her fanged teeth drip with blood. Her many arms are full of weapons, which are thought to be dangerous to enemies but protective of her children. Calcutta ("Kali's stairs") is named after her temple in this city.

The important role of the Divine Feminine is also seen in the female consorts who accompany many male deities. They are so much a part of the male god that the god cannot be active without them, and thus they are called *shaktis* ("energies"), because they allow the male gods to be effective in the human world.

The goddess Saraswati is the consort of Brahma and is far more popular than he. She is the patron of music, the arts, and culture and is often portrayed with a musical instrument in her hand. The shakti of Vishnu is the goddess Lakshmi, who is commonly dressed as a queen and sits on a lotus. As the consort of Vishnu, she dispenses good luck and protection. Shiva is portrayed with a variety of shaktis, the best known being Parvati and Uma. Sometimes Shiva is himself portrayed as androgynous: half of his body is masculine, while the other side shows a female breast. This androgyny represents the unity that underlies all the apparent opposites of reality—a unity also spoken of in the Upanishads and the Bhagavad Gita.

Female deities are frequently worshiped in Hinduism. This is a particularly fine sculpture of Shiva's companion, the goddess Uma.

Divinities of nature are frequently female. The goddess Ganga, who animates the Ganges River, is a good example. Tree spirits, too, are considered female, and frequently it is women who offer them worship.

The Guru as Object of Devotion

Because Hinduism is not organized in a hierarchical fashion, devotion to a guru (spiritual teacher) is a large and ancient component of Hindu spirituality. The etymology of the word *guru* is expressive: "the one who removes darkness." Anyone who seeks spiritual growth—no matter what his or her caste or station in life—may seek a guru, whom the individual can visit regularly to seek advice. Even gurus who have taken vows of silence can offer advice and insight to their disciples by writing on tablets or simply by looking at them with love.

Although the majority of gurus are men, female gurus are not uncommon. All that is necessary is that the guru be recognized as a person of holiness. Because a guru expects to be surrounded by students and devotees, he or she will frequently set up an ashram, a religious community for

As a man may be blindfolded, and led away, and left in a strange place; and as, having been so dealt with, he turns in every direction and cries out for someone to remove his bandages and show him the way home; and as one thus entreated may loose his bandages and give him comfort; and as thereupon he walks from village to village, asking his way as he goes; and as he arrives home at last—just so does a man who meets with an illumined teacher obtain true knowledge.

—Chandogya Upanishad[34]

disciples. Usually an ashram is a commune of people living in a single compound, separate from ordinary society, but it may also be in a town and made up of various buildings owned and used by the devotees. Most gurus stay within their communities, but some travel, even outside India, to set up additional ashrams elsewhere. Frequently an aging guru will designate a successor from among his or her closest disciples and those specially trained.

It is common to touch and even kiss the feet of a guru—an act of reverence that is also performed at times for parents and grandparents. To an outsider, such an act may seem excessive. However, many Hindus believe that the guru is both a saint and a living embodiment of the divine. Behind this conception is the recognition that although divine reality exists within all human beings, most people manifest their divine nature inadequately, because their ignorance and self-centeredness restrict its expression. Such people are compared to glass windows that are so dusty that only a little light shines through. However, some people, over many lifetimes of effort, have reached a stage of such achievement that their ego has disappeared and their charity has grown immense. In these rare people the innate divine light shines brilliantly. This view explains why Hindus believe that one need only be in the presence of the guru to benefit—like a plant in sunshine—from that person's spirituality.

It also explains the intriguing practice of *darshan* ("presence"). Because people of spiritual accomplishment are thought to radiate their divine nature, disciples find opportunities to be in the presence of the holy person. Sometimes also a holy person will sit or stand silently, allowing devotees to come forward one by one to look into the teacher's eyes and to experience the divine energy that shines out.[35]

Devotion to Animals

Hinduism is distinctive among world religions for its kindness to animals. A devout Hindu does not kill or eat animals. Cows often wander along Indian streets, and cars and taxis take care to drive around them. Furthermore, visitors to some Hindu temples may find monkeys and even mice well fed and running free. Several extremely popular gods, such as Ganesha and Hanuman, have animal features; and gods such as Shiva and Vishnu are regularly portrayed in the company of their animal companions. A Shiva temple would often be thought incomplete without a statue of Nandi, the bull who is Shiva's vehicle.

This devotion to animals in Hinduism has several possible origins: an ancient deification of certain animals, such as the elephant and tiger; the desire to neutralize dangerous or mischievous animals, such as the snake, rat, and monkey; and even a sense that human beings and animals have the same origin (a belief also common in oral religions). Belief in reincarnation has undoubtedly also played a role. When they see animals and insects, many Hindus see prehuman beings who in their spiritual evolution will eventually become human themselves. This brings a feeling of closeness to nonhuman forms of animal life.

In Hinduism, cows are treated with special veneration. They are often fed in public and ornamented with garlands at festivals.

Among the animals, cows receive special veneration. This tradition may stem from pre-Aryan worship in the Indus River valley of the bull or cow, a symbol of fertility and economic value. In rural India, to have a cow is to have milk and butter, fuel (dried dung), and the warmth and comfort associated with household pets. With a cow, one is never utterly destitute. Affection for the cow may also arise from the strong thread of ancient devotion to the Divine Feminine and thus may represent a vestige of earlier matriarchal society—hinted at by the commonly used term *gau mata*, "mother cow." (The fact that Muslims butcher cows is a source of terrible friction between the Hindus and Muslims in India.)

Other Forms of Religious Devotion

Indian thought loves multiplicity. "As many as the sands of the Ganges" is a description applied to a variety of subjects. One example of multiplicity is the Hindu recognition of immense numbers of gods. Realizing that each god or goddess may have several forms and may be accompanied by divine consorts and animal companions, we gain a dizzying sense of the limitlessness of devotional possibilities. In everyday life, every person is expected to have a religious practice involving at least one of these deities, but the exact form generally is not dictated, and virtually no form of devotion is rejected.

Pilgrimage is a common form of religious expression in Hinduism, as it is in many religions. India is dotted with sites that are held to be sacred to the

Hindu Celebrations

Religious festivals are frequent and usually joyous. Some are clearly associated with the seasons, such as a springtime fertility festival and a post-monsoon festival. Others are related to events in a god's life, such as the site of his birth or places he traveled to. Some festivals are regional, and some are national.

Although India is hot during most of the year, winters can be cold, especially in the north. The spring is therefore welcomed with the celebration *Holi*. It is traditional for boys and girls to playfully throw colored water on each other (nowadays some even use squirt guns), thus evoking images of Krishna's exploits with the milkmaids.

After the monsoons of the summer months, the land is green, the air is cool, and there is a sense of peacefulness. The season has the feeling of a second spring and a new beginning. People often spend time repairing any damages the rains may have caused. Holidays at this time reenact the power of goodness to conquer evil forces. For example, *Divali*, recalling the return of Rama and Sita, is a time when people clean their houses and illuminate them outside with candles and lights. Ganesha and Lakshmi, who are both associated with good fortune, are particularly honored at this time.

Durga Puja, held in December and particularly popular in northeast India, celebrates the goddess Durga's ability to overcome dangerous powers. People dance in front of her statues in the street, and in Calcutta the festival ends with the immersion of her statues in the river.

most popular gods and goddesses, and devotees of a particular deity will often try to visit all the important sites associated with that deity. Pilgrimages can also involve listening to a famous guru's sermons and meditating with the guru's followers.

 PERSONAL EXPERIENCE: A CREMATION IN BALI

A stream flows through tall bamboo at one end of the town, and rice paddies stretch out to the west. In the neighboring hills are several fine temples. The splendid setting of Ubud, this town in central Bali, has long attracted artists, and the town has two major museums of Balinese art, which are lovely buildings in their own right. The town is well located for the exploration of the rest of the island.

I was staying in a small hotel down a dirt road, on the outskirts of town. My second-floor room was up a steep outdoor staircase, but it had a large veranda that looked out over the rice paddies, and every day I heard two roosters crow from a house in the middle of the fields. Each morning the woman who lived next door brought out offerings of flowers and rice on green leaves, and she put the offering with incense at a small altar, dedicated to Brahma, in her garden. As soon as she had put out the rice, said her prayer, and left, birds swooped down to take their share.

People associate Hinduism with India, but it is the principal religion in Bali, as well, where it has blended with folk religion in a highly ritualistic form. When I arrived in Ubud, I went down to the main street to find a driver. (You don't want to be your own driver on Bali.) "I'm not interested in shirts or carvings," I said to the first driver who offered his help—"just temples and

The bodies of several people are cremated in a ritual bull at the end of an elaborate procession and ceremony in Ubud, Bali.

ceremonies." He laughed and we came to a rate quickly. Because his name, Nyoman, is so common in Bali, he had given himself a nickname: "Nyoman Blue." He even had business cards with the name. He said he liked the color and the sound of the word. Every morning he and I would meet on the main street, across from the Casa Luna, to plan our day's excursion.

One morning when we met he said, "We don't have to drive anywhere today. There's going to be a cremation just outside town. We can walk." He took me several blocks away to where the procession would begin. I had brought the sarong that I had to wear when visiting temples, and put it around my waist.

Already people had assembled and the street was packed. A life-sized red wooden bull, carved from a tree trunk, had been set atop carrying poles. Nearby was a wooden tower, at the base of which was a small "house" that contained the remains of the deceased person, once an important citizen of the town. Men in black-and-white checkered sarongs and gold headbands were chatting cheerfully and smoking Indonesian clove cigarettes. More people came, but no one looked sad. I tried to find shade as we waited, and then, not knowing how long the procession and cremation would last, I went off to buy a bottle of water.

Just as I returned, the men picked up the tower and the red bull on its poles. The procession began, the men weaving left, right, and sometimes in circles, often at a run—they wanted to make sure that the spirit of the dead man could not find its way back and cause difficulties. We started up a hill. The road curved to the left as it rose, then went down into a grove of tall trees beyond the town. At last we reached a grassy clearing. The men set down what they had carried. I stood under a banyan tree, trying to be unobtrusive. A priest dressed in white watched as the shrouded remains were placed within the red bull. The priest then rang a bell and sprinkled water, with a flower in his fingers. Women relatives of the deceased came forward to place offerings within the bull, and a man nearby held a rooster. Suddenly the red bull erupted in flames, which shot up to the leaves of the banyan tree under which I stood. The smoke was intense, and I moved to the other side of the clearing to escape from it. Several men went to burn the wooden tower, which had been set down in the back of the clearing, and they seemed to congratulate each other. People chatted—it reminded me of the social time after a church service—then drifted away slowly. As we went back, I realized at a bend in the road where I was. I could see the verandah of my hotel, which was just barely visible on the ridge across the rice paddy.

What had struck me was the absence of sadness. Not only was the cremation performed months after the man had died, but any mourning was dissipated by belief that the deceased had had other lives in the past and would probably have more in the future. The cremation had helped transform a body back to basic elements and would allow the deceased to move onward in the cycle of rebirths.

HINDUISM AND THE ARTS

Given Hinduism's tendency toward multiplicity, it is not surprising that Hindu temples, particularly in southern India, are often covered with statues, many with multiple faces and arms. The concept of multiplicity has a purpose. To illustrate this, think of a wheel that begins to turn. At first, each spoke of the wheel is visible, but as the wheel turns more quickly, the spokes disappear and dissolve into a unity. The profusion of images in Hindu art can be similarly hypnotic, with the experience of multiplicity frequently leading to an overarching sense of unity. Profusion thus fits in well with the mystical orientation common in Hinduism.

Behind this Hindu temple roofline in Benares stands the minaret of a mosque. Peaceful co-existence with other religions, especially Islam, is a major challenge for Hinduism today.

Another characteristic of Hindu artistic sensibility is symbolism. One of the clearest examples is the depiction in painting and sculpture of figures with multiple arms and faces, which are not literal but symbolic representations of power and wisdom. Specific symbols are associated with individual deities and allow them to be identified. Krishna, for example, is recognized by his flute.

Hindu painting can sometimes be disappointing. Much of what one sees in India is rather garish devotional art sold at temple gates. Many fine paintings of the past have undoubtedly vanished because of the fragility of the paper and cloth on which they were done. The murals that remain, however, demonstrate the heights Hindu devotional painting has sometimes attained; and some yantras—geometrical paintings used in meditation—are unforgettable.

Hindu sculpture, however, far outshines Hindu painting. Fine pieces of sturdy stone and metal are on display in India and in museums around the world. Metal sculpture advanced quite early. The finest generic example of Hindu sculpture is Shiva in his guise as "ruler of the dance" (*Nataraja*)—an image that was introduced in southern India more than a thousand years ago but is still produced today. For many, this sculpture represents the perfection of Hindu art, combining visual beauty with a symbolic meaning that intensifies the visual power.

The power of stone sculpture is often quite sensuous. Given the world-denying aspect of some Hindu thought, one might expect that the great stone sculpture of Hinduism would be ascetic—perhaps elongated and otherworldly. The opposite is true, however. Some of the best-known examples of stone sculpture are the figures of sensuous men and women, enjoying life and each other, on the temples of Khajuraho in central India. This sort of sculpture was influenced by Tantrism, the antipuritanical movement that teaches that everything in the world, including sex, can be used to attain higher states of consciousness.

Popular Hinduism has made use of hymns to many gods as expressions of bhakti yoga. Their regular rhythm and repetition help produce a state of altered consciousness in the worshiper, bringing a sense of selflessness and union with the divine. Instrumental music—especially involving drums and the harmonium, a hand-pumped reed organ—has also been an integral part of religious celebrations for centuries.

Classical Indian instrumental music is less obviously religious, yet much of it has an undeniable mystical quality. It makes use of *ragas,* elements of Indian music that blend features of both scales and melodies. Frequently these ragas are played and musically developed over deep tones that are played as a drone. (The *sitar,* the best-known Indian stringed instrument, has drone strings on its side.) The drone suggests the underlying timeless world of Brahman, against which changing melodies—suggestions of the world of time—move. Musical pieces often begin quite tentatively, then gradually speed up to a very quick pace, and suddenly stop, bringing to the listener (and players) an experience of release and peace.

Indian classical dance is more obviously tied to religion. It interprets stories derived from the tales of the gods, such as Krishna and Rama. Much of it also originated as a part of religious ceremony, performed at religious festivals and in or near temples. Dance is meant to produce delicate states of feeling, some of which are thought to assist contact with particular gods.

HINDUISM: MODERN CHALLENGES

India, as we have seen, is isolated from other lands by mountains and ocean. This has meant that its rural culture and ancient polytheism could develop undisturbed for centuries. But invasions did occur, inevitably bringing new beliefs and values. Many of these new elements were adopted, but others were fought.

An early invasion, as we saw, came when Aryan culture entered India from the northwest, bringing its own gods, priests, and social system. Eventually Aryan culture was absorbed, but there were strong opposition movements. (Buddhism and Jainism, which will be discussed in the following chapters, were two of the sturdiest.)

Another early invasion was only partially successful. Alexander the Great (d. 323 B.C.E.) brought his army from Greece and reached the Indus River, where he talked with sannyasin about religion and philosophy. He had hoped to conquer India and then reach China, too; but his men, sick and discouraged, forced him to turn back, and he died in Babylon on the way home. Had Alexander been able to fulfill his plans, his influence in India could have been immense. Despite his failure to carry them out, though, forms of Greek government and art, brought by the Greek invaders, profoundly influenced northwest India for centuries.

In the past millennium, two additional waves of influence washed across India: Islam and the British. Islam first came into India from Afghanistan, and a sultanate was set up in Delhi in 1206. After invasions from Turkmenistan, the sultanate was supplanted by the Mughal dynasty, beginning in 1398. The Mughal dynasty continued on into the eighteenth century, even as the British were consolidating their control over much of India.

There could hardly be two religions more in contrast than monotheistic Islam and polytheistic Hinduism. The contrast has produced intense conflict, which continues today. The more than five centuries of Islamic rule that began in 1206 were marked by a spectrum of attitudes toward Hinduism, moving back and forth between cruel oppression and complete tolerance. The attitude of the state depended on the opinions of the ruler of the time. For example, Akbar (d. 1605) was so tolerant that he invited members of other religions to speak at court, and he became convinced that India needed a new religion that would blend the best of all older religions. His great-grandson, Aurangzeb (d. 1707), however, was notoriously harsh in his zeal, destroying Hindu temples and sometimes demanding conversion on pain of death.

Of course, not all conversions to Islam were forced. Islam was very attractive to many people. It was appealing to those who appreciated its monotheistic simplicity, its architecture, its literature, and its way of life. (Many beautiful buildings were created by the Mughals; the Taj Mahal, for example, was built by Aurangzeb's father.) Islam was also appealing because it was the religion of the aristocratic ruling classes; and it was greatly attractive to lower-caste Hindus, who felt oppressed by the Hindu caste system. Consequently, by the end of the Mughal period, Islam was the religion of millions in north India. But this fact would later create great problems, particularly when India became an independent state, and it would remain as a major source of religious friction and violence.

European values have also, gradually, posed a major challenge to traditional Hinduism. This process began after 1500 C.E., when European powers took control of parts of India. Goa, on the west coast, became a center of Portuguese culture that lasted until 1960, when Goa was taken over by Indian army forces. Similarly, Pondicherry, on the southeast coast, was at one time a center of French culture. The most significant European influence on India, however, was English. Great Britain controlled most of the subcontinent for about two centuries. Although India became independent of Britain in 1947, British influence is evident in modern India's law, education, architecture, rail transportation, and military life.

Throughout India today one can find former British churches, mostly shuttered and closed, which only hint at both the positive and negative impact of British Christianity on India. The British were not successful in making many converts, but through their schools and colleges British Christian missionaries helped challenge and change some traditional Hindu beliefs and practices. Among those elements that were questioned were untouchability, child marriage, prohibition of remarriage for widows, polytheism, the content of education, and the role of women.

One of the earliest British-inspired Indian reformers was Ram Mohan Roy (1772–1833). He was typical of the many reformers who grew up in Calcutta, which was for a long time the capital of British India and the center of westernizing thought. While remaining a Hindu and even writing articles in defense of Hinduism, his thinking was influenced by both rationalism and Christianity.[36] He began a movement, the Brahmo Samaj, that adopted Christian-inspired elements: the belief in one God, the rejection of polytheism, congregational worship, and an ethical urgency that sought to better the lot of the oppressed. The Brahmo Samaj later split into three branches—all of which are still active.

Possibly as a result of contact with European values, one practice that was made illegal in the early nineteenth century was that of *sati* (or *suttee*, named after the first wife of Shiva). While there is no evidence to suggest that this practice was common, in sati a woman whose husband had died could volunteer, as a sign of her wifely devotion, to be burnt alive on her husband's funeral pyre. Although the British found the notion of sati horrible, they were unwilling to intervene at first. Reform-minded Indians, however, worked with the British to make the practice illegal. Instances of sati still happen today, but they are rare.

Mohandas Gandhi

Mohandas Gandhi (1869–1948) was born in the seaside town of Porbandar in western India, north of Bombay. Because Britain then controlled the country, many Indians advocated violence as a response to British domination. This historic turning point became a defining time in Gandhi's life.

As a young man, Gandhi learned basic ideas of nonviolence from Hinduism and Jainism (see chapter 5). He was a vegetarian because of his religious upbringing; yet in his day, young Indian boys believed that the British were strong because they ate meat. Young Gandhi tested this theory by eating meat for a year, but he had a dream of a goat crying in his stomach and was compelled to give up his experiment.[37] His marriage at the age of 13 was arranged by his family to a girl named Kasturbai, also 13.

During his late teen years, family members recommended that Gandhi study law in London. Because his pious Hindu mother feared the bad influences he would be exposed to there, he agreed to take a vow that he would not eat meat, drink wine, or touch a woman while abroad. A Jain monk administered the vow, and Gandhi left for London in the fall of 1888 at the age of 19. Kasturbai and their young son Harilal remained with Gandhi's parents.

Feeling rebellious at the time, Gandhi enthusiastically adopted English clothes and manners and even took dancing lessons; but in London he also began serious study. Becoming familiar with the Christian Bible, he was particularly moved by Jesus' call to forgiveness and nonviolence, which he found in the Sermon on the Mount (Matt. 5–7) in the New Testament.

It was in London, too, that he first read the Bhagavad Gita, discovering outside India the wisdom in Hinduism. He took to heart its ideal of the active but selfless human being. Such a person, Gandhi later wrote, is a person who is "without egotism, who is selfless, who treats alike cold and heat, happiness and misery, who is ever forgiving, who is always contented, whose resolutions are firm, who has dedicated mind and soul to God, who causes no dread, who is not afraid of others."[38]

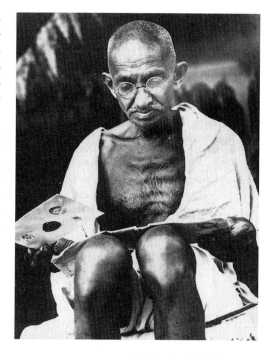

After obtaining his law degree in 1891, Gandhi returned to India but soon decided to accept an offer to practice law in South Africa. There he learned of the inequities of *apartheid* (the official system of racial segregation that endorsed legal restrictions against non-European people, including Indians), and he began to perfect the ideologies that he would later spread in India. His thinking was influenced by writings that advocated simplicity and nonviolence, such as the essay "On Civil Disobedience" by the American author Henry David Thoreau and the book *The Kingdom of God Is Within You* by the Russian writer Leo Tolstoy. A farm that Gandhi bought became something of an ashram, while his law office in Johannesburg became a center for nonviolent political action. He began to employ strikes and marches to publicize his goals and to wear Indian clothing (specifically the *dhoti*, a type of loincloth) as a way of identifying with the Indian cause.

Mohandas Gandhi adopted nonviolent strategies to win Indian independence from Great Britain.

Gandhi returned to India in 1915 and dedicated his life to seeking Indian independence from Britain. Although he was repeatedly imprisoned, Gandhi insisted that all his followers remain nonviolent. For him ahimsa (nonviolence) was fundamental. Gandhi not only believed in nonviolence for its own sake, but he felt that it gave a great moral power to its adherents and that it could sway those who were cruel, thoughtless, and violent. He called this power *satyagraha* ("reality force," or "holding onto truth"). Gandhi made use of every possible nonviolent technique: marches, hunger strikes, talks, demonstrations, and, of course, publicity. He argued that violence only begets further violence and brutalizes those who are violent, whereas nonviolence begets admiration, spiritual greatness, and ultimate freedom.[39]

One brilliant example of Gandhi's nonviolent techniques was the Salt March of 1930. At that time the British taxed all salt eaten in India and made it illegal to possess salt not bought from the government monopoly. Gandhi cleverly led a three-week march on foot from his ashram to the ocean, nearly 250 miles away. Fewer than a hundred people began the march with him, but thousands joined along the way. Reaching the sea, Gandhi collected the natural salt left on the beach by the waves—thus breaking the law. In seashore communities all around India, people came to do the same, and thousands were put into jail along with Gandhi. This march was the turning point. Weakened both by the Indian independence movement and by World

War II, the British forces at last agreed to leave India in 1947. Perceiving Gandhi's greatness following the Salt March, the writer Rabindranath Tagore earlier had called him *Mahatma* ("great spirit"). This became his title.

Gandhi believed so much in loving tolerance that he hoped it could keep a newly independent India free of religious battles. Muslim leaders, however, fearful that the Hindu majority would oppress Muslims, worked to create the new separate Muslim state of Pakistan. Some Hindu militants wanted revenge for what they perceived as wrongs done by Muslims to Hindus in the new Pakistan, and one of these Hindu militants assassinated Gandhi early in 1948. Gandhi's last words were *Ram, Ram* ("God, God").

Gandhi's example was so powerful that the idea of satyagraha spread to other countries and was adopted in the 1960s by the Baptist minister Martin Luther King, Jr., to help protest racial segregation in the United States. King insisted that activists march peacefully and sit in restaurants quietly, without responding to threats or cruelty. Their gentle persistence, magnified by publicity, brought success.

Contemporary Issues

The issues that moderate Hinduism faces, as it is evolving today, come from three sources: the conservative social teachings of traditional Hinduism, the centuries-old conflict with Islam, and the challenges of the contemporary world.

Conservative Hindus find religious justification for preserving rules about untouchability, keeping strictly the divisions of the caste system, and limiting women to traditional roles. The injustices of untouchability have long been recognized, but legal assistance for untouchables came only in the twentieth century. Untouchables, now allowed to enter all temples in India, have made great strides toward some social equality and opportunity. For example, there is a system whereby a quota of untouchables must be included in governmental hiring and university entrance policies. The reality, however, is that in the villages untouchables still must live separately from others. They do not feel free to use wells and other water sources that are used by higher-caste persons, and they feel threatened by violence if they should attempt to go beyond their traditional limits.

The caste system is weakening, especially in large cities. But a glance at a big-city Sunday newspaper is all it takes to find evidence of the caste system's continuing hold on contemporary life. It is common, for example, for Indian parents to place ads in the newspaper to find a spouse for their child, and these ads frequently detail the son or daughter's caste, educational background, and sometimes even complexion.

The role of women has expanded in modern India, but it remains a focus of heated debate. In India's distant, pre-Aryan past, it is possible that women played an important public role. The importance of female deities and the fact that there have been many female gurus may be a continuation of this early tradition. But the incoming Aryan culture was thoroughly patriarchal. Just as it has been canonized in other religions, so male domination in India was canonized by the law code of Manu (second century B.C.E.). This code made the female subservient to the male and the wife subservient to her husband. A good wife was expected to treat her husband as a god, no matter what his character or treatment of her. Women were not trained to read and write, as this was thought to be detrimental to their principal roles as wives and mothers. Nowadays Hindu women commonly learn to read and write, and many go on to higher education and important public roles. Critics, however, point out that women's education is often only basic, and that they are largely limited to a few career areas—teaching, secretarial work, nursing, and medicine. Critics also point out that in villages women are sometimes confined to traditional domestic roles under threat of violence from their husbands. A related problem comes from the practice in India of the bride's family having to pay a dowry to the family of the bridegroom. Wives whose families do not pay what is considered enough are threatened. Sometimes they are even killed by the family members of the husband, freeing the husband to marry again.

Conflict between Hindus and Muslims has been ongoing, particularly since the partition of India and Pakistan in 1947. Gandhi had hoped that India would not have to split into parts along religious lines, but Muslim leaders insisted on separation. Ironically, the Partition did not bring peace. Disagreement about the border between India and Pakistan, particularly in Kashmir, has never been resolved. Two wars have already been fought, and a third is a constant threat. Since both countries possess atomic weapons, the potential horrors of such a war are especially great.

Conflicts between the Hindus and Muslims within India itself have also continually flared up. Old wounds were reopened in 1992 when Hindu activists destroyed a mosque at Ayodhya in northern India. They argued that it was the site of the birth of Rama and that it had once been a Hindu temple, but that the Muslim ruler Babur had destroyed the temple and built a mosque on the site. Atrocities on each side have been the result. While India claims to be a secular state, the fact that eighty-five percent of its people are Hindu gives Hindu causes an undeniable weight, and Muslims argue that the government has not adequately protected them. Similar conflicts have occurred in Kashmir at the site of a Hindu shrine to Shiva. Just as fundamentalism has risen in several other religions, it is now influential in Hinduism. A militant form is even establishing Hindu military training camps for girls.

The third source of conflict comes from the intrusion of contemporary values, particularly individualism, women's rights, sexual freedom, modern fashion, and consumerism. Globalization has made instant some of the conflicts that once arose more slowly. There is now quick communication through e-mail and cell phones, and television brings new values irresistibly into the home (for example, a somewhat sanitized version of MTV can be seen in India today). The Western world of banking and financial credit is quickly moving many of its operations to India, where college graduates speak English but salaries are still comparatively low. It is already the case that an American consumer making a routine call for computer help will probably be talking with a computer specialist in Bangalore, Mumbai, or

Delhi. These jobs will provide greater economic opportunities for women as well as men, inevitably raising the potential for conflict between traditional values and new possibilities.

Hindu Influence beyond India

Over the centuries, Hinduism has spread to countries near India and afar, often by way of traders and immigrants. In a few places, it has remained strong, whereas in others it has surrendered to other religions. Hinduism is the state religion of Nepal, where about eighty percent of the population is Hindu. Hinduism was once widespread in Southeast Asia, but today only traces of it remain. In Cambodia (Kampuchea) is the great ruin Angkor Wat, originally a Hindu complex. In Thailand, vestiges of a Brahmanical priesthood are particularly active in court ceremony, and images of Brahma, Vishnu, and Ganesha are common. Some forms of ritualistic Buddhism in northern and eastern Asia have kept alive a few Hindu gods, such as Indra, in art and ceremony. Hinduism, of course, continues wherever Indians have immigrated. Outside India it is strongest in South Africa, Malaysia, Fiji, Singapore, and England.

Hinduism was once widespread in Indonesia, where it had been spread by Indian traders. During the Muslim invasions, however, the Hindu court was forced to retreat from the main island of Java and settled to the east on the small island of Bali, where a fascinating example of Hindu culture thrives.

The figures and architectural detail of this temple at Angkor Wat in Cambodia clearly show the temple's Hindu origins.

Dance retains an important role in traditional Hindu ceremonies in Bali.

Here, Hinduism lives on in a complicated, beautiful form that is mixed with folk religion and Buddhism. Each village has Hindu temples, where dances based on Indian tales (especially about Rama) are performed. Shadow-puppet plays tell Hindu stories, and Balinese wood carvings reproduce images of Hindu gods, goddesses, and heroes. The central temple of Bali, a complex of buildings on the volcanic Mount Agung, is dedicated to the Trimurti. Although the rest of Indonesia is primarily Muslim, some Hindu elements remain in Indonesian dance and puppet plays. Interestingly, the national airline of Indonesia, despite the country's primarily Muslim orientation, is named Garuda Airlines, after the magical bird that carries Vishnu through the skies.

Hinduism has had some influence on the West since the nineteenth century. The earliest impact was intellectual, a result of the translations of the Upanishads and the Bhagavad Gita into Latin, French, German, and English. The translations generated great interest among philosophers, scholars, and poets. In the United States, the New England movement called Transcendentalism owes a good deal to its literary contact with Hinduism. Ralph Waldo Emerson (1803–1882), Henry David Thoreau (1817–1862), and Walt Whitman (1819–1892) all spoke in their writings of a sense of the sacredness of nature and the ultimate unity of all things, and they sometimes even used terms demonstrating Indian influence, such as *Brahma* and *Oversoul* (another name for Brahman). This literary trend was expressed in another form in England, where composers such as Gustav Holst (1874–1934) and Ralph Vaughan Williams (1872–1958) put selections from the Rig Veda and Whitman's *Leaves of Grass* to music.

The next wave of influence occurred when Indian gurus began to travel to the West. The first of these gurus was Swami Vivekananda (1863–1902),

The International Society for Krishna Consciousness offers vegetarian food at its temples and restaurants around the world.

who represented Hinduism at the first World Parliament of Religions, held in Chicago in 1893. He was the successor to Ramakrishna (mentioned earlier), the noted mystic and devotee of the Great Mother. Vivekananda began the Ramakrishna Mission and set up Vedanta societies and Ramakrishna centers across Europe, India, and the United States. A Vedantist center has existed in Hollywood since the 1930s, and British writers such as Christopher Isherwood (1904–1986), Aldous Huxley (1894–1963), and Gerald Heard (1889–1971) all practiced meditation there. Isherwood, under the influence of his guru, Swami Prabhavananda, became a Vedantist and translated the Bhagavad Gita into English.

The third wave of Hindu influence in the West occurred in the late 1960s. The American counterculture embraced India as the fount of wisdom. Commercial air travel made it possible for Indian teachers to come to the West and for westerners to travel to India. Some westerners, such as the Beatles, studied in India with the guru Maharishi Mahesh Yogi and became enamored of Hinduism. (George Harrison's song "My Sweet Lord" was written to honor Krishna.) The Maharishi eventually came to the United States and established the Transcendental Meditation movement, which promotes regular daily meditation to achieve health and happiness. Some westerners who went to India became disciples of Sai Baba, a contemporary teacher in south-central India, and still others, such as the psychologist Richard Alpert (who took the name Ram Dass), studied with Indian teachers and returned to write about their experiences. Western visitors to India adopted forms of yoga, Hindu vegetarian cuisine, Indian clothing, and Indian music and then took them back to Europe, Canada, and the United States, where they entered the Western mainstream.

The movement called the International Society for Krishna Consciousness (ISKCON) was founded in New York in 1967 by Swami Bhaktivedanta Prabhupada (1896–1977) to spread a form of devotional practice among westerners. Commonly known as the Hare Krishna movement, ISKCON has succeeded in attracting westerners to live a traditional form of Hindu religious life. Its practitioners worship Krishna as the highest incarnation of the divine, chant daily, eat a vegetarian diet, and, if celibate, wear the traditional orange robe. The impact of this movement in the West has been particularly strong in the area of cuisine, prompting the opening of vegetarian restaurants across Europe, the United States, and Canada.

The largest recent influence of Indian culture has been due to the immigration into North America and Europe of millions of Hindus, ensuring that virtually every major city has a large Hindu population along with the associated temples, festivals, and art. As Hindus settle around the globe, we can expect the appreciation of Hinduism to grow.

What we have just discussed—the impact of Hinduism on Western thinkers, musicians, and poets—was in large measure achieved by non-Hindus inspired by Hindu culture. Now Hindus themselves, in and out of India, are producing internationally acclaimed works, especially novels and films. Their particular points of view result from experiences accumulated across centuries in one of the world's richest cultures. Those experiences will in time help global citizens, whatever their origins, to see themselves with an understanding that has been enriched by the Hindu worldview.

RELIGION BEYOND THE CLASSROOM

In the United States, Canada, and elsewhere, one can visit Vedanta Society centers and ISKCON temples. They exist primarily in major cities, and both organizations welcome all who are interested. Many ISKCON temples hold weekly public services that include chanting, a lecture, and frequently a vegetarian meal. An elaborate temple exists at New Vrindavan, West Virginia. In west Los Angeles, non-Hindus are welcome to visit the Self-Realization Fellowship Shrine, located on Sunset Boulevard near the Pacific Coast Highway. It has buildings in Indian style and a peaceful lake. Temples built by immigrant Hindu communities can be found in many major cities.

Outside North America, Hinduism can be experienced in four places that are available to the international traveler: India, Bali, Nepal, and Singapore. India, being the home of Hinduism, is filled with important Hindu temples and other religious sites. If the traveler has only a short amount of time, the most important religious sites to visit in conjunction with Hinduism are possibly Benares (Varanasi), to observe religious practices at the Ganges River, and Khajuraho, to see its elaborate temples. Museums with major collections of Hindu art are found in Mumbai (Bombay), New Delhi, and Kolkata (Calcutta).

Bali, as mentioned earlier, is a unique society, derived from the Hindu culture that once existed on Java. Each village has its own gamelan orchestra (consisting primarily of percussion instruments, such as gongs, xylophones, and drums) and regular dance ceremonies, many of whose stories are based on Hindu tales. Balinese painting and wood carving are similarly inspired by Hinduism. The temple complex on Mount Agung is the mother temple of Balinese Hinduism. Called Pura ("temple") Besakih, it is dedicated to Brahma, Vishnu, and Shiva. The offshore temple at Tanah Lot is scenic, though sometimes crowded. Other temples of note exist at Batuan, Tampaksiring, and Bedugul. The town of Ubud has several beautiful temples in its vicinity, and it is a good place to stay for exploring much of the island. Entry to temples is allowed to non-Hindus, but a sarong must be worn.

Much of the population of Nepal is Hindu. The capital city of Katmandu stands in a high valley that also contains two other towns, Patan and Bhadgaon (Bhaktapur), and all three have interesting temples. The traveler can rent a bicycle in Katmandu for visiting the towns and the rest of the valley.

Singapore, a thoroughly modern city and a financial center of Asia, affords an intriguing view of Hinduism active in an urban environment. Hindu temples of interest include Sri Mariamman Temple and Sri Srinivasa Perumal Temple.

FOR FULLER UNDERSTANDING

1. Investigate to see if examples of Hindu practice exist near your home or school. Visit a Hindu temple or center, and attend a service if possible; then write a short description to share with others.
2. Read one of the numerous excellent works by contemporary Indian novelists (such as V. S. Naipaul, Arundhati Roy, Amitava Ghosh, Vikram Seth, Sashi Tharoor, and Jhumpa Lahiri)—works that describe life in today's India or in the communities of Indians who have emigrated to the West. Make notes on the elements of Hinduism you find in the novel.
3. Read various selections from Walt Whitman's powerful group of poems *Leaves of Grass*. Copy three short pieces that seem to suggest Hindu teachings. Read these poems aloud to friends, and then discuss their possible parallels with Hindu teachings.
4. Research the life of Martin Luther King, Jr. Find out how and when he learned about the techniques of nonviolent resistance. Describe specifically how he made use of these techniques. What parallels do you see with the traditions of Hinduism and with the work of Gandhi?
5. Join two or three other students in a research project on the caste system in India today. How is it viewed within India today? (Be sure to consider views in Indian cities and in rural areas.) What have been its good and bad effects? What keeps it alive and what has made it change? How might it look in 2030? Pay particular attention to similarities and differences in the pronouncements of Hindu and secular leaders.
6. Consider a research project on the roles of women in India today, particularly as they have been shaped by Hindu beliefs and practices. (The internet provides access to some popular Indian periodicals, and video shops often carry Indian films.) Who are some of the principal voices in the debate within India on women's roles, and what are their opinions? Do Hindu and secular leaders hold identical views?
7. View one or two Indian films. Write reviews that focus on explicit references to Hindu religious tales, teachings, and values, as well as subtler echoes of Hindu ideas.

RELATED READINGS

Bhagavad-Gita: The Song of God. Tr. Swami Prabhavananda and Christopher Isherwood. New York: Signet, 2002. A justly famous translation with a valuable introduction by Aldous Huxley.

Deutsch, Eliot. *Advaita Vedanta: A Philosophical Reconstruction*. Honolulu: University of Hawaii Press, 1980. A clear philosophical explanation of the main ideas of Vedanta—Brahman, self, karma, jnana, and moksha.

Eck, Diana. *Darsan: Seeing the Divine*. New York: Columbia University Press, 1998. A readable study of the devotional importance in Hinduism of the images in pictures, statues, and film.

Gandhi, Mohandas. *The Essential Gandhi*. Ed. Louis Fischer. New York: Vintage, 2002. Gandhi's writings on politics, nonviolence, spirituality, and his own life.

Mesko, Sabrina. *Healing Mudras*. New York: Ballantine, 2000. A useful discussion of mudras (sacred hand gestures), with clear photographs and descriptions of their use, aimed at a popular audience.

Ramana Maharshi, Sri. *The Essential Teachings of Ramana Maharshi: A Visual Journey*. Matthew Greenblatt, ed. Carlsbad, CA: Inner Directions, 2002. Teachings of a great spiritual teacher, combined with photos of him and his ashram.

The Upanishads. Trans. Swami Prabhavananda and Frederick Manchester. New York: Signet, 2002. A readable translation of twelve basic Upanishads.

KEY TERMS

ahimsa (*uh-him'-sa*): "Nonharm," "nonviolence."

ashram (*ash'-ram*): A spiritual community.

Atman (*at'-mun*): The spiritual essence of all individual human beings.

avatar (*ah'-va-tar*): An earthly embodiment of a deity.

Bhagavad Gita (*bhuh'-guh-vud gee'-ta*): A religious literary work about Krishna.

bhakti (*bhuk'-ti*): Devotion to a deity or guru.

bhakti yoga: The spiritual discipline of devotion to a deity or guru.

Brahma (*bruh-mah'*): God of creation.

Brahman (*bruh'-mun*): The spiritual essence of the universe.

brahmin (*bruh'-min*): Member of the priestly caste.

caste: One of the major social classes sanctioned by Hinduism.

Devi (*deh'-vee*): "Goddess"; the Divine Feminine, also called the Great Mother.

dhyana: Meditation.

Durga: "Awe-inspiring," "distant"; a mother-goddess, a form of Devi.

guru: A spiritual teacher.

hatha yoga: The spiritual discipline of postures and bodily exercises.

jnana yoga: The spiritual discipline of knowledge and insight.

Kali: "Dark," a form of Devi; a goddess associated with destruction and rebirth.

karma: The moral law of cause and effect that determines the direction of rebirth.

karma yoga: The spiritual discipline of selfless action.

Krishna: A god associated with divine playfulness; a form of Vishnu.

kundalini yoga: A form of raja yoga that envisions the individual's energy as a force that is capable of being raised from the center of the body to the head, producing a state of joy.

mantra: A short sacred phrase, often chanted or used in meditation.

maya: "Illusion"; what keeps us from seeing reality correctly; the world, viewed inadequately.

moksha (*mohk'-shah*): "Liberation" from personal limitation, egotism, and rebirth.

puja (*poo'-jah*): Offerings and ritual in honor of a deity.

raja yoga: The "royal" discipline of meditation.

Rama: A god and mythical king; a form of Vishnu.

samadhi (*suh-mah'-dhee*): A state of complete inner peace resulting from meditation.

samsara (*suhm-sah'-rah*): The everyday world of change and suffering leading to rebirth.

sannyasin (*san-nyas'-in*): A wandering holy man.

Shiva (*shee'-vah*): A god associated with destruction and rebirth.

Trimurti (*tree-mur'-tee*): "Three forms" of the divine—the three gods Brahma, Vishnu, and Shiva.

Upanishads (*oo-pahn'-i-shads*): Written meditations on the spiritual essence of the universe and the self.

Vedas (*vay'-duhs*): Four collections of ancient prayers and rituals.

Vishnu: A god associated with preservation and love.

yoga: A spiritual discipline; a method for perfecting one's union with the divine.

CHAPTER **4**

Buddhism

 FIRST ENCOUNTER

Caught in Bangkok city traffic, the taxi you took from your hotel drives along slowly. Yet the leisurely pace allows you to look carefully at all the activities around you. On the sidewalk, a man fixes the heel of a shoe for a customer, and next to him a woman is sewing a dress on a Singer treadle sewing machine. In the next block, you see people on stools eating noodles at red tables; one man eats with one hand and talks on a cell phone with the other. Beyond, two women seated on the sidewalk sell small garlands of white flowers; next to them, a man is repairing false teeth. Your view, though, is suddenly cut off by five noisy motorcyclists who buzz past your cab.

Although Bangkok is not an old city, like Kyoto or Rome, it was planned on a grand scale as a royal city, with a fine palace and magnificent temples. One of these temples is Wat Bovorn, which a friend told you to see. She said that it is not far from Khao San Road (made famous by the film *The Beach*). She further explained that Wat Bovorn is next to a canal and is one of the greenest and most peaceful temples in Bangkok. At last the taxi stops to let you out. On top of the white gate, two cats lie asleep in the sun. Just inside the gate, you see an elderly lady chatting with a young couple. You nod politely and walk to the stairs, leaving your shoes next to the many pairs already lined up there. People are crowded together just inside and outside the door, watching the ceremony. You enter by a side door, and as you squeeze into a place on the red carpet, you are struck by the strong scent of flowers and incense. Electric fans revolve at each side of the room, moving the humid air.

Young men in fresh monks' robes stand facing two large statues of the Buddha, one behind the other. Beyond the would-be monks are rows of older men with shaved heads, dressed in similar brown monks' robes. The young men are being accepted into the order of monks. It does not look like an unhappy fate. You ask yourself, Why the shaven heads and bare feet? You wonder why they choose this type of commitment, and what kind of life Thai Buddhist monks live. This leads you to be curious about the life of the Buddha, the founder of this religion, and wonder where all of this began.

THE BEGINNINGS OF BUDDHISM: THE LIFE OF THE BUDDHA

In this joyous Thai depiction of the Buddha's birth, we see his mother Maya in the center (just having given birth from her side), while the newly born Buddha is shown to the world by a court of *apsaras* (Buddhist angels).

Buddhism is one of the world's oldest and most significant religions. It has spread through almost all of Asia, influencing the many cultures there, and is now gaining followers in the West. But it had its beginnings in India and arose from the experience of one person.

India in the fifth century B.C.E. was in a state of religious ferment. There was great enthusiasm for personal religious experience, leading people to experiment with meditation and deep breathing and to study with gurus. A growing number of schools of philosophy taught new ways of thinking, some of which opposed the growth of the priestly Vedic religion. Into this world came Siddhartha Gautama (c. 563–483 B.C.E.), who would come to be known as the Buddha, or the Awakened One.

Because so many devout legends have grown up around the story of the Buddha's life and teaching, it is sometimes hard to separate fact from fiction.[1] Although there is no single, authoritative biography of the Buddha, his legendary life follows these outlines. Siddhartha was born the son of a prince of the Shakya tribe in what is today Nepal, in the lower Himalaya Mountains. Legend says that his mother, Maya, dreamt that a white elephant

Siddhartha, a wealthy prince before he attained enlightenment, is here portrayed as the Buddha with princely crown and raiment. This depiction is frequent in the temples of Myanmar.

entered her side—this was the moment of conception of the future Buddha—and that Siddhartha was born miraculously from her side. Siddhartha's mother died a week after childbirth, and the boy was raised by his aunt.

When a sage inspected the child, he saw special marks on Siddhartha's body, indicating that he would be an illustrious person. At his naming ceremony, priests foretold that his life could go in one of two directions: either he would follow in his father's footsteps, inheriting his position and becoming a great king, a "world ruler"; or, if he were exposed to the sight of suffering, he would become a great spiritual leader, a "world teacher."

Siddhartha's father, wanting his son to succeed him, took measures to keep the boy from exposure to suffering. Kept in a large walled palace compound, Siddhartha grew up in luxury; married, at an early age, a young woman his father had chosen; and had a son. He was educated and trained as a warrior to prepare for eventually taking over his father's role.

All was going according to his father's plan until Siddhartha disobeyed his father's command not to leave the royal grounds. Visiting a nearby town, he soon witnessed the suffering of ordinary life. He saw—and was moved by—what are called the Four Passing Sights. He came across an old man, crooked and toothless; a sick man, wasted by disease; and a corpse being taken for cremation. Then he saw a sannyasin (a wandering holy man, a renunciate) who had no possessions but seemed to be at peace.

The paintings in Buddhist temples retell dramatically Siddhartha's response to what he saw. At 29, he realized that his life up until then had been a pleasant prison, and he saw the same programmed life stretching forward into his old age. The suffering he had just encountered, however, prompted him to question the meaning of human experience and threw him into a depression that kept him from enjoying his luxurious and carefree life any longer.

Siddhartha decided to escape. Legend tells how he took a last look at his sleeping family and attendants and rode to the edge of the palace grounds, where he gave his horse to his servant, removed his jewels, and cut off his long black hair. Putting on simple clothing, he went out into the world with nothing but questions. This event is called the Great Going Forth.

It is common in Indian spirituality to seek a teacher, and Siddhartha did just that. Traveling from teacher to teacher, he learned techniques of meditation and discussed philosophy, but he was ultimately unsatisfied. Begging for food and sleeping outdoors, Siddhartha spent about six years seeking answers to his questions—particularly about the troubling facts of suffering and death. His own mother had died young, a death that was apparently without meaning. Why, he often asked, is there suffering? Why do people have to grow old and die? Is there a God or unchanging divine reality behind the surface of things? Is there a soul and an afterlife? Are we reborn? Can we avoid suffering? How should we live? (Many of these questions were the common concerns of the period, and we therefore find many of the same topics discussed in the Upanishads of Hinduism [see chapter 3] and among the Jain doctrines [see chapter 5].)

Seeking answers to his questions, Siddhartha discovered that his teachers agreed on some issues but not on others. So, in the company of five other nomadic "seekers," he set out to find the answers he needed. To rid himself of distractions and to purify himself spiritually, Siddhartha also practiced great austerity, living on as little food, drink, and sleep as possible in the hope that he would find new insight and even gain spiritual powers.

Eventually, Siddhartha collapsed from weakness. He was found resting under a sacred tree by a kind woman who had come from the nearby town of Gaya to worship the spirit of the great tree. (Siddhartha was so emaciated that she may have thought him to be the tree spirit.) She offered him food, which he took gratefully. Once revived, Siddhartha realized that his austerities had not strengthened him or brought him any closer to the answers he sought. Moreover, because he had now rejected extreme asceticism by accepting food and had deliberately avoided the hot sun by sitting under a large shade tree, Siddhartha's five companions, when they discovered his apparent backsliding, abandoned him.

Being a practical person, Siddhartha decided to adopt a path of moderation—a middle way between self-indulgence and asceticism. He went to another tree, now called the Bodhi Tree,[2] and sat facing the east, resolving to remain there in meditation until he had the understanding he needed. Various traditions give different details: one says he sat for a week; another

This painting, on the wall of a rural Laotian temple, portrays Siddhartha under the Bodhi Tree at the moment he becomes the Buddha, the Awakened One.

says he remained there for forty-nine days—a week of weeks. Nevertheless, every version talks of his struggle with hunger, thirst, doubt, and weakness. Some stories describe the work of an evil spirit, Mara, and his daughters who tempted Siddhartha with sensuality and fear. But Siddhartha resisted all temptation. During one entire night, as he sat meditating under a full moon, Siddhartha entered increasingly profound states of awareness. Legend says that he saw his past lives, fathomed the laws of karma that govern everyone, and finally achieved insight into release from suffering and rebirth.

At last, at dawn, he reached a state of profound understanding, called his Awakening, or Enlightenment (**bodhi**). He saw suffering, aging, and death in a new way, recognizing them as an inevitable part of life but also seeing the possibility of release. We might wonder about the influence of the tree and the moon on Siddhartha. The tree overhead, with its thousands of leaves and twigs, despite its appearance of permanence, would change, age, and die; and the full moon, with its brilliant light, was a promise of new understanding. Whatever the cause of his enlightenment, Siddhartha arose and said that he was a man who had woken up. From this came his new name: the Buddha, the Awakened One, taken from a Sanskrit word meaning "to wake up."

A wonder of the world, this huge statue of the Reclining Buddha in Polonnaruwa, Sri Lanka, may be unsurpassed in conveying the serenity that is the core of Buddhist teaching.

From the site of his enlightenment at Gaya, the Buddha traveled west and explained his awakening to his five former companions at a deer park at Sarnath, near Benares. Although they had parted with him earlier for abandoning his ascetic habits, they reconciled with him and became his first disciples.

The Buddha spent the rest of his long life traveling from village to village in northeast India, teaching his insights and his way of life. He attracted many followers, and donors gave land, groves, and buildings to the new movement. The Buddha thus began an order (*sangha*) of monks and later of nuns. The Buddha's way was a path of moderation, a middle path, not only for himself but also for his disciples. It was midway between the worldly life of the householder that he had lived before leaving home and the ascetic life of social withdrawal that he had followed after his departure from home. But the specifics of monastic community life and its relation to the nonmonastic world—on whom the monks relied for food—had to be worked out over time.

Tradition tells of the warm friendship the Buddha shared with his disciples and of their way of life, wandering about begging and teaching.

The monks remained in one place only during the monsoon months of summer, when the rains were so heavy that travel was impractical. Looking on the Buddha's lifestyle from a modern vantage point, we can see that it was a healthy one: moderate eating, no alcohol, daily walking, regular meditation, pure air. Probably because of this, the Buddha lived to an old age.

When he was 80, legend says, the Buddha ate food offered by a well-meaning blacksmith named Chunda, but the food was spoiled and the Buddha became terribly sick. Sensing that he was dying, he called his disciples. To those who were crying over his impending death, he reminded them that everything must die—even the Buddha himself. He then offered these final words of advice: "You must be your own lamps, be your own refuges. Take refuge in nothing outside yourselves. Hold firm to the truth as a lamp and a refuge, and do not look for refuge to anything besides yourselves."[3] In other words, the Buddha's final instruction was this: Trust your own insights, and use self-control to reach perfection and inner peace.

Following this pronouncement, the Buddha turned on his right side and died. The many sculptures and paintings of the so-called Reclining Buddha may be images of his serene moment of death.[4] In any case, Buddhists idealize the Buddha's attitude toward death as a model for everyone.

THE BASIC TEACHINGS OF BUDDHISM

It is impossible to know exactly what the Buddha taught. He did not write down his teachings, nor did his early disciples. The only written versions were recorded several hundred years after his death, following centuries of being passed on orally—and of being interpreted in multiple ways.

The basic teachings that have come down to us are in a number of written languages, all of which are different from the language (apparently a variation of Magadhi) spoken by the Buddha. One of the most important languages through which Buddhist teachings have been passed down is Pali, a language related to Sanskrit; another is Sanskrit itself—often called the Latin of India because of its widespread use in earlier years for scholarly works.

At the core of what is generally regarded as basic Buddhism are the Three Jewels (Sanskrit: *Triratna;* Pali: *Tiratana*)—that is, the Buddha, the Dharma, and the Sangha. The Buddha is thought of as an ideal human being whom other human beings should imitate; the image of him, seated in meditation, is a constant model of self-control and mindfulness. He is not usually thought of as being dead but as existing in a timeless dimension beyond the world. The **Dharma** (Sanskrit), or Dhamma (Pali), means the sum total of Buddhist teachings about how to view the world and how to live properly. The **Sangha** is the community of monks and nuns.[5]

The Buddha's teachings are like the Buddha himself—practical. Surrounded in the India of his day by every kind of speculation about the afterlife, the nature of the divine, and other difficult questions, the Buddha concentrated on what was useful. He refused to talk about anything else—a benign neglect that has been called his noble silence. He said that a person who speculated about unanswerable questions was like a man who had been wounded by an arrow but refused to pull it out until he knew everything about the arrow and the person who shot it. The wounded man would die before he could get all the information he wanted.

The Buddha wished to concentrate on the two most important questions about existence: How can we minimize suffering, both our own and that of others? And how can we attain inner peace? The Buddha's conclusions are not just intellectual solutions but also recommendations for a practical way of living; Buddhist doctrines are meant to be accepted not on blind faith but rather only after they have been experienced as truths by each individual.

The Three Marks of Reality

Common to all forms of Buddhism is a way of looking at the world. Although this view may seem pessimistic at first, it is meant to be a realistic assessment of existence that, when understood, helps lead one, ultimately, to inner peace and even joy. According to this view, reality manifests three characteristics: constant change, a lack of permanent identity, and the existence of suffering. This view is the foundation for the Four Noble Truths and the Noble Eightfold Path, which we will discuss shortly.

Change One of the things the Buddha recommended is that we look at life as it really is. When we do, he said, the first thing we notice is life's constant change, or impermanence (Pali: **anichcha;** Sanskrit: *anitya*). We are often surprised by change—and pained by it—because we do not expect it, but the fact is that nothing we experience in life ever remains the same. We get used to things (our own face, family, friends, house, car, neighborhood), and they seem to remain basically the same every time we look at them. But that is an illusion, for they are changing daily, gradually. We usually only notice the changes over time.

Everyone knows the shock of change, such as seeing an old friend after many years apart, or looking at childhood photos. Even old movies on television and old songs on the radio—the performers now aged or even long gone—clearly convey the Buddhist sense of the inevitability of change. A family gathering can have the same effect: the death of a much-loved grandparent may be contrasted by the sight of a great-grandchild playing in a playpen in the corner.

People also change. Think of what the word *love* means to a five-year-old, a teenager, a new parent, or a person who has lost a spouse. Or imagine hearing the news of a divorce between two people you thought were well suited and happily married.

When we truly experience impermanence, we see that all of reality is in motion all the time, that the universe is in flux. As the kaleidoscope of reality slowly turns, its patterns change; and while old patterns disappear, new patterns are born, all of them interesting. As the Buddha taught, the wise person expects change, accepts it, and even savors it. The wise person might also reflect that just as pleasures do not last forever, neither do sorrows.

No Permanent Identity We know that the Buddha urged people to abandon egotism and a fixation on material objects. Related to this, he denied the existence of the permanent identity of anything. Thus, the second mark of reality is that each person and each thing is not only changing but is made up of parts that are also constantly changing, a concept referred to as the fact of "no permanent identity." In the case of people, it is called "no permanent soul" or "no self." The Pali term is **anatta;** in Sanskrit it is *anatman* ("no *Atman*") because of the Buddha's refusal to accept the Hindu notion of timeless, unchanging reality (*Atman*) underlying everything—people, things, essences, and gods.

For the sake of logical convenience, we often talk about each person or thing as if it were a single unified reality. Let us first consider something nonhuman, say, a car. We call it *a car* as if it were one single reality, but actually it is made up of many things—glass, aluminum, rubber, paint, headlights, belts, pistons, wires, and fluids—many of which are either going wrong right now or probably soon will be.

Then think of how each human being, though called by a single name, is actually made up of organs, body parts, instincts, memories, ideas, and hopes—all of which are constantly changing. Consider also one's self-perception. I naively think I am the same person from day to day, even if I get a haircut or lose weight or see a film. But if I recall myself at age 10 and then compare that person with who I am now, I seem now to be someone quite different.

To the Buddha, to believe that a person has some unchanging identity or soul is as mistaken as believing that a car has an unchanging essence. The car is not a car because it has a "car soul"; rather, it is a car because of a social convention that refers to its many related parts by a single word. This tendency is so strong that we sometimes think that a label (*car*) is the reality. Although the Buddhist view may seem strange at first, it is quite rational—and it helps eliminate surprise when my car won't start, when a friend becomes distant, or when a photo reveals the inevitability of aging. All these changes show the same process at work.[6]

Suffering The third characteristic of reality, known as **dukkha** (Pali), or *duhkha* (Sanskrit), is usually translated as "suffering" or "sorrow," but it also means "dissatisfaction" or "dis-ease." It refers to the fact that life, when lived conventionally, can never be fully satisfying because of its inescapable change. Even in the midst of pleasure, we often recognize that pleasure is fleeting. Even when all the bills are paid, we know that in a few days there will be more. Try as we might to put everything in our lives in order, disorder soon reasserts itself. In the midst of happy experiences, we may worry about the people we love. And there are times when ever-changing life brings misery: the death of a parent or spouse or child, divorce, sickness, fire, flood, earthquake, war, the loss of job or home.

Dukkha encompasses the whole range, from horrible suffering to every-day frustration. Someone once compared the inevitability of dukkha to buying a new car. Your car brings the pleasures of mobility and pride of ownership, but as you go for your first ride you know what lies ahead: insurance premiums, routine maintenance, and costly repairs.

The Buddha concluded that to live means inescapably to experience sorrow and dissatisfaction. But he analyzed the nature and causes of suffering much like a doctor would diagnose an illness—in order to understand and overcome them. Those who say that Buddhism pessimistically focuses on suffering do not see the hopeful purpose behind that focus. Indeed, no one can escape suffering, but each person can decide how to respond to it, as indicated in the Four Noble Truths.

The Four Noble Truths and the Noble Eightfold Path

Perhaps to aid in their memorization, some Buddhist teachings were grouped into fours and eights. The Four Noble Truths are a linked chain of truths about life: (1) suffering exists; (2) it has a cause; (3) it has an end; and (4) there is a way to attain release from suffering—namely, by following the Noble Eightfold Path. Let's look at each concept more closely.

The First Noble Truth: To Live Is to Suffer   To say it perhaps more descriptively, "birth is attended with pain, decay is painful, disease is painful, death is painful."[7] Having a body means that we can be tired and sick. Having a mind means that we can be troubled and discouraged. We have so many daily duties that our lives become a long list of things-to-do, and we feel like jugglers trying to keep too many balls spinning in the air. The past cannot be relived, and the future is uncertain. And every day, we have to decide what to do with the rest of our lives. (It has been remarked that adults so frequently ask children "What do you want to be when you grow up?" because the adults themselves are still trying to decide what to do with their own lives.)

To live means to experience anxiety, loss, and sometimes even anguish. In other words, "living means sorrow." Although the message sounds dark, this truth urges us to be realistic, not melancholy; it is also hopeful in the sense that if we recognize why suffering comes about then we can lessen it.

The Second Noble Truth: Suffering Comes from Desire   When he analyzed suffering, the Buddha saw that it comes from wanting what we cannot have and from never being satisfied with what we do have. The word *trishna* (Sanskrit), or *tanha* (Pali), which is often translated as "desire," might better be translated as "thirst"; it can also be translated as "craving," suggesting both an addiction and a fear of loss. Some of our desires are obvious: food, sleep, clothing, housing, health. Some desires are more subtle: privacy, respect, friendship, quiet, stresslessness,

The eight-spoked wheel is an ancient symbol of Buddhist teachings.

security, variety, beauty. And some desires are simply "wants" that are cultivated by our society: alcohol, designer clothes, tobacco, entertainment, expensive food. We all have desires, and because life around us is always changing, no matter how much we acquire we cannot be permanently satisfied. Desire is insatiable, and the result is discontent, dissatisfaction, and sometimes misery. But is there a way to be free of suffering?

The Third Noble Truth: To End Suffering, End Desire   It is hard to argue with the reasonableness of this truth, yet it goes against modern Western notions. The Western tendency is to strain to achieve every imaginable desire. This tendency seems to thrive in cultures—such as many modern ones—that emphasize individual legal and moral rights, competition between individuals, and individual success in school, in one's job, and in sports. Belief in a distinct and permanent self or an immortal soul may be the origin of such individualism. This tendency is rather different from the sense of self that comes from a worldview that values the individual's membership in the group—a view of self more common, traditionally, in tribal and Asian cultures.

To our modern way of thinking, the Buddha may seem to have been rather stark in his recommendations. Nevertheless, he himself left home and family and possessions because he believed—and taught—that *any* kind of attachment will bring inevitable suffering. The shaven head and special clothing of monks and nuns symbolize their radical detachment from worldly concerns.

Buddhists themselves recognize, though, that not everyone can be a monk. Consequently, this third truth is moderated for laypeople. It is commonly interpreted as a recommendation that everyone accept peacefully whatever occurs, aiming less for happiness and more for inner peace. The individual should concentrate on the present moment, not on the past or the future or one's desires for them. Because times of happiness are always paid for by times of unhappiness (the pendulum swings in both directions), a certain emotional neutrality is the best path.

Acceptance is a step to inner peace if I recognize that what I have right now is actually enough. Ultimately, I have to accept my body, my talents, my family, and even my relatives. Of course, some adjustments can be made: I can move, have plastic surgery, change my job, or get a divorce. Ultimately, though, much of life simply has to be accepted—and appreciated when possible.

The essence of the Third Noble Truth is this: I cannot change the outside world, but I can change myself and the way I experience the world.

Look within.
Be still.
Free from fear and
attachment,
Know the sweet joy
of the way.
—The Dhammapada[8]

The Fourth Noble Truth: Release from Suffering Is Possible and Can Be Attained by Following the Noble Eightfold Path   The ultimate goal of Buddhism is **nirvana.** (The term is Sanskrit; the equivalent in Pali is *nibbana*.) The term *nirvana* suggests many things: end of suffering, inner peace, and liberation from the limitations of the world. The word *nirvana* seems to

mean "blown out," or "cool," suggesting that the fires of desire have been extinguished. Upon attaining nirvana, the individual has self-control and is no longer driven from inside by raging emotional forces or from outside by the unpredictable events of life. It may not necessarily imply the elimination of anger (stories tell of the Buddha's getting angry at disputes within the monastic community), but it does suggest a general inner quiet. Nirvana is also believed to end karma and rebirth after the present life. (More will be said about nirvana later in this chapter.) To reach nirvana, Buddhism recommends following the Noble Eightfold Path.

The Noble Eightfold Path: The Way to Inner Peace   The eight "steps" of the path actually form a program that the Buddha taught will lead us toward liberation from the impermanence and suffering of reality. Together, they describe three main goals: to face life objectively, to live kindly, and to cultivate inner peace. Although they are often called "steps," the eight recommendations are not to be practiced sequentially but rather all together. As it is usually translated, the Noble Eightfold Path sounds so old-fashioned that readers may not immediately perceive its practicality. But keep in mind that the word *right* in the following list is a translation of a word that might better be translated as "correct" or "complete."

1. *Right understanding* I recognize the impermanence of life, the mechanism of desire, and the cause of suffering.
2. *Right intention* My thoughts and motives are pure, not tainted by my emotions and selfish desires.
3. *Right speech* I speak honestly and kindly, in positive ways, avoiding lies, exaggeration, harsh words.
4. *Right action* My actions do not hurt any other being that can feel hurt, including animals; I avoid stealing and sexual conduct that would bring hurt.
5. *Right work* My job does no harm to myself or others.
6. *Right effort* With moderation, I consistently strive to improve.
7. *Right meditation* I use the disciplines of meditation (**dhyana**) and focused awareness to contemplate the nature of reality more deeply.
8. *Right contemplation* I cultivate states of blissful inner peace (**samadhi**).

THE INFLUENCE OF INDIAN THOUGHT ON EARLY BUDDHIST TEACHINGS

It is uncertain whether the Buddha intended to begin an entirely new religion. Early Buddhist literature rejects certain elements of the common Vedic practice of the time, particularly its ritualism, its reliance on priests, its caste system, and its belief in any permanent spiritual reality. Non-Buddhists responded argumentatively when women and slaves entered the Buddhist monastic order. Such evidence leads us to think that early Buddhists saw themselves as outside the mainstream priestly Vedic culture—a fact that may

In Buddhism, the movement toward liberation is often symbolized by a rising architectural form. Pagodas and the more ancient stupa form rise above Shwedagon Paya, the most important temple in Yangon and all of Myanmar.   ◀

The great temple of Angkor Wat in Cambodia was built in the twelfth century as a Hindu temple but later was adapted for Buddhist use.

have assisted them in developing their own statements of belief and practice. Nevertheless, we do know that early Buddhist teachings accepted certain elements of Indian thought that are today shared to some extent by Hinduism, Jainism, and Buddhism.

Ahimsa: "Do No Harm"

Foremost among the elements adopted from the Indian worldview of the Buddha's day was the ideal of *ahimsa* ("nonharm"; see chapter 3). It is not clear how old this ideal is, and it has not always been followed. We do know that Vedic sacrifice at the time of the Buddha sometimes included animal sacrifice (and animal sacrifice in Hindu practice can still be found, particularly in Nepal and Bali). But we also know that the ideal of ahimsa was already prominent in India before the time of the Buddha and may have had ancient and pre-Aryan origins.

For Buddhism, ahimsa is fundamental. The ideal holds that to cause suffering to any being is cruel and unnecessary—life is already hard enough for each of us. Ahimsa discourages causing not only physical pain but also psychological hurt or the exploitation of another. Upon reaching a real understanding that every being that feels can suffer, the individual gains wider sympathy. It is then natural and satisfying for the individual to live with gentleness.

Ahimsa is a high ideal and not always easy to achieve. Furthermore, we must recognize that there will always be a gap between the ideal and actual practice in different Buddhist cultures and among individuals. Nevertheless, however murky the definition of the "best action" may be, the ideal is fairly clear. A compassionate person does everything possible to avoid causing suffering: "ashamed of roughness, and full of mercy, he dwells compassionate and kind to all creatures that have life."[9] This empathetic ideal has been interpreted as recommending, when possible, a vegetarian or semivegetarian diet, and it warns against involvement in any jobs or sports that would hurt others, such as being a butcher, hunter, fisherman, soldier, or weapon maker. The result is a way of life that is harmonious and free of remorse.

The Soul and Karma

The Buddha rejected the notion of a soul (an unchanging spiritual reality), but he accepted some notion of rebirth. How, we might then ask, can an individual be reborn if there is no soul? Buddhism holds that while there is no individual soul the elements of personality that make up an individual can recombine and thus continue from one lifetime to another. Buddhism offers the examples of a flame passing from one candle to another and the pattern caused by a breeze that passes over many blades of grass. The candles are separate, but only one flame passes between each candle; the blades of grass are rooted to separate places, but the pattern of the breeze travels across them and "unites" them in movement.

Closely related to the notion of rebirth is *karma*. As we discussed in chapter 3, karma determines how one will be reborn. In Hinduism and Jainism, karma is like something that clings to the soul as it passes from life to life in reincarnation. It works automatically: good actions produce karma that brings good effects, such as intelligence, high birth, and wealth; bad actions produce karma that brings the opposite, including rebirth into animal and insect life-forms. Because the Buddha rejected the existence of a soul, explaining how karma works is more difficult in Buddhism. It is thought to accompany and affect the elements of personality that reappear in later lifetimes. Regardless of their specific manner of functioning, karma and rebirth were already such powerful ideas in the India of the Buddha's time that they continued in early Buddhism and from there have spread well beyond India. They remain highly influential concepts in Buddhist countries today.

Nirvana

In Buddhism, as in Hinduism, the everyday world of change is called **samsara,** a term that suggests decay and pain. Liberation from samsara,

"Who Am I?"

Buddhist teachers often require their students to meditate on this question: "Who am I?" At first, giving an answer seems simple. I take for granted that I know who "I" am. After all, in English the word is just one letter and is even capitalized. Surely those facts must be a sign that the matter is clear. (But why don't we capitalize "you"?) Yet the question of who I am becomes more difficult the more I think about it. I start by thinking that finding the answer will be like opening a peach or avocado and finding a pit—a core—at the center. But the question turns out to be more like peeling an onion and finding one layer after another.

Who or what is this "I"? Is it my name? Is it my body? Is it my parents? Is it my tastes or talents? Is it my job? Is it my thoughts, my memories, or my hopes? Or could it just be my driver's license or my social security number? What makes me me?

The various religions and cultures answer the question of identity quite differently. A westerner will probably initially answer with his or her personal name (the fact that it is a first name is very significant). This way of answering may be influenced by the emphasis in Judaism, Christianity, and Islam on the importance of the individual. Believers within these three religions also often speak of having an immortal soul that was created by God. Ultimately, they may say, a person's identity comes from having a unique soul. And this unique soul, while giving human dignity, also makes us feel separate from every other individual human being.

Yet there are other ways of looking at identity. Someone from East Asia who has been influenced by Confucianism might answer the question of identity with his or her family name—which in East Asian cultures precedes the personal name. Or this person might give the name of a company or school. A person with a background in Taoist thought might say, "I am a part of the natural world, or I am a manifestation of the Tao." A person with a Hindu background could say, "I am God."

The Buddhist view is rather unusual and uncompromising. It derives entirely from questioning one's experience. Certainly each person has a sense of identity, but does it mean that there is a soul or permanent self as its cause? Is it possible that the sense of separate and permanent identity might be a fiction, something not ultimately real? Buddhism tells us to look inside carefully.

If I examine my inner experience, Buddhism says, I see that my consciousness is not permanent, but is more like a string of little events—one moment of awareness after another. As a result of this kind of examination, Buddhist thought differs from many other religious traditions, for it teaches that one's personal identity is constructed of changing parts and does not come from having a soul. As an example, think of a molecule. It is made of electrons, protons, and other particles of energy; but it is mostly empty space. Like a molecule—Buddhist teaching tells us—the human self is similarly a buzzing blend of many elements moving in empty space.

What are those elements? Let us think of a few that make up my sense of self, and then of their origins. The language that I speak and in which I think my thoughts comes from the people who raised me—but, since they didn't invent the language, it must come from a long chain of earlier people, too. My body comes from my parents—but it also is made up of the food that I eat every day, which was grown, transported, and sold by many people. I breathe oxygen—but that comes from the ocean, trees, and sky. In other words, everything that I am comes from somewhere or someone else. And each day, because I receive new parts and lose old parts, my "I" is constantly changing. If I examine my identity closely, I will see that it is made of layers and parts, which stretch out into the past and future and even into other parts of the world. Buddhism teaches that whatever "I" am is ultimately not separate but is intimately connected to the rest of the universe.

Was the Buddha an Atheist?

Philosophers often ask questions about the nature of reality. Is there a Creator? Is the universe eternal? Is the extent of the universe infinite?

The Buddha witnessed intense wrangling over such questions in the India of his day and apparently disliked the tendency of debate to inflame anger. He thus avoided paying too much attention to the "unanswerable questions." His teachings and the earliest monastic rules do, however, clearly use reason to address such questions.

What, then, did the Buddha believe and teach about the existence of God? To answer this requires two more questions.

- Is there a Creator God? Early Buddhism explicitly rejects such a belief, as did other religious movements in India at that time. For example, we know that Jainism and a philosophical school of the time, the Lokayata, both rejected the notion of a Creator. (The Buddha, however, did believe in the existence of what were sometimes called *gods*—superhuman beings who lived above the earth but who were also subject to karma and rebirth.)

- Is there an Unchanging Divine Reality? Regarding such a belief—called *Brahman* in the Upanishads—early Buddhism exhibited a similar skepticism. Apparently the Buddha saw *everything* to be in constant change, and his experience did not recognize anything whatsoever that was unchanging, thereby precluding a belief in Brahman.

Perhaps the Buddha would best be called a nontheist. Although details of the Buddha's thought are not entirely clear, what is obvious is the extreme practicality of his focus. He opposed religious dogmatism, blind devotion to a guru, and the power of a priestly caste. From his point of view, birth as a human being was a rare opportunity, and one's focus in life should be on living in such a way as to bring enlightenment. Regarding all questions, the Buddha asked disciples to experience things for themselves and then to trust their own judgment.

---

however, is attained in nirvana. The notion has many similarities with the Hindu goal of *moksha* ("liberation"; discussed in chapter 3). Nirvana is thought of as existence beyond limitation. Many people in the West associate nirvana with a psychological state, because it is described as evoking joy and peace; but perhaps it is better to see nirvana as being indescribable and beyond all psychological states. Although reaching nirvana occurs rarely, it is theoretically possible to attain during one's lifetime; the Buddha is said to have "entered nirvana" at the time of his enlightenment. Once a person has reached nirvana, rebirth is finished, and in a culture that believes that individuals have already been born many times before this current life, an end to rebirth can be a welcome thought.

THE EARLY DEVELOPMENT OF BUDDHISM

Buddhism might have remained an entirely Indian religion, much as Jainism has, if it were not for an energetic king named Ashoka, who flourished about 250 B.C.E. (Timeline 4.1). Ashoka's plan to expand his rule over a large part of India naturally entailed much fighting. After a particularly bloody battle in eastern India, as Ashoka was inspecting the battlefield, he saw the scene very differently than he had before. The whole experience was so horrifying that Ashoka converted to the ideal of nonviolence.

TIMELINE 4.1

	c. 563–483 B.C.E.	Life of Siddhartha Gautama, the Buddha
Life of Ashoka, Indian king who spread Buddhist values	c. 273–232 B.C.E.	
	c. 50 C.E.	Entry of Buddhism into China
Creation of the Lotus Sutra	c. 100 C.E.	
	c. 300 C.E.	Beginning of the spread of Buddhism in Southeast Asia
Entry of Buddhism into Korea	c. 400 C.E.	
	c. 520 C.E.	Introduction of Bodhidharma's Meditation School of Buddhism to China
Acceptance of Buddhism in Japan	c. 552 C.E.	
	c. 630 C.E.	Entry of Buddhism into Tibet
Founding of Tendai and Shingon Buddhism in Japan by Saicho (767—822) and Kukai (774—835), respectively	c. 820 C.E.	
	c. 845 C.E.	Third great persecution of Buddhism in China, which permanently weakened Chinese Buddhism
Revival of Theravada Buddhism in Sri Lanka and Southeast Asia	c. 1000 C.E.	
	c. 1100–1500	Decline of Buddhism in India
Life of Honen, founder of the Pure Land sect in Japan	1133–1212	
	1158–1210	Life of Chinul, founder of Korean Chogye order
Beginning of the growth of Zen in Japan	c. 1200	
	1222–1282	Life of Nichiren, founder of Nichiren Buddhism in Japan
Life of Tsong Kha-pa, Tibetan Buddhist reformer°°	1357–1419	
	1644–1694	Life of poet Matsuo Basho
Beginning of World Fellowship of Buddhists	c. 1952	

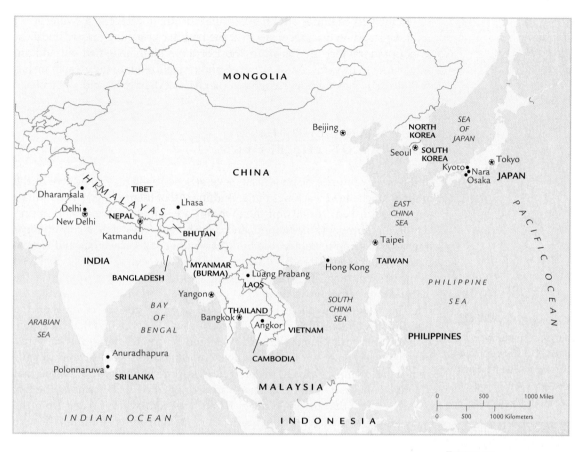

FIGURE 4.1

The birthplace and traditional home of Buddhism: India, China, Japan, and Southeast Asia.

Although it is uncertain whether Ashoka became a Buddhist, he did make political use of Buddhist moral values. A cynic might note that forbidding violence is a practical move for any ruler who wishes to remain on the throne. In any case, the principle of nonviolence is most effective when it is embraced widely; otherwise, the few people who are nonviolent will be preyed upon by the violent.

To bring a large number of the population around to his new nonviolent way of thinking and acting, Ashoka decided to spread the principles of nonviolence throughout India and possibly even beyond. To do this, he erected many stone columns inscribed with his principles, placing some at sites important in the Buddha's life. A number of these columns still exist today.

Our historical knowledge of Ashoka is quite limited, but he looms large in Buddhist legend. One story tells us that Ashoka sent as a missionary to Sri Lanka a son or nephew named Mahinda (also called Melinda, Mahendra, and Menander). Whatever the truth of this story, it is a fact that Sri Lanka is largely Buddhist today. Indeed, it may have been Ashoka who gave Buddhism its urge to spread and helped to make it one of the world's great missionary religions (Figure 4.1).

Timeline of significant events in the history of Buddhism. ◀

In the first centuries after the Buddha's death, in response to widespread and long-standing disagreements over the Buddha's teachings, many Buddhist schools and splinter groups arose. Most of these ultimately died out and are only names to us today. A few survived and crystallized into the great branches of Buddhism that we now recognize: Theravada, Mahayana, and Vajrayana.

THERAVADA BUDDHISM: THE WAY OF THE ELDERS

In the early centuries of Buddhism, several schools claimed to adhere to the original, unchanged teachings of the Buddha. All of them shared the Buddha's opposition to Vedic ritual and the brahmin priesthood, as well as his appreciation for simplicity, meditation, and detachment. They took a conservative approach, hoping to protect the Buddha's rather stark teachings and simple practice from being altered. Of all the conservative schools, one has survived to the present day: Theravada. Its name is often used today to refer to the entire conservative movement.

The lotus flower, here in a bucket awaiting use as an offering during ceremonies, is associated with the full flowering of the mind that occurs at enlightenment.

The Theravada school takes its name from its goal of passing on the Buddha's teachings unchanged. Its name means "the way (*vada*) of the elders (*thera*)." Theravada monks originally passed on the teachings in oral form, but they eventually wrote them down. Although the school's claim to have kept its teachings relatively unchanged over time is doubtful, it is true that Theravada has a deliberately conservative orientation. Furthermore, the fact that its home in Sri Lanka was somewhat isolated from the changes occurring within Buddhism in India may have protected the original Theravada teachings from altering greatly.

The heart of Theravada Buddhism is its community of monks. As a school, it has always stressed the ideal of reaching nirvana through detachment and desirelessness achieved through meditation. (This of course is an ideal that some would point out has been contradicted by the Sangha's having courted wealth and temporal power.) Although Theravada does accept that laypeople can attain nirvana, the life of the monk offers a surer path. The notion is enshrined in the ideal of the **arhat** (Sanskrit; Pali: *arahat,* meaning "perfect being," "worthy"), a person who has reached nirvana.*

The Theravada monastic community had its distant origins in the wandering sannyasins and in the groups of Hindu ascetics who lived in the forests. A sign of this

---

*In the discussion of Theravada Buddhism, it would be more accurate to use the Pali terms *nibbana, arahat,* and *sutta,* as opposed to the Sanskrit terms *nirvana, arhat,* and *sutra;* however, for the sake of consistency, the text throughout this chapter will reflect the terminology (whether Pali or Sanskrit) that is most familiar in the West.

Theravada monks receive their food from devout Buddhists. Here, monks at Mahagandhayon Kyaung, a large monastic school in Amarapura, Myanmar, line up with their rice bowls during Buddhist Lent, when laypeople bring food to the monks in order to earn beneficial karma.

connection is the orange robe of the Theravada Buddhist monk, also worn today by Hindu monks and ascetics. But even during the Buddha's lifetime, his monks began to live a settled life during the summertime monsoon season, giving their time to discussion and inhabiting caves or groves and parks donated by lay followers.

Theravada had spread very early from India to Sri Lanka, where it coexisted for centuries with other forms of Buddhism before becoming dominant in the twelfth century of the common era. By the fourth century, it had been carried—along with other elements of Indian culture—to Myanmar (Burma) and to Thailand. Theravada did not become predominant in Myanmar until the mid-eleventh century, when Bagan began to flourish as a great Buddhist city and center of Theravada under King Anawratha. Fourteenth-century Thailand, having freed itself of Khmer domination, also adopted Theravada Buddhism. The conservatism of Theravada was politically appealing to rulers for its moral rigor. Today it is the dominant religion in Sri Lanka, Myanmar, Thailand, Laos, and Cambodia.

Theravada monks must beg daily for their food, which has meant that they, like the Buddha's early followers, have to live close to laypeople. In fact, Theravada monasteries are often in the middle of towns. When Theravada monks go out on their begging rounds, people who wish to donate food

Buddhism in Thailand

Theravada Buddhism is the state religion of Thailand, and more than ninety percent of Thais are Buddhists. Thai Buddhists, however, practice a religion that blends elements from Buddhism, Hinduism, animism, and folk belief. Perhaps because Buddhism so emphasizes tolerance, it is particularly rich with elements from different religious traditions that have been allowed to flourish alongside traditional Buddhist beliefs and practices.

Buddhism's prevalence in Thailand is evident in everyday life. Thais frequently act publicly on the assumption that doing good deeds will "make merit"—bring good karma for this life and for future lives. To make merit, Thais offer coins to the needy on the street, give food and robes to monks, attend Buddhist services, and help animals. And Buddhist monks can be seen everywhere—walking in the streets and riding in the back of buses (which they ride free), in *tuk-tuks* (three-wheeled cabs), and on riverboats.

Yet equally visible are animistic "spirit houses." These look like miniature temples, and they are erected on high posts at the corner of a piece of land, on high-rise rooftops, or under large, old trees. Spirit houses are dedicated to the guardian spirits of the property and to the spirits of former owners. Worshipers offer food and flowers to them daily.

Frequently the Hindu god Brahma is the figure inside the spirit houses, and small images of dancing girls—derived from Hindu temple worship—are left as permanent offerings. In shops a visitor might see a statue of Ganesha, the elephant-headed Hindu god associated with success. Another influence of Hinduism is readily apparent in Thai art and dance, which tell the stories of Rama, Sita, and Hanuman, whose tales are retold in the Ramakien, the Thai version of the Ramayana.

A strong magical dimension is part of Thai Buddhism as well. Thai males often wear a necklace of Buddhist amulets to defend themselves against sickness and injury (the owners will describe in happy detail the origin and power of each of the amulets). Tattoos, often with images of the Buddha, Rama, and Hanuman, are thought to have a similar effect. Certain monks are firmly believed to have special powers; those monks are even consulted to find out winning lottery numbers. And taxi drivers—not to mention their often anxious passengers—hope that the multiple Buddhist images on their dashboards will offer needed protection in traffic.

freely offer them cooked rice and vegetables. Donors believe they are receiving beneficial karma from their acts of generosity, and people support the monasteries much like other societies give to libraries and other social agencies. In return for donations of food and clothing, many monasteries run schools, meditation centers, and medical clinics, as well as care for stray animals. Monks are honored guests at both civic and family occasions. They are role models of gentleness and insight and are often consulted for advice.

Theravada Teachings and Literature

The Theravada collection of the Buddha's teachings is called the Pali Canon. As a whole, this mass of material is called *Tipitaka* (Pali), or **Tripitaka** (Sanskrit), which means "three baskets." The name comes from the fact that the writings were divided according to their subject matter into three groups.

The first collection (called *vinaya*—Pali and Sanskrit) outlines the procedural rules for monastic life. These include rules on begging, eating, relations with monks and nonmonks, and other disciplines.[10]

The second collection comprises sayings of the Buddha in the form of sermons or dialogues. This type of material is called *sutta* (Pali), or **sutra** (Sanskrit), and it is subdivided into five groups: Digha Nikaya ("long teachings"), Majjhima Nikaya ("middle-length teachings"), Samyutta Nikaya ("connected teachings"), Anguttara Nikaya ("graduated teachings"), and Khuddaka Nikaya ("small book collection"), which includes the Dhammapada.

A third collection, developed later, is called *abhidhamma* (Pali), or *abhidharma* (Sanskrit), meaning "the works that go beyond the elementary teachings." It systematized the doctrine presented more or less randomly in the sutras.

Theravada temples sometimes have the steeply pitched rooflines that we see on this prayer hall in Luang Prabang, along the Mekong River in northern Laos. Monks gather around four o'clock in anticipation of the afternoon recitation of sutras.

Theravada Art and Architecture

Images of the Buddha did not appear in the earliest centuries of Buddhism; instead, artists used symbols to represent him and his teachings. One symbol was the eight-spoked wheel, which derived from the Noble Eightfold Path and represented all the basic Buddhist teachings, the Dharma. (The wheel may have been suggested either by the disk of the sun, symbolizing light and health, or by the wheel of a king's chariot, a symbol of royal rulership.) The umbrella, often carried to protect an important person from the hot sun,

This Reclining Buddha at Wat Po in Bangkok is one of the most revered images in Thailand. Note the Buddha's feet near the door at the far end of the hall.

symbolized the Buddha's authority. Other common symbols included a set of footprints, a lotus flower, and an empty throne. Many types of **stupa,** which began as a large mound, arose over the remains of Buddhist monks and at important Buddhist sites. Symbols may have been used at first simply because artists were struggling with the basic challenge of depicting simultaneously the humanity of the Buddha and his great spiritual attainment, his enlightenment. By the first century of the common era, however, images of the Buddha began to appear. (Scholars debate the possible influence of Greek sculptural traditions.[11]) In Theravada countries we now frequently see statues of the Buddha meditating, standing (with hand outstretched in blessing), walking, or reclining. Some of the most beautiful sculptures are the Reclining Buddhas of Sri Lanka and Thailand.

MAHAYANA BUDDHISM: THE "BIG VEHICLE"

The second great branch of Buddhism is called Mahayana, a word that is usually translated as "big vehicle." It suggests a large ferryboat in which all types of people can be carried across a river, and it hints at the broad scope of the Mahayana vision, which can accommodate a wide variety of people seeking enlightenment. Mahayana emphasizes that nirvana is not only attainable by monks but is a possibility for everyone. Mahayana also stresses that enlightenment is a call to compassion, for "the Mahayana tradition maintains that a person must save himself by saving others."[12]

Some critics of Mahayana Buddhism claim that it has allowed ritual and speculation—which had been deemphasized by the Buddha—to creep back in. It is possible that the Indian love of ritual and imagery remains alive in a new form in Mahayana. For example, the fire ceremony of some Mahayana sects certainly derives from Vedic practice. But this is really to say that Mahayana initially was thoroughly Indian and sought to express its truths in very Indian ways.[13]

It is possible that some practices or attitudes of early Buddhism did not always fulfill the religious needs of many laypeople who appreciated ritual. Mahayana Buddhism, however, has abundantly met almost every religious and philosophical need.[14] It is the source of some of the most extraordinary creations of the human mind—in its art, architecture, philosophy, psychology, and ceremony.

New Ideals: Compassion and the Bodhisattva

In Mahayana Buddhism, the religious ideal broadened: from the exemplar of the monastic person, fairly detached from family life, it expanded to include nonmonks, women, and the married. Mahayana began to explore the possibilities of following a religious path that was active in the world. This difference signaled a shift in the notion of what is virtuous. It might have represented a reaction against Indian asceticism and the cult of the

The Hindu ritual of anointing sacred objects became a part of Mahayana devotional practice as seen here in the anointed dome of Boudhanath in Nepal.

sannyasin, or it might have indicated a new form of devotionalism and love of ritual. It might also have come from a widening of the concept of nirvana. Nirvana was now thought to be found within samsara, the everyday world of change. This devotional shift began in India and in central Asia, but it grew in strength when Mahayana entered China, a culture that has long valued nature and the physical world in general. In Mahayana, the human body and the material realm are viewed positively, and there is a great openness toward art and music. Mahayana grew as the senses and emotions were increasingly viewed as means of spiritual transformation, and as the gulf between sacred and nonsacred (typical of Vedic practice) was bridged.

In Mahayana, wisdom remained an important goal, but the pairing of wisdom and compassion was central to its teachings. Compassion became an essential virtue and the preeminent expression of wisdom. The term for this compassion is **karuna,** which may also be translated as "empathy," "sympathy," or "kindness." Karuna is somewhat different from the Western notion of kindness, in which one separate human being, out of an abundance of individual generosity, gives to another separate human being. Rather, karuna implies that we all are part of the same ever-changing universe. Deep down, the individual is not really different from anyone or anything else. To be kind to others is actually to be kind to oneself. Karuna in action simply means living out this awareness of the unity of the universe. With this perception of the interrelatedness of all beings, including animals, compassion comes naturally: if I am kind, my kindness must be shown toward anything that can feel pain. The great prayer of Buddhist compassion is this: May all creatures be well and happy. It is a common Mahayana practice to mentally project this wish to the world every day.

The esteem for karuna influences the human ideal in Mahayana. Instead of the Theravada ideal of the arhat, who is esteemed for detached wisdom and unworldly living, the ideal in Mahayana Buddhism is the person of deep compassion, the **bodhisattva** ("enlightenment being"). Because a bodhisattva embodies compassion, it is often said that a bodhisattva will refuse to fully enter nirvana, in order to be reborn on earth to help others. A person may even take the "bodhisattva vow" to be constantly reborn until all are enlightened.

The same kind of openness to a variety of religious paths that we saw in Hinduism is also typical of Mahayana Buddhism. Mahayana recognizes that people differ greatly and find themselves at different stages of spiritual development. For example, a person who would not benefit from study or meditation might be able to achieve a new level of understanding through the use of ritual, imagery, and religious objects. It is possible to find the influence of bhakti yoga (see chapter 3) in Mahayana, because Mahayana even endorses devotion to deities. Some critics who appreciate the historical Buddha's rejection of such religious practices may label them as superstition. Regardless, Mahayana is open to anything that can lead to greater spiritual awareness, a concept known as "skillful means" (Sanskrit: *upaya*).

Mahayana Thought and Worldview

Mahayana has encouraged a vision of reality that is imaginative, wide, and often profound. A legendary story tells of a Chinese emperor who began reading certain Mahayana sutras; he then said in astonishment that the experience was like looking out over the ocean. He sensed the vastness of the Mahayana vision as he experienced both the quantity and the quality of the sutras that he was attempting to understand.

Several key notions must be introduced here. They show a worldview of a universe populated by holy personalities and full of the divine. These notions may seem dry when they are only read about, but they will become very meaningful when a person is experiencing Mahayana art in temples and museums. These ideas underlie Mahayana sculpture, painting, and belief.

At Boudhanath in Katmandu, Nepal, these eyes represent the omnipresent Buddha nature.

The Three-Body Doctrine (Trikaya Doctrine) In Mahayana, the Buddha nature can express itself in three ways. This is called the **trikaya** ("three-body") doctrine. The historical Buddha who lived in India came to be considered the manifestation of a divine reality, "the cosmic Buddha nature." The Sanskrit term for this is *Dharmakaya* (often translated as "law body," "form body," or "body of reality"). According to Mahayana Buddhism, the cosmic Buddha nature, although invisible, permeates all things. (It sometimes has been compared to the Hindu notion of Brahman, and may have been influenced by it.) In people, the cosmic Buddha nature frequently presents itself as potential. In fact, it is our true nature that we need to recognize and realize. Dharmakaya also exists in the natural world, for all things are a sacred manifestation of the cosmic Buddha nature. When we experience the mystery of the natural world, we experience the Dharmakaya.

Siddhartha Gautama's physical body, because it is considered an incarnation of this divine reality, is called Nirmanakaya ("transformation body"). The notion that the historical Buddha was a divine manifestation reminds us of the Hindu notion of the multiple incarnations of Vishnu, and this Mahayana notion may have been influenced by that Hindu belief.

In keeping with the notion of many incarnations, many Mahayana schools believe in more than one transformation body of the Buddha. We might recall that both Theravada and Mahayana schools describe the Buddha's knowledge of his past lives. Both branches of Buddhism also believe that another historical Buddha, **Maitreya** (Sanskrit; Pali: Metteya), will appear on earth in the future to inaugurate a golden age. In several

Mahayana cultures, this belief has taken on great importance. In China and Vietnam, the Buddha who will come is called Mi-lo-fo and is often shown as an overweight, joyful, "laughing Buddha." In Korea, the notion of Miruk (as Maitreya is known there) has been especially influential in generating belief in a messianic future, which has prompted the creation of many beautiful statues in his honor. He is often shown seated on a stool or raised platform in the so-called Western style, with one leg down on the floor and the other crossed over it, his head resting thoughtfully on one hand as he contemplates the future.

In Mahayana philosophy, the cosmic Buddha nature has also taken bodily shape in supernatural Buddhas who live in the heavens beyond our earth. These Buddhas have radiant, invulnerable bodies and live in constant happiness. In Sanskrit, they are called Sambhogakaya Buddhas ("perfect-bliss-body" Buddhas). Mahayana Buddhism envisions many Buddhas existing simultaneously, each with his own sphere of influence (called a Buddha Land). Particularly important is the bliss-body Buddha who created a Buddha Land in the western direction of the setting sun. There he receives the dying who wish enlightenment after death. His name in India was **Amitabha Buddha** (Chinese: Amito-fo; Japanese: Amida Butsu). Many devout Buddhists hope to be reborn in his paradise. After attaining enlightenment there, they can return to the world to save other beings. Their devotion to Amitabha Buddha has inspired a great body of fine painting and sculpture that depicts a large Buddha seated on a lotus flower, surrounded by peaceful disciples in pavilions set in gardens full of flowers.

Heavenly Bodhisattvas We have already discussed the focus of Mahayana on the earthly bodhisattva, a saintly person of great compassion. But Mahayana Buddhism also holds that many bodhisattvas who are eager to help human beings also exist in other dimensions beyond the earth. They, too, are beings of great compassion. Some once lived on earth and have been reborn beyond this world, but they retain an interest in it. They may appear miraculously on earth when needed or possibly may even be reborn to help others.

The most significant of the heavenly bodhisattvas has been Avalo-kiteshvara, who looks down from a location above in order to give help. In India, Avalokiteshvara was portrayed as male, but in China this bodhisattva was conceived as feminine because of her association with compassion and mercy. Her name in Chinese is Guanyin (Kuan-yin,* "hears cries"). She first

---

*Two systems are currently used for transcribing Chinese words into English: the *pinyin* and Wade-Giles systems. Because the mainland Chinese government and the United Nations have adopted pinyin, it has become the most commonly used system. The older Wade-Giles was the standard transcription system until pinyin was adopted, and it is still frequently encountered (as in the spelling of *Kuan-yin* and *Taoism*). For major Chinese terms in this book (both here and in chapter 6), the pinyin spelling is given first and the Wade-Giles spelling second.

In Mahayana, compassion is especially manifested in the many-armed form of Guanyin.

began to be shown in early depictions as having both male and female characteristics; but eventually she became entirely feminine. (As an object of devotion, she plays a role in Asia similar to that of Mary in Europe.) East Asian paintings and sculpture frequently show her with a very sweet face, dressed all in white, holding the jewel of wisdom or a vase of nectar, with the moon under her feet or in the sky behind her. Other artistic renderings of her, particularly in temple sculpture, show her with a halo of many arms (she is said to have a thousand), representing her many powers to help. In the palm of each hand is an eye, symbolizing her ability to see everyone in need. In temples, Guanyin is frequently paired with the Buddha. He is often in the front and center of the sanctuary, and she is located immediately behind him; or she may be a member of a triad, sitting to one side of the Buddha, with another bodhisattva or disciple of the Buddha on the other side. In China and Japan (where this bodhisattva became popularly known as Kannon), many temples were dedicated to her alone.

Shunyata One Mahayana doctrine asserts that all reality is *shunya* ("empty"; that is, empty of permanent essence). Literally, **shunyata** may be translated as "emptiness" or "zeroness." But what does this mean? The notion is an outgrowth of the basic Buddhist view of reality that everything is constantly shifting, changing, taking new form. If we consider an individual person, we can say the "individual" is a pattern, made of parts in continuous change. If we broaden our scope, larger patterns appear, such as the patterns of a family, a city, or a society. Similarly, nature is a combination of smaller patterns making larger patterns, like wheels within wheels. And even the parts themselves ultimately disintegrate as new parts are born. To better understand this concept, think of clouds, which look large and substantial but are forever appearing and disappearing, moving past each other and changing shape and size. Because everything is in constant change, each apparently individual person and thing is actually "empty" of any permanent individual identity. The notion of shunyata also suggests the experience that everything is a part of everything else, that all people and things exist together. To get this idea across, translators have suggested using terms like *clearness* and *transparency* instead of *emptiness*. (Interestingly, the character that the Chinese have often used for translating the word shunyata is the character for *sky*.) All of these translations suggest that there are no barriers between things.

Tathata Literally translated, the word **tathata** means "thatness," "thusness," or "suchness." This is a rich notion that invites each person's experience and interpretation. Tathata represents a view of experience that says that reality is revealed in each moment, as we savor patterns, relationships, and change. Because no moment is exactly the same, and no object is exactly the same, each can be observed and appreciated as it passes. Thus, simple, everyday events reveal the nature of reality. We may experience "thatness" when two elements come together in an unexpected way—for example, when a small child says something childlike but wise. Sometimes it comes when we notice a moment of change, such as when, after a long string of muggy summer days, we get up to add a blanket to the bed on the first crisp autumn night. Or it might be when we notice random elements coming together—for example, when a bird drinks from a water fountain or a dog joyously sticks its nose out of the window of a passing car. It might be when we recognize the uniqueness of a simple object or event, such as the beauty of a particular

The Mahayana teaching of tathata tells that all reality, like this encounter between a butterfly and a flower, is transitory.

apple in the supermarket, or the special way that the shadow of a tree falls on a nearby building at this particular moment. The experience can also come from something funny or sad. Although tathata involves the mundane, it is also a poetic moment that will never return in exactly the same way.

The wonder that can be seen in everyday life is what the term *tathata* suggests. We know we are experiencing the "thatness" of reality when we experience something and say to ourselves, "Yes, that's it; that is the way things are." In the moment, we recognize that reality is wondrously beautiful but also that its patterns are fragile and passing.

Mahayana Literature

Mahayana Buddhism in India used a Sanskrit version of the Tripitaka, but to these works it added a host of other materials. (Consequently, the Mahayana Tripitaka is longer than that of Theravada.) Many of the new Mahayana works were called sutras because they purported to be the words of the Buddha, but in reality they were imaginative, colorful creations written at least several centuries after the Buddha lived, from about 100 B.C.E. to about 600 C.E. The teachings of these sutras, however, may be seen as a natural development of basic Buddhist insights.

Primary among these texts are the Prajnaparamita Sutras ("sutras on the perfection of wisdom"), the earliest of which may have been written about 100 B.C.E. These sutras attempt to contrast ordinary understanding with the enlightened understanding that everything in the universe is interdependent.

The influential Vimalakirti Sutra teaches that it is possible to live a devout Buddhist life without necessarily becoming a monk. The hero of the sutra is the man Vimalakirti, who was, as historian Kenneth Ch'en describes

Worshipers are dwarfed by the Buddha image in this Mahayana temple of southern China.

him, "a layman rich and powerful, a brilliant conversationalist, a respected householder who surrounded himself with the pleasures of life, but was also a faithful and wise disciple of the Buddha, a man full of wisdom and thoroughly disciplined in his conduct."[15] Because the main figure is not a monk but more like a devout gentleman, we can see why this sutra became popular with laypeople. Its purpose, though, was serious. It showed that individuals can work successfully amidst the dangers of worldly life, can avoid causing harm, and can actually help themselves and others.

Two works that would have great influence on East Asian Buddhism were the Pure Land Sutras (two versions of the Sukhavati Vyuha Sutra, "sutra of the vision of the happy land"). The sutras speak of a heavenly realm, the Pure Land, established by the merciful Amitabha Buddha, where human beings can be reborn. All that is necessary for rebirth in the Pure Land is devotion to this Buddha, as shown by repetition of his name as a sign of total trust in him. These sutras would eventually give birth to a wildly successful movement, the Pure Land movement, which is still popular today. (We will discuss the Pure Land school of Mahayana a little later in this chapter.)

The monastery of Hengshan hangs on a hillside in Shanxi Province in China, a witness to the Buddhist desire for detachment from the world.

One of the most widely loved works of Mahayana was the Saddharma Pundarika Sutra ("lotus sutra of the good law"), known simply as the Lotus Sutra. In this sutra, the Buddha shows his transcendent, cosmic nature. As he preaches to thousands of his disciples, his light and wisdom extend out into the universe. Using parables, the sutra insists rather democratically that all people have the Buddha nature and that all, therefore, can become Buddhas. Many of its parables talk of the "skillful means" that can lead people of differing types and mentalities to enlightenment.

Mahayana in China

Mahayana Buddhism spread out of India to central Asia and to China, which it entered in the first century of the common era. As Buddhism spread to China and its neighboring regions, the Sanskrit canon was translated bit by bit into at least thirteen central Asian languages. In China, several Chinese versions were made of most of the major works. At first the translations were rough, but later versions were more exact, once translators had a better knowledge of Buddhist ideas and how to convey them in the Chinese idiom. By the eighth century, an enormous number of Buddhist works had been translated into Chinese.[16]

The appeal of Mahayana Buddhism in ancient China is worth considering. In some ways, the Buddhist ideal of monastic celibacy went against the grain of the Chinese Confucian culture, which (1) saw moral demands existing within family relationships, (2) venerated ancestors, and (3) valued continuity of the family line (see chapter 6). Yet Mahayana Buddhism had virtues that would appeal to a wide spectrum of the population. It accepted local cults and continued their practice of using rituals that promised magic, healing, and fertility for the masses of ordinary people. It created great temples with beautiful art and ceremony. It promoted peace and family harmony. It answered questions about the afterlife and performed funeral and memorial services for the dead. It provided a secure way of community life for people not interested in having children or creating their own families. It offered philosophical insights not already present in Chinese culture. And it provided many rulers with prayers and rituals that would help protect the nation and the rulers themselves.

Mahayana Buddhism had great success in China in the four centuries after its introduction, but its adherents repeatedly clashed with Taoists and Confucianists over issues of government influence and social values. As a result, Buddhism in China suffered three major persecutions between the fifth and the ninth centuries, when monasteries and temples were destroyed by the government and monks and nuns were forced back into lay life. There were several reasons for these persecutions. Buddhism was sometimes considered a dangerous foreign import, teaching antisocial thought and practice. Because monks and nuns had no children, they were thought to be neglecting a necessary religious role as parents, and their monastic life did not allow them to take care of their own aged parents—a fact that seemed unfilial. Furthermore, monks and nuns were not taxed and could not be employed in public work projects. And because so much metal (especially copper) was used for statues and religious implements, there was sometimes not enough to mint coins.

After the third great persecution, Buddhism never entirely recovered its strength in China. Most individual schools lost their popularity; however, two forms of Mahayana survived and flourished. The school of meditation (Chan, Ch'an) became popular among monks, and the Pure Land movement, focused on devotion to Amitabha Buddha, became important for laypeople. The beliefs and practices of many Mahayana schools that had begun in China were transmitted to Japan and continue to some extent there (as we will see in a later section). Ultimately, especially after later Mongol and Manchu control, Buddhism would become (along with Confucianism and Taoism) one of the Three Doctrines—a strand in a Chinese religious mixture of the three religions and folk belief.

Mahayana in Korea

Buddhism and its literature were carried into Korea from central Asia and China as early as 372 C.E.[17] Buddhism was adopted widely for its supposed powers to protect the three kingdoms then ruling the peninsula. Monasteries

Buddhist Festivals

The most important Buddhist festivals focus on the birth of the Buddha, his enlightenment, his death, the celebration of the New Year, and sometimes the commemoration of the dead. The exact dates for these celebrations and memorials differ from culture to culture.

In Theravada Buddhist countries, one great celebration (Vesak) recalls the birth, the enlightenment, and the death of the Buddha. It is celebrated at the time of the full moon in May.

In Mahayana Buddhism, the three festivals of the Buddha's life are separate. His birth is celebrated on the eighth day of the fourth month; his enlightenment is commemorated in winter on Bodhi Day, the eighth day of the twelfth month; and his death is recalled in early spring on the fifteenth day of the second month. (Chinese and Korean Buddhists follow the lunar calendar, while Japanese Buddhists use the Western calendar.)

Celebration of the New Year often includes a visit to a temple to end the old year and the sharing of a vegetarian meal to welcome the new year. (The Japanese keep the Western New Year, while the Chinese celebrate their lunar New Year in February.)

In Japan the dead are remembered in a mid-summer festival called O-Bon, derived from older Chinese practice. It has blended with Shinto elements and a belief in the Mahayana bodhisattva Jizo, who guides the dead back to the spirit world. If possible, the spirits' return is lighted with candles that drift down a stream or out into the ocean.

Festive lanterns are part of the Buddha's birthday celebration in Seoul.

In July and August, O-Bon is celebrated across the world at Buddhist temples that have origins in Japan. O-Bon dances welcome the temporary return of ancestors.

were thought of as powerhouses, sending monks' prayers to powerful Buddhas and bodhisattvas and receiving their celestial care in return. Korea was unified by the Silla kingdom, producing the Unified Silla dynasty (668–918 C.E.), and this unification led to a blending of religious elements from Taoism, Confucianism, shamanism, and Buddhism. Buddhism became the state religion and primary practitioner of official ritual.

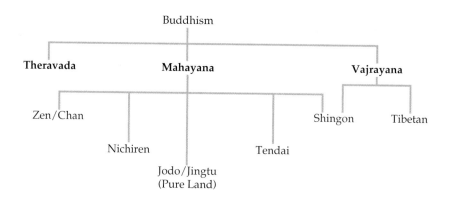

Buddhism in Korea reached its apogee during the Koryo dynasty (918–1392 C.E.). During this time, 80,000 wooden blocks were carved for the printing of all Korean and Chinese Buddhist texts of the Korean Tripitaka. After the first set of blocks was burned during a Mongol invasion, another set, which still exists, was finished in 1251. One of the greatest exponents of Korean Buddhism at this time was the monk Chinul (1158–1210). Given to a monastery as a young boy, he began meditation and textual study early. He had three great experiences of insight, all prompted by his reading of Mahayana materials. He founded the Chogye order, which combines textual study with regular meditation. It is still influential today.

Buddhism was supplanted by Confucianism as the state religion during the Yi dynasty (1392–1910). Nevertheless, although the aristocracy identified with Confucianism, the common people remained Buddhist. The Japanese takeover of Korea, beginning in 1910, was marked by efforts to force monks to marry. After the Japanese occupation ended in 1945, the Chogye order reverted to complete celibacy, and married monks entered the T'aego order.

Mahayana in Japan

Buddhism entered Japan in the sixth century C.E., where it began to grow after some initial resistance. It became so powerful in the early capital of Nara that in 794 the new capital city of Kyoto (then called Heian-kyo) was founded partly in order to be free from the influence of Buddhist clergy. The new capital was designed on a grid pattern, after Chinese models, and Japanese culture imported many elements of the Chinese culture of the time. Because the founding of the new capital coincided with a vibrant period of Mahayana Buddhism in China, Japanese Buddhism also imported Chinese Buddhist schools.

The history of Buddhism in Japan shows a movement toward increasing the power of laypeople. The first period, when the capital was at Nara, was dominated by essentially monastic Buddhist schools. In the second period, after the capital moved, the dominant schools (Shingon and Tendai; Figure 4.2) were ritualistic and appealed to the aristocracy. Their prominence lasted for about four hundred years. In the thirteenth century, however, two

Mahayana often absorbed pre-Buddhist gods. Here, at the entrance to a Japanese temple, we see a wooden sculpture of such a deity, intended to ward off evil spirits.

schools (Pure Land and Zen) particularly appealed to commoners and the military. Because Zen was adopted by many in the military, which controlled Japan until 1868, it became enormously influential in Japanese culture in general. (The separate schools are described in the following section.)

Some Major Schools of Mahayana

The many ideals of Mahayana Buddhism contain the seeds for a variety of schools of intellectual interpretation and practice. One such ideal—the notion that kindness is the supreme sign of enlightened awareness—has allowed many pre-Buddhist beliefs and practices to continue within Mahayana Buddhism: old gods receive new names, making them into heavenly Buddhas and bodhisattvas; old beliefs are absorbed; and old practices persist with new meanings. As we discussed earlier, Mahayana Buddhism (as well as other religions) also recognizes that people find themselves at different stages of spiritual evolution. Thus, whatever helps a person move to the next stage of awareness may be religiously acceptable. This is the notion of "skillful means": some people need images to look at and gods to pray to; other people need a community of devout friends; and a very few need only silence and emptiness. Finally, the multiplicity of Mahayana texts invites many philosophical and practical approaches, as one Buddhist group focuses on one text and another Buddhist group focuses on another. The sects of Mahayana Buddhism thus show a wide variety of attitudes toward the use of art and ritual, toward the acceptance of pleasure, and toward worldly success.

These interesting differences are exhibited in the major sects of Japan, described in the following pages. All of these sects (except one) came originally from China. They were carried to Korea and Japan, both by missionaries from China and by students from Korea and Japan who had traveled to China to study. A look at the sects that came from China to Japan suggests what the separate sects were once like in China. Over time, Buddhist sects in China and Korea that did not die out tended to borrow from each other and to blend. In Japan, however, the sects have remained fairly separate, and there they may be most easily experienced by interested travelers today. Because several of the following schools no longer exist in China, their Japanese names are given first.

Shingon   The name of this school is Shingon (Chinese: Zhen-yan, Chen-yen) and means "true word" or "word of truth." The title refers to the use of sacred chants, called mantras. We might recall that the spread of Mahayana Buddhism in China was due in part to the magical effects that were thought to come from Buddhist ritual. People believed that Buddhist ritual, if carefully performed, would provide security for rulers, children for married couples, and more favorable agricultural conditions for farmers.

Behind Shingon ritual is a focus on experiencing union with the cosmic Buddha nature. This can be accomplished through the chanting of mantras, accompanied by a multitude of rituals and ritual objects. Foremost among these rituals is a fire ceremony, the *goma,* a continuation of the Vedic fire ceremony. In this ceremony, the priest builds a fire within a square sacred space bounded by colored cords. The priest throws wood and leaves slowly into the fire, symbolically destroying all egotistic hindrances to mystical union.

Shingon uses two **mandalas,** which are geometrical designs, usually painted on cloth, that present reality in symbolic form. One mandala, the Kongo-kai ("diamond-world") mandala, shows the universe from the point of view of the wise person as a universe of oneness and perfection. It represents the universe seen as nirvana. The other mandala, the Tai-zo ("womb") mandala, shows the universe from the point of view of the compassionate person. It sees the universe as samsara, a place of suffering and growth that needs our help.

Shingon originated from the growth of a type of magically oriented Buddhism that developed in India. This esoteric tradition would be carried to China by the eighth century (and, in a slightly later form, to Tibet). It

An image of the bodhisattva Jizo is backed by a painting of the Shingon Kongo-kai mandala.

flourished in China for no more than two hundred years, but luckily it survived in Japan.

Shingon was brought to Japan from China by Kukai (774–835 C.E.), a Japanese monk who studied in China and returned to Japan with a knowledge of ritual and with books, mandalas, and altar implements. As Kukai became influential among the aristocrats of the new capital of Japan, he instituted a network of Shingon temples, which spread his sect across southern Honshu and the island of Shikoku. The monastic center that he founded is located at Mount Koya, near Osaka. After his death, he received the name Kobo Daishi ("the Great Master who spreads the Dharma"), and under that name he has become a venerated cultural hero in Japan. Shingon, because of its love of ritual, has inspired many arts, particularly sculpture and painting. It has similarities with Tibetan Buddhism, and it thus contains some elements of Vajrayana Buddhism (discussed later in this chapter).

Tendai The Tendai (Chinese: Tiantai, T'ien-t'ai) sect is named for the great Chinese monastic institution at Mount Tiantai ("heavenly terrace"), where the sect began in eastern China. A large complex of monasteries arose there.[18]

By the eighth century C.E., there were many varied Buddhist texts, some written up to a thousand years after the time of the Buddha. When they had been translated into Chinese, the result was great confusion. How could the Buddha have uttered so many sermons, some with apparently contradictory ideas? The solution was to organize the teachings according to levels of complexity. It was taught that the Buddha had revealed his most basic insights to everybody, but that he had revealed his most difficult thoughts only to those disciples who could understand them. The Tiantai (Tendai) sect attempted to categorize all the teachings and present them in a meaningful way, as a kind of ladder of steps leading to full enlightenment. Naturally, its own special teachings were at the top.

In Japan, this sect was favored by the emperor and his court for the expected benefits and protection it would bring to the country. The Japanese monk who went to China and returned with skills in Tendai Buddhism was Saicho (767–822 C.E.), who later received the honorary title Dengyo Daishi ("the Great Master who transmits the teachings"). Tendai's center, Enryaku-ji, is located on Mount Hiei, north of Kyoto. Although the earlier complex of more than 1,200 monastery buildings was burned in the late sixteenth century, what has been rebuilt is quite extensive. (It is a pleasant day trip by bus from Kyoto and should not be missed by travelers to that city.)

Saicho borrowed from many sources. In addition to his use of ritual, he and his followers accepted various devotional practices, such as regularly chanting the name of Amitabha (Amida), the Buddha of the Western Paradise. Another practice was to take walks that lasted many days, a tradition that grew out of the austerities of Japanese ascetics living in the mountains.

Jodo, or Pure Land The Pure Land (Chinese: Jingtu, Ching-t'-u) school created a devotional form of Buddhism that could be practiced by laypeople as well as monks. The cult of bodhisattvas already existed in India and central Asia, but it had great appeal in China too. Pure Land Buddhism in China can be traced back to the monk Tan Luan (T'an Luan, c. 476–542). Legend says that he instituted the devotion to Amitabha Buddha as the result of a vision. Complete devotion to this Buddha, the monk thought, would result in the believer's rebirth in Amitabha's Pure Land, the Western Paradise. Devotees regularly repeated a short phrase, derived from Mahayana scriptures and praising Amitabha Buddha. At first the repetition of the Buddha's name was a monastic practice, but it then spread to the laity. In Chinese, the phrase is *Namo Amito-fo;* in Japanese, it is *Namu Amida Butsu*. Both mean "Praise to Amitabha Buddha." Daily repetition and recitation at the moment of death were thought to ensure the believer's rebirth in the Western Paradise.

In China, devotion to Amito-fo, the Buddha of the Western Paradise, became an important feature of all Buddhist practice, which it still is today. (A common everyday greeting for centuries was *Omito-fo*, based on the Pure Land mantra.) Belief in a paradise might also have counteracted the fear of purgatorial "hells," which had also become a common belief in Chinese Buddhism. We might reflect, finally, that Pure Land Buddhism was highly democratic. Because it did not demand meditation, ceremony, scripture study, or even literacy, it offered a form of Buddhism open to everyone.

In Japan, the Pure Land movement was spread by the monk Honen (1133–1212), who was originally a Tendai monk at Mount Hiei. His movement became a separate sect called Jodo Shu ("Pure Land sect"). Shinran (1173–1262), a disciple of Honen, continued the laicization of the *nembutsu,* as the chant is called in Japanese. He taught that human actions to attain salvation were unimportant in comparison to the saving power of the Buddha. Convinced that monastic practice was unnecessary, Shinran married. (He has often been compared with Martin Luther, who also married and emphasized simple trust as the way to salvation.) The movement that Shinran began eventually grew into the Jodo Shin Shu ("True Pure Land Sect"). Pure Land sects have been extremely popular in China and Japan, and this popularity has made them the largest form of Mahayana Buddhism.

It was once common to think of the Pure Land as a real location somewhere beyond the earth. Today, however, it is often considered a metaphor for a compassionate and joyful way of living in the everyday world.

Pure Land Buddhism has inspired—and continues to inspire—the arts. In sculpture and painting, Amida (Amitabha) is often shown at the center of a triad. At his left is Kannon (the bodhisattva Avalokiteshvara), and at his right is Seishi (the bodhisattva Mahasthama-prapa). Amida is also seen alone, surrounded by beams of light, descending from the sky to offer help and receive the departed. The same images, sometimes drawn in gold on indigo paper, often appear in manuscripts of the Lotus Sutra.

Nichiren Unlike the other sects discussed thus far, Nichiren Buddhism began in Japan. Its founder was a Tendai monk, Nichiren (1222–1282). After being trained at Mount Hiei, Nichiren sought a simpler path than Tendai, which used many sutras and practices in the search for enlightenment. Out of the thousands of Mahayana texts, Nichiren wanted to find one that contained all the essential teachings of Buddhism. Following the lead of the Tendai tradition, which had already given much attention to the Lotus Sutra, Nichiren asserted that the Lotus Sutra was indeed the embodiment of all essential religious teaching. He thought of himself as a reincarnation of a minor Buddha in the Lotus Sutra (his monastic name Nichiren means "sun lotus"). His sect uses a chant that honors this sutra: *Namu Myoho Renge Kyo,* meaning "Praise to the mystic law of the Lotus Sutra." Devout followers repeat the mantra many times a day, especially in the morning and evening. They believe that doing so will connect them with the divine power of the universe.

Nichiren Buddhism has produced several branches. Among the most important are Nichiren Shu ("Nichiren sect"), Nichiren Sho-Shu ("True Nichiren sect"), and Soka Gakkai ("Value Creation Educational Society"). The Nichiren sect treats its founder as a bodhisattva, or Buddhist saint. The Nichiren Sho-Shu elevates Nichiren to the role of a reincarnation of the Buddha, "the Buddha of the present age." The Soka Gakkai branch was formerly a lay arm of Nichiren Sho-Shu. However, an angry split occurred in 1991–92, and Soka Gakkai became fully independent. There is in all of these branches an acceptance of the material world and an attempt to improve it. Soka Gakkai particularly works to reform society through political means, seeking peace through intercultural understanding.

Nichiren Buddhism was little known outside Japan until after World War II. It has now established itself all around the world. The goal-oriented chanting of some Nichiren groups has been very attractive to some westerners, and several celebrities (such as Tina Turner) practice a form of this faith.

As teachers, monks pass on the traditions they received from their own teachers, including knowledge of the arts. Here a Vietnamese monk teaches calligraphy.

ZEN BUDDHISM: ENLIGHTENMENT THROUGH EXPERIENCE

Zen Buddhism, a school of Mahayana Buddhism, began in China and was carried to Japan, like most of the schools just mentioned. Its influence is so significant that it needs to be discussed apart from the other schools of Mahayana Buddhism. Zen takes its name from the seventh step of the Noble Eightfold Path—*dhyana* ("meditation"). In Chinese the word is *chan (ch' an),* and in Japanese it is *zen.* (In the discussion here, Chan refers to the sect in China, and Zen refers to the sect as it developed in Japan.) The complexity that had overtaken Chinese Buddhism helped create a counterbalancing movement toward simplification. For the Chan sect in China, simplification came from looking directly to the enlightenment experience of Siddhartha Gautama. Siddhartha had become the Buddha, the Enlightened One, through his practice of meditation. Although he did not deny the value of ritual, the Buddha did not think that it led to enlightenment. Taking after the Buddha, the members of the Chan movement, in their desire for enlightenment, favored the technique of seated meditation, just as Siddhartha Gautama had.

Chan Buddhism traces itself back to a Buddhist monk named Bodhidharma, who is said to have come to China (about 500 C.E.) from India or central Asia and in China began his Meditation school. Bodhidharma is often shown sitting in meditation, with Western facial features, swarthy skin, a light beard, and an earring. In paintings, he faces a wall to indicate his strong desire to block out anything that would distract him from his meditation. It has been said that he meditated for so long that his legs became withered. He is the embodiment of patience and persistence.

The native Chinese religious and philosophical movement called Taoism (see chapter 6) undoubtedly paved the way for Chan Buddhism and influenced it. Taoism had similar ideals: silence, detachment, acceptance, distrust of symbolization, and union with the universe. Taoism also practiced meditation. Taoism may have added to Buddhism its own esteem for the natural world and its appreciation for humor, although exactly how Taoism influenced Chan is debated. There are also Confucian elements in Chan and Zen, such as the communal nature of monastery life and the transmission of realization from master to disciple.

In the long history of Buddhism, some teachers have emphasized the importance of regular meditation and the effectiveness of meditative techniques, saying that they produce enlightenment gradually but inevitably, like the coming of dawn. Others have stressed that enlightenment can occur as a sudden awakening to one's true nature, like a flash of lightning, anywhere and at any time. One Chinese school, the "northern school," is thought to have taught a gradual method of attaining enlightenment, while the "southern school" advocated methods aiming at a sudden experience of enlightenment. In China, the northern school eventually died out, and Chan and Zen later assumed the possibility of sudden enlightenment. Both of the two main Zen schools of Japan today—Rinzai and Soto—descend from the southern school of Chan Buddhism. The Soto school values meditation, which it calls "just sitting." Consequently it is considered to be a bit more relaxed than the stricter Rinzai school, which focuses on the ideal of sudden enlightenment and makes use of additional techniques (discussed in the following section).

The enlightenment experience (called **satori**, or *kensho*) brings an awareness of the unity of oneself with the rest of the universe. The enlightened person knows that human distinctions and separations—mine, yours; this, that; one, many—are distinctions that societies and individuals' minds create and then project onto other people and things. Such distinctions are not ultimate, though, for all human beings consist of the same basic energy of the universe, appearing in many varied shapes. This experience of ultimate unity brings new insights and emotions to the art of living: less anxiety over attaining goals, less concern about death, and an appreciation for the preciousness of everyday life.

Zen Techniques for Enlightenment

The most fundamental Zen technique for reaching enlightenment is regular "sitting meditation," called *zazen.* In Zen monasteries, zazen is normally done for several hours in the morning and evening. It involves sitting in silence with one's back straight and centered, keeping the body still, and taking deep and regular breaths. These are just simple techniques for quieting the mind and focusing on the moment. The mind becomes more peaceful, and ideally, with long practice, a state of simple awareness takes over as one's "true nature" is revealed.[19]

A question, called a **koan,** is another technique for attaining awareness. Its origin is uncertain, but the name derives from the Chinese *gong-an* (*kung-an*), translated as "public discussion." The koan is not a question that can be easily answered using logic. It demands pondering. Consider, for example, the question, Why did the monk Bodhidharma come from the West? An appropriate answer could be, "the bush in the garden"—or any response that mentions an ordinary object. The meaning of this apparently odd answer is that Bodhidharma's whole purpose was to make people wake up to the wondrous nature of even simple objects in everyday life. Sometimes a good answer to a koan need not be a verbal response but rather an appropriate action, such as lifting up a hand, taking off a shoe, holding up a flower, or even raising an eyebrow.[20]

Manual labor is also essential to Zen training. In a Zen monastery, work in the garden and kitchen and the repair and cleaning of the monastery are techniques to combat the inadequacy of words to describe reality. Zen, influenced here by Taoism, maintains that words are often barriers that keep us from immediate contact with the true nature of things. Silent meditation blended with direct experience of the physical world can take us beyond words and thoughts to experience reality itself.

Buddhism and the Arts of Japan

Many people assume that Buddhism has had a role in shaping the arts of Japan. As a matter of fact, what we think of as "Japanese style" is a mixture of Shinto (chapter 7), Buddhist influences (especially Zen), and traditional Japanese attitudes toward nature. Although Zen has indeed influenced Japanese arts, the extent of its influence will always be debated. After all, the various arts were developed not only by monks but more often by craftsmen and talented amateurs under the influence of Buddhism. And over the past three hundred years, these arts have taken on a life of their own, carried on by laypeople and in several branches of Mahayana Buddhism.

Haiku A *haiku* is an extremely short poem. In Japan, longer Chinese poetic forms were telescoped and refined. The model haiku in Japanese is a seventeen-syllable poem written in three lines (the first in five syllables, the second in seven, and the third, again, in five). The ideal traditional haiku should mention or suggest the season, and, like a good photograph, it should capture the essence of a moment before it passes.

Manual labor, here practiced in a Korean temple, is a Zen technique for emptying the mind. ◄

Matsuo Basho (1644–1694) is considered the greatest of Japan's haiku writers. The following poem is widely quoted and considered to be his masterpiece:

Old pond:
A frog jumps in.
Sound of water.

Why, we may wonder, is this poem held in such esteem? On first reading, it seems simple, insignificant. But on closer inspection, it reveals intriguing balance and contrast. There are many possible interpretations. The old pond suggests timelessness, but the splash is momentary, representing every daily event when seen against the backdrop of eternity. Or the frog could represent a human being; the pond, the mind; and the splash, the sudden breakthrough to enlightenment. Perhaps the frog signifies the Buddhist monk in meditation, while the pond suggests all of Buddhist teaching. Or maybe the frog symbolizes the poet himself and the splash is the poet's insight. Thus, the imagery can be taken both literally and in several equally valid symbolic ways.

Tea Ceremony   The making, drinking, and offering of tea to guests has developed into a fine art in Japan, called *chado* (or *sado*, "the way of tea"). Bringing guests together for a ritual tea ceremony in Japanese is called *cha no yu* ("hot water for tea"). The drinking of tea had first been used in Chinese monasteries for medicinal purposes and as an aid for staying awake during meditation. There, tea drinking also developed some ritual elements. Tea drinking was then carried to Japan and was practiced assiduously by both Zen monks and lay disciples. Under the tea master Sen no Rikyu (1522–1591), the tea ceremony took on its current highly stylized form.[21]

The essence of the Japanese tea ceremony is the gathering of a few guests, the preparation of green tea, and the offering of tea and sweets. The tea ceremony normally takes place in a tea pavilion, whose design is inspired by a rustic country hut, often mentioned in Chinese poetry.

Guests approach the tea pavilion along a garden path of stones, where they wash their hands at a stone basin with a bamboo ladle. They enter the room and kneel before the *tokonoma,* an alcove at the front of the room adorned with a hanging scroll and a flower arrangement. After pausing to appreciate the scroll and flower arrangement, the guests proceed to cushions on one side of the room. At the other side of the room, the host kneels in front of a lighted charcoal brazier and ritually cleanses the tea bowl and serving implements. A plate of sweet cakes is then offered, to balance the taste of the green tea. Next, the host stirs boiling water into the powdered green tea and offers some to each guest. Conversation is usually limited to appreciative remarks and questions about the scroll, the tea, the tea bowl, and other objects in the room. The purpose of the ceremony is to create and enjoy together an atmosphere of harmony and beauty, where each object, action, and word contributes to the tranquil experience.

Ceramics   Bowls used in the tea ceremony look deliberately natural, almost as if they were dug up out of the ground. They often look rough and unfinished, with earth-colored glazes dripping down their sides. The rims

The head of the Urasenke School of Tea prepares tea for the Japanese political leader Junichiro Koizumi.

sometimes are not quite even, and colors are not always uniform. Sometimes there are even bubbles and cracks in the ceramic. All this is deliberate. The accidents of firing the bowls in the kiln are appreciated, as are the subtle shades of earth tones that are produced. The aim is, paradoxically, to create pieces that exhibit deliberate naturalness and a calculated spontaneity.

Ikebana The word for Japanese-style flower arrangement—*ikebana*—means "living flower." Each arrangement is designed to suggest flowers in their natural state, as if a piece of garden were brought inside a home—even if the suggestion of "natural state" is artfully accomplished with clippers and wire!

Flower arrangement can be traced back to the offerings of flowers placed on altars in the temples of China and Japan. But ikebana grew into a unique art form of its own, and examples of ikebana now are found in restaurants, offices, and homes.

Ikebana is quite different from Western flower arrangement, which tends to be dense, symmetrical, and colorful. Ikebana is the opposite. The arrangements are airy, asymmetrical, and generally of no more than two colors. Effective ikebana is temporary art, lasting but a few days and changing every day. Thus, some see ikebana as a manifestation of Buddhist insight into impermanence. Ikebana is Buddhist sculpture.

Garden Design In China and Japan, gardens have long been an essential part of architecture, planned along with the buildings they complement. Garden designers are ranked as highly as poets and artists. Some gardens are created for strolling, others for seated contemplation from under an eave. They are not essentially Buddhist, of course, and not all monasteries have a garden. But they are found frequently enough in Buddhist environs for us to say that gardens have been used to present Buddhist ideals.

The monastery garden of Ryoan-ji expresses the peaceful simplicity that is the hallmark of Zen.

A famous example is the rock garden at Ryoan-ji, in northwest Kyoto. Ryoan-ji garden, enclosed on two sides by a low earthen wall, consists of five clusters of large boulders set in raked white gravel. The rocks and gravel suggest mountain peaks rising through clouds or islands in a river. The fascination of the garden is the relation between the clusters of boulders. Viewed this way, the boulders seem more like ideas in a great mind. The only vegetation in the garden is the moss at the base of the stones and the trees beyond the wall. Really more like an x-ray of an ideal garden, Ryoan-ji would seem to be unchanging because of its stony nature; but it changes a great deal, depending on the season, the weather, the light, and the time of day.

Calligraphy and Painting Calligraphy (Greek: "beautiful writing") is a highly prized art form in China and Japan. Because the characters used in Japanese and Chinese writing are closer to pictures and to drawing than they are to alphabet letters, they have a great range of vitality and beauty. The Zen ideal is to produce what is spontaneous but also profound, and because writing is done with an inkbrush, great expressiveness in darkness, weight, movement, and style of characters is possible. Furthermore, the ink cannot be erased, and the result is thought to be the immediate expression of the writer's personality and level of awareness. When fine calligraphic talent is employed to write a striking phrase or poem, the result is doubly powerful.

Painting is closely related to calligraphy, because both are done with the same type of brush. Frequently, calligraphy and pictures are combined in the same work, so that one reinforces the other. Zen-style painting is done quickly, often taking nature as its subject and ordinarily using black, white, and intermediate shades of gray. Some Zen-inspired painting is almost cartoonlike, as exhibited in satirical drawings of Zen personages and quick sketches of everyday objects, such as brooms and buckets.

The epitome of Zen simplicity in art is the *enso,* a black circle, almost always done in a single, quick stroke on paper or a piece of wood. The empty circle represents the emptiness of all reality.

Zen does not have the kind of popularity that Pure Land Buddhism enjoys. However, because Zen was taken up by the military class, which ruled Japan for almost seven hundred years, it has had extensive influence on Japanese culture. Among the Zen-inspired elements that became a part of the culture are the ideal of simple elegance, the use of natural wood in interior design, and the nearly empty Zen-style rock garden. Over the past one hundred years, Zen has had global impact as well—in architecture, art, interior design, and fashion. It is apparent, for example, in the domestic architecture of Frank Lloyd Wright and his followers, which popularized the use of large windows and natural stone. It seems even to have influenced retail chains such as The Gap and Banana Republic, where we see natural wood floors, uncluttered space, and clothing in muted earth tones.

VAJRAYANA BUDDHISM: THE "DIAMOND VEHICLE"

Mahayana Buddhism in India developed practices and beliefs that have sometimes been called esoteric (hidden, not openly taught), such as the use of special chants and rituals to gain supranormal powers. When some of these traditions entered Tibet, Indian Mahayana Buddhism joined with Tibetan shamanism to create Tibetan Buddhism, a complex system of belief, art, and ritual. Although Vajrayana actually includes other forms of esoteric Buddhism, Tibetan Buddhism is its most prominent expression.

The name *Vajrayana* means the "vehicle of the diamond" or "vehicle of the lightning bolt." The name suggests strength, clarity, wisdom, and flashes of light, all of which are associated with the enlightened awareness that this vehicle seeks to transmit. Vajrayana is considered by some to be simply a special form of Mahayana. But most consider Vajrayana to be a third branch of Buddhism, because of its complexity and unique elements.

Origins, Practice, and Literature of Tibetan Buddhism

The pre-Buddhist Tibetan religion worshiped the powers of nature. As was the case with many native religions, these powers were often envisioned as

The most prominent missionary of Vajrayana was Padmasambhava, known in some areas as Guru Rimpoche ("precious jewel"). Here, the abbot of Kurjey Lhakhang in central Bhutan dresses as Guru Rimpoche and processes among the faithful as part of the celebration of the Guru's birthday.

demons that had to be appeased. Shamanistic rituals involving animal sacrifice and the use of bones, dance, and magical incantations were intended to control the demonic powers.

This Tibetan religion was challenged by a new religion, a special type of Buddhism practiced in northeast India, named Tantric Buddhism for its scriptures, the Tantras ("spread out"). Tantric Buddhism opposed the original Buddhist detachment from the world and its negative attitude toward bodily pleasure. The Tantras taught that the body and all its energies could be used to reach enlightenment. For Tantric Buddhism, enlightenment is an experience of ultimate oneness that occurs when a practitioner unites all opposites. Sexual union is a powerful experience of unity, and Tantric Buddhism uses the imagery and (rarely) the practice of sexual union to help attain enlightenment. In its imagery and belief system, Tantric Buddhism shows influence from Hinduism—particularly its tendency to pair a male and a female deity and its love of multiple deities. Vajrayana believes the divine Buddha nature expresses itself in a multitude of male and female deities.

A form of Tantric Buddhism first entered Tibet in the seventh century and was spread by Indian missionaries. Tradition holds that a king named Song-tsen-gam-po (active c. 630) became its patron and made it the national religion. In the beginning, native priests fought against this new religion, but

Long trumpets, bells, and drums often accompany chanting in Vajrayana ceremonies.

a legendary Buddhist monk named Padmasambhava, who came from India in the late eighth century, reconciled the two religions and turned the native demonic gods of Tibet into guardian deities of Buddhism.

The resulting religion blended shamanistic interests, the sexual imagery of Tantric Buddhism, and traditional Buddhist elements such as the chanting of sutras, meditation, the ideal of nonviolence, and the search for enlightenment. Monks thus were called upon not only as teachers but also as doctors and shamans; they were expected to bring health, control weather, and magically protect worshipers from death. A Tibetan spiritual teacher is often called **lama** (a Tibetan translation of the word *guru*), and this title is thus frequently used as a title of honor for all monks.

Although the Indian ideals of the wandering holy man and cave-dwelling solitary did not die out in Tibetan Buddhism, they were not well suited for a climate as severe as that of the cold and barren Tibetan plateau. More compatible, it seemed, were the large monastic complexes that had grown up in late Indian Buddhism. The Tibetan version of such a complex often looked like a fortified hilltop castle and was in effect a complete city for sometimes thousands of monks, containing libraries, prayer halls, kitchens, storage areas, and large courtyards used for public performances. A written form of the Tibetan language was created for the translation of Buddhist scriptures from India. It also made possible the writing of scriptural commentaries and other treatises.

Over time, the practice of celibacy declined, and the heads of Tibetan monasteries frequently passed on their control to their sons. The consumption of meat and alcohol became common as well. A reform movement, however, emerged under the monk Tsong Kha-pa (1357–1419), demanding that monks be unmarried and that strict monastic practice be reinstituted. His sect, as a result, came to be known as Gelug-pa, meaning "party of virtue." (It is also commonly called the Yellow Hat sect because of the tall, crested yellow hats that the monks wear during religious services.) This sect grew powerful. It helped create many of the greatest monasteries, full of art and complete sets of Buddhist scriptures, and it provided Tibet with its political leadership for several centuries. The executive head of the Gelug-pa is called the Dalai Lama ("ocean superior one").

It became a common belief in Tibetan Buddhism that certain major lamas are reincarnations of earlier lamas, who in turn are considered emanations of Buddhas and bodhisattvas. (A belief in reincarnation thus solved the problem of transmission of leadership, which in a celibate monastic order cannot pass to a son.) The lineage of the Dalai Lama, for example, traces itself back to a nephew of Tsong Kha-pa, the first of the line of succession. Each Dalai Lama is considered to be an emanation of Avalokiteshvara, the heavenly bodhisattva of compassion. When a major lama dies, his reincarnation is sought, found, and trained. The current Dalai Lama, for example, was found in eastern Tibet. A delegation of monks, after consulting a state oracle about the place of rebirth, took objects (such as prayer beads) that had been used by the previous Dalai Lama and mixed them with similar objects. The boy who was recognized as the current Dalai Lama selected only those objects used by the previous Dalai Lama, helping to prove his identity. (The movies *Kundun*, *Seven Years in Tibet*, and *Little Buddha* give vivid pictures of the selection of the Dalai Lama and other Vajrayana practices.)

The literature of Tibetan Buddhism consists of two large collections of writings. The Kanjur is the core, made up of works from the Tripitaka (mostly Mahayana sutras and the vinaya, with Tantric texts). The second part, the Tenjur, comprises commentaries on scripture and treatises on a wide variety of disciplines, such as medicine, logic, and grammar. The collection exceeds four thousand works.

Ritual and the Arts

Vajrayana Buddhism is interested in the acquisition of both internal and external powers and holds that such powers may be attained through proper ritual. The ritual allows the individual to become identified with a particular Buddha or heavenly bodhisattva, thus giving the individual the power and protection of that heavenly being.

Because correctly performed ceremony brings identification with a powerful deity, ceremonial objects play significant roles. We noted earlier that some devices, such as the mantra and mandala, were used in Mahayana practice. These devices were subsequently adopted by Vajrayana. But in Vajrayana these objects and techniques take on special importance. Among the significant ritual objects is the **vajra,** a metal object somewhat like a divining rod or scepter that represents a stylized bolt of lightning. The vajra is associated with diamond-hardness, power, and insight. It is held in the

A huge thondrol (Buddhist tapestry), here portraying Guru Rimpoche in his many manifestations, is unfurled for a few hours once a year at Bhutan temple ceremonies. Viewing the thondrol is said to liberate one from the cycle of rebirths.

right hand and suggests kind action. A bell is held in the left hand and symbolizes wisdom. When used together, one in each hand, they represent the union of wisdom and compassion. The vajra and bell are essential to Tibetan Vajrayana ritual in a way that other religious objects (mentioned in the following paragraphs) are not.

Another important Tibetan Buddhist object is the prayer wheel, which comes in all sizes—from very tiny to as tall as a two-story building. A prayer wheel is a cylinder that revolves around a central pole. Inside the cylinder are pieces of paper inscribed with sacred phrases. It is believed that the turning of the written prayers creates as much good karma as if one were to recite them. Believers often carry small prayer wheels and turn them as they walk, while the devout push or pull large prayer wheels at temples and in public places. Some prayer wheels are placed in streams, where the flowing water turns them. The same principle applies to the wind blowing through prayer flags, which consist of square or triangular pieces of cloth containing inscriptions.

Certain ritual objects evoke awe at first because of their connection with death. They are meant to inoculate the believer against the fear of dying by forcing the individual to accept death long before it comes. For example, human thighbones are used to make small trumpets, and half of a human skull, decorated with gold or silver, might be used as a ceremonial bowl. Paintings and statues of fierce deities often have a similar function.

Prayer wheels, cylinders that contain written prayers and chants, appear in many locations and are turned by passersby as an act of devotion.

Music and dance, used by shamans to protect against demons, also play an important role in Tibetan Vajrayana. Drums, long trumpets, bells, and cymbals are used to accompany a deep, slow droning chant. The effect is hypnotic and evokes the sacredness that underlies reality.

In Vajrayana as well as Mahayana, a mantra is chanted or written to bring power and wisdom through repetition. The most highly revered mantra in Tibetan Vajrayana is *Om mani padme hum!* (literally translated, "Om—the jewel—oh lotus—-ah!"). One translation employs Tantric sexual symbolism: "The jewel is in the lotus." The jewel and lotus represent sexual opposites, and the mantra represents sexual union—symbolic of enlightenment. In yet another symbolic translation—"The jewel *is* the lotus"—the jewel represents the divine Buddha nature, and the lotus represents the everyday world of birth and death. Hence, the mantra means that this world of suffering is the same as the Buddha nature and that the enlightened person sees that they are the same. Both symbolic translations and their messages are valid. (The ordinary user of the mantra, however, may well be unaware of these meanings and may think of it only as a powerful prayer.) In addition to this mantra, there are many others, each of which is believed to be sacred to a particular Buddha or bodhisattva or which is valuable for obtaining a certain result.

Symbolic hand gestures (**mudras**) on statues of the Buddha are common throughout all forms of Buddhism. For example, the right hand extended with the palm outward and the fingers pointing up is a mudra of blessing; if the palm is open but the hand is turned downward, the mudra symbolizes generosity. In Vajrayana, a large number of mudras have evolved to convey more esoteric meanings, such as the unity of opposites. Mudras also help distinguish individual Buddhas and bodhisattvas within the large pantheon of deities. Moreover, mudras can be performed to a chant, with the two hands simultaneously forming mudra after mudra to create a harmonious balance of opposites.

The mandala (geometrical art form) that is used in some forms of Mahayana takes on great variety and complexity in Tibetan Buddhism. We might recall that a mandala is a sacred cosmic diagram, often used in meditation. It may represent in symbolic form the entire universe, the palace of a deity, or even the self. A common form is a circle within or enclosing a square, or a series of circles and squares that grow smaller and smaller as they come closer to the center of the design; another form looks like a checkerboard of many squares. A mandala usually appears as a painting on cloth, but it may take many forms. For some ceremonies, monks create a mandala in sand and then destroy it at the end of the ritual, expressing vividly the Buddhist teaching that everything must change.

Any painting on cloth is called a *thangka* (pronounced *tan'-ka*). In addition to mandala designs, a wide variety of subjects can appear on thangkas. Common images are Buddhas, bodhisattvas, and guardian deities, painted in both benevolent and terrifying forms (the terrifying forms both frighten away demons and chasten the believer). The female deity Tara, who represents mercy, appears in two major forms (white and green) and in several minor forms. We also find frequent representations of the monk Padmasambhava and other noted teachers. The existence of so many celestial beings and saints—with their attendants and symbolic objects—provides artists with a multitude of subjects to paint and sculpt.

PERSONAL EXPERIENCE: VISITING THE DALAI LAMA

For many in the West, a visit to the Dalai Lama means a visit with the most renowned teacher of Buddhism alive. As the religious leader of Tibetan Buddhism, the current Dalai Lama is fourteenth in the line. Until 1959, when he fled to escape advancing Chinese Communist soldiers, he was also the political leader of Tibet. With the permission of the Indian government, he and his advisors settled in Dharamsala, a hill town in northern India, where he continues to live today. He received the Nobel Peace Prize in 1989 for his promulgation of nonviolence and peace.

Through the kindness of a friend, I got a letter of introduction so that I could visit the Dalai Lama at his home. It was late spring when a colleague and I traveled on a packed and noisy bus into the foothills of the still-snowy Himalayas to Dharamsala. Dharamsala is actually two towns, Upper and Lower, and was once an English hill station where British colonials relaxed in

The Dalai Lama, the head of Tibetan Buddhism and Nobel Peace Prize Laureate, speaks frequently both to followers and to the world community.

the hot summer months. Now the English are mostly gone. Lower Dharamsala is inhabited by Indians, and Upper Dharamsala is primarily Tibetan.

After arriving, I called the monk-secretary of the Dalai Lama to confirm my appointment and then went out for a walk around Upper Dharamsala. In the center of the town, a group of large prayer wheels drew a small crowd of men and women in bright Tibetan clothing who moved from one wheel to the next. I stopped in a small store, where I bought a white scarf to present to the Dalai Lama the next day. This is a traditional offering in high-altitude Tibet, where flowers are not easily obtainable. When I was making my purchase, I asked the shop owner if he were a Buddhist, like so many others in town. "Oh, no," he laughed. "I'm a Parsee, but I'm happy to sell to anyone!" I had not expected to meet a Zoroastrian in that Tibetan Buddhist enclave, and I reflected on how many religions coexist in India, where religion is taken quite seriously.

The Dalai Lama lives in a modest villa near a large, modern Tibetan temple. At 2:00 P.M. we were ushered into a reception room. After five minutes, the Dalai Lama and his secretary entered. Both wore dark Tibetan monks' robes.

The Dalai Lama seemed a mixture of opposites. His handshake was firm but his manner gentle. His voice was deep, but his frequent laugh was high and bell-like. He seemed reserved behind his lively eyes. His accented English was good, but he would often speak to his secretary in Tibetan, checking on the proper translation of a word into English.

Our conversation was almost entirely about religion. We spent nearly an hour discussing the role of religion in the modern world. "Why does religion exist?" I asked. He said that religion was only a means to an end, which is human goodness.

"Is there any difference between a good person and a holy person?" I asked. "There is no such difference," he declared.

He said that it is quite possible to become trapped by the forms of religion, which should really lead beyond themselves to kindness and insight. "It is necessary to go further, beyond individual religions, and not be limited by the forms themselves. It may also be necessary to find new forms for religion," he said.

I began to ask him which of his teachers had been most influential. "I have been influenced by great pundits [sages]," he said. I nodded, thinking he was referring to special teachers he had encountered in his youth as a student. "The great pundits of the last few centuries," he added. I nodded again, now thinking he meant the great teachers discussed in books that he had read. But when he explained further, it was clear to me that these pundits who had personally influenced him were the teachers who had taught the previous Dalai Lamas, his earlier incarnations. I continued to nod but suddenly was aware that we had two very different ways of looking at existence.

We talked about the symbolism of colors and their use in Tibetan Buddhism. He pointed to my shirt, which was turquoise. "That is my favorite color," he exclaimed with a laugh.

At the end of the interview, we went out into the garden. I left with the scarf I had brought—returned to me by the Dalai Lama as a memento of the visit. I also left with the feeling that I had met someone who showed me clearly that a good man is a holy man, too.

BUDDHISM, THE WEST, AND MODERN CHALLENGES

People in the West have been attracted to Buddhism for a long time. They appreciate its basically rational approach to understanding reality, which fits in well with a scientific orientation. Some appreciate what they see as its emphasis on awareness, self-reliance, and psychological development (even if, as critics argue, "using" Buddhism this way turns it into just another form of ego gratification). Many in the West are also attracted to the Buddhist ideal of nonviolence as a standard for civilized behavior in a multicultural

Buddhist Meditation

Because meditation is a core practice of Buddhism, many kinds of meditation have developed. Some of them have made their way to the West, where they have occasionally been modified.

In the Theravada tradition, one approach to meditation is especially significant. It is called Vipassana (insight), because it emphasizes being fully attentive to the present moment. This attentiveness, sometimes called mindfulness, is primarily accomplished by sitting quietly and paying attention to one's exhalation and inhalation. The same type of meditation may also be done while walking. The meditator walks extremely slowly on flat ground, being aware at each moment of the motion of the right, then left, foot. (In Sri Lanka and elsewhere, some monasteries have special walking tracks for this type of meditation.)

Seated meditation, particularly cultivated by Chan and Zen, is the most significant form of Mahayana meditation. Like Vipassana, it begins with a focus on breathing. It may then include reflections on a question given by a master or on the meaning of a line of poetry. It may also make use of silent repetition of a single meaningful word or phrase.

The Vajrayana tradition, with its love of art and ritual, has developed many complex meditations. Vajrayana meditation tends to make use of ritual objects (bells, candles, butter lamps), images, mandalas, Sanskrit words (mantras), hand gestures (mudras), and visualization exercises. Frequently the meditation involves reconstructing in one's imagination the image of a favorite deity. The meditator then takes on the identity of that deity for the duration of the meditation. Other meditations involve contemplating the moon, clouds, or water.

Some meditations make use of imaginative techniques; the meditator mentally creates a lotus, a moon disc, a written Sanskrit syllable, an altar of deities, colors, or rays of light, often imagining these in a certain order.

All three traditions also have some form of what can be called a meditation of compassion. The meditator reflects on the many different kinds of sentient beings—human, animal, and insect. The next step of the meditation is to recognize that all of these beings are struggling to survive, that all are trying to avoid pain, and that many are suffering. The meditation ends when the meditator projects outward the wish that all sentient beings may be well and happy. This wish is sometimes accompanied by a mental image of light and warmth radiating outward.

Beginners who are interested in Buddhist meditation can try simple seated meditation. A quiet spot is best, and the meditator should sit on a cushion or sofa, with legs drawn up. (If that is not possible, then one may sit on a chair, with the feet flat on the ground.) Some people like to face outside, looking into a garden. The back should be straight, the position comfortable, and the breathing deep, slow, and regular. Eyes may be either open or closed. The meditator should remain as still as possible. Focus should be on breaths in and out. Thoughts need not be banished, but should simply be "watched," like seeing clouds passing. One can start by meditating a short amount of time—even as little as five minutes per day. Soon it will be possible to meditate for longer periods once or twice a day. Many report that the exercise leaves them with a greater sense of inner peace and often even oneness with their surroundings.

world—an attraction that was magnified by the Dalai Lama's selection for the Nobel Peace Prize in 1989.

Buddhism's first contact with the West occurred in the late eighteenth century, when translations of primarily Theravada material were brought back to Europe from Sri Lanka and Myanmar by English colonials and missionaries.

The opening of Japan to foreigners in the second half of the nineteenth century created a second wave of interest in Buddhism. French, English, and American people began to read about Japanese culture and to see photographs of early Buddhist temples and examples of Buddhist-inspired art. Foreign interest dovetailed with anti-Buddhist government actions in Japan after 1868, which forced many Buddhist temples to sell some of their art. Japanese art was then collected widely in Europe and America, both by private collectors and by museums.

Just as many see Buddhism's influence on Japanese art, so Buddhism has influenced Western art via Japan. There is no doubt that the Japanese influence on Western art has been extraordinary since Japan opened to the West. French art of the late nineteenth century was invigorated by the discovery of Japanese prints and scrolls, which flooded into France after 1880. Asymmetry, a love of nature, and an appreciation for the passing moment—features of much Japanese art—began to appear in the work of the Impressionists and Postimpressionists, particularly Vincent van Gogh (1853–1890), Henri de Toulouse-Lautrec (1864–1901), and Claude Monet (1840–1926). (One of van Gogh's self-portraits was almost certainly influenced by pictures of Buddhist monks that he had seen.) Monet's Japanese-style water garden, with its pond of water lilies at Giverny, near Paris, is a good example of the influence Japan had at the turn of the century in France.

Haiku and other forms of Japanese poetry began to influence Western poetry at the same time. We see this particularly in the Imagist school, which produced short poems that depended on a few strong images presented in simple language. Poets who exemplified this style include Ezra Pound (1885–1972), e. e. cummings (1894–1962), H. D. (Hilda Doolittle, 1886–1961), and William Carlos Williams (1883–1963).

A third wave of Buddhist influence came in the decades just after World War II, when U.S. soldiers returned from the American occupation of Japan. The great interest of the time was Zen (perhaps only loosely understood), which influenced the poetry of the Beat movement and the lifestyle of the counterculture. The novels of Jack Kerouac (1922–1969) show a Zenlike love of the spontaneous. His book *On the Road,* about a cross-country trip with friends, inspired readers to make similar explorations. Zen love of the moment is also evident in the jazz–like poetry of Allen Ginsberg (1926–1997) and the ironic poetry of Lawrence Ferlinghetti (b. 1930). San Francisco, where many of the Beat writers were based, became an early headquarters of Zen thought and practice in America, as it still is today.

Zen centers, often under lay leadership, were established at this time in major cities in North and South America and Europe. These centers have allowed westerners to learn directly about Zen through both instruction and meditation. Some centers have also opened bookstores, vegetarian restaurants, and retreat centers.

A fourth wave of Buddhist influence is more recent and involves several types of Buddhism. Tibetan Buddhism has established communities of immigrant Tibetans and converts in many places in the United States (California, Colorado, New York, Hawai`i) and in Europe (Switzerland, France, Great Britain), and Tibetan Buddhist art is now regularly acquired and exhibited by museums. Forms of Pure Land and Nichiren Buddhism have made many converts, particularly in large cities of North America. And Asian immigrants from Taiwan, Hong Kong, and Southeast Asia have all begun their own temples and celebrations where they have settled.

From the middle of the nineteenth century to the middle of the twentieth century, Buddhism outside Asia was primarily made up of ethnic Buddhists (mostly immigrants) and so-called elite Buddhists (non-Asian intellectuals and academics). These two groups have interacted and been joined by a large middle-class following. A new type of Buddhism is emerging from the interaction of the three groups: "engaged Buddhism." This movement comprises a wide variety of people who, as Buddhists, work for social betterment. Some emphasize that compassion must show itself practically as help for the poor, sick, and oppressed. Others see in the Buddhist principles of moderation and nonharm the bases for work in the areas of animal rights and environmental protection. A broadly based Western Buddhism, in Europe, North America, and Australia, is taking on such a life of its own that it is beginning to be called the "fourth vehicle" (*yana*) of Buddhism.

Ironically, even as it gains followers in the West, Buddhism has been weakened in many countries and regions that have been its traditional home. When Communist governments took over Mongolia (1921) and China (1949), Buddhism was severely repressed, and many temples and monasteries were destroyed. This pattern continued when Tibet was taken over by the Chinese government (1959). The Dalai Lama went into exile and at least a million Tibetans are thought to have died in the ensuing persecution. In China, several thousand monasteries were destroyed, particularly during the Cultural Revolution (1966–76), causing both human suffering and an incalculable loss to the world of art. In recent years there has been a modest amount of rebuilding in all these regions, with the financial support of Buddhists from abroad. On the one hand, governments fear that monasteries can become centers of anti-government activity; but governments also recognize the importance of Buddhist sites both to the inhabitants and to tourists, whose goodwill (and foreign exchange) they wish to encourage. In Sri Lanka, the separatist movement in the north leads Hindus and Buddhists to fight against each other, straining the tradition of nonviolence in both religions. In Myanmar (Burma), the government officially supports Buddhism, yet Buddhist human rights activists have been jailed.

On the other hand, relations with the non-Buddhist world have brought new vigor to Buddhism in its traditional areas. For example, we now see Buddhist environmental groups in Thailand. (Members of one group place monks' orange robes around trees they hope to save.) There is a growing interest in Buddhist monastic life for women and in female leadership roles in Buddhism. These movements have been spurred on by Buddhist nuns in Taiwan, who have arranged for the ordination of women from countries (such as Nepal, India, and Sri Lanka) where full ordination of women is not yet practiced. And although Buddhists have long been associated with certain types of compassionate work, they are now turning to newly perceived areas of need. In Thailand, Buddhist monasteries have established hospices for patients with AIDS. In Taiwan, the Tzu Chi Foundation was begun in 1966 by Master Cheng Yen, a Buddhist nun, who saw the need for a Buddhist relief society. The Foundation now has more than four million

A monk in China offers the universal Buddhist gesture of greeting. ▶

devotees on many continents, who help victims of accidents, crimes, earthquakes, and other misfortunes.

Buddhism is clearly entering a new phase in its long journey. In part, Buddhism can predict what that phase will bring: the one constant, as always, is change.

RELIGION BEYOND THE CLASSROOM

Buddhism has now spread widely enough in North America that it is easily accessible to those interested in experiencing it, including non-Buddhists, who are welcomed. (The popular Buddhist magazines *Tricycle* and *Shambhala Sun* have directories at the back that list centers across North America.) Almost every large city has a Zen center, as well as temples for Chinese, Japanese, Thai, and Tibetan Buddhist practice. The West Coast and Hawai`i are particularly rich with people and places to visit. The largest Buddhist temple in North America, called Kuang Shan Shi Temple, was built by Buddhists from Taiwan and is in Hacienda Heights in the Los Angeles area. Japanese gardens are open to the public in such places as the Golden Gate Park in San Francisco, the Botanic Garden in New York City, and the Butchart Gardens in Victoria, British Columbia.

Travel in Asia allows the visitor to see Buddhist art in its traditional environs, where monks reside and hold services. Five countries in Asia offer westerners particularly rich experiences of Buddhism: Thailand and Sri Lanka for Theravada, Japan and South Korea for Mahayana, and China for both Mahayana and Vajrayana.

Thailand is easily accessible, because Bangkok is an airline hub for all of Southeast Asia. Although Bangkok is not an old city, it has several temples on a grand scale. At Wat Po, one can walk around a large but charming Reclining Buddha. Wat Phra Keo houses the famous Jade Buddha statue. Wat Bovorn (Bovornivet) is a picturesque complex of large trees, old buildings, and canals. And visitors can take an easy day trip by boat from Bangkok upriver to Ayutthaya, an old capital full of temples and sculpture in various states of preservation.

Sri Lanka is a tropical island south of India. One of the most moving statues of the Buddha anywhere is at Polonnaruwa. The statue, cut from the rock of a cliff, depicts the Buddha lying peacefully on his right side. The Buddha's face—certainly not the face of an 80-year-old—is serene. The serenity is reinforced by the drapery of his robe, which looks like sheets of water smoothly cascading over the Buddha's body. The delicacy of the face and clothing contrasts with the large, squarish feet, placed firmly together, which convey a sense of determination and strength. The other major sight in Sri Lanka is the ancient, great white stupa at Anuradhapura, a monument that exhibits the origins of the stupa shape.

Japan is dotted with thousands of Buddhist temples. The greatest concentration of historic temples is in the former capital cities Kyoto and nearby Nara. In Kyoto, essential sights include Ryoan-ji, the most famous Zen garden in the world; Kiyomizu-dera, a temple set on wooden pillars high on a hillside; Kinkaku-ji, the Gold Pavilion; and Tofuku-ji, a temple complex full of maple trees and wooden bridges. But this is only a small sample. Nara contains one of Japan's greatest statues of the Buddha, the Daibutsu, housed in the largest wooden building in the world.

South Korea is not well known to tourists but should be because of the exceptional natural beauty of this country's mountains and forests. South Korea's east coast has fine temples, many of which are located in the scenic national parks of Odae-san and Sorak-san. The greatest temple complex is Pulguk-sa, at Kyongju, in the southeast.

China has so much Buddhist art and architecture that one could spend years visiting its sights. Because most visitors arrive in Beijing, they can easily visit the Lama Temple (Yonghegong, a Vajrayana temple) in the city and hire a taxi to visit two temples in the Fragrant Hills (Xiangshan): Reclining Buddha Temple (Wofusi) and the Temple of the Azure Cloud (Biyunsi). Major cities all contain Buddhist temples, and the cave art at Datong and Dunhuang is famous. A visit to the city of Lhasa in Tibet offers a melancholy glimpse into the formerly vibrant center of Tibetan Buddhism. The Dalai Lama once lived at the Potala, part of which is open to the public. The Jokhang, the former "cathedral" of Lhasa, can also be visited. More hopeful examples of Tibetan Buddhism can be experienced in Tibetan refugee communities in Nepal (such as at Patan in the Katmandu Valley) and in India (such as at Dharamsala).

In Asia, although Buddhist art can usually be seen in a religious setting, some of the most important Buddhist works are now displayed in museums—in Tokyo, Bangkok, Seoul, Taipei, New Delhi, and Beijing. Outside Asia, museums in large cities often have collections of Buddhist art. In North America, major museums are located in New York (Metropolitan Museum), Washington, D.C. (Freer Gallery), Kansas City (Nelson Gallery–Atkins Museum), Boston (Museum of Fine Arts), Cleveland (Cleveland Museum of Art), Chicago (Art Institute), San Francisco (Asian Art Museum), Los Angeles (Los Angeles County Museum of Art), Seattle (Seattle Art Museum), Honolulu (Honolulu Academy of Arts), and Toronto (Ontario Art Museum). Museums in many European cities also have significant collections of Buddhist art, particularly in London (British Museum, Victoria and Albert Museum) and in Paris (Musée Guimet).

FOR FULLER UNDERSTANDING

1. Many immigrants to the United States from traditionally Buddhist countries continue to celebrate their cultural festivals and are usually quite welcoming of visitors. If your area has such festivals, participate and make notes on (or photograph or videotape) examples of Buddhist influences on the festivities.

2. Do a virtual journey over the internet of Buddhist websites, which range from semiprivate devotional websites to museum-based libraries of Buddhist art. Prepare an annotated bibliography of the websites you found most valuable, and describe some of the insights and questions that occurred to you as you explored.

3. Read a biography of the Dalai Lama and other books about Tibetan Buddhism. Prepare a written report on how the Dalai Lama's beliefs and actions earned him the Nobel Peace Prize. The Dalai Lama consistently preaches nonviolence. Is this realistic? Please give arguments for your position.

4. Find out if there is a Buddhist meditation center in your area. Visit it with another classmate, gather information, and then make a report to your class.

5. Do some library research on American architect Frank Lloyd Wright (1867–1959) and his connections with Japan. Is there any evidence to suggest that Wright was influenced by Buddhist ideas or forms?

6. Around New Year's or the Chinese New Year, phone Chinese restaurants in your area to see if any of them serves the seasonal meal *jai* ("monk's food"). If you find such a restaurant, go with a group of classmates or friends for the feast. Ask the manager or waiter about the tradition's origins, and report (perhaps after additional library research) on what you learned.

7. Buddhism has sometimes been accused of being too passive and of over-emphasizing detachment from the world. Do you think that these are fair criticisms? If the criticisms are fair, what suggestions would you have for change in Buddhism? How might change be brought about?

8. Read one of the books in the list of Related Readings. Write a review in which you show how the book expanded your knowledge of basic teachings or practices covered in this chapter.

RELATED READINGS

Batchelor, Martine. *Meditation for Life.* Somerville, MA: Wisdom, 2001. Meditations with excellent photos by Stephen Batchelor.

Boucher, Sandy. *Opening the Lotus: A Women's Guide to Buddhism.* Boston: Beacon, 1998. An account of the author's personal experience in Buddhism, her understanding of its meaning, discussion of Tara and Kwan Yin, and a directory of female Buddhist teachers.

The Dalai Lama. *The Path to Tranquility.* New York: Penguin, 1998. A collection of daily readings about peace, gratitude, and compassion.

Friedman, Lenore. *Meetings with Remarkable Women: Buddhist Teachers in America.* New York: Random House, 2000. Portraits of the author's encounters with seventeen women teachers, giving insight into the growth of roles for women in modern Buddhism.

Goldberg, Natalie. *Writing Down the Bones: Freeing the Writer Within.* Boston: Shambhala, 1986. A Zen-inspired book of anecdotes and exercises about writing.

Gross, Rita. *Buddhism After Patriarchy: A Feminist History, Analysis, and Reconstruction of Buddhism.* Ithaca: State University of New York, 1993. A review of the historical distrust of women in Buddhism, an analysis of essential Buddhist concepts, and a call to a new Buddhism of equality.

Kabat-Zinn, Jon. *Wherever You Go, There You Are.* New York: Hyperion, 1995. Short meditative chapters about topics such as patience, doing chores, and breathing—meant to help bring mindfulness to everyday life.

Kamalashila. *Stages of Meditation.* Ithaca: Snow Lion, 2001. A selection from Kamalashila's *Stages of Meditation,* with commentaries by the Dalai Lama.

King, Winston. *Zen and the Art of the Sword.* New York: Oxford University Press, 1993. A fine introduction not only to the influence of Zen on the samurai but also to many elements of Japanese culture.

Kornfield, Jack. *A Path with Heart.* New York: Bantam, 1992. A valuable discussion of Buddhist concepts, such as lovingkindness, attention, and self-acceptance, written by a westerner who underwent Buddhist monastic training.

Lopez, Donald, Jr., ed. *Religions of Tibet in Practice.* Princeton, NJ: Princeton University Press, 1997. A varied and scholarly collection of readings from Tibetan Buddhism, including sermons, monastic rules, history, and biography.

Morreale, Don, ed. *The Complete Guide to Buddhist America.* Boston: Shambhala, 1998. A large directory of Buddhist groups and meditation centers, divided according to the three branches of Buddhism.

Okakura Kakuzo. *The Book of Tea.* Boston: Shambhala, 2003. A succinct classic about tea and the tea ceremony.

Paul, Diana. *Women in Buddhism.* 2d ed. Berkeley: University of California Press, 1985. A study of Buddhist texts that present images of women.

Rapaport, Al, comp. *Buddhism in America.* Rutland, VT: Tuttle, 1998. A thick collection of talks that were given at a Boston conference on Buddhism, with a wide range of topics, from the predictable (monasticism, meditation) to the unexpected (Buddhism in the media, Zen in prisons).

KEY TERMS

Amitabha (*ah-mee-tah'-buh*): The Buddha of the Western Paradise, a bliss-body Buddha in Mahayana.

anatta (*un-nah'-tuh*): "No self"; the doctrine that there is no soul or permanent essence in people and things.

anichcha (*uh-nee'-chuh*): Impermanence, constant change.

arhat (*ahr'-hut*): In Theravada, a person who has practiced monastic disciplines and reached nirvana, the ideal.

bodhi (*boh'-dee*): Enlightenment.

bodhisattva (*boh'-dee-suh'-tvah*): "Enlightenment being"; in Mahayana, a person of deep compassion, especially one who does not enter nirvana but is constantly reborn to help others; a heavenly being of compassion.

Dharma (*dhur'-mah*): The totality of Buddhist teaching.

dhyana (*dee-yah'-nuh*): "Meditation"; focusing of the mind; sometimes, stages of trance.

dukkha (*doo'-kuh*): Sorrow, misery.

Guanyin: A popular bodhisattva of compassion in Mahayana.

karuna (*kuh-roo'-nuh*): Compassion, empathy.

koan (*koh'-ahn*): In Chan and Zen Buddhism, a question that cannot be answered logically; a technique used to test consciousness and bring awakening.

lama: A Tibetan Buddhist teacher; a title of honor often given to all Tibetan monks.

Maitreya (*mai-tray'-yuh*): A Buddha (or bodhisattva) expected to appear on earth in the future.

mandala (*mun'-duh-luh*): A circular design containing deities, geometrical forms, symbols, and so on that represent totality, the self, or the universe.

mudra (*moo'-druh*): A symbolic hand gesture.

nirvana (*nir-vah'-nuh*): The release from suffering and rebirth that brings inner peace.

samadhi (*suh-mah'-dee*): A state of deep awareness, the result of intensive meditation.

samsara (*suhm-sah'-ruh*): Constant rebirth and the attendant suffering; the everyday world of change.

Sangha (*suhng'-huh*): The community of monks and nuns; lowercased, *sangha* refers to an individual monastic community.

satori (*sah-toh'-ree*): In Zen, the enlightened awareness.

shunyata (*shoon'-ya-tah*): The Mahayana notion of emptiness, meaning that the universe is empty of permanent reality.

stupa (*stoo'-puh*): A shrine, usually in the shape of a dome, used to mark Buddhist relics or sacred sites.

sutra (*soo'-truh*): A sacred text, especially one said to record the words of the Buddha.

tathata (*taht-ha-tah'*): "Thatness," "thusness," "suchness"; the uniqueness of each changing moment of reality.

trikaya (*trih-kah'-yuh*): The three "bodies" of the Buddha—the Dharmakaya (cosmic Buddha nature), the Nirmanakaya (historical Buddhas), and the Sambhogakaya (celestial Buddhas).

Tripitaka (*trih-pih'-tuh-kuh*): The three "baskets," or collections, of Buddhist texts.

vajra (*vuhj'-ruh*): The "diamond" scepter used in Tibetan and other types of Buddhist ritual, symbolizing compassion.

CHAPTER **5**

Jainism and Sikhism

 FIRST ENCOUNTER

While you are traveling from Delhi to Mumbai, which many still call Bombay, you cannot help overhearing a conversation in your train compartment. Two young Americans are explaining to a middle-aged Indian gentleman that they are traveling to the ashram of a Hindu guru just outside the city.

"She has many disciples in California, where we live. We'll stay in her ashram for six months, practicing hatha yoga and meditation," says the young woman, "then we'll travel. We'll be in India for almost a year. What do you recommend we see here in western India?"

"Let me think," says the gentleman. "Well, you might enjoy Elephanta Island near Bombay, known for its statue of Shiva. You would enjoy Goa, too; it's like a bit of Portugal on the Indian coast, with large old churches and fine beaches. And there are the caves of Ajanta and Ellora, famous for their sculpture." He tells the couple about the ferryboat that goes to the island and the bus transportation to the caves.

"Have you been yet to Amritsar, the sacred city of the Sikhs?" the gentleman asks. "It is to the

185

north of here. The Golden Temple there is lovely and sits in the middle of its own small lake." The couple responds that they have not been there but that they've heard of the Sikhs. "Sikh men let their hair grow long and wear turbans, I think," says the young man. The older gentleman confirms that many do.

The conversation then turns to the Jains. "Some live in the south, but there are also a good number in west and northwest India, with some beautiful temples and fine statues," the gentleman says. "The Jains, you know, were a big influence on Mahatma Gandhi, who came from Gujarat, north of Bombay. Jains teach strict nonviolence and are vegetarian, like the Hindus. In fact, I am a Jain myself," says the gentleman.

"Wasn't it hard for you to give up meat?" asks the young man.

"My dear sir, not at all," exclaims the man with shock. "You see, I have never even tasted it!"

The train arrives at the couple's station on the outskirts of the city, and the conversation closes abruptly. "Here is my card, with my address and business number in Bombay," says the gentleman. "Call me if I can be of further help. I would be happy to give you a tour of the city."

"Thank you very much. We'll be in touch with you after our stay at the ashram," says the young woman. They scramble to gather their backpacks and other things. When they are gone, the gentleman raises his eyes in wonder, and your eyes meet. He smiles beatifically.

SHARED ORIGINS

India is now home to two religions that are not well known in the West: Jainism and Sikhism. The first is ancient, and the other is relatively young. Adherents of the two religions can be found in limited numbers around the world, but the majority live in India.

Both religions have some connection with Hinduism, sharing with it certain characteristics, such as a belief in karma and rebirth. Furthermore, both of them, having developed in opposition to Hindu polytheism and ritualism, strive toward greater religious simplicity. In spite of their similarities, however, Jainism and Sikhism differ in their views of reality and in their emotional tones. It is therefore interesting to look at them side by side. Jainism rejects belief in a Creator and sees the universe simply as natural forces in motion, yet it also recognizes the spiritual potential of each person. Like early Buddhism, Jainism emphasizes the ideals of extreme nonattachment and nonharm (*ahimsa*). Sikhism, to the contrary, embraces a devout monotheism and accepts meat eating and military self-defense. Regardless of their differences, both religions stress the importance of the individual's struggle to purify the self, to act morally, and to do good to others.

JAINISM

BACKGROUND

As the Aryans and their Vedic religion expanded eastward into the Ganges River valley, they naturally created opposition. As we saw in chapter 4, some people rebelled against the growing strength of the caste system, and non-brahmins, especially the aristocrats, felt threatened by the power of the priests. Moved by compassion, some people opposed the animal sacrifices that were often a part of the Vedic ritual. Two great religious movements grew out of this opposition. One—Buddhism, which we studied in chapter 4—is well known because it spread beyond India. The other movement—Jainism—has remained less well known because, until recently, it has not sought converts in other lands. When they arose, both Buddhism and Jainism were influenced by some early Hindu ideas, but they may have also practiced much older ascetic traditions.

It is possible that Jainism has not spread widely because it is uncompromising: in it we find an extremist quality that is fascinating, thought provoking, and often noble. Tendencies toward nonviolence and austerity apparent in Hinduism and Buddhism are carried to their logical endpoint in Jainism, and the skepticism of early Buddhism is practiced rigorously. The study of Jainism, in fact, gives greater clarity to our understanding of those two other Indian religions.

Although Jainism did not spread widely, its strong ideal of nonviolence has attracted interest throughout the world. We see its influence directly in the thought and work of Mahatma Gandhi and, indirectly, in the thought and work of Martin Luther King, Jr.

MAHAVIRA AND THE ORIGINS OF JAINISM

Jains date the origins of their religion to the distant past. They believe that in the present cycle of the universe twenty-four great people have reached perfection; and though living in quite different centuries, these saints have been role models and guides who have shown the way to others. These saints are called **tirthankaras,** which can be translated as "crossing makers" or "ford finders"—a *ford* being a section of a river that allows people to cross through the moving stream to the other side. It is notable that the term does not convey the image of a bridge. The point of the term is that people cannot cross to the other side without getting wet and going through the river itself. The historical existence of most of these tirthankaras cannot be proven, but the twenty-third one, Parshva, may have been a real person who lived in India, possibly between 850 and 800 B.C.E. (Timeline 5.1).

The most recent tirthankara is considered to be the greatest of them all and is often thought of by outsiders to be the founder of Jainism. His name was Nataputta Vardhamana, but he is usually referred to by an honorary

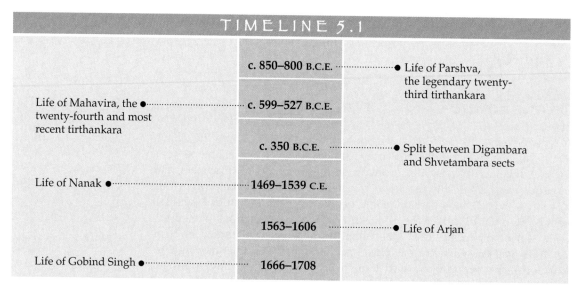

	c. 850–800 B.C.E.	Life of Parshva, the legendary twenty-third tirthankara
Life of Mahavira, the twenty-fourth and most recent tirthankara	c. 599–527 B.C.E.	
	c. 350 B.C.E.	Split between Digambara and Shvetambara sects
Life of Nanak	1469–1539 C.E.	
	1563–1606	Life of Arjan
Life of Gobind Singh	1666–1708	

Timeline of significant events in the history of Jainism and Sikhism.

title: Mahavira, meaning "great man" or "hero." When he lived is not entirely certain. An older dating, accepted by Jains, puts his life entirely in the sixth century B.C.E. (c. 599–527 B.C.E.), but some scholars believe he lived a bit later (540–468 B.C.E.), as a contemporary of the Buddha.

Mahavira's life story is surrounded by legend, although the basic outline—which somewhat resembles the story of the Buddha—seems clear. He was born into an aristocratic family of a noble clan. Luckily, he was the second son and thus had fewer responsibilities to care for his parents than did his older brother. One branch of Jains holds that he never married; another says that he married and had a child. But all agree that he left home at about age thirty to live the life of a wandering holy man.

After leaving home, Mahavira embraced extreme asceticism, and legend tells of his harshness toward himself and of the harshness received from others. He is said to have pulled out his hair when he renounced the world, and villagers taunted him during his meditations by hurting him with fire and with pins that they pushed into his skin. Dogs attacked him, but he did not resist. In order to avoid all attachments to people and places, he moved to another place every day; and after losing his loincloth, he went entirely naked for the rest of his life. He lived as a wandering holy man, begging for his food along the way. He was so gentle that to avoid causing injury to any living thing he strained whatever he drank to keep from swallowing any insect that might have fallen into his cup, and he stepped carefully as he walked down a road to avoid crushing even an ant.

After twelve years of meditation, wandering, and extreme mortification, Mahavira, at the age of 42, had an experience of great liberation. He felt completely free of all bondage to the ordinary world—no longer being troubled by pain, suffering, shame, or loss. He now felt fully in control of himself, sensing that he had won out over all the forces that bind a person to the world. As a result of his liberating experience, Mahavira is called a **jina** ("conqueror"). It is from this title that the religion Jainism takes its name.

Mahavira spent the next thirty years of his life teaching his doctrines and organizing an order of naked monks. He died at about 72 at the village of Pava, near present-day Patna, in northeastern India.

WORLDVIEW

Jainism, like Buddhism, rather starkly rejects belief in a Creator God. The Mahapurana, a long Jain poem of the ninth century C.E., states that "foolish men declare that Creator made the world. The doctrine that the world was created is ill-advised and should be rejected."[1] Jainism offers the following philosophical arguments: If God is perfect, why did God create a universe that is imperfect? If God made the universe because of love, why is the world so full of suffering beings? If the universe had to be created, did not God also need to be created? And where did God come from in the beginning?

Jains respond to these questions by denying any beginning and asserting instead that the universe is eternal. Although the universe has always existed, it must continually change, and in the process of eternal change, structure arises on its own. Jainism (like Hinduism) teaches that the universe goes through regular great cycles of rise and fall. During the periods when human beings exist, there first is moral integrity, followed by inevitable moral decay; luckily, however, in each human age, tirthankaras appear to point the way to freedom.

According to Jainism, everything is full of life and is capable of suffering— a view of reality (called **hylozoism,** "matter alive") that may be quite ancient. In addition, Jain philosophy is dualistic, for Jains teach that all parts of the universe are composed of two types of reality, which are intermixed. There is spirit, which senses and feels, and there is matter, which is not alive and has no consciousness. Jainism calls these two principles **jiva** ("soul," "spirit," "life") and **ajiva** ("nonsoul," "nonlife"). Jains, however, see life and consciousness where others do not—even in fire, rocks, and water. Thus they extend the notion of spirit and feeling beyond human beings, animals, and insects. They are also aware of the minuscule life-forms that live in earth, water, and wood. Their way of looking at reality makes Jains cautious about injuring anything—even that which does not at first appear to have the capacity to suffer.

Jainism sees the human being as composed of two opposing parts. The material side of the human being seeks pleasure, escape from pain, and self-interest, while the spiritual side seeks freedom and escape from all bondage to the material world and from the limitation of ego. Because other forms of reality are not aware of their two opposing aspects, they can do nothing about the essential incompatibility of the two parts. Human beings, however, have the ability to understand their dual nature and to overcome their limitations. With discipline, human beings can overcome the bondage of the material world and the body, liberating their spirits through insight, austerity, and kindness.

Enriching this vision of the human situation are the Jain beliefs in karma and reincarnation. Like Hindus, Jains believe that spirits are constantly being reborn in various forms. A spirit can move up or down the scale of rebirth, as well as free itself entirely from the chain of rebirths.

What controls the direction of rebirth is karma, which is produced by every action. As discussed earlier, karma is an important notion in Hinduism and Buddhism; but for Jains, karma has a quite physical quality: it is like a powder or grime that settles on and clings to the spirit. The level of rebirth is determined automatically, according to one's state of karma at the time of the death of one's current body.

Jains traditionally have believed that superhuman beings exist in realms of the universe above the earth. Often these beings are called gods or deities, but such terms can be misleading. We must recall that Jains believe that these superhuman beings are also subject to karma and change. When the karma that has brought them rebirth as gods has run out, they will be reborn in lower parts of the universe. Some Jains, however, do believe that when these celestial beings are in their superhuman form they can be of help to people on earth who pray to them. Jains also believe that some beings exist in painful realms below the earth, and Jains hope to avoid being reborn there.

The Jain goal is to reach a state of total freedom. Liberated spirits, at last freed of their imprisoning material bodies, live on in the highest realm, which is thought to be at the very top of the universe. Mahavira and other tirthankaras dwell there, and although they cannot assist human beings (as deities might), they are role models whom human beings devoutly recall in order to gain strength and courage.

JAIN ETHICS

Jainism has five ethical recommendations, which monks and nuns are expected to keep quite strictly. Laypeople, however, have the flexibility to adjust their practice to their particular life situations. (We must also recall that these are ideals that are not always lived out perfectly by individuals.)

> The saint, with true vision, conceives compassion for all the world. . . . The great sage becomes a refuge for injured creatures, like an island which the waters cannot overwhelm.
>
> —Acaranga Sutra 1:6, 5[2]

Nonviolence (ahimsa) A more accurate English translation of *ahimsa* might be "gentleness" or "harmlessness." Ahimsa is the foundation of Jain ethics, and Jains are best known for their extreme measures in this regard. Believing that Mahavira swept the ground in front of him as he walked and before he sat down, Jain monks and nuns sometimes use a small, soft brush to move ants and other insects out of the way so that no life-form—even the tiniest—will be crushed. Feeling a kinship with the animal world as well, Jains have established hospitals to care for sick animals. They have been known to buy caged animals and set them free. Jains are also strict vegetarians, and some reject the use of animal products such as leather, feathers, and fur.

Because Jain laypeople avoid occupations that would harm insects or animals, hunting and fishing are forbidden, as are slaughtering or selling animal flesh. And although some Jains are farmers, farming is often avoided because the necessary plowing could hurt small animals and insects living in the fields. Jains, instead, have gravitated to jobs that ideally cause no hurt, such as being doctors, teachers, lawyers, accountants, and businesspeople. As an indirect result, the Jains in

Jain nuns carry begging bowls and whisks.

India make up a powerful business class whose reputation for virtue earns them the trust of others.

Nonlying Jainism discourages the telling of any falsehood and avoids exaggeration, even when meant humorously. Lying and exaggeration are dangerous, Jains think, because they often cause hurt. Although these ideals are not always followed, Jains' general mindfulness of their speech and their reputation for honesty in their contractual agreements have earned them great respect.

At the same time, Jainism teaches that "absolute truth" is impossible to find or express, because everyone sees a situation from a unique point of view. A famous story illustrates the relativity of truth. In this story, several blind men touch the same elephant but experience it quite differently. The first man touches the ear and says it is a fan; the second man touches the leg and says it is a tree trunk; the third man touches the tail and says it is a rope; and so on. (Although this story is popular among Jains, it is doubtless older than Jainism itself.)

Nonstealing Jains may not take from others that which is not given. Stealing arises from improper desire and causes pain to others.

Chastity For the monk or nun, this means complete celibacy, and for the married individual, this means sexual fidelity to one's spouse. Mahavira saw sex as a danger, because it strongly binds a person to the physical world, strengthens desires, and can create passions that harm others. For those who are sexually active, improper sex is that which hurts others.

Jains and a Holy Death

Because it so values nonattachment, Jainism defends a person's right to end his or her own life. (This is also true of Hinduism but not so for many other religions—although most religions are indeed concerned with a good and holy death.) Jain scriptures even teach that Mahavira and his parents died by self-starvation. We must be cautious here, however, in using the word *suicide.* Jains do accept ending one's own life, but we must understand the practice from the Jain point of view and within that context. Jains see all life as a preparation for the liberation of the spirit (jiva) from the body, and when a person is sufficiently evolved spiritually, that person can make the final choice to no longer create more karma.

The Jain ideal thus allows and esteems ending one's life only after a long life of virtue and detachment, and it must be done with consideration for others. Gentle methods of ending one's life are the best, such as walking into an ocean or lake. The most highly esteemed method, however, is self-starvation, called **sallekhana,** "holy death." Jains prepare for sallekhana over the years by practicing fasting. When a person is old and growing weak, eating less and less is seen as an appropriate way to hasten the end. Self-starvation, or "the final fast," involves giving up food but continuing to drink liquids; death comes in about a month. This kind of death by self-starvation is considered an ultimate, noble expression of non-attachment and freedom.

Nonattachment Human beings form attachments easily—to family, to home, to familiar territory, to clothes, to money, and to possessions. Jainism asserts that all attachments bring a certain bondage and that some attachments, especially to money and to possessions, can take complete control of a person. For laypeople, the ethical requirement of nonattachment suggests cultivating a spirit of generosity and detachment and limiting one's possessions to what is truly necessary. For monks and nuns, this requirement is interpreted more severely. Jainism teaches that Mahavira abandoned all attachments—family, possessions, even his clothing—and that monks and nuns must imitate him to the best of their capacity.

THE DEVELOPMENT OF JAINISM AND ITS BRANCHES

Jainism first developed in northeastern India, in the same area that gave rise to Buddhism. Both Mahavira and the Buddha rebelled against aspects of Vedic religion: they refused to accept the authority of the Vedas, the Vedic gods, or the importance of a priestly class, and they placed emphasis, instead, on meditation and self-purification.

Although Buddhism followed a deliberate path of moderation—a "middle way"—Jainism gloried in austerity. While the Buddha rejected both nakedness and suicide as well as all extreme austerity, Mahavira's breakthrough experience of liberation, most Jains believe, was due to his extreme harshness toward himself. He was successful precisely because he accepted—and even sought—cold, heat, poverty, nakedness, and humiliation.

The way of extreme austerity, however, is for rare individuals only. For most people, even for monks and nuns, the harshness must be softened according to life's circumstances. Because Jainism spread to different parts

FIGURE 5.1
Branches of Jainism

of India, with their differences in culture and climate, several branches of Jainism arose, which interpret the basic principles and teachings with some variations (Figure 5.1).

Digambaras

The name of this sect is beautiful and means "clothed in sky" or "atmosphere-clad." It is a pleasant way of referring to the monks' ideal of going completely naked, even in public. The **Digambara** branch holds that everything must be renounced, including the last scrap of clothing and the consequent shame of nakedness.

Most members of this branch live in southern India today. As tradition explains, a famine that occurred in the north drove many Jains southward. Divergences developed between those who had remained in the north and those who had moved south. Thinking that northern followers had lost an essential seriousness, the southern branch became conservative, continuing to insist on renunciation of the most literal type. Its conservatism shows itself in many ways. For example, Digambara Jainism does not accept women into monastic life, holding that they may become monks only when they have been reborn as men. Possibly because of its high regard for celibacy, it also rejects the tradition that Mahavira was ever married.

Shvetambaras

The name of this sect means "clothed in white" and comes from the fact that its monks dress in white robes. The **Shvetambara** branch allows women to enter monastic life as nuns and to dress in white as well. (Being clothed was allowed not only in deference to modesty but also because it was demanded by the colder climate of northern India.) Shvetambara Jainism teaches that Mahavira was indeed married at one time but left home to find liberation. Nowadays this branch has members not only in the northeast but also in western and northwestern India.

Sthanakavasis

By the standards of India, the **Sthanakavasi** branch is fairly young, having grown up within the past few hundred years. It is a reform movement that emerged from the Shvetambara branch in the early eighteenth century. Popular Jainism had increasingly developed the practice of venerating statues of Mahavira and other tirthankaras, influenced by the Hindu practice of **puja** (devotional ritual performed in front of statues and at altars). Some Jain reformers opposed this practice because it seemed to turn the tirthankaras into deities to be prayed to for help. The Sthanakavasis, therefore, do not make use of either temples or images. (Their name comes from the simple buildings—*sthanakas*—in which they meet.) Rather than concentrate on temple ceremony, Sthanakavasis focus on meditation and individual austerities.

Terapanthis

An even newer reformist movement is the **Terapanthi** branch. It was founded in 1817 by Acharya Bhikshu (1788–1860), also called Swami Bhikkanji Maharaj. The origin of the name Terapanthi, which means "thirteen," is debated. It may come from the thirteen moral principles outlined by the founder or from the number of persons in the group of the earliest disciples. Like the Sthanakavasis, the Terapanthis reject the use of images. To ensure discipline, the founder instituted a hierarchical structure with a supreme guru, the *Acharya*, at the top who oversees all operations. The Terapanthis, while being strict in their practice, have been at the forefront in spreading Janism outside of India and in spreading basic Jain principles among non-Jains, both within India and beyond.

JAIN PRACTICES

Because they emphasize the ability of individuals to purify themselves and to perfect their own characters, Jains do not stress that devotional acts—directed toward gods or deceased leaders—bring help. Nonetheless, the practice of puja—offered to both the tirthankaras and to deities—has been adopted by most Jains (with the exception of the Sthanakavasis and Terapanthis). There is a general feeling that the devotional acts have a good effect on one's state of karma and that they focus the mind on saintly behavior. Jain temples, therefore, contain statues of the tirthankaras, especially Rishaba (the first tirthankara), Nemi (the twenty-second), Parshva, and Mahavira. The temple statues often look the same. In Digambara temples, the statues are unclothed and simple; in Shvetambara temples, they may be clothed and more ornate. Puja is performed before statues regularly, both by Jains and (in some places) by brahmin Hindus employed for the task. Puja ordinarily involves the offering of food, incense, the flames of oil lamps, and flowers, and sometimes the statues are bathed and devotees circumambulate (walk around) the statues. In some areas, there are large outdoor statues, which are bathed in milk and other liquids on special occasions. Many Jains also maintain home altars where they perform puja.

Fasting is regularly practiced by monks and nuns, particularly at the times of full and new moons. Laypeople join the monks in fasting on the last days of the Jain year in late summer, before the celebration of the New Year begins (in August or September). This period of fasting (*paryusana*) lasts fifteen days for the Digambaras and eight days for the Shvetambaras. The religious year ends with a confession of wrongdoing and a plea for pardon from anyone the devotee might have offended.

A devotee anoints the feet of a Jain statue. The vines on each side (showing at the top corners of the photograph) hint at the immobility and perseverance of the tirthankara.

Pilgrimage is an important part of Jain spirituality, and the village near Patna, where Mahavira died, is a great pilgrimage center. Jains also visit the great temple complexes (some of which are on mountaintops in western India) and attend the bathing of large statues. Jains celebrate the birthday of Mahavira in the spring and his experience of liberation in the autumn.

JAIN SCRIPTURES

Jains speak of ancient scriptures, the Purvas, that exist no longer in their entirety, but only as limited quotations in later scripture. Disagreement exists among the sects over what is to be accepted as canonical (authoritative). The literature preserved by the Shvetambara sect consists of forty-five works, divided into the canonical scriptures and later noncanonical works. At the heart of the canonical material are the eleven Angas ("limbs"). (A twelfth is said to have existed at one time.) Jainism holds the Angas to be the teachings of Mahavira, although they were not given final form until two centuries

While Jainism emphasizes simplicity, some of its most noted architecture is quite elaborate, as here in the Sitambara Jain Temple of Kolkata (Calcutta).

after his death. There are also twelve Upangas ("lesser limbs"), a collection of laws, rituals (particularly associated with assistance in dying), and other miscellaneous texts. Later noncanonical works include biographies of holy persons, commentaries on canonical works, and books of philosophy and science.[3] The Digambara sect does not fully accept the authenticity of the Angas, maintaining that the words of Mahavira were remembered and transmitted imperfectly after the first division of the Jains had taken place. The Sthanakavasis do not recognize any literature as scripture.

JAIN ART AND ARCHITECTURE

The most striking examples of Jain art are the statues of Mahavira and other tirthankaras. Although the seated statues resemble Buddhist sculpture, other sculptural forms contrast greatly with their Buddhist counterparts. Buddha figures are often gentle looking, with a preternatural sweetness in the faces; Jain figures, however, tend to be bold, powerful, and imposing. This is particularly true of statues of tirthankaras shown naked and standing: their nakedness somehow adds to their strength, and the standing figures are often presented with their legs and arms surrounded by vines, their immobility suggesting persistence and strength of character. The tirthankara seems to dare the viewer to be equally as strong.

Jain temple architecture does not echo the simplicity of the sculpture. Some Jain temples (such as the temple complex on Mount Abu, in western India, famous for its carved ceilings) show as much love for richness and decoration as some Hindu temples do. Sometimes, as in Calcutta, the temples also feature exuberant elements borrowed from European architecture, such as Corinthian columns and stained glass.

SIKHISM

BACKGROUND

Sikhism grew up in an area called the Punjab, which today is part of northwestern India and eastern Pakistan. Although the region has a long history of religious conflict between Hindus and Muslims, it is also an area in which significant attempts have been made to bridge division and misunderstanding. It is not surprising, then, that Sikhism, nurtured in the midst of conflict and resolution, exhibits elements reminiscent of both groups.

It is hard to imagine two religions more divergent than Hinduism and Islam. Hinduism recognizes many gods, while Islam recognizes only one; Hinduism cherishes religious images, whereas Islam prohibits them; and Hinduism promotes vegetarianism, but Islam, although it has dietary restrictions, allows the killing and eating of many animals, including cows.

Both religions, though, share an appreciation for religious devotion and value the attainment of mystical consciousness. In Hinduism, these traditions have been cultivated by the devotees of bhakti yoga, and in Islam they have been cultivated by Sufis (see chapter 10). (Some scholars maintain that Sufism in fact derived much early inspiration from Hinduism.) Both religions also recognize the important role of a spiritual master—a *guru* or a *shaykh*. And while Islam is known for its rejection of images, some Hindus have also spoken against an exaggerated love of images.

Before Sikhism began, there were already people, called *sants*, who practiced a spirituality that drew from both religions and that sought to overcome religious divisions. The greatest exponent of the sant tradition was the mystic Kabir (1440–1518), whose poetry has had enormous influence in India. It is from this interest in a mystical spirituality beyond the restrictions of any one religion that Sikhism emerged, and it was in the Punjab, where two often-opposing religions collided, that the founder of a new religion was born.

NANAK AND THE ORIGINS OF SIKHISM

The founder of Sikhism, Nanak, was born in 1469 in what is today Pakistan. He grew up in a Hindu family, married, had two children, and held several jobs—first as a herder and then as a clerical assistant to a sultan. Because Nanak's life as a householder was accompanied by a strong religious interest, he and a Muslim friend named Mardana created a devotional association and met in the evenings to sing hymns and to discuss religious ideas.

One day Nanak had an experience so powerful that he saw it as a revelation. After bathing and performing religious ablutions in a nearby river, Nanak went into the adjacent forest and did not reemerge for three days. During that time, he felt himself taken into the divine presence. He would later say that he had experienced God directly. This shattering experience revealed to him that there is but one God, beyond all human names and conceptions.

Nanak referred to the fundamental divine reality as the True Name—signifying that all names and terms that are applied to God are limited, because the divine is beyond all human conception. Nanak now understood that Hindus and Muslims worshiped the same God and that a distinction between the two religions was mistaken. Nanak became famous for insisting that when the True Name of God is experienced, rather than just talked about, there is no "Hindu" and there is no "Muslim."

Nanak's revelation is similar to stories of the life-changing prophetic calls of Isaiah, Zarathustra, and Muhammad (as we will see in later chapters). His revelatory experience resolved his earlier doubts and was the great turning point of his life. Having decided to spread his new understanding, Nanak left his family and home, accompanied by his friend Mardana. As homeless wanderers, they visited holy sites throughout northern India. Wherever they went, Nanak preached and sought disciples, which is the meaning of the word **Sikh** (disciple). As a part of his preaching, Nanak sang devotional songs while Mardana, who was from a social class of musicians, played musical accompaniment.

Particularly startling was Nanak's style of clothing, which deliberately blended Hindu and Muslim elements. He wore the Hindu *dhoti* (a cloth drawn up between the legs to form pants), along with an orange Muslim coat and Muslim cap. He adorned his forehead with Hindu religious markings. The combination of elements was an important prophetic statement, predictably causing consternation among both Hindus and Muslims.

Nanak and Mardana continued their devotional teaching together until Mardana's death in his late sixties. Not long after, when Nanak sensed his own end approaching, he passed on his authority and work to a chosen disciple. He died in 1539 at age 70. Nanak is commonly called Guru Nanak and is recognized as the first of a line of ten Sikh gurus ("spiritual teachers").

THE WORLDVIEW AND TEACHINGS OF NANAK

Just as Nanak's clothing combined elements of Hinduism and Islam, so too did his worldview, at least on the surface. Earlier commentators spoke of Sikhism merely as a combination of Hindu and Muslim elements, yet Sikhs themselves—and more recent scholars—see Sikhism as an entirely unique religion. They speak of Nanak as having rejected both Islam and Hinduism, and they hold that Sikhism comes from a totally new revelation.

Nanak accepted—as does Hinduism—a belief in reincarnation and karma. His view of the human being was similar to that of the Sankhya school of philosophy, which views the human being as a composite of body and spirit. Because the body and physical world by nature bind and limit the spirit, the spirit must overcome physicality as it seeks freedom and absorption in the divine. This process may take many lifetimes to accomplish.

In spite of Nanak's acceptance of reincarnation and karma, there were other elements of Hinduism that he rejected. From a very early age, for example, he resisted Hindu love of ritual, criticizing it for taking human attention away from God. Similarly, he disdained Hindu polytheism, particularly Hindu devotion to images of various gods and goddesses. It is possible that Nanak's views in this regard were influenced by Islam. Islamic practice also supported Nanak's acceptance of meat eating. (Nanak thought of the animal world as having been created for the use of human beings.)

According to Nanak's view of God, although God is ultimately beyond personhood, God does have personal qualities, such as knowledge, love, a sense of justice, and compassion. As such, God can be approached personally by the individual. God, according to Nanak, is the primary Guru; and although Nanak saw himself as God's mouthpiece, he preached that God dwells within each individual and can be contacted within the human heart.

Despite his emphasis on finding the divine within the individual, Nanak believed that true religion has a strong social responsibility. He criticized both Islam and Hinduism for their deficiencies in helping the poor and the oppressed. In response to his convictions, Nanak organized religious groups, called *sangats,* which were to offer both worship to God and assistance to fellow human beings.

THE DEVELOPMENT OF SIKHISM

Sikhism has gone through several stages of development. In its earliest stage, Sikhism was not defined as a distinct religion. It was simply a religious movement that sought to coexist peacefully with other religions. In the next stage, Sikhism was forced to adopt a militant, self-protective stance toward the world, and it took on some of the elements of a more formalized religion—a sacred book, a sacred city, and clearly defined religious practices. After that period of self-definition and consolidation, Sikhism, in its third and final stage, was able to move beyond its land of origin and to make converts elsewhere.

The earliest stage was that of the first four gurus—Nanak, Angad, Amar Das, and Ram Das. During this period, hymns were written, numerous communities were organized, and a village headquarters was created at Amritsar, in northern India.

The next stage—of consolidation and religious definition—began with Guru Arjan (1563–1606), a son of Ram Das. In his role as fifth guru, Arjan built the Golden Temple and its surrounding pond at Amritsar. Collecting about three thousand hymns—written by himself and earlier gurus and saints—Arjan created the sacred book of the Sikhs, the **Adi Granth** ("original collection"). Because he resolutely resisted attempts by the Muslim emperor Jahangir to make him adopt Islamic practice, Arjan died of torture.

The Golden Temple at Amritsar enshrines the Adi Granth and is the spiritual center of the Sikh faith.

Arjan's son, Har Gobind, steered Sikhism in a more self-defensive direction. As a result of the persecution of his father, Har Gobind enlisted a bodyguard and an army to protect him and his followers. He adopted the practice of wearing a sword and thus abandoned the Hindu ideal of ahimsa. The growing militancy of evolving Sikhism was successful in averting persecution during the tenure of the next gurus, Har Rai and Harkishan.

The ninth guru, Tegh Bahadur, however, was imprisoned and decapitated by the Muslim emperor Aurangzeb, who saw Sikhism as a serious threat to his control. In response, the tenth guru, Gobind Rai (1666–1708) idealized the sword. Because of his military power, Gobind Rai came to be known as Gobind Singh ("Gobind the lion"). He inaugurated a special military order for men, called the Khalsa, and devised a ceremony of initiation, called the baptism of the sword, which involved sprinkling initiates with water that had been stirred with a sword. The Khalsa was open to all castes, for Gobind

The "Five K's" of the Sikh Khalsa

In India and in big cities of the West, Sikhs today are often associated with turbans. In fact, their characteristic dress reflects not one but five practices. These practices are not observed by all Sikhs, however, but only by those who have entered the Khalsa, the special Sikh military order. The five practices were originally adopted by members of the Khalsa to promote strength and self-identity.* Because the names of the practices each begin with the letter *k*, they are called the Five K's:

- *Kesh:* uncut hair and beard—in association with the lion and its power; the hair on the head is

usually worn in a topknot and covered with a turban or cloth.

- *Khanga:* hair comb—to hold the long hair in place.
- *Kach:* special underwear—to indicate alertness and readiness to fight.
- *Kirpan:* sword—for defense.
- *Kara:* bracelet of steel—to symbolize strength.

---

*In addition, members of the Khalsa were required to avoid all intoxicants. For a long time, the Khalsa was open only to men, but eventually it was opened also to women.

Singh had ended all caste distinctions among Sikhs. Every male within the Khalsa took the name Singh ("lion").

Over time, Gobind Singh suffered the deaths of his four sons and was left without a successor. Possibly foreseeing his own assassination, he declared that the Adi Granth was to be considered both his successor and the final, permanent Guru. The sacred book, both in Amritsar and in Sikh temples (**gurdwaras**), is therefore treated with the same reverence that would be shown a living guru. As such, it is called Guru Granth Sahib. At the death of Gobind Singh, Sikhism was now clearly defined as a religion, with the means to spread beyond its place of origin.

SIKH SCRIPTURES

The primary book of Sikh scripture, the Adi Granth, is divided into three parts. The first and most important part is the **Japji,** a moderately long poem by Guru Nanak that summarizes the religion. It speaks of the indescribability of God and the joy of union with him. Its opening words declare, "There is only one God whose name is true, the Creator, devoid of fear and enmity, immortal, unborn, self-existent."[4] The second part consists of thirty-nine *rags* ("tunes") by Guru Nanak and later gurus. The third part is a collection of varied works, including poems and hymns from Hindu, Muslim, and Sikh gurus and saints.

Because the Adi Granth is believed to contain the living spirit of Nanak and his successors, it is treated with utmost reverence and given personal honors as the embodiment of the gurus. At the Golden Temple in Amritsar, it is brought out in the early morning by a gloved attendant, set on a cushion under a canopy, read from aloud by professional readers, fanned throughout the day, and then "put to bed" at night. In gurdwaras, copies of the Adi Granth are enshrined and read. It is consulted for solutions to problems by opening it freely and reading from the top of the left-hand page. (Even children are named by this method, being given names corresponding to the first letter read at the top of the left-hand page when the Adi Granth

Meals and hospitality are an important part of Sikh religious events. Here devotees in Southern California celebrate the anniversary of the birth of Guru Gobind Singh.

is opened randomly.) Sikh homes may have a room to enshrine the Adi Granth, and devout Sikhs daily read or recite its passages from memory.

An example of the poetic nature of the Adi Granth is the following canticle by Nanak in praise of God:

> Wonderful Your word, wonderful Your knowledge;
> Wonderful Your creatures, wonderful their species;
> Wonderful their forms, wonderful their colors;
> Wonderful the animals which wander naked;
> Wonderful Your wind; wonderful Your water;
> Wonderful Your fire which sports wondrously;
> Wonderful the earth . . . ;
> Wonderful the desert, wonderful the road;
> Wonderful Your nearness, wonderful Your remoteness;
> Wonderful to behold You present.[5]

SIKHISM AND THE MODERN WORLD

Because of their military training, Sikhs were employed by the British as soldiers. After the British left the Indian subcontinent in 1947, however, the Sikhs experienced painful dislocation. More than two million left Pakistan to avoid conflict with the Muslim majority, and most settled in northwestern

India, where today some Sikhs hope to create an independent state. Antagonism has flared up between the Sikhs and the Indian government over this matter, and although Sikh separatists have taken over the Golden Temple at Amritsar, Indian government forces have repeatedly taken it back. In retaliation for her support of Indian government troops during the first of these takeovers, Prime Minister Indira Gandhi was assassinated in 1984 by Sikhs who were among her bodyguards.

Sikhs have begun to settle widely outside India, particularly in countries open to Indian immigration, such as England and former British territories. (There is a considerable community, for example, in Vancouver, British Columbia.) They have established gurdwaras, which serve as daily prayer centers as well as charitable kitchens and social meeting places. Although Sikhs do not have a tradition of making converts, their simple and self-reliant lifestyle has attracted many new members. Their success and continued growth is likely.

PERSONAL EXPERIENCE: A VISIT TO THE GOLDEN TEMPLE

The Golden Temple of Amritsar sits in the midst of a busy Indian city on an island in an artificial lake. On the day that I visited, however, the water of the lake had been drained, and about thirty workers were moving about and chatting down below as they cleaned and made repairs. While I surveyed the scene, I overheard what sounded like American English being spoken nearby. A man with black hair and a short black beard, his blond wife, and his young daughter were taking photos and discussing the restoration work. I offered to take their photo against the backdrop of the Golden Temple, and then we fell into conversation. The man introduced himself and his family. Mr. Singh and his wife Marianne were not American, he said, but Canadian.

"I was born in Vancouver just after my parents immigrated to Canada from India. We've come here to visit my grandparents and to see the Golden Temple," he explained. "And I'm from Alberta, originally," added Mrs. Singh. "I'm not a Sikh—at least not yet. I was raised Catholic. My parents immigrated to Canada from Poland and have a farm north of Calgary. My husband and I met in college at the University of British Columbia." She turned to the girl, "This is our daughter, June." After shaking hands, we went across the walkway together into the Golden Temple.

The interior was hot and muggy, but a feeling of devotion overcame my discomfort. A venerable-looking man with a long white beard was reading from the Adi Granth while an attendant waved a feather fan overhead. People moved very slowly in line, but our time inside was actually short, because the crowds kept us from staying too long. Outside, we decided to have lunch together. We found a restaurant not far away where we ate and talked.

Mr. Singh pointed to his short hair and neatly clipped beard. "As you can see, I do not practice all the traditions of my religion. I am proud of my religion, though, and particularly proud of the emphasis it puts on strength and endurance."

Workers regularly clean and restore the Golden Temple and its pond.

Mrs. Singh nodded. "Being in a mixed marriage, we've certainly needed strength at times, and we've found elements in both our religions that help us. I think, though, that we are typical of many Canadian couples, and our mixed marriage has been a rich experience for both of us."

"For our parents, too," Mr. Singh added, and both laughed and shook their heads knowingly. "My name means `lion,'" he continued. "I want to use my strength to be a strong individual, not just a representative of a single religious path. Where I live, there's a large Sikh community, and it would be easy to deal exclusively with people of my own religion and ethnic background. But I want to be more universal, while keeping my religion in my heart."

As we got up to leave and were saying our good-byes, Mr. Singh lifted his arm. "Though I cut my hair and beard, I always wear this." He pulled back the cuff of his long-sleeved shirt and proudly showed me his kara—his steel Sikh bracelet.

RELIGION BEYOND THE CLASSROOM

Jainism The great sites of Jainism are in India. Elaborate temples are located in several cities, particularly Calcutta, Ajmer, and Mumbai (Bombay). There are temple complexes on several mountains, the most famous of which are on Mount Shatrunjaya near Palitana and on Mount Abu, in western India. The place of Mahavira's death, at Pava, near the city of Patna in northeastern India, is a center of pilgrimage.

Sikhism The greatest site of Sikhism is its religious center, the Golden Temple, set in a large artificial pond in the city of Amritsar, in the Punjab region of northwestern India. Sikh temples can be found in many cities throughout the world and may be visited by non-Sikhs.

FOR FULLER UNDERSTANDING

1. Study present-day India, and mark on a map the places where Jains and Sikhs are to be found.
2. Construct arguments for and against the Jain acceptance of religiously inspired self-starvation.
3. Jainism preaches complete vegetarianism—eating no fish or animals. Is this reasonable for all people, or only for a small minority? Support your assertions with evidence.
4. Find out where Sikh communities exist in North America. If there is a Sikh community in your area, learn more about it, visit its temple, and give a report.

RELATED READINGS

Dundas, Paul. *The Jains.* London: Routledge, 1993. A fine modern introduction to Jainism.

Jacobi, Hermann, trans. *The Gaina Sutras. The Sacred Books of the East,* vols. 22 and 45. London: Oxford University Press, 1884. A classical selection of material from two Angas and other works.

Jaini, P. S. *The Jaina Path of Purification.* Berkeley: University of California Press, 1979. An explanation of Jain belief and practice by a prominent Jain scholar.

Koller, John. *The Indian Way.* New York: Macmillan, 1982. A philosophical discussion of Indian schools of thought, including Jainism.

McLeod, W. H. *Guru Nanak and the Sikh Religion.* New York: Oxford University Press, 1969.

———. *Textual Sources for the Study of Sikhism.* Chicago: University of Chicago Press, 1990. A good selection of Sikh scripture and more recent writing.

Pal, P. *The Peaceful Liberators: Jain Art from India.* London: Thames & Hudson and the Los Angeles County Museum of Art, 1994. A well-illustrated presentation of Jain art, particularly sculpture and manuscript illumination.

KEY TERMS

Adi Granth (*ah'-dee grahnth*): "Original collection"; the primary scripture of the Sikhs.

ajiva (*uh-jee'-va*): Matter without soul or life.

Digambara (*di-gam'-ba-ra*): "Clothed in sky"; a member of the Jain sect in which monks ideally do not wear clothing.

gurdwara (*gur-dwa'-rah*): A Sikh temple.

hylozoism: The belief that all physical matter has life and feeling.

Japji (*jahp'-jee*): A poem by Guru Nanak that begins the Adi Granth; the poem is recited daily by pious Sikhs.

jina (*jee'-na*): "Conquerer"; the Jain term for a perfected person who will not be reborn.

jiva (*jee'-va*): Spirit, soul, which enlivens matter.

puja (*poo'-ja*): Ritual in honor of a tirthankara or deity.

sallekhana (*sahl-lek-hah'-nuh*): "Holy death"; death by self-starvation, valued in Jainism as a noble end to a long life of virtue and detachment.

Shvetambara (*shvet-am'-ba-ra*): "Clothed in white"; a member of the Jain sect in which monks and nuns wear white clothing.

Sikh (*seek*): "Disciple"; a follower of the Sikh religion.

Sthanakavasi (*stun-uk-uh-vuh'-see*): "Building person"; a member of a Jain sect that rejects the use of statues and temples.

Terapanthi (*teh-ra-pahn'-tee*): A member of the newest Jain sect.

tirthankara (*tihr-tahn'-kah-ruh*): "Crossing maker"; in Jainism, one of the twenty-four ideal human beings of the past, Mahavira being the most recent.

CHAPTER **6**

Taoism and Confucianism

 FIRST ENCOUNTER

You have gone to Taipei to see one of the world's greatest collections of Chinese art at the National Palace Museum and to experience the color and complexity of Chinese culture. City life is indeed as colorful as you hoped it would be. Taipei is a jumble of sights and sounds. Half the city's population seems to be riding motorbikes. More than once you've seen a whole family—father in front, mother and child in the middle, grandmother at the rear—balanced on a single scooter.

Wandering alternately along bustling boulevards and back streets, you come upon a large Taoist temple, seeing first its walls and then behind them its tall, sloping tile roofs with ceramic dragons and other figures at the corners. You know you are approaching the entrance when you reach sidewalk stalls selling temple offerings: oranges, grapefruit, red candles, flowers, and long sticks of incense bunched in red-and-gold paper packets. You decide to buy some incense.

Inside the gates, you feel as if you have just walked into a fair. People cluster to talk and then break off, walking in random directions. Near you someone is taking a plate with fruit to a large table, one of several in the center of the big open courtyard. Standing next to the table, a man with a boat-shaped red hat blows on an animal horn. Around a great central brazier, smoke rises in clouds. The smell of incense is so over-powering you have to move away to breathe some fresh air.

At each side of the central courtyard are two lines of people who seem to be waiting for some sort of medical treatment. A woman in a blue smock stands at the front of each line and pats and rubs people on the shoulders and arms and back as they come forward. You stop to watch. A friendly gentle-man nearby, happy to practice his English with you, turns and explains, "These women are healing. They used to suffer themselves but were healed, and now they pass on the healing to others."

You notice a young couple putting a few sticks of incense in each of sev-eral braziers that front different altars. The gentleman, who is now walking along with you, explains, "They are going to get married and are seeking help from all the gods here in the temple."

You stop at a painting of a young woman in flowing robes. Below her are high ocean waves. Your new friend tells you that this is Ma-tsu, a Chinese girl who died young but became a goddess. She is especially powerful as a protector of fishermen. The gentleman calls her Heavenly Mother.

A group of elderly people, each carrying incense sticks and fruit, fol-lows a shirtless young man who appears to be in some kind of trance. He leads the group around to the rear of the temple. "They are here from the south to ask advice," the gentleman says. "The young man has special gifts. He can speak with the main god of this place."

You and your companion continue walking around together, talking about the images and placing your lighted incense sticks at several altars. In front of a small altar, a bent old woman throws what look like two large, wooden, crescent-shaped beans on the floor in front of her. "She is seeking help with her future," says your friend. Behind the scenes, along side corri-dors, you notice men stretched out asleep, some propped against bright red pillars. Near the exit, you say good-bye and offer thanks to your kind guide. He bows and shakes your hand at the same time.

As you exit through the large gates, you see someone burning silver paper money on the sidewalk. No one else seems to take notice. The vendor from whom you bought your incense smiles and nods, and you smile back as you turn to walk down another crowded, noisy street.

BASIC ELEMENTS OF TRADITIONAL CHINESE BELIEFS

Confucianism, Taoism*, and Buddhism have been collectively called the Three Doctrines, and together they have had a profound influence on Chinese culture and history. Buddhism, as we saw in chapter 4, was an import to China, with roots in Indian belief. Confucianism and Taoism, on the other hand, sprouted and grew up, side by side, in the soil of indigenous

Chinese belief. We thus begin our study of these two Chinese religious systems by considering some of the features of traditional Chinese belief and practice.

Early Chinese belief was a blend of several elements. Some of them, such as a belief in spirits, can be traced back more than three thousand years. The following elements provided a basis for later developments in Chinese religion and were especially important to the development of Confucianism and Taoism.

Spirits Early Chinese belief seems to have been polytheistic and animistic; that is, spirits were thought to be active in every aspect of nature and the human world. Good spirits brought health, wealth, long life, and fertility. Bad spirits caused accidents and disease. Disturbances of nature, such as droughts and earthquakes, were punishments from spirits for human failings, but harmony could be restored through rituals and sacrifice.

Tian During the Shang dynasty (c. 1500?–c. 1100 B.C.E.) the omnipotent power that was believed to rule the world was called Shang Di (Shang Ti) and was thought of as a personal god, capable of being contacted by diviners. Perhaps Shang Di was the memory of an ancestor, and the veneration of Shang Di was part of the ancient practice of honoring ancestors. In the Zhou (Chou) dynasty (c. 1100–256 B.C.E.), a new political regime—the Zhou kings—ignored the Shang belief and began explaining life in terms of a different conception, Tian (Tíen), which is usually translated as "Heaven." It appears that Tian was envisioned both as an impersonal divine force that controls events on earth and as a cosmic moral principle that determines right and wrong.

Veneration of ancestors The same cautious reverence that was shown to spirits was also naturally felt for ancestors. Ancestors at death became spirits who needed to be placated to ensure their positive influence on living family members. Veneration of ancestors provided the soil for the growth of Confucianism.

Seeing patterns in nature China's long and mighty rivers, high mountain chains, distinct seasons, and frequent floods, droughts, and earthquakes all influenced the Chinese view of the natural world. To survive, the Chinese people had to learn that while they could not often control nature they could learn to work with it when they understood

---

*As mentioned earlier, the pinyin spelling will precede the Wade-Giles spelling of major Chinese words throughout this book. (Pinyin pronunciation is generally similar to English usage, except that the pronunciation of c is *ts*, q is *ch*, and x is *sh*.) For the words *Taoism, Tao,* and *Tao Te Ching,* however, the Wade-Giles spellings have been used so widely in English publications that they have in effect become standard English and are thus retained here. (In the pinyin system, for those who would prefer to use it, these terms are Daoism, Dao, and Daodejing.)

At the Temple of Heaven, in Beijing, the emperor performed ceremonies to honor Tian ("Heaven").

its underlying patterns. Some of the patterns were quite easy to discern, such as the progression of the seasons, the paths of the sun and moon, and the cycle of birth and death. Others were more subtle, like the motion of waves and the ripple of mountain ranges, as well as the rhythm of the Tao (which we will discuss shortly) and the alternations of yang and yin. Taoism may be traced back to this concern for finding—and working within—natural patterns.

Yang and yin After about 1000 B.C.E. the Chinese commonly thought that the universe expressed itself in opposite but complementary principles: light and dark, day and night, hot and cold, sky and earth, summer and winter. The list was virtually infinite: male and female, right and left, front and back, up and down, out and in, sound and silence, birth and death, "strong" foods (meat and ginger) and "weak" foods (fish and rice), and "dynamic" (odd) numbers and "stable" (even) numbers. The names for the two complementary principles are **yang** and **yin.**

These principles are not the same as good and evil. Yang is not expected to win over the force of yin, or vice versa; rather, the ideal is a dynamic balance between the forces. In fact, the emblem of balance is the yin-yang circle, divided into what looks like two intertwined commas. One half is light, representing yang; the other is dark, representing yin. Inside each division is a small dot of the contrasting color that represents the seed of the opposite. The dot suggests that everything contains its opposite and will eventually become its opposite. Both forces are dynamic and in perfect balance as they change, just as day and night are in balance as they progress. We can think of yang and yin as pulsations or waves of energy, like a heartbeat or like breathing in and out.

Divination Divination (a system of methods for knowing more about the future) was an integral part of early Chinese tradition. The oldest technique involved the reading of lines in bones and tortoise shells. Later, an elaborate practice was developed that involves the **Yi Jing (I Ching,** The Book of Changes; discussed later in this chapter), an ancient book that interprets life through an analysis of hexagrams. A hexagram is a figure of six horizontal lines. There are two kinds of lines: divided (yin) and undivided (yang). A hexagram is made of two trigrams (figures consisting of three lines each) and is "constructed" by tossing sticks or coins and writing down the result, beginning with the bottom line. Thus sixty-four different hexagrams are possible. The hexagrams are thought to represent patterns that can develop in one's life, and the Yi Jing gives an interpretation of each hexagram. With the help of the Yi Jing, a person can interpret a hexagram as an aid in making decisions about the future.

We now turn to two great systems of Chinese religious thought, Taoism and Confucianism, which many consider to be complementary traditions. Taoism is often thought to emphasize the yin aspects of reality and Confucianism the yang. Together they form a unity of opposites. While we here treat them separately and one of them must be discussed before the other, separate treatment is something of a fiction. The two systems grew up together and actually, as they developed, helped generate each other. We must keep this in mind as we study them.

Yang and yin, symbolized by a circle of light and dark, represent the complementary but opposing forces of the universe that generate all forms of reality.

This hexagram for "contemplation" is made from two trigrams. The lower trigram means "earth," and the upper trigram means "wind."

TAOISM

Because it incorporated some of the previously mentioned elements and many others from traditional Chinese belief and practice, Taoism is really like a shopping cart filled with a variety of items: observations about nature, philosophical insights, guidelines for living, exercises for health, rituals of protection, and practices for attaining longevity and inner purity. We should note, however, that Taoism and Chinese folk religion are not exactly the same thing, although the terms are often used interchangeably, and in some cases the border between the two is not clear.

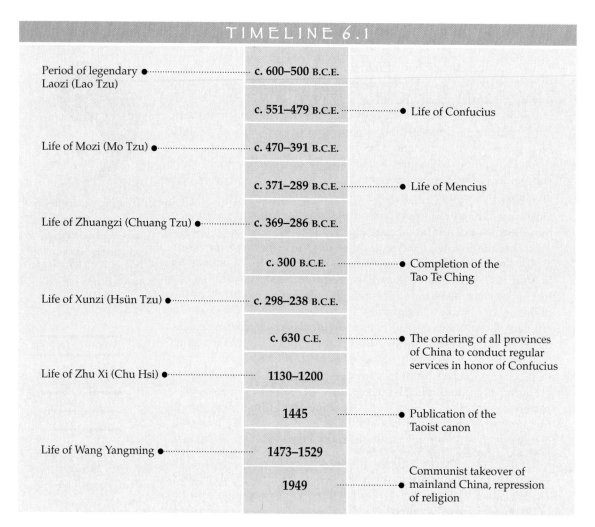

Period of legendary ●	c. 600–500 B.C.E.	
Laozi (Lao Tzu)		
	c. 551–479 B.C.E.	● Life of Confucius
Life of Mozi (Mo Tzu) ●	c. 470–391 B.C.E.	
	c. 371–289 B.C.E.	● Life of Mencius
Life of Zhuangzi (Chuang Tzu) ●	c. 369–286 B.C.E.	
	c. 300 B.C.E.	● Completion of the Tao Te Ching
Life of Xunzi (Hsün Tzu) ●	c. 298–238 B.C.E.	
	c. 630 C.E.	● The ordering of all provinces of China to conduct regular services in honor of Confucius
Life of Zhu Xi (Chu Hsi) ●	1130–1200	
	1445	● Publication of the Taoist canon
Life of Wang Yangming ●	1473–1529	
	1949	● Communist takeover of mainland China, repression of religion

Timeline of significant events in the history of Taoism and Confucianism.

Taoism as we know it today includes ideas and practices both from the early philosophical phase of Taoism and from the later development of Taoism as a religion. It is common to differentiate between the philosophical Taoism that we find in the Tao Te Ching (which we will discuss in the following section) of about 300 B.C.E. (Timeline 6.1) and the later, ritualized, Taoism that arose after 100 C.E. We will do that here for purposes of discussion, though without making too strong a distinction between the two. It is now thought that philosophical Taoism may have emerged, at least in part, from ritualistic origins; and later ritualistic Taoism is now commonly seen as an expression in ritual of the philosophical insights of Taoism. Thus a strong separation of the two is incorrect.

THE ORIGINS OF PHILOSOPHICAL TAOISM

Early Taoism, while possibly influenced by shamanism, created literature that was philosophically oriented. Later, an organized religion emerged. Here we look at some early thinkers and writings.

Laozi (Lao Tzu)

Taoism as a body of teachings is often traced back to a legendary figure named **Laozi (Lao Tzu),** whose name means "old master" or "old child." In the traditional story, Laozi's birth (c. 600 B.C.E.) resulted from a virginal conception. According to legend, the child was born old—hence the name "old child." Laozi became a state archivist, or librarian, in the royal city of Loyang for many years. (Legendary stories also relate how Confucius came to discuss philosophy with the old man.) Eventually tiring of his job, Laozi left his post and, carried by an ox, traveled to the far west of China. At the western border, Laozi was recognized as an esteemed scholar and prohibited from crossing until he had written down his teachings. The result was the Tao Te Ching, a short book of about five thousand Chinese characters. After Laozi was finished with the book, he left China, never to be seen again.

The Tao Te Ching

The **Tao Te Ching** is the great classic of Taoism, accepted by most Taoists as a central scripture, and one of the world's greatest books. Its title can be translated as "the classical book about the Way and its power." Sometimes the book is also called the Laozi (Lao Tzu), after its legendary author. Possibly because of its brevity and succinctness, it has had an enormous influence on Chinese culture.

The book seems to have taken several centuries to develop before attaining its current form, which probably did not occur until about 300 B.C.E. (We know that the material is very old, however, because two silk manuscripts, dated to about 100 B.C.E., were discovered in 1973.) In the eighty-one chapters of the Tao Te Ching we can recognize passages that seem to hint at early shamanistic elements, such as passages that seem to be about attaining invulnerability and reaching trance states (in chapters 10, 16, 50, 55). We also see philosophical passages that clearly grew up in opposition to Confucianism, for they use Confucianism's own terms to oppose its emphasis on education and legislated morality (in chapters 18–20, 38). Scholars continue to debate the age of the two traditions and their mutual influence.

The eighty-one short chapters of the Tao Te Ching are probably a compilation of the work of many people, rather than a single author. The book shows some repetition, has no clear order, and exhibits a deliberate lack of clarity. In form, each chapter is more poetry than prose.

What was the original purpose of the book? One theory holds that its overall purpose was political, that it was meant as a handbook for rulers; another sees it primarily as a religious guidebook, meant to lead adherents to spiritual insight; and still another views it as a practical guide for living in harmony with the universe. It is possible that the Tao Te Ching fulfilled all these purposes and that its passages can have several meanings at the same time. Part of the genius of the book is its brevity and use of paradox: its meaning depends on who is interpreting it.

Tradition says that Laozi, when leaving China, disappeared on the back of an ox.

Throughout the Tao Te Ching are references to the **Tao.** The book speaks of its nature and operation; it describes the manner in which people will live if they are in harmony with the Tao; and it gives suggestions for experiencing the Tao. The book also provides images to help describe all of these things. What, though, is "the Tao"?

The first chapter of the Tao Te Ching begins by saying, "The Tao that can be told is not the eternal Tao."[1] In other words, we cannot really put into words exactly what the Tao is—a fact that is ironic since the book itself uses words. Yet the book goes on to tell us that the Tao is "nameless;" that is, it is not any individual thing that has a name—such as a *door,* a *tree,* a *bird,* a *person.* The Tao cannot be named because it has no form. But the Tao *can* be experienced and followed by every individual thing that has a name. The Tao Te Ching says the Tao is the origin of everything and that all individual things are "manifestations" of the Tao.

Although the Tao is the origin of nature, it is not "God," because it does not have personality. It neither cares about human beings nor dislikes them—it only produces them, along with the rest of nature. Because the Tao makes nature move the way it does, it can be called the way or the rhythm of nature.

To experience the Tao, we must leave behind our desires for individual things, a concept that runs counter to everyday concerns—how much something costs, what time it is now, whether something is big or small. In fact, the Taoist way of seeing things is so odd to some people that at first it seems like trying to see in the dark, as the end of the first chapter of the Tao Te Ching describes:

> Darkness within darkness.
> The gate to all mystery.

The Taoist sees things differently. To illustrate, there is an intriguing example in the twentieth chapter of the Tao Te Ching: A Taoist is observing a group of people who are in a park, celebrating a holiday. They all seem happy as they climb up to the top of a terrace where a ceremony will occur. They appear to know what they are doing and where they are going. Not the Taoist, though, who feels "formless" and "like the ocean"—adrift.[2] The Taoist is troubled by the contrast. The others seem happy and sure of themselves, but the Taoist can only watch, and feels strangely like an outsider. Then the chapter ends with a sudden, extraordinary affirmation. The Taoist recognizes something intensely personal and difficult, but willingly accepts the sense of separateness from the others and from their conventional way of seeing things. The Taoist accepts, and concludes,

> I am different.
> I am nourished by the great mother.

Thus, the Tao cannot be "known" in the same way that we see a car or hear a sound, for example. It cannot be perceived directly but rather by intuition. Perhaps it is like the difference between hearing only musical sounds and recognizing a song.

The Tao Te Ching presents several powerful images wherein the Tao seems most active and visible. Contemplating them can help us experience the Tao, and by taking on some of the qualities of these images, we begin to live in harmony with the Tao that inhabits them. Several common images follow:

Water Water is gentle, ordinary, and lowly, but strong and necessary. It flows around every obstacle. Chapter eight praises it: "The highest good is like water."[3] It assists all things "and does not compete with them."[4]

Woman The female is sensitive, receptive, yet effective and powerful.

Child The child is full of energy, wonder, and naturalness.

Valley The valley is yin, and it is mystery.

Darkness Darkness can be safe, full of silence and possibility.

Zhuangzi (Chuang Tzu)

Taoism was enriched by the work of **Zhuangzi (Chuang Tzu),** who was active about 300 B.C.E. What we know of him comes from the writings he left behind. His personality seems playful, independent, and in love with the fantastic. The book of his writings, called the Zhuangzi (Chuang Tzu), is

The Seasons of Life

A famous story illustrates what it means to live in harmony with nature: Upon hearing of the death of Zhuangzi's wife, a friend, Huizi (Hui Tzu), goes to offer sympathy. Although he expects to find Zhuangzi crying and in ritual mourning, Huizi finds Zhuangzi instead singing and drumming on a bowl. Huizi is shocked—and says so. Responding in a thoughtful way, Zhuangzi says that at first his wife's death saddened him terribly, but then he reflected on the whole cycle of her existence. Before his wife was a human being, she was without shape or life, and her original self was a part of the formless substance of the universe. Then she became a human being. "Now there's been another change, and she's dead. It's just like the progression of the four seasons, spring, summer, fall, winter."[5] When winter comes, we do not mourn. That would be ungrateful. Similarly, a human being goes through seasons. Zhuangzi describes his wife as now being like someone asleep in a vast room. "If I were to

follow after her bawling and sobbing, it would show that I don't know anything about fate. So I stopped."[6]

In this story, note that Zhuangzi is singing and playing on a bowl. Rather than mourn passively, he does something to counteract his sorrow. His singing is a profound human response, quite believable. And Zhuangzi does not say that as a result of his insight he no longer feels sad. Rather, he says that as far as mourning is concerned, "I stopped." In other words, despite his feelings, he deliberately behaves in a way that seems more grateful to the universe and therefore more appropriate than mourning.

This tale suggests that to live in harmony with nature means to accept all its transformations. The great Tao produces both yang and yin, which alternate perpetually. The story says that yin and yang are our parents and we must obey them. If we cannot embrace the changes, we should at least observe them with an accepting heart.

---

composed of seven "inner chapters," which are thought to be by the author himself, and twenty-six "outer chapters," whose authorship is less certain. It is possible that the inner chapters were written before the Tao Te Ching itself was complete.

The Zhuangzi, unlike the poetry of the Tao Te Ching, contains many whimsical stories. It continues the themes of early Taoist thought, such as the need for harmony with nature, the movement of the Tao in all that happens, and the pleasure that we can gain from simplicity. It underscores the inevitability of change and the relativity of all human judgments. It also adds to Taoism an appreciation for humor—something that is quite rare in the scriptures of the world.

Perhaps the most famous of all the stories in the book tells of Zhuangzi's dream of being a butterfly. In his dream he was flying around and enjoying life, but he did not know that he was Zhuangzi. When he woke up he was struck by a question: Am I a person dreaming that I am a butterfly, or am I a butterfly dreaming that I am a person? This story hints that the boundary between reality and the imaginary is not really as clear as we might think.

Another story makes fun of people's judgments and the arbitrariness of their joy and anger. A trainer gave his monkeys three acorns in the morning and four at night. When the monkeys conveyed their dissatisfaction with receiving too few acorns in the morning, the trainer obliged, giving them four acorns in the morning and three at night. As a result, "the monkeys were all delighted."[7]

The Zhuangzi rejects every barrier, including that between the ordinary and the fantastic, between the normal and the paranormal, as hinted by the story of the butterfly dream. But the love of the marvelous really shows itself best in some stories that talk of the supernatural powers that a wise person can attain. The Zhuangzi tells of an exceptional person who could tell everything about one's past and future, another who could ride on the wind, and another who was invulnerable to heat or pain. The Zhuangzi thus elaborates the potential results of being one with the Tao.

THE BASIC TEACHINGS OF PHILOSOPHICAL TAOISM

The main teachings of the Tao Te Ching and the Zhuangzi can be summarized as follows:

Tao This is the name for whatever mysterious reality makes nature to be what it is and to act the way it does. The Chinese character for *Tao* is commonly translated as "way," but it has also been translated as "existence," "pattern," and "process." Primarily, the Tao is the way that nature expresses itself—the natural way. Human beings can unite themselves with the Tao in the way they live.

Wu wei: The ideal of effortlessness To have commandments would go against the nature of Taoism; but it does offer recommendations about how to live—recommendations that do not come from a divine voice but from nature, the model of balance and harmony. The recommendation most often mentioned in the Tao Te Ching is **wu wei**, which literally means "no action." Perhaps a better translation is "no strain" or "effortlessness." The ideal implies the avoidance of unnecessary action or action that is not spontaneous. If we look at nature, we notice that many things happen quietly, effortlessly: plants grow, birds and animals are born, and nature repairs itself after a storm. Nature works to accomplish only what is necessary, but no more. Consider the plain strength of the ordinary bird nest. Birds build homes according to their needs, and what they make is simple and beautiful; they don't require circular driveways, pillars, or marbled entryways. The ideal of "no strain" is the antithesis of all those sweat-loving mottoes such as "No pain, no gain" and "Onward and upward."

Simplicity Taoism urges its followers to eliminate whatever is unnecessary and artificial and to appreciate the simple and the apparently ordinary. In this regard, Taoists distrust formal education because of its inherent complexity and artificiality. (This was one of their major complaints against the Confucians, who put so much trust in education.) In a passage that has delighted students for centuries, the Tao Te Ching in the twentieth chapter states its opinion: "Give up learning, and put an end to your troubles."

The boatman who goes with the river's flow is an example of wu wei in practice.

Gentleness Because Taoists pursue the gentle way, they hate weapons and war. The wise person loves peace and restraint and avoids all unnecessary violence. The wise person "does not regard weapons as lovely things. For to think them lovely means to delight in them, and to delight in them means to delight in the slaughter of men."[8]

Relativity People see things from a limited point of view that is based on their own concerns. They see things in terms of divisions: I-you, good-bad, expensive-cheap, valuable-worthless, beautiful-ugly, and so forth. Taoists believe that it is necessary to attain a vision of things that goes beyond these apparent opposites.

TAOISM AND THE QUEST FOR LONGEVITY

Taoism has absorbed many practices that are thought to bring a person into union with the Tao. These practices help the person feel the flow of nature, attain spiritual purity, and live a long life.

To use the word *yoga* to describe Taoist exercises could be misleading, because *yoga* is a Sanskrit word. But this word is useful for conveying to nonspecialists the physical aspect of Taoism. The canon of Taoist literature includes recommendations for many types of arm and body movements, breathing regulation, diet, and massage.

One "yogic" practice is called *internal alchemy*. It aims at transforming and spiritualizing the life force (**qi, ch'i**) of the practitioner. Some later forms of internal alchemy teach exercises that move the life force from its origin at the base of the spine upward to the head. From there it circles back, via the heart, to its origin. This movement is accomplished through certain postures, muscular exercises, and practices of mental imagery. Some Taoists have held that these techniques of internal alchemy can create an entity—the "immortal embryo"—that can survive the death of the body.

Another technique of internal alchemy is the cultivation of a new way of breathing, the ideal being the gentle breathing of a sleeping child. To achieve this ideal, breathing can be adjusted to the beat of one's heart and slowed down by taking fewer and fewer breaths in relation to the number of heartbeats.

In ancient China, some people experimented with physical alchemy, hoping to create an elixir that could extend life and even make a person immortal. Because gold did not rust, individuals attempted to make gold either into a liquid that could be drunk or into a vessel from which an elixir could be drunk. Jade, pearl, mother-of-pearl, and compounds of mercury were also utilized. Some people undoubtedly died as a result of these experiments. When there seemed to be little success in this direction, the alchemical search became a metaphor for the development of the type of internal alchemy just described. In Chinese culture there remains, however, a great interest in pills, foods, and medicines that are believed to prolong life. Some of these (such as ginseng, garlic, and ginger) seem to have genuine medical benefits.

RELIGIOUS TAOISM

Early Taoism was not an "organized religion." Many of its earliest practitioners lived alone, as some still do today. The eremitical (reclusive) way of life dates back to ancient China, and some chapters of the Tao Te Ching may have emerged from it.

As time went on, however, the movement became more organized. At first, groups of like-minded individuals came together to pool their experience in the search for longevity and special powers. From these groups sprang organizations headed by charismatic individuals—something like religious orders. One group, called the Yellow Turbans, was led by a man named Zhang Jue (Chang Chüeh, who lived during the first century C.E.), but it eventually died out. Another, led by Zhang Daoling (Chang Tao-ling, c. 150 C.E.), developed an organization that allegedly helped Taoism survive into the present. The organization created a hierarchical structure, based on the son, grandson, and successors of the founder, and set up a system of parishes. Because the successors of Zhang Daoling carry the title "heavenly master," the sect is called the "way of the heavenly masters." It is most active in Taiwan, but has come to life again in mainland China, especially in the southeast.

Taoism also produced monasteries and orders of celibate monks. Although this form of Taoism was suppressed in the early days of the

Taoist monasticism, though once widespread on the mainland, never emerged in Taiwan. It is growing, however, on the mainland. This is an example of an old Taoist monastery in Xi'an.

Communist government, it has come to life again, and there are now several hundred active Taoist monasteries on the mainland. This monastic sect is known as the Complete Perfection order, which deliberately blends elements of Buddhism, Confucianism, and Taoism. Its prayer book was reprinted in 2000, and services that make use of the prayer book may be experienced in the morning and evening at the White Cloud Monastery (Baiyunguan) in Beijing.

One of the stimuli that influenced Taoism to take an organizational path was Buddhism, which entered China by the first century C.E. Buddhism was brought by a monastic clergy who imported and translated a large number of written works and set up monasteries and temples that had impressive rites. In order to survive, Taoism began to imitate these elements. By the fifth century C.E., religious Taoism had grown into an organization with significant political influence.

Taoism also imitated Buddhism in its production of a vast number of sacred books. The range of topics was wide: guidebooks on meditation, breathing exercises, and sexual yoga; stories of wonder-workers and of ecstatic excursions made to the stars; recipes for longevity and magical powers; manuals of alchemy; and descriptions of ritual. Collectively, these works form the Taoist canon—a collection of more than a thousand books, similar in authority to the multiple sutras of Buddhism. Publication of the canon took place in 1445, but supplements continued to be added later.

There is consensus among scholars that religious Taoism absorbed many of the elements of the Chinese worldview and brought together various strands and schools interested in philosophy, meditation, and immortality. Ultimately, Taoism embraced everything that is believed to bring physical health and spiritual elevation.

Religious Taoism also developed a pantheon. It honors Laozi and other great people of the past who are thought to be immortal and part of a heavenly court—based on the Chinese imperial bureaucracy—that is ruled by the mythic Jade Emperor.

Religious Taoism is still far stronger in Taiwan than in mainland China. This is partly due to the initial repression of all religion in mainland China by the Communist regime. It is partly due, too, to the fact that the sixty-third heavenly master moved to Taiwan after the Communist takeover of the mainland. Nonetheless, over the past two decades religious Taoism has revived on the mainland, resulting in much interchange between Taiwan and the mainland. A large statue of Laozi was erected in 1999 in southeastern China, and pilgrims from Taiwan routinely travel to the mainland to honor the goddess Ma-tsu at her island pilgrimage site.

Although Heavenly Master Taoism is the major form of ritualized village Taoism and has as many as fifty thousand priests active today, Complete Perfection (monastic) Taoism is growing, with an estimated twenty thousand priests. It also currently has the support of the mainland government.

Many Taoist clergy do ministerial work, attending to the needs of the public. Exorcists—called Red Heads because of their red hats or scarves—work to heal and restore harmony. Taoist priests—called Black Heads because of their black caps—are also able to perform exorcisms, but they are primarily involved in performing blessings, funerals, and other rites such as the Jiao (Chiao), an esoteric rite of cosmic renewal. The Jiao lasts at least three days and combines indoor ritual, closed to the laity, and a large public outdoor celebration, which includes puppet shows, performances, music, processions, banquets, and food booths. The Jiao, regularly performed on Taiwan, is beginning again to be performed on the mainland as well.

Taoist practices and beliefs are kept alive in part by the Chinese tendency to blend beliefs of several systems. It is common, for example, to find Taoist images in Chinese Buddhist temples. In the mind of most Chinese, there need be no argument. In ordinary practice, elements from folk religion, Taoism, Confucianism, and Buddhism are combined. They are mutually supportive—as members of all Three Doctrines have generally agreed.

TAOISM AND THE ARTS

It is possible to see Taoist influences in many Chinese art forms, although the extent of the influence is impossible to determine with precision. Paintings of Laozi riding on an ox are clear examples of Taoist influence, as are

Taoism influenced Chinese painting in its portrayal of nature, as seen here in a fourteenth-century painting of weathered pine trees.

This moongate expresses yin (the circle) within yang (the garden wall). Together, the two create harmony.

references to Zhuangzi in poetry, but beyond that it is perhaps more accurate to say that poetry and the arts share many of the same concerns of Taoist thought—just as they do of Chinese Buddhist and Confucian thought.

As we know, the immensity, flow, and mystery of nature are common themes in the Tao Te Ching, and some of the book's most important images are flowing water, the valley, and the uncarved block of stone. These themes and images are abundant in Chinese painting.

The Chinese Garden—Bridge to the Infinite

The philosopher Wing-Tsit Chan has written of the union of house and garden and of the semireligious role that a Chinese garden can play:

> Nature is never looked upon by the Chinese as chaotic or disorganized. Heaven and earth co-exist in harmony, and the four seasons run their course regularly. Thus the Confucians and the Taoists unite in reminding the Chinese that there is a universal principle pervading all things, whether in the realm of physical nature or in the sphere of human life. This universal principle expresses itself in two aspects, the Yin and the Yang, or the negative and the positive forces. In casting away regularity in favor of irregularity for his garden, the Chinese never violates the regularity of nature. Natural order is religiously preserved. . . . Over and above irregularity and informality, there reigns a higher order, the order of nature. . . .
>
> This harmony of man and nature in the flow of the great stream of rhythm makes the Chinese garden more than something merely secular. It is true that no one would look upon the Chinese garden as a religious structure. . . . But in spite of all this, we cannot deny the fact that the garden is regarded as an ideal place for meditation. Meditation may be purely moral, an effort at self-introspection. Intense and sincere meditation, however, inevitably leads to the absorption in the Infinite.[9]

In the house man is in the society of his fellow beings, but in the garden he is in the society of nature. Inside the house he is a Confucian with all his moral codes, conventions, and a prescribed way of life, whereas in the garden he is a Taoist, a romantic, primitivistic, carefree "new-born child." . . . But the garden is more than the supplement to the house. It fulfills a higher function of life, the function that only art can fulfill. . . . It is here that man becomes natural, spontaneous, and sincere.

—Wing-Tsit Chan[10]

In Chinese nature painting, perspective is important. Images drawn from nature are often presented either very close up or at a great distance. Paintings of a bird or a stalk of bamboo seen close-up help the viewer see the mysterious energy at work in these nonhuman forms of life: a bird perches in a certain way on a branch, and a stalk of bamboo emerges in its own special way into the sunshine. These paintings make us look more closely at the humbler elements of nature—cats, rabbits, birds, deer—and recognize that they, too, have their own interests and patterns of living and that our human patterns are only a small part of the much wider repertory of nature.

The great genius of Chinese nature painting is particularly evident in the paintings of landscapes seen at a distance. These paintings often depict hints of mountains far away and, beyond them, infinite space. Some portray a person gazing far into the distance, even beyond the painting itself. What we most notice in these works is the fascinating use of empty space. Some of the paintings are almost half empty, but they do not feel unfinished, as if something were missing. Ma Yuan (fl. c. 1190–1230) was a master of this effect. In his painting entitled *A Scholar and His Servant on a Terrace*, a gentleman looks out past pine branches into the distance; the upper left half of the painting, in the direction of the man's gaze, is entirely empty. In his painting *Walking on a Mountain Path in Spring*, a man strolls into an emptiness—virtually the entire right side of the painting—inhabited only by one small bird. The space of the paintings is the positive emptiness to which the Tao Te Ching draws our attention.

Chinese poetry frequently praises themes also found in the Tao Te Ching and the Zhuangzi: the joy of life in the countryside, away from the complications of the city; the change of seasons; simplicity; and harmony with nature. The poet who is often praised for his fine expression of Taoist ideals is Li Bo (Li Po), who lived during the Tang dynasty and died about 762 C.E.

Roofline of a Taoist temple in Taiwan.

Little is known about his life, but his death is famous. According to tradition, he died as the result of a poetic accident. Sitting drunk in a boat one night, Li Bo reached out to embrace the moon's reflection on the water, but he fell in and disappeared beneath the surface. One of his poems is about Zhuangzi's dream of being a butterfly. Another is about Li Bo's being so absorbed in nature that he did not notice dusk coming on; when he stood up at last, flower petals fell off his clothes. His poems are so highly regarded that they have been memorized and recited by the Chinese for centuries to express their own deepest feelings.

Chinese garden design is an art form that complements and completes Chinese architecture. The house is yang, the realm of the square and the straight line; the garden is yin, the realm of the circle and the curve. Inside is family harmony; outside is harmony with nature. One realm supports the other.

The importance of nature requires that traditional house design include and even incorporate the garden in its creation. At a minimum, if the family can afford it, the traditional Chinese house features one or several courtyards, with trees, plants, rocks, and possibly even a small pond. In the case of larger constructions, such as mansions and villas, the designs might also include natural or artificial lakes, waterfalls, streams, hills, and grottoes. Chinese garden design differs from that of common Western design. Instead of straight lines and symmetry, walkways meander, and bridges may zigzag. Gates, in imitation of the moon, may be round. And water moves in its natural manner—that is, not upward, as in a fountain, but only gently down.

TAOISM AND THE MODERN WORLD

Religious Taoism will continue for the foreseeable future in Taiwan and in overseas communities of people of Chinese background. And as the government of mainland China continues to relax its antireligious stance, we can expect Taoist ritual to fully revive there and take the same form that we see in Taiwan. There are many indications of such a trend, although the mainland government still strictly controls religion and often treats clergy primarily as custodians of historical sites that are important to tourism. In mainland China, Taoist ritual is now allowed on some traditionally Taoist mountain sites (such as Mount Tai), in urban Taoist temples, and in many villages. Taoist ritual seems to be reviving particularly in southeastern China because of its geographical proximity and many business contacts with Taiwan. Other Taoist practices live on as well: in his charming book *Road to Heaven: Encounters with Chinese Hermits*, Bill Porter recounts in photographs and writing his recent meetings with some Taoist hermits living in mainland China.

In world culture, Taoism as a philosophy continues to spread its influence. Or, to be more precise, we might say that popularized Taoist notions—conveyed in the many English translations (and mistranslations) of its classical books—are invoked by a spectrum of the world's citizens, from members of the environmental movement to producers of science-fiction movies. Fans—new and old—of the Star Wars films who can also quote from the Tao Te Ching may see Taoist thought in this line from the movies: "May the Force be with you." For many, "the Force" is yet another way of referring to the unnamed Tao.

Confucianism: Philosophy or Religion?

Should Confucianism be treated as a philosophy or as a religion? Those who wish to call it a philosophy point out its lack of interest in a God or gods and its lack of focus on any world beyond this one. And although they recognize that some Confucian religious ritual exists, they argue that ritual is not essential and has been largely abandoned in public life.

It is possible, though, that the particular standards some people use to downplay Confucianism as a religion have been taken unconsciously from Western notions of religion and then applied to all systems, Western and non-Western alike. Other people, applying different standards, point out

that Confucianism is more than simply a philosophy. If Theravada Buddhism can be treated as a religion, they argue, so too can Confucianism. Like Theravada Buddhism, Confucianism is a moral system that functions as a religion in providing meaning and order in people's lives. Confucianism can also be said to have its scriptures (the Confucian classics), as well as a mystical dimension that enables people to experience their unity with the universe through inner equilibrium and harmony with society. These facts invite us to treat Confucianism from a religious point of view, as we do in this book.

CONFUCIANISM

Taoism, as we just saw, seeks to bring human beings into union with the Tao, particularly through imitating certain qualities in nature—its harmony, lack of strain, and flowing mystery. The complex of ideals and beliefs that helped give shape to Laozi's teachings also influenced Confucius, the major teacher of the second great Chinese school of thought. Thus, it is not surprising to find Confucianism as concerned with the Tao as Taoism is; as one Confucian classic says, "He is the sage who naturally and easily embodies the right *way*."[11] This "way" is the cosmic Tao that permeates the entire universe—the Tao that we see in the everyday life of the noble person also "in its utmost reaches, . . . shines brightly through heaven and earth."[12]

THE TAO IN CONFUCIANISM

There is a difference, however, between Taoist and Confucian notions of the Tao. For Confucians, the Tao of primary interest is the Tao within the *human* world, manifested in "right" relationships and in a harmonious society. It was social harmony Confucius described when he listed his particular wishes: "[In] regard to the aged, to give them rest; in regard to friends, to show them sincerity; in regard to the young, to treat them tenderly."[13]

In Taoism, everything is a part of the rhythm of nature—the Tao. In Confucianism, however, although birds and clouds and trees are what they should be, human beings do not automatically become what they should be. The sweet, spontaneous infant can quickly turn into the selfish child. The Confucian would say that training in virtue is necessary in order to enable the Tao to manifest itself clearly in the human being.

The Master said, "At fifteen, I had my mind bent on learning. At thirty, I stood firm. At forty, I had no doubts. At fifty, I knew the decrees of Heaven. At sixty, my ear was an obedient organ for the reception of truth. At seventy, I could follow what my heart desired, without transgressing what was right."

—from the Confucian Analects[14]

The Doctrine of the Mean, an important Confucian text (discussed later in this chapter), recommends several types of training, including training in the cultivation of personal equilibrium and harmony. We should recall that Taoists avoid such "training," feeling that formal education has a potential for distorting one's originally pure state. Confucians, however, hold that the best training does not contaminate character but, by cultivating virtues, gives it definition and clarity.

THE LIFE OF CONFUCIUS

Confucius was born in 551 B.C.E., at a time when China was not a single empire but a group of small kingdoms. His name was Kong Qiu (K'ung Ch'iu). He later became known by the title of Kong Fuzi (K'ung Fu Tzu), meaning "Master Kong," but he is known in the West by the Latin version of his name, which was created and spread by European Catholic missionaries.

Tradition relates that Confucius was from a once-noble family that had fled at a time of political danger to the state of Lu (south of present-day Beijing). His father died when Confucius was a child, and despite their poverty, his mother raised him as an educated gentleman. He enjoyed chariot riding, archery, and playing the lute. In his teens, he became seriously interested in pursuing scholarship. He is said to have held a minor government post as tax collector, probably to support his mother and his

This image of Confucius, which presides over the Temple of Learning in Hanoi, expresses the ideal of human nobility.

studies. His mother died when he was in his late teens, and he entered into a state of mourning. When the period of mourning was over, he began his public life as a teacher.

Despite his eventual success as a teacher, Confucius had always wanted to play an influential part in government, and it is possible that for a time (c. 500–496 B.C.E.) he became a government minister. Confucius married and is believed to have had a son and a daughter. He lived for about fifteen years outside of his home state but eventually returned to Lu to take a somewhat ceremonial post as senior advisor. He died about 479 B.C.E.

LIVING ACCORDING TO CONFUCIAN VALUES

The period in which Confucius was born was a time of social turmoil because of the disintegration of the feudal system. Seeing families and individuals suffering from the social disorder, Confucius concluded that society would function properly only if virtues were taught and lived.

The ideals of Confucius were two: he wanted to produce "excellent" individuals who could be social leaders, and he wanted to create a harmonious society. He believed that these ideals were complementary: excellent individuals would keep society harmonious, and a harmonious society would nurture excellent individuals.

Confucius believed that each human being is capable of being good, refined, and even great; but he differed from the Taoists because he was convinced that a human being cannot achieve those qualities in isolation. In his view, a human being becomes a full person only through the contributions of other people and through fulfilling one's obligations to them. These other people include parents, teachers, friends, aunts and uncles, grandparents, ancestors, and even government ministers.

Confucius also believed that more than social interaction (which even animals have) is needed. For Confucius, that "more" is what makes *ordinary* human beings into *excellent* human beings, "superior persons." What constitutes that "more"? What are the sources of human excellence?

According to Confucius, excellence comes partly from the cultivation of an individual's virtues and intellect. Thus, education is essential. We should recognize, though, that for Confucius education meant more than knowledge; it also involved the development of skills in poetry, music, artistic appreciation, manners, and religious ritual. Confucius valued education because it transmitted the lessons of the past into the present. He believed that much of the wisdom required to produce excellent human beings is already expressed in the teachings of the great leaders of the past. Convinced that the past provides fine models for the present, Confucius thought that education could show the way to wise and happy living.

Moreover, Confucius saw civilization as a complicated and fragile creation; because of this, he believed that civilized human beings must be full

The Ideal Human Being

Confucianism is often thought of as a system for the regulation of social groups. Yet Confucianism is also a system for the transformation of the individual. Undergirding Confucianism is not just the ideal of an orderly society but also the ideal of a perfect human being.

This perfect person is the **junzi (chün tzu)**—a term usually translated as "superior person," although a better translation may be "noble person." The following quotations give a sense of the virtue that guides the junzi—the person who shows humanity at its best. In such a noble human being the Confucian ideals have been inculcated since childhood, and the virtues have been practiced for so long that the whole Confucian manner of relating to the world has become completely natural. The "noble person," as Alfred Bloom nicely describes, is

> distinguished by his faithfulness, diligence, and modesty. He neither overpowers with his knowledge, nor is afraid to admit error. He looks at all sides of any issue, is cautious and not concerned for personal recognition. Carrying himself with dignity, he appears imperturbable, resolute, and simple. He is exemplary in filial piety and generous with his kin. In his relations with others he looks for good points, though he is not uncritical. As a leader, he knows how to delegate

responsibility and when to pardon or promote. He is sensitive to the feelings and expressions of others.[15]

A subtle portrait of such a person has been given by George Kates, who describes the man who became his personal tutor in China. Kates writes about the civilized manner that manifested itself in all his tutor's actions, even in the cultivated way the tutor entered a room and sat in a chair. The tutor, Mr. Wang,

> had contrived to make his humdrum life, composed of a daily routine of monotonous teaching and domestic privation, symmetrical and reasonable indeed. . . . His eyes were kind; and his glance could at times glow when some new thought would catch and hold him. His side-face made you like him. . . . He . . . remained closed and therefore secure, if only because he knew so well by indirection how to turn aside effectively any indiscreet remark or lolloping conduct on the part of some new and immature pupil. . . . When Mr. Wang became assured that we thus had the same sense of decorum, barriers fell. Yet I remained more unwilling than ever now to press in upon his carefully guarded privacies; and upon this base we built a tranquil relation, partial it is true, but one that lasted us peaceably through many years. He became my formal teacher.[16]

of respect and care. Care must be given to the young, who will continue human life on earth, and to the elders, who teach and pass on the traditions. There should be reverence for everything valuable that has been brought from earlier generations.

Confucius's idea of a perfect society was one in which every member of society would be cared for and protected, and no one would feel abandoned. (Modern Western reality provides a possible contrast: in a city full of people an individual can feel utterly alone.) Confucius believed that a perfect society could come about if people played their social roles properly. His sense of social responsibility was codified in the five great relationships.

The Five Great Relationships

In Confucianism, relationships are just as real as any visible object. Human beings are not individuals but interwoven threads of relationships with many people. To a great extent, in Confucian thinking human beings *are* their relationships.

Today, as in past centuries, the Chinese devote themselves to study—here in a study hall of the former Confucian Imperial Academy in Beijing.

All relationships, however, are not equal. The level of a relationship may be determined by personal factors, such as friendship or family connection, or by more formal social factors, such as age or socioeconomic status. Confucianism recognizes this inequality and actually lists relationships according to a hierarchy, beginning with the most important:

1. *Father-son* Family is the foundation of society for Confucians, with the relationship between father and son at its core. (This relationship also represents all parent-child relationships.) The father must be responsible for the education and moral formation of the son, and the son must be respectful and obedient and must care for the father in his old age. Confucians have extended this ideal in ways that some people in more individualistic societies today might not appreciate; for example, the father must help in the selection of a career and a marriage partner for his son. Also, the relationship of obligation is mutual and does not end until the death of the father. The parent-child relationship is so fundamental that it can function as the model for similar relationships, such as that between employer and employee.

2. *Elder brother-younger brother* Languages such as English, French, and Spanish do not distinguish between an elder brother and a younger brother. But the Chinese, Korean, Vietnamese, and Japanese languages—which all have been strongly influenced by Confucian thought—have different words for the two kinds of brothers. In their cultures, the distinction is important. An elder brother must assume responsibility for raising the younger siblings, and the younger siblings must be compliant. The practicality of this arrangement becomes clear when we appreciate the possibility of an elderly father dying before

The hierarchy of human relationships determines the roles of spouses, parents, and offspring.

all his children have been raised. The paternal responsibility then would shift to the eldest son, who has a unique status in the family.

3. *Husband-wife* Each person in this relationship is responsible for the other's care. In Confucian thought, the relationship is hierarchical. The husband is an authoritative protector, and the wife is a protected homemaker and mother. The Confucian notion of marriage also implies much less romantic expectation than does the modern Western notion; in Confucian societies wives, over time, can even become quite motherly toward their husbands.

4. *Elder-younger* All older people have responsibility for younger people, because younger people need care, support, and character formation. This means, as well, that younger people must show respect to those older than themselves and be open to their advice.

   Important to this relationship is the role of the mentor, which is taken very seriously in Confucian cultures. The elder-younger relationship exists between a teacher and a student, between a boss and an employee, between older and younger workers, and between an expert and an apprentice. (The traditional characters for *teacher* in Chinese and Japanese literally mean "earlier-born." The term suggests the relationship of master-disciple and has overtones of strong mutual obligation.)

In some versions of the Five Great Relationships, the friend-friend relationship is listed fourth. The relationship between elder and younger and that between friend and friend are actually quite close, however. In friendship there is often a certain hierarchy: the friends may differ in rank, health, wealth, or knowledge. And if the difference is not evident at first, time will bring it about. In this relationship, the more powerful friend has a responsibility to assist the other friend, who is in need. The relationship between friends, especially male friends, has meant to China what romantic love has meant to post-Renaissance Europe and to the West in general. In Confucian culture, a friendship entails serious commitment, and a friendship made in youth is expected to last a lifetime.

5. *Ruler-subject* It might seem that this relationship should be listed first, and sometimes it is.[17] However, more often it appears last in the lists, reflecting the Confucian perspective on the role of the ruler: above all, a ruler must act like a father, assuming responsibility and care for the subjects who are like his children. Thus, the father-son relationship is primary in that it is the model for most other relationships. Confucianism holds that social order begins in a harmonious home and then extends outward—to town, province, and country. This last relationship, then, brings the list full circle, back to the smallest unit of society—the family.

The Five Great Relationships signify that each person must live up to his or her social role and social status. This has been called the *rectification of names*. I have only to consult my social role and title to know my duty. For example, a father must be a caring father, a manager must be a responsible manager, and a friend must be a good friend.

In Confucian societies, consequently, people see each other quite strongly in terms of their relationships and social roles, and because the family is the primary model for all groups, age determines position. We see interesting implications of the Five Great Relationships in Confucian countries today. For example, modern Japanese and Korean companies often act like large families, and management plays a fatherly role. Similarly, an employee's identity comes largely from his or her place in the company, and job titles are significant. The exchange of business cards—on which the person's title is prominently featured—is a careful ritual. Seniors have responsibility for juniors, and one's pay and role are largely based on seniority. Privacy and individual rights are not highly emphasized, and there is far more togetherness. Harmony is all-important.

The Confucian Virtues

Just as social harmony comes from the living out of the Five Great Relationships, so personal excellence comes from the manifestation of five virtues. Although they emphasize harmony between people, the Confucian virtues do not lead to antlike conformity. Some Confucian virtues, such as love of education and the arts, help individuals develop their unique talents. But the virtues most prized by Confucianism are indeed largely social virtues. Individual uniqueness, although valued by Confucianism, is expected to be muted, subtle, and considerate of others.

Ren (jen) The Chinese character for **ren (jen)** illustrates the word's meaning by blending two simpler pictographs—for "person" and "two." When we look at the Chinese ideogram for the virtue of ren, we understand its meaning: to think of the other. It is translated in many ways: "sympathy," "empathy," "benevolence," "humaneness," "kindness," "consideration," "thoughtfulness," and "human-heartedness." It does not mean to drop one's own self-interest or to be mindlessly generous. It simply means that one must be considerate of the other person through one's actions and words.

Some people, though, do not know how to be kind, or they have difficulty in certain situations being kind spontaneously. In Confucian thinking, to follow social conventions is an important way for such people to show ren. After all, underlying all worthy social conventions is considerateness. A motto that reflects the essence of ren is, "If you want to be kind, be polite."

Li This word is often translated as "propriety," which means "doing what is appropriate" or "doing what is proper to the situation." Originally, **li** referred to carrying out rites correctly. More generally, it means knowing and using the proper words and actions for social life. For each situation, there are appropriate words to say, proper ways to dress, and correct things to do. Sometimes propriety entails the control of one's own desires. The **Analects,** which record the sayings of Confucius, assert, "To subdue one's self and return to propriety, is perfect virtue."[18] In Western culture, which values what is different and individualistic, the notion of li may seem oppressive and suggest personal weakness. Confucianism, on the contrary, sees self-control as a sign of strength—and practicality. We all recognize that every social situation has its hidden structure. Chew gum at a job interview and you will not get the job; wear shorts to a funeral and you will probably cause hurt to the mourners. Li means good manners. It is putting ren into practice.

Shu The usual translation of **shu** is "reciprocity," but its essence addresses the question, How will my action affect the other person? It is putting ren into practice. It is also another version of the Golden Rule: Do unto others as you would have them do unto you. The Confucian version, interestingly, is stated in negative terms: "Do not do unto others what you would not wish done to yourself."[19] It is therefore often called the Silver Rule. Logically, we may argue that the two formulations mean the same thing. But there is something gentler

In this memorial to a great teacher, Confucian, Buddhist, and folk elements blend. Here, words carved on a pillar rest on the back of a tortoise, a symbol of long life and wisdom. ▶

This shop window displays writing brushes and, to the left, stones that are to be incised with owners' personal seals. Proper use of these materials exhibits cultivation.

about the Confucian version. The Golden Rule can be misleading. For example, I may love wine, but this does not mean that I should "do unto others" by serving wine to everyone who comes to my home. The Silver Rule helps me consider my actions from the other person's viewpoint.

Xiao (hsiao) The word **xiao (hsiao)** is usually translated as "filial piety" (devotion of a son or daughter to a parent). It also means the devotion that all members have to their entire family's welfare. It encompasses several notions: remembrance of ancestors, respect for parents and elders, and care for children in the family. Xiao means doing what would please one's parents and bring them respect, such as getting a good education. It means caring for siblings. It can also mean feeling a sense of responsibility to marry in order to continue the family line. Ideally, it means valuing the entire extended family—of past, present, and future.

Wen The term **wen** means "culture" and includes all the arts that are associated with civilization. Confucianism has a special love for poetry and literature, as well as a fondness for calligraphy, painting, and music. The educated person is expected not only to have a knowledge of these arts but to have an amateur skill in them as well. Wen can also entail the general notion of art appreciation, or connoisseurship. A connoisseur has a highly developed aesthetic sense and is able to know and appreciate beauty in its many forms.

Confucianism stresses other virtues, too—particularly loyalty, consensus, hard work, thrift, and emotional control. One virtue frequently mentioned is sincerity. The Confucian notion of sincerity, however, is not the same as the Western notion; in fact, it is virtually the opposite. The Western notion of sincerity concerns something that an individual says or does that is personal and "from the heart," free of social control. The Confucian notion of sincerity, however, means to choose naturally and automatically to do what is correct for society. It teaches that the individual should restrain selfish desires in order to fulfill job duties and social obligations properly. Through this kind of unselfish sincerity, the noble person becomes united with the force of the universe, which is already—according to Confucian thought—sincere. "Sincerity is the way of Heaven. . . . He who possesses sincerity is he who, without an effort, hits what is right. . . . He who attains to sincerity is he who chooses what is good, and firmly holds it fast."[20]

CONFUCIAN LITERATURE

Confucius considered himself primarily a transmitter of wisdom. Consequently, much of what is called the literature of Confucianism actually preceded him and was subsequently edited and added to by Confucian scholars. Thus, it is not always possible to separate with certainty the teachings of Confucius, his predecessors, and his followers.

Confucian literature, divided into the **Five Classics** and the **Four Books,** includes pre-Confucian works of poetry, history, and divination; the sayings of Confucius and his disciples; and the sayings of Mencius, a later Confucian teacher. The canon of Confucian literature has varied, but it became settled during the Song dynasty (960–1279 C.E.).

Confucian literature became the "core curriculum" for almost six hundred years in China, from 1313 until 1912. China was the first country in the world to have regular examinations to enter the civil service; but these were based on the Confucian books and their commentaries. Any male could take the examinations, and success in them often guaranteed a post with the government. The common practice in families who could afford it was to select at least one boy in the family to receive a Confucian education and to prepare him for the examinations. In aristocratic families, all boys were given a Confucian education.

Because the Confucian books were part of the established educational system, the sayings of Confucius and Mencius came to pervade Chinese culture. They have been quoted as authoritatively in China as the Bible is quoted in the West or the Qur'an is quoted in Muslim societies. They also have put a heavy stamp on the neighboring cultures of Korea, Japan, and Vietnam, as well as overseas Chinese communities everywhere. Although the literature is no longer an essential part of the educational curriculum in Asia, Confucian values continue to be taught both formally in school and less formally in the family and surrounding culture.

The Five Classics and the Four Books

The Five Classics

The Book of History (Shu Jing, Shu Ching) is an anthology of historical material about kings from earliest times up until the early Zhou (Chou) period (c. 1100–256 B.C.E.).

The Book of Poetry (Shi Jing, Shih Ching) is a collection of three hundred poems of the Zhou period, once believed to have been selected by Confucius.

The Book of Changes (Yi Jing, I Ching) speaks of the basic patterns of the universe. It is used to understand future events and to work with them properly. It is also an important Confucian document because it tells how the noble person will act in the face of life's events.

The Book of Rites (Li Ji, Li Chi) lists ancient ceremonies and their meaning. Another classical book, The Book of Music, is said to have once been a part of the classics but no longer exists separately. Part of it may perhaps survive, embedded in The Book of Rites.

The Spring and Autumn Annals (Chun Qiu, Ch'un Ch'iu) comprises historical records of the state of Lu, where Confucius lived, and ends with a later commentary.

The Four Books

The Analects (Lun Yu, Lun Yü) are the sayings of Confucius and his conversations with followers.

Tradition holds that his followers collected his sayings and wrote them down, but this work may better be attributed to the disciples of his followers. It is possible that some sayings are much later additions. The twenty sections of the Analects contain little stories and short sayings—sometimes only a sentence or two long—that often begin with the phrase "The Master said." They cover a wide variety of topics but often discuss the character of the noble person. Here are two typical sayings: "The Master said, a gentleman takes as much trouble to discover what is right as lesser men take to discover what will pay";[21] and "A gentleman covets the reputation of being slow in word but prompt in deed."[22]

The Great Learning (Da Xue, Ta Hsüeh) is a short discussion of the character and influence of the noble person. Its introductory section is traditionally attributed to Confucius and the remainder to a disciple, but this attribution is dubious. It contains many quotations from the Book of Poetry, which are given a moral interpretation. Although it was at one time within the Book of Rites, The Great Learning has been printed separately since the thirteenth century C.E. It was the very first book to be memorized and studied by Chinese students. This book

THE DEVELOPMENT OF CONFUCIANISM

Schools of Philosophy

The basic nature of human beings has been one of the great topics of discussion throughout the history of China. Is human nature good or bad or somewhere in between? This is not a theoretical question at all, because how one answers this question has crucial practical results. If human nature is basically good, it should be left on its own and trusted, and moral training, laws, and punishments are of little importance. If human nature is basically evil, human beings need strict moral education, stern laws, harsh punishments, and a strong ruler. A middle position is also possible: if human nature is neutral, human beings need education that is not coercive and a ruler who governs primarily through example.

Before Confucianism was adopted as official state policy during the Han dynasty (206 B.C.E.–220 C.E.), major schools of thought on this topic already had emerged, reflecting a full spectrum of opinion. The Confucian schools

For centuries, the Chinese have acquired personal copies of Confucian sayings by making rubbings of stone columns into which the sayings have been carved.

stresses that one must begin with self-cultivation and personal virtue if one wishes to produce order in the family and state. "From the Son of Heaven [the emperor] down to the mass of the people, all must consider the cultivation of the person the root of everything besides."[23]

The Doctrine of the Mean (Zhong Yong, Chung Yung), another work once part of the Book of Rites, speaks in praise of "the mean," or equilibrium. Its beginning—with its references to "heaven" and the "way"—hints at the mystical side of Confucianism. "What Heaven has conferred is called the nature [of humanity]; an accordance with this nature is called the path of duty; the regulation of this path is called instruction. The path may not be left for an instant."[24] A human being who follows "the way of Heaven" avoids extremes and remains in harmony. This balance unites the individual with the balance of the universe. "Let the states of equilibrium and harmony exist in perfection, and a happy order will prevail throughout heaven and earth, and all things will be nourished and flourish."[25]

The Mencius (Mengzi, Meng Tzu) is a long collection of the teachings of Mencius, a Confucian who lived several centuries after Confucius. Like the Analects, the sayings of the Mencius frequently begin with the phrase "Mencius said." Sometimes the tone seems quite gentle, such as in this saying: "Mencius said, The great man is he who does not lose his child's-heart."[26]

took a middle course between extremes, recognizing both the great abilities of human beings and the need for their formation.

The most liberal of the thinkers were the Taoists, who were so optimistic about the natural goodness of human beings that they rejected moral or intellectual education of any kind. The Tao Te Ching shows clearly the Taoist rejection of Confucian education.[27] The entire book presents instead a vision of people living simple lives in small villages, governing themselves with natural good sense.[28] Laws should be few, because if life is lived simply, order will arise spontaneously.

Closer to the center, but still to the left, was the teaching of Mencius, a Confucian who flourished about 300 B.C.E. (His name is the Latin version of his Chinese name—Mengzi, Meng Tzu.) The teachings of Mencius were ultimately so acceptable to many that his writings, named after him, became one of the Four Books.

Mencius did not merely repeat the thoughts and values of Confucius; it seems he was a bit more optimistic about human nature, perhaps because of his contact with Taoism. There are innumerable Taoist-sounding passages among his sayings. One of them, for example, uses an image loved by Taoists: "The people turn to a benevolent rule as water flows downward."[29]

Mencius was struck by the many virtues that could be found in ordinary people: mercy, kindness, conscience. "The feeling of commiseration belongs to all men; so does that of shame and dislike; and that of reverence and respect. . . ."[30] In human beings, he thought, there is an "innate goodness," and virtues exist in everyone, at least in seedling form. The sprouts need only the proper nurturing, which education can provide by helping naturally good tendencies in a child to grow properly and to flower. Education does not radically redirect human nature, but helps it to become what it already potentially is.

Mencius was aware of the ideal of universal love but thought that such an ideal was impossible and unwise. According to Mencius, in society there is a hierarchy of love and responsibility: we must love our families first, then our friends and neighbors, and then the rest of society; and to reject that structure would bring about social disorder. Education is valuable in making the natural order clear and in helping individuals live with it dutifully.

Confucius's position on human nature seems to have been fairly close to the center of the spectrum. We have already seen this in his view on the importance of education. Confucius was also optimistic; he believed that human beings respond to kindness and good example.

A darker view of human nature was held by Xunzi (Hsün Tzu), who was active about 250 B.C.E. He is also considered a Confucian, but because of his pessimism about human nature his thought did not ultimately receive the official support that was eventually given to Mencius. Mencius and Confucius tended to view Heaven, the power that rules the universe, as ultimately benevolent. But for Xunzi (as for the Taoists), the universe is totally uncaring; it works according to its own nature and patterns.

Xunzi viewed human nature and human beings as functioning in a similarly mechanistic way. Human beings will veer toward self-interest unless they are taught differently. Consequently, education is not social refinement of an already good person; instead, it must be a radical moral and social reformation of human tendencies that are primarily selfish and individualistic. Education must inculcate proper ceremonies, manners, laws, and customs, for these artificial rules help transcend selfish individual interest and make civilization possible. "All propriety and righteousness are the artificial production of the sages, and are not to be considered as growing out of the nature of man. It is just as when a potter makes a vessel from the clay . . . or when another workman cuts and hews a vessel out of wood. . . ."[31]

Holding a view of human nature similar to Xunzi's was the **Mohist** school, although its exact position is not easy to categorize. Mozi (Mo Tzu, c. 470–391 B.C.E.) was known as a self-disciplined, idealistic person who lived simply and worked actively against war and for the betterment of common people. He thought that without laws people are predatory, and that with laws, although there is order, society is inequitable. He held that social problems arise because people's love is graded and partial. The answer, he thought, is to practice equal love for everybody. "Who is the most wise? Heaven is the most wise. And so righteousness assuredly issues from Heaven. Then the gentlemen of the world who desire to do righteousness cannot but obey the will of Heaven. What is the will of Heaven that we should all obey? It is to love all men universally."[32]

The **Legalists,** who were influential from about 400 to 200 B.C.E., also had a view of human nature like Xunzi's and Mozi's but possibly even starker. For the Legalists, human beings are fundamentally selfish and lazy. They will lie, cheat, steal, and kill whenever it is in their interest. "Civilization" is just a very thin veneer, easily shattered; and without stern laws and punishments, people will destroy one another. According to the Legalists, the education of children should consist mainly of warning and punishment, and society must continue these sanctions with adults, because adults are really just children in disguise.

For several centuries after the time of Confucius, the various philosophical schools strove for influence. Legalism triumphed for a time in the third century B.C.E. The foundation of the Han dynasty, however, provided an opportunity to find a school of thought that could make the greatest contribution to social order. Around 135 B.C.E., a scholar proposed to the emperor that Confucianism would help unite the country. This scholar, Dong Zhongshu (Tung Chung-shu), also recommended that the emperor set up a Confucian school for the education of government officials. The emperor followed his advice, and Confucian thought began to gain recognition as an important political philosophy.

The Development of Confucianism as a Religious System

Confucianism grew in response to many needs and interests. In its first phase, as we have just seen, it was challenged by rival philosophies. Next, it was challenged by religion.

When Buddhism entered China in the first century C.E., it brought new ideas and practices (as we saw in chapter 4). One radical idea was a general deemphasis of worldly human concerns and duties, as exemplified by unmarried Buddhist monks. Monks did not have children to continue the family line, nor could they take care of their parents in old age—another deficiency that seemed counter to the virtue of filial piety (xiao). Buddhism appeared to focus on the topics of death, karma, nirvana, past lives, and future lives, and it built expensive temples and practiced elaborate ceremonies. It is important not to overstate the case, but to some Confucians these tendencies were socially deficient.

Of course, the aspects of Buddhism that some Confucians discounted were what made it so appealing to many people. Buddhism was colorful, imaginative, and ritualistic, and it gave people hope that there were supernatural

Laozi, the Buddha, and Confucius (and sometimes their followers) are frequently pictured together in harmony.

beings who could help them. Chinese who became monks and nuns also benefited because they had a fairly secure life and paid no taxes.

Partially in response to Buddhism's success, Confucianism entered a second phase and took on explicitly religious characteristics. The family of Confucius had made sacrifices to the spirit of Confucius at his tomb long before Buddhism entered China. Several Han emperors did likewise. But in succeeding centuries, Confucius received posthumous titles, and in the seventh century, every province of China was expected to establish a Confucian temple and to support regular ceremonies. Statues of Confucius were set up, along with pictures of his disciples; and elaborate ceremonies, with sacrifice, music, and dance, were conducted in spring and autumn. Authorities began to place Confucianism on a par with Buddhism and Taoism; and the three traditions were viewed as a religious triad. The three systems (which, many agreed, complemented each other) were compared to the sun, the moon, and the planets, each one a necessary part of a complete religious cosmos. Pictures and statues of the three founders—Laozi, Confucius, and the Buddha—began to appear, with the three figures side-by-side in friendly poses. This practice continues today.

In its third phase, after 1000 C.E., Confucianism was enriched by scholarship and philosophy. The movement, called Neo-Confucianism, clarified texts and codified the elements of Confucian thought. It attempted to determine which Confucian schools taught doctrine that was consistent with the views of Confucius. It also sought to provide a metaphysical vision of all reality for Confucianism, akin to that found in Taoism and Buddhism.

The greatest exponent of Neo-Confucianism was Zhu Xi (Chu Hsi, 1130–1200 C.E.), a scholar who gave Confucianism its mature shape as a complete system of thought and action. In judging the teachings of Confucian thinkers after Confucius, Zhu Xi concluded that Mencius belonged among the orthodox but that Xunzi did not because of his notion that human nature was inherently bad. The prestige of Zhu Xi's commentaries on the Four Books helped the Four Books, along with his commentaries, become the basis for the civil service examinations.

Zhu Xi attempted to formulate a general vision of reality by using notions found in the teachings of Confucius and Mencius. He rejected the Mahayana Buddhist notion of ultimate emptiness and instead adopted a view of reality that was closer to the Taoist notion of the constant generation of reality. His view, though not scientific in the modern sense, was positivistic and stressed the natural order of things. Trying to discover the source of change, Zhu Xi spoke of two fundamental principles: qi (ch'i), "vital force" or "energy"; and li, "law" or "rational principle." Although they are distinct, the two principles work together. Li impels qi to generate the permutations of yang and yin. Zhu Xi called li the Great Ultimate (Tai Ji, T'ai Chi), because he saw the one principle of li working everywhere in the world. In human beings, it is "the mind," which is one with the mind of the universe. "Fundamentally there is only one Great Ultimate, yet each of the myriad things has been endowed with it and each in itself possesses the Great Ultimate in its entirety. This is similar to the fact that there is only one moon in the sky but when its light is scattered upon rivers and lakes, it can be seen everywhere."[33]

Another Neo-Confucian of importance was Wang Yangming (1473–1529). Unlike Zhu Xi, he did not stress the need to look outward. Rather, he believed that truth could be discovered through intuition (whether this was mystical insight or conscience or something different is not entirely clear). Wang Yangming compared the mind to a mirror, which had the native ability to reflect but needed polishing and cleaning to keep it working properly. He saw a close connection between knowledge and virtue, holding that innate insight gives a person not only an understanding of fact but also an appreciation for virtue. Those who know about goodness, he said, will practice it.

An attempt to purify Confucian ceremony came during the Ming dynasty (1368–1644), when an imperial command dictated a simplification of Confucian temples and their ritual. Statues of Confucius and his disciples were replaced by tablets inscribed with their names and titles. Ritual became simpler in order to conform to what were considered ancient patterns, and the Confucian temples took on an archaic spareness that seemed truer to the spirit of Confucius. This spareness is still quite moving today.

If we look back at the 2,500-year history of Confucianism, we can see general patterns and turning points. In the first 500 years after Confucius, Confucianism began to emerge as an officially endorsed philosophy. Over the next 1,000 years, state temples and ritual were organized. In the succeeding millennium, Confucianism absorbed philosophical elements from Taoism and Buddhism but moved toward greater simplicity in its ceremonial life. And in the twentieth century, formal Confucian education and ritual lost most of its governmental support. However, as we shall see later, many of its values live on in family, corporate, and government life.

CONFUCIANISM AND THE ARTS

Confucianism has been a great patron of the Chinese arts. The ideal human being, the junzi, does not need to be rich, but he or she must be a well-rounded lover of history, art, poetry, and music. Because of Confucianism's high esteem for education and books, the noble person must cultivate in particular all aspects of writing—the premier art form of Confucianism.

Confucianism so values the written word that the greatest influence of Confucianism on the arts has been in calligraphy. In the West, calligraphy is not valued in the same way that it is in China and the countries China has influenced. The importance of artistic writing is easily apparent to any visitor of a country in east Asia.

(Calligraphy can appear in unexpected places. I remember a bus driver in China who was deeply pleased with a purchase he had made. We had

Ancestors' names are frequently inscribed on small tablets that are displayed on an altar, in keeping with Confucian values. This memorial is in Korea, a country still very much under the influence of Confucianism.

stopped for lunch in a small, dusty town in western China. After lunch, as the passengers climbed back on board, the bus driver held a rolled-up scroll he had just bought at a tiny shop. With just the faintest urging, he unrolled the scroll carefully. The Chinese passengers were hot, tired, and ready to sleep, but everyone at the front of the bus strained to look over each other's shoulders at the scroll. The Chinese characters were solid but lively, with fine balance between the heavy black ink of the characters and the white paper. On the narrow scroll the vertical Chinese message was this: "To see the view, climb higher." I could easily envision the same scene playing out a thousand years earlier, only in an ox cart.)

The tendency to place Chinese calligraphy on the walls of homes, restaurants, and hotels is still strong wherever Chinese culture has penetrated, both in and out of China. It is sometimes even done where ordinary laypeople (such as in Korea) can no longer read many of the Chinese ideograms.

Calligraphy came to be considered one of the greatest of the Chinese arts because it combines so many elements of value. A work of calligraphy can show physical beauty, as well as intellectual and moral beauty. It manifests the cultivated nature of the person who wrote it, shows respect for poets and thinkers of the past, and inspires the viewer to scholarship and virtue.

Confucian influence might also be seen in the common practice of adding written material to a painting. We should note that the same kind of brush is used for both painting and calligraphy. Consequently, the artist might include a poem at the side of the painting, and a later owner might even add an appropriate poem to indicate his or her appreciation for the painting.

Just as Taoism has considerably influenced Chinese art—particularly in nature painting—so too has Confucianism, most notably in its portraiture of ancestors. It was common in the past for Chinese families to commission paintings of parents and immediate ancestors and to keep these in the home to represent the presence of the deceased person. (Nowadays a photo is used, and sometimes a wooden plaque with the ancestor's name is a suitable substitute.) Other genres of painting that were influenced by Confucianism were the court paintings of honored officials, which show both artistic skill and psychological insight. Paintings that under Taoist influence might have shown only mountains, mists, and streams may depict central groups of people performing activities in houses and pavilions, the ideal being a harmonious blending of the three essential elements—Heaven, earth, and humanity.

Not only did Confucianism influence the arts; it seems the sensual nature of the arts may have softened the sharp edges of Confucianism. One cannot love the arts and hate the physical world, because the arts celebrate its beauty. But Confucianism has recognized that all artworks have a moral aspect. At the lowest level, the morality of an artwork can be judged in a way that depends on the obvious. A simple person, for example, may think that an art object is automatically moral if it has a proverb written on it. At a more sophisticated level, however, we recognize that an artwork conveys morality by its quality. Thus we say that there is "bad art" and "good art." It is interesting that we use the terms *bad* and *good* to describe both art and human behavior. Confucians would say that this usage is quite correct and that good art makes good people.

PERSONAL EXPERIENCE: AT A CONFUCIAN TEMPLE

In my visits to Confucian temples in Korea and Taiwan, I was struck by their austere beauty. They are quite different from many Taoist and Buddhist temples, which have fantastic numbers of statues, throngs of visitors, and enough incense rising from huge braziers to turn the air blue-gray.

In Confucian temples, I would find peaceful courtyards with ponds and old trees enclosed by red-pillared colonnades. As I entered the temples, the noise of the street would give way to deep silence. Few other people would be there. Walking along the covered porches, I could peer in windows and see the old-fashioned musical instruments still used in Confucian ceremonies. In other windows I would see yellowing photos of celebrations held in years past, in which people in robes and antique hats stood in rows, some

The entrance to Beijing's Confucian temple Kongmiao. ▶

holding long feathers and others playing musical instruments. After going through smaller courtyards and walkways, at last I would arrive at the main temple building, far in the back. Inside, on top of tall dark tables would be wooden tablets inscribed with the names of Confucius (in the very center) and his disciples. A few sticks of incense would be burning in a single small incense holder. The deliberate simplicity, along with the absence of even one statue, provoked much thought about the values of that teacher who had lived more than two thousand years ago.

I was eager, on my first trip to China, to see in Beijing the Confucian Temple (Kongmiao) and former Confucian Imperial Academy (Guozijian). Maps showed them close to the Vajrayana Buddhist Lama Temple in an old section of the city. I was told that the Confucian Temple was now officially a museum, and no services were held there anymore. The current government on the mainland, I learned, allows Confucian ceremonies only at the place of Confucius's birth. The Confucian temples and ancestral temples that survive have been given new uses as storehouses, community centers, and small factories. But I was hopeful.

I took a taxi, choosing one among the many that were waiting for foreign customers at the entrance to my hotel. The Confucian Temple stood behind walls on a narrow street in an old-fashioned residential area of one-story houses. There were lovely trees and no traffic. Beyond the entrance, the garden looked overgrown.[34] Just inside the garden stood tall, wide columns of stone—carved with Chinese characters—that had once been white but were now gray-green. These columns were among the many tablets in the complex that contained the names of Confucian scholars, the texts of Confucian classics, and records of Chinese history. They had been placed there long ago as a public service for anyone who wished to read and copy them. Some of the columns had obvious cracks through the middle. Although once broken, they appeared to have been repaired and set up again.

I walked up the stairs to the wide uneven stone platform in front of a main building. I tried to look inside, but the old wooden doors were locked with a chain and rusty padlock. I couldn't even find a crack wide enough to look through. On the platform in front of the building a net for badminton or volleyball had been set up some time ago, its posts leaning crookedly.

The building that housed the old Confucian Imperial Academy was nearby, and I made my way there, wondering about its state of repair. Had it survived? Would it even be open? As I came close, I could hear the sound of electric fans, but otherwise there was complete silence. Doors were open, and a large room was illuminated by dim, bluish fluorescent lights. It was absolutely packed full of students—all studying at long desks. Almost every seat was taken, but the room was so quiet that I wondered if the students were taking an examination. I ascertained that they were not. Not a person moved or coughed, and no one came in or out. Not wanting to disturb the students, I retraced my steps back to the temple grounds. It was clear that Confucianism as temple ritual here had been abandoned, but

Confucianism as a value system and a way of life in many ways seemed quite alive.

I walked again around the marble tablets. While I had been in the academy, a student had entered the temple grounds. He stood on a short stepladder next to one of the columns. Placing a large piece of white paper on the carved Chinese characters, he began to do a rubbing. He was so intent in making his copy of the characters that he did not see or hear me as I quietly went out the gate.

CONFUCIANISM AND THE MODERN WORLD

The modern world has been hard on government-sponsored Confucianism. In 1911 the Qing (Ch'ing) dynasty collapsed and with it also collapsed the public system of Confucian ceremony and education. When faced with the new scientific knowledge introduced to China from Europe, Confucianism as a total educational curriculum seemed desperately inadequate. As young Chinese sought a whole new form of education, traditional Confucianism could not compete. Confucian temple ritual also came to an end in China, having always relied on support from the state.

Early attacks on Confucianism were made by the New Culture movement, beginning in 1916. While some members wished to hold on to basic Confucian ethics, others thought that all vestiges of Confucianism should be destroyed. Some of the leaders of the movement had studied in the West. Among these was Hu Shih (1891–1962), who studied at Columbia University under the philosopher John Dewey (1859–1952) and returned to China to teach and write. The movement looked to pragmatic thinkers, such as William James (1842–1910), John Dewey, and Bertrand Russell (1872–1970), and criticized Confucianism on many counts. Confucianism was accused of enslaving women to their fathers and husbands, of subjugating sons to tyrannical fathers, and of keeping alive a culture and literature that only looked to the past.

The Communist takeover of mainland China in 1949 further weakened Confucianism as a belief system. Continuing the earlier anti-Confucian themes, Communism has been highly critical of Confucianism for several reasons. First, Confucianism preaches elitism rather than egalitarianism. Although Confucianism maintains that anyone can become a junzi (noble person) through training, in fact Confucian education has often been limited to only those whose parents could afford it. Communism, in contrast, proposed to educate all equally.

Second, the Communists accused Confucianism of valuing males over females, reserving education and power for males, and providing no official power to wives and daughters. With only one exception in all of Chinese history (the empress Wu, who ruled from 683 to 705 C.E.), the official role of emperor has been confined to males. Women's roles have been traditionally concerned with childbearing, and women have derived much of their social identity from men. Communism has preached (at least in theory) that Confucianism's sexist tendencies have created oppression and a loss of talent for society.

Third, the Communists criticized Confucianism for focusing on the old rather than the new and on the humanities rather than the sciences. To Communism this focus on the past reflects a backward vision, like driving a car by looking through the rearview mirror.

Many Communists thought that only when Confucianism was destroyed could China move forward. On the mainland, these views led to either the destruction of Confucian temples or their use for other purposes, and to the development of a Western-based curriculum for education and government jobs. Mao Zedong (Mao Tse–Tung), the leader of the Communist Revolution, hated the rigidity and old-fashioned thinking that he saw in Confucianism. Mao's anti-Confucian ideals were particularly destructive during the Cultural Revolution (1966–1976), when students reviled their teachers and destroyed much that was considered to be antiquated. On the other hand, Mao also cultivated the image of himself as a benevolent Confucian ruler and father figure; he was a poet and writer; and many of the virtues he encouraged in his people are reminiscent of Confucian ideals—particularly duty, sacrifice, and self-cultivation.

The system of Confucianism has fared better in neighboring Asian countries and regions, such as South Korea and the island of Taiwan. There Confucian temples and ritual are maintained, although in diminished form, by the government or private families. But in every country influenced by China, such as Japan and Singapore, we find the Confucian system of virtues and behaviors still very much alive. Although these countries have adopted Western science into their curriculums, their cultures maintain an ethic that is Confucian. They highly value the extended family, education, personal discipline, and public order.

Ironically, according to many scholars, Confucian virtues may have helped lead many Confucian countries to modern economic development. This fact has not been lost on the government of mainland China, which has begun to soften its earlier anti-Confucian stance. What will probably become more common there is a growing public respect for Confucius, a restoration of some Confucian materials to the curriculum, and the teaching of Confucian virtues in modified form—all blended with a Western interest in science, mathematics, and computer technology.

The leaders of Confucian countries are horrified by what they have seen of the chaotic individualism and violence in some Western countries. They see the Confucian ethic as an antidote to social ills and therefore continue to view education as character building, not merely as intellectual formation. Singapore has already developed a national educational curriculum that explicitly teaches Confucian virtues, and this may become a model elsewhere. Confucian virtues continue to be promulgated in schools, companies, and government work in many East Asian countries. It is also intriguing to see how much Confucian instruction appears on television in East Asian countries. There, behavior expressing the values of harmony, loyalty, and filial piety is visible both in historical dramas and in many stories of modern life. Television instruction in Confucian virtues may become a deliberate technique used by some Asian governments to attain their goals.

Confucian teaching is, in practice, being modified for modern life. The lesser status of the female is being abandoned widely as women are beginning to demand equal opportunity. Confucian societies everywhere now offer curriculums that blend science and a focus on the future with studies of the past. Greater latitude is gradually being given to individual needs and personalities. With these modifications, Confucianism is gaining a renewed attractiveness.

Rather than dying, Confucianism is possibly beginning a new stage in its long life. The core of Confucianism is unassailable. It is primarily ethical, because it focuses on correct behavior. Yet it is more, because it rests on a vision of human unity and a connection with the harmony of the universe.

RELIGION BEYOND THE CLASSROOM

For a view of popular Taoist religion the temples of Hong Kong, Singapore, and Taiwan offer a mixture of Taoist and folk elements. In mainland China, two Taoist temples in Beijing are open to the public: White Cloud Temple (Baiyunguan) and the temple of the god of Taishan (Dongyuemiao). Regular Taoist services are offered at the White Cloud Temple.

A location that has inspired much Chinese landscape painting is Guilin (Kwei-lin). A boat trip on the River Li is a good way to experience this surreal landscape of high mountains. Places of Taoist interest in the vicinity are the White Cloud Temple and Reed Pipe Cave (Ludiyan). Chinese gardens of special beauty are located in southern China in Hangzhou, Suzhou, and Shanghai.

For a view of Confucianism, visitors can go to the Confucian Temple (Kongmiao) and former Confucian Imperial Academy (Guozijian) in Beijing. Traditional Confucian ritual has been restored at the Temple of Confucius in the town of Qufu, which also contains the tomb of Confucius and the Confucian Family Mansion.

Although Confucianism as a value system is alive throughout much of East Asia, traditional Confucian ritual and training are most visible in South Korea and Taiwan. Rituals are common in September and October, in honor of Confucius's birthday (often marked on or near September 28). Some places also have festivities in springtime, particularly at the spring equinox.

Traditional Confucianism is still influential in South Korea. In Seoul, one should visit the impressive Chongmyo Royal Ancestors' Shrine. A Confucian ceremony (called Cherye) occurs there each year on the first Sunday of May. Songgyun'gwan University contains a Confucian shrine, and Confucian music and ritual are performed there in spring and autumn.

Beyond Seoul, Confucian academies are located throughout South Korea, although nowadays they are used for a variety of educational purposes. In Andong there is the Tosan Sowon, and near Angang is the Oksan Sowon. In Kangnung, visitors can visit the Hyangkyo and Taesungjon Confucian Academy and Shrine at Myungnung School. Six miles from Kangnung is the Ojuk-hon Confucian Shrine, with a festival on October 26. Chunghak-dong, in the hills near Chinju, is a Confucian village where the Confucian classics are taught in traditional style. Some families also maintain private Confucian shrines for the veneration of Confucius and their ancestors.

In Taiwan, sizable Confucian temples can be found in major urban areas. The Confucian temples in Taipei and Tainan are especially beautiful. Ceremonies are conducted at most Confucian temples early on the morning of Confucius's birthday (September 28), which is called Teacher's Day.

FOR FULLER UNDERSTANDING

1. Based on what you have read, describe the personality of Confucius. Can you think of any recent historical figure who displays a similar character and values? Compare the two.
2. Describe how Taoism and Confucianism complement each other.
3. List the differences that you see between the Confucian junzi (noble person) and the Theravada Buddhist monk.
4. Do you see any contradiction between the Taoist ideal of gracefully accepting death, suggested by the Tao Te Ching, and the Taoist search for long life and immortality? Can the two goals be reconciled? Explain your answer.
5. Do some research on contemporary life in Korea and Japan. Look particularly for evidence of Confucian virtues that seem to contribute to their economic growth.
6. Consider your own "home culture." If Confucianism became an influence there, how would its principles or rules be expressed in everyday language and activity?
7. Investigate whether your area has a Chinese garden, and visit it if you can. Find books in the library with photographs of Chinese gardens. What common Taoist themes and images do you find there?

RELATED READINGS

Confucius. *The Analects.* Trans. D. C. Lau. New York: Penguin, 1979. A clear translation of the sayings of Confucius.

Kates, George. *The Years That Were Fat.* Cambridge, MA: MIT Press, 1960. A beautifully written appreciation of the elements of traditional Chinese life.

Kidd, David. *Peking Story.* New York: Clarkson Potter, 1988. A description by a unique individual of life in an aristocratic family at the time of the Communist Revolution. Excerpts from this book originally appeared as sketches in the *New Yorker.*

Kohn, Livia. *Daoism and Chinese Culture.* Cambridge, MA: Three Pines Press, 2001. A summary of the history and essentials of the religion, with attention to new interpretations that have emerged in the past thirty years.

———. *The Taoist Experience: An Anthology.* Albany: State University of New York, 1993. A wide selection from about fifty texts of the Taoist canon and other Taoist sources.

Liu I-Ming. *Awakening to the Tao.* Translated by Thomas Cleary. Boston: Shambhala, 1988. Meditations on seeing and living the Tao, written in 1816 by a Taoist sage at the age of 80.

Lopez, Donald, Jr., ed. *Religions of China in Practice.* Princeton, NJ: Princeton University Press, 1996. An anthology of unusual selections from Chinese religions, including poetry, folk tales, chants, and visions.

Nosco, Peter, ed. *Confucianism and Tokugawa Culture.* Honolulu: University of Hawaii Press, 1996. Essays on the influence of Confucianism in Japan from the seventeenth to the nineteenth centuries.

Porter, Bill. *Road to Heaven: Encounters with Chinese Hermits.* San Francisco: Mercury House, 1993. The journal of a search for and conversations with Taoist and Buddhist hermits in modern China.

Saso, Michael. *Taoist Master Chuang.* Rev. ed. Cambridge, MA: Sacred Mountain Press, 2000. The author presents Taoist history and ritual, drawing on the teachings of his master and his own training as a Taoist priest in Taiwan.

Schipper, Kristofer. *The Taoist Body.* Berkeley: University of California Press, 1993. A detailed description of Taoist religious thought and practice by a European scholar who was ordained a Taoist priest.

KEY TERMS

Analects: The book of the sayings of Confucius.

Five Classics: The classical literature of the time preceding Confucius, including poetry, history, and divination.

Four Books: The major Confucian books, which include the sayings of Confucius and Mencius.

junzi (chün-tzu; *joon'-dzuh*): "Noble person," the refined human ideal of Confucianism.

Laozi (Lao Tzu; *lau'-dzuh*): The legendary founder of Taoism.

Legalists: The strictest of the Chinese philosophical schools, which advocated strong laws and punishments.

li (*lee*): Appropriate action, ritual, propriety, etiquette.

Mohists: A Chinese school of philosophy that taught universal love.

qi (ch'i; *chee*): The life force.

ren (jen; *ren*): Empathy, consideration for others, humaneness; a Confucian virtue.

shu (*shoo*): Reciprocity; a Confucian virtue.

Tao (*dau*): The mysterious origin of the universe, which is present and visible in everything.

Tao Te Ching (*dau duh jing*): The classic scripture of Taoism.

wen: Cultural refinement; a Confucian virtue.

wu wei (*woo'-way'*): "No action," "no strain"; doing only what comes spontaneously and naturally; effortlessness.

xiao (hsiao; *shyau*): Family devotion, filial piety; a Confucian virtue.

yang (*yahng*): The active aspect of reality that expresses itself in speech, light, and heat.

Yi Jing (I Ching; *ee jing*): An ancient Confucian book of divination, one of the Five Classics, still in use today.

yin: The receptive aspect of the universe that expresses itself in silence, darkness, coolness, and rest.

Zhuangzi (Chuang Tzu; *jwang'-dzuh*): Author of the Zhuangzi, a book of whimsical stories that express themes of early Taoist thought.

CHAPTER 7

Shinto

 FIRST ENCOUNTER

In a lush park of Tokyo stands Meiji Shrine, a Shinto shrine created in the early twentieth century to honor the spirit of the emperor who had opened Japan to the rest of the world. After the emperor died in 1912, schoolchildren all over Japan contributed trees for the grounds. The trees, which have since grown very tall, surround spacious beds of purple and white Japanese iris that bloom thickly in the summer.

You enter the shrine by walking through a **torii,** a simple, tall wooden portal. As you move toward the compound of shrine buildings, you see large stone basins of flowing water. You watch visitors dip bamboo ladles into the basins, pour a bit of water over their hands, touch their faces, and then dry their hands with white handkerchiefs before proceeding. The worshipers walk quietly along the gravel path toward the main buildings. They climb the steep stone stairs, stand reverently on the landing before the entrance to the shrine hall, and clap their hands several times. They bow their heads silently before descending the stairs. Off to the side, two women attach small pieces of white paper to a tree, while other visitors crowd in front of booths that sell amulets, mementoes, and poetry that was written by the emperor. Meanwhile, five men in white robes, wearing stiff black hats and large, oddly shaped black shoes, stride silently across the courtyard single file.

You wander slowly to the iris garden. It is so full of people admiring the flowers that you must inch your way along the gravel and stone paths that wind between the gardens and ponds. Several people, to your amazement, have set up easels in front of the irises and are actually painting, despite the crush of people trying to take photos behind them.

You take a vacant seat on a stone bench and pause to look at the flowers and the people. What was meant by the clapping of hands? Why did people pour water over their hands at the entrance to the courtyard? Who were the men in the white robes and what does all this have to do with the spirit of an emperor? Why does the complex look more like a park than a church or temple?

THE ORIGINS OF SHINTO

Like most indigenous religious traditions, Shinto has no known person or group as its founder. In fact, its mysterious origins date back to the ancient people of Japan and their stories of how the world came into being. Like many people long ago, the people of the Japanese islands (Figure 7.1) lived close to nature, and Shinto as a religion reflects that reality in its worship of the spirits who are believed to inhabit the natural world. Shinto seems to have arisen from a human awareness of the power of nature and the need to be in harmony with it. Shinto retains elements of shamanism, contact with nature spirits, and mysterious healing. While most of the world's old religions of nature have disappeared, Shinto still exists in modern Japan, a fact that is sometimes marked by a shrine tucked between concrete skyscrapers.

Shinto is more, however, than a nature religion. It also has ethnic and family dimensions. The spirits that are worshiped include the spirits of departed family members, distant ancestors of one's clan, and great leaders—such as the emperor for whom the Meiji period is named, who did so much to modernize Japan.

The name *Shinto* emerged when Buddhism came from China to Japan. Before that time, there was no need to name the native religion—it was simply what everyone did. In fact, the Japanese name for Buddhism, *Butsu-do* ("the way of the Buddha"), helped give a name to the native religion. The indigenous Japanese religion came to be called the *shen-dao* ("the way of the gods") in Chinese, pronounced *shin'-to* in Japanese. ("The way of the gods" is also expressed in the Japanese language by the phrase *kami-no-michi*.)

Like the origin of Shinto, the origin of the Japanese people is also mysterious. Although Japanese often think of themselves as a single "race," they apparently descended from several immigrant groups who came from the northwest, possibly Siberia and Korea, and from the south, possibly from the Malay Peninsula. Although the immigrant groups may have focused their primary worship on different natural forces (such as the sun and the

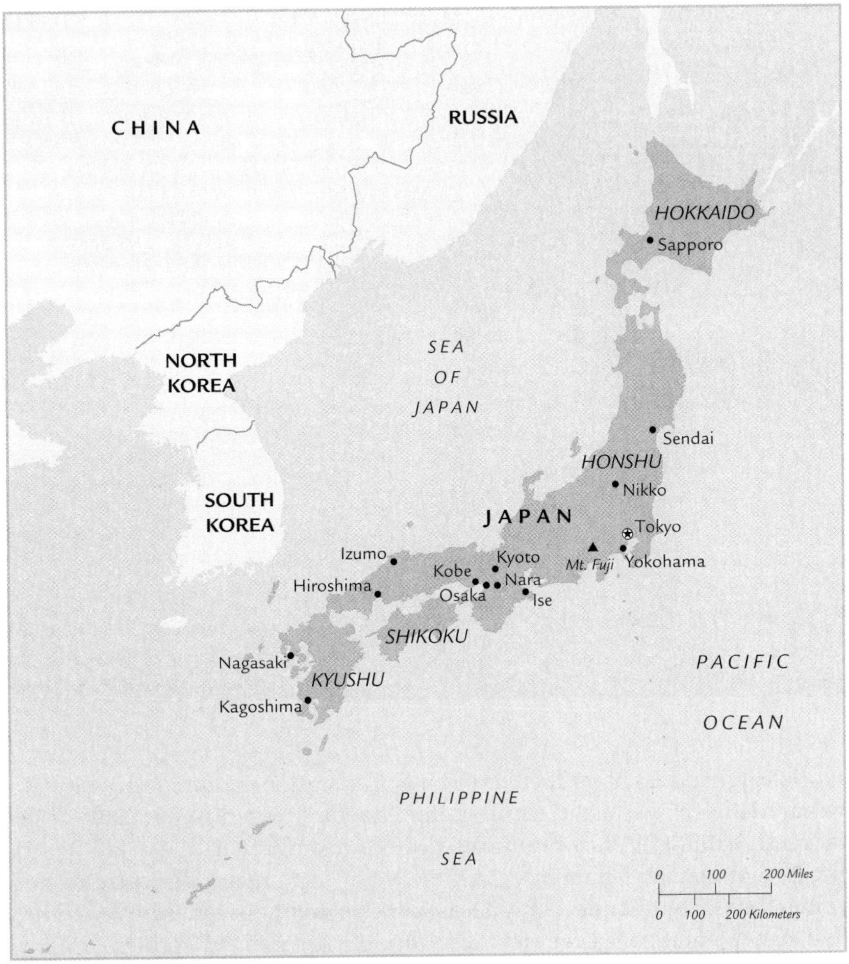

FIGURE 7.1

Islands of Japan

moon), it seems their traditions eventually mixed, ultimately blending a large number of gods into a pantheon and yielding a single creation myth.

In the beginning, as the creation myth relates, there was primeval chaos, which came to be populated by several generations of deities, or spirits, called **kami** (possibly, "sacred").[1] Two of these kami—**Izanami** ("female who invites") and **Izanagi** ("male who invites")—became the cosmic parents who created the first islands of Japan. According to an ancient chronicle, the Kojiki, "Hereupon all the Heavenly Deities commanded the two Deities His Augustness the Male-Who-Invites and Her Augustness the Female-Who-Invites, ordering them to 'make, consolidate, and give birth to this drifting land.' Granting to them an heavenly jeweled spear, they deigned to charge them. So the two Deities, standing upon the Floating Bridge of Heaven, pushed down the jeweled spear and stirred [the ocean] with it . . . ; the brine that dripped down from the end of the spear was piled up and became an island."[2]

Personal purification is necessary when entering a shrine.

Izanagi and Izanami then gave birth to additional kami, many of them nature deities. One of the nature deities was a fire god. As a result of his birth, Izanami was horribly burned, died, and went to the underworld. Because of Izanagi's immense grief, he traveled to the underworld to find Izanami, but she rebuffed him because of her ugliness caused by the burn and decay—maggots even crawled through her body. Horrified, Izanagi returned alone to the everyday world. Dirty from his contact with the underworld and with death, he cleansed himself in the ocean to regain a state of purity. As he washed, from his tear-filled eyes emerged the spirit of the sun, **Amaterasu** ("shining in heaven"), and the spirit of the moon, Tsukiyomi ("moon night possessor"). From his nostrils came the spirit of the wind, Susanowo ("impetuous male").[3] Eventually, the sun goddess Amaterasu sent her grandson to bring order to the islands of Japan. From him, the myth continues, came Jimmu, the first human emperor of Japan. As a result, the imperial house mythically traces its origin back to the goddess of the sun.

This story is intriguing for a number of reasons. It puts the kami of sun, moon, and wind into a family relationship, thus harmonizing the stories of several kami who might have once been worshiped separately by different tribes. It declares the emperors of Japan to be divine in origin (which, as we shall see, has had serious ramifications throughout Japan's history). It also portrays Amaterasu as female, while the kami of the moon, Tsukiyomi, is male. (This is unusual in traditional belief systems; usually the deity of the moon is female and the deity of the sun is male.)

This story also expresses a concern with purity—a major focus of Shinto. Pollution (*tsumi*) comes especially from contact with death, but purity can be restored by washing and ritual expiation (*harai*).

Another significant aspect of this creation story is that the islands of Japan are believed to be the creation and the home of divine spirits. Japan is thus a sort of "this-worldly" heaven, which human beings share with divine beings. (Traditional Japanese belief maintains that the spirits live in an "upper world" but that their realm is not separate from this world and thus they can exist and appear in this world.) Such a view differs significantly from those religions that see this world not as a paradise but as a place of suffering—a prelude to a heaven that can be reached only after death. In the more optimistic Japanese view, the task of human beings is to live up to the heavenlike world into which they have been born.

THE HISTORICAL DEVELOPMENT OF SHINTO

As we have already mentioned, the entry of Buddhism into Japan in the sixth century (Timeline 7.1) forced Shinto to define itself. It was a process that was complicated by the tendency of Mahayana Buddhism not only to tolerate but also to absorb native religious elements. Buddhist monks viewed Shinto kami simply as different forms of Mahayana buddhas, bodhisattvas, and other heavenly beings, and they preached that the Buddhist deities were already being worshiped in Japan under Shinto names. This approach made the introduction of Buddhism fairly easy. At first there was some resistance, and the new religion was viewed as dangerous and foreign. But over time elements from both religions were drawn upon, and a certain blending of religious practice occurred.

Along with Buddhism came a torrent of cultural elements from China. Before contact with the mainland, Japan already had a culture of its own, but it was fairly simple in comparison to that of China. Contact with China introduced a system of writing, which the Japanese began to adapt for their own use. It also introduced Chinese architecture, poetry, ceramics, art, and all sorts of new ideas—from philosophy to cuisine, from clothing design to city planning. The Japanese were fascinated by all these novelties, and the importation of Chinese culture continued, with some interruptions, for a thousand years.

Accommodation with Buddhism and Confucianism

Despite the enthusiasm for Buddhism and the accompanying aspects of Chinese culture, Shinto did not disappear. Instead, the two religions reached an accommodation. Although there were many exceptions, several patterns emerged: Shinto was often associated with agriculture, fertility, and birth,

	c. 660 B.C.E. · · · · · · · · · · · · · ● Period of the legendary Emperor Jimmu
Ritual worship of sun ● · · · · · · · · and fertility	**PRE–c. 350 B.C.E.**
	c. 350–550 C.E. · · · · · · · · · · ● Unification of clans and of kami worship
Introduction of ● · · · · · · · · · · · · · · Buddhism to Japan	**552 C.E.**
	712 C.E. · · · · · · · · · · · · · · · ● Writing of Kojiki
Writing of Nihongi ● · · · · · · · · · · · · · ·	**720 C.E.**
	c. 1650–1850 · · · · · · · · · · · ● Shinto scholarly revival
Life of Nakayama Miki ● · · · · · · · · ·	**1798–1887**
	1836–1918 · · · · · · · · · · · · · ● Life of Deguchi Nao
Beginning of the Meiji ● · · · · · · · · Restoration and modernization of Japan	**1868**
	1882 · · · · · · · · · · · · · · · ● Beginning of State Shinto
End of State Shinto ● · · · · · · · · · · ·	**1945**
	1946 · · · · · · · · · · · Emperor Hirohito rejects ● title of divinity

Timeline of significant events in the history of Shinto.

while Buddhism was called on for philosophy, help with serious sickness, funerals, and the afterlife.

The accommodation was signaled in various ways. Shinto shrines frequently contained a Buddhist place of worship or had some Buddhist rites for the kami, while Buddhist temples often had a Shinto shrine on their grounds. Shinto also adopted the Buddhist practices of preaching sermons, venerating statues, and using incense. Furthermore, Shinto shrines featured Chinese architectural details, such as tile roofs and red paint. Often the mixture was so thorough that a place of worship was neither exclusively Shinto nor Buddhist. Although the two religions were forced in the nineteenth century to disentangle themselves, one can still see many examples of their mutual influence.

Confucianism was also introduced to Japan along with Chinese culture. It meshed nicely with Japanese practices such as the veneration of

Early in the typical Shinto ceremony, priests and people bow to be cleansed by a purification wand.

ancestors, who were thought of as kami, and the loyalty given to family and clan. As it had in China, Confucianism in Japan began to play the role of an ethical system that supported education, family, and government. The whole nation began to view itself as being joined in a family relationship, with the emperor as father and the government ministers as elder brothers. Family and school instilled the Confucian virtues of respect for the emperor, reverence for ancestors and elders, care for juniors, loyalty, discipline, and love of learning. Many of these values were subsequently reinforced by Shinto.

Shinto and Japanese National Identity

Japan tends to swing back and forth between a great enthusiasm for outside cultures and a strong desire to assert Japanese uniqueness. Chinese cultural imports, which were strong in the seventh and eighth centuries, weakened but then returned again in another wave in the thirteenth century. Western influence, which arrived with the Portuguese in the sixteenth century, was

Kamikaze Pilots and Shinto

During World War II, Japanese pilots who made suicidal crash attacks achieved such notoriety in the West that a new word entered the English language: **kamikaze.** Containing the word *kami,* it means "spirit wind." Does it have a connection to Shinto?

We know that Shinto priests blessed the planes and the kamikaze pilots. The blessings were part of the larger governmental use of Shinto to further the military effort. But we might also see elements of Buddhism and Confucianism in the creation of the kamikaze pilot. Buddhism teaches the need to accept bravely the transience of life. Confucianism stresses loyalty to government leaders and superiors. Both of these helped to generate the warrior code of loyalty, duty, and honor, called **bushido** ("warrior way"). Although bushido developed as the code of the fairly small **samurai** class, it had immense influence throughout the Japanese military.

During certain periods Shinto has been utilized to promote war, and it is possible to argue that Shinto has sometimes lent itself to nationalistic use. (The veneration of the spirits of deceased military at Yasukuni Shrine in Tokyo is a current source of debate.) In fairness, we should note that most Buddhist sects in Japan also supported Japan's role in the war effort.

---

considered so dangerous that Japan largely sealed itself off from the outside world until the mid-1800s. After that came a great wave of Western influence that strengthened over the rest of the nineteenth century. Except for the years just before and during World War II, direct Western influence has continued through to the present.

In the face of these strong influences from other shores, the Japanese have relied on Shinto to help give them a sense of identity. When Buddhism threatened to nearly swallow up Shinto, priests at the shrine of **Ise** in the fourteenth century demanded an independent Shinto, separated from Buddhist influence. They argued that the "original" gods of Japan were Shinto and that the Buddhist deities associated with them were at best only later manifestations of the Shinto kami.

The movement for an independent Shinto grew stronger from the seventeenth to the end of the nineteenth century. Thinkers and writers such as Kamo Mabuchi (1697–1769) and Motoori Norinaga (1730–1801) wrote about the early myths and kami of Shinto, hoping to divest it of later additions. They wanted to restore a purified, original Shinto that would be separate from the ritual and beliefs of Buddhism and the ethics of Confucianism.

When the West challenged Japan to modernize in the late nineteenth century, Shinto was enlisted as a cultural counterweight that would preserve the "Japanese spirit." In 1868 a young man, Mutsuhito, came to the throne and assumed real, rather than merely symbolic, power. Known to history as the Emperor Meiji, he began a deliberate process of bringing Japan into the modern world. He imported European and American experts to build up the governmental, military, and educational systems according to Western models. It was a turning point in Japanese history, known as the Meiji Restoration. Shinto was forced to separate from Buddhism, and places of worship had to decide whether to declare themselves Shinto or Buddhist. For a short time Buddhism even suffered persecution, as Japan's leaders emphasized the divine origins of the emperor and began to tie Shinto to a growing spirit of nationalism.

Shinto was now a tool in the national buildup, and in 1882 a national religion called State Shinto was set up. Thousands of shrines received a special national status, with government financial support and control by the Home Ministry. Priests at these shrines were official government employees, and in return for financial support, they were supposed to represent the imperial household and maintain traditional values. All other nongovernmental Shinto shrines and organizations were treated as independent, self-supporting institutions and together were called Sect Shinto.[4]

Unfortunately, these developments set the stage for the exploitation of Shinto during the militaristic expansion that occurred after Japan's victory (1905) in the Russo-Japanese War. The government increasingly used State Shinto to generate patriotism, both during the military buildup of the 1930s and then during World War II. The divinity of the emperor—the descendant of Amaterasu—was officially taught in schools, and schoolchildren memorized and recited daily a special statement endorsing this view, the Imperial Rescript on Education.

When World War II ended, the Occupation forces demanded that Japan become a secular country. State Shinto was abolished by the government; the emperor renounced his divine status; Shinto shrines were returned to private religious practice; and all religions were placed on an equal footing. In theory Shinto became a strictly private religion, but in reality Shinto retains a special place in national life.

ESSENTIALS OF SHINTO BELIEF

The heart of Shinto is a sensitivity to the mysterious powers of nature. Kami are not thought of so much as beings living in another, distant realm, but rather as powers in or near this world whose presence might be felt, for example, when we are standing in a grove of trees or looking at a waterfall or contemplating a distant mountain. The kami can also cause dread, such as one might feel in the midst of a terrible storm or being lost on an ocean. The kami are the energies that animate nature: they cause rice to grow and wind to blow; they cause volcanoes to spew lava and earthquakes to split the land. The kami of nature are especially seen in places of natural power and beauty.

Kami are treated as persons and are given names—a fact that enables human beings to approach them and feel closely related to them. We have already learned the names of the major kami: Izanagi, Izanami, Amaterasu, Tsukiyomi, and Susanowo. In addition there are lesser kami. Among them are the god of fire, the goddess of grain, ocean spirits, mountain spirits (among whom the god of Mount Fuji is preeminent), and spirits of great trees, rivers, and waterfalls. There are also animal spirits, particularly of animals thought to have mysterious cunning, such as the badger, the fox, and the snake.

Ancestors—who have also become kami—live close by, ready to return to see how their descendants are faring.[5] Shinto is thus a way of maintaining a connection with family and clan members. Respect for the dead comes both from a love of deceased family members and from the natural fear of the unknown. In Shinto, ancestors are believed to be capable of influencing a family's earthly life. The spirits of great leaders—especially past emperors, artists, teachers, and scholars—are particularly venerated; and Confucianism, as we have seen, strengthened this Shinto respect for ancestors and for other great people of the past.

After Buddhism entered Japan, influential members of the court sought to record the early myths, both to preserve them and to defend the religious foundation of aristocratic claims. In the early eighth century, at imperial request, the myths were written down, using the new script that had come from China. The ancient myths appear in the beginnings of two core works, the **Kojiki** ("chronicle of ancient events," 712 C.E.) and the **Nihongi** ("chronicle of Japan," 720 C.E.).[6] These works also contain genuinely historical material. Ancient Shinto ritual and prayers (*norito*) were recorded in the tenth century.

Although Shinto has no clearly defined code of ethics, a type of morality does flow from the Shinto system of values and its way of looking at life. The Western notion of internal guilt is not found in Shinto. There is no moralistic God who gives commands or judges a person, nor is there a sense of original sin or of any basic sinful tendency. Instead, human beings are fundamentally good, the body is good, and this earthly life is good. Shinto worships fertility and new life, and sex is viewed positively, without guilt. Sexual imagery—particularly phallic rocks and wood carvings—can be seen at many shrines.[7]

Unlike many other religions, Shinto tends to turn its focus away from death, which is thought of as the opposite of life and growth.[8] Because Shinto worships the life force, it works to counteract whatever brings sickness or death. Just as dirt is removable, so too are all other pollutants. According to Shinto, we must keep our bodies, houses, and clothes clean and bright; and when they become dirty or contaminated, we must wash them, get rid of the dirt, and purify them with blessings. In Japan, washing, sweeping, and cleaning—seen everywhere daily—have religious implications. One's character must be unstained, too, and human relations must be kept healthy. Similarly, the human character must have "sincerity" (*makoto*)—it must be pure, without egotism, committed. (Many of Emperor Meiji's poems, available for sale at Meiji Shrine, are about the importance of sincerity.) Human beings conserve and restore their purity by fulfilling all obligations, repaying debts, and apologizing for misdeeds.

Because kami are everywhere, living with them demands that we show them reverence. One way is to visit them at their shrines, which are their homes. Another way is to show respect for nature, which is one reason for Japan's high esteem for farming and carpentry and for the architectural use of elements such as wood and stone in their natural state. Respect for nature also means maintaining a harmony with nature and all its processes.

The head priest, here in red, officially greets the kami by chanting prayers handwritten on a scroll.

SHINTO RELIGIOUS PRACTICE

Shinto practice occurs at several levels. It encompasses formal worship and blessings by priests at shrines; blessings by priests away from the shrine; Shinto observances of holidays, the seasons, and nature; everyday practice by individuals in their homes; and the ceremonial practice of Shinto by the emperor and other authorities. Active shrines have a priest—a job that is frequently hereditary.

Worship at Shrines

People visit shrines to pray for health, for success in school and career, and for the well-being of those they love. A visit begins by passing under the torii, which looks like a ceremonial entrance or gateway and is sometimes tall and magnificent.[9] Worshipers wash their hands and mouth at a water basin just inside the entrance. They proceed through an open courtyard to the building—the *haiden*—where the kami is worshiped. Behind the haiden (and often visible from it) is a small hall or cabinet where the kami is enshrined. In smaller shrines, there may be no front worship hall but only a small place where the kami is enshrined. (It is possible that the earliest shrines had no buildings at all.[10])

Priests place offerings of food and drink in front of the kami. Here, they offer tangerines.

Worshipers ascend the stairs to the haiden or to the space in front of the room where the kami is enshrined. They bow, donate a coin, then often ring a bell and clap several times to gain the kami's attention. They bow again and pray, either silently or by chanting. Then they bow again and leave. Sometimes they tie small wooden plaques (*ema*) or pieces of paper, with their requests written on them, to fences or to the branches of a nearby sacred tree.

When worshipers visit a shrine for a blessing, a priest waves over them a branch or wand adorned with paper streamers. This implement is used to purify the devotee and the surrounding area.

Shrines sometimes have shrine "treasures," which possibly originated as gifts from visiting dignitaries. Most commonly these are antique metal mirrors, swords, and symbolic jewels—mirrors are considered particularly important. It is believed that kami sometimes present themselves in these treasures. The treasures are not shown publicly, however, and many shrines do not have them.

Shown here is a typical local shrine, with offerings of fruit, sake, and mochi. The mirror behind the jars of sake represents the kami of the sun. ▶

Each shrine has its special festival days (*matsuri*). These may be celebrated with grand processions and various types of entertainment. Sometimes, to honor the kami, celebrants parade the kami in a hand-carried

Shrine visitors often take charms home with them. These brocaded amulets at Jishu Jinja in Kyoto promise happiness in love.

litter, an *omikoshi*. On festival days, temporary booths are set up to sell foods and religious souvenirs. (Large shrines, such as Meiji Shrine, have permanent booths.) Among the souvenirs are amulets of various kinds, some in brocade bags, which are thought to bring good luck. Some amulets are kept in the home, and small ones are kept in a car for protection.

People visit shrines for blessings at important times in their lives. Babies are brought for a blessing a month after birth. Children are brought for additional blessings when they are young, when special protection is thought to be valuable. This practice is known as "7-5-3"; girls are brought at ages 3 and 7, and boys are brought at age 5.

Shinto priests also perform ceremonies, such as weddings, away from the shrine. Once held in homes, weddings nowadays often occur in large hotels or reception rooms, because they are usually followed by a banquet. Priests also bless construction sites, houses, and cars, as well as perform exorcisms at locations that have come to be associated with misfortune, in order to make people feel comfortable there again.

Shinto priests wear long robes (often white, symbolizing cleanliness and purity), which are based on old Chinese aristocratic design that became popular in the court of the Heian period. Priests' shoes are made of carved wood (like Dutch wooden shoes) and covered with black lacquer, and they wear high caps of black lacquered horsehair. The hats of dignitaries have a long flexible extension, which is attached at the top or back of the hat. The extension, created in China, is believed to represent the tail of the horse. (Thought of as a symbol of energy and strength, the horse came to be considered a sacred animal. A few Shinto shrines have even kept stables of horses.)

Some shrines also have female attendants (*miko*), who wear bright red skirts. They assist in ritual, play a short metal musical instrument covered with bells, and represent a vestige of early shamanism.

Celebration of the New Year

New Year's is a very special time in Shinto practice. The home must be thoroughly cleaned before New Year's in order to make it attractive to the spirits, who are invited to visit. The main gate or door is decorated with a special arrangement called the *kadomatsu* ("entry pine"), which is made up of three pieces of cut green bamboo, a small branch of pine, and if possible, a sprig of plum. The bamboo signifies persistence; the pine, freshness and life throughout the winter; and the plum, the first sign of life in early spring. Together, the branches of greenery in the kadomatsu symbolize human virtue.

During New Year's, rice is pounded into a soft dough called *mochi,* then made into round shapes that are piled on top of each other and topped with a tangerine. Rice signifies wealth and fertility, and the mochi anticipates the planting of rice in the spring. On New Year's eve, the family gathers to eat a special soup made of vegetables and mochi, called *ozoni,* which is thought to promote health. On New Year's day, men and women dress in kimono, take offerings to Shinto shrines, and pray there for success in the coming year. Over the following days they make formal visits to relatives and friends and renew relationships. The themes of the whole holiday season are cleansing and the renewal of life.

Observances of the Seasons and Nature

Traditionally, Shinto has marked the seasons with special practices, particularly for planting and harvesting rice. In the industrial nation of Japan today, however, these rituals are becoming less important.

Because respect for nature is at the heart of Shinto, reverential objects and small shrines are sometimes placed in the midst of forests, in fields, or on mountains. Among these are torii (which can even be found in the ocean), a pile of stones (possibly phallic in origin), or a sacred rope. Respect for the spirits of ancestors is shown by pouring water or tea over gravestones and by leaving offerings of food and flowers.

One noteworthy Shinto practice is purification with water, a practice that must be very ancient because it appears in several myths about the kami. As we have already mentioned, devotees always wash their hands with water at the entrance to a shrine. A related ritual, called **misogi,** involves standing under a waterfall as a ritual act of purification. Before entering the water, the devotee does calisthenics and deep-breathing exercises. The practitioner is then cleansed with a bit of salt. Backing into the water, the person stands for some time as the water falls full-force on his or her shoulders. The practitioner may shout and cut the air with a hand to enhance the experience of purification. The ritual ends with a drink of *sake* (rice wine) and possibly a meal, if it is performed with others. Misogi combines the ritual of cleansing with the ideal of self-discipline and probably began in the practices of ascetics who lived in the mountains.

Another Shinto practice is the climbing of a sacred mountain to gain union with the spirit of that mountain. The climb up Mount Fuji, for example, is something that many Japanese hope to accomplish at least once in their lifetime, and several Shinto sects specifically worship the kami of Mount Fuji.

Other Practices

Daily worship occurs in the home, where a small Shinto shrine called the **kamidana** is maintained, often on a high shelf. It may contain a mirror, and

Shinto ceremonies often include reception of a personal blessing that is conveyed by a priest's touching of the head with the gohei. This gesture represents contact with the kami.

Visitors to Kiyomizu-dera catch and drink water from a sacred stream. ▶

offerings are made there, especially of rice and water. It is common to offer prayers at the kamidana at the beginning of each day. Some homes also maintain an outdoor shrine in the garden.

A semiofficial form of Shinto that is practiced by the emperor and his household is also still part of the religion. The emperor has traditionally been considered the high priest of Shinto, and his reign is inaugurated with Shinto rites. He participates every spring in Tokyo in a ceremonial rice-planting on the palace grounds in order to guarantee the fertility of the rice harvest for the entire nation. He and his family also visit the shrine of Ise annually to pray for the country. An emperor, when he dies, is buried with Shinto rites— something quite rare, because among ordinary Japanese people funeral services are conducted by Buddhist priests.

**PERSONAL EXPERIENCE: A TEMPLE
HIGH ABOVE KYOTO**

On my first trip to Kyoto, I had planned to spend a full day walking in its
beautiful eastern hills. My ambitious plan was to begin at the north end, to
continue south through the eastern part of the city, and to end finally at the
Buddhist "mother temple" of Kyoto, Kiyomizu-dera ("clear water temple").
I had heard that it was a wonderful spot for watching the sun set.

As sunset grew near, I arrived at the stairs that lead up to the temple.
To call the place a single "temple" is misleading. It is really a large complex
of wooden buildings scattered across a wooded hill. The main part of the
temple is built on top of an enormous deck that extends far out over the hillside, supported by wooden pillars that rise high above the treetops.

Standing on the deck, I could see across all Kyoto. Other people were
there, too, standing patiently at the railing waiting for the sunset. All of us
watched reverently as the sun slipped beneath the horizon; then the clouds
turned pink, and the city was engulfed in an orange haze. As daylight faded
and the gray city turned blue, nighttime Kyoto was being born. It was
easy to imagine, down below, the dinner restaurants, noodle shops, and
tiny bars all coming to life. Up here, however, the antique atmosphere of
Kiyomizu-dera embraced us with its distance from the world.

On the way out was a triple stream—the "clear water" that gave the temple its name. As I walked down the high temple stairs, I could see, far below,
the three thin streams of water that cascaded into a pool. Coming closer, I
noticed in the twilight the bamboo ladles that lay there for visitors to use to
take a drink. As I reached the bottom of the stairs, I looked again. There, at the
base of the three waterfalls, obscure in the dimness and plunging water, a man
in a white robe stood motionless, knee-deep in the water. I saw that his palms
were held together in a gesture of prayer. I took a drink from the waterfall,
then retreated toward the path that leads out into the valley below the temple.
I looked back one last time at the falling water. The man had not moved.

I'd gone to Kiyomizu-dera expecting a beautiful sunset, perhaps the
scent of incense and the sound of a Buddhist chant. What I hadn't expected
to find, near the temple's base, was the practice of the Shinto ritual misogi.[11]
Yet how fitting, I thought, that a religion in Japan that grew up in close contact with the native religion should today have, as the basis for its name and
at the base of this grand temple's frame, waters sacred to a Shinto kami.

SHINTO AND THE ARTS

Shinto worships beauty, but the influence of Shinto on art is not immediately clear. There is no strong Shinto tradition of figurative art, in which gods
are portrayed in paintings and sculpture. There are some exceptions, but
kami are thought of almost universally as invisible presences, not to be portrayed. Instead, the defining features of Shinto art are openness, a use of natural elements, and a deliberate simplicity.

It can be argued that Shinto's high esteem for nature has had a profound influence on Japanese art and architecture. The Japanese screens and scrolls that portray nature that are often said to be the product of Taoism or Zen are equally the product of Shinto. This can also be said of all the fine and decorative art forms, such as ceramics and kimono design, in which elements of nature are a primary inspiration. Traditional Japanese architecture, with its floor of rice matting and its unpainted wooden walls, also shows Shinto influence.

Perhaps because Shinto places almost no emphasis on doctrines and ethical demands, it has focused instead on the beauty of ritual, giving Shinto an important relationship with the arts. Its love of ceremony has demanded that attention be paid to all objects and clothing used in its sacred ritual, to the places where the ritual takes place, and to the exact way the ritual is performed.

Architecture

The traditional architecture of shrines (**jinja**) is a primary expression of Shinto artistic expression. These structures seem to have begun as storehouses for grain and other foods, which were raised off the ground for protection from water and insects. These granaries functioned as the natural and comfortable homes of the gods who served as protectors of the stored foods. The original pattern of the shrine called for walls made of wood and roofs made of thatch, which would be renewed regularly. Roof beams often extended high above the roof, in a style that is also found in South Pacific island architecture. This feature of extended roof beams (*chigi*) and the fact that the construction materials seem to be appropriate for a warm climate lead many to think that the Shinto shrine originated possibly in Malaysia and islands farther south.

As discussed earlier, Shinto architecture today reflects Japan's history. The Chinese influence, a force since 500 C.E., is evident in symmetrical compound design, curving roofs, and roof tiles. The Shinto scholarly revival of the seventeenth century, as well as the nationalistic Meiji Restoration of the later nineteenth century, produced efforts to rid Shinto of Buddhist (and therefore Chinese) influences. These efforts were only partially successful. "Pure" Shinto style, with uncurving gabled thatch roofs, unpainted and uncarved wooden walls, and nailless construction, is most evident at Ise. Because the wood and thatch need to be replaced regularly in order to keep them bright and fresh, the maintenance of this style can be afforded at only a few sites.

The shrines of Ise, which are rebuilt every twenty years, are striking because of their extreme simplicity. They sit on a ground of white stones in the midst of tall cedar trees, and to reach the inner shrine, the visitor must cross a river. In the summer, the cicadas fill the air with cricketlike sounds, adding to the sense of primordial mystery.

The earliest torii, or ceremonial entryway, was probably made of three logs lashed together, though we don't know its exact origin. From this basic

A large torii marks the entrance to a neighborhood Shinto shrine on King Street in Honolulu.

shape, many graceful variations emerged. The original torii were certainly made of unpainted wood, although today many are painted white, red, or orange. The torii usually signify sacred landmarks, but they can also be set in water. (The enormous orange torii standing in the ocean at Miyajima island near Hiroshima is the best-known example.)

At some shrines, so many torii are set up as thanksgiving offerings that over many years they create a tunnel (as seen at Fushimi Inari Shrine, in Kyoto). Tied to the torii or to the front of a shrine is often a ceremonial rope (**shimenawa**), from which may be hung white paper streamers, particularly on festival days. Special shimenawa, occasionally very thick and elaborate, are created for New Year's celebrations. These shimenawa have become an art form in their own right, appearing at New Year's time not only on shrines but also over the doors of shops and homes. Because kami are considered to reside in any place in nature that is awe-inspiring, shimenawa may also adorn exceptional trees and rocks.

274

A miko offers dance (*kagura*) to entertain the kami.

Music and Dance

Shinto is also known for its distinctive music called **gagaku.** Originally played in the Chinese imperial court of the Tang and Song dynasties, gagaku was adapted by Shinto and so slowed down that it creates an impression of ancient solemnity. The instruments that are used make a flutelike, reedy sound that sounds close yet far away, fresh and new, but also timeless. Gagaku is a perfect accompaniment to Shinto ritual.

One story in the Kojiki tells of how Amaterasu was lured out of a rock cave by music and dance. Shinto shrines often include dance at festival times to entertain the resident kami. From this shrine dance evolved the stately **Noh** dance dramas, which tell the stories of people and their contacts with the spirits. The making of masks and exquisite robes for Noh performers has become a fine art.

SHINTO OFFSHOOTS: THE NEW RELIGIONS

The fact that Shinto is not a strongly institutionalized religion is both a weakness and a strength. It is a strength because anyone can set up a Shinto shrine and even begin a Shinto-inspired movement; it is a weakness, however, because Shinto generally has not had the organizational structure necessary to make converts or spread the religion beyond Japan. Shinto shrines do belong to confederations, however, which help them with staffing; and many smaller shrines are affiliated with one of the old, large national shrines.

Shinto, possibly helped by its lack of institutional structure, has produced (and still produces) an amazing variety of sects, especially over the past two centuries. Some are more traditional than others. Some worship all the major kami or focus on just one of them. Some borrow from Confucianism, Buddhism, or Christianity and speak of a divine parent (or parents)

A priest presents a symbolic offering of sake at the entrance to a haiden at Omoto headquarters in Kameoka, Japan.

and of the human race as a single family. Some utilize traditions derived from mountain asceticism. Some emphasize healing. Some venerate a charismatic founder who is thought to be a kami and the recipient of a divine revelation.

It is possible to group Shinto sects and offshoots into (1) those that are the most traditional, (2) those that emphasize mountain spirituality, (3) those that stress purification, and (4) those that have emerged from shamanistic revelations. The last group is especially prominent. Offshoots that consider themselves separate religions are sometimes called the New Religions.

Japan, like Korea, has had a long history of shamanism; and in both countries the shamans are often female. We might recall that the shaman acts as an intermediary between the gods and human beings. The shaman helps bring physical and emotional healing. This openness to shamanism has helped produce the offshoots of Shinto that revere an inspired leader who was the recipient of a divine revelation. These offshoots illustrate the ability of Japanese religious traditions to take on new forms.

One of the New Religions is **Tenrikyo** ("heavenly reason teaching"), founded by Nakayama Miki (1798–1887), who discovered her religious abilities by accident. When Miki called in a shaman to perform rites to improve her unhappy life and miserable marriage, she intended only to act as the shaman's assistant but instead went into a trance that lasted several days. During the trance a kami spoke through her, saying, "I am the True and Original God. . . . I have descended from Heaven to save all human beings, and I want to take Miki as the Shrine of God. . . ."[12] When Miki came out of the trance, she explained that many kami had spoken to her. The greatest, she said, was the parent kami (*Oya-gami*) of all human beings. The name of the kami was Tenri-o-no-mikoto ("Lord of divine wisdom"). This kami wished her to disseminate teachings to people about how to live properly so that they might have health and long life.

The notion that physical health comes from mental health is strong in Tenrikyo, which preaches healing by faith. This religion is exceptional for its institutional structure and other traditional religious elements that allow it to spread beyond Japan. It has sacred scripture—the poetry that Nakayama Miki wrote as a result of her revelations.[13] The sect has even created a city near Nara, called Tenri City, where its ideals are put into practice. Tenri City contains a university, library, and museum; religious services are offered twice daily in the main hall.

Another New Religion is called Omotokyo ("great origin teaching"), or simply **Omoto.** It was founded by Deguchi Nao (1836–1918), a woman who experienced terrible poverty and misfortune. Of her eight children, three died and two suffered mental illness. Nao's husband died when she was 30, and she was reduced to selling rags. In her despair, she experienced a vision of the creation of a new, perfect world. Working with a man she adopted as her son, Deguchi Onisaburo, Nao established a religion that she hoped would begin the transformation of society.

Nao's vision grew out of the traditional Shinto view of earth as a heavenly realm of the spirits and its shamanistic trust in the spirits to bring healing to human life. Like many other New Religions, Omoto aims to better *this* world rather than accumulate rewards for an afterlife. It wishes to bring happiness to the individual and peace to society.

Omoto is of particular interest because it sees in the creation of art the essence of religious manifestation. For Omoto, all art is religious. To spread its belief about the connection between art and religion, Omoto began a school at its headquarters in Kameoka, near Kyoto, to teach traditional Japanese arts to non-Japanese. To encourage world peace, Omoto has promoted the study of Esperanto (a universal language) and sponsored contacts with members of other religions, such as Muslims and Christians. Omoto has even held services in New York's Cathedral of Saint John the Divine, where Shinto ritual objects remain on display.

Omoto has itself produced offshoots. One is the Church of World Messianity (Sekaikyuseikyo). It was founded by Okada Mokichi (1882–1955), who was believed to be able to heal by means of a source of light within his body. He thought that he could share this healing light by writing the character for light (*hikari*) on pieces of paper, which he gave to his followers. Devotees work for the coming of a time on earth when the world will be free of war, poverty, and disease. Elements of Buddhism can be seen in this religion, for the supreme deity is called Miroku (the Japanese name of Maitreya, the Buddha expected to come in the future).

Other Shinto offshoots include Seicho-no-Ie ("house of growth") and P. L. Kyodan ("perfect liberty community"), which emerged from Omoto, and Honmichi ("true road"), which emerged from Tenrikyo. The goals of all these groups are similar: harmony, beauty, health, happiness, and the creation of a paradise on earth.

The New Religions are the object of some interest for what they may foretell about the direction of religions in the future. They tend to be practical, peace-oriented, and "this-worldly." Many value the contributions of women, and many esteem the arts. Borrowing valuable elements from other religions, they are moving in new directions.

SHINTO AND THE MODERN WORLD

Shinto could have died out under the onslaught of Buddhism, or it could have easily faded away when Japan adopted Western science and technology. Yet Shinto is a unique example of an early nature religion that is still vital in the modern world.

Why does Shinto seem to maintain its relevance in modern life? Four of its elements have particular modern significance:

An esteem for nature Because much of our natural world is threatened by overpopulation, pollution, and exploitation, we may have something to learn from the Shinto attitude toward nature.

The stance of benevolent silence on most moral and doctrinal questions For modern democracies that attempt to blend many viewpoints, Shinto

This shrine and torii, set amid modern office buildings in Tokyo, stand as testimony to the robust nature of Shinto.

provides a religion that does not fragment society over doctrinal and moral issues.

Aesthetically pleasing ritual Some religions have downplayed the importance of ritual, ranking it below doctrine and morality. But for many people who question traditional ethics and doctrines, the nonjudgmental ritual of Shinto appears all the more valuable.

Eclecticism Shinto does not exclude other religions, but allows their practice and sometimes absorbs their teachings and various elements. The eclecticism of Shinto reflects its inclusive viewpoint.

> Art is the mother of religion.
> —Omoto saying

Shinto has gone wherever Japanese people have settled: Brazil, Peru, the United States (particularly Hawai`i and California). Some believers in Shinto see its potential as a universal religion of nature and would like to see it spread among non-Japanese people. But Shinto is not a missionary religion, nor does it generally have the institutional structure to do missionary work. It is possible, however, that some well-organized Shinto offshoot, such as Tenrikyo, will spread far beyond its country of origin.

It may be that traditional Shinto derives much of its vitality from the specific terrain, climate, and geographical isolation of Japan—from its mountains, waterfalls, thick forests, and myriad islands, all in continual change from the procession of the seasons. If so, then Shinto will remain restricted to that country. Nonetheless, it is easy at least to imagine the spread of traditional Shinto, especially to areas in which its special elements might take root in a welcoming, supportive community.

RELIGION BEYOND THE CLASSROOM

Every town and village in Japan has at least one shrine, and most have many more. The neighborhood shrines are full of charm and worth visiting, particularly during a fair or festival (*matsuri*). (Check guidebooks and local English-language newspapers in Japan for dates and times.)

In Tokyo, Meiji Jingu is the preeminent shrine. Sundays, New Year's, and midsummer are especially good times to visit. Yasukuni Jinja is another large shrine in Tokyo. (Because it is dedicated to military personnel who died in war, it is sometimes a center of controversy for those who fear a resurgence of Japanese militarism.) Both shrines are in traditional Shinto style. An example of "baroque" Shinto style can be seen just outside Tokyo; located at Nikko (an easy day trip from Tokyo), Toshogu Shrine is a large complex of elaborate buildings.

Kyoto, the ancient capital, has several shrines of beauty and interest. The most imposing is Heian Jingu, painted red in the Chinese style. Gion Jinja, Kitano Jinja, and Yasaka Jinja are also located in Kyoto.

Ise, in southeastern Honshu, is not easily accessible to the foreign visitor because it is off the usual tourist route, but it can be reached by train from Tokyo, Osaka, or Kyoto. In pure Shinto style, its shrine is one of the greatest architectural sights in the world.

Mount Fuji is the most important and possibly most beautiful mountain of Japan. Several Shinto sects worship its kami, and many Japanese climb Mount Fuji once in their lives as a semireligious pilgrimage. Visitors commonly travel to Mount Fuji, stay overnight, and walk up to experience dawn from a lookout spot near the top of the mountain. (Consult the Japan National Tourist Organization for help in making all travel plans and reservations.)

Because of the immigration of Japanese to Hawai`i, Shinto is quite evident there. The main shrine of Honolulu is Izumo-Taisha-kyo, near the downtown area and Chinatown. It is in fairly pure Shinto style. Another is Kotohira-Jinsha, near the Bishop Museum in Kalihi. Wakamiya Inari Shrine is located in the Plantation Village at Waipahu Cultural Garden Park. This red shrine is typical of a small, local shrine. Also worth visiting, especially at New Year's, is Hawai`i Daijingu, in Nu`uanu.

FOR FULLER UNDERSTANDING

1. Design a "new" religion that builds upon some of the elements of Shinto and perhaps incorporates traditions from other religions and institutions.
2. Research one of the Shinto New Religions. Look into its origins, its current status, and its spread. Use your research to predict its future course.
3. Most of the New Religions, such as Omoto and Tenrikyo, have offices dedicated to international outreach. At a library, find out the address of the Japanese headquarters of one of these religions, and send a written request for information in English. Share the information with your class.

4. Using a library, an architects' association, and/or the Internet, research recent trends in Japanese architecture, both grand (public spaces) and small (private homes). Write a report that highlights the connections between recent trends and traditional Shinto attitudes and arts.
5. Shinto's roots and history are very much tied to Japan. How great is the likelihood that Shinto can follow the paths charted by, for example, Christianity and Islam and become a worldwide religion?

RELATED READINGS

Blacker, Carmen. *The Catalpa Bow*. New York: Japan Library, 1999. A literate study of Japanese shamanism.

Kitagawa, Joseph. *On Understanding Japanese Religion*. Princeton, NJ: Princeton University Press,

1987. A good introduction to Japanese religions, including the New Religions, by a major scholar.

Littleton, C. Scott. *Shinto: Origins, Rituals, Festivals, Spirits, Sacred Places*. New York: Oxford University

Press, 2002. An excellent, well-illustrated introduction to Shinto.

Nelson, John. *A Year in the Life of a Shinto Shrine.* Seattle: University of Washington Press, 1996. A firsthand account of the rituals carried on during each of the four seasons at a shrine in Nagasaki.

Picken, Stuart, and Yukitaka Yamamoto. *Shinto Meditations for Revering the Earth.* Berkeley: Stone Bridge Press, 2002. Reflections on the power and beauty of thunder, rain, and other phenomena of nature.

KEY TERMS

Amaterasu (*ah'-mah-te-rah'-soo*): "Shining in heaven"; goddess of the sun.

bushido (*boo'-shee-doh*): "Warrior knight way"; military devotion to a ruler, demanding loyalty, duty, and self-sacrifice; an ideal promoted by State Shinto.

gagaku (*gah'-ga-ku*): The stately ceremonial music of Shinto.

Ise (*ee'-say*): Location in southeastern Honshu of a major shrine to Amaterasu.

Izanagi (*ee-za-nah'-gee*): "Male who invites"; primordial male parent god.

Izanami (*ee-za-nah'-mee*): "Female who invites"; primordial female parent god.

jinja (*jin'-ja*): A Shinto shrine.

kami (*kah'-mee*): A spirit, god, or goddess of Shinto.

kamidana (*kah-mee-dah'-na*): A shelf or home altar for the veneration of kami.

kamikaze (*kah'-mee-kah'-zay*): "Spirit wind"; suicide fighter pilots of World War II.

Kojiki (*koh'-jee-kee*): The earliest chronicle of Japanese history.

misogi (*mee-soh'-gee*): A ritual of purification that involves standing under a waterfall.

Nihongi (*nee-hohn'-gee*): The second chronicle of Japanese history.

Noh: Dramas performed in mask and costume, associated with Shinto.

Omoto (*oh'-mo-to*): A New Religion, which stresses art and beauty.

samurai (*sah'-moo-rai*): Feudal soldier.

shimenawa (*shee-may-nah'-wa*): Twisted rope, marking a sacred spot.

Tenrikyo (*ten'-ree-kyoh*): A New Religion devoted to human betterment.

torii (*to-ree'*): A gatelike structure that marks a Shinto sacred place.

CHAPTER **8**

Judaism

 FIRST ENCOUNTER

After spending two days in Tel Aviv, you leave for Jerusalem and arrive at your hotel near the old part of the city. Once there, you can't wait to begin exploring. The Old City is a place for walking and wandering, with wonderful sights in its narrow streets.

Drawing you like a magnet is the site of the ancient temple, destroyed by Roman soldiers nearly two thousand years ago. Only its foundation stones remain. On the mount where the temple once stood is now a glittering golden dome. Built by Muslims, the Dome of the Rock covers the great stone beneath it, which is venerated by Muslims and Jews alike, who hold that their ancestor Abraham came to this spot.

You decide to walk down from the city, to view the mount from below, after which you plan to turn back and travel, like a true pilgrim, "up to Jerusalem." You buy food for a picnic lunch at stalls as you walk inside the city. Soon you are beyond the Old City gate. Luckily, the day is sunny but not hot. You see a large stone tomb in the valley below and beyond it, in the east, Mount Scopus.

	c. 1800 B.C.E. ··········	● Traditional date of Abraham, the legendary first patriarch
Traditional date of the Exodus of the Hebrews from Egypt, led by Moses ● ··········	c. 1250 B.C.E.	
	c. 1000 B.C.E. ··········	● Establishment of Jerusalem as the capital of the Israelite kingdom by King David
Completion of the First Temple by Solomon ● ··········	c. 950 B.C.E.	
	721 B.C.E. ··········	● End of the northern kingdom, destroyed by Assyria
Destruction of the First ● ·········· Temple and exile of Israelites in Babylonia	586–539 B.C.E.	
	515 B.C.E. ··········	● Dedication of the Second Temple
First public reading of the Torah ● ··········	c. 430 B.C.E.	
	c. 200 B.C.E. ··········	● Completion of the last books of the Hebrew scriptures
Destruction of the Second ● ·········· Temple of Jerusalem by the Romans	70 C.E.	

Timeline of significant events in the history of Judaism.

At last it is time to stop for a rest and to eat your lunch. You sit under a tree and look back, thinking to yourself about the events this site has witnessed. Your mind becomes crowded with the names of biblical kings, prophets, and priests associated with Jerusalem: David, Solomon, Melchizedek, Isaiah, Jeremiah. As the sounds of everyday traffic filter through your thoughts, you imagine the many battles over this holy city and the successive waves of conquerors—Babylonians, Greeks, Romans, Arabs, and European crusaders—who took possession of it in the past, and you think of the more recent battles and problems here. You cannot help thinking of the contrast between the violence that this place has seen and the root of the city's name—*salem*. Like *shalom* and *salaam*, words to which it is related, the word *salem* means "peace" and "wholeness."

You start back, walking uphill thoughtfully. You see the small tombstones in front of the walls, the high walls themselves, and a beautiful double stone gate, now sealed. Slowly, you make your way back through the city streets around to the western side, to what is left of the great temple. The immense foundation stones, set there during an enlargement ordered by King Herod the Great, were too solid to be knocked down and too big to be carted off. An open area at their base, the **Western Wall,** is now used for contemplation and prayer—on the left stand men, and on the right, women.

	c. 90 C.E.	● Completion of the canon of Hebrew scriptures
Completion of the Mishnah ●	c. 200 C.E.	
	c. 400 C.E.	● Completion of the Palestinian Talmud
Completion of the ● Babylonian Talmud	c. 600 C.E.	
	1135–1204	● Life of the philosopher Moses Maimonides
Creation of the *Zohar* ● by author Moses de León	c. 1280	
	1492	● Expulsion of the Jews from Spain
Life of Baal Shem Tov ●	1700–1760	
	c. 1800	● Beginning of the Reform movement in western Europe
The Holocaust (Shoah): the destruction of much of European ● Judaism by the Nazis	1937–1945	
	1948	● Beginning of Israel as an independent Jewish state

Some hold prayer books, and many touch their hands and foreheads to the wall. You see little pieces of paper, which have prayers written on them, rolled up or folded and placed in the cracks between the stones. These have been left here by people who have come to speak with God and to remember their family members in prayer. You reflect on the historical events that led up to the building of the temple, whose foundation stones are all that remain. You think of the long and great history of the Jews, who developed and flourished in spite of persecution in lands far away. It is deeply moving to be here, and you stay a long time in silent contemplation.

AN OVERVIEW OF JEWISH HISTORY

Jewish history goes back two thousand years or far longer, depending on one's point of view. This difference of opinion revolves around a major historical event—the destruction of the Second Temple of Jerusalem by the Romans in 70 C.E. (Timeline 8.1), which brought about the end of the temple-based ceremonial religion of that region and the widespread dispersion of its people to lands far away from Israel. Following the calamity of the temple's destruction, the earlier religion had to develop in new ways to survive.

From the centralized, temple-based religion practiced in Israel, another form of religion arose that could be practiced among the Jews who lived outside of Israel. Jews anywhere in the world could now practice their religion in the home and synagogue. In recognition of this fundamental religious reorientation, a distinction is often made between **biblical Judaism** and **rabbinical Judaism.** When we study the Judaism practiced today, what we are really studying are the forms of Jewish belief and religious practice that largely came into existence after the destruction of the Second Temple.

The two great spans of time—before and after the destruction of the Second Temple—are also commonly subdivided into two periods each. Over the first great span of time, a landless people established a homeland in Israel and made Jerusalem the capital of its kingdom. Great change occurred and another period began, however, when the kingdom of Judah and its First Temple were destroyed by the Babylonians (586 B.C.E.), forcing the Israelite people into exile in Babylonia (present-day Iraq) for nearly fifty years. These events made clear to the exiled people that religious law and history had to be put in written form to guarantee their survival. As a result, the Hebrew Bible was created, and study of the scriptures and prayer in synagogues became important, even after the temple was rebuilt.

The second great time span comprises the two thousand years of the development of Judaism in the common era. It also can be subdivided into two periods. The first period marks the evolution of rabbinical Judaism and traditional Jewish life, from about 100 C.E. to approximately 1800 C.E., the beginning of the modern period. About two hundred years ago, a movement began in Judaism as a response to (1) the new thinking of the European Enlightenment, (2) the liberal thought of the American and French Revolutions, and (3) the laws of Napoleon, which were carried widely beyond France. The movement, called the **Reform,** questioned and modernized traditional Judaism and helped produce the diverse branches within Judaism that exist today. The Reform also raised the issue of Jewish identity. Who is a Jew? What is essential to Judaism? These are two questions to which we will return later.

The Hebrew Bible records that the roots of Judaism go back far into the past, to a landless people sometimes called Hebrews and more commonly called Israelites, who traced themselves to an ancestor named Abraham. Because much of what we know of the first span of Hebrew history comes from the Hebrew Bible, we will examine it first. We should note, however, that the Hebrew Bible is not a history book in the modern sense; it presents instead what might better be called sacred history. It is the Israelites' view of their God's relationship with them in the midst of historical events.

We should note, too, that the Hebrew Bible is significant not only in terms of the history of the Hebrews but also in terms of its role in the development of Judaism over the past two thousand years. When the ceremonial religion of the Jerusalem Temple ended in the first century C.E., it was the Hebrew scriptures that provided a foundation for the development of rabbinical Judaism. The scriptures offered a firm basis for Jewish **rabbis** (teachers) to offer their **midrash** (interpretation) of biblical laws and practices: the books outlined the Ten Commandments and other ethical teachings; they established the major yearly festivals that would guide and sanctify the lives of Jews; and they contained the psalms that became the everyday prayers of Jews everywhere.

Thus, we turn first to the Hebrew Bible, to understand its structure and to examine the laws and history of the Hebrew people. After looking at the Hebrew Bible and at Hebrew and Jewish history, we will then consider Jewish belief, practice, and influence.

THE HEBREW BIBLE

Judaism is often associated with the land of Israel, but Judaism is perhaps better associated with its most important book, the Hebrew Bible. Although nowadays the Hebrew Bible is published as a single volume, it is made up of individual "books," which were once separate written scrolls. The word *Bible*, in fact, comes from the Greek term *biblia*, which means "books." The individual books were originally oral material that was subsequently written down in some form perhaps as early as 900 B.C.E., although the final form was not achieved until about 200 B.C.E. It was once thought that Moses wrote the first

Traditional Jews open a Torah scroll in Jerusalem.

Books of the Hebrew Bible

TORAH

Genesis (Bereshit)

Exodus (Shemot)

Leviticus (Vayiqra)

Numbers (Bemidbar)

Deuteronomy (Devarim)

THE PROPHETS (NEVI'IM)

Joshua (Yehoshua)

Judges (Shofetim)

Samuel (Shemuel)

Kings (Melakhim)

Isaiah (Yeshayahu)

Jeremiah (Yirmeyahu)

Ezekiel (Yehezaqel)

Book of the Twelve (Tere Asar): Hosea, Joel, Amos, Obadiah, Jonah, Micah, Nahum, Habakkuk, Zephaniah, Haggai, Zechariah, Malachi

THE WRITINGS (KETUVIM)

Psalms (Tehillim)

Proverbs (Mishle)

Job (Iyyov)

Song of Songs (Shir Hashirim)

Ruth (Ruth)

Lamentations (Ekhah)

Ecclesiastes (Qohelet)

Esther (Ester)

Daniel (Daniel)

Ezra-Nehemiah (Ezra-Nehemyah)

Chronicles (Divre Hayamim)

five books of the Bible—the Torah—but this is no longer commonly held. Instead, scholars see the Torah as composed of four strands of material, which arose in different periods but have been skillfully intertwined by later biblical editors.[1]

The Hebrew Bible is divided into three sections: the **Torah** (the Teaching), **Nevi'im** (the Prophets), and **Ketuvim** (the Writings). Considered as a whole, it is often called **Tanakh** (or Tanak), which is an acronym made up of the first letters of the Hebrew names for the three sections: *t, n, k*.

The Torah is the sacred core of the Hebrew Bible, with its stories of the creation, Adam and Eve, Noah, and the Hebrew patriarchs and matriarchs—the early ancestors of the Hebrew people. It introduces Moses, the great liberator and lawgiver, and his brother Aaron, the founder of the priesthood. It includes laws about daily conduct and religious ritual—material that would be of great importance to the later development of Judaism. Because the Torah comprises five books, it is sometimes called the Pentateuch (Greek: "five scrolls"). (We should recognize that the term *Torah* is also used more widely to refer to all teachings, both written and orally transmitted, that are thought to have been revealed by God.)

The second part of the Tanakh, called the Prophets, is named for those individuals who spoke in God's name to the Jewish people. The books that concentrate on the history of the Israelite kingdom are called the Former Prophets, followed by additional books, which are more strongly visionary and moral in tone, called the Latter (or Later) Prophets. In the Latter Prophets, the voices of the individual prophets tend to predominate.

The third part of the Tanakh, called the Writings, is closer to what we think of as imaginative literature. Although it includes some late historical books, it contains primarily short stories, proverbs, reflections on life, hymn (psalm) lyrics, and poetry.

We will use the term *Hebrew Bible* for all of this material. (Jews do not refer to the Hebrew scriptures as the Old Testament, as do Christians, because the title implies that the Jewish books have meaning only in relation to the Christian books, collectively called the New Testament. Also, the order of books in the Hebrew Bible, in the format that it assumed by the end of the tenth century C.E., differs somewhat from the general order that is found in Christian Bibles.) The commonly used titles of some of the books are Greek, based on early Greek translations.[2]

The historical accuracy of the Hebrew Bible is not always certain, because not all biblical accounts can be verified by archeological finds or references in other historical records. Although we can presume that many of the accounts (particularly those of events after the Jewish kingdom was established) are based on historical fact, we must also recognize that they were recorded by the Jews themselves, who naturally viewed historical events from their own special perspective. Furthermore, many accounts were transmitted orally long before they were written down or assembled in final form, thus affecting the way they were recounted.

BIBLICAL HISTORY

Whatever its historical accuracy, the heroic and mythic power of the Hebrew Bible cannot be denied. It is filled with astonishing people and powerful images. Adam and Eve, for example, stand naked and suddenly aware among the trees and streams of the Garden of Eden. Noah and his wife are surrounded by animals in their big wooden boat, riding out a long flood. Moses climbs to the top of cloud-covered Mount Sinai to speak with God and receive the Ten Commandments. These images and ideas are not only unforgettable, but they are also part of Western culture and have influenced its laws, art, literature, and ways of living.

In the Beginning: Stories of Origins

The earliest stories of the Hebrew Bible, given in Genesis 1–11, have a mythic quality that is universally appealing. The story of the origin of the world presents God as an intelligent, active, masculine power who overcomes primeval chaos. To create order, God imposes separations—separating light from darkness and land from water—and completes his work of creation in stages, spread over six days. At the end of each day, God views what he has done and sees that it is good. Finally, satisfied with the result of all his labor, God rests on the seventh day.

Paradise, by Marc Chagall (1962), captures Adam and Eve, caretakers of the Garden of Eden, just before they partake of the fruit.

This account (which shows parallels with the creation story in the Babylonian epic poem *Enuma Elish*) appears in the first chapter of Genesis, the first book of the Bible. This first account is cosmic and measured—possibly written that way in order to be read out solemnly by a priest at temple ceremonies. The second account (perhaps written earlier than the first) begins in the second chapter of Genesis. This account is more human, utilizes colorful dialogue, and focuses on the first human parents, Adam and Eve, and on their moral dilemma.

The Garden of Eden, which God has created for his refreshment, is based on the pattern of a walled garden, complete with fruit trees, birds, exotic animals, a central fountain, and streams to cool the air. God creates Adam to live in the garden as its gardener and caretaker, forming his body from the dust of the earth and breathing life into Adam with his own breath. In some way, Adam is a copy of God himself, for the human being, the Bible says, is made "in the image of God" (Gen. 1:27),[3] bearing some of the dignity of God. Soon, though, because Adam is lonely, God decides to give him a companion. Taking a rib from Adam while he is in a deep sleep, God forms Eve around that rib. In the first account of creation, male and female were created simultaneously, but in the second account, the male is created first and the female afterward—leading to the interpretation that while the male is a copy of God, the female is only a copy of the male.

Interestingly, the conception of God in the creation stories is somewhat different from many later views. For one thing, although the biblical God has no apparent rivals, he does not appear to be alone, and when he declares "Let *us* make man" (Gen. 1:26),[4] he is most likely addressing his heavenly counselors, some of whom are identified in later texts (such as Psalms and Job). In addition, God is not represented as pure spirit. The account in chapter two of Genesis says that God walks and eats; and having made the garden to enjoy, he strolls in it when he wants to enjoy its cool breezes. God allows Adam and Eve to eat from almost all the trees but forbids them to eat fruit from one of the trees that he especially needs to nourish his supernatural life and insight. Eve, tempted to eat from the forbidden tree, does so, then urges Adam to do the same. For their disobedient act, they are exiled from God's garden. God can no longer trust them, knowing that if they were to remain they might become his rivals. Now they must live outside the garden, work, and suffer for the rest of their amazingly long lives.

To some, the portrait of Eve—a temptress who brings down punishment on Adam and herself—is distressing. But it should be pointed out that Eve is the one with ambition and personality, while Adam seems far less colorful. Whatever the interpretation—and there have been many—the story of Adam and Eve has influenced Western views of women, men, and marriage for several thousand years.

Next is the story of Adam and Eve's children, Cain and Abel (Gen. 4:1–16), whose sibling rivalry ends in Cain's murder of Abel. This tale may reflect ancient rivalries between farmers and herders.

Following this is the story of the Great Flood (Gen. 6–9), which echoes a Mesopotamian tale, the *Epic of Gilgamesh.* Disgusted with the rapidly growing, immoral human population, God sends a flood to do away with humanity—all of humanity, that is, except the righteous Noah and his family. He warns Noah to build a large wooden boat (an ark) and fill it with animals, because only those in the boat will survive the coming downpour. At the end of the flood, God makes a pact with Noah never again to destroy the earth by water. As a sign of this promise, God places his "bow" (perhaps an archer's bow) into the sky. The rainbow is a reminder of his solemn promise. Like several of the early stories, this account gives an explanation for a natural phenomenon. This story also explains how, from the three sons of Noah, different races arise.

Chapter eleven of Genesis tells the story of the tower of Babel (or Babylonia). Wanting to reach the heavenly realm that was believed to exist above the skies, people begin building a very tall tower. God, not willing to have his private world invaded, stops the construction by making the builders speak different languages. Because they can no longer understand each other, they cannot finish their tower. This story also gives a convenient answer to the question, Why are there different languages in the world?

Did Adam, Eve, Cain, Abel, Noah, and the others really exist? For centuries, Jews have thought of them as historical figures. Now, however, influenced by the views of scholars, many Jews view them instead as symbolic figures who set the stage for the events that follow. The first eleven chapters of Genesis are, in effect, a great allegorical introduction to the rest of the Hebrew Bible. There are many indications of this nonhistorical, symbolic purpose. For example, Adam and his immediate descendants are described as living to great ages—Adam is said to have lived to be 930 years old (Gen. 5:5) and Methuselah, the longest-lived, 969 years old (Gen. 5:7). Moreover, many names are apparently symbolic; for example, *Adam* means "humankind" and *Eve* means "life." Scholars also now point out that the stories of the creation and the flood derive from earlier Mesopotamian tales. What is important to understand, though, is that these stories were given new meanings by the Israelite scribes who adapted them.

The World of the Patriarchs and Matriarchs

Abraham is the first Hebrew patriarch (Greek: "father-source"). He is introduced in chapter twelve of Genesis, the point at which the book becomes more seemingly historical. Abraham, first known as Abram, is called by God to leave his home for another land. Originally from Ur (in present-day Iraq), Abraham migrates via Haran (in Turkey) to the land of **Canaan.** "Now the Lord said to Abram, 'Go from your father's house to the land that I will show you. I will make of you a great nation'" (Gen. 12:1–2a).[5] This passage is significant to Judaism because it is seen as establishing a claim to the region now called Israel. Abraham's migration becomes a pilgrimage of great importance, making him, his son Isaac, and his grandson Jacob the patriarchs of Judaism.

After assuring Abraham of land and many descendants, God enters into a solemn **covenant,** a contract, with Abraham. God promises to provide land, protection, and descendants, but in return Abraham and his male descendants must be circumcised as a sign of their exclusive relationship with God (Gen. 17).

The most famous story of Abraham concerns his son Isaac. Abraham has long been unable to have a son by his wife, Sarah. At Sarah's urging, he fathers by her maid, Hagar, a son named Ishmael. But then, to the amazement of all, Sarah herself has a son (Gen. 19). Soon, though, Sarah jealously demands that Ishmael and Hagar be sent away. (This aspect of the story will be important later on in Islam.) Shockingly, God then asks (in Gen. 22) that Abraham offer Isaac, the beloved son of his old age, as a sacrifice. (Perhaps this is a vestige of an earlier practice of human sacrifice.) Abraham agrees and sets out with his son to Mount Moriah, believed by Jews to be the hill on which Jerusalem now rests. Just before the boy is to die, God stops Abraham, and a ram, whose horns had become tangled in a bush nearby, is used as the sacrifice instead. God has thus tested Abraham's devotion, and in so proving his absolute loyalty to God, Abraham has shown himself worthy of land, wealth, fame, and the joy of knowing he will have innumerable descendants. (This passage may show the replacement of human sacrifice with the sacrifice of animals.)

Genesis also contains stories about some extremely memorable women, the matriarchs of the Hebrew people: Sarah, Rebecca, Rachel, and Leah.

Marc Chagall's *Abraham Preparing to Sacrifice His Son* (1931) shows Abraham just as he is on the point of offering his son as a sacrifice. An angel stops his hand and a ram becomes the substitute for sacrifice. This story, also important in Christianity and Islam, shows the obedience of both Abraham and his son.

Although these women are always linked with their husbands, they all have strong and carefully drawn personalities. Sarah, for example, stays modestly inside the tent when strangers arrive but laughs so loudly that they hear her and then question her about why she is laughing (Gen. 18:10–15).

The stories in Genesis also tell of mysterious contacts with God—called **theophanies**—which are sometimes friendly in nature but at other times fierce and frightening. God appears to Isaac, for example, and promises him protection and many descendants (Gen. 26:24). One of Isaac's sons, Jacob, has a vision of God in a dream (Gen. 28). He sees a stairway leading from earth into the sky. God is at the top, and angels are ascending and descending, linking heaven and earth. A more unusual theophany occurs when Jacob wrestles all night long with a mysterious stranger—God or God's angel. At dawn the fight is over, and Jacob receives from the stranger a new name: Israel ("wrestles with God"). Because Jacob and his sons would settle the land of Canaan, it came to be called Israel after his new name. Jacob, with

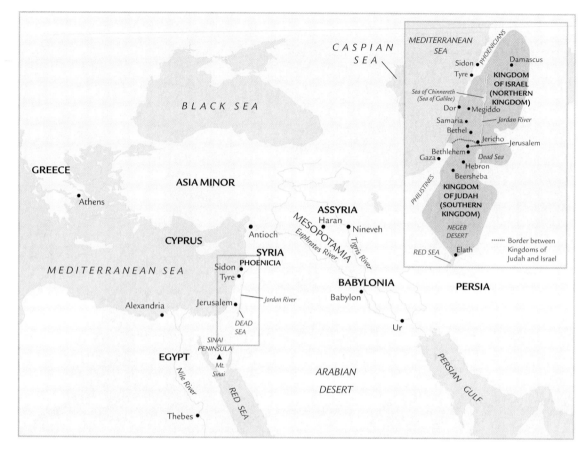

FIGURE 8.1

The eastern Mediterranean with an inset of the two kingdoms (c. 900 B.C.E.)

his two wives and two concubines, has many sons, who would become the ancestors of the twelve tribes of Israel.

Joseph, Jacob's next-to-last son, is the focus of the final section of Genesis. Because Joseph's brothers sense that his father loves him best, they scheme to have him killed. Ultimately, though, they sell him as a slave, and he is taken to Egypt (Figure 8.1). There, through his special gifts, he rises in importance to become a government minister. When a famine in Israel brings his brothers down to Egypt to look for grain, Joseph is not vengeful but invites his brothers to bring their father to Egypt and to settle there permanently. They do so and settle in the land of Goshen in northeastern Egypt. The book of Genesis ends with the death of Jacob.

Before proceeding, we must draw attention to an ongoing debate in biblical studies alluded to earlier in this chapter: How historically true are these stories, especially that of Abraham? Traditional believers and some scholars think that the stories surrounding Abraham do express historical truth, though shaped by oral transmission for many centuries before being written down. Other scholars, however, argue that the Israelites arose in Israel itself, possibly as a landless peasant class that revolted against its rulers. If that view is true, then the story of Abraham and his entry into Israel from else-where may not be historically accurate. In addition, no archeological evidence has yet been found to prove the existence of Abraham. The debate about the historical existence of Abraham may never be resolved.

Moses and the Law

After several centuries, the population of Hebrews in Egypt had grown so large that the Egyptians saw them as a threat. The Book of Exodus tells about the proposed solution: the pharaoh commands that all baby boys be killed at birth. However, the baby Moses (whose name is probably Egyptian) is spared by being hidden. After three months, when his Hebrew mother is afraid to keep him any longer, she and her daughter fashion a watertight basket, put him inside, and place the basket in the Nile River. There he is discovered by an Egyptian princess who raises him as her own. As a young adult, Moses sees an Egyptian foreman badly mistreating an Israelite slave. In trying to put an end to the cruelty, Moses kills the foreman. Moses then flees from Egypt.

Our next glimpse of Moses comes when he has found a new life beyond the borders of Egypt, where he is now a herdsman for a Midianite priest named Jethro, whose daughter he has married. One day, when Moses is out with his father-in-law's herds, he sees a strange sight: a large bush appears to be burning, but it is not consumed. As Moses approaches the bush, he hears the voice of God, who commands Moses to return to Egypt to help free the Hebrews.

Living in a world that believes in many gods, Moses is curious to know the name of the divine spirit speaking to him. The deity, however, refuses to give a clear name and says mysteriously, "I will be who I will be," and then commands Moses to tell the Hebrews "that 'I will be' sent you" (Exod. 3:14).[6] In Hebrew the mysterious answer provides an etymological clue to *the* name for God. The name for God, usually associated with the verb *hayah* ("to be"), is Yhwh. The name is usually written Yahweh, but the exact pronunciation is unknown.

As mentioned, Moses lived in an age when people believed in many gods, and he had grown up in the polytheistic culture of Egypt. People everywhere believed in multiple gods who were thought of as guardian deities of particular groups and regions. Could Moses—or the patriarchs and matriarchs before him—have really been monotheistic? Probably not. A strong possibility is that Moses and the Hebrew patriarchs and matriarchs believed in the existence of many gods, of whom one, possibly a major deity, declared himself the special protector of the Israelites. If this is true, monotheism was not the original belief system of the Israelites but evolved over time. Some scholars wonder whether the actions of the Egyptian pharaoh Akhenaten (Ikhnaton, reigned c. 1352–1336 B.C.E.) influenced the development of Jewish monotheism. Akhenaten gave sole worship to the god Aten, symbolized by the sun, and he unsuccessfully attempted to suppress the worship of all other Egyptian gods. Despite later efforts to undo Akhenaten's work, a hymn in honor of the sun-god Aten was found at Tell-el-Amarna, Akhenaten's capital, and it shows remarkable similarities to the biblical Psalm 104.

Ultimately, the god of the Jews would come to be proclaimed "the one true God." We see two traditions in the Torah. In one (possibly older) tradition, Yahweh is embodied and appears directly to human beings. In another (possibly later) tradition, Yahweh exists as a spirit, existing apart from human beings. The notion of God as being transcendent and distant strengthened over time, and the transformation was complete when Yahweh came to be considered pure spirit and any reference to his body was considered to be metaphorical. In addition, God's name eventually was thought of as being too sacred to be pronounced; instead of speaking the name *Yahweh*, priests and lectors substituted the Hebrew word *Adonay* ("the Lord").[7] Ultimately, all other gods were considered false gods; images of anything that could be construed as a god were prohibited, and Yahweh at last was considered the one God of the entire universe.

But these changes would all occur after the time of Moses. In the book of Exodus, Yahweh, the god of the Hebrews, simply needs to show himself to be more powerful than any of the gods of the Egyptians (Exod. 12:12). It is by his power that ten plagues strike the Egyptians and convince the pharaoh (possibly the great builder Ramses II, c. 1292–1225 B.C.E.) to let his Israelite slaves leave.

The last and greatest of the plagues is the death of the first-born sons of the Egyptians. The Israelites' sons are spared because they have followed Yahweh's warning and have marked the doors of their homes with the blood of a substitute—a sacrificial lamb (Exod. 12:13). Because God has "passed over" Egypt, the event is thereafter called the **Passover** (*Pesach*), and its yearly memorial has become one of the major Jewish festivals (which we will discuss later).

The Bible tells of the Hebrews' journey out of Egypt through a large body of water, the Red Sea, on their way to the Sinai Peninsula. (The Hebrew term may be translated as either "Red Sea" or "Reed Sea." The second translation may refer to the reed-filled marshes of northeastern Egypt.) Movies have dramatized the event, showing two walls of water held back as the Hebrews marched between them. But the reality was possibly less dramatic. Although Egyptian records do not mention it, the exodus from Egypt has become a central theme of Judaism. A whole people, protected by God, leaves a land of oppression and begins the march toward freedom.

The Books of Exodus and Numbers describe in detail the migration back to Israel—a migration that lasted a full generation, about forty years. The most significant event during this period of passage is God's encounter with Moses at Mount Sinai. (The location of the mountain, also called Mount Horeb, is unknown, although tradition has placed it in the southern part of the Sinai Peninsula.) The Book of Exodus (chap. 19) paints a terrifying picture: the mountain is covered with cloud and smoke; lightning and thunder come from the cloud; and the sound of a trumpet splits the air. The people are warned to keep their distance, for only Moses may go to meet God at the top of the mountain. Moses enters the cloud and speaks with God.

The Ten Commandments, symbolized by the Roman numerals, appear on this synagogue in Prague (Czech Republic), along with the six-pointed star of David, another common symbol of Judaism.

When Moses descends, he returns to his people with rules for living—the Ten Commandments (Exod. 20). The strong moral orientation of Judaism is apparent here, for Moses does not return with an explanation of the universe, with science, or with art, but rather with ethical precepts. Parallels have been drawn to several other early codes, particularly that of the Babylonian King Hammurabi (c. 1792–1750 B.C.E.).

Undergirding the commandments is the conviction that a covenant—a contract—exists between Yahweh and his people. He will care for them, but they must fulfill their half of the bargain by following his laws and giving him sole worship. Such an agreement had already been made between God and Noah and later with Abraham. The covenant is reaffirmed with Moses and solidified by the laws and commandments, which give it legal form.

Following the Ten Commandments, the Book of Exodus outlines obligations regarding the treatment of slaves, animals, and property. (These instructions were probably deliberately placed here to share in the respect given the Ten Commandments.) We see here important texts that were mined by later teachers for their insight into fairness, justice, and compassion. They take up quite specific cases. In one story, for example, when a landowner begins a fire in his field that spreads to and destroys another landowner's field, the first landowner must pay damages to the second landowner (Exod. 22:6). In another situation, a neighbor's cow or donkey has run loose and the person who sees the animal is obligated to take it back to its owner (Exod. 23:4).

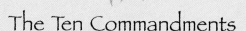

The Ten Commandments

I am the Lord your God who brought you out of Egypt, out of the land of slavery. You shall have no other god to set against me.

The Ten Commandments[9] begin with a reminder that Yahweh is the protector of the Hebrews and that because of his help they owe him their obedience. There seems to be an understanding, however, that other peoples have their own gods.

You shall not make a carved image for yourself nor the likeness of anything in the heavens above, or on the earth below, or in the waters under the earth. You shall not bow down to them or worship them; for I, the Lord your God, am a jealous god. I punish the children for the sins of their fathers to the third and fourth generations of those who hate me. But I keep faith with thousands, with those who love me and keep my commandments.

The commandment not to make images was meant to prevent worship of any deity but Yahweh, and it has been observed quite strictly over the centuries. Although a few early synagogue paintings of human figures have been found,[10] the prohibition has restrained in general the development of Jewish painting and sculpture. Only in the past hundred years have Jewish artists emerged, and many have been nonrepresentational artists.

You shall not make wrong use of the name of the Lord your God; the Lord will not leave unpunished the man who misuses his name.

The commandment against misuse of Yahweh's name opposes using God's name to bring misfortune on people, as by curses and black magic. Eventually, it was considered unacceptable to pronounce the name of Yahweh for any purpose whatsoever. Only the high priest had this privilege and did this but once a year.

Remember to keep the Sabbath day holy. You have six days to labor and do all your work. But the seventh day is a Sabbath of the Lord your God; that day you shall not do any work, you, your son or your daughter, your slave or your slave-girl, your cattle or the alien within your gates; for in six days the Lord made heaven and earth, the sea, and all that is in them,

and on the seventh day He rested. Therefore the Lord blessed the Sabbath day and declared it holy.

The commandment to keep the Sabbath was a humane commandment, intended to give regular rest to servants, slaves, children, workers, and animals.

Honor your father and your mother, that you may live long in the land which the Lord your God is giving you.

The commandment to honor one's parents offers a reward: long life. We should note that Hebrews generally thought of rewards and punishments as being given on earth and in one's lifetime. The notion of rewards given in a future life or an afterlife was a later development.

You shall not commit murder.

This commandment does not prohibit all killing but prohibits murder—that is, unlawful and undeserved killing of human beings. Killing human beings in wartime and in self-defense was allowable, and execution was expected as the punishment for many types of crime.

You shall not commit adultery.

The commandment against adultery is only incidentally concerned with sex. Primarily it is a property law, because a man's wife was legally considered his property. This commandment is linked with the commandments immediately before and after it, because all three refer to property rights. To murder is to take unlawful possession of another person's body; to commit adultery is to disregard a man's right to sole possession of his wife; and to steal is to take unlawful possession of another person's goods.

You shall not steal.

You shall not give false evidence against your neighbor.

You shall not covet your neighbor's house; you shall not covet your neighbor's wife, his slave-girl, his ox, his ass, or anything that belongs to him.

In this last commandment, property rights are linked together and spelled out clearly.

The Book of Leviticus begins with detailed laws about animal sacrifice (chaps. 1–7) and then takes up the complexities of ritual purity. In addition to laws about general honesty and humaneness, Leviticus outlines many special laws that would be important to the later development of Judaism: laws specifying which animals may and may not be eaten (chap. 11), laws prohibiting the consumption of meat with blood in it (17:10) or the cutting of one's beard (19:27), and laws governing the observance of the major religious festivals (chap. 23). The Book of Numbers returns to historical themes, recounting specifically the years of wandering before the Hebrews entered Canaan but also spelling out laws about ritual purity and the keeping of vows. The Torah ends with the Book of Deuteronomy, which repeats the Ten Commandments and describes the death of Moses, an event that occurs just before the Hebrews enter the Promised Land of Canaan.[8]

The historicity of Moses is, like that of Abraham, another focus of debate. Virtually all Jews believe him to have been a real person. So far, however, no Egyptian archeological records have been found that mention Moses, a slave rebellion, or an exodus from Egypt; and no archeological evidence has yet been found to give proof of the forty years of wandering in the desert. This lack of evidence, however, does not disprove the historicity of Moses. A common view sees the biblical account as representing basic historical truth that has been magnified and embellished over time.

The Judges and Kings

After Moses' death, the Israelites were led by men and women who had both military and legal power, called judges. To think of them as military generals is more accurate than to envision them as modern-day courtroom judges. The Books of Joshua and Judges describe this period.

Joshua, the Hebrew Bible records, is the general who leads the Hebrews across the Jordan River after Moses' death. (The historical accuracy of this account, which so closely resembles the story of Moses' crossing the sea, is often debated.) Under Joshua's leadership, the Hebrew tribes take the town of Jericho, with the help of spies and the assistance of Rahab, a prostitute of the town, who hides them. After this victory, the Israelites take additional territory, and the land of Canaan is divided up among eleven of the tribes. Only the tribe of Levi is not given land, because members of this tribe are to serve as priests and assistants in worship; instead of land, members receive a portion of religious offerings and other forms of regular support. Realizing that they need to be unified for their protection, the people of Israel soon establish a king, select a capital city, impose a system of laws, and build a temple for centralized worship. The biblical Books of 1–2 Samuel and 1–2 Kings describe the process.

The first king, Saul (whose reign began c. 1025 B.C.E.), became a tragic figure, suffering repeatedly from depression and then dying after a battle— one tradition says from suicide (1 Sam. 31:4). After a civil war divided the country's allegiance, a new king emerged to lead Israel. David (c. 1013–973 B.C.E.) was a young man from Bethlehem, a town in the tribal area of Judah.

As an accomplished military leader, David oversaw the buildup of the kingdom. Recognizing the need for a central city, he took over the hilltop town of Jebus, renaming it Jerusalem and establishing it as the national capital. Because David was described as a musician, many psalms are attributed to him, and because he had a strong interest in religious ritual, he is also said to have planned to build a temple in Jerusalem where national religious ceremonies could be carried out. He died, however, before he could accomplish that goal. No certain archeological evidence for David has yet been found, but his historicity is not generally doubted. Archeological evidence does exist, however, for his son Solomon.

David's son Solomon built and dedicated the First Temple in Jerusalem, thus creating a home for Yahweh, whose presence it was hoped would protect the kingdom. The exact design of Solomon's temple is not certain, but it was probably a long, tall, rectangular building—designed according to similar temples in the region—that featured an interior sanctuary and outdoor courtyards for sacrifices and gatherings. Services included prayers by priests, with hymns sung by choirs and accompanied by musical instruments, such as trumpets, lyres (harplike stringed instruments), and cymbals. Incense and grain were common offerings, and animals were ritually killed and offered as burnt sacrifices to Yahweh. Some sacrifices, called holocaust offerings, demanded that all the animal be burnt and thus transported upward to God. Other sacrifices involved the offering of the animal's blood and fat to God, thus allowing the priests and the offerer to share in a meal of cooked meat from the animal parts that remained.[11]

Having a royal palace and the national temple in Jerusalem unified the separate Hebrew tribes for a time, but the taxes required to fund these and other extensive building projects made the people rebellious. After the death of Solomon, the northern tribes broke away from the control of the king in Jerusalem and set up their own kingdom.

Division weakened the two kingdoms, and in 721 B.C.E. Assyria, an expanding power in the northeast, took over the northern kingdom. A theological explanation for the destruction of the northern kingdom came from prophets of the time. **Prophets** (human beings who spoke in God's name) were significant figures—both as groups and as individuals—from the earliest days of the kingdom; but individual prophets became important in the three hundred years after 800 B.C.E. Typically the prophet experienced a life-changing revelation from God and then felt commissioned by God to speak his message to the people. The prophet Isaiah, who was active in the eighth century B.C.E., is possibly the best known. He had a vision of God in the temple of Jerusalem, which he described as being filled with smoke (symbolic of the divine presence) and the voices of the angels crying out "Holy, holy, holy" in the presence of God (Isa. 6). His feeling of unworthiness dissolved when an angel touched a lighted coal to his lips, thus purifying and empowering Isaiah. From then on, he could speak his message. Isaiah and other prophets explained that political losses were punishment from Yahweh for worshiping other gods and for not having kept his laws. The losses were not a sign of God's weakness but rather of his justice and strength.

What's in a Name?

Just one example of the immense cultural influence of the Hebrew Bible is evident in many commonly used names. Following are some personal names from the Hebrew Bible, along with their original meanings:

Aaron	("exalted one")	Jonathan	("The Lord has given")
Abel	("breath")	Joshua	("The Lord's help")
Abigail	("father is rejoicing")	Malachi	("my messenger")
Abraham	("father of many")	Micah	("Who is like [God]?")
Adam	("humankind")	Michael	("Who is like God?")
Amos	("carried [by God]")	Miriam	("rebellion")
Benjamin	("favorite son")	Naomi	("my delight")
Caleb	("dog," meaning "faithful")	Nathan	("gift")
Daniel	("God is my judge")	Noah	("rest")
David	("beloved")	Oprah	(re-spelling of Orpah: "back of the neck")
Deborah	("bee")		
Esther	("[the goddess] Ishtar")	Rachel	("ewe")
Eve	("life")	Rebecca	("noose")
Isaac	("laughter")	Reuben	("behold, a son")
Isaiah	("The Lord is my salvation")	Ruth	("companion")
Jacob	("seizing by the heel")	Samuel	("name of God")
Jared	("descent")	Sarah	("princess")
Jeremy	("The Lord frees")	Seth	("appointed")
Joel	("The Lord is God")		

The southern kingdom, the kingdom of Judah, carried on alone, although with constant anxiety, for more than a century. Unfortunately, another power had emerged—Babylonia—and at first the remaining southern kingdom paid tribute; but when tribute was refused, Babylonia took control. In 586 B.C.E. Nebuchadnezzar II destroyed Solomon's temple, tore down the city walls of Jerusalem, and took the aristocracy and a great part of the Jewish population off to Babylonia into an exile that would last almost fifty years. Because the kingdom had ended and temple worship was no longer possible, the religion of Israel seemed to lose its heart.

Exile and Captivity

The period of exile in Babylonia (586–539 B.C.E.) was a monumental turning point and one of the most emotional chapters in the history of Judaism. Psalm 137 is a manifestation of the sorrow felt by the Jews during their captivity. It tells of their inability to sing happy songs as long as they were in exile: "By the rivers of Babylon—there we sat down and there we wept when we remembered Zion."[12]

Zoroastrianism

Although Zoroastrianism today is a small religion (found mostly in India), it was once a religion of millions, and its influence spread far beyond its home in Persia. It was begun by the prophet Zarathustra (or Zoroaster), who was born (c. 650 B.C.E.) in what is now Iran. Zarathustra was surrounded by the worship of nature gods, common to the Aryan religion, which was also practiced in India. As in Indian Vedic religion, the religion of Zarathustra's culture involved the worship of gods at fire altars, the use of a ritual drink (*haoma,* like the Vedic *soma*), and a hereditary priesthood. Like the Buddha after him, Zarathustra was distressed by the sacrifice of animals at the fire altars and by the power of the priests.

At about the age of 30, Zarathustra experienced a vision that changed his life. He felt himself transported heavenward by a spirit he called *Vohu Manah* ("good mind"), into the presence of the High God *Ahura Mazda* ("wise lord"), a god associated in Zarathustra's mind with cosmic justice. Like the calls of Isaiah and Muhammad (see chapter 10), this revelation led Zarathustra to preach his new message. At first, Zarathustra was met with strong rejection, which he blamed on demons (*daevas*) and the satanic head of evil forces, *Angra Mainyu* ("wicked spirit"). Zarathustra's bitter experiences deepened his sense that evil forces constantly oppose the forces of goodness. He was undaunted, however, and his preaching eventually converted an Iranian king, Vishtaspa, who used his power to spread Zarathustra's new religion. Zarathustra condemned animal sacrifices, but he maintained the ceremonial use of the Aryan fire altar. Although fire was not to be worshiped, Zarathustra considered it to be symbolic of divine goodness. Tradition relates that Zarathustra died in his seventies, killed by invaders while praying at his fire altar.

What we know of Zarathustra comes from the most ancient part of the Avesta, the Zoroastrian scriptures. They teach of a high God, Ahura Mazda, who expresses himself through good spirits whose names are virtues. Whether these spirits are simply aspects of Ahura Mazda or independent beings is unclear. The most important is called *Spenta Mainyu* ("holy spirit"). Others, for example, have names that mean "power," "devotion," "immortality," and "obedience." (We find some tantalizing similarities in the Jewish mystical literature of the Kabbalah, in Gnosticism, and in some New Testament letters.)

Although Zoroastrianism is ultimately monotheistic, it sees the universe in morally dualistic terms. Forces of good are in perpetual conflict with forces of evil—a conflict that mysteriously began at the start of time. Each person is involved in this cosmic struggle and thus must make moral choices between good and evil. Good actions include telling the truth and dealing honestly with others—in the Avesta, good actions include cultivating farmland and treating animals kindly. There is a belief in divine judgment and in an afterlife of reward or punishment, which begins at death when each individual's soul must cross a bridge that can lead to paradise. If the individual has been good, the bridge is wide and the journey to paradise is easy; but if the individual has been evil, the bridge becomes so narrow that the soul falls into the depths of hell.

Zoroastrianism also presents an apocalyptic vision of the end of time: when the world comes to an end, there will be a resurrection of all bodies and a great general judgment; at this time the world will be purified by fire, which will punish the evil but leave the good untouched. Because Zoroastrianism was widespread in the Near East and Middle East for centuries, some see its influence in the worldviews of the Essenes (a semimonastic faction of Judaism), in some later books of Jewish scripture (such as Job and Daniel), in early Christianity, and in Islam.

Zoroastrianism has long been a highly ritualistic religion. At the center of its worship is the fire altar, where priests dressed in white attend an eternal flame. To keep the flame from impurity, an attendant must wear a white cloth (*padan*) that covers his nose and mouth. Believers who come to pray take off their shoes and touch the door frame reverently.

Several rites of passage are significant in this religion. Perhaps the most important ceremony is a coming-of-age ceremony (*Navjote*), performed for both boys and girls near puberty. The young person is given a white muslin shirt (*sudreh*) as a symbol of pure intention and a cord (*kusti*) to be worn around the waist as a symbol of dedication. The marriage ceremony is another rite of passage, important to the whole community. The marriage is performed by a priest in the bride's home. The bride and groom, both dressed in white, have their hands tied together during the ceremony to show the bond between them. Finally, there is the funeral rite. Because death is considered a form of corruption of the body, the corpse is disposed of in a way that will least contaminate the elements of nature. Traditionally, Zoroastrians have tried to avoid cremation (which they believe contaminates the element of fire) or burial (which they believe contaminates earth and water). Instead, they are famous for the low circular towers (*dakhma*), where dead bodies are exposed to birds of prey and to the elements of nature. These towers exist in Iran and India, but in places where no burial towers exist, contemporary Zoroastrians do make use of burial or cremation.

The central festival is NoRuz, a New Year festival that is held at the time of the spring equinox, on or near March 21. It is celebrated not only by Zoroastrians but by Iranians of many faiths, who do spring cleaning, wear new clothing, and eat festive meals. Jumping over outdoor fires is a unique practice—it is thought to bring health during the coming year. Because seven is a sacred number, people create side tables at home with seven ritual items, many of which are symbolic of new life. These may include new green shoots of wheat, colored hardboiled eggs, garlic, wine or vinegar, candles, a mirror, and a bowl of goldfish. Meals made of seven other foods, such as apples, pudding, dried fruit, and pastries, are also eaten. These groups of seven originally recalled Ahura Mazda and the six Holy Immortals, the spirits through whom Ahura Mazda expresses himself.

Contemporary Zoroastrianism is in something of a state of crisis because of its dwindling numbers. Although Zoroastrianism was once the widespread state religion of Persia, only about fifty thousand Zoroastrians live in Iran today. Large numbers moved to India more than a thousand years ago, where they settled in Mumbai (Bombay) and created their own distinctive culture. In India they are called Parsees ("Persians") and number about a hundred thousand. Because of their regard for education and hard work, their contributions to science, industry, and music in India have been extraordinary. As a result of recent emigration, perhaps another fifty thousand live in large cities in North America, England, and Australia. Among believers, debate rages about intermarriage with people of other faiths, about conversion, about whether the priesthood should be only hereditary, and about translation of the sacred texts for services. Conservatives believe that strict keeping of traditional practices will protect their religion, while liberals believe that the religion will die unless there is change.

Without a temple, public ritual had come to an end, but in its place the written word took on new importance. During their exile in Babylonia, the Jews began to meet weekly to discuss the scriptures and to pray. What developed was the **Sabbath** service of worship, study, sermon, and psalms, performed in a meetinghouse, or *synagogue* (Greek: "lead together"). The period of exile also made it clear that the oral Hebrew religious traditions had to be written down if the Jews were to survive.

During their exile, the Jewish people began to assimilate influences from the surrounding Babylonian culture. Knowledge of the Hebrew language declined, while Aramaic, a sister language, emerged as the common tongue. (Aramaic eventually even crept into the sacred literature. While Hebrew is the canonical language of scripture, a few passages, and in some cases whole chapters, are in Aramaic, although the reason for the latter is not clear.[13]) Also emerging at this time was a growing sense of an active spirit of evil, often called Satan, and of a cosmic antagonism between good and evil. The sense of moral opposition, while present in the Israelite religion from an early time, may have been sharpened from this time on, both by the pain of exile and by subsequent contact with the Persian religion of Zoroastrianism.

Return to Jerusalem and the Second Temple

In 540 B.C.E., Cyrus came to the throne of the Persian Empire and, after taking over Babylonia, allowed the Jews to return to their homeland. The returning exiles rebuilt their temple, dedicating it in 515 B.C.E., and the sacrificial cult was reestablished. The Book of Psalms, containing the lyrics of 150 hymns, is often called the hymnbook of the Second Temple, and when we read in the closing psalms of all the instruments used in temple worship, we get a sense of the splendor of the ceremonies performed there.

The new temple inaugurated an era, called the period of the Second Temple, in which the work of priests took on great importance. Priests worked out in detail the ceremonies of the Second Temple, because it played an expanded role as the religious center not only for the land of Israel but also for all Jews who lived abroad. Some Jews, we might note, had remained in their adopted country of Babylonia; as a result, a significant Jewish presence was established there that would last more than a thousand years. There was also a large population of Jews living in northern Egypt, and Jews who lived outside Israel often made pilgrimage to the temple in Jerusalem, as long as it existed.

At the same time, the work of recording oral traditions and editing written material also grew in importance. Scribes did not want the history of their people to be lost, and the result of their work was to become the Hebrew Bible. A final edition of the Torah (Pentateuch) was made, the prophetic books were compiled, and new books were written as well. Several of the last books written were literary—such as Ecclesiastes, a dark meditation on life, and the Song of Songs, a collection of love poetry. One work, the Book of Daniel, was apocalyptic, envisioning a final judgment at the end of the world—a vision possibly influenced by Zoroastrianism. Among these late literary works, the Book of Job is one of the world's first written attempts to understand the suffering of an innocent person. Possibly reflecting a Zoroastrian sense of a cosmic struggle between good and evil, in Job the role of Satan is important. (The name might be better translated as "the Satan," because the word means "adversary" or "prosecutor.") The books that would eventually be accepted into the Hebrew canon were finished by about 200 B.C.E.[14]

CULTURAL CONFLICT DURING THE SECOND TEMPLE ERA

The historical record in the canonical Hebrew scriptures ends with the building of the Second Temple. But the history of the region did not end here. Because of the geographic location of Israel, it seemed that the Jews in Israel would continually have to contend with invasions—and in some cases conquests—by foreign powers.

The Seleucid Period

When the army of Alexander the Great was on its way to conquer Egypt, it made Israel part of the Greek Empire, and after Alexander's death in 323 B.C.E, his generals divided up his empire. Israel at first was controlled by Egypt, which was ruled by the descendants of Alexander's general Ptolemy. Later, Israel was controlled by Syria, ruled by the descendants of Alexander's general Seleucus.

In 167 B.C.E. a Seleucid ruler, Antiochus IV (Antiochus Epiphanes) took over the temple, apparently with the intention of introducing the worship of the Greek god Zeus to the site. His deliberately placing pork (a forbidden meat) on the altar and his prohibition of circumcision caused such hatred among the Jews that they rebelled. Led by a Jewish family of five brothers, the Maccabees (or Hasmoneans), the Jews took back the rule of their country, and the temple was rededicated to the worship of Israel's one God. (The winter festival of **Hanukkah,** widely kept today, is a joyous memorial that recalls that rededication of the Second Temple.) The country retained its autonomy for almost a century, until the Roman general Pompey took control in 63 B.C.E.

Antagonism between Jewish culture and the growing Greek-speaking culture in the region was inevitable, because Jewish culture had values and practices that made absorption into Greek culture difficult, if not impossible. For example, all Jewish males were circumcised, which meant they were easily identified in the public baths or while exercising in gymnasiums. There were also Jewish dietary restrictions that forbade the eating of pork and shellfish and strict prohibitions against work on the Sabbath. These practices conflicted with the sophisticated Greek-speaking culture called Hellenism (from *Hellas,* meaning "Greece"), a culture that was becoming dominant in the entire Mediterranean area, even after the Romans took control of the region. Greek plays and literature were read everywhere around the Mediterranean; Greek history, science, medicine, and mathematics were considered the most advanced of their day; and Greek architecture and city planning were becoming the norm. Because of its sophistication, Hellenistic culture was hugely attractive to educated people.

Responses to Outside Influences

Contact with Hellenistic culture led to a variety of responses. Some welcomed and adopted it, either in whole or in part; some rejected it, clinging passionately to their own ethnic and religious roots; and the rest took a position in between. Tensions led to the rise of several religious factions among the Jews in Israel during this period, after 165 B.C.E.

The **Sadducees** were the first of the factions to emerge.[15] They were members of the priestly families, living primarily in Jerusalem, and were in charge of the temple and its activities. The fact that they derived their living from temple worship would have made them traditional—at least in their public behavior. They accepted the Torah as sacred but generally did not accept other books as being equally inspired—a position that brought them into conflict with other groups.

The **Pharisees** were the second faction that arose.[16] Their focus was on preserving Hebrew piety through careful observation of religious laws and traditions. Because of their emphasis on daily religious practice, the Pharisees relied heavily on the scriptures for devotional guidance. They accepted as canonical a wider number of books than did the Sadducees—a source of conflict with the priests—and they valued the oral tradition that accompanied the written Torah, a tradition they traced back to Moses. (Later rabbinical Judaism would develop from and continue the work of the Pharisees.)

A third faction, eventually called the **Zealots,** was opposed to foreign influences and after 6 C.E. was bitterly opposed to Roman rule of Israel. The Romans called them "robbers." The name Zealots—from the Greek word for *zeal*—was given to them when wars began between the Jews and the Romans. The patriots sometimes used violent means to achieve their ends.

The **Essenes** were the fourth group. Not a great deal is known with certainty about them, although current interest in them is intense. They were written about by three authors of the classical world: Philo (c. 10 B.C.E.–50 C.E.), a Jewish theologian of Alexandria; Josephus (c. 37–100 C.E.), a Jewish general and historian; and Pliny the Elder (23–79 C.E.), a Roman writer. These classical writers indicate that the Essenes numbered several thousand; lived a communal, celibate life, primarily in the desert area near the Dead Sea; rejected animal sacrifice; and avoided meat and wine. We also are told that the Essenes were skilled in medicine; dressed in white; followed a solar calendar that was different from the lunar calendar used in the temple; studied the scriptures assiduously; and kept separate from the rest of society. Moreover, we now recognize that there may have been several varieties of Essenes and that a strict celibate core at Qumran (called the Covenanters) was supported by a non-celibate network of supporters and sympathizers throughout Israel.

A common theory holds that the Essenes began as a breakaway group of priests opposed to the Maccabee family's takeover of the high priesthood. They saw themselves as an advance guard, preparing for the time when God would end the old world of injustice and bring about a new world of mercy and peace. They described themselves as "sons of light" who were fighting against the forces of "darkness."[17] Because their center was no more than fifteen miles east of Jerusalem, they would have had some contact with the political currents of their day, and they may have shared some of the ideals of the Zealots and Pharisees.

Scrolls and scroll fragments, called the Dead Sea Scrolls, were uncovered between 1947 and 1955 in caves near Qumran, above the northwestern shore of the Dead Sea. It is possible that the scrolls constituted the library of the Essenes or that they were a more general library of Jewish sacred books brought from Jerusalem for safekeeping during the rebellion against the Romans that began in 66 C.E. Besides containing all or part of nearly every book of the Hebrew scriptures, the cache of scrolls contained works that commented on scriptural books, gave details about the organization and practices of the Essenes, and spoke of a coming judgment and end of the world. The Dead Sea Scrolls show that during the later part of the Second-Temple period, there was no universally accepted norm of correct religion, and the canon of scripture was still in the process of formation. Instead, there were many books and interpretations of correct practice, each competing for acceptance.

Although the Second Temple was flourishing, the older, ceremonial, temple-based religion was in fact giving way to a more decentralized

Inside the Shrine of the Book in Jerusalem, a visitor inspects examples of the Dead Sea Scrolls. The building is or in the shape of one of the jars in which the scrolls were stored.

The Dead Sea Scrolls were preserved for 2,000 years in these caves near Qumran.

religion, based on the Hebrew scriptures, on the practice of the Pharisees, and on religious practice in the synagogues.

THE DEVELOPMENT OF RABBINICAL JUDAISM

The Roman Empire assumed direct political control of much of Israel in 6 C.E, and it ruled with severity. Consequently, there was much anti-Roman fervor and a widespread hope that, as in the time of the Maccabees, the foreigners could be expelled and a Jewish kingdom reestablished. A major revolt broke out in 66 C.E., but Roman legions crushed it brutally in 70 C.E., when they destroyed the temple and much of Jerusalem.

The end of the Second Temple was a turning point for the Jewish faith, producing two major effects. It ended the power of the priesthood, whose sacrificial rituals were no longer possible. It also forced the religion to develop in a new direction away from temple ritual, moving Judaism toward a central focus on scripture and scriptural interpretation.

The Canon of Scripture and the Talmud

Once the temple-based religion had been destroyed, it was necessary to clearly define which religious books—of the several hundred being revered and read by various groups—constituted the sacred canon. Although scholars now question it, an old tradition holds that in about 90 C.E., twenty years after the destruction of the Second Temple, Jewish rabbis gathered together in Israel at the town of Yavneh (Jamnia). There, it is said, they examined each book individually to decide which books would be included in the canon. (Some books, such as the Song of Songs and Ecclesiastes, were hotly debated and were almost excluded.) The canon of the land of Israel resulted from this process of selection. A slightly larger number of books had already been accepted by Jews in Egypt and came to be known as the Alexandrian canon.

Another revolt began in Israel in 132 C.E. Some declared its leader, Bar Kokhba, to be the **Messiah,** the long-awaited savior sent by God to the Jews. (We might note that the Jewish concept of a Messiah was generally that of a general or kinglike ruler who would have military powers.) In 135 C.E., the Romans put down this second revolt even more cruelly than the first, with many public executions. Jerusalem was demolished and rebuilt as a Roman city, with a new name, Aelia Capitolina, and Jews were forbidden to live there. Jewish families who had remained in Israel even after the destruction of the Second Temple now fled. They went not only to Egypt but settled around the Mediterranean, expanding the number of Jews living in the **diaspora** (dispersion of Jews beyond Israel). The existence of a canon of scripture, which could be copied and carried anywhere, brought victory out of apparent defeat. Rabbinical Judaism, based on interpreting sacred scripture and oral tradition, could spread and flourish.

Once the Hebrew scriptures were declared complete, the next logical development was their protection and explanation. Interpretive work, called midrash ("seeking out"), became a central focus of evolving Judaism. Some

Jewish teachers held that the teachings of God had been passed on not only in the written Torah but also in an oral form to Moses, who came to be called "our Rabbi." Rabbis held that the "oral Torah" was passed on by Moses to Joshua and from him to others in an unbroken line. This concept of an oral Torah given by God as a counterpart of the written Torah is sometimes called "the dual Torah," and it helped give great authority to later rabbinical commentary.

The work of interpreting the Hebrew scriptures and applying their principles to everyday problems went on in stages. By about 200 C.E. there existed a philosophical discussion in six parts of specific biblical laws and their application, called the Mishnah ("repetition"). By about 400 C.E., the Mishnah had received further commentary (the Gemara, "supplement"), and the result was the Palestinian **Talmud** ("study"), or Talmud of the Land of Israel.

When people use the word *Talmud*, however, they usually are referring to a second, larger collection of material—called the Babylonian Talmud to distinguish it from the earlier, shorter commentary—completed by about 600 C.E. and compiled by religious specialists in Babylonia. It consists of the earlier Mishnah and an extensive commentary. After the Hebrew Bible itself, the Babylonian Talmud became the second most important body of Jewish literature, and it continued to be commented on over the centuries by rabbinical specialists. (A modern edition by Rabbi Adin Steinsaltz is the most recent example.)

The Babylonian Talmud is vast, sometimes being compared to an ocean in which a person can sail or swim. In the Babylonian Talmud, rabbis of different generations added their insights and solutions to problems. The growth of opinion is visible, because the earliest material is printed in the center of each page, and later commentary is arranged around it. The Babylonian Talmud contains legal material (*halakhah*, "direction") and nonlegal anecdotes and tales (*haggadah*, "tradition"). It is really a large encyclopedia, organized into sections, or tractates, according to subject matter. Its size and complexity, along with the difficulty of mastering it, would contribute to a strong scholarly orientation in later Judaism.

Islam and Medieval Judaism

The diaspora introduced Jewish vitality to places far from Israel, such as Spain and Iraq. After the ninth century, this Jewish presence was possible because of the tolerance with which Islam—now dominant in Spain, North Africa, and the Middle East—usually treated the Jews. Islam has held that Jews and Christians have a special status: called "peoples of the Book," they are members with Muslims in the same extended religious family. The result was that cities such as Alexandria, Cairo, Baghdad, and Córdoba became havens for Jewish thought.

Jewish academies in Babylonia continued the tradition of learning that had produced the Babylonian Talmud. The great scholar Saadia ben Joseph (Said al-Fayyumi, 882–942 C.E.) translated the Hebrew scriptures into Arabic

Two rabbis speak:
Hillel used to say: If I am not for myself, who will be for me? Yet if I am for myself only, what am I?

Shammai said:
Set a fixed time for thy study of the Torah; say little and do much; and receive all men with a cheerful countenance.

—from The Sayings of the Fathers[18]

and wrote commentaries that synthesized Jewish and Greek thought. He also composed a prayer book, which has been used throughout the Jewish world. The other great center of learning was in Islamic Spain. Saadia's thought was carried there, providing a matrix for the philosophy and poetry of the Jewish Academy of Córdoba, which flourished in the tenth and eleventh centuries.

Foremost among the Jewish medieval thinkers was Moses Maimonides (called Rambam, 1135–1204), who was born in Córdoba but who fled that city with his family when it was occupied by Muslim forces hostile to both Jews and Christians. He eventually settled in Cairo, where he practiced medicine at the court of Salah-al-Din (Saladin). The work that made him famous was his book *The Guide of the Perplexed,* in which he argued that Judaism was a rational religion and that faith and reason were complementary. He wrote this work in Arabic in order to make it accessible to a wide readership. Maimonides is also known for his *Mishneh Torah,* a scholarly work written in Hebrew, which is a religious code of fourteen books that summarizes the legal formulations of the Talmud and other rabbinical writings. Maimonides is renowned for his list of the basic principles of Jewish belief, which we will discuss later in this chapter.

Jewish thought has consistently shown several approaches in its interpretation of the Hebrew Bible. The more conservative tendency, which produced the Talmud, has interpreted the Hebrew scriptures fairly strictly, using them as a guide for ethical living. This tendency has generated much written commentary about the application of principles that had developed in an earlier agrarian society to later, often urban lifestyles.

Another trend has been speculative, using the scriptures imaginatively as a way to understand more about the nature of God and the universe. Out of this second tendency came works of Jewish mysticism, which we look at next.

The Kabbalah

The Middle Ages saw renewed interest in Jewish mysticism. The whole body of Jewish mystical literature, called **Kabbalah** ("received," "handed down"), began to emerge even before the common era in works that speculated on mysterious passages of the Hebrew Bible. For example, kabbalistic literature speculated about Enoch (an early descendant of Adam) and the prophet Elijah, who had not died but had simply been transported upward to God's realm (Gen. 5:24 and 2 Kings 2:11). It also speculated about Yahweh's throne (*merkebah*) and the sound of the surrounding angels (see Isa. 6:2), using the scriptures as a tool for understanding more about the reality of God and the hidden structure of the universe. A frequent mystical assumption was that the Hebrew Bible was written in coded language that could be interpreted only by those who knew the code. Much biblical language, this view held, was to be read not literally but symbolically.

A special key for mystical interpretation was *gematria*—the practice of transposing words into numbers. (The term *gematria* is related to the word *geometry.*) For example, *aleph,* the first letter of the Hebrew alphabet, would be given a value of 1; the second letter, *beth,* a 2; and so on. In this way, the letters of every word could be added up and correspondences between similar sums could be found.

New mystical speculation arose in the medieval period, sometimes as a response to the growing persecution of Jews. Common themes were the divine origin of the world, God's care for the Jews, and the eventual coming of the Messiah (spoken of in Dan. 7 and elsewhere). The human world was frequently seen as the microcosm of a greater heavenly world beyond the earth and the human being as a microcosm of the universe: "the superior and inferior worlds are bound together under the form of the Holy Body, and the worlds are associated together."[19] What was learned about the microcosm would then give insight into the larger realm, and vice versa.

The most famous book of the Kabbalah is the *Zohar* ("splendor"). It was long believed to have been written in the first centuries of the common era, but in actuality it was probably written about 1280 in Spain by Rabbi Moses de León. The *Zohar* sees the universe as having emerged from a pure, boundless, spiritual reality. From the divine Unity come the ten *sefiroth*—ten active, divine powers, such as wisdom, intelligence, love, and beauty. The *Zohar* compares these sefiroth to individual colors: "from the innermost center of the flame sprang forth a well out of which colors issued and spread upon everything beneath, hidden in the mysterious hiddenness of the Infinite."[20] The sefiroth of God manifest themselves in the structure of the physical world and are a bridge between the world of God and the human world. Human beings are particularly significant in creation, blending the divine and the earthly, for within their bodies is a spark of divine light that seeks liberation and return to God. Other texts included the *Sefer Yetzira* and the *Sefer HaHasidim*. Some Jewish circles valued the mystical texts of the Kabbalah as much as, or even more than, the Talmud.[21]

Christianity and Medieval Judaism

The mystical movements gave comfort to European Jews as their persecution increased. Christianity had become the dominant religion in all Europe by the late thirteenth century, but Christianity carried with it an anti-Jewish prejudice that had been present since the first century C.E., when Christianity was separating—sometimes angrily—from its Jewish origins (see, for example, Matt. 27:25 and Acts 7:31–60 in the Christian New Testament).

The dominant position of Christianity in medieval Europe also had political implications, because Christians were thought of as loyal citizens, whereas Jews were treated as suspicious and even traitorous persons. Because so much of Jewish religious practice was carried out in the home, superstitious stories circulated among Christians that Jews needed the blood of Christian children for their Passover meal or that they stole and misused the consecrated Christian communion bread. Because Jews were often forbidden to own farmland, they were excluded from agriculture; and because they were kept out of the guilds (the medieval craft unions), they were excluded from many types of urban work. Furthermore, because

Beginning in 1215, Jews were often forced to live in separate sections of towns, called ghettos. Here we see the Jewish cemetery in the old ghetto of Prague.

Christians in the Middle Ages were generally prohibited from lending money at interest, this role became a Jewish occupation, but it generated much ill will among those to whom money was lent. In many places, Jews were forced to wear a special cap or display some other identifying detail. They were sometimes also forced to live in a separate section of town, called a *ghetto*, which might be walled so that Jews could be locked in at night.

Jews were persecuted regularly. At the time of the First Crusade, for example, many were killed by crusaders who were on their way through what is now Germany to Israel. During the period of the bubonic plague, also known as the Black Death (1347–1351 and sporadically afterwards), Jews sometimes were blamed for the deaths. In retaliation, many Jews were killed; some were even burned alive in their synagogues.

Beginning in the late Middle Ages, European Jews were forced into exile. Often the motive was economic as much as religious, because exiling the Jews would allow the Christian rulers to confiscate their property and to be freed of debt to them. Over a period of two centuries, Jews were expelled from England, France, Spain, and Portugal. In Spain, they were forced in 1492 to become Christians or to leave. Some Spanish Jews converted to Christianity but continued Jewish practice in their homes. As a result of the Spanish Inquisition, which sought out Jews who had converted only in order to remain in Spain, Jews fled elsewhere—to Morocco, Egypt, Greece, Turkey, Holland, central Europe, and the New World. It is at this time that two great cultural divisions of Judaism emerged—Sephardic Judaism in the Mediterranean region, North Africa, and the Middle East, and Ashkenazic Judaism in Germany, central Europe, and France. We will look at their cultural differences later, when we examine the branches of Judaism.

QUESTIONING AND REFORM

The Renaissance of the fifteenth and sixteenth centuries began a new era for Europe. As people began to travel more, they were exposed to a multitude of previously unknown religions, cultures, and regions of the world. The invention of printing with moveable type quickened this process by making written material widely available. Discoveries in science and instruments such as the telescope revolutionized people's perception of the earth and its relationship to the larger universe. These changes, which presented challenges to the Christian worldview, also affected Judaism.

After the Renaissance, Judaism began to move in two directions, both of which continue today. One direction cherished traditional ways; the other saw a need for modernization. The traditionalist way, strong in eastern Europe, offered refuge from an uncertain world. In central Europe, traditionalism expressed itself both in Talmudic scholarship and in the devotional movement *Hasidism* ("devotion," "piety"). The Hasidic movement was founded by Israel ben Eliezer (c. 1700–1760), a mystic and faith healer known affectionately as the Baal Shem Tov (the "good master of the Holy Name"). He felt that living according to the rules of the Torah and Talmud was important, but he also felt that devout practice should be accompanied by an ecstatic sense of God who is present everywhere.[22] Hasidism emphasized the beauty of everyday life and the physical world, teaching that "only in tangible things can you see or hear God."[23] Hasidism continued to inspire Jews over the past centuries and remains one of the most vital movements in Judaism today.

The other direction in which Judaism moved was toward modernization. The liberal direction, which was strongest in Germany and France, urged Jews to move out of the ghettos, to gain a secular education, and to

> The creator and the object of His creation are a Unity inseparable.
>
> —Hasidic saying[24]

enter the mainstream of their respective countries. In Germany, the modernizing movement, called the Reform, began in the late eighteenth century. With the goal of making worship more accessible, the Reform movement translated many of the Hebrew prayers into German and introduced musical elements (such as organ and choir music) that derived from current Protestant Christianity. (Choir music and instrumental accompaniment had existed much earlier, however, in the religious practice of the temple, as we see in Psalm 150.) In France and Italy, legal liberation began at the time of Napoleon. In many places, Jews were no longer barred from entering universities, which helped to enlarge the pool of highly educated, generally liberal, thinkers in Judaism. The Reform movement, however, generated many counterresponses—among them, an attempt to preserve traditional Judaism (Orthodox Judaism) and an attempt to maintain the best of tradition with some modern elements (the Positive-Historical School and Conservative Judaism). We will look at all these movements later in more detail.

JUDAISM AND THE MODERN WORLD

The growth of freedom for European Jews over the nineteenth century did not end anti-Jewish activity. The Russian Empire, where Eastern Orthodox Christianity was the established religion, continued its restrictions on Jews, with occasional outbreaks of persecution. In response, Jews from Russia, Poland, and the Baltic area emigrated, and from 1880 to 1920 more than a million Jews came to the United States, most coming to or through New York City. Their children and grandchildren sometimes moved further, settling in Los Angeles, Chicago, Miami, and elsewhere. Jews also immigrated to other large cities in North America and Latin America, such as Montreal, Toronto, Mexico City, and Buenos Aires—bringing a new freedom to Judaism, but at a price. Jewish identity was compromised because many Jews wished to assimilate with the surrounding culture, and intermarriage grew in frequency.

Traditional Jewish life continued in Europe until the end of the 1930s, particularly in Poland and the Baltic region, where there were still more than three million Jews. Beautiful evocations of this warm, traditional lifestyle are evident in the paintings of Marc Chagall and in the book that he and his wife Bella created together, *Burning Lights*.[25] This centuries-old culture, however, would be destroyed within ten years by Adolf Hitler.

Hitler and the Holocaust

The rise of Adolf Hitler in 1933 as German chancellor and head of the Nazi Party began a prolonged wave of anti-Jewish activity that ended in the most dreadful sufferings. Hitler was fueled by several irrational notions. One was a theory of racial classes, which imagined Jews and Gypsies to be subhuman polluters of a pure but mythical Aryan race. Another was Hitler's belief that Jewish financiers and industrialists had conspired against Germany and

The path to death
at Auschwitz.

helped make possible the Allied victory over the Germans during World War I. Hitler sought both an imaginary racial purity and political revenge.

At first, the Nazis put pressure on Jews to emigrate by forcing them out of government and university positions, by boycotting their stores, and eventually by physically persecuting them. Many Jews did emigrate, particularly to North America—Albert Einstein is a well-known example. After the annexation of Austria and the invasion of Poland (1939), Nazi control eventually spread to Holland, Norway, northern France, and Czechoslovakia; and as Nazi domination spread to these countries, so too did the persecution of Jews. Jews who wanted to flee found it hard to find refuge, because many countries, including the United States, refused to take in large numbers of Jews. Moreover, France and England did not forcefully protest Hitler's policies against the Jews, and the Catholic leader Pope Pius XII had signed a concordat of understanding with Hitler. The Jews were without defenders, and when World War II was declared, they were caught in a trap.

Hitler began plans to exterminate all European Jews. Jews in countries under Nazi control were officially identified, made to wear a yellow star in public, and eventually deported via train to concentration camps. Because there was a large number of Jews in Poland, most major concentration camps were constructed there. Some camps are well known—Auschwitz, Bergen-Belsen, Maidanek, Mauthausen—but there were also hundreds of smaller camps, such as Melk (in Austria, on the Danube River) and Dachau (in Germany, near Munich).

Upon arrival at the extermination camps, Jews were often divided into two groups: (1) those who were strong enough to work and (2) the rest—mostly women, children, the sick, and the elderly—who were to be killed immediately. (The psychologist Viktor Frankl has described the process in his book *Man's Search for Meaning*.) At first, internees were shot to death; but as their numbers increased, gas chambers and crematoria were constructed to kill them and incinerate their bodies. Those who were kept as workers lived in horrible conditions and were routinely starved, insufficiently clothed, and attacked by all kinds of vermin and disease. Few ultimately survived.

By the end of World War II in 1945, about twelve million people—Jews, Gypsies, homosexuals, Jehovah's Witnesses, prisoners of war, and political enemies—had died in the concentration camps. Of these, it is estimated that as many as six million were Jews, and of that number about a million and a half were Jewish children. This immense loss is called the **Holocaust** (Greek: "completely burned") or *Shoah* (Hebrew: "extermination"). It is one of the greatest crimes ever committed against humanity.

The extermination has left a shadow on civilization and a great scar on Judaism. About a third of the world's Jews had been killed, and of those who died, a large number had been devout traditional Jews. Their death, under such painful circumstances, raised haunting questions about the faith and future of Judaism.

Creation of the State of Israel

A major result of the Holocaust was the creation of the state of Israel after more than a century of hope, thought, and work. Centuries of virulent anti-Jewish restriction and persecution had created in many Jews a desire for a Jewish nation, where they could live without fear, in the traditional historic home of their faith. The movement came to be called **Zionism**, after Mount Zion, the mountain on which Jerusalem is built.

The state of Israel emerged through several steps. The first was the notion of a separate Jewish nation, popularized by the influential book *The Jewish State,* written by the Hungarian-born Austrian writer Theodor Herzl (1860–1904) following an outbreak of antisemitism in France. The second step was the Balfour Declaration, a political statement issued in 1917 by the British government, which endorsed the notion of a Jewish homeland. When World War I ended, the British received control of the area then called Palestine and authorized a limited immigration of Jews to their territory, the British Mandate of Palestine. The third step came after World War II. Impelled by the Nazi slaughter of Jews, the newly created United Nations voted to divide the old British Mandate of Palestine, and from this territory, a new Jewish state of Israel was created. Palestinians who left or who lived in surrounding areas, however, sometimes became a very hostile part of the neighboring population.

The difficult relationship between Jews and Palestinians has continued to the present day. There have been repeated wars and an exchange of terrorist activities between Israel and Palestinians, and the conflict has grown more horrifying in recent years. On the one hand, Jews everywhere have gained pride through the resurrection of their homeland and of the Hebrew language. But, on the other hand, there is great distress at the human cost and at the fact that so far the conflict has not been resolved.

Because European Judaism was almost completely destroyed, Jewish life today has two centers: Israel and the United States. The estimated Jewish population of Israel is about five million and that of the United States is roughly six million. Judaism in the United States is largely liberal and enjoys general freedom of practice. In Israel, Judaism presents a wide spectrum of opinions and practices, ranging from liberal and even atheistic to highly conservative and traditionally religious. Some important control of government policy and daily life is in the hands of traditionalists, but for perhaps a majority of the population Judaism is more a culture than a religion.

PERSONAL EXPERIENCE: A VISIT TO ANNE FRANK'S HOUSE

In high school I read the diary of Anne Frank, a teenage Jewish girl of Amsterdam who had hidden with her family and others throughout most of World War II. Her sensitive diary covers her years from age 13 to 15. In August of 1944, Nazi soldiers found the family and took them away to the concentration camp of Bergen-Belsen, where Anne died in March of 1945—just months before the war ended. Her father was the only family member who survived, and when he returned to Amsterdam he was given her diary, found on the floor of the house where they had hidden.

In her diary she wrote of her discovery of the beauty of nature—something she'd never appreciated before. Hiding in the attic rooms, she began to look out an upstairs window for long periods of time. One night she wrote: "the dark, rainy evening, the gale, the scudding clouds held me entirely in their power; it was the first time in a year and a half that I'd seen the night face to face."[26] Anne described having fallen in love there and her first kiss—with her friend Peter, who was also in hiding. As she described it, "suddenly the ordinary Anne slipped away and a second Anne took her place, a second Anne who is not reckless and jocular, but one who just wants to love and be gentle."[27] She wrote as well of God, religion, and belief.

During my first trip to Europe, near the end of my college years, I sought out the narrow house beside the canal in Amsterdam where Anne and her family and others had all lived in hiding. After climbing the steep, narrow stairs, I looked out through the same window that Anne had looked out many times, and I realized that the life and young intelligence that had once lived here had been so meaninglessly destroyed. As I stood there in thought, gazing through the open window, the bells of a nearby church rang out. What feelings, I wondered, had the sound of those bells evoked in her? As for me, I could feel only loss and emptiness.

Afterwards, when reading her diary again, I marveled at the sweet hopefulness she expressed there, near the end of the book, and near the end of her short life: "in spite of everything I still believe that people are really good at heart."[28]

Anne Frank and her family hid in a secret annex beyond this door in a house in Amsterdam. ◀

JEWISH BELIEF

There is no official Jewish creed, but there is a set of central beliefs, first formulated by the medieval scholar Maimonides. Among them are

- Belief in God. God is one, formless, all-knowing, and eternal. God is master of the universe as its creator and judge. God is both loving and just.
- Belief in the words of the prophets.
- Belief that God gave the law to Moses.
- Belief that the Messiah, the savior to be sent by God, will come someday.
- Belief that there will be a resurrection of the good "in the world to come."

Regarding these beliefs, there is no universal agreement about the precise meaning of the Messiah, the resurrection of the good, or "the world to come." In the past, these were understood literally. The Messiah would be a heaven-sent, powerful leader who would inaugurate a new age, and at that time the deceased who had followed God's laws would come back to life. Some Jews no longer interpret these beliefs literally but see them as symbols of the ultimate triumph of goodness in the world.

Belief in personal immortality or in the resurrection of the dead has been a frequent topic of debate among Jews. One can find several references in the Hebrew scriptures to an afterlife and to a resurrection of the good (see 1 Sam. 28:13–14 and Dan. 12:2), but other passages express doubt about any afterlife at all (Eccles. 3:20). In the postbiblical period, however, the Pharisees defended the notion of a future resurrection of the good, and rabbinical Judaism accepted this position. Although the notions of resurrection and even of an immortal soul have been defended by many within the Jewish faith, Judaism more strongly emphasizes the kind of immortality that comes from acting virtuously in this world, living on in one's children, and leaving behind some charitable contribution to the world.

In Judaism, human beings have a special role. Because they are created in God's image, they have the ability to reason, to will, to speak, to create, and to care; and they have the responsibility to manifest these divine characteristics in the world. Jews believe that among human beings, the Jewish people have a special role—a role that some believe is to witness to the one God and to do his will in the world. Others believe that their role is to suffer for a purpose known only to God. And others have said that their role is to bring a sense of justice to a world that often has none. Although there is no agreement about *the* Jewish role, there is general consensus among Jews that they hold a unique place in this world, and there is great pride in knowing that they have contributed so much to world culture.

RELIGIOUS PRACTICE

To be a Jew, however, does not come only from holding a set of beliefs; it is even more a way of living. Scholars explain this by saying that Judaism is less interested in *orthodoxy* (correct belief) and far more interested in *orthopraxy*

Jewish Meditation

Meditation has long been practiced in Judaism, particularly as a part of the Jewish mystical tradition. Because the Hebrew Bible has sometimes been believed to contain esoteric knowledge about the nature of God and his plan, it has been mulled over repeatedly for hidden messages.

The repetition of certain words and phrases has long been regarded as a method for attempting to unlock hidden messages and deeper meanings. Thus, it is not surprising that meditation involves such repetitions in ways that unite both intellectual and emotional elements. Among the objects of meditation have been the names of God, their constituent Hebrew letters, each letter of the Hebrew alphabet, the exact order of words in the biblical text, and the possible mystical connections between biblical words. The Torah and Psalms are particularly mined for their insights. The person is blessed, say the psalms, who meditates on the Torah day and night (Ps. 1).

Meditation can of course be done at home, but has also been common in the hour before, and the hour after, synagogue services. Standing and bowing are a common posture of both prayer and meditation in Judaism.

(correct practice). The Ten Commandments, of course, are at the heart of Jewish morality, and they direct behavior; but there are many additional laws and specific customs that dictate how time is to be used, what foods are to be eaten, and how prayer is to be conducted. And although Judaism promotes congregational worship, many Jewish celebrations are carried on in the home. Moving like wheels within wheels, the week, month, and year all have their devotional rhythms, established by religious laws and customs. The goal of all laws, however, is the recognition of God's presence and the sanctification of human life.

The Jewish Sabbath

Central to all forms of Judaism is keeping the Sabbath, the seventh day of the week, as a special day. The Sabbath, when kept properly, is felt to sanctify the entire week. Recalling the royal rest of God after the six laborious days of creation, the Sabbath is a day of special prayer and human relaxation (see Exod. 20:11 and 31:12–17).[29] In earlier times, before watches and clocks were invented, a "day" began in the evening at sundown; thus the Jewish Sabbath begins on Friday at sunset and lasts until Saturday at sunset.

The traditional purpose of the Sabbath was a compassionate one: it was to allow everyone, even slaves and animals, regular rest. The prohibition against work has been interpreted variously over the centuries. Shops, of course, would be closed. Traditionally, fires could not be built on the Sabbath because of the work involved; and related to this, some traditionalist Jews today will not turn light switches or kitchen stoves on or off during the Sabbath. The prohibition against making fires meant that food consumed during the Sabbath period would have to be cooked beforehand or eaten uncooked (see Exod. 35:1–3). Interpreting the requirement of rest in the modern world, some Jews do not drive a car or use a telephone during the Sabbath. Although some restrictions might seem excessive, their purpose is to separate the everyday world of labor from the one day of the week in which everyone can enjoy leisure.

The Sabbath is meant to be joyous and is often remembered that way by adults who have grown up in traditional households. The Talmud recommends that the mother of the household welcome the Sabbath on Friday night by lighting candles, and it recommends that the family drink wine at the Sabbath meal as a sign of happiness. During the Jewish exile in Babylonia, synagogue study and worship became a regular way to mark the Sabbath, and today it is common for religious Jews to attend a synagogue service on Friday night or Saturday morning. Friends are often invited over to share the main Sabbath meal, and on Saturday evening the Sabbath is at last bid farewell. There is an old Jewish adage: More than the Jews have kept the Sabbath, has the Sabbath kept the Jews.

Jews speak with pride of their observance of the Sabbath, pointing out that the great gift of Judaism to the world has not been the creation of a beautiful temple in physical space but rather the creation of a beautiful "temple" in time. Jews were once called lazy by the Romans for stopping their work one day out of every seven. But the Jewish practice has triumphed, and one day of the week is generally set aside as a day of rest throughout the world.

Holy Days

Just as the week is sanctified by the Sabbath, so the months and the entire year are sanctified by regular holy days and periods, each marked by a distinctive emotional tone—happiness, sadness, repentance, gratitude.

Before speaking of specific festivals, we must point out that the Jewish religious calendar is lunar, meaning that each month begins with the new moon. However, adjustments must be made in order to keep the lunar years in general harmony with the regular, solar calendar. Because a year of twelve lunar months lasts 354 days, one lunar year is eleven days shorter than one solar year. Therefore, in the Jewish religious calendar an extra month is added approximately every three years. The lunar months of the Jewish year thus vary somewhat, as do the holy days.

Like the lunar calendar, many Jewish holy days derive from an earlier time when most Jews lived an agricultural life. The earliest holy days arose at seasonal turning points, but later, additional holy days were instituted to recall important events in Jewish history.

The Jewish New Year, **Rosh Hashanah,** recalls the creation of the world and occurs during autumn, in the seventh lunar month (see Lev. 23:23–24). Coming at the end of the agricultural season, this celebration allows people to consider their obligations and to pay off their debts. It is preceded by a month of daily blowing of the *shofar* (a ram's horn), which produces a solemn tone of warning to remind people that they stand before God.

Ten days later comes the most sacred day of the year, **Yom Kippur,** the Day of Atonement (see Lev. 16). To atone means to make up for one's faults, and this day has traditionally been kept by prayer and strict fasting, with no food or drink during the entire day. Devout Jews spend most of the day in the synagogue or in quiet private prayer at home, seeking God's forgiveness and making resolutions to better their lives. Rosh Hashanah and Yom Kippur are called the High Holy Days, and otherwise quite secular Jews frequently keep them in some way, refraining from work or school and often attending synagogue. The entire period is called the Days of Awe, because of the mood of solemn judgment.

Not long afterward, and complementing the Days of Awe, comes a joyful harvest celebration, called **Sukkot** ("shelters," "booths"; see Deut. 16:12–15). In early days it was common for families to sleep outdoors in the fields during the autumn harvest season—which enabled them to begin work in the fields early, to stay late, and to protect what they had harvested. The small sleeping shed that was used began to be built and slept in as part of the celebration, and eating or sleeping in the shelters came to symbolize the period of wandering in the desert, before the Israelites entered the land of Canaan. Today, a shelter made of light wood (referred to in Hebrew as a *sukkah*) is set up in or near the home and is commonly decorated with branches and fruits to suggest the bounty of the earth. (The biblical description of this harvest festival helped to shape the first American holiday of Thanksgiving.) The eighth day of Sukkot, called the day of Rejoicing in the Torah (*Simhat Torah*), ends the festival, with readings from the end of the Torah—the final chapters of Deuteronomy. The cycle of readings from the Torah can then begin again. Men carry the Torah in procession, kiss the Torah scrolls, and sometimes even dance with the scrolls to show gratitude for the guidance of the Torah.

Hanukkah, the Feast of Dedication, is an early-winter festival full of joy. Often called the Feast of Lights, it is a welcome celebration during the growing gloom of winter. Each day, over an eight-day period, one more candle is lit on a nine-branched candelabrum—a special form of **menorah**—until at the end of the festival, all are alight. (The ordinary menorah has seven branches.) The festival commemorates the time in 165 B.C.E. when after a period of desecration by the Syrian forces of Antiochus IV, the Second Temple was rededicated. Tradition says that oil that should have lasted only one day miraculously kept burning for eight days. Consequently, over an eight-day period, families gather in the evening, light the Hanukkah candles, and play traditional games with their children, and children receive small gifts each night.

A late-winter feast just before spring commemorates another important event. **Purim** recalls a time when the Hebrews were in danger of annihilation in Mesopotamia, as told in the book of Esther. When Haman, a government minister, wished to destroy the Hebrews, they were saved by Esther, the queen, and her uncle, Mordecai.[30] This happy festival is marked by the reading of the book of Esther, by costume plays that reenact the story, and by parties.

The weeklong festival of Passover (Pesach) occurs in the first lunar month and may have originally begun as a springtime nature festival of renewal.[31] Its primary role now, however, is to recall the Hebrews' exodus from Egypt and to symbolize their liberation (see Deut. 16:1–8). The blood of the lamb killed for the Passover meal, as the book of Exodus relates, was

The Passover Seder includes unleavened bread, wine, haroseth, and bitter herbs.

placed over the doors of the Hebrews (Exod. 12), thus keeping the angel of death from entering their homes while the power of God "passed over" Egypt. The most significant event of Passover is a memorial meal, the **Seder** ("order"), at which Jews eat several symbolic foods. The bread is a thin, flat bread (*matzah*), made without yeast, which helps recall how there was no time for bread to rise in the Hebrews' rush to leave Egypt. The meal also includes a shank bone of lamb or other animal, representing the sacrificial lamb. A salad of nuts and fruits (*haroseth*) recalls the mortar used by the Hebrews in their forced labor. Diners dip parsley in salt water and eat bitter herbs to remind themselves of the suffering of the Hebrews during their oppression. During this memorial meal, the story of the exodus is retold. An additional place is set at the table for the prophet Elijah, and a cup of wine is reserved for him—actions representing the hope that he will return to earth to announce the coming of the Messiah. A delicious meal follows the ritual part of the supper. Today, many Jews invite non-Jews to share in their Seder and celebration of Jewish customs.

The Holocaust, or Shoah, is memorialized on the day of Yom Hashoah in April or May. It is a new memorial, kept in late spring, and rituals for it are still being worked out, including services in honor of those who died. Television programs show films documenting the Holocaust, and memorial concerts feature music by Jewish composers (such as Leonard Bernstein). The theme of the memorials is "Never again!"

The period after Passover is kept with general austerity until the summer festival of Shavuot, called the Feast of Weeks because it occurs at the end of a week of weeks—fifty days after Passover (see Deut. 16:9–12). It began as a summer grain-harvest festival. Later, Shavuot gained a special religious meaning as an invitation to renew the covenant, because it was believed that God gave Moses the Ten Commandments at this time of year.

Nine weeks after Shavuot there is a day of fasting that recalls the destruction of the two temples. Called Tisha Be-Av, this fast, and the week preceding it, have traditionally been marked by lamentations and a very serious mood; but since the creation of the state of Israel, this period of solemnity is not as widely observed.

The month before Rosh Hashanah is marked by the daily blowing of the shofar, and with Rosh Hashanah the religious year begins anew.

Jewish Dietary Practices

From its earliest biblical origins, Judaism has valued cleanliness and care regarding food. What were once basic rules of hygiene developed into rules about ritual purity—rules about what is, from a religious point of view, considered to be clean and unclean. Traditionally, these rules were intended particularly for those who conducted the temple services, but they came to be expected of all Israelites, who thought of themselves as a "nation of priests." In recent centuries, some Jews have relaxed their observance of certain dietary rules, keeping them to a greater or lesser degree as they think suitable and according to the branch of Judaism to which they belong.

One of the basic tenets of traditional Jewish dietary practice is that food consumption and food handling be done according to religious laws. The term **kosher** (Hebrew: *kasher*) means "ritually correct" and particularly applies to food preparation and consumption. In regard to meat, all blood must be drained before the meat is cooked and eaten, because blood, which gives life, is sacred to God. In temple services, blood was offered on the altar separately from the rest of the sacrificed animal, and only meat without blood could be eaten by the priests and sharers in the sacred meal (see Lev. 17). This rule also ensured that animals that had died in the field or were killed by larger animals—carcasses that might be unsafe to eat—could not be consumed (see Exod. 22:31). In practice, there are very specific methods of kosher slaughter, inspection, and preservation.

Pork and shellfish are forbidden (see Lev. 11), probably because these animals were considered scavengers and thus easily contaminated by what they ate. (Pork sometimes contains a parasite, *Trichinella spiralis*, which can be killed only by cooking at high temperatures.)[32] For traditional Jews, meat and dairy products may not be mixed or eaten together at the same meal. This also means that a household that "keeps kosher" must maintain separate sets of cooking implements, pans, dishes, and utensils—one for meat and one for dairy products. Some households even have separate sinks and refrigerators. These practices derive from a rule of uncertain origin that forbids the cooking of a baby goat or lamb in its mother's milk (Exod. 34:26). It is possible the practice was forbidden for being cruel; some fetal animals, cut from the womb before birth, were considered tender delicacies. The practice of cooking a kid in its mother's milk may also have been associated with non-Hebrew religious practice and therefore forbidden.

Other Religious Practices

Regular daily prayer is practiced by devout Jews at dawn, noon, and dusk, and private prayer is often done at bedtime as well. When they pray in the morning during the week, traditionalist males use the **tefillin,** or *phylacteries,* which are two small boxes containing scriptural passages; one is attached to the forehead by leather straps tied around the head, and the other is attached

A traditional Jewish man, wearing the tefillin and talit, reciting morning prayer.

to the upper left arm by straps wound down around the arm and hand. They signify quite literally that God's law is in the mind and heart of the person at prayer (see Deut 6:8). The **talit** (a prayer shawl)—usually white, with dark stripes and fringes—covers the man's head and body during prayer and signifies humility in the sight of God. In less traditional forms of Judaism, the prayer shawl is sometimes not used, but men wear the skullcap (*kippah* in Hebrew and **yarmulke** in Yiddish, the old language of eastern European Jews). Devout males sometimes express their reverence before God during their waking hours by covering their heads continually with a skullcap.

Remembrance of God is also assisted by the presence of a *mezuzah,* which is placed on the doorpost of the entrance to a home and sometimes on the doorposts of interior rooms (see Deut. 6:9). Like the tefillin, the mezuzah is a small container that holds scriptural words; it can be touched upon entering the house or room. Unlike the tefillin, it is used even by secular Jews.

Perhaps because sexuality and the origin of life are considered especially sacred, Judaism has a number of practices relating to them. Eight days after birth, when a male receives his name, he is circumcised—the foreskin of the boy's penis is cut off by a specialist. The ceremony recalls God's covenant with the Hebrew people (see Gen. 17 and Lev. 12:3). The origin of the practice of circumcision in Judaism is uncertain. It began possibly as a health measure, to prevent infection commonly brought about by hot climates; but it is also possible that circumcision began as a way of recognizing divine control over sex and generation. Males mark puberty with a coming-of-age ceremony at age 13, when a young man legally becomes an adult, or "son of the commandment" (**bar mitzvah**).

In some branches of Judaism, girls age 12 to 18 are honored in a coming-of-age ceremony, called a *bat mitzvah.* For women, menstruation and childbirth have also been considered special times, involving use of a ritual bath (*mikvah*) and purification.

Although in ancient days priests on duty in the temple and soldiers in the field were expected to be temporarily celibate, sex has been viewed positively in Judaism. With the exception of the Essenes, Jews have honored marriage and considered children a major goal of life (see Gen. 1:28 and 12:2).

Devout Jews place a mezuzah, containing words from the Torah, beside their doors and touch it reverently when they enter.

DIVISIONS WITHIN CONTEMPORARY JUDAISM

We find in Judaism both cultural differences and differences in the observance of traditional rules. Some commentators, as a result, talk not of "Judaism" but of "Judaisms."

Culturally Based Divisions

The great ethnic diversity among Jews has resulted in a number of cultural divisions within Judaism. It is important to understand these divisions in order to appreciate the richness of Judaism, as well as the challenges that face Israel, where members of these groups have come to live together.

Sephardic Jews The name *Sephardic* comes from a mythic land of Sephar (or Sepharad), once thought to exist in the distant west of Israel and often identified with Spain. After the Roman victories over the Jews in Israel (70 and 135 C.E.), Jews emigrated from Israel and settled in lands far away. Southern Spain particularly became a center of flourishing Jewish life, especially under Muslim rule, but this ended with the expulsion of the Muslims and Jews by the Christian rulers in 1492 C.E. Sephardic Jews (**Sephardim**) carried their language and culture to Morocco, Greece, Turkey, Egypt, and elsewhere in the Mediterranean region, as well as to Holland and England. The common language of the Sephardic Jews, termed Ladino in recognition of its ultimate derivation from Latin, was a type of Spanish mixed with Hebrew words and often written in Hebrew characters. Sephardic Jews lived in significant numbers in Morocco until recent times, when most immigrated to Israel. More than half of the Jews of Israel are of Sephardic background.

Ashkenazic Jews The name *Ashkenazic* comes from Ashkenaz, a descendant of Noah who settled in a distant northern land (see Gen. 10:3). The term **Ashkenazim** refers to those Jews who at one time lived in or came from central Europe. A very large population of Jews flourished for centuries in Poland, the Ukraine, Lithuania, Latvia, Germany, and Hungary, and before the Holocaust three million Jews lived in Poland alone, where sometimes entire towns (called *shtetls*) were Jewish.

The origin of Ashkenazic Judaism is unclear, but the most common opinion is that it arose when Jews migrated from France and other countries of western Europe to central Europe, after 1000 C.E. Another theory, advanced by Arthur Koestler in his book *The Thirteenth Tribe*, holds that a whole kingdom in southern Russia, called Khazaria, converted to Judaism after the seventh century C.E. This theory argues that the conversion to Judaism was a highly political decision: conversion to Christianity would have brought absorption into the Byzantine Empire, and conversion to Islam would have brought control by Muslim forces. Invasions from the north that occurred several centuries later forced the Jewish Khazars into Hungary, Poland, and the rest of central Europe.

The common language of central European Judaism was *Yiddish* ("Jewish"), a medieval form of German mixed with Hebrew words and written in Hebrew characters. While it flourished, Ashkenazic Judaism produced a rich culture of books, stories, songs, and theater in Yiddish. Ashkenazic culture virtually ended in Europe with the Holocaust, but Yiddish language and culture lived on in the United States, Canada, and Israel, and although they once seemed to be rapidly declining, there are recent signs of revival. Yiddish-speaking culture has contributed Yiddish words and ideas to American life. (For example, television has made popular the Yiddish terms *shlemiel* and *shlemozzel*—names for two types of laughable characters. The first term comes from the name Samuel.) Yiddish literature is now being translated into many languages.

Other Jewish Cultures A mysterious form of Judaism exists in Africa among the Falashas of Ethiopia. The Falashas practice a religion that accepts as canonical only the five books of the Torah—a sign that Ethiopian Judaism could be quite ancient. Possibly an archaic form of Judaism, once practiced in Arabia or southern Egypt, penetrated into Ethiopia and continued there, cut off from contact with later Jewish development. However, there may be other explanations for the existence of the Falashas. In 1990, when they were subject to Marxist persecution in Ethiopia, many Falashas were airlifted by the Israeli government to Israel. Judaism established itself in a small community on the western coast of India, though today it is very small. Distinctive Jewish cultures also exist in Yemen, Iraq, and elsewhere.

Observance-Based Divisions

Within Judaism today, divisions also exist based on variations in religious observance. As described earlier, a movement for reform began in eighteenth-century Germany with a questioning of traditional Jewish practices. This created a distinction between traditionalist Jews and those who wished to modernize Jewish practice. Although some Jews have held to traditional practices, other branches have developed out of the conviction that Judaism will stay vital only if it reinterprets its traditions, just as it did after the destruction of the First and Second Temples. Those who reinterpret Judaism have naturally come to varied conclusions about what should be kept, discarded, or viewed symbolically rather than literally. Disagreements abound about observance of the laws of the Torah and Talmud, the use of Hebrew in services, the role of women in traditionally male roles, support for the nation of Israel, and the relationship of Judaism with the non-Jewish world. Four branches have emerged. We begin with the most traditional and move to the least traditional, although the branches did not emerge in this order.

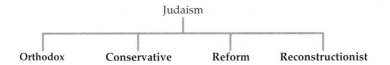

FIGURE 8.2
Observance-based branches of Judaism

Orthodox Judaism   Traditional Judaism is often called **Orthodox** (Figure 8.2), but we might recall that until the Reform movement began there was no need to give a special name to traditional Judaism, because all Jews were traditional in belief and practice. In a sense, Orthodox Judaism came into being only after the Reform began, and as a response to it. When we use the term *Orthodox* to refer to traditional Jews, we should also recognize the great variety among Orthodox Jews—particularly regarding social and political positions. Some, termed integrationists, seek to play a role in civil society, while others, called separatists, want to live their traditional lifestyle apart from society, sometimes without political activity. Most Orthodox Jews support the state of Israel, and many accept the need for secular education in addition to traditional learning, but some are opposed to both.

Traditional Jews in
Jerusalem buy branches
for Sukkot.

With this said, we can describe Orthodoxy as a branch of Judaism committed to retaining traditional practice and belief. Orthodox Jews are hesitant to discard any traditional practices, even those not demanded by the Torah but simply revered as reasonable later developments that are said to "guard" the Torah from being lost or misinterpreted. Some specific practices follow.

- Orthodox synagogues separate males and females, with females often sitting in an upstairs gallery.
- For a service to take place, there must be a quorum (*minyan*) of ten Jewish males.
- Services are conducted completely in Hebrew and led by male rabbis.
- Only males may celebrate the coming-of-age ceremony (bar mitzvah).
- Men at prayer use the talit and at weekday morning prayer use the tefillin.
- Males must keep their heads covered (with the skullcap, prayer shawl, or hat) as a reminder that God is above all.
- Social roles (especially among ultraorthodox Jews) are strictly separate. Men are the breadwinners of the family, and women are responsible for running the household.

- The hair of the beard and in front of the ears is sometimes left uncut by males, in response to a command in the Torah (Lev. 19:27).
- Some Orthodox Jewish males (and particularly those affiliated with a specific Hasidic community) also wear a style of dress that developed in central Europe during the nineteenth century—a black hat and black coat (originally a beaver-skin hat and a black smock).
- Orthodox women who are married sometimes cover their heads with a kerchief when outside the home. (Some cut their hair short and wear a wig, although this practice is condemned by certain rabbis.) The hair is covered as an expression of modesty, because a woman's hair is considered to be seductive to men.
- The Orthodox household keeps strictly the traditional laws about diet.
- Orthodox Jews closely follow rules that prohibit any manual labor on the Sabbath. Cooking is not allowed, nor is driving a car, walking long distances, dialing a telephone, or even turning on an electric light.

Outsiders might consider the strictness of this lifestyle burdensome. But the Orthodox themselves—particularly those who have been raised as Orthodox—say that it is not difficult. They say that it is even fulfilling, because every waking moment is consciously devoted to the worship of God.

In continental Europe, Orthodox Judaism was nearly destroyed by the Nazis. In Israel, although only a tenth of the population can be considered traditionalist or Orthodox, that segment has considerable political power. In the United States, Orthodoxy is a small minority among those who practice Judaism, but it has gained recognition and visibility particularly through the efforts of Hasidic communities.

Conservative Judaism   For some Jews, the European movement for reform seemed too radical. **Conservative Judaism** traces itself back to the Positive-Historical School of Judaism in Germany, but it took strong root in the United States among Jews who desired moderate change that was coupled with a protection of beloved traditions, such as the use of Hebrew in services. Conservative Judaism recognizes that change has always been a part of the religion, that the centuries have seen many gains and losses—for example, the temple sacrifices ceased but the Talmud was written. Thus this branch of Judaism accepts change but uses study and discussion to guide change carefully, valuing all traditions and weighing them thoughtfully. Conservativism itself has also changed over time by altering its positions on several important issues. For example, it once opposed Zionism and forbade the ordination of women as rabbis, but it has reversed itself in both instances. In the United States, almost half of all practicing Jews belong to this branch.

Reform Judaism   Reform Judaism began in Germany out of a desire of some Jews to leave ghetto life completely and enter the mainstream of European culture. An early influence on this movement was Moses Mendelssohn (1729–1786), a major thinker and writer. Mendelssohn, although he was not a Reform Jew, had influence on Reform and Orthodox Judaism. He argued for religious tolerance, held that Judaism could be combined with civil culture, and embraced many of the ideals of the European Enlightenment of the eighteenth century—human dignity, equality, individual liberty, democracy, secular education, and the development of science. These ideals brought radical changes in the Jewish circles that espoused them, because in the name of reform, every traditional Jewish belief and practice could be questioned.

The result has been that in Reform synagogue worship, women and men do not sit separately, services are conducted in both the native language and Hebrew, choirs and organ music are common, and use of the talit and tefillin has either been dropped or made optional. Traditional ways of dressing, common among the Orthodox, have disappeared. Perhaps more important, equality is espoused for men and women. As a result, women may become rabbis, and girls have coming-of-age ceremonies in which they are declared "daughters of the commandment" (bat mitzvah).

The goal of the Reform movement has been to thoroughly modernize Judaism, in the hope that it will survive in the contemporary world. However, because several of the Reform ideals are considered to be injurious to traditional Judaism, Orthodox Jews view the Reform with suspicion and see it as a dangerous dilution of Judaism.

Reconstructionist Judaism   This newest and smallest branch of Judaism grew out of the thought of its founder, Mordecai Kaplan (1881–1983), a Lithuanian who came to the United States as a child. Kaplan was influenced by the American ideals of democracy and practicality. As a leader in the Society for the Advancement of Judaism, Kaplan promoted a secular vision that encourages Jews to become familiar with as many elements of traditional Judaism as possible but that allows them the freedom of individual interpretation. Elements of belief that traditional Jews interpret literally (such as angels, prophecy, revealed law, and the Messiah) are taken as useful symbols by **Reconstructionism;** even the notion of God is seen from a pragmatic viewpoint as "the Power which makes me follow ever higher ideals."[33] Instead of searching for a minimum number of beliefs and practices that are the unchanging essence of Judaism, Reconstructionism sees Judaism as a changing cultural force, with many elements and manifestations. Judaism, in this view, is a whole civilization "which expresses itself . . . in literature, art, music, even cuisine. It never stands still but evolves."[34]

THE CONTRIBUTIONS OF JUDAISM

Judaism's unique contributions to civilization are products of the Jewish view of life. Although postbiblical Judaism embraced a belief in a resurrection of the dead who had lived holy lives and in their life "in the world to come," the focus of Judaism has been primarily on the importance of loving—and contributing to—*this* world. As described in the Book of Genesis, the world has not only been created by God but is also the object of his admiration, and human beings, an important part of God's plan, are of unique value. Just as when God speaks, acts, and gives form to the universe, human beings imitate him when they shape the world and better it.

The emphasis on living fully in this world has shaped the ways in which members of the Jewish faith achieve fulfillment. Jewish culture values the following:

Individuality and independence

The body, medicine, and medical care

Marriage, family life, and children

Psychology, psychotherapy, and counseling

Education, books, journalism, and debate

Economics, business, and finance

Law and social justice

Philanthropy and social contribution

Comedy and humor

Musical composition and performance

As a consequence, prestige in the Jewish community has attached itself historically to vocations that express the preceding values—physician, professor, scientist, writer, merchant, manufacturer, musician, entertainer, producer, comedian, lawyer, and counselor.

Several vocations are represented less frequently by Jews, either for religious reasons or because of past social restrictions. For example, until recent times the label "Jewish artist" was almost a contradiction in terms. We might recall that one of the Ten Commandments forbids the making of human and animal images. Although this commandment has not always been interpreted strictly (and some examples of religious Jewish image making do exist), the visual fine arts in general were not thought of as appropriate forms of religious expression for devout Jews. The area of nonfigurative decorative arts, however, was acceptable. Judaism has produced beautiful religious objects, such as candelabra, wine cups, Sabbath bread plates, and scroll covers. (Many fine examples can be seen in the Jewish Museum in New York City.)

Until the past century, however, artistic instincts generally have been channeled into other paths, such as music and architecture. We should, though, be aware of the artistry that exists in the images, records of visions, and patterns of sound to be found in Jewish religious literature and poetry.

Although Jews are a small minority in every country except Israel, their achievements on the world stage, especially over the past two centuries, have been exceptional. Jews often feel a justifiable pride in their contributions in many areas.

Philosophy was enriched by the thought of Martin Buber (1878–1965), whose book *I and Thou* has become one of the seminal works of modern thought. In it, Buber described the "I-Thou" relationship with someone or something in the world as a relationship of openness and dialogue. Buber held that in every I-Thou relationship in the world the divine is encountered.

All real living is meeting.
—Martin Buber[35]

Albert Einstein (*left*) is considered by many to be the preeminent scientist of the modern world. Elie Wiesel (*right*) was imprisoned in a concentration camp as a teenager. His writings about the Holocaust helped earn him the Nobel Peace Prize.

Buber also pointed scholarly attention to mysticism and Hasidic wisdom through his anthologies of Hasidic stories.

Many great Jewish authors have contributed to literature: Saul Bellow (b. 1915), Elie Wiesel (b. 1928), Chaim Potok (1929–2002), and Isaac Bashevis Singer (1904–1991), to name just a few. Their themes have often been religious—spiritual self-discovery, individuality in interplay with religious tradition, and the Jewish response to the Holocaust.

The fairly new discipline of psychology owes its advancement to the great work of people of Jewish background, such as Sigmund Freud (1856–1939), Abraham Maslow (1908–1970), and Viktor Frankl (1905–1997). (The striking examples of dream analysis in the Books of Genesis and Daniel are ancient precursors to psychoanalysis.) All three thinkers concerned themselves with the role of religion—Freud being nonreligious and quite skeptical, but Maslow and Frankl seeing the significance of religion in bringing essential meaning to human life.

In recent times, classical music has been particularly enriched by notable Jewish composers who have brought an explicitly religious dimension to their music. Ernest Bloch (1880–1959) is known for his works inspired by Judaism, especially his *Schelomo.* Leonard Bernstein (1918–1990), although best known for his secular musical *West Side Story,* also created serious works on explicitly Jewish themes—such as his *Jeremiah Symphony,* his *Chichester Psalms,* and his *Kaddish Symphony,* which is a disturbing memorial to an ancient, dying God.

The image-making restrictions that discouraged the development of Jewish painting began to weaken for some artists in the late nineteenth century. Marc Chagall (1887–1985) had to leave his small hometown in Russia in order to learn to paint, but in his imagination he re-created the Jewish world he had left behind. His paintings are full of the Jewish figures he learned about in childhood—angels, rabbis, Jewish violinists, Jewish brides and grooms.

Possibly the most important influence of Jewish values on world culture over the past one hundred years has come through film. (The traditional Jewish prohibition on the making of human images apparently did not apply to filmmaking.) In California, the film industry was built up largely by men of Ashkenazic background, whose Orthodox parents and grandparents had emigrated from Europe. It is significant that *The Jazz Singer* (1927), the first successful talking film, is a Jewish story that tells of a young Jewish man eager to make a career singing popular songs. To do this, he must oppose his own father, a cantor in a synagogue who wants his son to have the same career as he. The story epitomizes the struggle in the life of every young Jewish man of the time: to live a traditional life in a Jewish world or to find a new style of life within the secular world. (The story is so powerful that it has been remade several times. The first version featured Al Jolson and another, Neil Diamond. The last and possibly best version was a segment of *The Simpsons,* in which the character Krusty, a clown, is at last accepted by his father, Rabbi Krustowsky.) The advent of the talking film opened up a whole new area for development—the written, sung, and spoken word of film—and unleashed the potential of scriptwriters, songwriters, lyricists, and comedians, many of whom were (and are) of Jewish background. They brought into their work the traditional Jewish values, particularly the love of home and family, of words and books, of humor and song.

Modern feminist values are sometimes in conflict with Jewish tradition. This conflict can be seen in some film work of Barbra Streisand (b. 1942). The film *Yentl,* for example, is a demand for gender equality in Judaism. Set in eastern Europe in 1904, it tells the story of the daughter of a rabbi who cuts off her hair and pretends to be a male—all so she can enter a rabbinical school. The film *Hello, Dolly* also presents Streisand (in the character of Dolly Levy) as a strong Jewish woman and role model.

Similar talent at writing and entertaining was called for with the arrival of television. Today, television writers of Jewish background often introduce elements of Jewish culture, such as Jewish rituals, Yiddish words and phrases, scriptural references, and insider jokes (in such television shows as *The Simpsons*). Television series sometimes address quite sensitive issues that face modern Jews. One program, for example, showed an interreligious married couple—in which the husband was Jewish but the wife was not—trying to decide whether to have the ritual of circumcision performed after their boy is born. (They did.) Another showed how a woman converted to Judaism in order to marry her Jewish boyfriend. Programs like these make welcome use of the powerful medium of television to explain Judaism to a wide audience.

JEWISH IDENTITY AND THE FUTURE OF JUDAISM

Judaism today is particularly concerned with two great questions, which are inescapably linked. What is essential to being a Jew? Will Judaism survive?

Appreciating the cultural and religious divisions among Jews demonstrates how difficult it is today to define what makes a Jew. Three hundred years ago, the question of identity was nonexistent, because Jews were those people who practiced traditional Judaism. Now, however, Jewish identity is no longer so easy to ascertain. Although Orthodox Judaism holds that a person is born a Jew if his or her mother is Jewish, this does not address the matter of practice, and today there are many nonobservant Jews. A person may also convert to Judaism. (Celebrities such as Elizabeth Taylor and Sammy Davis, Jr., made the possibility of conversion quite well known when they accepted the Jewish faith.) However, some Orthodox rabbis have refused to accept conversions to non-Orthodox branches of Judaism. Judaism is certainly a religion, but there is great disagreement about the essentials of belief and practice, and many people consider themselves Jews even though they do not practice the religion.

Furthermore, any attempt to define a Jew as a person belonging to a single culture or ethnic group is virtually impossible. Jews are as ethnically diverse as they are ideologically diverse, a fact that becomes quite clear when one visits Israel. Although there is as yet no clear answer to the question of Jewish identity, the topic becomes more important as Jews increasingly intermarry with non-Jews.

The history of Judaism has been marked by displacement and disasters. In the past century, nearly a third of the world's Jewish population was destroyed. Nevertheless, Jewish history has also been marked by the will to endure. The resilience of Judaism has in large part resided in its ability to adapt to changing circumstances and environments. This ability suggests that in the decades ahead, Judaism will again take new forms and gain new life.

RELIGION BEYOND THE CLASSROOM

Because Judaism is a religion that emphasizes practice, to experience Judaism one should see how it is and has been lived. This can be done by attending services and visiting with Jewish families. If travel is possible, touring North America, Europe, and Israel, in particular, is an unforgettable way to experience Jewish life.

North America Jewish life is vibrant in the United States and Canada. People with specifically religious interest may visit most synagogues to experience their Sabbath prayer. (It is thoughtful to phone beforehand to make arrangements.) There are architecturally significant synagogues in some major cities, especially New York and Los Angeles.

Some Jewish families are happy to include non-Jews in Passover Seders; this can sometimes be arranged through synagogues in one's area. Non-Jews are frequently invited, too, to bar mitzvah and

bat mitzvah celebrations and to weddings; such celebrations are wonderful opportunities for non-Jews to experience the visual and oral richness of Jewish practice. Jewish contributions to the arts can be seen in several places, such as the Jewish Museum in New York City. The Holocaust Museum in Washington, D.C., provides powerful insight into the buildup of antisemitism in Germany and the virtual destruction of European Judaism during World War II.

Europe The continent is dotted with significant sites and museums, particularly where there was once a strong Jewish presence. Jewish museums (some housed in former synagogues) are located, for example, in Vienna, Prague, Copenhagen, Berlin, Budapest, Toledo, and Amsterdam. Amsterdam is also the city of the Anne Frank house—which should have particular meaning for anyone who has read her diary. Former ghetto areas in some cities still retain a flavor of Jewish life, for example, in Venice (near the train station), Paris (the Rue des Rosiers area in the Marais district), Amsterdam (Jodenbuurt, around Jodenbreestraat), Prague (five synagogues and a cemetery in the Josefov area), and Córdoba (the Judería, Synagogue, and Plaza Juda Levi). A few former concentration camps have been kept intact as museums and memorials to the Holocaust, such as Dachau (near Munich), Theresienstadt (near Prague), and Auschwitz (Oświęcim, near Krakow).

Israel This country is, of course, full of significant Jewish sites, of which Jerusalem is the most important. (It is wise to check on safety precautions when making travel plans for Israel.) The Western Wall of the Second Temple is a place for prayer; the Shrine of the Book displays examples of the Dead Sea Scrolls; and Yad Vashem is a memorial to the Holocaust. Other places in Israel are also worth visiting, time permitting. One such site is the fortress ruins of Masada, where Jewish Zealots resisted Roman soldiers, even to the point of suicide. The tomb of Abraham is venerated at Hebron, and Mount Carmel (near Haifa) is associated with the life of the prophet Elijah. Finally, visitors might be interested in arranging to visit, stay in, and even work at one of Israel's many communes (*kibbutzim*).

FOR FULLER UNDERSTANDING

1. If your area has a synagogue or a museum that chronicles Jewish history, visit it and make an oral report to your class on what you learned.

2. With a few classmates, undertake a comparative study of women's roles in several religions, including Judaism. Pay particular attention to changes that took place during the twentieth century, and speculate on changes that might occur during the twenty-first century.

3. Using library and computer-lab resources, examine architectural models and diagrams of the Second Temple. Prepare an illustrated report in which you explain the various temple courts and the services held there.

4. Choose an artist, composer, or writer whose work suggests the influence of Jewish thought and practice. Study several of that person's works, making note of any elements on which Judaism has left its mark.

5. Read one of the books listed in the bibliography. Write a review in which you show how the book expanded your knowledge of basic teachings or practices covered in this chapter. Conclude your review by explaining ways in which the book may be relevant in today's world.

6. Jewish sacred texts, like texts in the Hindu, Christian, and Islamic traditions, show a God who at times commands violent action. If you were a rabbi in today's world, how would you treat such texts in your teaching and preaching?

RELATED READINGS

Buber, Martin. *I and Thou.* New York: Simon & Schuster, 1984. An influential book that speaks of the holiness of the close personal relationship, which Buber calls the I-Thou relationship.

Chagall, Bella, with drawings by Marc Chagall. *Burning Lights.* New York: Holmes & Meier, 1996. A book that evokes through words and drawings the warm Orthodox Jewish world of central Europe before the Holocaust.

Flanders, Henry Jackson, Robert Wilson Crapps, and David Anthony Smith. *People of the Covenant.* 4th ed. New York: Oxford University Press, 1996. A good introduction to Hebrew scriptures and history, from Abraham to the Second Temple period.

Frank, Anne. *Anne Frank: The Diary of a Young Girl—the Definitive Edition.* New York: Doubleday, 1995. The unexpurgated diary of a young Jewish girl who hid with her family in Holland during World War II.

Frankl, Viktor. *Man's Search for Meaning.* Rev. ed. New York: Washington Square Press, 1997. A two-part book that describes the author's horrifying experiences in several concentration camps and then gives his reflections on the human need for meaning.

Friedman, Maurice. *Martin Buber: The Life of Dialogue.* 4th ed. New York: Routledge, 2002. A lucid explanation of the thought of Buber, by a leading disciple.

Kaplan, Aryeh. *Jewish Meditation: A Practical Guide.* New York: Schocken, 1995. Instructions by an Orthodox rabbi on contemplation, use of biblical mantras, visualization, and prayer.

Kushner, Harold. *When Bad Things Happen to Good People.* New York: Avon, 1997. A compelling book in which a rabbi tackles the question of evil in a world created by a good God. See also his recent related work, *The Lord Is My Shepherd,* a book of reflections on Psalm 23.

Scholem, Gershom. *Major Trends in Jewish Mysticism.* New York: Schocken, 1995. A classic by a major specialist in Jewish mystical literature.

Singer, Isaac Bashevis. *Collected Stories.* New York: Noonday, 1983. A collection of almost fifty stories by a Jewish writer and Nobel laureate, including the story of Yentl, the girl who wished to be a rabbi, on which the movie of the same name was based.

Umansky, Ellen, ed. *Four Centuries of Jewish Women's Spirituality.* Boston: Beacon, 1992. An anthology of stories, poems, journal entries, and prayers by Jewish women.

KEY TERMS

Ashkenazim (*ash-ken-ah'-zeem*): Jews who lived in or came from central Europe.

bar (bat) mitzvah: "Son (daughter) of the commandment"; the coming-of-age ceremony that marks the time when a young person is considered a legal adult within the Jewish community.

biblical Judaism: Judaism before the destruction of the Second Temple (70 C.E.).

Canaan (*kay'-nun*): An ancient name for the land of Israel.

Conservative Judaism: A branch of Judaism that attempts to blend the best of old and new Judaism.

covenant: A contract; the contract between the Hebrews and their God, Yahweh.

diaspora (*dai-as'-po-rah*): The dispersion of Jews beyond Israel, particularly to Persia, Egypt, and the Mediterranean region.

Essenes: A reclusive semimonastic Jewish group that flourished from c. 150 B.C.E. to 68 C.E.

Hanukkah (*ha'-nuk-kah*): An early-winter festival recalling the rededication of the Second Temple, celebrated with the lighting of candles for eight days.

Holocaust: The destruction of European Judaism by the Nazis; also known as *Shoah* (Hebrew: "extermination").

Kabbalah (*kab-bah'-luh* or *kab'-bah-luh*): "Received," "handed down"; the whole body of Jewish mystical literature.

Ketuvim (*ke-tu-veem'*): "Writings"; the third section of the Hebrew scriptures, consisting primarily of poetry, proverbs, and literary works.

kosher (*koh'-shur*): "Ritually correct"; refers particularly to food preparation and food consumption.

menorah (*me-noh'-ruh*): A candelabrum usually containing seven—and occasionally nine—branches, used for religious celebrations.

Messiah (*mes-sai'-uh*): A savior figure to be sent by God, awaited by the Jews (see Dan. 7:13–14).

midrash (*mid'-rash*): "Search"; rabbinical commentary on the scriptures and oral law.

Nevi'im (*ne-vee-eem'*): "Prophets"; the second section of the Hebrew scriptures, made up of historical and prophetic books.

Orthodox Judaism: The most traditional branch of Judaism.

Passover (Pesach): A joyful spring festival that recalls the Hebrews' exodus from Egypt and freedom from oppression.

Pharisees: A faction during the Second Temple period that emphasized the observation of biblical rules.

prophet: A person inspired by God to speak for him.

Purim (*poo'-reem*): A joyous festival in early spring that recalls the Jews' being saved from destruction, as told in the Book of Esther.

rabbi (*rab'-bai*): A religious teacher, Jewish minister.

rabbinical Judaism: Judaism that developed after the destruction of the Second Temple (70 C.E.).

Reconstructionism: A modern, liberal branch of Judaism that emphasizes the cultural aspects of Judaism.

Reform: A movement beginning in the nineteenth century that questioned and modernized Judaism; a liberal branch of Judaism.

Rosh Hashanah (*rosh ha-sha'-nah*): "Beginning of the year"; the celebration of the Jewish New Year, occurring in the seventh lunar month.

Sabbath: "Rest"; the seventh day of the week (Saturday), a day of prayer and rest from work.

Sadducees (*sad'-dyu-sees*): A priestly faction, influential during the Second Temple period.

Seder (*say'-dur*): "Order"; a special ritual meal at Passover, recalling the Hebrews' exodus from Egypt.

Sephardim (*se-far'-deem*): Jews of Spain, Morocco, and the Mediterranean region.

Sukkot (*soo-koht'*): "Booths"; a festival in the late autumn that recalls the Jews' period of wandering in the desert after their exodus from Egypt.

talit (*tah'-lit*): A prayer shawl worn by devout males.

Talmud (*tahl'-mood*): An encyclopedic commentary on the Hebrew scriptures.

Tanakh (*ta-nak'*): The complete Hebrew scriptures, made up of the Torah, Prophets (Nevi'im), and Writings (Ketuvim).

tefillin (*te-fil'-in*): Phylacteries; two small boxes containing biblical passages that are worn by Orthodox males on their head and left arm at morning prayer during the week.

theophany: A revelation or appearance of God.

Torah (*toh'-rah*): "Teaching," "instruction"; the first five books of the Hebrew scriptures; also, the additional instructions of God, believed by many to have been transmitted orally from Moses through a succession of teachers and rabbis.

Western Wall: The foundation stones of the western wall of the last temple of Jerusalem, today a place of prayer.

yarmulke (*yar'-mool-kah*): The skullcap worn by devout males.

Yom Kippur (*yohm kip-puhr'*): Day of Atonement, the most sacred day of the Jewish year.

Zealots: An anti-Roman, nationalistic Jewish faction, active during the Roman period of control over Israel.

Zionism: The movement that has encouraged the creation and support of the nation of Israel.

Christianity

 FIRST ENCOUNTER

On a Sunday morning in Rome you make your way by taxi to Saint Peter's Basilica, perhaps the best-known church in the world. You plan to attend the Pope's Sunday Mass. You enter the piazza on foot, passing the tall columns that form two encircling arms around a great open space. The first thing that you see is the dome over the church, which was designed by Michelangelo and refined by others. The dome is a work of special beauty: it is not a half-circle as you might expect but, stretching upward, is shaped more like an egg. The rise of the dome is accentuated by the "lantern," or viewing room, on top, which ties the dome to the sky.

Walking toward the entrance, you pass one of two huge tiered fountains. The breeze throws some of the falling water onto the stones of the pavement, and you feel mist on your face. As you get closer to the church and ascend the stairs, the dome overhead, now hidden by the porch, disappears. You pass two eagle-eyed guards who inspect you and the hundreds of others entering the church to make sure that every person's arms and legs are clothed modestly.

Once inside the church you see two famous sights. The first, just inside the door, is Michelangelo's marble statue called the *Pietà*. It portrays Mary holding the body of her crucified son Jesus across her lap. The second, to the right as you approach the high altar, is a thirteenth-century bronze statue of Saint Peter (attributed to Arnolfo di Cambio), whose right big toe shines from having been touched by so many visitors. Wonderful as these statues are, once your eyes adjust to the light inside the body of the church itself, you are taken by the true magnificence of this vast room. The interior space is so enormous that the view to the far end of the church is softened by a kind of mist. Sunlight streams down diagonally through windows in the dome, caught in beams by the atmospheric haze of the air. Above the high altar is a huge copper roof (called a *baldachin* and designed by Giovanni Bernini), supported by four pillars that twist upward into space. At the very back of the church, a magnificent oval window of yellow and white glass portrays the Holy Spirit of God as a dove in flight.

The church fills with people. After candles are lit on the high altar, the pope enters and begins the ceremony called *Mass*. The choir sings in Latin as the pope slowly carries a silver pot of incense around the altar. You watch the smoke rise in clouds through the air. There are readings from a large book, and finally wafers of bread are blessed and offered to the people. As the ceremony moves solemnly through its stages, you wonder about the origins of it all. You know that the Mass originated as a simple meal—the Last Supper of Jesus with his twelve followers. The high altar, up a multitude of stairs, you know is essentially a table. But the incense, the robes, the chant sung in Latin—where did these originate, and why are they still used?

After Mass, you walk around the church, absorbing it from different angles and perspectives. You stand under the dome. Why, you wonder, are high ceilings so common in churches? You go outside and wait in the piazza with tens of thousands of other visitors of every nationality and origin. Precisely at noon the pope appears to the right of the church in a high window of his apartments. He speaks, then blesses the crowd. What thoughts, you wonder, would Jesus have if he were with you now? How have these ceremonies come to be? What will be the future of this church and of Christianity?

The grandeur of Saint Peter's basilica becomes clear when you enter it for the first time. ◀

THE LIFE AND TEACHINGS OF JESUS

Christianity, which grew out of Judaism, has had a major influence on the history of the world. Before we discuss its growth and influence, we must look at the life of Jesus, who is considered its originator, and at the early scriptural books that speak of his life.

At the time of Jesus' birth and long before that, the land of Israel had been taken over repeatedly by stronger neighbors. During Jesus' time, Israel was called Palestine by the Romans and was part of the Roman Empire—but not willingly. The region was full of unrest, a boiling pot of religious and political factions and movements. As we discussed in chapter 8, patriots wanted to expel the Romans. The Sadducees, a group of priests in Jerusalem, kept up the Jewish temple rituals while accepting the Roman occupation as inevitable. Members of a semimonastic movement, the Essenes, lived an austere life in the desert and provinces; for the most part, they deliberately lived away from Jerusalem, which they thought was corrupt. The Pharisees, a lay movement of devout Jews, preoccupied themselves with meticulously keeping the Jewish law.

Many Jews in Jesus' day thought that they were living in the "end times." They expected a period of turbulence and suffering and a final great battle, when God would destroy all the enemies of pious Jews. God, they believed, would then inaugurate a new age of justice and love. Some expected a new Garden of Eden, where the good people who remained after the Judgment would eat year-round from fruit trees and women would no longer suffer in childbirth. Most Jews shared the hope that the Romans would be expelled, that evildoers would be punished, and that God's envoy, the **Messiah,** would appear. The common expectation among the Jews of Jesus' day was that the Messiah would be a king or a military leader who was descended from King David. (The name *Messiah* means "anointed" and refers to the ceremony of anointing a new king with olive oil.) Many held that the Messiah had been foretold in some of their sacred books—such as Isaiah, Micah, and Daniel—and they expected him to rule the new world.

Into this complicated land Jesus was born about two thousand years ago (Timeline 9.1). Traditional teaching tells of a miraculous conception in Nazareth, a town of northern Israel, and of a birth by the virginal mother Mary in Bethlehem, a town in the south not far from Jerusalem. It tells of wise men who followed a guiding star to the baby soon after his birth. The traditional portrait of Jesus, common in art, shows him in his early years assisting his foster father Joseph as a carpenter in the northern province of Galilee. It is possible that the truth of some of these traditional details—as it is regarding the lives of many other religious founders—may be more symbolic than literal.

There have been many attempts to find the "historical Jesus." Although artists have portrayed Jesus in countless ways, no portrait that we know of was ever painted of Jesus while he was alive. Of course, we can guess at his general features, but we cannot know anything definitive about the individual face or eyes or manner of Jesus.

Timeline of significant events in the history of Christianity. ▶

	c. 4 B.C.E.– c. 29 C.E.	Life of Jesus
Life of Paul	c. 4–64 C.E.	
	313 C.E.	Issuance of the Edict of Toleration by Constantine, making Christianity legal
Life of Augustine	354–430 C.E.	
	476 C.E.	Collapse of the Roman Empire of the West
Life of Benedict	c. 480–c. 547 C.E.	
	638 C.E.	Muslim conquest of Jerusalem
Split between Eastern and Western Christianity	1054 C.E.	
	1099	Conquest of Jerusalem during the First Crusade
Black Death	1347–1351	
	1453	Conquest of Constantinople by Muslim forces
Life of Martin Luther	1483–1546	
	1492	The expulsion of Jews and Muslims from Spain
Life of John Calvin	1509–1564	
	1517	Beginning of the Protestant Reformation
Founding of the Church of England by King Henry VIII	1534	
	1565	Christianity enters the Philippines
Life of composer Johann Sebastian Bach	1685–1750	
	1805–1844	Life of Joseph Smith
Founding of the World Council of Churches	1948	
	1962–1965	Modernization of Catholicism by the Second Vatican Council

Almost everything we know of Jesus comes from the four Gospels of the New Testament. (**Testament** means "contract" or "covenant," and **gospel** means "good news.") The Gospels are accounts, written by later believers, of the life of Jesus. The Gospels, however, tell very little of Jesus until he began a public life of teaching and healing. He probably began this public life in his late twenties, when he gathered twelve disciples and moved from place to place, teaching about the coming of what he called the Kingdom of God. After a fairly short period of preaching—no more than three years—Jesus was arrested in Jerusalem at Passover time by the authorities, who considered him a threat to public order. From the point of view of the Sadducees, Jesus was dangerous because he might begin an anti-Roman riot. In contrast, Jewish patriots may have found him not anti-Roman enough. From the Roman point of view, however, he was at least a potential source of political unrest and enough of a threat to be arrested, whipped, nailed to a cross, and crucified—a degrading and public form of execution. Death came from shock, suffocation, and loss of blood.

Dying on a Friday, Jesus was buried quickly near the site of his crucifixion shortly before sunset, just as the Jewish Sabbath was to begin. No work could be done on Saturday, the Sabbath. On the following Sunday, the Gospels report, the followers who went to care for his body found his tomb empty. Some followers reported apparitions of him, and his disciples became convinced that he had returned to life. Forty days later, the New Testament says, he ascended into the sky, promising to return again.

This bare outline does not answer many important questions: Who was Jesus? What kind of personality did he have? What were his teachings? For the answers to these questions we must turn to the four Gospels. They are the core of the Christian New Testament.

Jesus in the New Testament Gospels

The four Gospels describe the life and words of Jesus, but the New Testament is not the equivalent of a well-documented research report. The Gospels are instead written remembrances of Jesus' words and deeds, recorded some years after his death by people who believed in him. All the books of the New Testament are strongly colored by the viewpoints of their writers and by the culture of the period, and scholars consequently debate how much they reflect the views of later Christian believers as opposed to the actual teachings of Jesus. In fact, it is difficult to establish the historical accuracy of New Testament statements about Jesus or the words attributed to him. (Perhaps an analogy can clarify the problem: the Gospels are like paintings of Jesus, not photographs.) In compiling our picture of Jesus, we must also recognize that the Gospels are not a complete record of all essential information. There is a great deal we cannot know about Jesus. Nevertheless, although we accept a possibly irresolvable uncertainty about the historical Jesus, a definite person does emerge from the Gospels.

However obvious it may seem to point this out, Jesus believed and trusted in God, just as all contemporary Jews did. But while Jesus thought of God as creator and sustainer of the universe, he also thought of God in

Although never portrayed during his life, Jesus has been the subject of innumerable paintings. This fresco of Jesus appears in a dome of the monastery dedicated to Saint John of Rila in Bulgaria.

a very personal way, as his father. It is Jesus' extremely special relationship to God that is central to Christianity.

Raised as a Jew, Jesus accepted the sacred authority of the Law and the Prophets (the Torah and the books of history and prophecy). As a boy, he learned the scriptures in Hebrew. He kept the major Jewish holy days common to the period, and he traveled to Jerusalem and its temple for some of these events. He apparently kept the basic food laws and laws about Sabbath observance, and he attended synagogue meetings on Saturdays as part of the observance of the Jewish Sabbath (Luke 4:16). It seems he was a devout and thoughtful Jew.

Nonetheless, one striking personal characteristic of Jesus, alluded to frequently in the Gospels, was his independence of thought. He considered things carefully and then arrived at his own opinions, which he was not hesitant to share. Jesus, the Gospels say, taught differently: "unlike the scribes, he taught them with authority" (Mark 1:22).[1]

Perhaps Jesus' most impressive characteristic was his emphasis on universal love—not just love for the members of one's own family, ethnic group, or religion. He preached love in many forms: compassion, tolerance, forgiveness, acceptance, helpfulness, generosity. When asked if a person should forgive up to seven times, he answered that people should forgive seventy times seven times (Matt. 18:22)—in other words, endlessly. He rejected all vengeance and even asked forgiveness for those who killed him (Luke 23:34). He recommended that we respond to violence with nonviolence. "But I tell you who hear me: Love your enemies, do good to those who hate you, bless those who curse you, and pray for those who mistreat you. If anyone hits you on one cheek, let him hit the other one too; if someone takes your coat, let him have your shirt as well. Give to everyone who asks you for something, and when someone takes what is yours, do not ask for it back. Do for others just what you want them to do for you" (Luke 6:27–31).[2]

Although Jesus' nonviolent, loving message has often been neglected over the centuries, it is spelled out clearly in the Sermon on the Mount sections of the New Testament (Matt. 5–7, Luke 6). In the world of Jesus' day, which esteemed force and exacted vengeance, his message must have been shocking.

Jesus was wary of an overly strict observance of laws that seemed detrimental to human welfare. About keeping detailed laws regarding the Sabbath, he commented, "The sabbath was made for man, not man for the sabbath" (Mark 2:27).[4] He did not confuse pious practices, common among the Jews of his day, with the larger ideal of virtue. He disliked hypocrisy and pretense (Matt. 23:5–8).

From what we can see in the Gospels, Jesus showed many human feelings. He had close friends and spent time with them (John 11:5) and was disappointed when they were less than he had hoped for (Matt. 26:40). He wept when he heard of the death of one of his dearest friends (John 11:33–36).

Jesus urged simplicity. He recommended that people "become like little children" (Matt. 18:3). He liked directness and strived to go beyond details to the heart of things.

Much of Jesus' advice is good psychology, showing that he was a keen observer of human beings. For example, we are told that as you give, so shall you receive (Matt. 7:2) and that if you are not afraid to ask for what you want, you shall receive it (Matt. 7:7).

Jesus showed an appreciation for nature, in which he saw evidence of God's care (Matt. 6:29). But Jesus did not look at nature with the detached vision of a scientist. He knew scripture well but was not a scholar. As far as

Do not judge others, and God will not judge you; do not condemn others, and God will not condemn you; forgive others, and God will forgive you. Give to others, and God will give to you. Indeed, you will receive a full measure, a generous helping, poured into your hands—all that you can hold. The measure you use for others is the one that God will use for you.

—Luke 6:37–38[3]

we know, he was not a writer, and he left behind no written works. He showed almost no interest in money or in business. In adulthood he probably did not travel far from his home territory, between the Sea of Galilee and Jerusalem. While he may have spoken some Greek in addition to his native Aramaic, he did not apparently have much interest in the Greco-Roman culture of his day.

Whether Jesus had a sense of humor is hard to know. The four Gospels never mention that he laughed, thus giving him an image of solemnity. But some of his statements come alive when we see them as being spoken with ironic humor and even laughter (see, for example, Matt. 15:24–28). We do know that although he sometimes sought seclusion Jesus seems to have enjoyed others' company.

Some people would like to see Jesus as a social activist. He cared strongly about the poor and the hungry, but he apparently was not a social activist of any specialized type. For example, the Gospels do not record words of Jesus that condemn slavery or the oppression of women. Perhaps, like many others of his time, Jesus believed that the world would soon be judged by God, and this may have kept him from working for a specific reform. Instead, he preached basic principles of humane treatment, particularly of the needy and the oppressed (Matt. 25).

For those who would turn Jesus into a protector of the family and family values, the Gospels present mixed evidence. When asked about the divorce practice of his day, Jesus opposed it strongly. He opposed easy divorce because it meant that a husband could divorce his wife for a minor reason, often leaving her unable to support herself or to remarry. He stated that the marriage bond was given by God (Mark 10:1–12). And at his death, Jesus asked a disciple to care for his mother after he was gone (John 19:26). But Jesus himself remained unmarried. If Jesus had had a wife, that fact almost certainly would have been mentioned somewhere in a gospel or other New Testament book or would have survived in tradition. Moreover, there is no mention anywhere that Jesus ever had children.

Indeed, Jesus spoke highly of those who remained unmarried "for the sake of the kingdom of heaven" (Matt. 19:12).[5] As an intriguing confirmation of Jesus' unmarried state, we now recognize that celibacy was valued by the Essenes, the semimonastic Jewish movement of that era, which may have had some influence on him.[6] In any case, Paul—one of the most influential of the early Christians and missionaries—and generations of priests, monks, and nuns followed a celibate ideal that was based on the way Jesus was thought to have lived. In fact, the ideal of remaining unmarried for religious reasons has survived over the centuries and remains influential in several branches of Christianity today.

The Gospels mention Jesus' brothers and sisters (Mark 6:3). Some Christian traditions have held that these relatives were cousins or stepbrothers and stepsisters, hoping thereby to preserve the notion of his mother Mary's permanent virginity. But it is now widely accepted that Jesus had actual brothers and sisters who were children of his mother Mary and of Joseph. When we inspect his relationship to his family members, it seems that Jesus at times was alienated from them. They quite naturally worried about him and apparently wished he were not so unusual and difficult. But Jesus, irritated by their claims on him, said publicly that his real family consisted not of his blood relatives but of all those who hear the word of God and keep it (Mark 3:31–33). After Jesus died, however, because of their blood relationship with Jesus his family members were influential in the early Church, and the earlier disharmony was downplayed.

The Two Great Commandments

What then was Jesus' main concern? His teachings, called the Two Great Commandments, combine two strong elements: a love for God and an eth-ical call for kindness toward others. These commandments already existed in Hebrew scripture (Deut. 6:5 and Lev. 19:18), but Jesus gave them new emphasis by reducing all laws to the law of love: Love God and love your neighbor (Matt. 22:37–40). Being fully aware of God means living with love for all God's children. Like prophets before him, Jesus had a clear vision of what human society can be at its best—a Kingdom of God in which people care about each other, the poor are looked after, violence and exploitation are abandoned, and religious rules do not overlook human needs.

It may be that Jesus' emphasis on morality was tied to the common belief in an imminent divine judgment. This belief seems to have been a par-ticularly important part of the worldview of the Essenes, who thought of themselves as preparing for this new world. It was also essential to the think-ing of John the Baptizer (also called John the Baptist), whom the Gospel of Luke calls the cousin of Jesus. John preached that the end of the world was near, when God would punish evildoers. As a sign of purification, John immersed his followers in the water of the Jordan River. Jesus allowed him-self to be baptized, and when John died, Jesus had his own followers carry on John's practice by baptizing others. Whether Jesus shared John's view of the coming end of the world is debated. Some passages would seem to indi-cate that he did (see Mark 9:1, 13:30; Matt. 16:28). This vision of impending judgment is called **apocalypticism.** In the apocalyptic view, the Kingdom of God would soon be a social and political reality.

Whatever Jesus' views about the end times, his focus was on bringing about the Kingdom of God in each human heart. This would occur when peo-ple followed the Two Great Commandments and lived by the laws of love. Some of Jesus' closest followers were among those who seem to have expected him to be a political leader, wanting him to lead the fight against the Roman overlords to establish a political kingdom of God. But Jesus refused. The Gospel of John records him as saying, "My kingdom is not of this world" (John 18:36).[7] Instead of political violence, Jesus chose a path of nonviolence.

EARLY CHRISTIAN BELIEFS AND HISTORY

The Book of Acts records that after Jesus' ascension to heaven forty days fol-lowing his resurrection, his disciples were gathered, full of fear, wondering what to do next. The Book of Acts then tells how the Spirit of God came

The Apostles Saint Peter and Saint Paul, by El Greco, is a famous portrait that gives human faces to the apostles who did much to spread Christianity. It emphasizes Paul's contribution to New Testament writings.

upon them in the form of fire, giving them courage to spread their belief in Jesus as the Messiah. As they began to preach, they found that people of different countries and languages understood them, even though they did not necessarily speak the same language (Acts 2). This symbolic scene conveys the Christian belief that the spread of the Christian message was guided by God. The Book of Acts sees it as a reversal of the disunity that had afflicted human beings since the emergence of separate human languages (Gen. 11). (As we discussed in chapter 8, the Book of Genesis tells of an ancient time when people had begun to build a tower to reach God. Because God was not too eager for their intrusion, he created separate languages so that people could no longer communicate with each other and thus could not continue building their tower.) This first preaching of the Christian message has been called the Birthday of the Church.

The early Christian message was not complex. It is summarized in the **apostle** Peter's speech in Acts 2, which says that God is now working in a special way; Jesus was the expected Messiah, God's ambassador; and these are the "final days" before God's judgment and the coming of a new world. Early Christian practice required those who believed to be baptized as a sign of rebirth, to share their possessions, and to care for widows and orphans.

The early Christian group that remained in Jerusalem seems to have been almost entirely Jewish and was led by James, called the Just because of his careful observance of Jewish practice. Being one of Jesus' real brothers, James carried great authority. This Jewish-Christian Church was a strong influence for the first forty years. However, it was weakened by the destruction of the Temple in 70 C.E., and it seems to have disappeared over the next one hundred years. Meanwhile, the non-Jewish, Greek-speaking branch of early Christianity, led by Paul and others like him, began to spread throughout the Roman Empire.

Paul and Pauline Christianity

As the Jewish Christianity of Jerusalem and Israel weakened, Christianity among non-Jews grew because of the missionary Paul. Paul is occasionally called with much seriousness the cofounder of Christianity because of the way that Jesus' teachings and Paul's interpretation of them blended to form a viable religion with widespread appeal. Paul's preaching in Greek, his energetic traveling, and his powerful letters spread his form of belief in Jesus far beyond the limits of Israel.

Originally named Saul, Paul was born of Jewish parentage in Tarsus, a town in what is today southern Turkey. He was earnest about traditional Judaism and went to Jerusalem for study. At that time he was a Pharisee. There, he was adamantly opposed to the new "Jesus movement," which he saw as a dangerous messianic Jewish cult that could divide Judaism.

Paul, however, came to a new understanding of Jesus. The book of Galatians says that he pondered the meaning of Jesus for three years in "Arabia" and "Damascus" (Gal 1:17). In a more dramatic, later account, the Book of Acts relates that while Paul was on the road from Jerusalem to root out a cell of early Christian believers, he experienced a vision of Jesus. In it Jesus asked, "Saul, Saul, why do you persecute me?"[8] (See Acts 9, 22, 26.) After several years of study in seclusion, Paul became convinced that Jesus' life and death were the major events of a divine plan, and that Jesus was a cosmic figure who entered the world in order to renew it. Consequently, as we will soon discuss, the focus in Paul's thought is less on the historical Jesus and more on the cosmic Christ.

Paul discovered his life's mission: to spread belief in Christ around the Mediterranean, particularly among non-Jews, whom he found more receptive to his message. Many of the Pauline Epistles (or letters) that are part of the New Testament are addressed to regions and towns in Asia Minor (now Turkey) and Greece, which were then part of the Roman Empire. Paul also preached in Rome, where, tradition says, he was executed. (He had hoped to travel as far as Spain, but he probably did not realize that ambition.) His use of the Greco-Roman name Paul, instead of his Jewish name Saul, shows his orientation to the non-Jewish world.

Paul's missionary technique was the same in most towns. If the Book of Acts is correct in its portrayal of Paul's missionary work, he would begin by visiting the local synagogue or other Jewish place of worship (in Philippi, for example, the Jews worshiped beside a river). There, Paul would use Jewish scriptures, such as the Book of Isaiah, to explain his own belief that Jesus was the Messiah whom Jews had long been awaiting. He was unsuccessful with most Jews, who expected a royal Messiah, not a poor man who had been publicly executed. And they sometimes treated Paul as a traitor, especially when he said that it was unnecessary to impose Jewish laws about diet and circumcision on non-Jewish converts to Christianity.

Whether all Christians had to keep Jewish religious laws was a subject of intense debate in early Christianity. Christianity had begun as a movement of Jews who believed that Jesus was the expected Messiah, but it soon attracted followers who did not come from a Jewish background. Questions about practice led early Christianity to differentiate itself from Judaism, to define itself on its own terms. Did adult males who wished to be baptized also have to be circumcised? (Needless to say, adult male converts were not always enthusiastic about the practice of circumcision.) Did new converts have to keep the Jewish laws about diet? Did they have to keep the Jewish Sabbath? Should they read the Jewish scriptures?

Some early Christian preachers decided not to impose Jewish rules on non-Jewish converts, while others insisted that all Jewish laws had to be kept. The faction that insisted on upholding all Jewish laws, however, did not prevail. Ultimately, some elements of Judaism were retained and others were abandoned. For example, circumcision was replaced by **baptism** as a sign of initiation, but Jewish scriptures and weekly services were retained.

These efforts to define what it meant to be a Christian signaled a major turning point in Christianity. Paul's conclusions, in particular, played a prominent role in shaping the movement. His views on the meaning of Jesus, on morality, and on Christian practice became the norm for most of the Christian world. This happened because of his extensive missionary activities in major cities of the Roman Empire and because he left eloquent letters stating his beliefs. Copied repeatedly, circulated, and read publicly, these letters (and letters imitating his thought and style) have formed the basis for all later Christian belief.

Paul's training as a scholar of Jewish law made him acutely aware of human imperfection. He wrote that "all have sinned and fall short of the glory of God" (Rom. 3:23).[9] He came to feel, in fact, that external written laws, such as those of Judaism, hurt more than they helped; the imposition of laws that could not be fulfilled could only make human beings aware of their inadequacies. For him, Jesus came from God to bring people a radical new freedom. Believers would no longer have to rely on written laws or to feel guilty for past misdeeds. Jesus' death was a voluntary sacrifice to take on the punishment and guilt of everyone. Human beings thereby found **redemption** from punishment. Believers need only follow the lead of the Spirit of God, which dwells in them and directs them.

Thus Paul preached that it is no longer by the keeping of Jewish laws that a person comes into right relationship with God (**righteousness**); rather, it is by the acceptance of Jesus, who shows us God's love and who

Christians from Ethiopia carry the Gospel book in this Palm Sunday procession at the Church of the Holy Sepulchre in Jerusalem.

God's love has been poured into our hearts.
—Rom. 5:5 [11]

was punished for our wrongdoing. What brings a person into good relationship with God "is not obedience to the Law, but faith in Jesus Christ" (Gal. 2:16).[10]

Despite his newfound freedom, Paul did not abandon moral rules. But his notion of morality was no longer based on laws that were imposed externally—and kept grudgingly—but rather on an interior force that inspired people to do good deeds spontaneously.

The life of Jesus was for Paul a proof of the love of God, because God the Father had sent Jesus into the world to tell about his love. According to Paul, our awareness of God's love will inspire us to live in a new and loving way.

Paul saw Jesus not only as teacher, prophet, and Messiah but also as a manifestation of divinity. For Paul, Jesus was a cosmic figure—the preexistent image of God, the Wisdom of God (see Prov. 8), and the Lord of the universe. Jesus was sent into the world to begin a process of cosmic reunion between God and his human creation. **Sin** (wrongdoing) had brought to human beings the punishment of death. But Jesus' death was an atonement for human sin, and the result is that the punishment of death is no longer valid. Jesus' return to life was just the beginning of a process of eternal life for all people who have the Spirit of God within them.

The New Testament: Its Structure and Artistry

What we know of Jesus and early Christianity comes largely from the New Testament. The New Testament, which is also at the core of Christianity, is used in religious services, read regularly, and carried throughout the world.

The New Testament is divided into four parts: (1) the Gospels, (2) the Acts of the Apostles, (3) the Epistles, and (4) Revelation. The Gospels describe the life and teachings of Jesus and are traditionally attributed to early followers of Jesus and their disciples—the **evangelists** (Greek: "good news person") Matthew, Mark, Luke, and John. The Acts of the Apostles tells of the initial spread of Christianity, although its historical accuracy cannot be confirmed. The Epistles are letters to early Christians, primarily by Paul. The New Testament ends with a visionary book, Revelation, which foretells in symbolic language the triumph of Christianity. Altogether, there are twenty-seven books in the New Testament.

The New Testament is history, literature, and artistic creation all together. We should recall that because Judaism generally forbade image making, Christians did not produce much art in the first century of the new era. This meant that the aesthetic impulse had to express itself in writing, rather than in painting or sculpture. And because Christianity was not a legal religion until the early fourth century, Christian architecture, which would later flourish in public church buildings, could not easily develop at first. A great deal of the writing in the New Testament, however, is genuinely artistic.

The New Testament has a structure that is similar to the structure of the Hebrew Bible (see chapter 8). For early Christians, the Gospels were considered the new Torah, equivalent to the teachings of Moses. The record of the buildup of the Hebrew kingdom in the historical books of the Hebrew Bible—called the Former Prophets—is paralleled by the record of the growth of early Christianity in the Book of Acts. The Epistles are like the Wisdom Literature, which constitutes a major part of the third section of the Hebrew Bible, called the Writings. And the Latter Prophets of the Hebrew Bible are paralleled by the Book of Revelation.

All the books of the New Testament were written in Greek, the language of culture and commerce in the classical Mediterranean world in the first century of the common era. The quality of the Greek varies; in the Book of Revelation the language is considered rough, while in the Books of Luke and Acts it is considered particularly graceful.

The Gospels   We know of the life of Jesus primarily from the Gospels, which are written in an extremely pictorial way. They are filled with powerful stories and images and have been the source of great inspiration for much later Christian art. Each of the Gospels is as unique in its artistry and style as four portraits of the same person painted by four different artists would be: the resulting portraits would certainly be recognizably similar but also different in such details as choice of background, clothing, angle of perspective, and so on. The same is true of the "portraits" of Jesus that are painted in the Gospels: each gospel writer shows Jesus in a different way.

The Books of the New Testament

GOSPELS

Synoptic Gospels

Matthew (75–80 C.E.)

Mark (65–70 C.E.)

Luke (85 C.E.)

John (90–100 C.E.)

HISTORY

Acts of the Apostles (85 C.E.)

EPISTLES

Pauline Epistles (c. 50–125 C.E.)

Romans

1–2 Corinthians

Galatians

Ephesians

Philippians

Colossians

1–2 Thessalonians

1–2 Timothy

Titus

Philemon

Hebrews

Universal Epistles (c. 90–125 C.E.)

James

1–2 Peter

1–3 John

Jude

PROPHECY

Revelation (c. 95 C.E.)

Because the first three gospels, despite their differences, show a family resemblance in stories, language, and order, they are called the Synoptic Gospels (*synoptic* literally means "together-see" in Greek, implying a similar perspective). The synoptic writers show Jesus as a messianic teacher and healer sent by God. It is generally thought that the Gospel of Mark was written first, since it seems to be the primary source for the later Gospels of Matthew and Luke. The Gospel of John, however, is recognizably different and relies on its own separate sources.

The Gospel of Matthew is thought to have been written (about 75–80 C.E.) for an audience with a Jewish background. For example, it portrays Jesus as the "new Moses," a teacher who offers a "new Torah." In the Sermon on the Mount (Matt. 5–7), Jesus delivers his teachings on a mountain, just as Moses delivered the Ten Commandments from another mountain, Mount Sinai. The gospel also contains many quotations from the Hebrew scriptures, showing that Jesus was their fulfillment.

The Gospel of Mark is the shortest of the four Gospels, which suggests that it is the oldest (written around 65–70 C.E.). This gospel contains no infancy stories and begins instead with the adult public life of Jesus. In the original version, it ends with an account of Jesus' empty tomb. The resurrection account in Mark was added later. Some have argued that pages were lost from the end of the gospel (a view that has virtually no scholarly support), while others hold that the original gospel ended without the resurrection account.

The Gospel of Luke (written about 85 C.E.) is filled with a sense of wonder, perhaps because it speaks repeatedly of the miraculous action of the Spirit

The birth of Jesus, described in two of the gospels, is here celebrated with a traditional Nativity scene. Marking such a scene with *farolitos* or *luminarias* (little lanterns) is a tradition in some southwestern states.

of God at work in the world. It has been called the "women's gospel" because of its delicate portraits of Mary (Jesus' mother), her cousin Elizabeth, and other women. This is a gospel of mercy and compassion, with a strong focus on the underdog. The story of the Good Samaritan illustrates this very well (see Luke 10:29–37). It tells how a man, who was robbed and beaten, is then left by the side of the road to die. People pass by, including officials from the temple in Jerusalem, but they do nothing. At last the beaten man is helped by a Samaritan, a member of a race of people who were looked down upon by many Jews. The audience of the story, probably Greco-Roman, would have appreciated the assurance that in God's sight all people are equal and everyone is a neighbor.

The Gospel of John stands by itself. The time of its writing is difficult to pinpoint. Traditionally, it has been dated quite late—about 90 to 100 C.E.— because of its apparent elaboration of Christian doctrines. But details that might have come from an eyewitness suggest that parts may have been written earlier. Because it views human life as a struggle between the principles of light and darkness, students of the Gospel of John have wondered whether it was influenced by one or more religious movements of the period, such as the Persian religion of Zoroastrianism (see chapter 8), Greek mystery religions, or

Gnosticism (see chapter 10)—a movement that saw human life as a stage of purification to prepare the soul to return to God.[12] The discovery of the Dead Sea Scrolls in 1947 near Qumran has shown many similarities of language between the Gospel of John and certain phrases found in the Qumran literature (for example, "sons of light and sons of darkness"). The Jewish origins of the gospel are now clear.

In the Gospel of John, the portrayal of Jesus is full of mystery. He is the **incarnation** of God, the divine made visible in human form. He speaks in cosmic tones: "I am the light of the world" (John 9:5). "I am the bread of life" (John 6:35). "You are from below; I am from above" (John 8:23).[13] Scholars frequently question the historicity of these exact words, seeing them more as representing the author's vision of the heavenly origin and nature of Jesus.

The central aesthetic image of the gospel is of a ray of divine light that descends like a lightning bolt into our world, passing through and lighting up the darkness, but ultimately returning to its heavenly source and enabling human beings to follow. Most people, the gospel states, do not really understand the truth; but the true nature of Jesus as divine light can be seen by those who have an open heart. Water, bread, the vine, the shepherd, and the door are additional symbols used in the Gospel of John to indicate aspects of Jesus and his meaning for the believer. These symbols later became regular features of Christian art.

Symbols for the four Gospels themselves eventually appeared in manuscript illustrations and other art forms. They derived from a vision of the prophet Ezekiel (Ezek. 1:10). The winged lion represents the Gospel of Mark because that gospel opens in the desert, the lion's home. The winged ox represents Luke because that gospel begins in the temple of Jerusalem, where oxen were sacrificed. The winged angel represents the Gospel of Matthew because that gospel tells of angelic help at the time of Jesus' infancy. The eagle represents the Gospel of John, which begins soaringly with an account of the heavenly origin of God's Word.

The Acts of the Apostles This book (dating from about 85 C.E.) is really the second part of the Gospel of Luke, and scholars sometimes refer to the two books together as Luke-Acts. It is possible that the single work of Luke-Acts was divided in two in order to place the Gospel of John after the Gospel of Luke. Just as the Gospel of Luke portrays Jesus as moving inevitably toward his sacrifice in Jerusalem, so Acts portrays Paul in a parallel journey to his final sacrifice in Rome. At the heart of both books is a single beautiful image of a stone, dropped in a pond, that makes ever-widening ripples. Similarly, the life of Jesus makes ever-widening ripples as it spreads in a growing circle from its origin in Jerusalem to the ends of the earth.

The Epistles The word *epistle* means "letter" and is an appropriate label for most of these works, which were written to instruct, to encourage, and to solve problems. Several epistles are long and formal; a few are brief and hurried. Some epistles seem to have been written to individuals; some to individual churches; and others for circulation among several churches. And it appears that a few of the epistles were originally treatises (for example, Hebrews) or sermons (1 Peter).

The wide category of works called the Epistles can be divided into two groups. The first includes those books that traditionally have been attributed to the early missionary Paul—the Pauline Epistles. The second group includes all the other epistles—called the Universal Epistles because they seem to be addressed to all believers. The genuine Pauline letters are the earliest works in the New Testament, dating from about 50 to 60 C.E. The dating of the other epistles is debated, but some may have been finished as late as about 150 C.E.

Of the so-called Pauline Epistles, it is now recognized that several were not written by Paul. Hebrews is most clearly not by Paul, because the Greek is quite different from that of Paul's genuine letters. And because the "pastoral" Epistles (1–2 Timothy and Titus) show strong interest in church organization, they were probably written after Paul's time. The authorship of several others (such as Ephesians, Colossians, and 2 Thessalonians) is debated. However, writing in the name of a famous teacher after that person's death was a common practice in the ancient world; it was meant not to deceive but to honor the teacher.

One factor that has made the Epistles so much loved is their use of memorable images, many of which come from the Pauline letters. For example, life is compared to a race with a prize given at the end (1 Cor. 9:24); good deeds are like incense rising to God (2 Cor. 2:15); and the community of believers is like a solid building set on secure foundations (1 Cor. 3:9–17). Effective images also appear in the non-Pauline Epistles: new Christians are compared to babies who long for milk (1 Pet. 2:2); and the devil is like a roaring lion, seeking someone to devour (1 Pet. 5:8).

The themes of the Epistles vary widely, but they focus generally on proper belief, morality, and church order. The topics include the nature and work of Jesus, God's plan for humanity, faith, good deeds, love, the ideal marriage, community harmony, Christian living, the conduct of the Lord's Supper, and the expected return of Jesus.

Revelation   This final book of the New Testament was originally written (around 100 C.E.) as a book of encouragement for Christians who were under threat of persecution. Through a series of visions, the book shows that suffering will be followed by the final triumph of goodness over evil. The last chapters show the descent of the New Jerusalem from heaven and the adoration of Jesus, who appears as a lamb.

The language of Revelation is highly symbolic, deliberately using numbers and images in a way that would make the meaning clear to early Christians but obscure to others. For example, the lamb (Rev. 14:1) is Jesus, and the dragon with seven heads (Rev. 12:3) is the empire of Rome, a city built on seven hills. The number 666, the mark of the beast (mentioned in Rev. 13:18), may be the name of Emperor Nero, given in the form of numbers. Although long attributed to the author of the Gospel of John, Revelation is plainly— because of stylistic differences—by another hand. Some of its images were seminal to the development of later Christian art—particularly the adoration of the lamb, the four horsemen of the apocalypse, the book of life, and the vision of heaven.

The Christian Canon

We should recognize that some of the books in the New Testament were not accepted universally for several centuries and that their status involved much debate—Hebrews, James, and Revelation are the most prominent examples. Agreement on which books belonged to the sacred **canon** of the New Testament took several hundred years.[14]

Early Christians continued for the most part to accept and read the Hebrew scriptures, particularly those books—such as Genesis, Exodus, Isaiah, the Psalms, and the Song of Songs—that they saw as foreshadowing the events of Christianity. The New Testament books, therefore, were added to the Hebrew scriptures already in existence. Christians thought of the Hebrew scriptures, which they called the Old Testament, as being fulfilled by the Christian scriptures, which they called the New Testament. The Christian Bible thus includes both the Hebrew scriptures and the New Testament.

There is a whole spectrum of ways in which the Christian Bible is read and interpreted by Christians. One approach emphasizes the subjective aspect of the scriptures, interpreting them primarily as a record of beliefs. A contrasting approach sees the Christian Bible as a work of objective history and authoritative morality, dictated word for word by God. To illustrate, let's consider how the two approaches interpret the stories of creation in the Book of Genesis. The conservative position interprets the six days of creation and the story of Adam and Eve quite literally, as historical records, while the liberal approach interprets these stories primarily as moral tales that express God's power, love, and sense of justice. There are similar contrasts between the conservative and liberal interpretations of miracles (for example, the virgin birth) in the New Testament.

Interpretation of the Bible causes much controversy among Christians. It poses a serious problem for them because it has major implications for their understanding of God's will and their understanding of the life of Jesus. It also affects the question of how strictly to apply rules of conduct, codified—for example, in the Torah and in the Epistles—for quite different cultures several thousand years ago. Most contemporary Christians hold a position that is somewhere in between the conservative and liberal poles of the spectrum. They believe that the Bible was inspired by God in its essentials, but they see it as requiring thoughtful human interpretation. Interpretation of the Bible has been and still is a major cause of conflict and division in Christianity; however, the debate has also been—and still is—a great source of intellectual vitality.

THE ESSENTIAL CHRISTIAN WORLDVIEW

Although the New Testament reveals the essentials of the Christian way of looking at the world, it also reveals in its twenty-seven books a startling diversity in early Christian thought. Some areas of early difference involved the nature of Jesus, his relation to God the Father, his resurrection, and the date of his expected return to earth. (We also know from some epistles that controversy existed about forms of worship, organization, and the validity of the Jewish scriptures and laws.) It took almost five centuries of debate for mainstream Christianity to fully develop. The essential Christian worldview was eventually defined in several statements of belief, called *creeds*, and they have remained authoritative for many Christian groups. We should realize, though, that over the past five centuries significant differences have arisen again about some of these areas of belief, and quite varied interpretations have reappeared, reminiscent of the diversity of early Christian thought. Despite the contemporary diversity among Christians, most share the following general worldview.

God Behind the activity of the universe is an invisible, intelligent power that is eternal. This being, God, created the cosmos as an expression of power and love, and human beings are an important part of the divine cosmic plan. They may not understand the reasons behind specific events in their lives, but there are underlying reasons that only God knows.

The Father Jesus spoke often of God, his heavenly Father. The wise and caring qualities of God the Father are symbolized in art by a robed and bearded man, elderly but powerful. Michelangelo's imagery in the Sistine Chapel in Rome is an excellent example. Despite the portrayal of God the Father as male, we should note that Christian doctrine actually teaches that God the Father, as pure spirit, has no gender.

Jesus Christ Jesus was an ideal human being, but even more he was the visible manifestation of God. He showed God's love in his healing and his performing of other miracles. Jesus is thus often called the Word and Image of God to emphasize his divine origin and nature. Throughout most of its history, Christianity has emphasized Jesus' divinity. In art, however, especially since the Renaissance, the humanity of Jesus has emerged. Moreover, scholarly interest in Jesus as a human being has grown in recent centuries as a result of insights from psychology and new directions in biblical studies.

Jesus' life as a human being and his death were part of God's plan, and during his earthly life Jesus taught about the mind and will of God. Jesus died voluntarily in order to take upon himself the punishment that justice demands should fall on other human beings who have done wrong. Some forms of Christianity also teach that Jesus' death redeemed a basic sinfulness in humanity, called **original sin,** inherited from Adam by his descendants. After his resurrection and ascension, Jesus continued to live physically beyond the earth. Although he is not physically visible now, he is alive and is therefore worthy of human adoration and prayer. He will return in the future to judge human beings and to inaugurate a golden age.

Jesus has been given many devotional titles. The best-known, *Christ,* means "anointed." (Anointment is a ceremony in which a leader is consecrated with olive oil, a symbol of health and strength.) To refer to

Jesus as *Christ*, therefore, means that he is a special leader, sent by God. This title is the Greek equivalent of the Hebrew title *Messiah*.

The Holy Spirit In Jewish and Christian thought, God makes use of his Spirit to create and vivify. The Gospel of John records Jesus as saying that although he himself must leave the earth, the Spirit of God will come to strengthen his followers (John 16). Traditional Christian belief speaks of the Holy Spirit (or Holy Ghost) as a divine power that guides all believers. In art, the Holy Spirit is usually represented as a white dove, appearing over the head of Jesus or coming to Mary at the time of her conception of Jesus.

The Holy Trinity The word **Trinity** does not appear in the New Testament. The term, in common use by the fourth century, expresses the belief that God, although one, has three "persons": Father, Son, and Holy Spirit. (The names of Father, Son, and Holy Spirit do appear together at the end of the Gospel of Matthew.) The doctrine of the Trinity is called a mystery, meaning that it is beyond complete human explanation or understanding, but it hints that the nature of God is essentially a relationship of love.

Angelic forces Invisible personal forces have a powerful influence on individuals and on events. They were created by God as intelligent but bodiless beings. Benevolent forces are called *angels* ("messengers"), and malevolent forces are called *devils*. Devils are said to be rebellious angels led by a former angel, once called Lucifer ("lightbearer") and now called Satan ("adversary"). In art, angels and devils are shown with wings to represent their spiritual nature and ability to appear anywhere.

The Bible God's will and his plan for human beings are expressed in the **Bible,** a collection of books written down by many human beings, all of whom were inspired by God. The first three-quarters of the Christian Bible is made up of the Hebrew Bible (in a somewhat different arrangement than that used by Jews), which Christians adopted and called the Old Testament. The last quarter of the Christian Bible is called the New Testament. It is called "new" because it is thought of by Christians as a new contract or covenant with God and as a fulfillment of the Hebrew scriptures. However, great variety exists among Christian groups in their use and interpretation of the Christian Bible.

Human life Human beings are a major part of God's plan. They are on earth to perfect themselves, to help other human beings, and to prepare for the afterlife. Suffering, when accepted and put to use, allows human beings to grow in virtue, and good people are eventually rewarded in the afterlife. God's Word became embodied in Jesus in order to show human beings God's solidarity with them and to provide a model for how to live in harmony with God's will. Human beings can pray to God the Father and to Jesus to receive help from them.

Life after death Almost universally, Christianity accepts the view of the human being as consisting of two realities: body and soul. After the

This image of the Trinity is found in the Vatican Museum's apartments. God the Father is above; Jesus is in the middle, surrounded by his twelve disciples; the Holy Spirit appears at the bottom as the traditional dove. ◀

death of the body, the soul of a person is believed to be rewarded or punished permanently for the way the individual has lived on earth. Heaven, the reward of the good, is the presence of God. In art, heaven is often shown as a place of angels, light, joy, dance, and song. Hell, the punishment of the wicked, is shown as fire, smoke, suffering, and despair. Many Christians believe in a temporary intermediate state of the afterlife, called *purgatory,* which prepares less-worthy but not wicked souls for heaven. At the end of the world, there will be a great public judgment, and at this time the bodies of all who have died will come to life again and be reunited with their souls. The theme of the last judgment is frequently presented in Christian painting, sculpture, and music. Michelangelo, for example, painted it above the altar in the Sistine Chapel, and Mozart portrayed it in his *Requiem.* With a few early exceptions, reincarnation has not been a Christian belief.

These basic beliefs, which allow a great deal of room for individual interpretation, were added to and further refined over many centuries by powerful personalities. Just as Christianity was initially influenced by Paul, it was later influenced by other major historical figures, such as Constantine, Benedict, Luther, and others. It has also been greatly shaped by historical events, whose influence we will now examine.

THE EARLY SPREAD OF CHRISTIANITY

As we have already seen, Christianity is a missionary religion. The Gospel of Mark tells how Jesus sent out his disciples in pairs to preach throughout the land of Israel (Mark 6:7). Then the Gospel of Matthew ends with Jesus' command, "Make disciples of all nations" (Matt. 28:19).[15] In the following discussion, we will see how Christianity spread in stages: from being a Jewish messianic movement in Israel, Christianity spread around the Mediterranean; then it became the official religion of the Roman Empire; and after the end of the empire in the West, Christianity spread to the rest of Europe. (Later, we will see how it spread to the New World, Asia, and Africa.)

Paul's eagerness to spread his belief in Jesus took him to Asia Minor (Turkey), Greece, and Italy. Tradition holds that Peter, one of the original twelve apostles of Jesus, was already in Rome when Paul arrived and that both Peter and Paul died there under the Emperor Nero about 64 C.E. At that point, early Christianity was only loosely organized, but it was clear even then that some kind of order was necessary. Influenced by the Roman Empire's hierarchical political organization, Christians developed the monarchical (Greek: "one ruler") model of church organization. Population centers would have a single **bishop** (*episkopos,* "overseer"), who would be in charge of lower-ranking clergy.

In those days, before easy communication, a truly centralized Christianity was impossible. The bishops of the major cities thus played a significant role for the churches of the neighboring regions. Besides Rome, several other great cities of the Roman Empire became centers of Christian belief—particularly Antioch in Syria and Alexandria in Egypt (Figure 9.1). Because

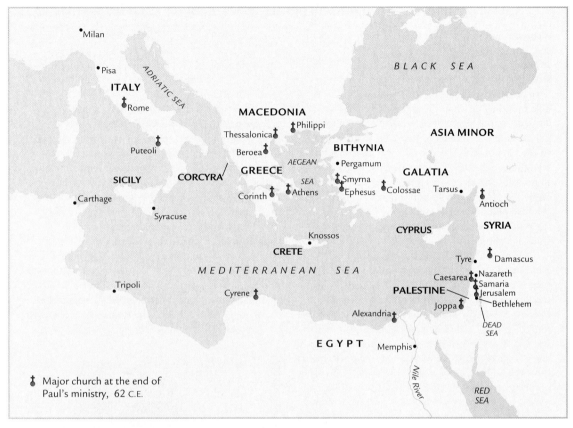

Major church at the end of
Paul's ministry, 62 C.E.

FIGURE 9.1

Historical centers of early
Christianity

the bishops of these important cities had more power than bishops of other, smaller, cities, four early patriarchates arose: Rome, Alexandria, Antioch, and Jerusalem. The word **patriarch** (Greek: "father-source") came to apply to the important bishops who were leaders of an entire region.

However, when serious questions arose about doctrine and practice, the early church leaders needed some way to answer them. On the one hand, they could seek a consensus from all other bishops by calling a church council—an approach that the churches in the eastern part of the Roman Empire held to be the only correct practice. On the other hand, they could designate one bishop as the final authority. The bishop of Rome seemed to be a natural authority and judge for two reasons. First, until 330 C.E. Rome was the capital of the empire, so it was natural to think of the Roman bishop as a kind of spiritual ruler, like his political counterpart, the emperor. Second, according to tradition, Peter, the head of the twelve apostles, had lived his last days in Rome and had died there. He could thus be considered the first bishop of Rome. The special title **pope** comes from the Latin word *papa* ("father"), a title once used for many bishops but now applied exclusively to the bishop of Rome.

The nature of papal authority and the biblical basis for it (Matt. 16:18–19) have been debated. Nonetheless, this hierarchical model of Christianity

Greek and Roman Religions and Early Christianity

If you are ever in Rome, be sure to take a walk from the Colosseum westward through the Roman Forum, along the *Via Sacra* (Sacred Way). Because the large stones of the ancient road are still there, between the bare pillars of many crumbled temples, you can't help but imagine what it must have been like about 100 C.E., at the height of the Roman empire, for a person who was coming to Rome for the first time. At the far end of the Forum rises the steep Capitoline Hill, the ancient center of government, where the Romans built a temple for Jupiter, the father of the gods. You also can't help but notice that just beyond the bare pillars are belfries and crosses—many of the Forum's buildings were long ago turned into Christian churches.

From its Middle Eastern roots, Christianity grew and spread within the Roman empire, where it displaced the established religions of the Greeks and the Romans only slowly. In fact, Christianity did not become the official state religion until the end of the fourth century. And since Rome in classical times was the largest city of the world, religions from faraway lands had also found their way there. (Rome in the imperial period was a great crossroads, much like London or Los Angeles today.) Like the temples that survive as Christian churches, elements from many of these religions were absorbed into the new religion of Christianity.

Since some of their gods came from the same source, the classical religions of the Greeks and the Romans show many similarities. But their religions were made of layers and were constantly evolving. The earliest layers, existing before recorded history, came from the veneration of local gods and nature spirits—often worshiped at sacred wells, groves, and roadside shrines. The next layer came from an array of sacred figures that was brought to Europe by the Aryans, who originated in southern Russia but flooded into Greece and Italy sometime around 2000 B.C.E. (The Aryan pantheon was also carried to India, and prayers to these gods may be found in the Vedas. Some of these Aryan gods are still worshiped by Hindus today.) Other layers were added when both the Greeks and the Romans absorbed gods from neighboring cultures. The growing Roman culture continued to borrow from the Greeks—both from those who lived in southern Italy and then from those in Greece itself. Sometimes major gods

absorbed the functions of lesser deities. Great heroes of the past could be declared to be gods. Later, so could emperors. (One, when he thought that he was dying, is said to have amusingly remarked, "I think that I am becoming a god.")

There were occasional attempts at creating a complete system of deities. We find one such attempt, for example, in the works of Homer. The Iliad and the Odyssey placed the major Greek gods on Mount Olympus, living in a kind of extended family under the care of the sky-god Zeus. Later, in the eighth century B.C.E., the writer Hesiod tried to establish detailed connections of birth and marriage between the many gods, and the Romans eventually borrowed those ideas from the Greeks. There were also attempts to bring statues of major gods together for worship in the same place. The Athenians put statues of their most important gods at the Acropolis—a fact that Paul noticed and mentioned when he preached in Athens (Acts 17:19–23). The Romans placed multiple temples in the region of the Forum, and then the

The Arch of Septimius Severus frames a Christian church tower.

The Forum's Via Sacra *today leads the visitor past remnants of temples dedicated to Roman gods, often incorporated into later Christian churches.*

emperor Hadrian created the circular Pantheon (Greek: *pan*, "all"; *theos*, "god"), which had altars for the deities that he thought most important. (Today the Pantheon—perhaps the most beautiful of all classical Roman buildings—is a Catholic church.)

Trying to give some order to the divine confusion, Romans began to teach that their gods and goddesses were the same as those worshiped under varied names in other cultures. Here, as an illustration, is a small sample of Roman deities that were seen as parallel with Greek gods and goddesses:

Jupiter/Zeus—sky and rain god, father of the gods

Juno/Hera—wife of Jupiter/Zeus, patron of wives and marriage

Venus/Aphrodite—goddess of love

Mercury/Hermes—messenger god and patron of business

Mars/Ares—god of war

The goddess Artemis is often associated with fertility.

Bacchus/Dionysus—god of intoxication and ecstasy

Pluto/Dis—god of the underworld and afterlife

Roman religious practice, along with the astrology that it borrowed from Syria and Greece, believed in hidden correspondences between gods, months, days, and planets. This belief shows its influence in the names of months that are still used in countries that have centuries of Christian history. Thus, we have,

January—named after Janus, a two-faced god of doorways, who was always invoked at the beginning of undertakings

March—named after the god Mars, associated with storms and war and priestly rites held in March to strengthen national defense

May—from Maia, a goddess of fertility

June—from Juno, wife of Jupiter and patroness of marriages

July—named for Julius Caesar, after he was declared a god

The days of the week showed similar correspondences: *Sunday*—sun; *Monday*—moon; *Tuesday* (Spanish: *Martes*)—Mars; *Wednesday* (Spanish: *Miércoles*)—Mercury; *Thursday* (Spanish: *Jueves*)—Jupiter, Jove; *Friday* (Spanish: *Viernes*)—Venus; *Saturday*—Saturn.

Despite their speculative forays, Greek and Roman religions involved practices as much as doctrine. In the days when medicine was undeveloped, charms and auspicious ceremonies were highly valued. Hence ritual, carefully performed, was essential. Ceremonies were held on festival days throughout the year. Romans had about thirty major festivals and many lesser ones—most with specific purposes, such as defense, fertility, and good harvest. These were largely acts of public religion, performed for the welfare of the nation. Thus, it is not surprising that Christianity continued such practices in developing its liturgical year, anchored in Christmas (the winter festival) and Easter (the spring rite of new birth). Saints' feast days, which were marked by special blessings and rituals, were similar to earlier veneration of the many gods.

Of great importance to the formation of Christianity were the Greek and Roman mystery religions. They have that name because initiates vowed not to disclose the details of their initiations and practices. These typically involved an instruction, purification rite, a sharing of sacred food or drink, and a revelatory experience. We see clear echoes in the early training of

would-be Christians (the "catechumens"), in baptism, and in eucharistic rites.

As the Roman empire expanded during the time of Jesus and early Christianity, it imported the exotic worship of gods from Asia Minor (Turkey), Persia, and Egypt. Among the first religious imports was worship of the goddess Cybele, "the Great Mother," and Isis, a mother-figure from Egypt. Such worship of goddesses undoubtedly influenced the growing Christian cult of Mary. From Persia came worship of the sun-god Mithras, which practiced baptism in the blood of a bull and a ritual sacred meal. Evidence of worship involving Mithras has been found as far away from Rome as London.

As you end your walk along the Roman Forum, you may think of other parallels. Early images of a beardless Jesus, found in Christian burial chambers, resemble images of Apollo and Dionysus. The tendency to treat Zeus or Jupiter as the supreme god—as was shown by the great Temple of Jupiter that crowned the Capitoline Hill—may have helped convert the Roman empire to monotheism. The ritual meal of Mithraism has echoes in the Christian Lord's Supper, and the ancient church of San Clemente in Rome is built upon a Mithraeum, a Mithraic place of worship.

The exact amount of Greco-Roman religious influence on Christianity's evolution will never be entirely clear. But the influences we've reviewed remind us that all world religions were once new religions that were built, in many different ways, upon what came before them. At the same time, the ability of a new religion to adapt existing religions could help the new religion to be accepted and understood—as we see so well in the case of Christianity.

became common in western Europe. Although the Protestant Reformation of the sixteenth century, which we will discuss later, weakened the acceptance of papal authority, the Catholic bishops of Rome have continued to claim supremacy over all Christianity, and the Roman Catholic Church maintains this claim. Christianity in eastern Europe, however, as we will see later in the chapter, developed and has maintained a different, less centralized form of organization.

The Roman Empire made many contributions to Christianity. In the first two centuries of the common era, Christianity was often persecuted because it was associated with political disloyalty. But when Constantine became emperor, he saw in Christianity a glue that would cement the fragments of the entire empire. In his Edict of Toleration, Constantine decreed that Christianity could function publicly without persecution, and he supported the religion by asking its bishops to meet and define their beliefs. This they did at the first major church council, the Council of Nicaea, held in Asia Minor in 325 C.E. By the end of the fourth century, Christianity had been declared the official religion of the Roman Empire.

Thus the partnership of Christianity with the Roman Empire marked an entirely new phase and a significant turning point for the religion. Christianity formalized its institutional structure of bishops and priests, who had responsibilities within the set geographical units—based on imperial political units—of dioceses and parishes. And because it now had the prestige and financial support that came with government endorsement, Christianity could enthusiastically adopt imperial Roman architecture, art, music, clothing, ceremony, administration, and law. Most important, through church councils and creeds, Christianity clarified and defined its worldview. And just as historians had written about the history of Rome, so writers such as Eusebius (c. 260–c. 339) came to record the history of Christianity.

Because Christianity in western Europe spread from Rome, much of it was distinctively Roman in origin—especially its language (Latin). Latin was the language of church ritual and scholarship in the West. The Bible had also been translated into Latin. Because of all this, scholars often say that though the Roman Empire disintegrated in the late fifth century, it actually lived on in another form in the Western Church. The emperor of Rome was replaced by the pope, but the language, laws, architecture, and thought patterns of Rome would continue fairly undisturbed in the West for more than a thousand years.

There are some fascinating examples of Roman influence on the Western Church. The typical design for church architecture, for instance, was the basilica—a long, rectangular, pillared building, originally used in Roman times for meetings and judicial proceedings. To the original design, Christian churches added one or two bell towers at the front of the building and a baptismal pool inside or outside. The clothing that Western Church clergy wore during worship ceremonies continued the fashions of the late Roman aristocracy. The undergarment was a long, white linen robe, called the *alb* ("white"), tied by a cloth belt, the *cincture*. Over the alb the priest wore the late-Roman *chasuble* ("little house"), which was originally worn as a poncho.

Roman influence was also incorporated in church ritual. Incense, once used by government dignitaries to purify the air, was used to symbolize prayer and the ascent of the spirit to God. Candles in tall candlesticks, originally carried to light the way for government authorities, were used in services to illuminate readings from scripture. Their light also came to symbolize spiritual understanding and new life. These are just a few of the many elements of the liturgy that were adapted from imperial court ceremony.

INFLUENCES ON CHRISTIANITY
AT THE END OF THE ROMAN EMPIRE

As the Roman Empire was collapsing in the West (it would end in 476 C.E.), new sources of energy and direction influenced the next stage in the development of Christianity. Two individuals who had a great impact on Christianity were a bishop, Augustine, and a monk, Benedict.

Augustine

Augustine (354–430 C.E.) was born in North Africa in the later days of the western part of the Roman Empire. Although we think of North Africa today as being quite different and separate from Europe, in Augustine's day it was still a vital part of the Roman Empire.

Augustine's mother, Monica, was a devout Christian, but his father was not. Like many others in his day, Augustine was pulled in two directions: he loved the classical non-Christian culture of Greece and Rome, but he was searchingly religious. As a young man, he became involved in a movement called Manicheism (influenced by Zoroastrianism), which saw the world as being strictly divided between the forces of good and the forces of evil. In this view, goodness expressed itself in the mind and spirit, and evil manifested itself in the body and the physical world. Although Augustine eventually rejected this movement, traces of its pessimistic view of the body and the physical world remain in Augustinian Christianity.

As an adult, Augustine left his home in North Africa for Italy to make his name as a teacher of rhetoric. After a short time in Rome, he acquired a teaching position in Milan. He became seriously interested in Christianity as a result of his acquaintance with Ambrose, the bishop of the city, and a priest named Simplicianus. While in his garden one day, Augustine thought he heard a child's singsong voice repeating the phrase, *Tolle et lege, tolle et lege* ("pick up and read").[16] Augustine, who had been studying the letters of Paul, picked up a copy of the epistles that lay on a nearby table. When he opened the book, what he read about the need for inner change pierced him to the heart, and he felt that he must totally reform his life. Augustine sought out Ambrose and asked to be baptized.

Augustine returned to North Africa to devote himself to church work. Ordained first as a priest and then as a bishop, he decided to live a monastic style of life in the company of other priests. Although he had had a child with a mistress before his conversion, Augustine now preached an attitude toward sex and marriage that encouraged a growing Christian suspicion of the body. A reversal of those attitudes began only a thousand years later with the thought and work of the reformer Martin Luther, who had been a celibate member of the Augustinian order but who later married and rejected its idealization of celibacy.

In the years after his conversion, Augustine wrote books that were influential in the West for centuries. His *Confessions* was the first real autobiography in world literature, and it details Augustine's growth and conversion.

The City of God was a defense of Christianity, which some people in his day blamed for the decline of the Roman Empire. *The Trinity* was Augustine's explanation of the relationship between God the Father, Jesus, and the Holy Spirit. He also wrote to oppose the priest Pelagius, a thinker who held a more optimistic view of human nature than Augustine did.

Augustine had incalculable influence on Western Christianity. He was *the* authority in Christian theology until the Protestant Reformation of the sixteenth century, and he was an influence, as well, on Reformation thinkers such as Martin Luther and John Calvin. In short, Western Christianity was basically Augustinian Christianity for over a thousand years.

Benedict and the Monastic Ideal

As mentioned earlier, Augustine, after his conversion, chose to become a priest and live with other priests and monks in a life devoted to prayer and study. This monastic way of life became a significant part of Christianity. It is important to remember that monastic life was not just a religious choice. In the days when life was less secure, when work options were severely limited, and when marriage inevitably brought many children (of whom up to half might die young), the life of a monk offered extraordinary freedom. The monastic life provided liberation from daily cares, leisure to read and write, a wealth of friendships with interesting people, and a strong sense of spiritual purpose and devotion. In fact, monks and nuns are found in many religious traditions today, and monasticism, far from being odd or rare, is a fairly universal expression of piety. Monasticism appears not only in Christianity but also in Hinduism, Buddhism, and Taoism; and in Judaism, the celibate monastic life was carried on among the Essenes for approximately two hundred years.

A monk is not necessarily a priest, nor need a priest be a monk. A monk is simply any male who chooses to leave society to live a celibate life of religious devotion; a priest is a person authorized to lead public worship. In the early days of Christianity, priests were often married and thus were not monks. However, under the influence of monasticism, Western priests were gradually expected to resemble monks and to be unmarried.

Christian monasticism probably sprang from a number of influences. One may have been the Essene movement and another was the fact that Jesus had never married. We might recall that he praised those who do not marry "for the sake of the kingdom of heaven" (Matt. 19:12).[17] Paul also was without a wife and recommended that state heartily for others (1 Cor. 7:32–35). Another influence on Christian monasticism came from Egypt, where hermits had been living in caves even before Jesus' time. Contact through trade between India and Egypt may have brought Buddhist literature and monks to Alexandria, and they might have influenced the Christian monastic movement as well. Lastly, once Christians were no longer being persecuted by the government, becoming a monk or nun was an important way for a Christian to show special religious fervor.

The first Christian monks that we know of are called the Desert Fathers: Paul the Hermit, Antony of Egypt, Paphnutius, Pachomius, and

Simon Stylite. There were also women (of apparently shady origins) among them: Saint Pelagia the Harlot and Saint Mary the Harlot. These individuals all turned away from the world to live what they thought of as a more perfect type of life. We can criticize the movement for its lack of interest in the needs of the world, but the movement also expressed a longing for the life of paradise—for joy, lack of conformity, individuality, and love of God. In fact, the monastic style of life was often called "the life of the angels."

The monastic movement in the West was greatly influenced and spread by a Latin translation of the *Life of Antony,* the Egyptian hermit. The movement took root in southern France and Italy. The real founder of Western monasticism was Benedict of Nursia (c. 480–c. 547 C.E.). Benedict was born into a wealthy family near Rome but fled to live in a cave, where he began to attract attention and followers who joined him in the monastic life. Eventually, Benedict and his followers built a permanent monastery on the top of Monte Cassino, south of Rome. From there the movement spread and became known as the Benedictine order.

Benedict's influence came from his *Rule for Monks.* Based on the earlier *Regula Magistri* ("rule of the master") and the New Testament, the *Rule* gave advice about how monks should live together throughout the year. It stipulated that monks should pray each week the entire group of 150 psalms (biblical poems), spend time in manual labor, and remain at one monastery. It opposed excess in any way, yet it was sensible; for example, it allowed wine, because, as it lamented, the monks could not be persuaded otherwise. The *Rule* became the organizing principle for all Western monasticism and is still followed today by Benedictines.[18]

> What can be sweeter to us, dear brethren, than this voice of the Lord inviting us? Behold, in His loving kindness the Lord shows us the way of life.
>
> —Saint Benedict's *Rule for Monks*[19]

Benedictine monks became the missionary force that spread Christianity—and Roman architecture and culture—throughout western Europe.[20] Among the great Benedictine missionaries were Augustine (d. 604 C.E.), who was sent as a missionary to England by Pope Gregory I, and Boniface (c. 680–755 C.E.), who spread Christianity in Germany.

From monastic ideals and practices have come several key elements of Christianity. For example, because monastic life segmented time into periods of work and prayer, it hastened the development of the clock. Even more significant was the ideal of celibacy. Living without family ties gave priests, nuns, and monks much mobility and freedom from care, yet it also promoted the ideal of a studious life somewhat detached from the outer world. It fostered the belief that the unmarried, celibate way of life was more perfect than noncelibacy—a belief that would not be seriously challenged in Christianity until the Protestant Reformation of the sixteenth century.

THE EASTERN ORTHODOX CHURCH

Up to this point, we have focused on Christianity in western Europe. But another form of Christianity, known as the Eastern Orthodox Church, developed and spread in Russia, Bulgaria, the Ukraine, Romania, Greece, and

Simple Gregorian chant evolved before 1000 C.E. as the form in which monks, and Christians in general, sang during liturgical celebrations. Here three men use Gregorian chant for the Passion account from John's Gospel on Good Friday at Rome's Basilica of Mary Major. ◄

elsewhere. These were regions that learned their Christianity from missionaries sent out from Constantinople, which Constantine had established as his imperial capital in 330 C.E.

The word **orthodox** means "correct belief" (from the Greek *orthos*, "straight," and *doxa*, "opinion," "thought"). It is used to designate Christianity in the East because of attempts by that church to define its beliefs and keep them unchanged.

Early Development

In the earliest centuries of Christianity, when communication was slow and authority was rather decentralized, the bishops of Jerusalem, Antioch, Rome, and Alexandria, though often at odds in their theology, were looked to for guidance and authority. They were eclipsed, however, when a small fishing village named Byzantion (or Byzantium, now the site of Istanbul in Turkey) was renamed Constantinople ("Constantine's city") and was made the new capital of the Roman Empire. The large population of Constantinople, its importance as a governmental center, and its imperial support of Christianity all united to elevate the status of the bishop of Constantinople. Now called a patriarch, he became the most influential of all the bishops in the East.

By moving the capital of the Roman Empire to Constantinople, Constantine had hoped to strengthen the empire by placing its capital closer to the northern frontier. From there, soldiers could be sent quickly to protect the frontier against the many barbarian tribes that lived in the north. But Constantine had in fact planted the seeds for an inevitable division of Christianity into Eastern and Western churches. For a time there were two emperors—of East and West—although this did not work well. The Latin-speaking Western empire, as we have seen, ended in the fifth century, and Western Christianity developed independently. The Greek-speaking Eastern empire, centered in Constantinople, spread its own form of Christianity and continued until its fall in the Muslim conquest of 1453.

The Orthodox Church is generally divided along ethnic and linguistic lines—Russian, Greek, Serbian, Bulgarian, and Romanian. But all these churches accept the statements of faith of the first seven Church councils, particularly those of Nicaea (325 C.E.) and Chalcedon (451 C.E.). The Orthodox Church has always held to a decentralized, consensus-based model. Although it does accept in theory that the bishop of Rome has a "primacy among equals," it holds that decisions concerning all of Christianity should be made collectively, in consultation with all patriarchs and bishops; thus, only Church councils are of ultimate authority.

Monasticism in the Eastern Church

As in the West, the monastic movement was an important aspect of the Eastern Church. It spread northward from Egypt and Syria into Asia Minor, where its greatest practitioners were the fourth-century church leaders,

Large Orthodox monasteries included monks' meeting and dining rooms, libraries, and sleeping quarters, along with a church and sometimes several chapels. Here we see part of the large monastic complex at Rila in Bulgaria.

Gregory of Nyssa, Gregory Nazianzen, and Basil of Caesarea, who set the pattern for the monastic movement in **Orthodoxy.** Basil (c. 330–379) wrote recommendations for monastic living that are still followed today in Orthodox Christianity. Greek-speaking monks of the eastern part of the Roman Empire carried Christianity from Constantinople into Russia and eastern Europe. The ninth-century brothers Cyril and Methodius are the most famous of these missionary monks, because they or their disciples are said to have been the authors of the Cyrillic alphabet, based on the Greek alphabet, which is in common use in eastern Europe and Russia today.

Eastern Orthodoxy has created great monastic centers. The most famous is on Mount Athos in Greece, the current center of monasticism in that region. All Orthodox branches have sent representatives there for monastic training, and to visit or study there is considered a great honor.[21] Other monastic centers grew up in Romania, Bulgaria, the Ukraine, and Russia. Because Kiev was the city where the first Russians were converted, it took on a role as a traditional religious center, and its monasteries were famous. The northeastern section of Romania contains extraordinary monasteries, many of whose walls are covered with frescoes. Other great centers of monasticism grew up in the regions around Moscow and Saint Petersburg. Many of these monasteries still exist and may be visited today.

Eastern Orthodox Beliefs

Several questions in its early development helped define and differentiate the Orthodox Church. One issue was the nature of Jesus Christ: How is Jesus related to God? Is God the Father greater than Jesus? If Jesus is divine as well as human, is he two persons or one person? And how did Jesus exist before his human life began? Some believers stressed the human nature of Jesus, while others stressed his divinity. The controversies eventually led to the creation and adoption in the fourth century of the Nicene Creed, which is accepted not only by the Orthodox but also by all traditional Western Christians. Because the creed was created to overcome several heresies, it speaks of the divine nature of Jesus in some detail:

> We believe in one God, the Father Almighty, maker of all things visible and invisible. And in one Lord Jesus Christ, the Son of God, begotten of the Father, the only-begotten; that is, of the essence of the Father, God of God, Light of Light, very God of very God, begotten, not made, being of one essence with the Father; by whom all things were made, both in heaven and on earth; who for us men, and for our salvation, came down and was incarnate and was made man.[22]

Even after the Nicene Creed, one school held that the divine and human natures of Christ were two separate persons, not one. Others argued that Jesus had only one nature, not two. The Council of Chalcedon (in 451 C.E.) declared that Jesus had two natures—divine and human—that were united in only one person.

After the major Church councils of the fourth and fifth centuries, certain groups of Christians, with differing views about the nature of Jesus, were labeled heretical. They continued to exist, however, though not in communion with the mainstream. The Nestorian Christian Church, existing primarily in Syria today, continues to teach that Jesus had two separate natures that were not united in a single person. The Coptic Christian Church, existing today primarily in Egypt and Ethiopia, maintains its belief that Jesus had only one nature, which was divine—a belief called *monophysitism* (Greek: "one nature"). The views of these two early churches exemplify the diversity of thought that existed among Christian groups in the first few centuries of the common era.

It is hard for some of us today to realize the vehemence with which these doctrinal battles were fought. The questions seem more like arguments over words. But at stake was the important question of the union of God and humanity. The insistence on the union of the divine and the human in Jesus left a strong mystical tendency in the theology of Orthodoxy, which equally emphasizes the potential for union between each human being and God. This mystical tendency expressed itself in every aspect of Orthodoxy—particularly in theology and art—and it still exists today.

Another defining controversy, which has had lasting influence, occurred over the use of images for religious practice. We might recall that one of the Ten Commandments prohibits the making of images (Exod. 20:4), and Jews,

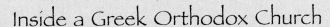

Inside a Greek Orthodox Church

In his book *Eleni*, Nicholas Gage documents his childhood in Greece during World War II and the civil war that followed it. His memories include this description of the Greek Orthodox church in his native village of Lia. The church was destroyed by the Nazis.

> For seven centuries the Church of the Virgin had nourished the souls of the [villagers of Lia]. Its interior was their pride and their Bible. No one needed to be literate to know the Holy Scriptures, for they were all illustrated here in the frescoes painted by the hand of monks long vanished into anonymity. In the soaring vault of the cupola, Christ the All-Powerful, thirty times the size of a mortal man, scrutinized the congregation below, his Gospel clasped in his hand. In the spaces between the windows, the prophets and apostles, painted full-length with bristling beards and mournful eyes, made their eternal parade toward the altar.

> The villagers of Lia never tired of staring at the wonders of the Church of the Virgin: the walls glowed with every saint and martyr, the twelve feast days, the Last Supper, the life of the Virgin, and as a final warning, on the wall near the door, the Last Judgment, where bizarre dragons and devils punished every sort of evil, with the priests in the front rank of the sinners.

> The jewel of the church was the magnificent golden carved iconostasis, the shimmering screen which hid the mysteries of the sanctuary until the priest emerged from the Royal Doors carrying the blood and body of Christ. The iconostasis held four tiers of icons, splendid with gold leaf and jewels, and between the sacred pictures the native wood-carvers had allowed their imagination to create a fantasy of twining vines and mythical birds and beasts perched in the lacy fretwork.[23]

as a result, have generally refrained from creating any religious images. Islam has a similar prohibition, as do some forms of Protestant Christianity today. The argument over making and using images reached a crisis when the Byzantine Emperor Leo III (680–740 C.E.) commanded the destruction of all images of Jesus, Mary, and the angels. It is possible that he did this for political as well as religious reasons, hoping to build bridges to Islam. But John of Damascus, a monk and writer, came strongly to the defense of religious images—or **icons,** as they are often called (the Greek term *eikon* means "image"). John argued that images served the same purpose for the illiterate as the Bible did for those who could read. He also argued that God, by becoming incarnate in Jesus, did not disdain the material world. Icons, he said, were simply a continuation of that manifestation of divine love shown through the physical world. Church councils later affirmed the use of images, thus putting an indelible stamp on the practices of the Orthodox Church, which glories in the veneration of religious paintings.

Cracks in the unity of Christianity appeared early, but the first great division occurred in 1054, when disagreements brought the bishops of Rome and Constantinople to excommunicate each other. The separation remains today. Although cultural differences assisted the separation, there were small doctrinal differences, as well. The most famous concerned the doctrine of the Trinity. Did the Holy Spirit come from the Father or the Son or from both? The oldest and traditional position held that the Father generated the Spirit, but it became common in the West to attribute the generation of the Spirit to both Father and Son together. The Latin word **filioque** ("and from the Son") was added to creeds in the West from an early period. The Eastern

Church rejected the notion as an improper addition to the Nicene Creed and cited it as a main reason for splitting off from the Western Church. Another dividing issue was the growing power of the pope and the claim that the bishop of Rome was the head of all Christians. Scholars today, however, point out the inevitability of separation because of other factors, such as distance, differences of language, and the political growth of northern and eastern Europe.

Orthodox belief is, in summary, quite similar to that which emerged in the West and eventually became mainstream Christianity. The doctrinal differences are quite small, but the Orthodox Church differs in emphasis. Mainstream Western Christianity (Catholicism and Protestantism) has focused on the death of Jesus as an atonement for sin. Some scholars have said that that focus indicates a more "legal" emphasis: God is viewed as a judge, and punishment and repentance are paramount. Eastern Christianity has put more emphasis on a mystical self-transformation that human beings can experience through contact with Christ. As a consequence, Orthodox Christian art and literature focus less on the crucifixion of Jesus and more on the resurrection.

With the collapse of Communism in Russia and eastern Europe, the Orthodox Church has regained some of its earlier strength. Church buildings that were banned from religious use have been transferred back to church ownership and restored. It is notable that after the fall of Communism Russian authorities decided to rebuild the Cathedral of the Holy Savior in Moscow, which Stalin had destroyed and replaced with a swimming pool. The Russian Orthodox Church was also successful in having laws passed in 1997 that affirmed its special status, thereby giving it assistance against the missionary efforts of some other religious groups.

 ## PERSONAL EXPERIENCE: INSIDE THE MONASTERIES ON MOUNT ATHOS

Mount Athos is a finger of rocky land, jutting into the Aegean Sea in the far north of Greece. The peninsula is a monastic state, where monks and hermits have lived for at least a thousand years. Although politically it is part of Greece, it is semi-independent and conducts its own affairs through a monastic council. At the center of the peninsula is a high mountain, and scattered around it, close to the shore, are twenty large monasteries. One spring, after getting the proper approvals from the government, I spent the week of Orthodox Easter at Athos.

From Athens I went to Thessaloníki, and from there I took a bus filled with people going back home to celebrate the festival. After staying the night in the village of Ierissos, I got on a ferry boat to Athos before dawn the next morning. In the small capital of Kariaí, where monks run the shops, I received my passport. Over its Greek words was a picture of the peninsula and of Mary, appearing protectively over its mountain. This passport allowed me to stay overnight in any monastery I visited.

The location of Dionysiou Monastery on Mount Athos reflects its monks' desire to pursue a life that is isolated from the distractions of everyday society.

Each day I walked from one monastery to the next, a trip of about four hours, and was received graciously everywhere. One day I even hitched a ride on the back of one of three donkeys that were being used to carry supplies to several monasteries for the Easter celebration. The two drivers of the animals gave me brandy and Easter candy as the donkeys ambled along. Spring flowers blossomed everywhere next to innumerable streams, which were fed by water from snow melting on the mountain. At one point, the drivers, no longer sober, began arguing with each other. They jumped off their donkeys and began to fight, and the donkeys fled. A monk who had been in a small rowboat came ashore, scrambled up the hill, and stopped the fighting. We recaptured the donkeys, which were feeding placidly farther up on the green hillside, and went on our way, as if nothing had happened.

The monasteries have high walls designed to protect the monks from the pirates who once roamed the coast. The lower half of each monastery is generally without windows, rising about 70 feet in height, and above that are as many as seven stories of wooden balconies. In the center of each monastery is a separate church building in the shape of a Greek cross, usually painted a reddish-brick color. Each arm of the church building is equal in size and is topped by a dome. At the intersection of all the arms is the large, central dome.

I can never forget the services of Easter, celebrated in those mysterious spaces. Being inside the churches felt like being in a group of caves. The floors were covered with sweet-smelling laurel leaves, an ancient symbol of victory. Chandeliers full of candles hung from the domes, illuminating the darkness like stars. For the predawn Easter service, monks used long sticks to make the chandeliers swing back and forth. As the chandeliers swayed, they lit up the murals and mosaics on the walls. I could see images of the prophet Elijah in his cave and the prophet Isaiah speaking with a six-winged angel. Jesus stood on a mountaintop, surrounded by an almond-shaped, rainbow-colored halo. Mary held her child and looked at me serenely. Above them all, an austere cosmic Christ held his hand up in blessing. Below him, each holding a lighted, orange beeswax candle that smelled like honey, monks on one side of the church began the Easter greeting. *"Christos anesti,"* they sang. "Christ is risen." Then monks on the other side answered back, *"Alithos anesti"*—"Truly, he is risen." They sang these two phrases back and forth for minutes. At last they stopped—except for one monk. He had a long white beard and was singing with his eyes closed. *"Christos anesti,"* he continued to sing loudly. *"Christos anesti."* The monks looked at each other in confusion, then smiled as a middle-aged monk came out and tapped the old monk on the shoulder. The old monk opened his eyes and there was silence.

CHRISTIANITY IN THE MIDDLE AGES

From its earliest days, when it was just another exotic "Eastern" religion in the Roman Empire, Christianity had made astonishing leaps—at first facing persecution, then becoming the official religion of the empire, and finally rising as *the* religion of all Europe. By 1200 C.E., the only non-Christians in Europe, including Russia, were small communities of Jews, primarily in cities; Muslims in Spain and Sicily; and followers of the old native religions in Scandinavia. Christianity also existed on a smaller scale, and in varied forms, in Ethiopia, the Middle East, and India.

There were many reasons for the growth of Christianity. It preached a gospel of mercy and hope, offered divine help, promised an afterlife, treated the sick, and aided the poor. It taught skills in agriculture and architecture, introduced books, and spread use of the technology of the time. Imagine how a candlelit church at Easter—with its music, incense, candles, jeweled books, glass windows, and gorgeously robed priests—must have appeared to people who were not yet Christians. The effect must have been intoxicating. A legendary story is told of Russian ministers who attended a service at Saint Sophia's Cathedral in Constantinople about 988 C.E. When they returned home to Kiev, they said that during the cathedral service they had not known whether they were on earth or in heaven.

Although many of the religious practices in both Rome and Constantinople were Roman in origin, the two centers, as we have seen, eventually split over differences. The existence of several patriarchates in the East kept any one of them from becoming a single ruling power. But the Roman

Church in the West had no competitors for power in its region and thus grew in authority and strength. The pope, as the bishop of Rome, asserted his dominion over all Christians, an assertion that was not widely opposed in the West until the Protestant Reformation of the sixteenth century. The long-term effect was that the practices of the Roman Church would set the standard for language, practice, doctrine, church calendar, music, and worship throughout western Europe and then beyond, wherever European influence traveled. (To get a sense of the far-reaching impact of Roman culture, consider the fact that the book you are now reading—long after the Roman Empire has ended and probably thousands of miles from Rome—is written in the Latin alphabet: the capital letters come from the classical Latin of Rome; the lower-case letters were created by Christian monks and clerics.)

The growing size of the Christian population and the increasing cultural dominance of Christianity created a climate for a wide variety of religious expression: devotional and mystical movements, the founding of new religious communities, the Crusades and the Inquisition, reform movements, and new interpretations of the Christian ideal. Over time, traditional church authority was questioned, giving rise to a search for new sources of authority.

Christian Mysticism

The word *mysticism* in theistic religions indicates a direct experience of the divine and a sense of oneness with God. Although not always approved of by church authorities, this sort of transcendent experience is nevertheless an important part of Christianity. Christian mystics have spoken of their direct contact with God, sometimes describing a dissolution of all boundaries between themselves and God. Accounts of their experiences speak of intriguing states of consciousness.

The fact that Jesus felt an intimate relationship with God, whom he called Father, provided a basis for seeing Jesus as a role model for all Christian mystics. The Gospel of John, which has a strong mystical tendency, sees Jesus in this light. We also see mysticism in some letters of Paul. For example, Paul describes himself as having been taken up to "the third heaven" and having heard there things that could not be put into words (2 Cor. 12:1–13). Many monks and nuns from the earliest days of Christianity yearned to experience God, and mystical passages are common in the writings of Origen, Augustine, and Gregory of Nyssa.[24] Origen (c. 185–254) was the first of many Christians who would interpret the biblical Song of Songs mystically. He saw the young lover as Jesus and his beloved as a symbol of the mystic, "who burned with a heavenly love for her bridegroom, the Word of God."[25]

Mystical experience was especially prized in the West during the Middle Ages and early Renaissance. Saint Francis of Assisi (1182–1226 C.E.) is possibly the best-known medieval mystic. Originally a playboy and son of a wealthy trader, Francis embraced a life of poverty in order to imitate the life of Jesus. He also showed a joyful love of nature, calling the sun and moon his brother and sister. One of the greatest Christian mystics was

Lord, make me an instrument of your peace. Where there is hatred, let me sow love; where there is injury, pardon; where there is doubt, faith; where there is despair, hope; where there is darkness, light; and where there is sadness, joy.

—Prayer attributed to
Francis of Assisi[28]

Bernini's sculpture of Teresa in a state of ecstasy attempts to capture a mystical experience that cannot be put into words.

Meister Eckhart (c. 1260–1328), a German priest whose description of God as being beyond time and space, as "void," and as "neither this nor that"[26] has captured the interest of Hindus and Buddhists as well as Christians.

Many mystics were women. In recent years, the mystical songs of the medieval Benedictine nun Hildegard of Bingen (c. 1098–1179) have become popular through the availability of numerous recordings. An Englishwoman, Julian (or Juliana) of Norwich (c. 1342–1416), had a series of mystical experiences, which she later described in her book *Revelations of Divine Love.* She wrote of experiencing the feminine side of God. "God is as really our Mother as he is our Father. He showed this throughout, and particularly when he said that sweet word, 'It is I.' In other words, 'It is I who am the strength and goodness of Fatherhood; I who am the wisdom of Motherhood.'"[27] One of the most famous female mystics was Teresa of Avila (1515–1582), a Spanish nun who wrote in her autobiography about her intimacy with God. A dramatic statue by Bernini at the Roman church of Santa Maria della Vittoria shows Teresa lost in ecstasy.

The mystical approach to Christianity was counterbalanced by Christian attempts to offer reasoned, philosophical discussion of primary beliefs. The religious communities of Franciscans and Dominicans (discussed later in this chapter) were especially active in this work. Thomas Aquinas (1225–1274), a Dominican priest, is the best known. In two major works, the *Summa Theologica* and *Summa Contra Gentiles,* he blended the philosophical thought of Aristotle with Christian scripture and other Christian writings to present a fairly complete Christian worldview. Even he, however, was swayed by the appeal of mystical experience. At the end of his life, after a particularly profound experience of new understanding brought on by prayer, he is said to have remarked that all he had written was "like straw" in comparison to the reality that could be understood directly through mystical experience.

The Crusades, the Inquisition, and the Founding of Religious Orders

During the fourth and fifth centuries and thereafter, Christians all over Europe made pilgrimages to visit the lands where Jesus had lived and died, and the Emperors Constantine and Justinian had built churches there to encourage this practice. But Muslims took control of Jerusalem in the eighth century, and by the eleventh century, Christian pilgrimage had become severely restricted. To guarantee their own safety in pilgrimage and their access to the "Holy Land," some Europeans felt they had a right to seize control over the land of Israel and adjacent territory. Attempts to take over the Holy Land were called the Crusades—military expeditions that today might be described as religious enthusiasm gone badly astray. At the time, however, the militant, crusading spirit was considered a high religious ideal.

The First Crusade began in 1095, and Jerusalem was taken after a bloody battle in 1099. Europeans took control of Israel and kept it for almost two hundred years, until they lost their last bit of Israel, at Acre near the port of Haifa, in 1291. Looking back on the events, we see the Crusades as a form of early colonialism, stemming from a questionable notion that European Christians had a right to control Israel. The suffering inflicted on Muslims and Christians alike was appalling, and most crusaders died not of wounds but of illness. Many Eastern Christians, too, died at the hands of crusaders because they were mistaken for Muslims. The Crusades also did ideological

This nun, a contemporary member of a religious order founded in the Middle Ages, engages in the traditional practice of teaching, here with Cambodian refugees in Thailand.

damage, for they injured Christianity in their promotion of the ideal of a soldier who kills for religious reasons—something quite foreign to the commandments of Jesus. The romantic notion of the Christian soldier, "marching as to war," has remained in some forms of Christianity ever since.

Benefits to the Muslim world were few. There were, however, unexpected benefits for Europe from its contact with the Islamic Near East. When crusaders returned home from Israel and Syria, they brought back foods and recipes, medicines, Persian carpets, architectural ideas, songs and musical instruments, poetry, and new ways of appreciating life. An early form of banking also emerged; because crusaders and pilgrims needed funds while far away from home, methods for transferring money had to be refined. Moreover, hospitals and religious workers to staff them were established along Crusade routes. Thus even though the Crusades did not succeed in their primary purpose, they were valuable for European culture in general and for European religion in particular.

One significant development in Christianity was the founding of nonmonastic religious communities, called *religious orders*. An order is a religious organization of men or women who live communal celibate lives, follow a set of written rules (Latin: *ordo*), and have a special purpose, such as teaching or nursing. The most famous medieval order was the Franciscan order, begun by Saint Francis of Assisi, who idealized poverty and worked to help the poor. Other orders were the Dominicans, who became teachers and scholars, and the Knights Templar, who protected the pilgrimage sites and routes. Most orders also accepted women, who formed a separate division of the order.

In another development of the times, as western Europe became almost fully Christianized, Jews, Muslims, and heretics were considered to be religiously and politically dangerous. Jews were forced to live a life entirely separate from Christians; nontraditional Christians who had emerged in southern France were destroyed; and an effort began that would rid Spain and Sicily of Muslim influence.

The Inquisition received its name from its purpose—to "inquire" into a person's religious beliefs. Church authorities set up an organization to guarantee the purity of Christian belief, and its aim was to root out variant forms of Christianity that were considered *heretical*—divisive and dangerous to public order. Heretics were ferreted out, questioned, tortured, and, if found guilty, burned to death.

The Inquisition was first active in southern France in the thirteenth century, and the same inquisitorial procedures were later employed in Spain. We might recall that in the fifteenth century there was a large scale attempt by Christian rulers to "reconquer" all of Spain. When all Spanish territory had been taken over by Christian rulers, Jews and Muslims were forced to convert to Christianity or to leave Spain, and many did leave, particularly for Morocco and Egypt. Those who stayed had to accept baptism and to publicly practice Christianity. Some of these new converts continued, however, to practice their old religions in private. The Inquisition attempted to discover who these "false Christians" were, and the religious order of Dominicans was especially active in this pursuit.

Tomás de Torquemada (c. 1420–1498), a Spanish Dominican, was appointed first inquisitor general by King Ferdinand and Queen Isabella in 1483 and grand inquisitor by Pope Innocent VIII in 1487. As he oversaw the Inquisition in Spain, he became notorious for his cruelty. The Reconquista, as the Christian movement was called, took over all Spanish territory in 1492. After this date, the Inquisition acted as a religious arm of the Spanish government both in Spain and in Spanish colonies in the New World.

The Late Middle Ages

The complete ousting of the crusaders from Israel (1291) marked the end of the Christian optimism that had been typical of the earlier Middle Ages. The loss was widely viewed as some kind of divine punishment for religious laxity. The feeling of pessimism deepened a half century later, when an epidemic of bubonic plague—called the Black Death for the black swellings that appeared on people's bodies—began to spread throughout Europe. The first major outbreak of disease occurred largely between 1347 and 1351. Beginning in France and Italy, as the plague swept throughout western Europe, whole towns were emptied, with no one left to bury the corpses. Priests often fled, refusing to attend the dying—a neglect that brought the church into great disrepute. Between a quarter and a third of the population died, and the plague continued to break out in many places for years afterward.

We now know that the disease was bacterial, caused by a bacillus found in fleas, which carried the disease to human beings. Rats that carried the fleas had arrived on ships that came from the Black Sea to ports in southern France and Italy. But the medical origin of the plague was not understood at the time, and people saw it instead as punishment from God. Some blamed the Jews, who were accused of poisoning wells or of angering God by their failure to accept Christianity. Others saw the plague as punishment for the lax behavior of church authorities.

It is natural that a successful institution will take its authority for granted, and by the late Middle Ages it was common for bishops and abbots to be appointed to their positions purely for financial or family reasons. Some even lived away from their monasteries or dioceses. Indeed, for most of the fourteenth century, the popes lived not in Rome but in southern France. This papal dislocation led to a weakening of church authority, until two and then finally three factions claimed the papacy.

The Middle Ages saw many changes in European society, as travelers to the Middle East and Asia returned home with new goods and ideas. New forms of trade and economy developed. Imagination and independence grew.

By far the greatest development of the late Middle Ages was the invention of printing with moveable type. Before that time, all writing had to be done, laboriously, by hand, making the Bible and other works available only to scholars and clergy. Although the first book to be printed (c. 1450) was a Latin Bible, translations were soon necessary. Printing also made possible the spread in modern languages of new and revolutionary ideas. As a result, a multitude of vital new forms of Christianity would emerge.

THE PROTESTANT REFORMATION

As institutions age, they naturally lose some of their earnestness and purity, prompting attempts at reform. The Eastern Church, weakened by the Muslim invasions and its own decentralization, had less need for reform. In contrast, the Roman Church in the West had been enormously successful, spreading throughout western Europe and building a centralized power structure that had not been seriously challenged in the first thousand years of its growth.

The Western Church establishment had become wealthy from bequests of the rich. To endow monasteries with land and money was a natural form of piety, which aristocrats hoped would benefit them in the afterlife. Collections in local parish churches also generated funds, some of which were sent to Rome, just as they are today.

By the late medieval period, people resented the lands and wealth of the church and its monasteries. Thoughtful people also were troubled by what seemed to be a multitude of superstitious practices—particularly the veneration of relics of saints. Significant relics included the bones of saints and any object supposedly touched by Jesus or Mary or the saints, such as Mary's veil and the nails used at Jesus' crucifixion. Many of these items were not genuine.

Other events also were leading the world in the direction of religious exploration and change. The fall of Constantinople to Muslim forces in 1453 drove Greek scholars to live in Italy. Their scholarly presence and their books sparked great interest in the Greek language, which contributed to an examination of the Gospels in their original language. The dissemination of printed Bibles encouraged anyone who could read to turn to the Bible—rather than to a priest, bishop, or pope—as the ultimate religious authority.

Earlier attempts at reform had not been successful. John Wycliffe (c. 1320–1384), an English priest, preached against papal taxation and against the special authority of the clergy. He labeled as superstition the doctrine of transubstantiation (the notion that the sacrament of bread and wine, when blessed at the Mass, literally turned into Jesus' flesh and blood). He also oversaw the first translation of the Latin Bible into English. Accused of heresy by Pope Gregory XI in 1377, he was forbidden to teach. He died a natural death by stroke, but after his teachings were condemned by the Council of Constance (1414–1418), his body was dug up and burned and the ashes were thrown into a river.

Jan Hus (c. 1369–1415), rector of the University of Prague, kept alive many of Wycliffe's criticisms. Excommunicated in 1410 and condemned by the same council that condemned Wycliffe, Hus was burned at the stake in 1415.

Reform was inevitable. Soon another great turning point would occur in Christianity. The north and south of Europe would painfully split along religious lines, and Western Christianity would divide into Protestantism and Catholicism.

This statue of Jan Hus, who made an early attempt to reform Christianity, appears in his birthplace near Prague.

Martin Luther

Martin Luther (1483–1546), a German priest, was the first reformer to gain a large following and to survive, and his success encouraged others who also sought reforms. Their joint influence ultimately created the Protestant branch of Christianity, so called because the reformers protested some of the doctrines and practices of the Roman Church.

Luther, convinced of his own personal sinfulness, entered religious life (the Augustinian order) as a young man because of a vow made during a lightning storm. To enter religious life, he had to disobey his father, who wanted him to be a lawyer.[29] But after ordination as a priest, Luther still did not experience the inner peace he had expected.

Luther became a college professor in the university town of Wittenberg, teaching courses in the Bible with a focus on the New Testament—particularly the Pauline Epistles. At a time when he felt overwhelmed by his own sinfulness, he was struck by Paul's words at the beginning of the Epistle to the Romans: "The just shall live by faith" (Rom. 1:17).[30] Luther admitted that upon reading this epistle he felt as if he had been "born anew" and sensed that now "the gates of heaven" were open to him.

What Luther came to believe was that no matter how great the sinfulness of a human being, the sacrifice of Jesus was enough to make up for all wrongdoing. An individual's good deeds could never be enough; to become sinless in God's eyes, a person could rely on the work of Jesus.[31] Luther also recognized the importance of his reading of the Bible as an important factor in receiving his new spiritual insight. Luther's main focuses have sometimes been summarized by the Latin phrases *sola scriptura* ("scripture alone") and *sola fides* ("faith alone").

Luther's teaching came at a time when the papacy was asking for contributions for the building of the new Saint Peter's Basilica in Rome. In return, donors were promised an **indulgence,** which would shorten the time after death that an individual would spend in *purgatory,* a preparatory state before the soul could attain heaven. Luther opposed the idea that anything spiritual could be sold.

To show his opposition and to stir debate, in 1517 Luther posted on the door of the Castle church of Wittenberg his demands for change and reformation in the form of *Ninety-Five Theses.* Despite reprimands, Luther was unrepentant, and in 1521 Pope Leo X excommunicated him. Luther's efforts at reform might have failed—and he also might have been burned at the stake—if he had not received the support of and been hidden by the prince of his region, Frederick III of Saxony. During this period of refuge, Luther translated the New Testament into German, and he soon translated the Old Testament, as well. Luther's translation of the Christian Bible was to become for the Germans what the King James Bible became for the English-speaking world—it had an incalculable influence on German language and culture.

After his insight into the sufficiency of faith, Luther firmly rejected celibacy and the monastic style of life. He married a former nun, Katharina von Bora, had six children, and opened his home to a wide range of visitors interested in his work on church reform.

Forms of Protestantism

The right of every individual to radically question and reinterpret Christian belief and practice is at the heart of Protestant Christianity. This so-called **Protestant Principle** has been responsible for the generation of major branches of mainstream Protestantism, a multitude of smaller sects, and many thousands of independent churches, which continue to proliferate miraculously. Their styles of organization and worship run the spectrum from ritualistic and structured to informal, emotional, and highly individualistic. Some Protestant denominations emphasize emotional conversion of individuals, while others stress broad social welfare. Some exclude people who are not in their denomination, while others are strongly inclusive, even inviting non-Christians to share in their services. Some have retained traditional ritual and an episcopal structure (that is, involving bishops and priests), while others have rejected all ritual and clergy. We must keep this variety in mind as we read about these denominations.

Emphases of Protestant Christianity

Protestantism seeks to find—and live by—what is essential to the Christian experience. It places great emphasis on the individual's own ability to establish a personal relationship with God.

Return to simple Christianity The New Testament outlines the essentials of Christianity, both in belief and in practice. Christians should imitate the early tradition and avoid unnecessary, later alterations.

Centrality of Jesus Jesus is the one way to God the Father. Devotion to Mary and the saints has distracted believers from their faith in Jesus and should be deemphasized or even abandoned. Trust in relics of Mary and the saints borders on superstition.

Guidance of the Bible The Bible is a divinely inspired guide for human lives. Believers should read it regularly, and ministers should explain it in sermons.

Importance of faith One's deeds alone cannot bring salvation. Faith in Jesus brings righteousness in God's eyes.

Direct relation to God Although ministers assist in religious services, they are not necessary as intermediaries between God and the individual. Every individual has a direct relationship with God.

Individual judgment The Holy Spirit helps each believer make decisions about the meaning of biblical passages and about how to apply Christian principles to everyday life. (The ability of each individual to radically question and rethink accepted interpretation is sometimes called the Protestant Principle.)

Lutheranism Martin Luther's version of the reform emphasized faith and the authority of the Bible. To encourage greater participation, Luther called for services to be conducted in German as well as in Latin. He also wrote hymns that were to be sung in German by the entire congregation, thus beginning a strong musical tradition in Lutheranism, which has particularly valued choral and organ music. (Johann Sebastian Bach [1685–1750] is the greatest composer of this tradition.)

Luther's version of the Protestant reform spread throughout central and northern Germany and then into Scandinavia and the Baltic states. It came to the United States with German and Scandinavian immigrants, who settled primarily in the upper Midwest. Over the years, Lutheranism has retained Luther's original enthusiasm for the Bible, a trust in God, and excellent church music.

Calvinism Once the notion of reform was accepted, it was adopted and reinterpreted by others who also sought change. Among them was the French theologian John Calvin (1509–1564). Calvin's thought is sometimes said to be darker than Luther's because he saw human nature as being basically sinful and almost irresistibly drawn to evil. He also took the notion of God's power to its logical end: if God is all-powerful and all-knowing, then God has already decreed who will be saved and who will be damned (a doctrine known as **predestination**). One's deeds do not cause one's salvation or damnation; rather, they are a sign of what God has already decreed.

Calvin's view of God as judge may have been influenced by his study of law at the university. Eager for reform, when he was only 26 he published a summary of his ideas in *The Institutes of the Christian Religion*. Persecuted in France, he was forced to flee and eventually settled in Geneva, Switzerland. Because of the work of the reformer priest Huldrych Zwingli (1484–1531), the

Swiss were already considering reforms. Calvin's great success in Geneva made the city a center for the expansion of the reform movement.

Where Luther had allowed much latitude in preserving elements of the Mass and other traditional Catholic practices, Calvin had a more austere view. Looking exclusively to the Bible for what might be approved, he encouraged the removal of all statues and pictures from the churches and the adoption of a style of congregational singing that had no organ accompaniment. The focus of the Calvinist service was on the sermon.

Ministers were not appointed by bishops—there were to be none in Calvinism—but were "called" by a council from each congregation. This practice, being highly democratic, threatened the political and religious leaders of the time, and believers were often forced into exile. Among such believers were the Puritans, who immigrated to New England, and the Huguenots (French Protestants), who were forced out of France in 1685 and settled in several areas of North America. Calvinism spread to Scotland through the efforts of John Knox (1514–1572), who had studied with Calvin in Geneva. It was in Scotland that a church structure without bishops was refined, providing a pattern for Calvinism in other countries. Calvinism ultimately became important in Holland, Scotland, Switzerland, and the United States. Later, in the nineteenth century, it began to become influential in sub-Saharan Africa, Korea, China, and the Pacific. The Presbyterian Church is the best-known descendant of Calvinism. It gets its name from the Greek word *presbyter,* meaning "elder" or "leader."

The Church of England (Anglican Church)   Another form of Protestantism, which originated in England under King Henry VIII (1491–1547), unites elements of the Reformation with older traditional practices. Some see the Anglican Church as a compromise between Catholicism and Protestantism. Perhaps it is a compromise, because it was born not so much out of Henry's interest in reform as it was out of his interest in marriage. His story is complicated. Henry's older brother, Arthur, had been married for political reasons to Catherine of Aragon, a Spanish princess. When Arthur died, Henry was forced to marry Catherine in order to continue the political relationship with Spain. This marriage produced a daughter but no living male heir—to Henry's terrible disappointment. When Henry fell in love with Anne Boleyn, a lady-in-waiting at the court, he sought to annul his first marriage. The pope and papal bureaucracy refused.

As a result, Henry began to dismantle papal power in England. He dissolved the monasteries, sold off their property, and added the funds to his treasury. He gave some of the lands to nobles and friends—an action that strengthened their loyalty to him. Henry had parliament declare that the "bishop of Rome" had no jurisdiction in England and that he, as the monarch, was the head of the Church in England. He maintained the traditional church structure of bishops and priests. (It is called an *episcopal structure,* from the Greek word *episkopos,* meaning "bishop" or "overseer.") He also kept the basic structure of religious services much as before, initially in Latin. He even maintained priestly celibacy, although this was abolished soon after he died. As a concession to reformers, Henry had an English translation of the Bible placed in each church for all to read. The Church of England had a shaky beginning, but Henry's daughter Elizabeth, when she finally became queen, established it firmly.

The Church of England produced several works of great significance in its first century of existence. *The Book of Common Prayer,* with all major prayers in English for church use, was issued in 1559. Its rhythmic sentences set a standard by which other works in English have been measured. Throughout the sixteenth century, composers were commissioned to write choral music in English for religious services. The result was a wonderful body of music, still in use today (a description appears later in this chapter). In 1604 the King James Bible was published, named for its sponsor, James I, who had succeeded Queen Elizabeth I. It became the single greatest influence on the English language.

The Church of England has been deliberately tolerant of a wide spectrum of interpretation and practice. Some churches have buildings and services of great simplicity (their style is called Low Church), while others use incense, statues of Mary, and stately ritual (called High Church). Furthermore, in spite of great opposition, the Church of England has recently accepted the ordination of women to the priesthood and episcopate.

Sectarianism   The powerful notion that every individual can interpret the Bible has encouraged—and still encourages—the development of an abundance of independent churches or sects. Most have been formed by a single, charismatic individual, and many have been small. Some have interpreted the Bible with literal seriousness, thus producing special emphases—among them, the rejection of the outside world and its technology; the adoption of an extremely simple lifestyle; total pacifism (rejection of war and violence); complete celibacy; and the expectation of the imminent end of the world. As a loosely defined group, this branch of Protestantism is called Sectarianism. Following are the most prominent sects:

> *The Anabaptists* (meaning "baptize again"), a Swiss movement that developed during the sixteenth century, stressed the need for believers to be baptized as a sign of their inner conversion—even if they had been baptized as children. Their worship was simple. From this general movement arose several Mennonite and Amish sects, some communities of which maintain a simple, agricultural lifestyle without the use of cars or electricity. (The movie *Witness* is set against a background of Amish life.)

> *The Baptists,* a denomination that began in England, have grown up as a major force in the United States. Baptists espouse some of the Anabaptist principles, including the need for inner conversion, baptism of adults only, simplicity in ritual, independence of personal judgment, and freedom from government control.

> *The Quakers* were founded by George Fox (1624–1691) in England. Those who came to the United States settled primarily in Pennsylvania.

Quakers are ardent pacifists; they have no clergy; and they originated a type of church service conducted largely in silence and without ritual. Their official name is Society of Friends, but the name Quaker came about from George Fox's belief that people should "quake" at the Word of the Lord.

The Shakers grew out of the Quaker movement. They were begun by an Englishwoman, "Mother" Ann Lee (1736–1784), who came from England to New York State. The Shakers accepted both women and men but preached complete celibacy. Their religious services were unusual because they included devotional dance, from which their name derives. Settling in New York State and New England, the Shakers founded communities primarily dependent on farming. Although there are only a handful of Shakers today, their vision of Christian simplicity lives on in their architecture and furniture, which is unadorned but elegant.

The Pentecostal movement, although it has ancient roots, has been especially active since the beginning of the twentieth century. It emphasizes the legitimate place of emotion in Christian worship. At such services one might encounter "speaking in tongues" (*glossolalia*), crying, fainting, and other forms of emotional response, which are thought of as gifts brought by the presence of the Holy Spirit.

The Methodist Church at first was simply a devotional movement within the Church of England. It was named for the methodical nature of prayer and study followed by Charles Wesley (1707–1788) and his followers at Oxford. But under the strong guidance of John Wesley (1703–1791), Charles's brother, Methodism took on an independent identity. Charles Wesley wrote more than six thousand hymns, which helped spread the movement.

THE DEVELOPMENT OF CHRISTIANITY FOLLOWING THE PROTESTANT REFORMATION

The Catholic Reformation (Counter Reformation)

The Catholic Reformation established the Roman form of the Mass as the standard Catholic ritual. Here that Mass is celebrated in Rome's ancient Basilica of John Lateran, which remains an architectural expression of the Catholic Church triumphant.

▶

Although the Protestant Reformation was a powerful movement, Roman Catholicism not only withstood its challenges but also grew and changed in response to it. That response, in the sixteenth and seventeenth centuries—called the Catholic Reformation or the Counter Reformation—strongly rejected most of the demands of the Protestant reformers. Protestants rejected the authority of the pope; Catholics stressed it. Protestants demanded the use of native languages; Catholics retained the use of Latin. Protestants emphasized simplicity in architecture and music; Catholics created churches of flamboyant drama.

Nevertheless, the Catholic Church recognized that some institutional reform was necessary. The church's first response was a long council, held in the northern Italian town of Trent between 1545 and 1563. The council set up

Emphases of Catholic Christianity

Catholicism accepts all traditional Christian beliefs, such as belief in the Trinity, the divine nature of Jesus, and the authority of the Bible. In addition, particularly as a result of the Protestant Reformation, it defends the following beliefs and practices.

Importance of good works The Christian must accompany faith with good works to achieve salvation.

Value of tradition Along with the Bible, church tradition is an important guide for belief and practice.

Guided interpretation of the Bible Individual interpretation of the Bible must be guided by church authority and tradition.

Hierarchical authority The pope, the bishop of Rome, is the ultimate authority of the church, and bishops are

the primary authorities in their dioceses (regions of authority).

Veneration of Mary and the saints Believers are encouraged to venerate not only Jesus but also Mary and the saints, who reside in heaven. As an aid to faith, believers may also honor relics (the bodies of saints and the objects they used while alive).

Sacraments There are seven **sacraments** (essential rituals), not just two—as most Protestant reformers held. They are baptism, confirmation, the **Eucharist** (the Lord's Supper, Mass), matrimony, holy orders (the ordination of priests), reconciliation (the confession of sins to a priest), and the anointing of the sick (unction).

a uniform seminary system for the training of priests, who had sometimes in the past learned their skills simply by being apprenticed to older priests; it made the Roman liturgy a standard for Catholic services; and it defended traditional teachings and practices (see the box "Emphases of Catholic Christianity"). This council took a defensive posture that erected symbolic walls around Catholic belief and practice.

Several new religious orders came into existence to defend and spread Catholic teaching, of which the most influential was the Society of Jesus, or the Jesuits. The Spanish founder of the Jesuits, Ignatius of Loyola (1491–1556), was a former soldier, and with this background, he brought a military discipline to the training and life of his followers. Ultimately, Jesuits made a lasting contribution through their establishment of high schools and colleges for the training of young Catholics, and many continue this work today.

Because of the varied interpretations of the Bible and of Christian doctrine that began to emerge as a result of the Protestant Reformation, a major part of the Catholic Church's response was to stress discipline and centralized authority. The First Vatican Council (1870) continued this emphasis when it declared that the pope is infallible when he speaks officially (that is, *ex cathedra,* "from the chair" of authority) on doctrine and morals.

The International Spread of Christianity

The New Testament contains the injunction to "baptize all nations" (Matt. 28:19). As a result of this order, powerful missionary and devotional movements arose within all branches and denominations of Christianity (Figure 9.2). Over the past five hundred years, these movements have spread Christianity to every continent and turned it into a truly international religion.

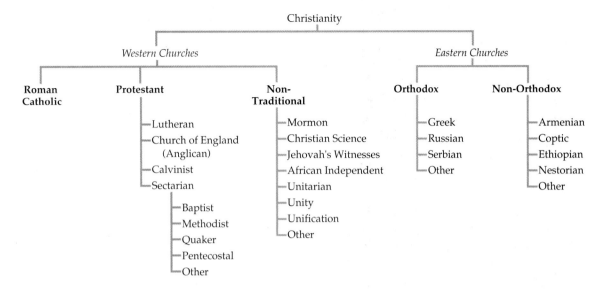

FIGURE 9.2

Branches and denominations of Christianity

An early wave of missionary work was conducted by the Catholic Church. Wherever Spanish, Portuguese, and French colonists took power, their missionaries took Catholic Christianity. The Jesuit Père Jacques Marquette (1637–1675) propagated Catholicism in Canada and the Mississippi River valley, and the Franciscan Padre Junípero Serra (1713–1784) spread Catholicism by establishing missions in California. In Asia, early Catholic missionaries at first had little success. Jesuit missionaries were sent out from such missionary centers as Goa in India and from Macau, an island off of southeastern China, to convert the Chinese and Japanese. The Spanish Jesuit Francis Xavier (1506–1552) and Italian Jesuit Matteo Ricci (1552–1610) were industrious, but their attempts in China and Japan were repressed by the government authorities, who wisely feared that conversion would bring European political control. Catholicism was, however, successful in the Philippines and Guam, where Spanish colonization contributed to the widespread acceptance of the religion. In the nineteenth century, French Catholic missionaries worked in Southeast Asia and the Pacific region. Tahiti, after being taken over by the French, became heavily Catholic; and Vietnam, too, now has a sizable Catholic population. In sub-Saharan Africa, wherever France, Portugal, and Belgium established colonies, Catholicism also took hold.

Catholicism in Latin America frequently blended with native religions. In Brazil and the Caribbean, African religions (especially of the Yoruba peoples) mixed with Catholic veneration of saints to produce Santería, Voodoo, and Candomblé (see chapter 11). In the southwestern United States, Mexico, Central America, and Spanish-speaking South America, cults of local deities were incorporated into Catholic practice. The cult of the Virgin of Guadalupe arose at the place where an Aztec goddess had been worshiped, and nature deities of the Mayans—gods and goddesses of the earth, maize, sun, and rain—are still venerated under the guise of Christian saints. Jesus' death on

Martin Luther King, Jr.

Martin Luther King, Jr., was born in Atlanta, Georgia, in 1929. The fact that both his father and grandfather were Baptist ministers led him naturally to religion. As a young man, he was troubled deeply by segregation and racism, and his studies in college and graduate school convinced him that Christian institutions had to work against racial inequality. His reading of Thoreau's "Essay on Civil Disobedience" and his study of the work of Mahatma Gandhi led him to believe in the power of nonviolent resistance. In 1959, following Rosa Parks's refusal to move from the white section to the back of a public bus in Montgomery, Alabama, King led a boycott of the buses there. Ultimately, the Supreme Court declared that laws imposing segregation on public buses were unconstitutional. As founder of the Southern Christian Leadership Conference, King mobilized black churches to oppose segregation. In 1964 he won the Nobel Peace Prize. He was assassinated four years later.[32]

King's powerful preaching and writing relied heavily on images taken from the Bible. His "I Have

Martin Luther King, Jr. led the Civil Rights Movement using principles of nonviolence based on the teachings of Jesus and Gandhi.

a Dream" speech is inspired by the stories of Joseph's dreams in the Book of Genesis (37:1–10). His "I Have Seen the Promised Land" speech is based on the story of Moses in the Book of Deuteronomy (34:1–4).

the cross was easy to appreciate in Mayan and Aztec cultures, in particular, in whose native religions offerings of human blood were an important part. Native worship of ancestors easily took a new form in the *Día de los Muertos* ("day of the dead"), celebrated yearly on November 2, when people bring food to graves and often stay all night in cemeteries lit with candles.

Protestant Christian missionaries and British conquests also spread their faith throughout the world. Protestant settlers who came to North America represented the earliest wave. The Church of England, Anglican Church, traveled everywhere the English settled—although in the United States at the time of the American Revolution the name of the church was changed to the Episcopal Church, to avoid the appearance of disloyalty to the new United States. The Anglican Church is widespread in Canada, Australia, New Zealand, and other former British colonies. It is also a major force in South Africa—as demonstrated by the campaign against apartheid (the former government policy of racial segregation) headed by Anglican Bishop Desmond Tutu in the late 1980s.

Protestant churches in the United States have played a large role in the lives of African Americans. When slaves were brought to the English colonies of North America, the slaves were (sometimes forcibly) converted to Christianity, usually Protestantism. Most African Americans became members of the Methodist, Baptist, and smaller sectarian denominations. In the nineteenth century, Protestant denominations split over the issue of segregation and slavery, and churches were divided along racial lines. In 1816 the American Methodist Episcopal (AME) Church emerged from Methodism to serve African Americans exclusively and to save them from having to sit in segregated seating at the services of other denominations. At the same time, some New England Protestant churches became active in the abolitionist (antislavery) movement, helping runaway slaves to escape to Canada and changing public opinion about the morality of slavery. Later, southern Protestant churches played a large role in the movement that fought segregation, and their pastors (such as Martin Luther King, Jr.) became its leaders.

Methodist and Presbyterian missionaries have spread their vision of Christianity to Asia and the South Pacific. About a quarter of South Koreans are now Christian, and Protestant Chinese have been prominent in the political life of Taiwan.

Missionaries have also spread Orthodox Christianity across Russia to Siberia and even into Alaska, where 40,000 Aleuts (Eskimo) belong to the Orthodox Church. (A Russian Orthodox church is located in Sitka, Alaska.) The Orthodox Church also spread to North America through emigration from Russia, Greece, and eastern Europe.

Christianity has been less successful in China, Japan, Southeast Asia (except Vietnam and the Philippines), the Middle East, and North Africa. But elsewhere it is either the dominant religion or a powerful religious presence.

Nontraditional Christianity

Because Christianity is a fairly old religion and has flourished in cultures far from where it originally developed, it has produced some significant offshoots. These denominations differ significantly from traditional Christianity, and although they are not usually considered a part of the three traditional branches of Christianity—Roman Catholic, Protestant, and Eastern Orthodox—they all sprang from Protestant origins. Although mainstream Christian churches often do not accept them fully, these offshoots manifest many Christian elements. Those that are growing rapidly present a special challenge to traditional Christianity.

Church of Jesus Christ of Latter-Day Saints   The Church of Jesus Christ of Latter-Day Saints, commonly known as the Mormon Church, is one of the fastest growing religious denominations in the world. Although Mormons consider themselves to be Christians who belong to a perfect, restored Christianity, mainstream Christian groups point out major differences between Mormonism and traditional Christianity. Consequently, we will consider Mormonism in some detail as an example of nontraditional Christianity.

Joseph Smith (1805–1844), the founder of the movement, was born in New York State. As a young man he was troubled by the differences and conflicts between Christian groups. When he was 14, he had a vision of God the Father and of Jesus Christ, who informed him that no current Christian denomination was correct, because true Christianity had died out with the death of the early apostles.

When Smith was 17, he had another vision. An angel named Moroni showed the young man to a hill and directed him to dig there. Mormonism teaches that Smith unearthed several long-buried objects of great religious interest. The objects were golden tablets inscribed with foreign words, a breastplate, and mysterious stones that Smith was able to use to translate the words written on the tablets. Smith began the translation work, dictating from behind a curtain to his wife Emma and to friends Oliver Cowdery and Martin Harris. The result of his work was the Book of Mormon. Later, John the Baptist and three apostles, Peter, James, and John, appeared to Joseph Smith and Oliver Cowdery, initiating them into two forms of priesthood—the Aaronic and Melchizedek priesthoods.

Hoping to be free to practice their religion, Smith and his early followers began a series of moves—to Ohio, Missouri, and Illinois. Opposition from their neighbors resulted from the new Church's belief in the divine inspiration of the Book of Mormon and its practice of polygamy, which Joseph Smith defended as biblically justified. At each new location the believers were persecuted and forced to leave. In Illinois, Smith and his brother were imprisoned and then killed by a mob that broke into the jail.

At this point, the remaining believers nominated Brigham Young as their next leader. Young organized a move to Utah, where he founded Salt Lake City. Prior to the move, a split had developed within the Church—in part over the matter of polygamy. Leadership of the smaller group, which did not travel to Utah, was taken over by Joseph Smith's son.

In Utah the Church faced regular opposition but grew in numbers. In 1890, a new revelation that disavowed polygamy was received by the fourth president of the Church. This rejection of polygamy (sometimes called the Great Accommodation) led to social acceptance of Mormonism. And in 1896, the Utah Territory won statehood.

The Mormon Church has always been a missionary Church, and it made its way very early to England and Hawai`i. The Church has spread so far through missionary efforts that it is now found worldwide. It has been particularly successful in the South Pacific.

Mormons accept as inspired the Christian Bible, which they usually use in the King James Version. They also believe that several other works are equally inspired. Most important is the Book of Mormon. Another inspired work is the Doctrine and Covenants, a list of more than one hundred revelations that were given by God to Joseph Smith and later heads of the Church. A last inspired work is The Pearl of Great Price, containing further revelations and a compilation of the articles of faith. These three additional works are all thought of as complements to the Christian Bible. More than 100 million copies of the Book of Mormon have been distributed.

While Mormons accept most traditional Christian beliefs, there are some differences. Mormons believe that God the Father has a glorified body, just as Jesus has, although they believe that the Holy Spirit is not embodied. Mormons believe that the souls of human beings once existed in spirit form

The Mormon Temple in Salt Lake City is the worldwide center of the Church of Jesus Christ of Latter-Day Saints (the Mormon Church).

before taking on earthly bodies and that these spirit-beings were sent into the physical world to perfect themselves.

The Mormon notion of the afterlife includes a belief in hell and in several higher levels of reward: the telestial, terrestrial, and celestial realms. The lowest level of reward is for souls who are imperfect but not wicked; the next is for generally good people; the highest is for devout Mormons and for Christians who have lived according to Christian principles, as those principles are understood by Mormonism. At the peak of the highest realm are Mormons who have performed all the special ordinances in one of the more than one hundred Mormon temples around the world. Couples who have had their marriages "sealed" in a temple service will continue as a married couple in the celestial realm and can become godlike, producing spiritual children there.

The Book of Mormon adds details to traditional biblical history. It teaches that some descendants of the people who produced the Tower of Babel (Gen. 11:1–9) settled in the Americas but eventually died out. It also teaches that a group of Israelites came to North America about 600 B.C.E. They divided into two warring factions, the Nephites and Lamanites, and Jesus, after his resurrection, came to preach to them. The Book of Mormon tells how in the fourth century C.E. the Nephites were wiped out in battles with the Lamanites, who are considered to be the ancestors of Native Americans.

While Mormons follow the Christian practice of using baptism as a ritual of initiation, they are unusual in that they also practice baptism by proxy for deceased relatives. This—along with a general interest in family life—is a major reason for Mormon interest in genealogy. In fact, Mormons maintain the largest source of genealogical records in the world.

Devout Mormons meet for study and worship each Sunday. Their Sunday meetings include a sacrament service (Lord's Supper), which is performed with bread and with water, rather than wine. Ordinary services are carried out in their local places of worship, and these services are generally open to the public. Special services, however, such as the sealing of marriages, are carried out in Mormon temples, and these temple services are closed to non-Mormons. For health reasons, devout Mormons do not smoke or drink alcohol, use illicit drugs, or drink coffee. Many also avoid all caffeinated drinks.

Because the Mormon Church emphasizes different gender roles for men and women, the hierarchy of the Mormon Church is male. Women, however, exercise leadership roles in their own organizations, which focus on domestic work, child rearing, and social welfare.

Mormons are well known for their emphasis on the importance of harmonious family life. In addition to expected family attendance at church services, there are numerous other Church-sponsored activities to engage family members. Mormons also support the tradition of setting aside one night each week for all family members to stay at home to enjoy their life as a family.

At the top of the Church hierarchy is the church president, who is called the Prophet (as well as Seer and Revelator), because he is considered capable of receiving new revelations from God. Below him is a group of men called the Quorum of the Twelve Apostles, and below that group are the first and second Quorum of the Seventies, who act as general authorities. Below them are area authorities and stake presidents (a *stake* is the equivalent of a diocese). Pastors are called bishops, and the males in their wards (parishes), when they reach the appropriate age, are ordained in various offices of the Aaronic and Melchizedek priesthoods. Young men are expected to give two years to preaching the religion, often in foreign countries. Young women are also invited to do missionary work, but the length of their missionary work is slightly less (usually a year and a half). At any one time, about 60,000 missionaries are active. Today the Church has about eleven million members, half of whom live outside the United States. The headquarters of the Church of Jesus Christ of Latter-Day Saints are in Salt Lake City, Utah.

Mormonism has a strong choral tradition. Hymns and solo works are sung at services, and the Mormon Tabernacle Choir, which gives regular concerts in Salt Lake City, performs a traditional repertory of hymns, oratorios, and other music.

In addition to the Mormons, who form the largest branch of the movement begun by Joseph Smith, there are at least a dozen offshoots. The most important is the Community of Christ, formerly known as the Reorganized Church of Jesus Christ of Latter-Day Saints (RLDS). It changed its name in 2001 in order to emphasize its closeness to mainstream Christianity. Smaller groups exist—some of them continuing the early practice of polygamy—primarily in Utah and western Canada.

Unitarian Church   The Unitarian Church takes it name from its emphasis on the oneness of God. It rejects the doctrine of the Trinity. For Unitarians, Jesus was an inspired human being who lived in a godlike way, but he was not divine. The Unitarian movement began in Europe during the Reformation, but remained a much-persecuted undercurrent. It had great success, however, in New England in the nineteenth century, particularly among Transcendentalist writers (such as Ralph Waldo Emerson and Henry David Thoreau), and it began to be influenced by the wisdom to be found in non-Christian traditions, especially Indian and Chinese. Reflecting this approach, its services use readings and songs from many sources. The Church speaks of its Judaeo-Christian background, but it prides itself on having no creed. Many of its members view traditional Christian beliefs as symbols rather than literal truths. Instead of emphasizing beliefs, the Church emphasizes values and actions, and it is dedicated to social justice, tolerance, and human rights issues. Its headquarters are in Boston, where it maintains a large complex of historic buildings devoted to the work of the Church. Because it merged with the smaller Universalist Church in 1961, its official name is Unitarian-Universalist (UU). (It is not to be confused with the Unity Church or Unification Church, which are described below.)

Christian Science and the Unity Church   The Christian Science, Unity, and other similar churches emerged in England and the United States in about 1880, coming from a larger movement called New Thought. The movement emphasizes positive thinking and the ability of the individual to grow through a belief in inner power. The use of positive affirmations is a technique that these groups share.

Christian Science, founded in 1879, has its mother church in Boston. The founder, Mary Baker Eddy (1821–1910), began the church following her recovery from a serious illness, a recovery she attributed to divine power. The book *Science and Health with Key to the Scriptures* gives her interpretation of biblical passages and is read along with the Bible in Christian Science services. Eddy emphasized the healing role of Jesus, and her church maintains that not only negative emotions but also physical sicknesses are the result of an inadequate understanding of the divine nature within each individual. Healing comes when the individual discovers that physical and mental evils are actually illusions. Christian Scientists generally avoid hospitals and doctors and instead seek healing through "practitioners," who visit and pray with the ill. The Christian Science Church supports reading rooms in urban locations, where passersby can acquaint themselves with the literature and religious views of the church.

Unity Church (or the Unity School of Christianity) is another religious denomination that emerged, like Christian Science, from the New Thought movement. It puts little stress on traditional Christianity, although it makes use of some of its language and practice. The Unity Church seeks wisdom in every religious tradition, and its groups often invite members of other religions to speak at their meetings. Services avoid mention of sin or punishment and instead rely on inspirational talks, peaceful music, and guided meditations to help individuals discover the hidden possibilities within themselves.

Jehovah's Witnesses   The Jehovah's Witnesses, founded by Charles T. Russell (1852–1916), are an apocalyptic group that puts the Bible, literally interpreted, at the center of belief and practice. The Witnesses hold that God (Jehovah), after punishing evildoers and nonbelievers with annihilation, will create in the near future a paradise-like world for virtuous believers. At one time the Witnesses thought this event would occur on earth in 1914, but they argue now that the process only began in 1914. Strongly influenced by the Book of Revelation, the members believe that 144,000 people of the past and present will be taken to heaven as a special reward, while all other good people of the past will rise from death and join the rest of the faithful on a restored earth. The Jehovah's Witnesses do not believe in the divinity of Jesus, the Trinity, or a permanent hell, which they say are not biblically based. Neither do they allow blood transfusions, because of the biblical prohibition against the ingestion of blood. They do not celebrate Christmas (or birthdays), which they consider to be non-Christian. And because they believe that the Bible demands freedom from the world, they are strongly nonpolitical, refusing to salute a flag or to give allegiance to any country. They spread their faith door-to-door as a part of their religious practice.

African Independent Churches   Christianity has been immensely successful in sub-Saharan Africa over the past one hundred years. Many of the churches there are in communion with the Roman Catholic Church or with mainstream Protestant churches. However, thousands of independent churches have arisen, both from Protestant and Catholic origins, with distinctively African characteristics. The Kinbanguist Church of Congo, for example, in its services uses sweet potatoes and honey instead of bread and wine. Physical and spiritual healing are an important goal in many churches, which often use water not only for baptism but for other forms of healing. Sacraments, however, are less important than powerful preaching and prophecy, and some churches either focus on a charismatic leader as a messiah figure or expect a messianic future. The Harrist Church in the Ivory Coast, for example, was founded in 1913 by a messianic leader, Richard Harris, who claimed to have received revelations from the angel Gabriel. The Harrist Church emphasizes faith healing. Another church, the Mai Chaza Church in Zimbabwe, was begun by a woman who claimed to have died and returned to life. A similar movement in the same area was begun by Johane Masowe, who also claimed to have died and returned to life and thereby gained special powers to heal. Other churches are the Balokole ("saved ones") in East Africa, the Catholic Church of the Sacred Heart in Zambia, and the amaNazaretha Church in South Africa.[33]

Unification Church   This church blends elements of Christianity and Confucian social principles. The founder, Reverend Sun Myung Moon, escaped from North Korea after great personal suffering and founded his church in South Korea in 1954. His church has associated Communism with demonic powers. Reverend Moon believes that evil forces will overtake the world unless they are opposed, and against these forces he hopes his church will help create "the kingdom of heaven on earth." He calls himself "the Jesus of the second coming." (This view might also be influenced by the Korean devotion to Miruk, the Buddha of the future.) Reverend Moon offers his vision of the new society as a great, well-ordered family. He and his wife claim to be the father and mother of the new just society, and in order to create this society, he arranges marriages between his followers, which he and his wife solemnize in large ceremonies. Outsiders see Confucian and Buddhist elements, conjoined with messianic Christianity, in the Unification Church.

CHRISTIAN PRACTICE

We have seen how Christian beliefs have developed and been interpreted in varied ways over two millennia. While Christianity is very much a religion of doctrines, it is also a religion of ritual, and after more than two thousand years, these rituals have become rich and complex. Although Christian ritual practice varies among branches and denominations, many elements are shared.

Sacraments and Other Rituals   *WHAT IS THE IMPORTANCE OF THE SACRAMENTS IN THE CHRISTIAN RELIGION.?*

The most important rituals are thought of as active signs of God's grace and usually are called sacraments. The rituals that are considered essential to the practice of Christianity are the following:

> *Baptism* This ritual cleansing with water is universally used in Christianity as an initiation rite. The ritual originally involved complete immersion of the body, but some forms of Christianity require that only the head be sprinkled with water. Baptism came to Christianity from Judaism, where ritual bathing was an ancient form of purification (see, for example, Lev. 14:8). It was also commonly used to accept converts to Judaism, and the Essenes practiced daily ritual bathing. John the Baptizer, whom the gospel of Luke calls the cousin of Jesus, used baptism as a sign of repentance, and Jesus himself

Some Christian churches perform baptism in lakes or rivers. The white garments and the water work together as symbols of purification.

was baptized and had his followers baptize others. Early Christians continued the practice as a sign of moral purification, new life, and readiness for God's kingdom. In early Christianity, because baptism was done by immersion in water, the act helped recall vividly the death, burial, and resurrection of Jesus. Although early Christians were normally baptized as adults, the practice of infant baptism became common within the first few hundred years. Catholicism, Orthodoxy, and the more ceremonial forms of Protestantism practice infant baptism. Other forms of Protestantism insist that the ritual be done only as a voluntary sign of initiation and, as such, that baptism be reserved for adults only.

Eucharist Another sacrament is the Eucharist (Greek: "good gift"), or Lord's Supper. Early Christians, particularly Paul's converts, met weekly to imitate the Last Supper, which was probably a Passover meal. At this meal of bread and wine, they prayerfully recalled Jesus' death and resurrection. Sharing the Lord's Supper is a symbolic sharing of Jesus' life and death, but beliefs about it are quite varied. Some churches see the bread and wine as quite literally the body and blood of Jesus, which the believer consumes; other groups interpret the bread and wine symbolically. All Christian denominations have some form of this meal, but they vary greatly in style and frequency. Catholic, Orthodox, and traditional

Signs and Symbols

In addition to the sacraments, a multitude of smaller devotional rituals has arisen over the two thousand years of Christianity. Making the sign of the cross—in which the fingers of the right hand touch the forehead, the chest, and the two shoulders—is used to begin and end prayer and to call for divine protection. Genuflection—the bending of the right knee—which originated as a sign of submission to a ruler, is a ritual performed by Catholics and some Anglicans on entering and leaving a church. Christians in general often pray on both knees as a sign of devotion to and humility before God.

Devotional objects are also widely used in Christianity. Blessed water (holy water) reminds one of baptism; it is used in the blessing of objects and in conjunction with making the sign of the cross on entering a Catholic church. Oil and salt are used in blessings as symbols of health. Lighted candles symbolize new understanding. Ashes placed on the forehead at the beginning of **Lent** (a time of preparation before Easter) recall the inevitability of death. Palms are carried in a procession on the Sunday before Easter to recall Jesus' triumphal procession into Jerusalem. Incense is burned to symbolize prayer and reverence. Statues and pictures of Jesus, Mary, angels, and saints are common in traditionalist forms of Christianity. Often the statues of saints have special insignia for identification, such as the X-shaped cross on which the apostle Andrew is believed to have been executed.

In addition to devotional rituals and objects, Christianity is a source of much religious symbolism. The fish is an ancient symbol of the Christian believer. It probably began as a reference to Jesus' desire that his followers go out "as fishers of men" (Luke 5:10), seeking converts. It was also used to represent the Greek word *ichthus* ("fish"), which could be read as an acronym for the Greek words that mean "Jesus Christ, God's son, savior." The cross is used to recall Jesus' death; when Jesus is pictured hanging on this cross, the cross is called a crucifix.

Letters of the Greek alphabet are frequently found in Christian art. Alpha (A) and Omega (Ω), the first and last letters of the Greek alphabet, symbolize God as the beginning and end of all things (Rev. 1:17). The logo IHS (from the Greek letters iota, eta, and sigma) represents the first three letters of the name *Jesus*. The logo XP (usually written as a single unit and called "chi-rho"—pronounced *kai-ro*) represents the first two letters of the name *Christ* in Greek. (It is also the basis for the abbreviation of *Christmas* as *Xmas*.)

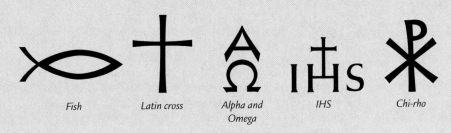

| Fish | Latin cross | Alpha and Omega | IHS | Chi-rho |

Protestant churches have a Lord's Supper service every Sunday. Less ceremonial churches prefer to focus their Sunday service on preaching and Bible study, but they usually have the Lord's Supper once a month. Virtually all churches use bread, but some use grape juice or water in place of wine.

In addition to these two main sacraments, accepted by all Christians, some churches count the following rituals as full sacraments:

Confirmation The sacrament of confirmation ("strengthening") is a blessing of believers after baptism. In the Orthodox Church, confirmation is often administered with baptism, but in Catholicism and in some Protestant churches, it is commonly administered in the believer's early teen years.

Reconciliation The sacrament of reconciliation (or penance) takes place when a repentant person admits his or her sins before a priest and is absolved.

Marriage This is the sacrament in which two people publicly commit themselves to each other for life. The two individuals administer the sacrament to each other while the priest or minister simply acts as a public witness of the commitment.

Ordination This sacrament involves the official empowerment of a bishop, priest, or deacon for ministry. (Some denominations ordain ministers but do not consider the action to be sacramental.)

Anointing of the sick In this sacrament (formerly called extreme unction), a priest anoints a sick person with oil—an ancient symbol of health—and offers prayers (see James 5:14).

The Christian Year

By the sixth century a fairly complete church calendar had evolved, which is still followed by most denominations of Christianity in varying degrees. The most important celebrations are Christmas and Easter. Additional festivals developed around these two focal points. The complete traditional calendar is kept by Catholic, Orthodox, and traditionalist Protestant churches (Anglicans and Lutherans). Because of the Reformation and later developments, many Protestants rejected parts of the traditional church calendar. (Because the Orthodox generally follow the old Julian calendar of the Roman Empire, Orthodox celebrations can occur up to several weeks after Catholic and Protestant celebrations.)

Easter The celebration of the resurrection of Jesus was the first Christian festival to develop. Its origins are in the Jewish Passover, a lunar festival of springtime during which Jews recall their exodus from Egypt. Christians have added another layer of meaning by using the festival to recall Jesus' return to life, which they believe occurred on the Sunday after the Jewish Passover. (The Western Church came to celebrate Jesus' resurrection on the first Sunday after the full moon that follows the spring equinox, while the Eastern Orthodox Church may celebrate Easter later.) Although there have been attempts—all unsuccessful—to give Easter a permanent date such as Christmas has, Easter is still an ancient moveable feast, connected with the full moon.

Christmas The celebration of Jesus' birth was a later development than the celebration of the resurrection. Although no one knows the exact date of his birth, it was once celebrated on January 6 and also on other dates in the spring. In Rome, however, Christians began to use the Roman midwinter solstice festival called Saturnalia to celebrate the birth of Jesus. Thus the festival of Christmas ("Christ-Mass") was

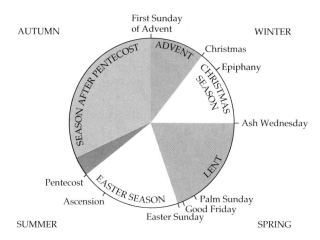

born and began its spread across the globe. The traditional celebration of Christmas lasts for twelve days. It ends with Epiphany (Greek: "showing"), which recalls the visit of the wise men to the child Jesus (Matt. 3:1–12).

From these two major festivals of birth and resurrection have grown two cycles of celebrations and memorial days. Two somber, reflective periods were introduced to help prepare for Christmas and Easter—Advent and Lent, respectively.

Advent The four-week preparation for Christmas that recalls the period before the coming of Jesus is called Advent (Latin: "approach"). It was once thought that the period from the Creation to the birth of Jesus was four thousand years, and each week of Advent thus represents one thousand years.

Lent The period of forty days of repentance and preparation for Easter is called Lent. The forty days recall the period of fasting and prayer that Jesus spent in the desert before his public life began. For many centuries, people were expected during Lent to do without meat, dairy products, and wine—all foods that were once associated with luxury.

The days just before Lent are given over to the last pleasures possible, before the abstinence of Lent begins. On the Tuesday before Lent, meat eating must stop at the end of the carnival (from the Latin *caro* "meat" and *levare* "to remove"). Because meat and butter are used up on that day, it came to be called *Mardi Gras* (French: "fat Tuesday") and is the day of a special pre-Lenten celebration in some countries.

Lent begins with Ash Wednesday, when the devout wear ashes on their foreheads to recall the inevitability of death and to show sorrow for wrongdoing. It has been customary during Lent for devout Christians to attend daily church services, to restrict their intake of food, and to give up pleasures. Secular entertainment, music, and marriage are sometimes forbidden until the end of Lent.

Palm Sunday, which commemorates Jesus' triumphal entry into Jerusalem, is still today celebrated with public processions.

Holy Week The week before Easter, called Holy Week, has particular meaning for Christians. Palm Sunday, celebrated on the Sunday before Easter, recalls Jesus' entry into Jerusalem and the acclaim he received in the form of people waving palm and olive branches. The Thursday before Easter recalls the Last Supper. Some churches mark this event by washing the feet of twelve people, in memory of Jesus' act of service to his followers. The Friday before Easter (called Good Friday) recalls his death, and services are often held between 12:00 P.M. and 3:00 P.M. in remembrance of the time that Jesus suffered on the cross. Saturday is a day of quiet but signals a strong change of mood, from sad to hopeful: on Saturday evening, a long vigil service is held, which ends with the first celebration of Easter at dawn.

Ascension and Pentecost Forty days after Easter, Jesus' ascension into heaven is celebrated. And ten days later the feast of Pentecost recalls the first preachings of the early Christians. The Sundays after Pentecost are devoted to meditations aimed at furthering the Christian life of the believer. Thus a whole church year centers around the drama of the life of Jesus and belief in him.

Saints' days and other practices The primary yearly cycle, mainly celebrated on Sundays, has been supplemented by a secondary yearly cycle that memorializes the saints—the heroes of Christianity. It is kept (with some variations) by Catholics, Orthodox, Anglican Protestants, and many Lutherans. Saints include Mary, Joseph, the twelve apostles, the four gospel writers, early bishops, leaders who were renowned for their holiness, and martyrs ("witnesses") who died in persecutions. In the West, Valentine's Day (February 14) and Saint Patrick's Day (March 17) are the best known of these saints' days and are celebrated in popular culture. Halloween derives from pre-Christian practice, but the name refers to the evening before All Saints' (All Hallows') Day, November 1. Almost every day of the year is dedicated to a special saint or saints, and in some countries children are still often named after the saint on whose feast day they are born.

Western Christianity has developed a symbolic system of colors to be used for church decoration and ministers' robes. White and gold, representing joy, are used for the greatest festivals, such as Christmas and Easter. Violet (or sometimes blue) is associated with Advent and Lent because of its more somber nature. Red represents the shedding of blood and consequently has been used for the feasts of martyrs—those who died for their faith. Because red is associated with the flamelike love of the Holy Spirit (see Acts 2), it is also used at Pentecost. Black was formerly used for adult funerals but has been replaced nowadays by white. Green, signifying growth in the Christian life, is used between Pentecost and Advent—appropriate during the agricultural summer months.

The cycle of festivals and use of symbolic colors weakened after the Protestant Reformation, when reformers eliminated what they felt was inessential in Christian practice. Vestiges of the color system, however, remain in weddings (in which the bride wears white) and at funerals (in which mourners wear black).

Devotion to Mary

Devotion to Mary, the mother of Jesus, appeared in Christianity quite early. In the Eastern Church, its strength was evidenced in the fifth century by arguments concerning the titles that could be given to Mary. For example, although some objected, Mary was called *theotokos* ("God bearer"). In churches she was pictured in frescoes and mosaics as a large figure holding a small infant Jesus. Sometimes she was paired with the adult Jesus. Icons and carvings began to show scenes from her life, and devotees prayed to Mary for their needs.

In the West, Roman Catholic devotion to Mary began to flourish in the Middle Ages. Many of the new churches built after 1100 C.E. in the Gothic style in France were named for *notre dame* ("our lady"), and statues of Mary, often tenderly holding her child on her hip, appeared in almost every church. Praying the *rosary* became common in the West after 1000 C.E. A rosary is a circular chain of beads used to count prayers, with the prayer *Ave Maria* ("Hail, Mary") said on most of the beads. (The use of rosaries for counting prayers is also found in other religions, such as in Hinduism, Islam, and Buddhism.)

Protestant reformers in the sixteenth century in the West criticized the devotion to Mary as a replacement for a devotion to Jesus. For this reason, devotion to Mary is less common in Protestant Christianity, although Lutheran and Anglican (including Episcopal) churches sometimes feature statues and pictures of her.

Today, devotion to Mary remains strong in Orthodox and Catholic branches of Christianity. In the nineteenth century, the Catholic Church declared that Mary's conception was an "immaculate conception," meaning that because she would be the mother of Jesus she did not inherit the original sin that came from Adam (Rom. 5:17). A sign of how important the veneration of Mary has become among Catholics is the fact that the Vatican has considered declaring Mary the "Co-Redeemer" of the world. Catholics believe that Mary appears in the world when her help is needed. The three most important sites where Mary is officially believed to have appeared are Lourdes (in southern France), Fatima (in Portugal), and Tepeyac (near

A woman holds a picture of the Virgin of Guadalupe, who is considered the protector of Mexico.

Mexico City). Lourdes, famous for its spring water, is a center for healing, and people hoping for a cure go there to bathe in its waters. Fatima, where Mary is believed to have appeared to three children, is another center of healing. And Tepeyac is the center of the veneration of Our Lady of Guadalupe, who is an important part of Hispanic Catholicism. Mary is believed to have appeared to a native peasant, Juan Diego, and to have left her picture on his cloak, which is displayed above the high altar in the church at Tepeyac. The site is particularly crowded on December 12, the feast day of Our Lady of Guadalupe. The festival is celebrated widely with Masses and processions in many cities and towns.

CHRISTIANITY AND THE ARTS

Particularly because of its ritual needs, Christianity has contributed much to architecture, the visual arts, and music. The stories and lessons of the Christian Bible and the rich symbols that are part of the tradition have inspired centuries of artists and composers. This artistic legacy is one of the greatest gifts of Christianity to world culture—a gift that can be experienced easily through travel, through visits to the great churches and museums of major cities, and through the experiencing of concerts and recordings of Christian music.

Architecture

When Christianity began, its services were first held in private homes. As it grew in popularity, larger buildings were needed to accommodate the larger groups, particularly for rituals such as the Lord's Supper. For their public services, early Christians adapted the *basilica,* a rectangular building used in the Roman Empire as a court of law. In larger Roman basilicas, interior pillars and thick walls helped support the roof. Windows could be numerous but not too large, because large windows would have weakened the walls. Rounded arches were placed at the tops of windows and doors and between the lines of pillars.

This style—known as Romanesque because of its Roman origins—spread throughout Europe as a practical church design and predominated across western Europe until about 1140. Sometimes two arms were added at each side of one end in order to allow more people to view the ceremonies. Adding two arms also gave the building the symbolic shape of the Latin cross (a cross with the lower part longer than the upper three parts).

Eastern Orthodox Christianity used the basilica shape but also developed another shape. The model was a perfect square covered by a large dome; it was based on the design of the Roman Pantheon. Soon four domed extensions were added on the sides of the main building, which allowed more people inside and offered better structural support to the roof. Like the two arms of the basilica, the four arms gave this building another symbolic shape—that of the Greek cross (a cross with all parts the same length). Because the windows around the domes had to be small, so as not to weaken the roof support, they shed little light, making the interior dark and mysterious. Mosaics with gold backgrounds help to magnify the sometimes dim light.

In the West, probably as a result of contact with Islamic architecture, a new style arose after 1140, known as Gothic style. (The designation *Gothic* was applied to this new style of architecture by a later age, which considered this style primitive and thus named it after barbarian Gothic tribes. The Gothic style, however, is neither primitive nor a product of Goths. It seems to have developed first in Persia, between 600 and 800 C.E., and elements of it may have been carried to Europe by Europeans returning from Syria and Israel.) The first example of Gothic architecture appeared in France—the cathedral of Saint Denis near Paris where it began, is still open to visitors today.

Gothic architecture is light and airy; it leaps upward toward the sky. Typical of Gothic style are pointed arches, high ceilings, elongated towers, and delicate stone carving. The walls and roofs are held up externally by stone supports (called *flying buttresses*) that extend outward from the walls and down to the ground. Because these supports do much of the work of holding up the roof, they allow the walls to be filled with large windows, frequently of colored glass. Smaller Gothic churches retain the rectangular shape of the basilica, but large Gothic churches add extensions on each side. Notre Dame Cathedral in Paris and Westminster Abbey in London are beautiful examples of this style. Gothic style was especially popular in France and England but also spread to Germany, Italy, Spain, and elsewhere. Most of the great European Gothic churches were begun in a single century, from about 1200 to 1300.

Gothic churches began springing up everywhere; any town of importance wanted to have a church built in the new style. This was especially true in towns that featured a cathedral. (A cathedral is a bishop's church and takes its name from the bishop's special chair, the *cathedra*, which symbolizes his teaching authority.) The great Gothic cathedrals were so impressive that Gothic style remains *the* style associated with Western Christianity. As a result, later grand churches outside Europe were built in Gothic style: for example, St. Patrick's Cathedral and the Cathedral of St. John the Divine in New York City; Grace Cathedral in San Francisco; the National Cathedral in Washington, D.C.; and the Notre Dame Basilica in Montreal.

In addition to the influence of the Gothic style in the West, other styles have also been important. The Catholic Reformation popularized the theatrical baroque style. The word *baroque* is thought to come from the Portuguese name for an irregular pearl, *barroco.* Baroque style uses contrasts of light and dark, rich colors, elegant materials (such as marble), twisting pillars, multiple domes, and other dramatic elements to create a sense of excitement and wonder. Beginning in Italy, baroque style also became popular in Austria and southern Germany, and because it was used by the Jesuits in their missions around the world, it is often called the Jesuit style. Fine examples are found in Rome, such as the church of Il Gesù and Santa Maria della Vittoria, and in Austria, such as Melk Abbey and Salzburg Cathedral. Other striking examples exist in Mexico, South America, and the Philippines.

While Catholicism was adopting the baroque style with enthusiasm, Protestantism generally moved in a more sober direction. Older Gothic churches were simplified and brightened by having much of their stained glass, statues, and paintings destroyed. Although the artistic loss was terrible, the result was a striking focus on basic architectural structure. Good examples of this can be found in the Netherlands and in the Protestant parts of Germany (the cathedral of Ulm is a fine example). With the focus of worship placed on hearing the Bible read aloud and listening to a sermon, new churches were built with pews, clear-glass windows, high pulpits, and second-floor galleries to bring people closer to the preacher. In larger churches, classical Greco-Roman architecture was drawn upon to produce the neoclassical style. Saint Paul's Cathedral in London, the masterwork of Christopher Wren (1632–1723), is the finest example of the style. Neoclassical

The soaring spaces of the Gothic cathedral (seen here in the hilltop cathedral of Prague) represent Christian faith—and human aspiration.

style became common in the United States, particularly in New England and the South, where it has been commonly used for both churches and other public buildings.

Mormon temples are architecturally interesting in that they are deliberately unlike older styles, such as Romanesque or Gothic or Byzantine. Instead, the building designs reflect an imaginative style that has been called Temple Revival. Elements of the style include large, flat building surfaces that are ornamented with elaborate grillework and decorated with tall, narrow spires. The temples in Salt Lake City and Los Angeles are good examples. Mormon art inside the temples and other public buildings tends to be realistic and representational, showing Jesus and scriptural scenes.

In the twentieth century, partly because new materials were developed (such as steel and concrete) or because old materials were used in a new way (such as large sheets of plate glass), experimentation led to innovations in church design, particularly in the United States. The Crystal Cathedral, designed by the noted architect Philip Johnson for a congregation in southern California, is made entirely of glass. (Robert Schuller, the minister who commissioned the church, began his preaching at a drive-in movie theater, and he said that it inspired him to want a church where he could see the sky.) The Wayfarer's Chapel at Palos Verdes, California, is made of plate glass and large beams of wood. Designed by Lloyd Wright, the son of Frank Lloyd Wright, it is set in a grove of tall trees on a bluff near the ocean and allows the worshiper an experience of closeness with surrounding nature. Concrete has been used as well to create unusual, modern soaring shapes, such as in the Catholic Cathedral of Saint Mary in San Francisco.

The Crystal Cathedral, an all-glass church near Los Angeles, was designed by Philip Johnson. Particularly well known for its Christmas and Easter presentations, it is a spectacular example of contemporary American Protestant architecture.

Art

Christianity has made immense contributions to art, despite the fact that it emerged from Judaism, which generally forbade the making of images.

This mosaic in the Church of Santa Maria in Trastevere dates from around 1140. Jesus is portrayed with his arm around his mother.

Mindful of the biblical prohibition against images (Exod. 20:4), a few Christian groups still oppose religious images as a type of idolatry. But because Christianity first began to flourish in the Greco-Roman world, it abandoned the prohibition of images and quickly embraced the use of statues, frescoes, and mosaics, which were common art forms there. By the second century, statues and pictures of Jesus had begun to appear, based on Greco-Roman models. The Christian Bible provided innumerable stories and images that could be depicted, and these illustrations, used in churches, served as both decoration and instruction.

Orthodox Christianity has tended to avoid statues but has concentrated instead on frescoes, mosaics, and icons (paintings on wood). A solemn style (sometimes called *hieratic*) was developed by Byzantine monks and painters in Constantinople and continues to be reproduced today. The unmoving, stylized figures often gaze full-face at the onlooker. They do not appear as ordinary human beings but more frequently as majestic universal types— prophets, monks, queens, kings. The backgrounds are usually gold, sometimes with stylized rocks and trees. The Orthodox depictions of Jesus emphasize his radiant divine nature and pay less attention to his human suffering than does Western art. Perhaps because of its emphasis on human beings' becoming divine through their contact with God, there is a strong otherworldly character to Orthodox art. Although the figures are rigid and sometimes not warmly human, they have an austere fascination that hints at a supernatural realm beyond, and the gold backgrounds of the artworks suggest timelessness and the light of eternity.

Icons play a special part in Orthodoxy. Churches usually have a high screen that separates the altar area from the body of the church. This screen is called an *iconostasis* ("image stand") because it is covered with icons. Doors through the iconostasis are closed during much of the service, cutting off the congregation's view of the priest and altar; the priest's chanting, however, can be heard as it comes over the screen. Thus the iconostasis becomes an important focus of attention for worshipers. Individual icons also stand around the church, and during services worshipers may kiss them and place candles nearby. Many homes also display icons.

In western Europe, Christianity favored artworks of sculpture, fresco, and painting (first on wood, later on canvas). Some of the earliest examples derived from older models; for example, statues of Jesus were based on earlier Roman sculptures. The Byzantine style of Constantinople was influential in frescoes and painting for many centuries, particularly in Italy, until the end of the Middle Ages.

New directions appeared in Western Christian art in the later Middle Ages, as wealth and population increased, and after 1300 an interest in the individual person and the human body is evident. This change in direction can be seen on the exterior statues of Chartres Cathedral in France: the earlier sculptures are elongated and unearthly, suggesting spirituality, while the later sculptures look more like real human beings. As the Middle Ages waned, statues and paintings of Mary began to show her less like a goddess and more like a human mother, and representations of Jesus began to emphasize his bodily suffering. The plain gold backgrounds of earlier paintings began to disappear, and the backgrounds became crowded with scenes of cities and of human activity, like farming, boating, and trading. Real people—such as donors with bowl-shaped haircuts—were painted kneeling in front of Jesus and Mary. This humanistic tendency eventually flowered in the Renaissance, when biblical persons often served as simply a pretext for quite secular painting and sculpture. Michelangelo's statue of David is a prime example.

During the baroque era, painting and sculpture tended toward the dramatic and showy. Paintings of saints often showed the saints' eyes lifted to the skies, the robes blown by wind, and sunlit clouds parted in the background. Sculptures were made of rich marble, and the figures employed dramatic gestures and poses. Paintings and statues were mixed together on the walls and in the domes of the churches, creating effects that often fool the eye. For example, an angel might be painted on the wall of a dome, with one of the angel's legs sculpted and dangling below. Sometimes the effect of baroque style is garish, but it can also be astonishingly beautiful.

Many Protestant groups rejected religious painting and sculpture as being unnecessarily sensual, wasteful, or idolatrous, and because artists in Protestant countries were not greatly patronized by churches, their subjects

ገጸሞ ቄ
ሞንቶ ስ

Modern Christian art has been enriched by the artistic traditions of many cultures. This Ethiopian painting portrays Jesus being tempted by the devil.

tended to be secular, often depicting home life, civic leaders, and landscapes. Christian art however, has begun to flourish again, particularly because it has increasingly been influenced by non-Western traditions and cultures. African artists, often showing Jesus and Mary with African features, have helped bring about a revival of Christian art, particularly in Uganda and other countries of central Africa.

Music

From the beginning, Christianity has been a religion of music. Jesus himself is recorded as having sung a psalm hymn (Matt. 26:30, Mark 14:26). Because of its early musical involvement, Christianity has contributed much to the development of both theory and technique in music. A Benedictine monk, Guido d'Arezzo (c. 995–1050), worked to help monks sing the notes of religious chants correctly; he is thought to have systematized the basic Gregorian musical notation system of lines, notes, and musical staffs, from which modern musical notation derives.

For the first thousand years, both Eastern and Western church music was chant—a single line of melody usually sung in unison without instrumental accompaniment. The origins of chant are uncertain, but it probably emerged from both Jewish devotional songs and folk music. Various modes developed, using scales of differing intervals. Each mode conveys its own feeling—some light, some sad, some exalted.

Music in the Orthodox Church is sung without accompaniment, thus remaining closer to ancient church music and to its origins in the synagogue and the Near East. The only instruments commonly found are bells and wooden clappers. The choral music of the Russian Orthodox Church tends to be done in harmony and is typified by extremely deep bass notes, so deep as to recall the pedal notes on an organ.

The ancient Greeks were familiar with the principles of harmony as they related to mathematics. But the use of harmony in terms of musical composition (called *organum*) seems to have first developed in Paris, in the cathedral of Notre Dame, about 1100. In the West, initial experiments with harmonized singing eventually led to the introduction of instruments, such as the flute, violin, or organ, which could easily be used to substitute for a human voice or to accompany the chant. Even though it is now considered a primarily religious instrument, the organ at first was opposed for use in some churches because it was considered a secular instrument.

Harmonic experimentation in church music continued in four directions: (1) voices alone (called *a capella* or "chapel style" because it was thought most appropriate for churches), (2) voices and instruments together, (3) organ alone, and (4) instruments in harmony (this was more common outside churches and eventually gave birth to the symphonic orchestra).

The most important early pattern for Western religious music was the Catholic Mass[34] (Lord's Supper), with its five sections of *Kyrie, Gloria, Credo, Sanctus,* and *Agnus Dei.* (The first section is in Greek, and the others in Latin.) The five sections vary greatly in mood. The Kyrie, which prays "Lord, have mercy" (in Greek, *Kyrie eleison*), is a plea for forgiveness. The Gloria, which begins "Glory to God in the highest places," is a joyous hymn of praise. The Credo ("I believe") affirms belief in God and recalls major events in the life of Jesus. The Sanctus ("holy") is the song of angels who are in the presence of God. The Agnus Dei ("Lamb of God") is a quiet prayer to Jesus for mercy and peace. On Sundays and at special celebrations, these five sections were traditionally sung, rather than spoken, and innumerable composers have put the five-part Mass to music.

A variant of the regular Mass is the Requiem ("rest") Mass, the Mass for the dead. It excludes the relatively cheerful Gloria and Credo and adds some more somber texts. Psalms and other short biblical passages were also put to music for the services. These relatively short works, usually in Latin, are called *motets.* All church music sounds best in the appropriate surroundings, such as in large stone churches, where sounds can resonate and echo.

After the Protestant Reformation, the tradition of composing Masses and motets was continued by Catholic composers. Renaissance composers, such as Giovanni da Palestrina (c. 1526–1594) and William Byrd (c. 1540–1623), composed Masses for voice alone. Later composers (such as Franz Joseph Haydn, Wolfgang Amadeus Mozart, Franz Schubert, and Ludwig van Beethoven) all made use of organ or orchestra in their Masses. Although the Catholic Church officially endorsed the purer musical style of unaccompanied singing, many dramatic Masses and motets were created; sometimes the line between sacred and secular music was hard to define. The dramatic style of church music reached an artistic peak in the luminous Masses of Mozart.

Continuing the Catholic tradition in the late-nineteenth and twentieth centuries, the French made notable contributions to both choral and organ music. Two Requiem Masses of extraordinary beauty are those by Gabriel Fauré (1845–1924) and Maurice Duruflé (1902–1986). Rather than grimly emphasizing divine judgment, they radiate joy and peace.

The Protestant Reformation greatly expanded the variety of religious music, as each branch created its own musical traditions. Luther, we might recall, wrote hymns in German, and although he encouraged some church use of Latin, he recommended that services be conducted primarily in the language of the people. The Lutheran tradition also supported the use of the organ, both on its own and to accompany hymns. The supreme genius of the Lutheran tradition was Johann Sebastian Bach. A church organist and choirmaster for most of his career, Bach composed many beautiful musical pieces for church use, both solo organ music and choir music. His *Saint Matthew Passion,* a musical reflection on the last days of Jesus, is one of the world's most complex and moving religious compositions. He also wrote in forms that derived from the Roman Catholic tradition, producing a *Magnificat* in Latin and his *Mass in B-minor,* which has been compared to a voyage in a great ship across an ocean.[35]

After the Church of England decreed that services be held in English, a body of church music began to develop in England. Much of this music was written for choirs, which traditionally have been supported by Anglican cathedrals. One of England's greatest composers, Ralph Vaughan Williams (1872–1958), often wrote religiously inspired music, some of which was intended for church performance. His *Fantasia on a Theme of Thomas Tallis* is a meditation on an Elizabethan hymn, and his soaring *Mass in G-minor* was used at the coronation of Queen Elizabeth II. (The written descriptions of all composers' works are as dry as mothballs; the only way to truly appreciate their music is to listen to these exceptional compositions. A short list of approachable music appears at the end of the chapter.)

Other forms of Protestant Christianity have been cautious about the types of music used in church services. Wanting to keep the music popular and simple, Protestant churches have supported the writing and singing of hymns but often have avoided more complex compositions. They have allowed use of the organ and piano but until recently have generally discouraged the use of other instruments. The churches that have been the most influential creators of hymns have been the Methodist and Baptist Churches, and as a result of the creativity of these and other sects there is now a whole genre called *gospel music.* Spirituals, based on biblical themes, are a distinctive African American contribution to Protestant Christianity.

In recent decades, a liberalization of practice has brought about great experimentation in both Protestant and Catholic church music. Guitars, synthesizers, and full rock bands are now common in church services. Christian songs are being created in a wide variety of styles, especially rock and reggae. The influence of church music on the secular musical world is also evident; Elvis Presley, Aretha Franklin, Stevie Wonder, Whitney Houston, and a multitude of others have risen to celebrity from a gospel-music background.

CHRISTIANITY FACES THE MODERN WORLD

Christianity—in spite of the strength of its varied interpretations and its international influence—faces obstacles that arise from new nonreligious worldviews.

The Challenges of Science and Secularism

The greatest challenge to Christianity as a whole has been the growth of science, and it will remain so. Along with science have come the demand for scientific proof and a nonsupernatural way of looking at the world. Biblical miracles, such as those written about in the Gospels, have been questioned and proof sought. Critical approaches to the study of scripture have also raised many questions, as have comparative religious studies. These tendencies appeared regularly in the eighteenth century, but the theory of evolution in the next century became a focus for angry public debate. At that time, the theory of evolution seemed to conflict with the biblical account of creation. Today, however, many churches have accepted evolutionary theory and see no conflict between it and the basic religious intent of the biblical story of creation. Perhaps this pattern of accommodation with science will repeat itself in other areas.

Related to science is the growth of secularism. Secularism refers to a worldview that shows interest in this world only and that refuses to refer to beliefs or values derived from any supernatural realm. The medical cures that were once sought from priests and prayer are now sought from doctors, hospitals, and pharmacies. Christians in earlier centuries expected their religion to provide them with art, music, and entertainment, but today people look for these art forms in movie theaters and on television. It is possible now to live one's life without any traditional religion, and this possibility makes some people question whether Christianity any longer has relevance. In western Europe, religious skepticism and low attendance at Sunday services are so common that European culture is routinely referred to by scholars as "post-Christian." As a result, the religion of contemporary Europeans—who were once the active figures behind Christianity—is often referred to as "cultural Christianity." This means that Europeans frequently are married and buried by Christian churches but are otherwise uninvolved with traditional religion.

While Christianity seems to be declining in Europe, it is acquiring many new converts in Asia and Africa. The religion places some emphasis on

The church at the Air Force Academy in Colorado Springs, seen by some as incorporating upswept jet wings into its design, symbolizes Christianity's attempt to confront the modern age.   ▶

improving the human condition in this world, a value that converts find appealing. The concern of Christians for the poor, the Christian willingness to battle against injustice, and the Christian promise that one can be "born again" to a new way of living are qualities that may give Christianity an enduring relevance.

Contemporary Influences and Developments

Mainstream Christian denominations now look for common ground and work together in a movement called **ecumenism,** from the Greek word for "household." Ecumenism sees all mainstream Christian groups as part of a single "household" of Christianity and tries to encourage dialogue between all its major branches. Marriages between partners of different Christian denominations are no longer discouraged and are sometimes witnessed by ministers of both churches. Several denominations often participate together in community welfare projects.

Cooperation and dialogue have occurred, too, at official and institutional levels. The best known of the ecumenical organizations is the World Council of Churches, which emerged from the Church of England. It now includes mainstream Protestant churches, all Eastern Orthodox churches, and observers from the Roman Catholic Church. Churches with similar beliefs have united or are discussing possible unions. At the international level, there have been formal meetings of many world religions. The first, held in 1893, was followed by a second parliament in 1993, which was represented by an even wider range of religions, including Native American religions. We can assume that an even more inclusive parliament will meet in 2093.

The Catholic Church, after four centuries of a defensive approach, took a new course in the mid-twentieth century. Pope John XXIII (Angelo Roncalli, 1881–1963), who had been elected as an elderly interim pope, convened a council of bishops in 1962. This council, named the Second Vatican Council (or Vatican II), proceeded to make the first major changes since the Council of Trent in the sixteenth century. The most obvious was to use the living languages of the people widely, in ordinary church services. Another change is that Catholic documents now endorse the value of other major religions and dialogue with Christian groups. More authority rests with laypeople, and consultation with them is officially encouraged. Modern approaches to understanding the Bible, pioneered by Protestant scholars, are now permitted. These changes have initiated intense debate over other elements of traditional Catholic life, such as the celibacy of priests, the ordination of women, the role of Catholic schools, and traditional positions on divorce, sex, and birth control. In other words, just about everything is being questioned.

What is happening in Catholicism can be seen as a new wave of the Protestant Principle of individual judgment that emerged in the sixteenth century. Some of the same events that occurred in Protestantism several centuries ago are happening again—but this time within Catholicism. Certain effects are predictable. There is already a spectrum of opinions, from ultraconservative

Christian Meditation

Inspired by the biblical admonition to "pray always," many forms of prayerful meditation have emerged in the long history of Christianity.

- In Russia, it became common to repeat some form of the Jesus Prayer: "Lord Jesus Christ, son of God, have mercy on me." That was done hundreds of times a day, until the repetition became almost as automatic as breathing.
- In Greece, monks practiced sitting quietly, putting their heads forward, and guiding their consciousness to the center of their bodies, where they used their imaginations to experience the inner light of God.
- In Europe of the Middle Ages, a form of walking meditation began to be done in labyrinths designed in the flooring of grand churches—such as we see at Chartres Cathedral in France. (This walking meditation is becoming increasingly popular today, and labyrinths may be found in many places—two are at Grace Cathedral in San Francisco, and another is at St. Andrew's Cathedral in Honolulu).
- Beginning in Egypt and the Near East, monks would recite the psalms very slowly, then silently reflect afterwards on the most meaningful verses.

In recent years, one particular form of meditation has been popularized by two Trappist monks, Thomas Keating and M. Basil Pennington. They call it Centering Prayer, and they explain that it was already described in the fourteenth-century classic The Cloud of Unknowing. "Contemplative prayer is the opening of the mind and heart, our whole being, to God, the Ultimate Mystery, beyond thoughts, words, emotions. . . . Centering Prayer is another word for a kind of prayer that has been around from almost the time of the apostles. In other times it's been known as the prayer of silence, the prayer of faith, the prayer of simplicity, the prayer of simple regard, pure prayer."[36] Keating and Pennington recommend that practitioners sit comfortably and quietly for twenty minutes, twice a day. They should choose a word from scripture to repeat internally, which will be the center of their meditation for one session—a word such as "love," "light," "peace," "wait," "taste," "child," "rebirth," "way," "wisdom." "One of the great advantages of Centering Prayer," says Keating, "is that it's like taking a vacation from the false self for twenty minutes twice a day. As the prayer continues in which we let go of thoughts for twenty minutes, we begin to experience a deep rest on the spiritual level. . . ."[37] The Centering Prayer will normally be practiced by individuals, but it may also be done in groups.

---

to extremely liberal, on every question, and there is more emphasis on the authority of the Bible and individual judgment. To prevent a breakup of the Catholic Church into factions, Church authorities have responded to these various questions with conservative policies in recent years. Although authorities have tried to lessen the debate, it is quite possible that Catholicism will eventually move in the same direction as many Protestant churches already have, with more liberal positions on most of these issues.

Christianity has a long tradition of helping the poor. A Catholic movement (which can be traced back to European ideas in the 1930s but only began in the 1950s) called Liberation Theology emerged in South America as a way of extricating the church from the power structure of politicians and landowners. Critics have accused the movement of identifying religion with social work, but it has done much to realign the Catholic Church with the poor. Evangelical and Pentecostal Protestant churches in South America have also been socially active against poverty.

A development in Protestant Christianity has been the emergence, beginning in the 1920s, of **evangelical** denominations. With an emphasis on the Bible, a conservative morality, and religious services that often encourage

Christians of all ages join to sing songs during a celebration in Pennsylvania.

the expression of individual emotion, this approach has helped Protestant Christianity develop in several often interrelated ways. One has been the rise of nondenominational churches, often begun by charismatic ministers who have little or no affiliation with established churches. Another has been the development of televangelism (television evangelism), which grew out of the work of radio evangelists (such as Billy Sunday, 1862–1935). Television evangelism, which often places an emphasis on healing, is significant because of the millions of people who can be reached by one minister. Lastly, because a great deal of Protestant religious television and radio programming is given to singing, Christian rock music and gospel music have entered the mainstream.

Some biblical passages, such as those that forbid women to preach (1 Tim. 2:13), have for centuries kept women out of public roles in Christianity. But women have assumed more leadership in Christian denominations over the past hundred years. The earliest examples of women in the ministry were in the charismatic and nondenominational churches. People like Aimee Semple McPherson (1890–1944), the founder of the Foursquare Gospel Church, advanced the cause of women in the churches. A vital radio preacher in Los Angeles in the early days of radio, McPherson accustomed people to the notion of a woman preacher.

Feminist theory is adding its insights to Christianity, which according to many is overly patriarchal and male-dominated. Some churches have responded by including more women in the ministry, and in some branches of the Church of England and the Lutheran Church women have recently become not only priests but also bishops. The male-oriented religious language that describes God in the Bible and in hymns ("king," "lord") is giving way to more inclusive language ("ruler," "creator").

The environment and the natural world were not strong concerns of Christianity in the past, but this is changing. Based on the notion that the world is the creation of God and reflects God's love, Christians are beginning to work out a theology of environmentalism. Expressing this interest, the design of some modern churches reflects a new interest in nature. For example, modern churches often feature large glass windows to reveal the surrounding sky and trees. The new cathedral of Evry, in France, designed by Mario Botta, even has trees growing on its roof!

Another current development is a renewed interest in Christian mysticism. The rereading of great medieval classics has also led to further interest in Hindu spirituality, Buddhist meditation, and other forms of mysticism. One form of mystically oriented Christian thought, called Creation Spirituality, is gaining renown. Begun by a priest, Matthew Fox, it unites contemporary concerns—mystical experience, feminism, ecology, and individual judgment—with traditional Christianity.

In summary, traditionalists see much to worry about, such as the scientific questioning of belief in the supernatural and the growth of secular values. But optimists see great vitality in Christianity because of its respect for the individual, its ethic of practical helpfulness, its love of the arts, and even its openness to debate.

RELIGION BEYOND THE CLASSROOM

Christianity has been a major patron and protector of the arts. The following list is long enough to highlight some of the significant examples of Christian art, but it represents a mere sampling of the multitude of artistic expressions produced by Christianity.

The best time to visit Christian churches is when they come alive, that is, during services or concerts. Almost every Christian church has at least one service on Sundays. In cathedrals and major churches the choral service is the most important and usually begins at about 10:00 or 10:30 in the morning. The great festivals, such as Christmas and Easter, are a particularly good time to attend a religious service. Concerts are often held in churches, too—usually in the evening. Consult local sources of information, such as newspapers, hotels, and travel bureaus.

North America Fine church buildings are located in many places, particularly in major cities. In New York: Saint Patrick's Cathedral, the Cathedral of Saint John the Divine, Saint Thomas Church (its choir school sings at services during the school year). In Boston: Trinity Church. In Washington, D.C.: the National Cathedral and the Shrine of the Immaculate Conception. In San Francisco: Grace Cathedral (which also has a choir school). In Los Angeles: the Wayfarer's Chapel (Palos Verdes) and the Crystal Cathedral (Orange County), which has special programs at Christmas and Easter.

There are many smaller churches of interest as well. Some historical churches include the Old North Church in Boston and the Franciscan missions of California (fine ones are located in Carmel, Santa Barbara, and San Juan Capistrano). Other churches are modern, designed by well-known architects, such as Frank Lloyd Wright's Unitarian Meeting House in Madison, Wisconsin, and Marcel Breuer's Abbey Church at Saint John's Abbey, Collegeville, Minnesota.

In Canada, of special beauty is the neo-Gothic Notre Dame Basilica in Montreal. In Mexico, the cathedral of Mexico City is exceptional and is on the site of an Aztec temple.

Europe The most important countries in Europe for visitors interested in the art and architecture of Christianity are England, France, Italy, Germany, Spain, and Greece. Below are some of their major religious sights.

In England, visitors should include in their itineraries Saint Paul's Cathedral and Westminster Abbey. The cathedrals of York, Durham, Lincoln, Wells, Salisbury, and Winchester are also fine buildings. Sunday services are usually held at about 10:00 A.M. (mattins) and 4:00 P.M. (evensong).

In France, organ concerts are held on Sunday afternoons at Notre Dame Cathedral in Paris. Other churches of interest in Paris are Sainte Chapelle (featuring exquisite stained glass), Saint Severin, Sacre Coeur (in neo-Byzantine style), and the Madeleine (in the style of a Greek temple). The cathedral of Chartres is a masterpiece of Gothic style, with much original stained glass and sculpture. Other significant Gothic cathedrals are located in Amiens, Rouen, Rheims, Laon, and Strasbourg. Major museums located in Paris are the Louvre and the Musée de Cluny.

Italy is the home to so much fine religious art and architecture that limiting examples to a small sampling is difficult. First-time travelers might want to visit the following in Rome, Florence, and Venice. In Rome: Saint Peter's Basilica (there is a papal blessing at noon on most Sundays), the Sistine Chapel, Saint Mary Major, Saint John Lateran, Il Gesù (a baroque church with a spectacular ceiling), Santa Maria della Vittoria (featuring Bernini's statue of Saint Teresa in ecstasy), and Santa Sabina (in very pure basilica style). In Florence: the cathedral (Duomo; with baptistery doors by Ghiberti and a bell tower by Giotto), Santa Maria Novella, Santa Croce, Orsanmichele, and the Convent of San Marco. In Venice: Saint Mark's Cathedral (featuring mosaics), Zanipolo, Salute, and Frari. Other noteworthy cathedrals are located in Milan, Siena, and Orvieto. Assisi and its basilica are wonderful to visit because of their association with Saint Francis and the frescoes attributed to Giotto. Major museums are located in Rome (the Vatican Museum), Florence (Uffizi Gallery, Pitti Palace, Bargello, San Marco, and Accademia), and Venice (Accademia).

In Germany, an especially fine Gothic cathedral (Dom) is located in Cologne. Other cathedrals of note can be found in Munich, Freiburg, Mainz, Dresden, and Ulm. Major museums are located in Berlin (Pergamon and Dahlem).

In Spain, the center of the Catholic Church is Toledo, one of the most beautiful hill towns in the world. Two sights not to miss there are the cathedral and the church of Santo Tomé. In Barcelona, of particular interest are the cathedral and the incomplete Sagrada Familia church (by Antonio Gaudí), which looks like melting ice cream. Other cathedrals of note are located in Seville (the location of one of the largest cathedrals in the world), Salamanca, and Madrid. The cathedral of Córdoba is a beautiful former mosque, still almost entirely intact. The major museum is the Prado in Madrid.

In Greece, two buildings of interest in Athens are the Little (Old) Cathedral and the New Cathedral. In Thessaloníki, visitors should see Agios Georgios, Agios Dimitrios, and Agia Sophia. Monastic life can also be experienced at the monasteries of Meteora, built on mountains. The Byzantine Museum in Athens contains many fine pieces of Christian artwork.

FOR FULLER UNDERSTANDING

1. Compile an inventory of questions (perhaps by rereading this chapter), and conduct interviews with pastors of different denominational churches. Write up a report that compares and contrasts the beliefs and practices of these churches.

2. Locate important examples of Christian art and architecture in your area. Prepare a self-guided tour tailored to a visitor who is interested in religious art and architecture.

3. Imagine that you have been offered an all-expenses-paid one-month trip to Europe in exchange for guiding a tour group to cities and sites that played major roles in the spread of Christianity. Do research to help you put together an itinerary. Then write a "script" of the history and details you will share with your tour group at each site.

4. See if there are any Christian nuns in your area. Arrange an interview with several nuns and, if possible, a visit to their convent. Ask the nuns to relate their personal stories of their choice to join the convent. Ask them also about their joys and their hopes. Write up your report as a collection of life stories or as part of a study on the status of women in various religions.

5. Experience the choral Sunday service at an Episcopal cathedral (or major Episcopal church) in your area. Make a report on the composers of the music performed.

6. In light of modern understandings of human sexuality, what religious meanings does celibacy have? Do you think that the practice of religious celibacy should be abandoned, retained, modified, or expanded among Christian groups? Please give reasons.

7. Read one of the books listed in the bibliography. Write a review in which you show how the book expanded your understanding of basic teachings, ideas, or practices covered in this chapter. Conclude your review by explaining ways in which the book you read may be relevant in today's world.

RELATED READINGS AND MUSICAL RECORDINGS

Books

Beard, Steve, et al. *Spiritual Journey: How Faith Has Influenced Twelve Music Icons.* Orlando: Relevant Books, 2003. A study of the role of Christianity in shaping several singers and groups, including Wyclef Jean, Moby, Johnny Cash, Al Green, Bob Dylan, Lauryn Hill, and Lenny Kravitz.

Burkert, Walter. *Greek Religion.* Cambridge, MA: Harvard University Press, 1987. Translation of a scholarly classic that gives a full range of information about sanctuaries, festivals, deities, and mystery religions, which in various ways influenced the development of Christianity.

Hale, Robert. *Love on the Mountain.* Trabuco Canyon, CA: Source, 1999. An insider's account of daily life as a hermit-monk.

Johnston, Robert. *Reel Spirituality: Theology and Film in Dialogue.* Grand Rapids, MI: Baker Book House, 2000. One Christian's perspective on the great questions that many films explore.

Keillor, Garrison. *Lake Wobegon Days* (New York: Penguin, 1995); and *Leaving Home* (New York: Penguin, 1989). Humorous sketches of Midwest life that provide serious insights into lived religion, by a writer with an unusual religious consciousness.

Kirk, Pamela. *Sor Juana Ines de la Cruz: Religion, Art, and Feminism.* New York: Continuum, 1999. A study of a seventeenth-century Mexican nun, whose thought and poetry are receiving increased attention.

Meehan, Bernard. *The Book of Kells.* London: Thames & Hudson, 1995. A richly illustrated introduction to the most beautiful of all European illuminated manuscripts.

Norris, Kathleen. *Cloister Walk.* New York: Putnam, 1996. A personal account by a Protestant writer who describes her discovery of monastic life and its rituals.

Perez, Nissan. *Revelation: Representations of Christ in Photography.* London: Merrell, 2003. A collection and discussion of many photographs that have offered interpretations of the life and meaning of Jesus.

Progoff, Ira, ed. and trans. *The Cloud of Unknowing*. Garden City, NY: Image/Doubleday, 1996. A modern translation of a medieval English classic of mystical experience.

Scheid, John. *An Introduction to Roman Religion*. Bloomington: Indiana University Press, 2003. A scholarly presentation of essential elements of Roman religion, organized by topics such as rituals, religious calendar, religious space, and deities.

Smith, Huston, ed. *Gregorian Chant: Songs of the Spirit*. San Francisco: KQED Books, 1996. An unusual collection of essays by many people on the topic of chant in general and Gregorian chant in particular, with many illustrations and a sample CD at the back.

Smoley, Richard. *Inner Christianity: A Guide to the Esoteric Tradition*. Boston: Shambhala, 2002. An overview of mystically oriented, non-mainstream interpretations of Christianity, from the Gnostic gospels to Swedenborgianism, by a former editor of the journal *Gnosis*.

Stockman, Steve. *Walk On: The Spiritual Journey of U2*. Orlando: Relevant Books, 2001. Examination of religious elements in the group U2, from its early days at Shalom Christian Fellowship to its Elevation tour.

VanderKam, James, and Peter Flint. *The Meaning of the Dead Sea Scrolls*. San Francisco: HarperSanFrancisco, 2002. A comprehensive discussion of the Dead Sea Scrolls and an explanation of their relation to Christianity.

Warrior, Valerie. *Roman Religion: A Sourcebook*. Newburyport, MA: Focus Publishing/R. Pullins, 2002. Translations of well-selected primary texts.

Ware, Timothy. *The Orthodox Church*. Baltimore: Penguin, 1993. A new edition of a classic on the history, beliefs, and practices of Orthodox Christianity.

Music

Christianity cannot be appreciated fully without experiencing some of its music. Following is a short list of selections, all available on CD by various recording houses. Especially approachable compositions are starred.

Bach: *Magnificat, Mass in B-minor, *motets
Britten: *A Ceremony of Carols
Byrd: Masses
Duruflé: *Requiem, Mass "Cum Jubilo," *motets
Fauré: *Requiem
Gregorian chant: *Masses of Christmas and Easter
Handel: *Messiah
Hildegard of Bingen: Hymns and antiphons
Mozart: *Coronation Mass, Requiem, *motets
Palestrina: Masses
Pärt, Arvo: *Fratres, Te Deum, *Magnificat
Rachmaninoff: *Evening Vigil* (other Orthodox music is available in collections)
Vaughan Williams: *Mass in G-minor, *Fantasia on a Theme of Thomas Tallis
Vivaldi: *Gloria
Zelenka: *Missa Dei Patris, Missa Dei Filii*

KEY TERMS

apocalypticism: The belief that the world will soon come to an end; this belief usually includes the notion of a great battle, final judgment, and reward of the good.

apostle (*a-paw'-sul*): One of Jesus' twelve disciples; also, any early preacher of Christianity.

baptism: The Christian rite of initiation, involving immersion in water or sprinkling with water.

Bible (Christian): The scriptures sacred to Christians, consisting of the books of the Hebrew Bible and the New Testament.

bishop: "Overseer" (Greek); a priest and church leader who is in charge of a large geographical area called a *diocese*.

canon (*kaa'-nun*): "Measure," "rule" (Greek); a list of authoritative books or documents.

ecumenism (*e-kyoo'-men-ism*): Dialogue between Christian denominations.

Eucharist (*yoo'-ka-rist*): "Good gift" (Greek); the Lord's Supper.

evangelical: Emphasizing the authority of scripture; an adjective used to identify certain Protestant groups.

evangelist (*ee-van'-je-list*): "Good news person" (Greek); one of the four "authors" of the Gospels—Matthew, Mark, Luke, and John.

filioque (*fee-lee-oh'-kway*): "And from the Son"; a Latin word added to the creeds in the Western Church to state that the Holy Spirit arises from both Father and Son. The notion, which was not accepted by Orthodox Christianity, contributed to the separation between the Western and Eastern Churches.

Gospel: "Good news" (Middle English); an account of the life of Jesus.

icon (*ai'-kahn*): "Image" (Greek); religious painting on wood, as used in the Orthodox Church; also spelled *ikon*.

incarnation: "In flesh" (Latin); a belief that God became visible in Jesus.

indulgence: "Kindness-toward" (Latin); remission of time spent in purgatory (a state of temporary punishment in the afterlife); an aspect of Catholic belief and practice.

Lent: "Lengthening day," "spring" (Anglo-Saxon); the preparatory period before Easter, lasting forty days.

Messiah: "Anointed" (Hebrew); a special messenger sent by God, foretold in the Hebrew scriptures and believed by Christians to be Jesus.

original sin: An inclination toward evil, inherited by human beings as a result of Adam's disobedience.

orthodox: "Straight opinion" (Greek); correct belief.

Orthodoxy: The Eastern branch of Christianity.

patriarch: The bishop of one of the major ancient sites of Christianity (Jerusalem, Rome, Alexandria, Antioch, Constantinople, and Moscow).

pope: "Father" (Latin); the bishop of Rome and head of the Roman Catholic Church.

predestination: The belief that because God is all-powerful and all-knowing, a human being's ultimate reward or punishment is already decreed by God; a notion emphasized in Calvinism.

Protestant Principle: The ability of each believer to radically rethink and interpret the ideas and values of Christianity, apart from any church authority.

redemption: "Buy again," "buy back" (Latin); the belief that the death of Jesus has paid the price of justice for all human wrongdoing.

righteousness: Being sinless in the sight of God; also called *justification*.

sacrament: "Sacred action" (Latin); one of the essential rituals of Christianity.

sin: Wrongdoing, seen as disobedience to God.

Testament: "Contract"; the Old Testament and New Testament constitute the Christian scriptures.

Trinity: The three "persons" in God: Father, Son, and Holy Spirit.

CHAPTER **10**

今日は 4/10/06
MEET WITH FRANCIE AND GRISELDA ON THURSDAY OF NEXT WEEK AT 11:AM

Islam

FIRST ENCOUNTER

With much anticipation you have taken a train from New Delhi to the town of Agra, not far away. You stop by your hotel room—with its slowly turning ceiling fan and its four-poster bed—long enough to drop off your bags. After bargaining with a driver in front of the hotel, you hop in a pedicab and merge with the currents of the Indian street. Alongside, in the human tide, you see what seem like a thousand bicycles and hundreds of other pedicabs, many filled with women with packages and schoolgirls with ribbons in their braided black hair. You see countless pedestrians, some of whom seem eager to collide with your pedicab. You pass tea shops and candy shops and photo shops and a movie theater, where a recording of a woman's song pierces the air and huge red and yellow posters advertise her latest film.

The pedicab turns suddenly and then stops next to a set of stairs. This must be it. You hop down and pay the driver. You then enter a gate into a dark enclosure and let your eyes adjust to the dim light. Beyond the darkness is a bright light at the end of a long channel of water. You see it—perhaps the most delicate domed building in the world: the Taj Mahal.

You have seen so many photos of this fragile-looking building, yet experiencing it firsthand evokes some unexpected feelings. The first is relief. You think to yourself: Here I am, at last. You also feel as if you are standing in a postcard. The building seems like a mirage.

After seeing the Taj Mahal for the first time, some people say, "It was huge!" And yet others say, "It was so much smaller than I expected." Part of its hallucinatory quality is that there is nothing to give it scale—no mountains or buildings behind it, which would give a clue to its size. (It is built on a riverbank, with the river invisible behind it.) Beyond the Taj Mahal is only open sky. The effect is dreamlike, a quality that is enhanced by the ambiguous color of the building. Covered in glistening white marble, the Taj Mahal takes on different light and hue, depending on the time of day. In the morning it is golden. At noon it is bright white. At sunset it grows pink. In moonlight it is a mysterious blue-violet.

To reach the building, you must walk through a long, formal garden, with grass and dark green bushes. The entire garden is enclosed by a wall with a fountain in the center, where channels of cooling water move in the four directions of a compass. The grass is being cut by a lawn mower pulled by two oxen.

Before you enter the Taj Mahal building itself, you must leave your shoes at the entry stairs. (In Islam, shoes are not allowed in holy places for reasons of respect and cleanliness.) As you enter, you see a filigree of Arabic writing and stylized flowers around the arches. Inside, there are no statues or pictures—only empty space under the great, tall dome. Two little boys come in with their parents just behind you and make loud birdlike calls, which echo wonderfully. They repeat their calls, listening for the echo. You want to experiment along with them but realize with a sigh the price of being an adult.

Although the Taj Mahal is not a place of worship, it is a sacred place, for it is a monument to Mumtaz Mahal, the best-loved wife of the Muslim ruler Shah Jahan (1592–1666), who built the monument in her honor. Their tombs are below, side-by-side. As you enjoy the sights, you ask yourself, How did such architecture come from a religion that emerged in desertlike Arabia? How did the Muslim religion get to India from Arabia? And why are there no pictures, paintings, or statues?

THE LIFE AND TEACHINGS OF MUHAMMAD

Muhammad[1] (570–632 C.E.) was born in Mecca, in what is today Saudi Arabia (Timeline 10.1). Much of what we know about him comes from his sermons and revelations in the Muslim sacred book, the **Qur'an** ("recitation"), and from the **hadiths** ("recollections," "narratives"), the remembrances of him by his early followers.

In the days before Islam arose, the religions of the Arabian Peninsula were Judaism, Christianity, Zoroastrianism, and traditional local religious practices. These local practices worshiped tree spirits, mountain spirits, tribal gods, and *jinni* (the origin of the English word *genie*)—capricious spirits that

	570–632 C.E.	● Life of Muhammad
Muhammad's first revelation ●	610 C.E.	
	622 C.E.	● Hijra: Muhammad's flight from Mecca to Yathrib (Medina); Muslim year 1
Muhammad's gain of control ● over Mecca	630 C.E.	
	680 C.E.	● Death of Husayn, grandson of Muhammad
Battle of Tours: ● Muslim incursion into France is halted	732 C.E.	
	922 C.E.	● Execution of the mystic al-Hallaj
Life of the Sufi ● scholar al-Ghazali	1058–1111 C.E.	
	1099	● Conquest of Jerusalem by Crusaders
Life of the Sufi poet ● Jalal-ud-Din Rumi	1207–1273	
	1291	● Muslim expulsion of the Crusaders from Israel
Muslim capture of ● Constantinople	1453	
	1492	● Expulsion of Muslims from Spain
Life of Shah Jahan, ● builder of the Taj Mahal	1592–1666	
	1947	● Independence of Pakistan as a Muslim nation
War between Arabs and Israelis ●	1966	

Timeline of significant events in the history of Islam

were thought to inhabit the desert and even to enter people. The supreme god Allah was an object of faith but not of worship. Allah "was the creator and sustainer of life but remote from everyday concerns and thus not the object of cult or ritual. Associated with Allah were three goddesses who were the daughters of Allah: al-Lat, Manat, and al-Uzza,"[2] goddesses related to nature, the moon, and fertility.

At the time of Muhammad's birth, Mecca (see map on page 453) was already a center of religious pilgrimage. Located in Mecca was a black

433

meteorite that had fallen to earth long before Muhammad's time. It was venerated because it was believed to have been sent from heaven. A squarish shrine had been constructed to contain it, called the **Kabah** ("cube").[3] By Muhammad's day, as many as 360 religious images of tribal gods and goddesses had been placed within the Kabah, and tradition tells that 24 statues, perhaps associated with the zodiac, stood around the central square of Mecca. By Muhammad's time, yearly pilgrimages to Mecca were already common, and a four-month period of regular truce among the many Arabian tribes was kept in order to allow this.

Muhammad's grandfather, Abd al-Muttalib, played an important role among the Quraysh (Quraish), the dominant tribe of Mecca, and is even thought to have been custodian of the Kabah. Muhammad's father died not long before Muhammad's birth, and his mother seems to have died when he was just a child. Muhammad then went to live with his grandfather, and after his grandfather's death two years later, he lived with his uncle, Abu Talib.[4]

As an adult, Muhammad worked as a caravan driver for a widow named Khadijah,[5] who had inherited a caravan company from her deceased husband. The friendship between Khadijah and Muhammad grew over time. They married in about 595 C.E., when Muhammad was 25 and she (tradition says) was about 40.[6] This marriage brought financial, spiritual, and emotional support to Muhammad; Khadijah proved to be his mainstay until her death. Together they had at least six children, but no boy—who could be Muhammad's hereditary successor—survived into adulthood. After Khadijah's death, Muhammad remarried a number of times. It is possible he married several of his wives out of compassion, because in his society widows of soldiers often needed a husband for financial support and legal protection.

From his travels as a caravan worker, Muhammad undoubtedly learned a great deal about several religions, including the differences within and among them. Although the monotheistic religions of his region believed in one "High God" and emphasized the need for morality, there was much disagreement as well. Jews and Christians disagreed about the role of Jesus and the nature of God. Christians disagreed with each other about the nature of Jesus. Jews and some Christians forbade image making, while other Christians allowed it. Many people also worshiped nature spirits. And the Persian religion Zoroastrianism, a major influence in the Near East of the time, so emphasized the moral struggle in human life that many people saw the world as being subject to two cosmic forces—good and evil.

As a religious person, Muhammad spent time pondering and meditating. To do this, he frequently went to caves in the hills surrounding Mecca that had long been used for prayer. When he was 40, during a religious retreat in a cave at Mount Hira, he received his first revelation, as recorded in the Qur'an. A bright presence came to him and held before his eyes a cloth covered with writing. It commanded three times that he recite what was written there:

> Recite in the name of the Lord who created—created man from clots of blood.
> Recite! Your Lord is the Most Bountiful One, who by the pen taught man
>   what he did not know.

Indeed, man transgresses in thinking himself his own master; for to your
  Lord all things return. . . .
Prostrate yourself and come nearer.[7]

At first, Muhammad doubted the nature of this revelation. Could it be madness or hallucination or some kind of demonic apparition? He confided in his wife Khadijah, who knew him well and encouraged him to accept his experience as a true communication from God. He became convinced that the bright presence was the angel Gabriel, and when further revelations came to him, Muhammad began to share them with his closest friends and family members—particularly his wife, his cousin Ali, and his friend, Abu Bakr. These were the first **Muslims,** meaning "people who submit" to God (Allah).

When Muhammad began to proclaim his revelations more openly, he was not well received. Although much of his message was unthreatening—Muhammad promoted the need for honesty, kindness, support of the poor, and protection of the weak—the revelations insisted that only the One God, Allah, should be worshiped. The revelations forbade the worship of other gods and demanded the destruction of statues and images. Muhammad also denounced usury (lending money at exorbitant rates) and the failure to make and keep fair contracts. These messages threatened businesspeople, particularly those involved in the pilgrimage trade, because the revelations denounced both common business practices and the multiple tribal gods whose images were kept in the Kabah. In 615 C.E., some of Muhammad's followers fled for safety to what is today Ethiopia. In 619 C.E., Khadijah died. When Abu Talib, Muhammad's protective uncle, died soon after, Muhammad became concerned for his safety. He and the rest of his followers considered eventually leaving Mecca.

During this stressful time, Muhammad, in 620 C.E., experienced himself being carried to Jerusalem and ascending from there into paradise. In this experience, called his Night Journey or Night of Ascent, the angel Gabriel guided him upward. As Muhammad ascended toward the highest heaven, he encountered angels and the great prophets of the past, including Abraham and Jesus, and at last entered into the presence of God. Muslims disagree about whether this event constituted a personal vision or an actual physical ascension from Jerusalem. Regardless, artistic tradition treats Muhammad's experience as a physical and bodily ascent from the city of Jerusalem.[8] He is pictured being carried on the back of the celestial steed Buraq, surrounded by flames and flying through the sky. This experience confirmed for Muhammad his vocation as a prophet and messenger of God.

Persecution of Muhammad and his followers in Mecca intensified. At the invitation of leaders of Yathrib, a city about three hundred miles to the north, Muhammad and his followers finally left Mecca in 622 C.E. Muhammad's migration, called in Arabic the **Hijra** (or *Hegira*, often translated as "flight" or "migration"), is a central event in Islam. It marks (1) the point at which Muhammad's message was favorably received and (2) the start of the Islamic

community (*umma*). For these reasons, the Muslim calendar dates the year of the Hijra as year 1. (In the West, dates according to the Muslim calendar are given as A.H.—*anno Hegirae*, Latin for "in the year of the Hijra.")

Muhammad's initial success in Yathrib was not complete. Jews there allied with his political enemies and rejected his beliefs because he recognized Jesus as a prophet and disputed the completeness and correctness of the Hebrew scriptures. Muhammad eventually banished or executed these enemies, and over time he gained control of the city. He set up the first Islamic **mosque** (*masjid*) in Yathrib, where many early rules about worship and social regulation were worked out. Yathrib is now called Medina (*madinat an-nabi*, "city of the prophet"). Along with Mecca and Jerusalem, Medina has become one of the three most sacred cities of Islam.

In spite of his success in Yathrib, Muhammad's goal was always to return to Mecca, the religious center of Arabia. In a battle in 624 C.E. at Badr between citizens of Mecca and Yathrib, Muslim soldiers triumphed against great odds. There were skirmishes and threats and a tentative treaty over the following few years until, finally, Muhammad returned as the victor to Mecca in 630 C.E. where he then took control of the city, destroyed all images in the Kabah and marketplace, and began to institutionalize his religious ideals.

Muhammad extended his control over further territory in Arabia; at the time of his death, he was planning to spread his religion into Syria. In his final sermon, he opposed merely tribal loyalties and preached the brotherhood of all believers. Muhammad died in Yathrib in 632 C.E.

Muhammad viewed himself, as did his followers, as the last of the long line of prophets who transmitted God's word to humanity. He did not consider himself to be divine but simply an instrument in the hands of God, a messenger transmitting God's will to the human world. Muslims view Muhammad as a man who showed perfection in his life, and they revere him as an ideal human being, a model for all believers.

ESSENTIALS OF ISLAM

Islam literally means "surrender" or "submission," indicating wholehearted surrender to God, and a Muslim is one who submits to God (Allah). The words *Islam* and *Muslim* are related to several words for peace, such as the Arabic word *salam* and the Hebrew *shalom*. They suggest the inner peace that is gained by surrendering to the divine. The word *Islam* also connotes the community of all believers, suggesting inclusion in a large family. As the Qur'an states, "the believers are a band of brothers."[9]

At the heart of Islam is a belief in an all-powerful, transcendent God who has created the universe and who controls it down to the smallest detail. Islam is thus a cousin to the other monotheistic religions of Judaism and Christianity, and all three religions worship the same God. It is possible, however, that the notion of God's power and transcendence receives the greatest emphasis in Islam. Some observers have commented that in Islam,

Muhammad, accompanied by angels, is portrayed during the Night of Ascent on the back of the steed Buraq. ◄

prostration of the entire body during prayer fittingly indicates a belief in divine power and the believer's submission to it—as compared to other characteristic prayer postures, such as kneeling (common in Christianity) and standing (common in Judaism). The physical posture of prostration illustrates well the Muslim attitude of total surrender to God.

Muslims refer to God as Allah. The word is a contraction of *al* ("the") and *ilah* ("God") and simply means "the God" or "God." (The Arabic word *Allah* is related to *El*, the general Hebrew word for "God.") Muslims explain that the word *Allah* is not the name of God—it simply means "God." It is said that Allah has ninety-nine names, among which are "the Merciful," "the Just," and "the Compassionate." These names demonstrate that Allah is not abstract—not just an impersonal force—but has characteristics of a personal being. In the Qur'an, Allah describes himself as personal and caring, as well as all-knowing, all-seeing, and all-powerful. Allah, because of this personal nature and the attribute of power, is referred to in Islam as being "male," although, strictly speaking, Allah has no gender.

It is sometimes hard for non-Muslims to understand the Muslim notion that God is omnipresent and controls every detail of life. The name of God is invoked in daily conversation, particularly in the frequently used phrase, "if God wills." People are called to prayer several times a day by a **muezzin,** a chanter who announces that Allah is great, greater than anything else. The chanted voice suggests that God is as active in the world as sound is active in the air, unseen but present. Some visitors to Muslim countries have remarked that people there live in a shared belief in God as easily as fish live in water or birds fly in air. God's active, present reality is taken for granted.

In Islamic belief, God has spoken repeatedly through human beings—prophets—revealing his mind and will. Muslims believe that divine revelation began just after the creation of the human race, when God spoke to Adam and Eve. It continued to occur, as when God spoke to patriarchs and prophets such as Abraham (Ibrahim) and Moses (Musa). Islamic belief also thinks of Jesus (Isa) as a prophet of God, although Muslims reject both the notion of Jesus' divinity and the Christian doctrine of the Trinity. Muslims believe that both Judaism and Christianity express true revelation from God but that in various ways those religions have contaminated God's word with human misunderstanding. It was Muhammad, Muslims believe, who freed the divine message from human error and offered it, purified, to all people. Because he is considered the last and greatest figure in the long line of prophets, Muhammad is called the "seal of the prophets."

Muslims trace their ancestry back to Abraham, the same patriarchal ancestor of the Jews, and to his son Ishmael (Ismail). Ishmael (as discussed in chapter 8) was conceived by Abraham and Hagar, who was a maid to Sarah, Abraham's wife. When Sarah, at an advanced age, became pregnant and gave birth to her son Isaac, Hagar and Ishmael were forced to leave Abraham's care, purportedly because of Sarah's jealousy. They survived in the desert only because an angel revealed to them a source of water, which Muslims believe was found near Mecca. Thus Islam and Judaism trace themselves back to a common ancestor, Abraham.

Muslims pray at Kuala Lumpur's Sultan Abdul Aziz Mosque, a modern adaptation of traditional architectural style. ◄

Muhammad learned about Judaism from the Jews who lived in Arabia. He also absorbed and considered religious elements from Christianity and Zoroastrianism—religions that share with Islam a belief in the soul, bodily resurrection, a final judgment (the Day of Doom), and an afterlife of hell for the wicked and paradise for the good.[10] All three religions also share with Islam a belief in angels and devils, who can have influence on human beings. Indeed, there are numerous similarities between Islam and other religions, and non-Muslims might speculate that Muhammad was influenced by these religions. However, Muslims hold that Muhammad's religious ideas came directly from God.

The overall worldview of Islam (as with the other three religions) is highly dramatic. Muslims believe that good and evil forces are in constant battle and that life on earth is filled with choices that lead to the most serious consequences. This conception goes hand in hand with the overall emphasis of all Western prophetic religions on morality. Religion is viewed as a strongly ethical enterprise; one of its most important purposes is to regulate human life. This moral emphasis appears clearly in the essential Five Pillars of Islam, which we will now consider.

The Five Pillars of Islam

All Muslims must accept and practice the following Five Pillars, so called because they support one's faith. The Five Pillars are mentioned in the Qur'an.

Creed (Shahadah)   "There is no God but Allah, and Muhammad is his messenger." This single sentence, when recited with belief, makes a person a Muslim. It is the first sentence whispered into the ears of a newborn infant; it is recited daily in prayer; and it is written in Arabic everywhere inside the domes of mosques and over their doors.

The most noticeable quality of the Muslim creed is its simplicity, for it emphasizes that there is only one God and that God is a unity. As the Qur'an says, "Your God is one God. There is no God but him."[11] The simplicity of the creed is in deliberate contrast to the rather long and complicated creeds of Christianity, and within it is a rejection of several Christian notions. It rejects the Christian doctrine of the Trinity, which Muslims see as a belief in three gods. It also rejects the idea that Jesus was divine or that any human being can be divine. It emphatically does not see Muhammad as a divine or supernatural figure but specifies his role as God's prophet and messenger.[12]

Prayer (Salat)   Much like the traditional Jewish practice of prayer at dawn, noon, and dusk, devout Muslims are called on to pray five times a day: before dawn and at midday, midafternoon, sunset, and nighttime.[13] Times for prayer are announced by a muezzin, who calls out from the top of a tower called a **minaret.** (Nowadays, recordings of the call to prayer are often played over loudspeakers.) The muezzin's call to prayer begins with *Allahu akbar* ("God is supreme"),[14] and it continues, "I witness that there is no God but Allah; I witness that Muhammad is the messenger of Allah; hasten to

Whether from a simple tower in a desert town or from this prominent minaret near the Atlantic Ocean, Muslims are called to prayer five times each day.

prayer." In towns and cities with many mosques, the call to prayer comes from the most prestigious mosque first and is then followed up by other mosques.

Before prayer, the individual is normally expected to perform a ritual purification with water, washing the hands, arms, face, neck, and feet. If water is unavailable, purification may be done with sand.

Those who pray face toward Mecca—inside a mosque the direction (**qiblah**) is indicated by a special arched niche (**mihrab**). In the earliest days of Islam, Muslims faced Jerusalem for prayer, but later revelations received by Muhammad in Yathrib changed this direction to Mecca. The Qur'an directs: "Turn your face toward the holy mosque; wherever you be, turn your faces toward it."[15] When several people are praying together, one person acts as the leader, standing at the head of the group in front of the mihrab. Passages from the Qur'an and other prayer formulas are recited from memory in Arabic, accompanied by several basic bodily postures: standing, bowing, prostrating, and sitting. Each time of prayer demands a certain number of sets (*rakas*) of prayers: two at morning prayer, three at dusk, and four at the other times of prayer.

Friday is the day of public prayer. On other days, people may pray privately, at home or at work, as well as in a mosque. Originally, the day of prayer was Saturday, following the Jewish practice; but Muhammad received a revelation that public prayer on Friday was God's will. In most Muslim countries, public prayer is performed at midday on Friday. Usually only men perform public prayer at a mosque, while women ordinarily pray at home; but where women are allowed to pray with men at a mosque, they are assigned their own area, separated by a curtain or screen or located in an upstairs gallery. The Friday service usually includes a sermon by a religious leader. Although Friday is a day of public prayer, it is not necessarily a public day of rest. In many Muslim countries, offices are open on Fridays, and because of European colonial influence, the public day of rest is Sunday. Some Muslim countries, however, recognize Friday as the weekly day of public rest.

Charity to the Poor (Zakat)   Muhammad was troubled by injustice, inequality, and poverty, and the demand that people give to the poor was a part of his overall vision of a more just society. Islamic practice demands that believers donate certain percentages of their total income, herds, and produce from fields and orchards each year to the poor. This is not a tax on yearly income, but rather a tax on all that one owns. The percentages vary, depending on what is taxed, but are commonly about 2.5 percent. Nowadays, government involvement in this taxation varies among Muslim countries. (In industrialized countries, government taxes commonly pay for systems of welfare, disability, social security, and other forms of assistance. This is a fairly recent phenomenon, however, that is practical only in money-based economies. Nonindustrial societies, which often use barter instead of money, depend much more on voluntary care for the poor.) In addition to established yearly donations, a good Muslim is expected to perform isolated acts of generosity and charity for the poor when such acts are called for in everyday life.

Fasting during Ramadan (Sawm)   To fast means to abstain from food for a specified period of time. The purpose of fasting is to discipline oneself, to develop sympathy for the poor and hungry, and to give to others what one would have eaten. Fasting is thought to be good for individual spiritual growth, and it is also an important bond that unites Muslims during the period of shared fasting known as **Ramadan.**

Ramadan, the ninth month of the Muslim calendar, is the time during which Muhammad first received his revelations. Fasting during this month, followed by a feast of celebration at the month's end, is considered a fitting way to remember this special event. During the month of Ramadan, devout Muslims avoid all food, liquid, tobacco, and sex from dawn until dusk. Exceptions are made with regard to food and drink for travelers, pregnant women, and the sick, but these people are expected to make up the days of fasting at a later time.

Because Islam follows a strictly lunar calendar, Ramadan occurs at a slightly different time each year, as measured by a solar calendar of 365 days. Twelve lunar months equal only 354 days; thus, Ramadan begins 11 days earlier each year than in the previous year. As a result, Ramadan can fall in any season. When Ramadan falls in winter, when the days are cool and short, it involves the least discomfort. But when the month of Ramadan falls in the summer, fasting can be a great hardship; when evening finally comes and the day's fast is ended, water and food seem miraculous.

We should note that periods of abstinence are common in many religions. The Christian observance of Lent, for about a month before Easter, is a well-known example, as is the Jewish practice of fasting on Yom Kippur, the Day of Atonement, in autumn.

Pilgrimage to Mecca (Hajj)   Pilgrimage—a religious journey by a believer to a sacred city or site—is a common practice in many religions. Besides fulfilling religious demands, pilgrimage offers other, less obvious rewards. It allows people to travel and experience new sights, brings people of different backgrounds together, and engenders a sense of unity. Best of all, it becomes a powerful symbol of an interior journey to the spiritual goals of new understanding and personal transformation. All Muslims, both men and women, unless prevented by poverty or sickness, are expected to visit Mecca at least once in their lifetime. Because Islam is central to the nature of Mecca, only Muslims may visit the city.

Pilgrimage to Mecca, or **Hajj,** was already a practice before Muhammad was born, possibly because worshipers wanted to visit the mysterious black meteorite that had fallen in the area. Muhammad, following divine revelation, continued the practice of pilgrimage to Mecca and many earlier aspects of that pilgrimage—including veneration of the black meteorite. Although this veneration might seem to contradict Muhammad's call for pure, non-idolatrous worship of the One God, the meteorite was thought of as a special gift from God. It was also connected with Abraham and even with Adam, who are said to have venerated it, and with the angel Gabriel, who was thought to have carried it to earth.

Because the present-day form of pilgrimage offers many deeply emotional experiences for believers, it deserves special description.[16] Contemporary pilgrims generally arrive by plane at Jiddah, the port city on the west coast of Saudi Arabia. In earlier times, people came by more romantic (and dangerous) methods—by boat or camel caravan. Air travel, however, has enabled people to come in great numbers. In the past, about 30,000 people visited Mecca each year; now 2,000,000 make the journey. In earlier days, the pilgrimage took months or even years. Some pilgrims died along the way, particularly when the special month of pilgrimage fell in the summer. Often it was the only long trip a person might ever take from a home village. Despite the numbers of pilgrims, to return home as a *hajji* (male pilgrim) or *hajjiyah* (female pilgrim) still confers much prestige.

Muslims distinguish between the "greater pilgrimage," which is made only during the special month of pilgrimage (*dhu'l-Hijjah*), and the "lesser

Worshipers pray facing the Kabah in the Great Mosque of Mecca.

pilgrimage," which can be made at other times of year as well. The lesser pilgrimage consists simply of a visit to Mecca and nearby holy sites. The greater pilgrimage, which is described in the following paragraphs, adds several days of arduous travel and ritual in the plains beyond Mecca; a trip to the city of Medina is often included.

Pilgrims first come to Mecca and are expected to arrive by the seventh of the month for the Hajj. For men there is special clothing, called the robe of Abraham, consisting of two pieces of white, seamless cloth. One piece is worn around the waist and lower body; the other covers the upper body and the left arm. (Women have no special clothing, but many dress in white. They do not veil their faces when they are participating in the pilgrimage.) The uniformity of clothing for males emphasizes their basic equality before God. In addition to the robe of Abraham and special prayers, all pilgrims are expected to refrain from sex, violence, and hunting. (It is easy to see how these pilgrimages and the associated practices drastically reduced intertribal warfare on the Arabian Peninsula.)

After settling into their hotels or hostels, pilgrims proceed to the great mosque. Inside the huge rectangle of the mosque area is a large courtyard, open to the sky. The four sides of the courtyard consist of pillared colonnades, which open out onto the central area and offer shade. At the center of the courtyard is the Kabah shrine. It is a building approximately 50 feet high and 40 feet wide and deep. It is covered with a black cloth, remade every year, whose edges are embroidered in gold with words from the Qur'an. The interior of the Kabah is empty and is entered only by caretakers and dignitaries, who ritually cleanse the interior with rosewater. The black meteorite, known as the Black Stone, is embedded in one external wall of the building and is visible on the outside from the courtyard.

After ceremonially purifying themselves with water, pilgrims immediately walk counterclockwise around the Kabah seven times. As they pass the eastern corner, they kiss or salute the Black Stone, which extends from the shrine about 5 feet above the ground. Today the Black Stone is surrounded by silver and has become concave from being touched and kissed over the years by so many millions of people.

Pilgrims reenact important events in the life of Abraham, their forefather. Islam holds that Hagar and Abraham's son, Ishmael, lived in the region of Mecca and that Abraham visited them here. Muslims believe that Abraham was asked by God to sacrifice his son Ishmael—not Isaac, as Judaism and Christianity teach—and that the near-sacrifice took place in Mecca. In their actions, they relive Abraham's spiritual submission as a means of emulating his close relationship to God.

After walking around the Kabah, pilgrims ritually recall Hagar. A long covered corridor nearby connects the two sacred hills of Safa and Marwah, which the Qur'an calls "signs appointed by Allah."[17] Between these two hills Hagar is believed to have searched desperately for water for her son Ishmael. Pilgrims walk speedily seven times along the corridor (the *Masa*), reenacting Hagar's thirsty search. They drink from the well of Zamzam in the mosque area, which is believed to be the well shown to Hagar by an angel.

On the eighth day of the month, after another visit to the Kabah, pilgrims go to Mina, a few miles outside Mecca, where they pray through the night. The next morning, the ninth day, they travel to the plain of Arafat, about 12 miles from Mecca, where Muhammad preached his final sermon. At noon they hear a sermon and stand all afternoon in prayer, exposed to the sun; the day of prayer at Arafat is often crucial to the experience of exaltation that the pilgrimage experience can bestow. That night is spent outdoors at Muzdalifa, halfway between Arafat and Mina.

The following day, the tenth of the month, is called the Day of Sacrifice (**Id al-Adha**). Pilgrims return to Mina, where they throw seven small stones at three square pillars, a ritual that recalls how Abraham responded to a temptation: when a demon tempted him to disobey God's command to sacrifice his son, Abraham threw stones at the demon and drove it away.

Pilgrims then select for themselves and their families one animal (sheep, goat, cow, or camel) to be sacrificed to reenact another important incident in Abraham's life: after showing his willingness to sacrifice his son Ishmael to God, Abraham was divinely directed to substitute a ram for his son. The slaughtered animal is then cooked and eaten. (This act of animal sacrifice is carried out throughout the Muslim world at the same time during the month of pilgrimage.) After the sacrifice, the men's heads are shaven, the women's hair is cut, and all fingernails and toenails are trimmed to signify a new,

The Islamic Religious Calendar: Festivals and Holy Days

Like other religions, Islam has developed a sequence of religious festivals and holy days. The main observances follow.

- The Day of Sacrifice, or Id al-Adha, is celebrated during the month of the Hajj (the twelfth lunar month). The head of every Muslim household is expected to sacrifice (or to pay someone to sacrifice) a sheep, goat, cow, or camel to recall Abraham's sacrifice of a ram in place of his son. The meat is cooked, eaten by the family, and shared with the poor.
- The Day of Breaking the Fast, or **Id al-Fitr,** is observed just after the month of Ramadan (the ninth lunar month) has ended. People have parties and often visit the graves of ancestors. Sometimes the festival goes on for up to three days.
- During Muharram (the first month of the Muslim year), believers remember the migration of Muhammad and his followers to Yathrib (Medina). For the Shiite branch of Islam, found primarily in Iran, Iraq, and Pakistan, the month has additional significance because it is associated with the death of Husayn, the son of Muhammad's son-in-law Ali. The first nine days of the month are solemn, and on the tenth day the devout reenact publicly the assassination of Husayn. Plays and processions vividly recall his death, sometimes with devotees cutting themselves and crying aloud during processions in the street.
- Muhammad's birthday occurs on the twelfth day of the third month of the year. In some countries it is a public holiday, and in some regions the whole month is given to celebrating and reading religious texts.
- Birthdays of other holy men and women are variously marked by devotees in different regions and groups. Shiites observe the birthday of Ali; religious communities honor the birthdays of their founders; and the birthdays of regional saints are celebrated locally.

purified life and a return to ordinary activities. Pilgrims then return to Mecca to again walk around the Kabah. Although this concludes the essential ritual of the Hajj, many pilgrims go on to visit Medina to honor the memory of Muhammad, who is buried there.

Additional Islamic Religious Practices

Islam aims at providing patterns for ideal living. Controls and prohibitions are imposed not to signify a love of suffering but to increase social order and happiness. Where outsiders might see only limitations, Muslims see instead the benefits that sensible regulations bring to individuals and societies. People who visit Muslim cultures often comment on the rarity of crime and the sense of security that people regularly feel on city streets.

Although it is strict, Islamic practice also values pleasure and happiness in this world. Believers must fast during the daylight hours of Ramadan, but each night families gather to enjoy a good meal together. The same general attitude applies toward sexuality. Although sex is regulated, Muslims do not value celibacy. Muhammad was no celibate and opposed celibacy as being unnatural. In this regard, Muslims are puzzled by Jesus' never having married and by the religious ideal of monasticism. It is within this framework of an ideal society that we should view some of the prohibitions of Islam.

Dietary Restrictions   The Qur'an forbids the consumption of pork and wine. Both Judaism and Islam view the pig as a scavenger animal, whose meat can transmit disease. Wine is forbidden because of its association with violence and frequent addiction. Although only wine is forbidden in the Qur'an, Islam has interpreted that prohibition to include all alcohol.[18]

Prohibition against Usury and Gambling   Charging interest on loans is not allowed. We might recall that in Muhammad's day money was lent at very high rates of interest, which impoverished and exploited the borrower. (Some Muslims today get around this prohibition by charging a "commission" for making a loan, although the loan itself is officially without interest.) Gambling is forbidden because it is considered a dangerous waste of time and money, as well as a potential financial risk for gamblers and their families.

Circumcision   Male circumcision is a religious requirement in Islam, although it is not actually demanded by the Qur'an. Circumcision at about age 7 or 8 is common. In circumcision, a small amount of loose skin (called the foreskin) is cut off from the end of a boy's penis. (We might recall that Jews circumcise boys on the eighth day after birth. Circumcision is also common among many Christians, although for them it is not a religious commandment; and it occurs frequently in native religions.) Explanations for the practice of circumcision vary. One is that the practice shows submission to the role of God in human procreation. Another relates to reasons of hygiene; in a hot climate, where daily bathing is not always possible, circumcision might have served as a preventive measure against infection. Perhaps both are true. In Islam, however, it is also done in imitation of Muhammad, who was circumcised.

In some primarily Muslim countries, particularly those in eastern Africa, Muslim girls are also circumcised at puberty. The act involves the removal of part or all of a girl's external sexual organs. A common explanation is that it decreases sexual desire in the circumcised young woman, helping her to remain a virgin before her marriage and to be faithful to her husband afterward. Non-Muslims in the West commonly criticize the practice as being repressive and dangerous; but some traditionalists see it as a valuable initiation rite and a preparation for marriage. In any case, we should recognize that it is not a Qur'anic command, nor does it have the same religious authority as does male circumcision.[19]

Marriage   In Islam, marriage is basically a civil contract, although a certain amount of ritual has grown up around it. In traditional Muslim societies, marriage is arranged by the parents and formalized by a written contract. Usually the bridegroom's family makes an offer of money or property to the family of the bride as a part of the contract. The marriage ceremony, which is held at home, is essentially the witnessing and signing of the contract. A passage from the Qur'an might be read, and there is usually a feast following the signing of the contract. Marriages can be annulled for serious reasons, and divorce is possible and can be initiated by a wife as well as by a husband. Neither annulment nor divorce, however, is frequent. After marriage, a woman takes on a new, more responsible role. As a wife she has left the protection of her father and is now the legal responsibility of her husband.

Women in Islam: Contrasting Notions of Liberation

Islam grew up within a culture that restricted many rights of women. The exact details of pre-Islamic Arabian culture are sketchy, but we know that female children, if unwanted, were routinely killed by being smothered or buried alive soon after birth. Wives were often treated as property, to be bought and sold, and a husband took as many wives as he pleased. Divorce meant that an ex-wife could be sent away with nothing for her financial support.

This background is important in understanding the new climate that Muhammad established for the rights of women:

- He forbade infanticide, thus saving many baby girls from death.
- He limited to four the number of wives a man could have and demanded that all wives be treated equally. Although this number of wives may seem excessive to non-Muslims, we should recall that in the past, marriage offered a woman economic and legal protection and was often entered into for these reasons. Today, most Muslim men have only one wife.
- He considered women and men equal in basic rights. Muhammad legislated that wives as well as husbands could institute divorce, and he demanded that a wife receive financial support in the event of a divorce. He also allowed remarriage for divorcées and widows. He affirmed property rights for women as well as men.

- Finally, he prescribed the basic religious duties, such as prayer, fasting, and the pilgrimage to Mecca, for both women and men.

Despite Muhammad's efforts on women's behalf, traditional Islam reinforces major social distinctions between women and men. While men may still have up to four wives, women may have only one husband. The Qur'an demands that both men and women dress modestly in public, but social custom dictates that women alone must cover their hair, because it is considered to be especially seductive; and although the Qur'an does not demand the veiling of a woman's face, it has become customary in some areas as an extension of the demand for public modesty. While men must wear the robe of Abraham during the pilgrimage, women have no special clothing for the pilgrimage. Women usually do not pray in the mosque with men at the Friday prayer, and if they do, it is in a separate section. In the past, women did not receive formal education; some countries even today have separate schooling for men and women. Women in general are still expected—even pressured—to play a role that is primarily domestic, centering around marriage and children. Public life is reserved for men, and men have greater freedom to enjoy themselves outside the home.

Some proponents of women's rights find certain passages in the Qur'an distressing. For example, in Sura 4 ("Women") we find the statement, "Men

Female Roles Islamic practice sees male and female social roles as different but complementary. Girls are prepared for traditional female roles, such as wife and mother, although in many Muslim societies today women also work as nurses, doctors, and teachers. Nevertheless, a woman is expected to be circumspect in public, particularly after marriage. In some societies, a woman must be veiled when she goes out of the house, and she allows only her husband and relatives to see her face. Quite conservative societies keep women from jobs outside the home, and women are expected to socialize only with female friends and relatives.

Death Rituals The same general simplicity of marriage ceremonies is also characteristic of death and funerals. Prayers from the Qur'an are recited for the dying person, and after death the body is buried in a plain white shroud. Ideally, for a male who has made the pilgrimage, the shroud is the white robe of Abraham that he wore in Mecca. The face of the deceased is turned

have authority over women because God has made the one superior to the other"; and the Qur'an states that although "good women are obedient," those women who could become disobedient are to be beaten.[20] Critics also point out that before Islam women derived some security from their clan or tribe, and they already had independent property rights and the right to initiate divorce. Islamic reform replaced that with the patriarchal nuclear family and female legal dependence on a male. As an example of this change in the status of women, critics point to the difference between Muhammad's first wife, Khadijah, who was a property owner and strong figure in her own right, and Muhammad's later wife A'isha, who was married at a young age and was expected to be secluded and submissive.

Positions on the role of women are moving in two directions. Under traditionalist pressure, the practice of covering the hair with a scarf (*hijab*) is spreading in some countries, such as Malaysia and Indonesia. At the same time, contemporary thinking in predominantly Muslim countries now makes it possible for women to receive public education, and growing numbers of women have careers and roles in public life.

Muslim women are typically fully covered and sometimes even veiled in public.

toward Mecca at the burial, and the headstone is usually an undecorated stone marker, which signifies equality of all people in death.[21]

Scripture: The Qur'an

The name *Qur'an* (*Koran*) means "recitation" and recalls the origins of these sacred writings in the sermons of Muhammad. The name also suggests the way in which the Qur'an is best communicated—by being recited. Although the Qur'an has been translated into many languages, only the Arabic version is considered to be fully authoritative. The beautiful sounds of the original are considered a part of its nature and are essential to its spiritual power.

The Qur'an is believed to be of divine origin, for it is God's Word, which was revealed to Muhammad during the approximately twenty years from his first revelation in 610 C.E. until the end of his life. Disciples wrote down the words of Muhammad's revelations, but after his death, when people

The simple gravestones of this Islamic cemetery surround a small shrine dedicated to a local saint. The desert location is a vivid reminder of the landscape from which Islam arose.

became concerned that variations would arise and spread, it was thought necessary to establish a single authorized version. Tradition holds that this work was begun by Abu Bakr, Muhammad's first successor, or **caliph** (*khalifa,* "successor"), and that the work was finished in the caliphate of Uthman, which ended in 656 C.E. However, recent scholars question this tradition, and the emergence of the authorized edition is now seen as more complex than was formerly thought. The authorized edition that did emerge became the basis for all later copies.[22]

There is a repetitive quality about the Qur'an, common to memorized material, due largely to the fact that the Qur'an is not a carefully constructed argument divided into segments, nor is it a series of stories. Rather, it is a body of sermons and utterances that repeats images and themes in a natural way.

The Qur'an covers a wide variety of topics and discusses figures who are also found in the Jewish and Christian Bibles: Adam, Eve, Noah, Abraham, Isaac, Jacob, Joseph, Moses, David, Solomon, Jesus, Mary, and others. It also gives practical admonitions about everyday life—about property rights, money, inheritance, marriage, and divorce. It refers to events in the life of Muhammad and to specifically religious beliefs and regulations—angels, divine judgment, fasting, and the pilgrimage. The topics and types of material are often blended together.

Children memorize verses from the Qur'an through group recitation in a Qur'anic school.

The Qur'an has 114 chapters, or **suras.** Each sura has a traditional name, derived from an image or topic mentioned in it, and many of these names are evocative: "The Elephant," "Light," "Dawn," "Thunder," "The Cave," "Smoke," "The Mountain," "The Moon," "The High One." The order of the suras does not reflect the exact order in which they were revealed. Except for the first sura, which is a brief invocation, the suras are arranged so that the longest is given first. This means that the last chapters are extremely short (and the easiest for beginners). The placement is generally, in fact, in reverse chronological order, with some intermixture of periods. The short suras are probably the earliest teachings of Muhammad, while the long ones are the products of his final years, when the details of Islamic life were being revealed to him. The suras of the Qur'an have been compared to leaves that have fallen from a tree: the first-fallen leaves are on the bottom.

Islamic art has been profoundly affected by the Qur'an. Indeed, some handwritten copies of the Qur'an are great artworks in themselves, often filled with gold letters and colorful geometrical designs. Because Islam generally prohibits the making of images, artists have developed the most wonderful calligraphy to record the sacred words of the Qur'an.

Frequently the words of a phrase from the Qur'an are also cunningly interlaced to make integrated designs, which are used to beautify mosques

In the name of God
The Compassionate
The Merciful.
Praise be to God, Lord
of the Universe,
The Compassionate,
the Merciful,
Sovereign of the Day of
Judgment!
You alone we worship,
and to You alone we
turn for help.
—Opening (Al-Fatihah)
of the Qur'an[23]

and religious schools (*madrasas, medersas*). On buildings, passages from the Qur'an are carved in stone or wood or set in mosaic. Of the many writing systems in the world, cursive Arabic, with its wondrous curves, is possibly the most visually beautiful of all. The fluid form of this writing is suggested nicely by the word *arabesque*, a French word that has entered the English language to describe a pattern of interlacing lines that are curving and graceful.

The repetition of phrases and images from the Qur'an is comforting to Muslims, who have heard them recited aloud in daily prayers and in sermons since childhood. Passages are recited regularly on the radio, particularly during Ramadan, and in some countries they are part of the signoff of television broadcasts. Present everywhere, every day, such phrases have a hypnotic resonance. Because Arabic is an especially beautiful language, chanting the Qur'an in Arabic is an art form, and some chanters have even become famous for the beauty of their voices and their interpretation of Qur'anic material.

THE HISTORICAL DEVELOPMENT OF ISLAM

Because his sons had died in infancy, Muhammad died without a clear hereditary male successor.[24] He apparently had not appointed anyone to succeed him,[25] and the result was confusion and an unclear line of succession—a fact that ultimately created significant divisions in Islam, whose effects remain today.

Muhammad had asked Abu Bakr, his friend and the father of his youngest wife, to be the principal leader of prayer. Because of this position, Abu Bakr was recognized as the first caliph. When Abu Bakr died two years later, he was succeeded by Umar, the second caliph, and followed by Uthman, both of whom were assassinated. The fourth caliph was Muhammad's cousin and son-in-law, Ali, the husband of his daughter Fatima. Ali was also assassinated, and control of Islam was taken over in 661 C.E. by his opponents, who ruled from Damascus. This period marks the first and most significant division of Islam, which broke into two factions, Shiite and Sunni (which we will discuss shortly).

The earliest stage of growth of Islam came during the time of the first four rulers, called the orthodox caliphs. These men had been close to Muhammad, and their home was Arabia. A major change occurred, however, as Islam spread outside Arabia. From an early, deliberate simplicity, Islam would now become more urbane and complex.

Expansion and Consolidation

Islam arose at a time (seventh century C.E.) that was congenial to the growth of a new political and religious power. The Byzantine Empire, ruling from Constantinople, had fought repeatedly with the Persian Empire, and both were weakened by the effort. Areas theoretically controlled by the Byzantine emperor, such as regions of northern Africa, were far away from the capital.

The weakness of the Byzantine and Persian Empires—and what Muslims believe was divine purpose—helped Islam quickly expand into their territory. Islamic armies took Syria in 635 C.E. and Persia in 636 C.E. They began to move

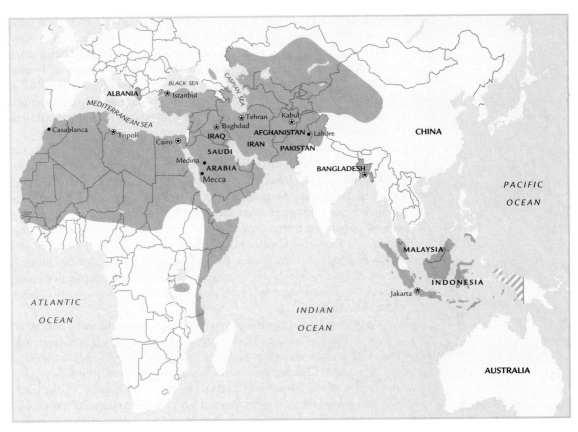

FIGURE 10.1
Map of the Islamic world.

westward, taking control of Egypt in about 640 C.E. The success was intoxicating. Islam spread across most of northern Africa over the next seventy years, and it spread across the Red Sea and Indian Ocean from Arabia to eastern Africa (Figure 10.1).

Islamic forces entered Spain in 711 C.E., when a Muslim general named Tariq landed in the south—the name of Gibraltar ("mountain of Tariq") recalls this event. In fact, Muslim forces might have spread Islam through much of western Europe if they had not been stopped in southern France by the Christian forces of Charles Martel, the grandfather of Charlemagne, in 732 C.E. at the Battle of Tours.[26] This battle—just a hundred years after the death of Muhammad—was one of the defining battles of world history because it prevented the further expansion of Islam into western Europe.

Although Islam was stopped from expanding northward, Islamic rulers remained in Spain for nearly eight hundred years, with capitals in Córdoba and Granada. The Islamic period in Spain is remembered with nostalgia and longing by many, for it is universally thought to have been a paradise-like time, when the arts flourished and Muslims, Jews, and Christians lived together in general harmony. The only other significant incursion into the West in these early centuries was into Sicily, where Islam was a force for about two hundred years.

From 661 C.E. to 750 C.E., Islam was controlled by the Umayyad dynasty—a period called the Damascus caliphate (the caliphate was now hereditary). During this period Islam adopted elements—from architecture to cuisine—that were introduced to Syria by the Roman Empire. It also adopted and refined the administrative and military apparatus of a political state. This fruitful contact with Roman-influenced Syria is just one example of the genius that Islam has shown in absorbing elements from other cultures and giving them new life.

Control of Islam shifted to Baghdad in 750 C.E. under the Abbasid dynasty—a hereditary line that claimed connection to Muhammad. It is often thought that this period, also known as the Baghdad caliphate, which did not end until 1258, was the golden age of Islam—its cultural peak. Just as the Umayyads had adopted Roman-inspired elements from Syria, so the Abbasids adopted much that was Persian—music, poetry, architecture, and garden design. Classical Greek texts on philosophy, science, and the arts were translated into Arabic. Under the influence of Indian artists, the pro-hibition on images was relaxed in court art, and miniature paintings and drawings of dazzling images were created. Baghdad became a world center of civilization and taste.

Islam continued to spread eastward into non-Arab cultures, and Arab domination of Islam waned as Islam spread to present-day Azerbaijan, Kazakhstan, Afghanistan, Pakistan, northern India, and Bangladesh. Islam also spread into western China, where millions of Muslims still live today.

After Baghdad was invaded and sacked by the Mongols in 1258, the polit-ical center of Islam shifted to Egypt. Then in 1453 Muslims captured the ancient Christian capital of Constantinople, making it the center of the Ottoman Empire as well as of the Muslim world until 1921, when the Ottoman Empire ended. During this long period Islam spread, primarily through trade, to southeastern Asia—to what is today Malaysia, southern Thailand, and Indone-sia, which presently has the largest Muslim population of any country in the world. Islam also spread to Mindanao, the southernmost island of the Philippines.

Because of the great size of Islamic territory—a span from Morocco and Spain to Indonesia and the Philippines—completely centralized control was impossible. Thus, secondary centers, which were sometimes totally inde-pendent caliphates, were established. In Spain, the cities of Córdoba and, later, Granada became local political capitals, until Muslims were expelled from Spain in 1492. In India, Delhi became the center of the Muslim Mughal (Mogul) Empire until the British took control of the subcontinent. The fiction of a single caliph ruling all of Islam, however, was kept alive until the Ottoman caliphate in Turkey was dissolved in 1924.

The Shiite and Sunni Division within Islam

Over the centuries of its growth, Islam has experienced several divisions. The most significant division is between the **Shiites** (from *shia*, "faction") and **Sunnis** (*sunna*, "tradition"). Today about ten to fifteen percent of Islam

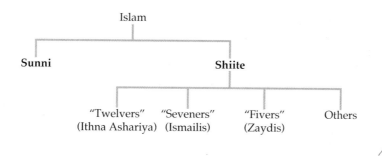

FIGURE 10.2
Branches of Islam

[handwritten notes in right margin: WHAT ARE THE SUNNIs AND THE SHIITs, AND HOW DID THE AS DIVISION OCCUR IN THE ISLAMIC RELIGION? DSQ DDU FRIDAY]

is Shiite, and the remaining majority is Sunni (Figure 10.2). The division began as a political argument over who should succeed Muhammad, but it has widened over the centuries into a division over belief, practice, and general religious approach.

The real argument over succession centered on different conceptions of the caliphate. Some thought that it should be held by a man of Muhammad's tribe (the Quraysh), someone chosen by his peers as being the person who was strongest and most capable of governing. This was a fairly practical notion of leadership. Others, however, saw the caliph as a spiritual leader, and they believed that God gave the spiritual power of the caliph to only those males who were descended directly from Muhammad's immediate family.

Shiite Islam   Shiites derive their name from the word *shia*, which means "faction"—namely, the faction, or party, of Ali, the son-in-law and cousin of Muhammad. We might recall that the legitimacy of the first four successors of Muhammad (Abu Bakr, Umar, Uthman, and Ali) was accepted by most early Muslims. Some early Muslims, however, held that Muhammad had assigned Ali to be his first successor but that a series of political and religious intrigues had initially kept Ali from the caliphate. These disagreements led to further arguments during the period of Uthman and continued even into Ali's eventual caliphate. Muawiya, leader of the Umayyad clan, rejected Ali's leadership, but when arbitration declared Ali to be the legitimate leader, Ali was assassinated. Following Ali's death, some believers held that succession rightfully belonged to his two sons, Hasan and Husayn. Ali's first son, Hasan, renounced his rights to succession; he was poisoned nonetheless by enemies. Ali's second son, Husayn (Hussein), fought against Umayyad control but was killed and beheaded after being defeated in 680 C.E. at the battle of Karbala (or Kerbela), in Iraq. Husayn's death allowed the Umayyad dynasty to maintain control for a hundred years, but it also created strong opposition, which became the Shiite movement. Shiites, who trace Muhammad's line of succession from Ali to Husayn, see Husayn as a martyr whose heroic death is a redeeming sacrifice that invites imitation. His burial site at the main mosque of Karbala in Iraq is considered a major holy place and, for Shiites, is a center of pilgrimage.

Shiite Islam believes that the legitimate succession was hereditary, descending from the immediate family of Muhammad. A God-given, hereditary spiritual power, called the Light of Muhammad, is thought by most

Shiites to have passed to a total of twelve successors, or **Imams.** For them, the first legitimate Imam was Ali. The line ended with the disappearance of the last Imam, Muhammad al-Mahdi, about 900 C.E. According to tradition, he did not die but entered a hidden realm from which he works by guiding Shiite scholars and leaders. Some Shiites believe that he will emerge from this state in the future to help restore Shiite Islam and that his reappearance in the world will usher in a messianic age, heralding the end of the world. There is much speculation about this figure, and he is thought to be sinless. The Ayatollah Khomeini (1900–1989) was considered by some in Iran to be the reappearance of this figure. Because Shiites believe that religious leaders are guided by the last Imam (hereditary successor of Muhammad), their leading clerics possess great authority. (The term *imam* is also used in both branches of Islam to refer to major religious leaders, but the term *ayatollah* is used exclusively in Shiite Islam to refer only to the most important imams.)

There are several divisions within Shiite Islam that differ on how many Imams there were and on the exact line of succession. Most Shiites believe in twelve Imams, as previously mentioned, and thus are sometimes called Twelvers—Ithna Ashariya. But members of one group, the Ismailis, are often called the Seveners because they disagree with the Twelvers about the identity of the seventh Imam; they trace descent from Ismail, whom they consider to be the seventh Imam. Disagreement over the fifth Imam produced a division called the Zaydis (named after Husayn's grandson, Zayd ibn Alia). They are commonly known as the Fivers and live predominantly in Yemen. An unusual group is the Alawites in Syria, whose practice has apparently been influenced by other religions. They believe in reincarnation and, in addition to Muslim holidays, they celebrate Christmas and Epiphany. Smaller groups also exist, some of which (like the Druze of Lebanon) are not considered orthodox Muslims.

Shiite Islam has been attractive to non-Arab Muslims, who have sometimes felt that they were relegated to an inferior role in a religion whose origins were in Arabia. Iran is the center of Shiite Islam because of its large Shiite population. But Iraq is the spiritual home because of the connection with Husayn. Slightly more than half of the Muslims of Iraq are Shiite; they are located primarily in the south of the country. Smaller populations exist in Pakistan, India, Lebanon, Syria, Yemen, and elsewhere.

Sunni Islam Sunni (or Sunnite) Islam, the other great division of Islam, takes its name from the word *sunna* ("tradition," "example"). It refers to the entire body of traditional teachings that are based on the life and teachings of Muhammad, as given in the Qur'an and the authoritative hadiths. Such a great majority of Muslims belong to this branch of Islam that the history of Islam is predominantly Sunni.

Sunni Islam developed to some degree in response to the claims of Shiite Islam. Because Sunnis accepted the legitimacy of the orthodox caliphates, they were compelled to develop a religious, political, legal, and cultural system that was consistent with their beliefs. The system included the caliphs, who were thought to rule in God's name; the Qur'an and hadiths, seen as expressing God's will; the schools and scholarly debate that interpreted the Qur'an and hadiths to apply to everyday life; and the scholars who carried on this debate. Traditional Islam does not separate political life from religious life; it aims to create a public life that is shaped by the Qur'an. Although scholarly debate has been a tradition of Shiite Islam, it is central to the ideology of Sunni Islam, which has often been distinctive in its openness to reason and practicality.

Sunni Islam does not have the clear divisions that we see in Shiite Islam. However, it does have its own divisions. Like any large-scale human development, Sunni Islam has generated interpretations of Islam that run the spectrum from ultraconservative to very liberal. Here we will speak briefly of the most important, and then will return to them at the end of the chapter, when we discuss Islam in the modern world.

One division that is frequently spoken of today involves the Wahhabi sect, a conservative movement. It is named after its founder, Muhammad Ibn Abd al-Wahhab (c. 1703–1791), who was born in Medina. The movement began in Arabia in the eighteenth century, experienced several declines, and underwent a revival in the past century. Its influence is now spreading throughout the Sunni world.

The Wahhabi movement was begun in order to return to an ideal purity that was thought to have existed in early Islam. The Wahhabi movement emphasizes doctrinal orthodoxy, and the name that Wahhabis themselves use for their movement may be translated as "Monotheism." Muhammad, as we know, opposed polytheism and emphasized that worship be reserved for God alone. A continual struggle therefore goes on in Islam over the veneration of deceased teachers, leaders, and holy men. Should they have shrines or special tombs? Should memorial days be celebrated for them? Should they be prayed to or referred to in prayer? The Wahhabis have opposed veneration of deceased people, no matter how saintly, saying that such veneration takes away from the unique worship of the one God. Thus Wahhabis do not even celebrate the birthday of Muhammad, and some oppose visiting his tomb in Medina. (Wahhabis earlier destroyed the shrines of Muhammad and his companions.) The Wahhabi movement also has a strongly moral dimension. Among its goals are simplicity, modesty, separation in public of males and females, and strict prohibition of alcohol.

Another reform movement began in India in 1867. The Deobandi movement is named after the town of Deoband, about 90 miles north of Delhi, where the first school was established. This sect resembles the Wahhabis in its emphasis on a simplified Islam: veneration given solely to God, rejection of devotion to saints, and strong differences between male and female social roles. But it gives great attention to the importance of Muhammad and his early companions, who are thought of as role models for Muslims. It argues that education should be entirely religious—it should be based only on the Qur'an and hadiths. Thus it opposes education in business and modern science.

These fairly stern movements have come into existence because Sunni Islam encompasses so many countries and individuals, with varied degrees of commitment. Within the immense numbers of Sunnis—who, we might recall, make up almost ninety percent of all Muslims—many are simply "cultural Muslims." They have been born into the faith but pick and choose the customs that they wish to follow. The most devout visit a mosque daily and follow all requirements about prayer, charity, and fasting. Others would call themselves moderate Muslims, attending the Friday prayer and doing some daily prayer, but not being otherwise involved. Some limit their practice to prayer at a mosque only on major festivals. Most observe the fast of Ramadan strictly, but some do not. Hence, the appeal of reformers. (We see something similar among Christians who attend church only at Christmas and Easter, or among Buddhists whose religious practice is confined to attending funerals.)

Another common pattern in some Sunni regions is the blending of Islam with older, local elements. One striking example of this is the traditional form of Islam in Indonesia, which is blended with Indonesian animism and Hinduism and includes ceremonies to honor spirits of nature. A news article described one recent service on the island of Java. "'In the name of God, the compassionate, the merciful,' the turbaned priest begins in the orthodox Muslim style. As the annual labuhan ceremony unfolds, he blesses the various offerings the Sultan of Yogyakarta has prepared for Loro Kidul, the goddess of the surrounding seas: silk, curry, bananas, hair and toenail clippings. The goddess, apparently, will be pleased with these items when they are carried in procession to the sea and thrown in, as will another local deity, who receives similar gifts tossed into a nearby volcano."[27] Clearly, this service—which resembles ceremonies that one might also see in Hindu Bali—owes much to the animism and Hinduism that preceded the coming of Islam.

Similar blendings can be found in many countries—particularly those that are away from the centers of orthodoxy, such as in western Africa and Southeast Asia. For many people, Islam is a veneer over much older practices. All mixed forms of Islam, however, can be—and often are—the object of reformers' criticism.

Liberal movements have also regularly emerged, although they have not yet coalesced into a clearly defined sect. Perhaps this is because they have spread largely from books espousing their ideas. These movements argue that Muhammad was a humanitarian reformer and that he himself would reinterpret his insights in light of modern needs. The liberal movements urge, in addition to religious studies, the study of science and business. They point out the early achievements of Islam in medicine, astronomy, and other sciences, and they encourage the continuation of this type of achievement. Perhaps the most influential of these liberal developments was the Aligarh Movement. Its founder, Sayyid Ahmad Khan (1817–1898), began a college at Aligarh, in India, which he devoted to principles of modern education. His ideas, promoted widely by his books and disciples, remain influential. Such ideas inspire like-minded groups in many countries.

Because Mecca is located in Saudi Arabia, it is one center of power in modern Sunni Islam. This (and the influence of a reformist movement) has meant that the government of Saudi Arabia expects its country to be a model of proper Muslim belief and behavior—as tourists and foreign workers who have been forbidden from importing alcohol have sometimes been shocked to discover. This has also led to occasional friction, particularly with Iran, which reflects the long-standing differences between Sunni and Shiite points of view.

Another center of power in the Sunni world is Egypt. Its universities, particularly Al-Azhar in Cairo, give it prestige as an interpreter of Islam; and its large Muslim population makes it politically important in the Muslim world.

SUFISM: ISLAMIC MYSTICISM

Islam began as a rather austere religion. But as it moved beyond Arabia, Islam came into contact with the luxurious lifestyle of the settled old cities in the Near East and northern Africa. The Umayyad dynasty, we recall, ruled Islam for one hundred years from Damascus, which even then was an ancient city. Damascus had become one of the most important cities in the eastern part of the Roman Empire, and it had retained its prominent role under the Byzantine Empire. The caliphate of Damascus simply carried on the aristocratic style of life already present.

Islam had contact not only with sophisticated city dwellers there, but also with the Christian monks and hermits who lived in Israel, Syria, and Egypt. Their simple lives made a great impression on Muslims, who seemed to desire something similar for Islam. Because Islam rejected celibacy as a religious ideal, the Christian model of monasticism could not be imitated exactly. What emerged, however, were lay individuals who cultivated the spiritual life on their own and groups of devotees, loosely organized around charismatic spiritual leaders.

Sufism is the name of an old and widespread devotional movement—or group of movements—in Islam. The name *Sufism* is thought to derive from the Arabic word *suf* ("wool"), because early Sufis wore a simple robe made of common wool. It is possible that this type of ordinary cloth was not only practical but also a visual statement opposing needless luxury. Sufism has been a religious movement that values deliberate simplicity.

But Sufism was not only a reaction against superficial luxury. The movement also grew out of a natural desire to do more than the merely formalistic. As Islam defined itself further, establishing religious practice in even the smallest areas of life, it was possible for some people to think that "keeping the rules" was all there was to being a good Muslim. Sufism, however, recognized that it is possible to "go through the motions" but to leave the heart uninvolved. As a result, Sufism sought the involvement of emotions. Because of this it has been called "the heart of Islam."

Sufi Beliefs

The core of the Sufi movement is its mysticism, its belief that the highest experience a person can have is a direct experience of God. Sufism holds that an individual can, on earth, experience God "face to face." Moreover, it teaches that experiencing God is the whole purpose of life, not something that has to wait until after death.

Sufi mysticism was encouraged by several religious movements that had been active in Egypt and Syria long before Sufism arose in the seventh and eighth centuries C.E. One was Neoplatonism, a mystical philosophical school that began in Alexandria in Egypt with Plotinus (c. 205–270 C.E.). Plotinus's work *The Enneads* spoke of the emergence of the entire cosmos from the One and the journey of the soul as it returns to its divine origin. Another movement that influenced Sufism was Gnosticism, which similarly saw life as a spiritual journey. Gnosticism produced its own literature and interpreted other religious literature symbolically. Christian forms of Neoplatonism and Gnosticism flourished in Syria not long before the Umayyad period and produced such books as *The Divine Names* and *The Mystical Theology* by Pseudo-Dionysius, who is thought to have been a Syrian Christian monk of the sixth century. It is also possible that influences from Hindu mysticism, coming from India into Persia, were behind a great flowering of mystical poetry.

Sufis saw in the Qur'an a number of passages that invited mystical interpretation. These became their favorites. A beloved passage says that Allah is so near to every human being that he is even "closer than the jugular vein."[28] Another favorite passage says, "Whether you hide what is in your hearts or manifest it, Allah knows it."[29]

The image of Muhammad also took on new meaning. To the Sufis, Muhammad was himself a mystic. He lived a life of deliberate simplicity, sought God, and had profound revelations. Because he submitted himself so fully to God's will, in his Night Journey he was carried up to the highest heaven, where he spoke with God as one friend speaking to another friend. This event, the scholar A. J. Arberry remarks, "for the Sufis constitutes the Prophet's supreme mystical experience and an example which they may aspire to follow."[31]

One of the great early Sufi saints was a woman mystic, Rabia (c. 717–801 C.E.), who left behind ecstatic writings that speak of God as her divine lover. She is famous for her statement that she sought God not because of fear of hell or desire for heaven but simply for himself alone. In other words, she sought God not for her sake but for his.

Sufis have commonly spoken about the sense of loss of self (**fana,** "extinction") that occurs in mystical experience: when the self is gone, all that remains is God. Some Sufis have spoken about this experience in language that has been shocking to the orthodox—their mystical descriptions seeming to weaken the distinction between God and his created world, which is strong in orthodox Islam, and even seeming to embrace pantheism, the belief that everything is God. Abu Yazid (d. 875 C.E.), when he was in ecstasy, is reputed to have said, "Glory be to me—how great is my majesty."[32] Al-Hallaj (d. 922 C.E.) was one of the most alarming Sufi figures; he publicly and repeatedly applied a name for God to himself, calling himself *al-Haqq*—"the Truth," "the Real," or "Reality Itself." His comments were so shocking to his contemporaries that they executed him.

Sufis continued to come into conflict with religious authorities who feared that Sufi meeting places would supplant the mosques and that a vague command simply to love would replace the clearer, specific commands of traditional Islam. The veneration of both living and dead Sufi masters also seemed to the orthodox to be opposed to the traditional demand to worship God alone.

Al-Ghazali and Sufi Brotherhoods

The conflict was softened when al-Ghazali (or al-Ghazzali, 1058–1111), a respected scholar and teacher of philosophy and theology in Baghdad, adopted Sufism. Al-Ghazali relates in his autobiography that despite the respect his job gave him he was deeply unhappy. What he was doing did not seem important to his own spiritual life. He was torn between leaving his post or staying on in comfort. At last, he followed an inner voice that demanded that he go "on the road." He did this for more than ten years, traveling in Syria and Arabia and living simply. He eventually returned to Baghdad and formed a brotherhood of Sufis, but he insisted on keeping orthodox law and practice as well. His blend of Sufism with traditional practice, his later books on Sufism, and his scholarly reputation made an indelible mark on Islam. He explained that the Sufi language of "extinction" (fana) is metaphorical, which he compared to "the words of lovers passionate in their intoxication,"[33] or to a diver lost in the sea.[34] His explanations of Sufism and his prestige gave a legitimacy to Sufism that it had not had before. Sufism and orthodoxy no longer needed to run like parallel lines, never meeting. Now they could enrich each other.

After al-Ghazali, more Sufi brotherhoods were founded and the religion became slightly more institutionalized. Disciples gathered around a master. The disciple—in Arabic called *faqir* and in Persian *darwish,* meaning "poor"— would learn a distinctive spiritual discipline (*tariqa*) from the *shaykh,* a Sufi expert. Often a master and his disciples lived in a compound of many buildings, and the life was semimonastic. Laypersons could also be associated with the religious order, even while living an outwardly secular life.[35]

Many Sufi orders emerged and spread widely. One of the most famous was the Maulawiya (in Turkish, Mevlevi), founded by Jalal-ud-Din Rumi (1207–1273). Born in Persia, Rumi eventually settled in what is today Turkey. Rumi's exquisite poetry is now well known beyond the Muslim world. His great work is called *Mesnevi* (or *Mathnawi*). The Maulawiya order became famous for its type of circular dance, which Rumi asserted could assist mystical experience. (The English phrase *whirling dervish* refers to a member of this order, and the Mevlevi dance is still performed in Konya on Rumi's birthday in early December.) Among other orders to emerge, with different emphases, were the Qadiri, Suhrawardi, and Naqshbandi.

Sufi Practice and Poetry

Sufism has incorporated many techniques to encourage spiritual insight, some possibly derived from Hindu yoga or from Christian monastic practice in the Near East. One technique involved jerking the head to encourage an upward flow of blood during prayer. Two other techniques were deep,

Sufis of the Mevlevi order
dance in Turkey.

regular breathing during meditation and the repetition of the ninety-nine names of Allah (**dhikr**), sometimes counted on a rosary, to enable a constant remembrance of God. Some groups used music and others used spinning or dancing in circles or occasionally ingesting wine and psychedelic plants to alter consciousness. Some groups reportedly howled and walked on fire, among other unusual techniques. And all groups made use of allegorical interpretations of Qur'anic passages and of Islamic practices (such as the pilgrimage to Mecca), which they saw as living metaphors for their mystical search.

Sufism has also used poetry in the same allegorical and symbolic ways. When read one way, a poem might resemble the lyrics of a romantic song. Read another way, the same poem might suggest a longing of the spirit for God, a search for God, or the ecstasy of final union with God. Sufism has inspired some of the world's greatest poets, as famous in the Muslim world as are Shakespeare and Goethe in Western countries.

Until recent decades, only one Muslim poet was well known in English-speaking countries. Omar Khayyám (c. 1048–1122), who was also an astronomer and mathematician, gained fame in the West from a late-Victorian translation (by Edward FitzGerald) of the long poem *The Rubaiyat*. Many people are familiar with "a loaf of bread, a jug of wine, and thou," which is paraphrased from the poem and brings to mind a romantic picnic. But a Sufi could interpret a loaf of bread symbolically as the depth of ordinary reality, the jug of wine (intoxicating but suspect) as ecstasy, and "thou" as the divine *Thou*—God. Through translations, many great Sufi poets, such as Rumi, Hafiz (c. 1325–1390), and Jami (1414–1492), are nowadays becoming better known and appreciated.

There is a warmth about Sufism that appeals to the ordinary layperson, and some Sufi groups have served as fraternal societies in people's lives—providing comfort, helping the poor, and even burying the dead. Sufism's characteristic warmth and practicality helped Islam spread to countries far from its place of origin, such as Malaysia and Indonesia.

The Sufi connection with common people, however, has sometimes made the orthodox think of Sufism as a superstitious folk religion. For example, Sufi practice has encouraged devotion to deceased shaykhs and has promoted visits to their tombs, hoping for miracles. To the orthodox, this recalls the Christian veneration of saints, who may be prayed to for favors—a practice that, according to the orthodox, takes attention away from the sole worship of God. Sufis also have sometimes substituted their spiritual practice for the regular daily prayer expected of all Muslims, and some Sufis have held themselves exempt from certain religious laws. Therefore, despite the esteem generated by al-Ghazali and the Sufi poets, Sufism is still held in disregard by some and is not always practiced openly by its devotees. Although mosques are plentiful and visible in the Islamic world, Sufi meeting places are hard to find, as are individuals who will actually admit to being Sufis. Luckily, however, Sufism has been buoyed in recent years by a growing appreciation of Sufi poetry and practice.

PERSONAL EXPERIENCE: RAMADAN IN MOROCCO

During my first trip to Europe as a college student, I found myself spending a very cold February in "sunny" Spain. No one had told me that snow falls in Madrid. But there it was, pure, white, everywhere. The air was so cold in our unheated youth hostel that everyone slept under mounds of blankets. Trudging back to the hostel one evening, ice in my veins, I realized that if I were to survive, I had to go south—quickly.

I took a train from Madrid, then a ferryboat across to Morocco, and finally a bus inland. At first the land was sandy, dry, and flat, but soon the countryside grew greener, with small hills and low trees. I saw children watching over flocks of sheep, and donkeys pulling carts and carrying food on their backs. Animals seemed to be as much a part of everyday life as cars are in Los Angeles. As I traveled south, Morocco appeared to be much like Spain, except that many of the men were dressed in long, hooded robes, and I could hear the call to prayer regularly during the day and early evening.

I reached Fès at the beginning of Ramadan. Old Fès is a traditional, Islamic-style city on a hill, brimming with mosques, shrines, and medersas (religious schools). Its streets, just wide enough for two people to pass, twisted and curved. Mules laden with saddlebags rushed past, their drivers yelling, "Balek!"—"Watch out!" On each side of the narrow streets, tiny shops sold fruit, vegetables, sweets, spices, perfumes, robes, brass, and leather. All kinds of fruit were piled high; spices were arranged in neat pyramids of red, yellow, and orange; and sweet desserts made of honey and almonds were heaped in thick stacks. People were buying for the evening meal that would end the day's fasting, but I never saw anyone eat or drink during the daytime. In the evening, the recitation of the Qur'an could be heard loudly, coming from radios placed in shops and on windowsills.

Many shops sold spiral candles with paper decorations on them, meant as offerings at shrines. At a shop where I stopped to buy a candle, the old owner was reading a copy of the Qur'an. I was hesitant to disturb him, but then two young customers came and helped. They each bought a candle, too, then introduced themselves. Moulay and Noureddine were students in Casablanca and were in Fès on vacation. Moulay was Berber, a member of the native tribal people of Morocco, and his parents lived in the north, near Oujda. Noureddine was Arab, from Ourzazate in the south. He told me proudly that his name (which he pronounced *nur-deen'*) means "light of religion." The two friends were making a pilgrimage together to the main religious sights of Fès, Meknes, and places in central Morocco. Soon their pilgrimage would end with a visit to the shrine of the saint after whom Moulay was named, in the hilltop town of Moulay-Idriss. They invited me to join them, and I accepted gladly.

All along the way we talked about religion—about my beliefs and theirs. They explained that their way of practicing Islam was not strict. They did not pray at all the times of daily prayer, and they did not keep all the customs. But, they told me, they prayed at the public prayer on Fridays, and they kept Ramadan. I could see that: they rose before dawn to eat and would not eat or drink again till after sunset. They kindly encouraged me to eat whenever I was hungry, thinking I must be weaker than they were. "You have no practice in fasting," Noureddine explained. They recommended, however, that during the day I not let others see me eat the bread and oranges or drink the water that I carried in my shoulder bag.

From our conversations, I discovered that Moulay and Noureddine were both interested in Sufism. Commenting on its teachings, Moulay said, "Allah is not something always clear and certain, like a tree or a mountain, that you only have to look at to see. Allah is a reality that you have to look for and discover for yourself. The word *Allah* is an invitation, like an invitation to a meeting or a party. You don't quite know what will happen until you go there yourself. I practice my religion to see what will happen. I think you have to do it in order to know it."

The large roofs of the main shrine stand out as one looks down upon the pilgrimage town of Moulay-Idriss.

Noureddine pointed to some boys on the road who were riding bicycles. "Maybe it's like that," he said. "You don't know how to ride a bicycle until you do it. In fact, it looks a little crazy. It even looks impossible. But when you do it, it works, and you get where you need to go."

Our first vision of Moulay-Idriss was from a distance: a white town at the top of two steep hills. "They say it's shaped like a camel's back," said Noureddine. When we arrived, the town was mobbed with people. Luckily, we found a small place to stay and left our things there. We then walked down to the entrance to the shrine, the burial site of Moulay Idriss I (d. 791 C.E.), a descendant of Muhammad and an early Muslim ruler of Morocco. My friends bought colorful green candles, decorated with cut paper, and asked me to wait for them. They went up a long corridor and disappeared; a small sign high up on the wall said, "No entry for non-Mussulmans." I passed the time observing people's faces and their clothing. One thing that struck me was the contrasting nature of some women's appearance: their faces were modestly veiled, almost to the point of being entirely covered, yet their gowns attracted one's attention because of their bright colors—purple, red, yellow, chartreuse.

When my friends returned, they took me up a seemingly endless flight of stairs to the top of the town. We looked down on square towers with roofs of green tile and across to the beautiful green mountains beyond. "That is the shrine down there," Moulay said, "but I'm sorry you cannot go inside."

465

Noureddine smiled but looked serious. Then he had an idea. He asked me, "Wouldn't you like to become a Muslim, too?"

ISLAMIC LAW AND PHILOSOPHY

Islamic thought focuses on both practice and belief. It asks, How should I live my life according to God's will, and how am I to understand and relate to God? Over the first five hundred years of Islam, these questions were debated intensely, and some basic principles were acknowledged. Islam also recognized that there could be reasonable disagreement. Thus, various schools of opinion emerged.

Because the Qur'an does not give specific laws for every possible human situation, Muslims have found it necessary to discuss how to interpret the Qur'an. Muslims believe that the Qur'an offers principles for correct guidance in all of human life; as such, regulations for specific instances have to be worked out by considering parallels and utilizing those basic principles.

In addition to the primary authority of the Qur'an, the hadiths—other people's recollections of Muhammad's words and actions—have been consulted. The most authoritative collection of recollections has been that of al-Bukari (died c. 870), which contains almost three thousand hadiths. The use of hadiths enlarged the body of material that could be drawn on for guidance, but it also created problems of its own. Disagreement about which hadiths were genuine prevented their universal acceptance. Also, even apparently worthy hadiths were not always consistent with each other.

Islam has a long history of scholarly debate. Over the centuries (from the eighth century on), four major schools of Islamic law have emerged in Sunni Islam and three schools in Shiite Islam, each school differing on what it has looked to as an authoritative guide for making judgments on particular cases: On what grounds may a wife request a divorce? Can a village without a mosque be taxed and forced to build one? How many witnesses are necessary to legitimize a marriage? and so on. In arriving at decisions, scholars have relied (to varying degrees) on a variety of things: the Qur'an (which has been interpreted both literally and symbolically), the hadiths, logic, precedents, analogy (*qiyas*), the consensus of early jurists, and the decisions of religious scholars.

Islamic Law and Legal Institutions

Islamic law, called **Sharia,** is the entire body of laws that guides the believer in this life. The legal ideal of Islam is different from what is now considered the norm in many countries. Most modern industrialized countries expect laws to reflect a kind of civilized minimum, something that all citizens, of any background or belief, can be expected to accept and obey in their public life. Often these laws have a distant religious background or origin, but they are framed for very diverse populations and are deliberately secular in nature. We see this distinction in the United States, for example, in debates about prayer in public schools. In industrialized countries, the two realms—secular and religious—generally exist somewhat apart.

The traditional Islamic ideal, however, does not separate religious and secular spheres, and this ideal is the subject of intense argument in strongly Muslim countries today. In the traditional Islamic ideal, laws bring everyday life into ever-closer harmony with the regulations of the Qur'an and traditional teaching.

Traditional Islam is theocratic, seeking the "rule of God" in all aspects of everyday life, for in its view there is one God and one correct religion. Nature is orderly because it follows the laws of God spontaneously—for example, gravitation governs the movement of the planets and the change of tides. Similarly, in Islamic thought God presents human beings with laws of human order. There cannot be different sets of laws for different human beings; otherwise, chaos would ensue. The laws of God must be obeyed not only because they are his commands but also because they lead to human fulfillment.

Of course, this ideal of a single religion guiding an entire society has rarely been attained. Muhammad himself recognized that there must be exceptions. Although he demanded that people who followed tribal folk religion convert to Islam, he was more lenient about Jews and Christians. In fact, he allowed Jews and Christians to continue their own laws and practices in the hope that they would eventually convert to Islam voluntarily. In Muhammad's eyes, Jews and Christians were "people of the book" and were thus considered as followers of the same general "religion of Abraham" as were Muslims—although living at a less perfect level.

Nonetheless, Islam has always held that the "rule of God," as presented in the Qur'an and Muslim tradition, is universally binding, and Islam teaches the ideal that the devout Muslim will spread knowledge and practice of the will of God. This ideal manifests itself in the common understanding of the goal of **jihad** ("struggle"), which because of its importance has sometimes been called the "sixth pillar of Islam." In fact, Muhammad distinguished two kinds of jihad: the "greater jihad," which is the struggle within oneself to overcome moral failings, and the "lesser jihad," which is the effort to spread Islamic belief and morality in the outside world. In reality, however, the notion of jihad has popularly been applied primarily to the second meaning. Sometimes the notion of jihad has been used to legitimize a militant fight for what is considered to be true and right.

Some governments, such as that of Iran since 1979, have imposed a theocratic rule. There and in a few other strongly Muslim countries, the rules of the Qur'an and the rulings of religious scholars have had great political power. Although Islam does not have an official clergy, it does have religious specialists and scholars (*ulama, mullahs*) who have various levels of influence, both religious and political.

Islamic Philosophy and Theology

Many profound questions emerged quite naturally as early thinkers began to consider the basic beliefs of Muhammad and of Islam. One of the first questions regarded intellectual investigation itself. Is a good Muslim allowed to question religious topics? Does the philosophical study of religion (*kalam,* "theology") hurt a person's spiritual life, or can it deepen it? Do faith and reason contradict each other, or can they coexist happily?

In theory, there is a distinction between philosophy and theology. Philosophy considers all questions by the light of reason alone, without making use of religious revelation. Theology, however, mixes philosophy and religion, for it uses philosophy to investigate religious doctrines. In reality, pure philosophy is rather difficult to find, for the religion of a surrounding culture will inevitably color both the questions and the methods of its philosophers. This happened frequently, as we will see, from the beginning of Islam.

Early thinkers posed important questions that had to be addressed. Some questions were simply intriguing, while others presented serious philosophical problems. For example, the Qur'an calls God both just and merciful. But how is it possible to be strictly just and also to be really merciful? Doesn't one virtue exclude the other? Or a second question: If God is truly all-powerful, how can a human being really be free to make a choice? Doesn't God make everything happen? And even when human beings think they are acting by their own choice, isn't God really doing the choosing? Or another question: If God is all-loving, why does he allow bad things to happen? Wouldn't an all-loving God prevent evil things from happening in the world? The list of many similar questions goes on.

Some philosophical questions arose early as a result of studying the Qur'an. Others, however, emerged as Islam encountered the philosophies and religions of its neighbors, such as when Greek philosophical works were first translated into Arabic and were then taught in the great schools of Baghdad, Córdoba, and Cairo. Aristotle, for example, taught that the universe was eternal. But didn't this conflict with the Qur'an's vision of God as Creator of the universe? Further questions arose when Islam moved into India and had contact with a monistic Hindu spirituality. Certain schools of Hindu thought taught that everything, ultimately, was God. But didn't this conflict with the Muslim notion that Allah, as Creator, is different from his creation?

In general, there have been two philosophical poles within Islam. The more liberal view values reason and maintains that everything can be examined intellectually. It argues that human beings are basically free and that reason is a God-given gift that illuminates and complements faith. The other, more conservative view is suspicious of reason, which it sometimes sees as an expression of false human pride. It therefore values intellectual submission, believing that ultimately neither God nor anything else can be explained fully by reason. It tends to see the entire universe, including human lives, as being strongly determined by God. Like a pendulum, the history of Islamic thought has swung back and forth between these two poles.

One of the first intellectual movements, the eighth-century Mutazilite school, was an early form of rationalism. In attempts to defend the young religion of Islam, this movement tried to answer several perplexing questions. When the Qur'an speaks of God in human terms (for example, the "face of God"), does this mean that God has a body, or is the language simply symbolic of God's characteristics? And regarding the Qur'an itself, what is its ultimate origin and nature? Is the Qur'an an earthly creation of

God? Or is the Qur'an—because it is God's thought and words—uncreated and eternal? The Mutazilites argued that the anthropomorphic speech of the Qur'an is symbolic and that the Qur'an is not eternal but was created by God. But the Mutazilites were opposed by other thinkers.[36]

The voice of conservatism responded firmly about a century later in the work of al-Ashari (died c. 935 C.E.). He spoke of God as being entirely sovereign and transcendent, and he stressed the power of God to determine human lives. It is said that al-Ashari was one of the most important influences on the common Muslim emphasis on the absolute power of God.

The value that Islam has placed on philosophical reasoning appears in the works of two Muslim thinkers who are considered prominent figures of world philosophy. They are Ibn-Sina (980–1037) and Ibn-Rushd (1126–1198), known in medieval European philosophy by their Latin names Avicenna and Averroës, respectively. Because of their interest in medicine and the natural sciences, as well as philosophy, they thought that using reason to explore nature would give insight into nature's Creator.

Perhaps the most influential philosophical formulations, however, were more conservative. They came from al-Ghazali (mentioned earlier) and his intellectual disciple al-Arabi (d. 1240), who rejected rationalism in favor of the conservative approach of al-Ashari. In his books *The Incoherence of the Philosophers* and *The Revival of the Religious Sciences,* al-Ghazali showed the inconsistency of several philosophers who based their thought on Aristotle's. He criticized philosophy for generating arguments and false pride, and he distanced himself from both rational theology and legalism. The elements that he thought to be the core of religion, instead, were submission of the heart to God and direct religious experience—ideals attainable by anyone, not just by philosophers.

Al-Arabi continued this line of thought, but, influenced also by Sufism, he moved even further in a mystical, monistic direction. For him, all apparently separate realities were images of God, and all activity was ultimately the activity of God.[37] Submission to God meant a lived awareness of God's active presence in all things.

ISLAM AND THE ARTS

Islam has had a unique influence on the arts. Its prohibition of much figural art, its love of the chanted word, its weekly public worship, and its focus on the Qur'an have channeled the inspiration of its artists in intriguing directions and helped create works of great imagination.

Architecture

Perhaps the greatest art form of Islam is its architecture. When we think of Islam, we envision tall towers and immense domes. It takes only a few visits—to the Umayyad Mosque in Damascus, to the Sultan Ahmet "Blue Mosque" in Istanbul, to the former grand mosque of Córdoba, or to the

Minarets were added to Istanbul's Aya Sofia when it was converted from a Christian church into a mosque. It is now a museum.

brand-new Hassan II mosque of Casablanca—to sense the architectural genius of Islam, whose uniquely shaped spaces express beauty in what is vast and empty.

Islamic architecture expresses itself most importantly in the place of public prayer, the mosque (*masjid,* meaning a space for prostration). Because a mosque can be any building or room where Islamic prayer is offered, its design can be quite simple, especially in villages or in cities where the Muslim population is small. Grand mosques, however, provide greater opportunity for artistic attention. A mosque has at least one formal entry to the compound, where shoes are to be taken off and left outside. Because purification is necessary before prayer, there is at least one fountain inside the compound for washing one's hands, face, neck, and feet. There is a high pulpit indoors or outdoors for sermons—although as an act of humility the speaker does not stand at the very top. Worshipers stand and prostrate themselves in rows, facing the mihrab (the special marker that indicates the direction of Mecca). The floor is usually covered with rugs or mats. Frequently, there are covered porches for protection from the sun and rain. Other wings or buildings—used for schoolrooms and libraries—are often a part of the complex. Outdoors there is also usually a minaret—a tall tower, either round or square, from which people are called to prayer. Although only one minaret is needed, there are frequently two;

Complex geometrical designs, the element of balance, and the color turquoise are characteristic features of Islamic architectural design.

in grand mosques there might be four or even six. Inside the minaret is a staircase, which leads up to a balcony near the top, from which the muezzin can chant his call.

Most styles of religious architecture in the world emphasize ornamentation, but the aesthetic principles of Islamic religious architecture are more austere. This simplicity enhances one's appreciation of space and balance, particularly in the mosque and its attendant structures.

The value of empty space is one of an art student's first lessons. Some paintings, for example, are partially devoid of paint or drawing, and although those parts seem to have no function, the student learns that the empty space actually acts in harmony with whatever is depicted. The space gives rest to the eye and directs the viewer's focus. In art this necessary emptiness is called *negative space*. In architecture, negative space is the space above or beside or around a building. The building shapes the space within and without, and both the space and the building work together to balance each other. Large mosques especially demonstrate a skillful use of negative space, such as in the shaped space between a dome and a minaret.

Because many mosques, particularly in dry climates, have extensive open courtyards, the negative space of most importance is the sky. It is beautifully balanced and complemented by the columns, arches, and walkways below. Other types of mosques, particularly in wetter climates, are almost entirely enclosed, frequently covered with one or more domes. But even

inside, a person can experience the beauty of negative space—especially in the large mosques of Turkey that are primarily domed buildings. A vast dome, although it shelters one from the sky, is itself like the sky in its feeling of expansiveness. The internal and external shaping of space also helps one experience the divine, for in Islam space is an important symbol of God, invisible but present everywhere.

In Islamic architecture, balance is another important feature, especially as it relates to the use of color. Perhaps because Islam spread throughout hot, sunny regions, the most typical color of its architecture is white, to reflect the sunlight. White is balanced by black, particularly in the dark shadows that are created by windows and doors, covered porches, and colonnades. Sometimes, too, alternating lines of black and white are painted on walls for decorative effect.[38] This white-black contrast is a fundamental theme of much Islamic architecture. A second color scheme contrasts blue with gold, often in the form of ceramic tiles on domes, where the dome is covered in one color and its base is covered in another. (Good examples are the golden Dome of the Rock in Jerusalem and the blue domes of Isfahan in Iran.) The blue can vary in shade from sea-blue to blue-green. The Islamic tendency toward the color blue-green is hinted at by the original meaning of the word *turquoise*, which in French means "Turkish."

◀ The interior design of the Taj Mahal (*left*) and the elaborately grilled door and window of a mosque in Casablanca (*right*) show elements of Islamic art intended to create a paradise in the imagination.   ▶

Fine Art

To talk of "Islamic art" might seem a contradiction in terms, owing to the prohibition in Muslim religious art against making images of human beings or animals. Nonetheless, Islam has created a rich tradition of pictorial art.

Paradise as a Theme in Art One theme that seems to have inspired much Islamic art—as well as architecture and garden design—is the theme of paradise. In the Qur'an and the Muslim imagination, paradise is quite concrete and sensuous. It is not just a heaven of diaphanous angels, singing hymns and resting on wispy clouds. Paradise is more like a fertile oasis or an enclosed garden. The Qur'an repeatedly says that paradise is "watered by running streams."[39] Wildflowers are at our feet, and we sit under date palms and other fruit trees, whose fruit is ready to be eaten.[40] In the afternoon, we feel cooling breezes. Paradise is safe, too. (Literally, the word *paradise,* from Middle Iranian, means "wall around.") We can stay outdoors in this garden, enjoying nature without fear.

This image of paradise in Islamic art often appears in symbolic form in the prayer carpet. Although the prayer carpet is not usually recognized as religious art, it is to Islam what stained-glass windows are to Christianity. Both are objects of contemplation for people at prayer. Interestingly, both manifest the same fundamental color scheme—every shade of red and blue. A major difference between the stained-glass window and the prayer carpet is that the latter does not depict human images. Instead of portraying figures of saintly persons, prayer carpets often contain a symbolic image of the garden of paradise. At the center of the carpet might be a stylized fountain that sends water in straight lines to each of the four directions and then around the entire border, the four sides of the border representing the walls of the garden. The rest of the carpet might be filled with stylized flowers. To walk into a large mosque where immense carpets are laid out side by side, such as the Umayyad Mosque in Damascus, gives the feeling of entering a magical garden.

The paradise theme is carried over in Muslim architecture as well: slender pillars resemble the trunks of trees, and arches that come to a point suggest adjoining tree branches. Ceilings often suggest a night sky full of stars: blue ceramic tiles may form a backdrop for golden six-pointed stars, clustered in complex patterns. Or delicate wood and plaster stalactites hang from the ceiling, suggesting light coming from heaven. The paradise theme is sometimes evident in and around mosque buildings, shrines, palaces, and even homes. It may express itself in fountains and narrow canals, in a grove of orange trees, in a garden full of fragrant plants (such as rose and jasmine), or in a decorated porch from which one can enjoy the sights and sounds of the garden.

The Islamic love of the Qur'an often continues the theme of paradise. The words of the Qur'an are symbolically the sounds of heaven: they are the voice of God, heard not only by human beings but also by angels. In spoken and chanted form, they fill the air and remind us of God and paradise. In written form, they decorate the domes, doors, walls, and windows

The Generalife gardens, constructed when Granada was the center of Islamic power in Spain, illustrate the Muslim ideal of paradise.

to remind us of the divine presence. The care and beauty that are lavished on handwritten copies of the Qur'an extend the sense of paradise: because the Qur'an is the book of God's speech, to open the Qur'an is to psychologically enter God's presence. Thus, beautiful writing has become an integral part of the Islamic art of creating paradise on earth.

Despite what has been said about the Islamic love of simplicity, Islamic art, particularly in manuscript writing and illustration, demonstrates an appreciation for ornamentation. Extremely fine, handwritten copies of the Qur'an feature pages surrounded by filigree. Similarly, geometrical designs on doors and walls create an effect of hallucinatory complication. Although Islamic ornamentation is complex, it is usually also subtle, allowing the eye to wander and inviting the mind to lose itself in the experience. Because many geometrical designs have no visual center, experiencing them can be like looking at stars or waves, inducing a gentle ecstasy.

Exceptions to the Prohibition against Image Making The prohibition against the making of images has been widely observed in Islam, but there have been three important exceptions. One is the imagery surrounding Muhammad's Night Journey—his ascent to the highest heaven. As shown by many Muslim artists, Muhammad rises through the air on his human-headed horse Buraq. Both are surrounded by golden flames and by hovering angels. As a bow to the Muslim prohibition against image making, however, Muhammad's face often appears as a rather ghostly blank space.

The second exception to image making is a whole category of art called Persian miniatures. (This tradition was continued in Turkish and Indian Mughal art as well.) Influenced by artistic traditions from nearby India, the Persian court commissioned innumerable small paintings of its personages and its activities—rulers on horseback, picnicking courtiers, and lovers enjoying the afternoon in a garden pavilion. The topics are usually secular, but the treatment has that same hallucinatory quality—evoked by complex designs—that we see in Islamic mosaic, stucco, and woodwork. Thousands of tiny flowers seem to carpet the meadows, and tens of thousands of leaves cover the trees. The eye becomes lost in infinity.

The third exception to image making belongs to the realm of folk art. Pilgrims who return successfully from Mecca have a natural pride in their accomplishment, as have their families. Often they will make or commission a picture of their pilgrimage on the way to or from Mecca—nowadays looking happily out of an airplane. Sometimes this picture is even placed outside the house, near the front door, where it cannot be missed.

Over the past century, the prohibition against making images has begun to break down. Statues are still not made, but photographs are common, often of religious leaders and family members. It is possible nowadays to see carpets and wall hangings woven with recognizable human figures.

ISLAM AND THE MODERN WORLD

Modern life presents great challenges to traditional Islam. Industrial work schedules make daily prayer and other religious practices difficult; women are demanding total equality with men and complete independence; and individualism is weakening family ties and social responsibility. Islam is being pulled in many directions.

Islam and Contemporary Life

Soon after its beginnings, Islam became and remained a world power for about eight hundred years. During that period, Islamic universities—in Baghdad, Córdoba, and Cairo—were among the great centers of learning and scientific investigation in the world. Islamic cities were centers of civilized living. During this period, Islamic strength contrasted with the general weakness of western Europe: the Roman Empire had ceased to exist in the West by the late fifth century, not long before Muhammad was born. Ruling from Constantinople, the Byzantine emperors continued the Eastern Roman Empire in weakened form. Islam's last great military victory was the conquest of Constantinople, and thus of the Eastern Roman Empire, in 1453. Islam continued to spread and consolidate eastward, as far as Indonesia and the Philippines, but after that its expansion slowed.

Toward the end of the fifteenth century the pendulum of power swung in the opposite direction. While Islam became fairly settled in its territory, western Europe began to expand its control. Significant turning points were Columbus's journeys to the New World, beginning in 1492, and Vasco da

Gama's journey around Africa and his arrival in India in 1498. These explorations changed the patterns of trade. Before then, trade was conducted primarily by land routes, which were frequently controlled by Muslim rulers. Now journeys could be made by ship, a form of travel that greatly enlarged the opportunity for travelers to influence others. These journeys were just the beginning of powerful waves of expansion by European traders, soldiers, political figures, and Christian missionaries. Coupled with circumnavigation were the growth of scientific understanding during the European Renaissance of the fifteenth and sixteenth centuries, the Enlightenment of the seventeenth and eighteenth centuries, and the development of technology during the Industrial Revolution of the eighteenth and nineteenth centuries. As Islamic and European cultures came into more frequent contact with each other, their differing values and social ideals led to conflict. That conflict continues today, although now the sources are less military and more cultural. The spread of European-American culture (called Coca-Colonization by some critics) is manifested in many forms: clothing (blue jeans, T-shirts), food (hamburgers, pizza, french fries), music (rock and rap), technology, modern Western medicine, and sociopolitical philosophy (industrial capitalism, democracy, nationalism, and individualism). Although Muslim countries have adopted Western technology and medicine, individualistic Western social behavior has caused them alarm. Modern Islam is an often unwilling partner in a tug-of-war that has been going on with European culture for hundreds of years.

Here, through one of the gates of the ancient city of Fès, we see the juxtaposition of the traditional minarets with a universal symbol of modern culture—bottled soft drinks.

The Challenge of Secularism   The most difficult of the Western models for Islam to accept is secularism. The word *secularism* comes from a Latin word for "world" (*saeculum*) and implies a focus on this world, without reference to values or entities beyond this world. Secularism seeks to create political institutions that are independent of any established religion.

Secularism is not necessarily antireligious. In its political form, it actually developed in part for religious reasons—to avoid religious fights and to enable all religions to flourish. The point of the secular model was not to destroy religion but to allow all religions to exist without hindrance from any one religion or from government. But secularism is based on a governmental system of laws, courts, and legislatures that operate independently from any religion. That ideal of independence from religion has caused dismay in many Islamic countries.

Science has also promoted secularism. Although investigators such as Isaac Newton (1642–1727) once looked into the properties of light in order to better understand the nature of God, scientists nowadays rarely carry on their work in this spirit. Science pursued for its own sake has led to a view of the universe that does not include God, as either its creator or its moral guide. In this worldview, God is not necessarily excluded but is simply not mentioned. (To appreciate this fact, look for the word *God* in a textbook on biology, chemistry, or physics.) But Islamic tradition holds that to view the universe apart from God is to live without God.

A Range of Solutions   One of the great challenges for Islam, therefore, has been to adopt from the West what is obviously useful, to avoid what is dangerous, and to continue holding on to what it thinks valuable. There are a variety of intriguing solutions to this challenge—a few are extreme responses, yet the majority are attempts at compromise.

Turkey has arrived at the most clearly secular solution. For centuries, Islam had a caliph, God's representative on earth, who united in himself religious and political power. As we discussed earlier in the chapter, the last caliphate existed for centuries in Istanbul. But in 1924, trying to build a modern country, Kemal Atatürk (1881–1938) dissolved the caliphate and created a new secular nation, modeled after the European pattern. He replaced the Arabic alphabet with the Roman alphabet for writing Turkish; he created a legal system independent of Muslim religious authorities; and he set up a democratic form of government that allowed women to vote. In his desire to Europeanize, he even outlawed men's wearing the fez (a traditional round hat) and women's wearing the veil, and he encouraged European styles of clothing. Turkey has generally kept to this secular vision, although religious conservatives make regular attempts to establish an Islamic government. Furthermore, Atatürk's hope of transforming Turkey into a European-style nation has not yet been fully realized.

At the other end of the spectrum is Saudi Arabia. When Saudi Arabia was declared an independent nation in 1932, the Qur'an was named the constitution of the country and the strict Wahhabi interpretation of Islam became dominant. There are no movie theaters and alcohol is forbidden. Women may not drive, they must be covered by the cloak-like *abaya* in public, and they go to their own schools, separated from men. Religious police (*mutawa*) ensure conformity to these rules. The Wahhabi emphasis on simplicity can be seen in its recommendation that followers dress simply and that their mosques be plain, with no minarets or decoration. They have carried this to Bosnia, where Wahhabi Muslims from abroad are in charge of rebuilding mosques damaged or destroyed by war. Because of the influence and financial aid of Saudi Arabia, the Wahhabi interpretation of Islam is spreading in many countries, particularly in those where religious schools have been financed by Saudi citizens and government agencies.

Iran, because it no longer has a king (shah), is even more clearly a theocracy. It has been influential in the Muslim world as a modern attempt to create an Islamic state. The situation was once quite different. For decades, Iran seemed to be moving inexorably toward westernization. After World War II, the ruling families of Iran traveled regularly to Europe (particularly to France) and adopted European ways of thinking and living. For example, the royal family spoke French and English fluently, and for the 1971 celebration of the twenty-fifth centennial of the Persian Empire, the food for the reception was flown in from Maxim's restaurant in Paris. Iran also had close political ties to the United States, and Tehran was an international city, a hub for most major airlines. All this ended in 1979, when an exiled mullah, the Ayatollah Khomeini, returned to Iran and Shah Mohammad Reza Pahlavi went into exile himself. Iran rapidly became a Muslim theocracy. A new constitution was written by the religious authorities, who also held a majority of the seats in the legislature. Khomeini had a new post created for himself as "legal guide," from which he could oversee and validate all legal and political developments. Mosques became centers of civil as well as religious activity; women were forced to veil themselves in public; and alcohol was strictly forbidden. Iran thus became a fully Muslim state.

Most countries that are primarily Muslim, however, lie uncomfortably between the two poles of secular government and theocracy. Increasingly, conservative Islamic groups nudge them in the direction, like Iran's, of becoming Islamic states. Liberal movements in Islam are accused of giving in too much to modern secular thought and abandoning Islam. Consequently, countermovements, sometimes violent, have arisen; they attempt to create a path that makes Islam relevant and active in the modern world. This was the goal, for example, of the Islamic Brotherhood, founded in Egypt in 1928. Blamed for the assassination of President Anwar Sadat in 1981, it is now officially banned in Egypt, but it is active there nonetheless.

Egypt is typical of those countries that have to work out a compromise, partly out of necessity. At least ten percent of its population is Coptic Christian, and Jews and Greeks living primarily in Alexandria play an important role in Egyptian shipping and business. Moreover, because Egypt is dependent on foreign tourism for its economic survival, it has at least a limited acceptance of alcohol in tourist hotels. The Egyptian government has generally recognized that solely Islamic laws would not work well for everyone. However, fundamentalist groups (such as the Muslim Brotherhood) offer a different vision—of an Egyptian Islamic state, governed by Sharia. Because they believe that tourism brings influences that are considered corrupting, these groups tolerate or even sponsor attacks of the sort that have sometimes been made on tourist groups in the past decade.

In many countries the debate is becoming broader and the volume rising. In India, conflict between Muslims and Hindus has broken out frequently, particularly over the status of Kashmir (which is predominantly Muslim, but ruled by India) and about mistreatment of each group by the other. The destruction of a mosque at Ayodhya by Hindus in 1992 became a flashpoint. Mob violence at the time caused the death of about two thousand people, and another thousand people were killed in 2002.

In Pakistan, the government tries to find a balance between official tolerance of all religious groups and support for Qur'anic schools, some of which preach extreme fundamentalism. The population of Pakistan is both Sunni (77%) and Shiite (20%), and there is a small but important minority of Christians, Hindus, and Parsees (Zoroastrians); unfortunately, attacks on mosques and churches are increasing.

In Indonesia the fundamentalist view is in conflict with the Western influence that comes from tourism and business. (Bombings at a bar in Bali in 2002 and a hotel in Jakarta in 2003 were violent responses.) It is also in conflict with the traditional Indonesian form of Islam that blends Islam with Hinduism and animism. Reformers (sometimes called *santri*) oppose the traditional practitioners (*abangan*), and they criticize traditional Indonesian practice as impure. Some of this reformism is also caused by the fact that great masses of people can now make the pilgrimage to Mecca; they learn there that their own form of Islam is considered to be imperfect.

The conflict between two visions—of a secular government and of an Islamic state—has been clearest in Afghanistan. The country was taken over in 1996 by the puritanical Taliban. The core of their movement came from students in Deobandi schools in Pakistan. ("Taliban" literally means "seekers of truth"—religious students—but we should note that the Taliban's views were even stricter than those of the founders of the Deobandi school itself.) The goal of the Taliban was to create the world's purest Islamic state, and they followed their own strict interpretation of the Qur'an. Taliban regulations about gender forbade men to cut their beards. Women were restricted solely to domestic roles. When the Taliban took control in Afghanistan, women were no longer allowed to work outside the home, they had to be totally covered when in public, and when away from home they were to be accompanied by a male relative.[41] The Taliban forbade all nonreligious music and destroyed tapes and CDs in public demonstrations. Films, television, e-mail, and the Internet were banned. Public executions and amputations were performed in soccer stadiums. The destruction at Bamian, northern Afghanistan, of two Buddhist statues, each more than a hundred feet high, was believed by the Taliban to be necessary to purify Afghanistan of idolatrous images. The statues, cut into a cliff, dated back to at least the fifth century and had been written about by a Chinese monk, Xuanzang (Hsuan Tsang), who visited Bamian in 630 C.E. Many Muslim political and religious leaders joined in world protests, but they were unable to stop the shelling of the statues in 2001. The loss brought a response of shock and horror around the world. The Taliban were soon ousted from power by Western forces but are still active in many parts of the country and in Pakistan.

Other countries that are being pressed by mostly conservative Muslim groups are Algeria, the Philippines, and Malaysia. In Algeria a civil war has been raging since 1992 between the groups that seek to establish an Islamic state and the old-guard government that has refused to hand over power. In the Philippines, Muslim groups are fighting for the independence of Mindanao, the large southern island, which is home to almost five million Muslims.

Malaysia is perhaps the most successful of all predominantly Muslim countries in integrating Islam with the modern industrial world. Malaysia is now the tenth largest trading nation in the world, and its national income has gone up every year for the past thirty years.[42] Its educational system is excellent, corruption has been controlled, private property is protected by law, and the courts are generally trusted. About a quarter of the population is Chinese and eight percent is Indian, and the government works actively to minimize racial or religious conflict. Passages from the Qur'an are emphasized that support private property, women's rights, and tolerance. There is a system of affirmative action in place for Malays. However, religious groups are gaining success in promoting the wearing of the head scarf (*hijab*) by Muslim women, the keeping of the fast during Ramadan, and other Islamic practices.

Islam in the West and Beyond

Islam has begun to spread to the West through immigration and conversion. It has spread to England, Canada, and Australia through emigration from some former British colonies, particularly Pakistan and India; and many French cities have large populations of emigrants from Algeria. Large cities in North America have also attracted Muslim emigrants, particularly from Iran, Lebanon, and Africa; for example, there are now more than 300,000 Muslim émigrés from Iran living in Los Angeles. Islam is also spreading in Chicago and Detroit, where it has had special appeal to minorities.

Because of its simplicity and strong moral guidance, Islam has been successful in attracting converts in places far away from traditionally Muslim regions. For example, Koreans who worked in the oil fields of Saudi Arabia have taken Islam back to South Korea. It is also growing strongly in sub-Saharan Africa, where it is attractive to some converts because it is a way of expressing a deliberate rejection of Christianity, which many people associate with European exploitation. Islam is also attractive in sub-Saharan Africa because of its acceptance of the traditional practice of polygamy.

Some relatively new forms of Islam have emerged that are not as inclusive as orthodox Islam, and their relation to mainstream Islam has occasionally been questioned. The movement known at first as the Nation of Islam, for example, was begun as an Islamic religious movement meant exclusively for African Americans. Its founders were Wali Farrad Muhammad (W. D. Fard, born c. 1877; he mysteriously disappeared in 1934) and his successor Elijah Muhammad (Elijah Poole, 1897–1975), who set up the first centers of worship in Detroit and Chicago. The Nation of Islam, whose members are known as Black Muslims, attempted to bring pride to African Americans by instilling the virtues of thrift, hard work, education, and self-defense. It created an organization for young men, called the Fruit of Islam, and one for young women, called Muslim Girl Training.

The Nation of Islam's original vision was anti-white, but this emphasis has softened due to the preaching of one of its most important members, Malcolm X. Under Wallace Deen Muhammad, the son of Elijah Muhammad, the Nation of Islam has renounced its purely racial basis, changed its name to the American Muslim Mission, and worked to integrate itself into mainstream Sunni Islam.

A follower of the early views of Malcolm X, Louis Farrakhan (b. 1933), has attempted a revival of the Nation of Islam, particularly through preaching the values of hard work and social responsibility. His Million-Man March on Washington in 1995 and his Million-Family March in 2000 were

Malcolm X

Malcolm X, originally Malcolm Little, was born in 1925 in Nebraska. His father was a Baptist minister who had been influenced by the thought of Marcus Garvey (see chapter 11), a Jamaican who preached the importance of pride in African descent.

Malcolm spent his teen years in Boston, living with his sister. While there, he was imprisoned for four years for theft. In jail he became a convert to the Nation of Islam. It was then that he changed his name to Malcolm X. The X was both a symbol representing the destruction of African families by slavery and a sign of a new way of living.

After release from prison, Malcolm X helped to found temples of the Nation of Islam and became a minister of the faith, first in Boston and then in New York. After conflict with Elijah Muhammad, he left the Nation of Islam. He made the pilgrimage to Mecca in 1964, where he experienced a profound change of thought. Prior to his pilgrimage, Malcolm X held violently anti-white views. During his visit to Mecca, though, he met Muslims of many races and ethnicities. His journey gave him new understanding of the spiritual implications within Islam for universal brotherhood.

Upon his return to the United States, Malcolm X devoted himself to working for racial equality and

Malcolm X at the National African Bookstore in 1964.

was vitally interested in spreading knowledge not only of Islam but also of African culture. He founded his own group, the Organization for Afro-American Unity, whose focus was political change. Tragically, he was assassinated in 1965, but his life story, *The Autobiography of Malcolm X*, has become a classic and keeps his ideals alive.[43]

successful attempts to generate self-pride and political activism among African Americans.

It is hard to predict the development of Islam over the next few centuries. The model of the democratic, secular state with a written constitution guaranteeing individual rights seems to be taking hold worldwide. Although some conservatives would like to unify Islam, it seems doubtful that there will ever again be a unified Islam or a single caliph. There are simply too many areas of possible disagreement. Islam will probably remain divided into nation-states, each with its own interpretation of the Muslim religion and its own path.

On the other hand, fundamentalist Islamic groups are becoming increasingly influential in the policy-making of their governments. Because the Qur'an contains a great many specific laws about such things as property rights, marriage, divorce, and sanctions for crimes, some Islamic groups wish to replace the laws of their country with Qur'anic laws (Sharia). Saudi Arabia has followed Sharia since its beginnings in 1932, and the establishment of a Muslim theocracy in Iran in 1979 has encouraged people to seek the introduction of Sharia elsewhere—particularly in Algeria, Egypt, Sudan, and Pakistan. Increasingly we will see a struggle between those who wish

American Muslims increasingly participate in political activism, as was evident during Louis Farrakhan's Million-Man March in Washington, D.C.

to have a secular system of laws, modeled at least to some extent on Western practice, and those who wish to follow Sharia instead.

This struggle is actually part of a larger struggle between fairly different cultures, and conflict perhaps will be inevitable. Islam has several important areas in which it differs strongly from mainstream European and American culture. Public prayer must be performed on Friday—which is a workday in Western countries. Interest on loans is forbidden—a demand that opposes a cornerstone of Western business practice. Wine (as well as other alcohol) is forbidden—whereas in traditional Western cuisines wine or beer plays an important role. (We might recall that both Judaism and Christianity use wine in religious services, and the New Testament explicitly recommends wine for health [1 Tim. 5:23].) Meat eaten by Muslims must be *halal* (slaughtered according to religious rules). Gambling is forbidden.

The area of greatest cultural conflict, however, regards the treatment of women. Islamic seclusion of women (which actually was patterned on Persian and Byzantine practice) is in conflict with the principles of women's liberation. The demand for modest dress (commanded by the Qur'an) and for covering of the hair (not explicitly commanded by the Qur'an) both are opposed by modern fashion. And, although monogamy is the norm in Islamic countries, marrying as many as four wives is allowed by Islamic law.

In addition to these areas of difference, Sharia considers criminal a greater number of acts than secular laws typically do—including, for example, adultery and blasphemy. Also, sanctions are likely to be different—for example, public stoning to death for adultery, and amputation of the right hand for obstinate theft.

An intractable problem that adds fuel to the conflict is resentment within the Muslim world over the Palestinian issue. The problem areas include Palestinians' poverty, the land that Palestinians lost when Israel was created in 1948, Israeli control of the West Bank, and the lack of a Palestinian state. There can probably be no peace until the Palestinian issue is resolved. Resentment has led to regular clashes and bombings, both in Israel and beyond, and those countries that are perceived as supporting Israel have become targets.

The destruction of New York City's World Trade Center in 2001 was perhaps the most horrifying single instance of cultural conflict. That and the simultaneous attack on the Pentagon were aimed at crippling the United States. The bombing in Bali in 2002 was aimed at Australia. The conflict has now become an us-versus-them situation that can escalate out of control. Many Muslim laypeople and clerics, though, decry what has happened. They particularly oppose any violence against civilians.

The religious and cultural conflict is further exacerbated by the fact that Islam can be embraced for political reasons. We must recall that virtually all Muslim regions were once colonized by European powers. Colonization began when the British began to take over India in the eighteenth century and Napoleon invaded Egypt (1798). During the nineteenth and twentieth centuries France colonized Morocco, Algeria, Tunisia, Lebanon, and Syria. At the same time, England colonized Libya, Egypt, Jordan, India, and Malaysia; and the Dutch took Indonesia. (The invasion of Iraq in 2003 by the United States and Britain is viewed by many Muslims as just another instance of the same pattern of colonization.) Muslims in once-colonized countries will quite naturally utilize Islam to emphasize their own national identity.

On the other hand, it can now no longer be a matter of enemies looking at each other from opposite, distant trenches. Islam is already a major part of Europe and North America. At least five million Muslims now live in France, making up one tenth of the population, and France has at least 1,500 mosques. It is estimated that, by the end of this century, Muslims will make up one third of the French population. In England there are perhaps two million Muslims today, with about 600 mosques, and the Muslim presence in England may eventually pressure the government to disestablish the Church of England. A large minority of Germans, whose parents came from Turkey, are Muslim. In the United States, the size of the Muslim population is uncertain, but probably at least five million; that population will be increasingly influential.

Approaches to reducing conflict vary. In England, the emphasis is on accepting differences as legitimate forms of multiculturalism. In France, the official approach has been to maintain a secular ideal and force people to assimilate to that (a current focus of debate concerns the wearing of the head scarf by girls in public schools). The approach in North America, though less clearly formulated, seems to be closer to the British model.

Adding to the complexity is an uncertainty: the role that popular culture will play in the cultural and religious mix. Popular culture is spreading everywhere. There have been attempts to shut it out, of course. Saudi Arabia allows no movie theaters—but videos and DVDs abound. Iran legally banned Hollywood films (a move that helped its film industry, which is creating films of quality and depth). Iran has also legally banned satellite dishes, but the success of this ban is limited—people hide them. The Taliban in Afghanistan banned movies, CDs, and the Internet, but those all began to return when the Taliban fell in 2001. The cultural influx is especially evident in Muslim countries of northern Africa, where people watch satellite-broadcast quiz programs, rock videos, and soap operas from Europe. In Europe and North America, Muslims, of course, are inundated with popular culture. It is already changing the way young people act, dress, and entertain themselves. Those responsible for making the films and creating the television programs that people watch may ultimately have the greatest influence on the future of Islam.

Some people focus on the differences between traditional Islamic culture and the dominant cultures of Europe and North America. They fear the conflicts that will necessarily arise. Yet religions show a strong tendency not only to change over time, but to change radically when they enter new cultures. Those who are fearful about the ability of Islamic and Western cultures to mix should reflect on the blending that has already occurred since the Middle Ages. Scholastic philosophy was made possible by translations of Aristotle made from Arabic into Latin. Gothic architectural style is thought to have originated in the Muslim world, and Western mathematics, chemistry, and astronomy were all enriched by Muslim thinkers. We get a sense of the contributions of the Islamic world to many areas of our Western world if we consider some of the words that have come into English from or through Arabic. A good number of English words that begin with *al* come from Arabic (*al* means "the"): *alcove, algorithm, alchemy,* and (ironically) *alcohol.* We might note the number of words used in science. But we also find many foods that were once delicacies in Europe: *orange, lemon, lime, sugar, sherbet, syrup,* and *coffee.* Other words with Arabic origins refer to objects that have added, in their own way, to human life: *lute, lacquer, mattress,* and *magazine.* The West has been greatly enriched by Muslim cultures.

There are elements of Western culture that orthodox Islamic societies will wish to avoid: alcohol abuse, gambling, high divorce rates, and urban violence. There will be regular debate about the roles and dress of women. And Muslim nations will continue to grapple over how much traditional Islamic law can be imposed in a modern society. Particularly under pressure from conservative movements, Islamic countries will do what they can to oppose what they see as dangerous elements. In the long run, however, we should expect them to maintain long-standing practices—regular prayer, charity, the Ramadan fast, pilgrimage to Mecca, and the ideals of generosity and justice.

RELIGION BEYOND THE CLASSROOM

Great Islamic art and architecture can be experienced most easily today in Egypt, Turkey, and Morocco—countries with well-developed infrastructures for travelers. Southern Spain also has much Islamic architecture, although the mosques have been converted to other uses.

Note that some mosques are open only to Muslims (especially in Morocco); a few have tours for non-Muslim visitors, however, and all of course can be viewed from the outside. Only Muslims may visit Mecca.

Egypt In spite of being a modern city, Cairo has much that is old and traditionally Islamic. Among its Islamic treasures are the al-Azhar Mosque and University and the Mosque of Ibn Tulun.

Turkey Istanbul is one of the most fascinating cities in the world. Its skyline, although constantly changing, is dominated by domes and minarets. Aya Sofia, built first as a cathedral and then serving as the central mosque of the city, is now a museum; but its architecture set a pattern for much subsequent mosque design. The Mosque of Sultan Ahmet is famous for its six minarets; it is called the Blue Mosque for its interior tilework. The Süleymaniye Mosque is also famous for its size and domes.

Morocco One of the greatest sights in Morocco is the new Hassan II Mosque at the edge of the ocean in Casablanca. The mosque—whose interior is as impressive as its exterior—is open for morning tours. Although most mosques in Morocco are closed to non-Muslims, visitors are welcome at the many medersas (religious schools). The cities of Fès and Marrakesh should not be missed and have good museums of Islamic art.

Spain Southern Spain is rich in Islamic art. One of the world's architectural masterpieces is the Alhambra palace in the hilltop city of Granada; worth visiting nearby are the gardens of Generalife, a thirteenth-century country estate. In Córdoba, the cathedral is a former mosque (called Mezquita); its interior is a forest of columns and Islamic arches. In Seville, the minaret of the former central mosque remains in use as the cathedral bell tower, called La Giralda.

United States Many of the more than 1,000 mosques in the United States are small and are often converted houses or stores. But large mosques and Islamic centers exist in some places, such as in Perrysburg, Ohio (near Toledo), in Washington, D.C., in Los Angeles, and in New York. Mosques in the United States often provide guided tours for Muslim and non-Muslim visitors alike.

FOR FULLER UNDERSTANDING

1. List some differences in attitudes toward women in Islam, Protestant Christianity, and Hinduism. Organize a panel to discuss this topic.
2. Research the differences in the attitudes toward death in Islam and Hinduism.
3. The Qur'an, like the Hebrew and Christian Bibles, shows a God who at times commands violent actions. If you were an imam in today's world, how would you treat such texts in your teachings and preachings?

4. Islam is becoming an important presence in Europe and North America. Discuss what contributions Islam might make there. Also discuss how non-Islamic cultures might influence or change the practice of Islam. (For example, could Islamic worship begin to adopt regular congregational music of some kind?)

RELATED READINGS

Akbar Ahmed. *Living Islam.* New York: Facts on File, 1994. A popular, nicely illustrated appreciation of Islam by a knowledgeable believer.

Dawood, N. J., trans. *The Koran.* London: Penguin, 1993. A clear translation of the Qur'an.

Dunn, Ross. *The Adventures of Ibn Battuta: A Muslim Traveller of the 14th Century.* Berkeley: University of California Press, 1990. A description of the cultural world and the travels of a man who set out from Morocco to go on the pilgrimage to Mecca, and ended up traveling to China and India as well.

Esposito, John. *Islam: The Straight Path.* 3d ed. New York: Oxford University Press, 1998. A book that is especially helpful in its discussion of contemporary developments in Islam.

Frager, Robert. *The Wisdom of Islam.* New York: Barron's Educational Series, 2002. A beautifully illustrated introduction to Islam by a specialist in Sufism who is also a practitioner.

Goldziher, Ignaz, et al. *Introduction to Islamic Theology and Law.* Princeton, NJ: Princeton University Press, 1981. A classic, scholarly study of the development of Islamic religious thought.

Khan, Hazrat Inayat. *The Mysticism of Sound and Music.* Boston: Shambhala, 1991. A poetic discussion in the Sufi tradition about how the beauty of music can reveal the divine.

Lewis, Bernard. *The Crisis of Islam.* New York: Modern Library, 2003. A review of Islamic history, with the conclusion that Islamic countries need to embrace the future.

Malcolm X. *The Autobiography of Malcolm X.* Orig. pub. 1964. New York: Random House, 1989. The story of the development of a young African American—a convert first to the Nation of Islam and then to traditional Islam—who has been a major influence on American political thinking.

Murphy, Caryle. *Passion for Islam: Shaping the Modern Middle East.* New York: Scribner, 2002. Experiences and conclusions about Islam in Egypt, written by the former bureau chief of the *Washington Post* in Cairo.

Schimmel, Annemarie. *Islam: An Introduction.* Albany: State University of New York Press, 1992. A study that focuses on Islamic mysticism, theology, and piety.

Turner, Howard. *Science in Medieval Islam: An Illustrated Introduction.* Austin: University of Texas Press, 1997. A volume that shows the many contributions made in Islamic countries to medicine, mathematics, geography, astronomy, optics, and other fields.

KEY TERMS

Caliph (*kay'-lif*): (Arabic: khalifa) "successor"; a religious and political leader.

dhikr (*tik'-ur*): A devotional remembrance of Allah through the recitation of his ninety-nine names and other devotional practices.

fana (*fah-nah'*): "Extinction"; the sense of loss of self in mystical experience.

hadith (*huh-deeth'*): "Recollection"; remembrance of an act or saying of Muhammad.

Hajj (*hahj*): Pilgrimage to Mecca.

Hijra (*hij'-ra*): "Flight"; Muhammad's escape from Mecca to Yathrib (Medina).

Id al-Adha (*eed' ahl-ahd'-hah*): The Day of Sacrifice during the month of the Hajj when an animal is sacrificed to recall the submission of Abraham.

Id al-Fitr (*eed' ahl-fee'-tur*): The festival at the end of the month of Ramadan during which people feast and visit friends and often the graves of ancestors.

Imam (*ee-mahm'*): A religious leader; specifically, one of the hereditary successors of Muhammad, venerated in Shiite Islam.

Islam: "Submission"; the Muslim religion and the community of believers who have submitted themselves to Allah.

jihad (*jee-hahd'*): "Struggle"; the ideals both of spreading Islamic belief and practice and of heroic self-sacrifice.

Kabah (*kah'-bah*): "Cube"; the square shrine at the center of the great mosque of Mecca.

mihrab (*meeh-rahb'*): The decorated niche inside a mosque that indicates the direction of Mecca.

minaret (*min-a-ret'*): A tower used by a chanter to call people to prayer.

mosque (Arabic: *masjid*): a Muslim place of worship.

muezzin (*mu-edz'-in*): A chanter who calls people to prayer.

Muslim: A person who submits to Allah.

qiblah (*kib'-lah*): The direction toward Mecca; the direction toward which Muslims pray.

Qur'an (*koor'-ahn*): "Recitation"; God's words as revealed to and recited by Muhammad; an authorized edition of the written words that appeared after Muhammad's death.

Ramadan (*rah'-mah-dahn*): The month of fasting; the ninth month of the Muslim calendar.

Sharia (*shah-ree'-uh*): "Path"; the whole body of Islamic law, which guides a Muslim's life.

Shiite (*shee'-ait*): A minority branch of Islam, which holds that Muhammad's genuine successors descended from his son-in-law Ali.

Sufism (*soof'-ism*): A group of devotional movements in Islam.

Sunni (*soon'-ee*): The majority branch of Islam, which holds that genuine succession from Muhammad did not depend on hereditary descent from his son-in-law Ali.

sura (*soo'-rah*): A chapter of the Qur'an.

11

Alternative Paths

 FIRST ENCOUNTER

After years of thinking about traveling to Asia, you finally take the plunge. Following a tour of the major cities of China, you are now in Vietnam on your own. During your first days there, you explore Hanoi, a beautiful city of two-story pink and yellow buildings, red-pillared temples, lakes, and large old trees. You visit its Confucian Temple of Literature, where a genial statue of Confucius seems to focus its glass eyes directly on you. Afterward, you fly south to Hué, a former royal city that sits beside the Mekong River, whose slow-moving water is so thick with brown silt that it looks like chocolate pudding. When you visit Hué's square of old palaces, you are amazed by the extent to which its royal enclosure was patterned after the Forbidden City of Beijing. Clearly, you think, China has had a profound influence on Vietnam.

Eventually you arrive in Ho Chi Minh City, formerly Saigon. In your hotel lobby, you see a poster advertising tours to the underground tunnels at Cu Chi that were used by the North Vietnamese soldiers during the Vietnam War. You walk over to talk with the agent at the tour desk, and she tries to interest you in additional tours. "Have you heard of Cao Dai?" she asks. You hadn't till now. "It is a big religion here in Vietnam," she explains. "Its cathedral is not far from the tunnels, and there is a Mass every day at noon. Why don't you go there, too?"

At 11:30 the next morning, you arrive at Tay Ninh, a quiet town of yellow stucco buildings, gravel roads, and people dressed in white. You can't miss the cathedral; it is an immense, churchlike yellow building with two tall towers that face the main road. Upon entering the building, you are directed up a long flight of stairs to a narrow visitors' gallery that runs along three sides of the interior. Looking down from the observation gallery to the front of the church's interior, you see a huge eye painted on a large blue globe that seems to hover in the sanctuary. Around you, decorative green dragons climb tall pillars to the sky-blue ceiling. Just before noon, people dressed in robes of red, blue, yellow, and white take their places in groups on the shining marble floor below. Chanting starts. The service begins.

What, you wonder, does the large eye represent? What are the people chanting, and what is the significance of the variously colored robes? Why are there Chinese dragons on the pillars inside a building that looks like a Christian cathedral? Why do they call their service a "Mass"?

ORIGINS OF NEW RELIGIONS

One of the most fascinating things about religions is that, like all forms of life and culture, they are constantly changing. Change occurs for many reasons. Sometimes followers of one religion move into another culture, and their religion mixes with a locally established religion, thereby producing a hybrid faith. Sometimes social problems lead to the emergence of a new religion, one that helps people cope with the new social issues they face. Sometimes followers of an older religion argue with each other and then separate, creating a new branch or, occasionally, an entirely new religion. And sometimes individuals have life-changing insights, attract followers, and create a new religion around themselves. We should recognize that many of the major religions and denominations began in similar ways—as new, small, and sometimes persecuted religious movements. In this chapter, we will look at some of the vital new religious movements that are currently small but that, after growing and changing for one or two thousand years, might someday become venerable old religions. (The vitality of these new religious movements is apparent from their many websites.)

In the religions that we examined in previous chapters, we sometimes saw the emergence of religious variants that were close enough to their origins to be considered modern interpretations of an older religion. In Shinto, for example, we reviewed the New Religions of Tenrikyo and Omoto. In Christianity, we looked into the Mormons and Christian Science. In Buddhism, we considered Soka Gakkai.

There are, however, some movements that begin within one religion and take on such an independent form that they ultimately constitute new, even if small, religions: Baha'i, which in the nineteenth century grew out of Shiite

"Cults," "Sects," and New Religious Movements

Possibly because they are small and different, new religious movements are sometimes looked down upon by members of larger and older religions. This is particularly true when a new movement wins converts from an established religion. Some movements are accused of too much control over their followers, and some are even seen as a threat to an entire society. Thus, it is not surprising that emotionally colored words—in particular the terms *sects* and *cults*—are used to describe new religious movements.

The term *sect* (related to *dissect* and *section*) literally means "division." The word *sect* can suggest a dangerous threat to social unity; however, the emotional weight of the term is not usually negative. Nowadays scholars use the term simply to designate an offshoot or branch that has emerged from an established religion, as in "orthodox sect" or "reformed sect." Sects also tend to be somewhat loosely structured.

Literally, the word *cult* has no negative meaning (it comes from the same Latin root that gives us the words *cultivate* and *culture*); however, it often has pejorative connotations. The word *cult* is frequently used to describe a group that is small, isolated, and under the control of a charismatic and dictatorial leader. Cults tend to have highly structured rules for living and to regulate contact with outsiders.

When we read of groups that have urged their followers to suicide or other pathological behavior, there seems to be some justification for the use of a word with a negative connotation. We might think, for example, of the People's Temple community that moved from San Francisco to Guyana and committed suicide there in 1978, or of the Aum Shinrikyo group in Japan that in 1995 released poison gas on the Tokyo subway. Looking at groups like these, we can see that some religious beliefs and leaders can indeed wield dangerous power over their followers. For the good of society, such groups need to be watched carefully, and individuals should approach them with caution.

At the same time, we should remember that societies often view a new religious movement as dangerous simply because it is different. We should remember that Christianity in the early Roman Empire was considered a dangerous Jewish cult and that Buddhism in China was once feared as a dangerous import from India.

Because of the emotional overtones of some words that describe smaller religious movements, scholars of religion have deliberately tried to find and use terms that are emotionally neutral. One of the most common terms, *new religious movement,* is now so frequently used that it is often abbreviated as NRM.

Islam, is a good example. And then there are other movements that emerge independent of established religions and eventually are recognized as distinct religions; Scientology is an example of such a religion.

Quite often, a new religious movement is *syncretic*—a blend of religions. The Vietnamese religion of Cao Dai, for example, blends Christianity with Buddhism, Taoism, and Confucianism. Santería and other related religions, prominent in the Caribbean, mix Christianity with elements from West African religions. We also see syncretism in religious movements that have grown out of Shinto, Buddhism, and Hinduism.

In this chapter we will consider some of the most significant new religious movements, along with a few older alternatives that are generating new interest. (We should note that some of the "new religious movements" have actually been in existence for quite some time.) The complexity of new religious movements becomes apparent when we try to find patterns among them. The movements are virtually impossible to categorize; thus, in this chapter we will consider them in generally the same order that we followed in earlier chapters. We will begin with religious movements that share features with indigenous religions (Contemporary Paganism and the Yoruba-tradition religions) and then proceed to religions that appear to have elements of Indian spirituality (such as Theosophy and Scientology). Next, we will take a look at religions that are close to traditional Chinese religions (Falun Gong and Cao Dai) and then end with religions that have some roots in Christianity and Islam (Rastafarianism and Baha'i).

CONTEMPORARY PAGANISM: WICCA AND DRUIDISM

The past hundred years have seen both a great growth in world population and a depletion of natural resources. As a result, many people sense an urgent need to reestablish harmonious relationships with the global environment. At the same time, developments in genetics, anthropology, and psychology have brought human beings to a clearer understanding of their closeness to the animal world. Perhaps for these reasons, new religious movements that reclaim ancient nature-based religions or that promote new environmental sensitivity are attracting many followers. Some of these followers are reacting against the insensitivity to native cultures and values that some mainstream religions exhibit. Others find the philosophies of these old-yet-new religious movements to be more compatible with their views on various social issues, including gender equality and environmentalism.

Contemporary Paganism is a general name for religious movements that attempt to return to earlier, nature-based religions, primarily religions associated with early cultures of Europe. Followers point out that the term *pagan*, although often used in a demeaning way to mean "uncivilized" and "debased," more properly refers to early, nature-based religions; they note

Celebrants light candles during Samhain, the festival that in Wicca marks the end of the old year and the beginning of the new.

that the term *pagan* actually comes from a Latin term for "countryside" (*pagus*) and that the term was used simply because nature religions lived on longer in rural areas than they did in cities. Followers of Contemporary Paganism claim that when Christianity spread throughout western Europe older pagan practices did not entirely die out. At least some of the practices went underground or took on a Christian appearance in order to survive.

Although small movements exist that attempt to re-create early Scandinavian and Germanic religions, the most common forms of Contemporary Paganism look back to Celtic mythology as their foundation. The best-known manifestation of the Contemporary Pagan movement is **Wicca.** *Wicca* is an Old English word that suggests association with magic, separation, and holiness. Its modern practitioners focus on Wicca's practical uses by calling it the Craft. Sometimes they also call their path simply the Old Religion.

Several strands or traditions of Wicca exist, but they tend to agree on many points. Like many of the world's religions, Wiccans worship both goddesses and gods whose sacred imagery is rooted in nature. Some Wiccans speak of multiple deities, while others prefer to speak of a single divine reality that has male and female aspects and images. Some groups personify the female aspect of the divine as "the Goddess" and the male aspect as "the God." Wicca teaches that the divine manifests itself in opposites that are reminiscent of yin and yang—dark and light, female and male, and so on. Yet, as in Taoism, some traditions of Wicca emphasize the female aspect of reality, perhaps because it has been underemphasized by some other religious traditions. In Wicca, women play a prominent role as bearers of knowledge and as leaders of ritual.

For Wiccans both the moon and the sun are sacred symbols, and the Wiccan yearly calendar receives its structure from their movement. Each year Wiccans celebrate the solar cycle by keeping as many as eight seasonal turning points, called **Sabbats,** which include the **solstices** and **equinoxes.** Wiccans celebrate the lunar cycle at the new and full moons. The times of the full moon, called **Esbats,** are often marked by gatherings and ceremony. The seasonal festivals and holidays mark both turning points in the world of nature and changes in the inner world of the practitioners. Regarding initiation and entry into higher levels of knowledge, Wiccan groups tend to recognize three stages. The first stage is initiation, and at the second or third stage the practitioner is considered competent to start an independent coven (worship group). Contemporary Wiccans call themselves Witches, and they use this term for both females and males.

Wicca has an ethical dimension. The primary commandment, called the Wiccan **Rede** (Advice), is a gentle form of the "Golden Rule." The Wiccan Rede is a rule of tolerance: "An [if] it harm none, do what you will." In other words, the individual is free to do anything except what harms others. This command, though, includes not harming animals, and many Wiccans are therefore vegetarians. It also prohibits harming the earth; thus Wicca has strong moral interest in protection of the natural environment. Another Wiccan moral belief is expressed as "the Law of the Triple Return." It states, "Whatever you do, good or bad, will return to you threefold." Wiccans

Wicca's Eight Seasonal Celebrations

Wiccan celebrations are called by several names; the most common terms follow. The seasonal dates pertain to the northern hemisphere.

Samhain (around October 31) Thought to mean "summer's end," **Samhain** marks the end of the old year and the beginning of the new. It is a time for recalling one's ancestors, whose spirits are believed to return temporarily to earth. Samhain is the origin of the modern holiday Halloween (see chapter 2).

Yule (December 21) The name *yule*, which derives from an Old Norse name for the midwinter solstice celebration, is appropriately related to the word *jolly*. This celebration marks the time when the darkness recedes and the light of the sun begins to gain strength.

Imbolc (February 1 or 2) This festival marks the end of winter and the first stirrings of spring. It is also called *Candlemas* because of special candles that traditionally were lit during Christian services.

Ostara (around March 21) This spring equinox festival is named after the goddess of the dawn (the word *Easter* has the same derivation).

Beltane (May 1) This is a day of celebration of fertility. It is probably named after the Celtic god Bel, a deity of the sun associated with Apollo.

Litha (June 21) During this feast of the summer solstice, Wiccans celebrate the warmth of summer and the beginnings of the harvest.

Lughnasad (August 1 or 2) Pronounced *loo'-na-sah* or *loon'-sar,* the name means "the games of Lugh," a Celtic god of music, crafts, and healing. It is a festival celebrating the grain harvest, when the first loaf of wheat from the harvest is baked. It is also called *Lammas,* after the new loaves of bread that traditionally were offered at Mass.

Mabon (around September 22) The autumn equinox coincides with this major harvest festival (much like Thanksgiving), during which Wiccans eat appropriate harvest foods.

believe that the energy that an individual sends out will return triply to the sender—that deeds bring their own punishment or reward.

It is possible that some of the beliefs and practices of contemporary Wicca are genuinely old, such as the rituals of Halloween and of May Day. The anthropologist Margaret Murray (1863–1963) provided strong evidence for the view that earlier forms of Witchcraft existed in Europe up to modern times. Her book *The Witch-Cult in Western Europe* quotes extensively from early sources in Latin, French, and English, written during the Middle Ages and Renaissance, that testify to the presence of earlier forms of a nature religion akin to Wicca. Her later book *God of the Witches* establishes the same points in more approachable style. In the United States, the Wiccan writer and political activist Leo Martello (1931–2000), whose work helped to open the way for the practice of Wicca in North America, traced his own knowledge back to ancient practices of his Sicilian ancestors.[1]

Some scholars, however, argue that Wicca is an artificial, quite new creation, a "mythic reconstruction." They point to the work of three people who did a great deal to establish contemporary Wicca: Gerald Gardner (1884–1964), Alex Sanders (1926–1988), and Doreen Valiente (1922–1999; see Timeline 11.1). In writings and practice these three recommended—and often created—rituals, phrases, and other elements that are now a part of modern Wicca. Yet other commentators see them as adapters of an older religious tradition who attempted to bridge the gap between a rural culture and a modern, urban

Timeline of significant events of new religious movements. ▶

	1503	Slaves from West Africa first arrive in Haiti
Development of religions of the Yoruba Tradition	**c. 1550–1850**	
	1817–1892	Life of Baha'u'llah, founder of Baha'i
Life of Madame Helena Blavatsky	**1831–1891**	
	1844	Beginning of the Babist Movement, precursor to Baha'i
Founding of Theosophical Society	**1875**	
	1884–1964	Life of Gerald Gardner, major influence on modern Wicca
Life of Marcus Garvey, African Jamaican activist	**1887–1947**	
	1891–1975	Life of Ras Tafari (Haile Selassie)
Life of Jiddu Krishnamurti	**1895–1986**	
	1911–1986	Life of L. Ron Hubbard, founder of Scientology
Founding by Marcus Garvey of the UNIA (Universal Negro Improvement Association)	**1914**	
	1922–1999	Life of Doreen Valiente, writer who helped establish modern Wicca
Life of Alex Sanders, major influence on modern Wicca	**1926–1988**	
	1928	Beginning of Cao Dai in Vietnam
Life of Bob Marley, reggae musician	**1945–1981**	
	1954	Founding of Scientology by L. Ron Hubbard
Visit of Emperor Haile Selassie to Jamaica	**1966**	
	1994	Beginning of Falun Gong
Repression of Falun Gong in mainland China	**1999**	

Druids gather for a ceremony at Stonehenge, a 5,000-year-old monument in southwest England.

one. (This process continues, as this self-proclaimed ancient religion does so much of its teaching through the very modern Internet!)

Although Wicca is the best-known form of Contemporary Paganism, there are others. Particularly popular in England is the **Druid** movement, which began in the eighteenth century as an attempt to reintroduce the religion practiced in France and England by the Celts about two thousand years ago. Early information on Druidic practice came from classical Roman literature, mainly from the writings of the emperor-general Julius Caesar and the historian Tacitus. Although Roman description of the Druids was undoubtedly colored by prejudice, its details certainly portray some actual practices and events. In fact, archeological finds have confirmed the truth of much early description.

Druids were an elite group of professionals who acted as judges, teachers, counselors, doctors, and priests. Their preparation lasted up to twenty years before full initiation. They were polytheists who worshiped about thirty major deities of nature and many lesser deities (about three hundred names of deities are found in the remaining literature). The sun and fire were important symbols of the divine. Druids conducted their services in groves of sacred oak trees; in fact, although the exact origin of their name is uncertain, *Druid* is commonly thought to mean "oak-tree wisdom."

Because so little is known of the ancient Druids, the modern Druidic movement has not only had to borrow from the data of literature and archeology, it has also had to rely on imaginative re-creations of organization and ritual. The Druids recognize three paths of practice, which may also be seen by some as stages of knowledge: **bards, ovates,** and druids. Modern Druids generally follow the same eight-part seasonal calendar as the Wiccans, and also celebrate the period of the full moon. Although Stonehenge in England predates the Druids, it is commonly associated with the modern Druids, who use the ancient circular stone complex for celebrations of the summer solstice.[2]

RELIGIONS OF THE YORUBA TRADITION: SANTERÍA, VOODOO, AND CANDOMBLÉ

When people from one culture enter another culture, they bring their religion with them. It sustains them and provides a bridge into their new lives. Sometimes elements of the two cultures mix in interesting ways. This is the case with the new religions that have their roots in the indigenous Yoruba tradition of Africa.

As the Americas were being colonized, a large slave trade arose. Enslaved Africans, largely from West Africa, were subsequently carried to South America, the Caribbean, and North America. Among the descendants of these slaves, new syncretic religions emerged that blended elements from indigenous African religions and the colonizers' Christianity.

Of the West African religions that were brought to the New World, those of the Yoruba people, who live in what is today Nigeria and Benin, were the most influential. (Other peoples whose religions were influential during the colonization of the Americas included the Fon, Nago, Kongo, and Igbo.) While **Santería** is perhaps the best-known religious movement to result from the mixture of Yoruba religions and Christianity, **Voodoo (Voudun)** and **Candomblé** are also prominent. These three related religions are sometimes referred to as religions of the Yoruba tradition.

These Yoruba-based religions are now several hundred years old, but for a variety of reasons they are today the focus of renewed interest. One reason is that an influx of Cuban and Haitian immigrants over the past thirty years has introduced these religious traditions to the United States. Another reason is that many African Americans today are interested in exploring their cultural and religious heritage. We should note, however, that there are significant historical differences among the three religions. Santería was influenced by Spanish colonial Catholicism and grew up in Cuba; Voodoo, influenced by French Catholicism, developed in Haiti; and Candomblé, influenced by Portuguese Catholicism, developed in Brazil.

There is some disagreement about the names given to two of these religions. Although the term *Santería* ("saint-thing" or "saint-way") was originally a negative way of identifying the movement, it is used here because most of the religion's practitioners accept it and use it themselves. The alternate name *Lukumí* or *Lucumí* (from the Yoruba language), however, is gaining some acceptance. The word *Voodoo* comes from the Fon word *vodun* ("mysterious power"), but because the word *voodoo* has taken on so many negative connotations, some authorities prefer to use the word *Voudun* instead. We also find in all three religions a variety in spellings of terms and of the names of gods.

At a sunset ceremony that marks the baptism of Jesus, celebrants bring offerings to the altar during this Voodoo ceremony in New Orleans.

In Santería, Saint Lazarus is the Christian *santo* of Babalú-Ayé, protector of the sick. Here, a statue of Lazarus is carried in a Santería procession in Cuba.

Although the three religions are a mixture of native African religions with Roman Catholicism, describing how elements have mingled is far from easy. Sometimes the terms *syncretism, synthesis,* and *symbiosis* are used to describe the mixture; however, such terms suggest a happy blend of complements, while the environment in which these three religions emerged was one of coercion and fear. Slaves were often forcibly baptized into Roman Catholic Christianity, and African religious practice was suppressed—sometimes harshly.

Major Orishas (Ochas) of Santería

Elegguá (also called *Elegbara* or *Eshu*) has knowledge of destiny and is therefore the first orisha to be prayed to in ritual. He is a messenger god as well as a trickster. Because of his knowledge of past and future, he is associated with corners and crossroads (turning points). His symbol is a clay head with eyes and mouth made of shells. Elegguá's colors are black and red. His parallel Catholic *santo* (saint) is usually Saint Anthony, whose festival is June 13.

Oshún is the goddess of love, fertility, and marriage. **Oshún** is associated with rivers, and her symbols are boats and mirrors. Her colors are yellow and white. Her Catholic parallel is Our Lady of Charity (celebrated on September 8 as the birth of Mary).

Shangó (*Changó*) is thought to have been a Yoruba king who was deified. He is envisioned as young, passionate, powerful, handsome, and vain. **Shangó** is associated with powerful storms, lightning, and thunder, and his symbol is the two-edged axe. His colors are red and white. Saint Barbara (December 4) is his most common parallel santo, because her image often holds a sword and is associated with storms.

Babalú-Ayé is imagined as a compassionate old man with a crutch, dressed in rough cloth, carrying a bag. He is called on to heal serious bodily afflictions, such as cancer, leprosy, and paralysis. Babalú-Ayé's symbol is a crutch. His colors are white and blue, and his parallel is Saint Lazarus, whose feast is December 17. (Some might recall hearing his name in a song sung by Cuban-born Desi Arnaz, who played Ricky Ricardo in the old *I Love Lucy* series.)

Obatalá is associated with intelligence, because at God's command he formed the earth and human beings. He is in charge of the mind and the head, and his symbol is the horsetail whisk, a symbol of authority. Because Obatalá is also associated with purity, his color is white, and he loves white things. His Catholic parallel is Our Lady of Mercy, whose festival is September 24.

Ochosi is envisioned as a hunter, dressed in purple, his favorite color. His symbol is the crossbow. Because Ochosi spends time in the woods, he knows plants and herbal medicine. Saint Norbert (June 6) is his parallel saint.

Oggún is a metalworker whose symbols are the knife and pick. He is the patron of barbers, butchers, and all who work with knives and metal. Because Oggún is rough and dangerous, he is considered to be responsible for war and vehicle accidents. His colors are black and green. Saint Peter (June 29) is the *santo* most associated with him, because Saint Peter is usually shown holding two metal keys (the keys to the Kingdom of Heaven).

Yemayá is the protector of women and is called on to help with motherhood. She is associated with the ocean, and her symbols are coral and seashells. Yemayá's colors are white and blue, and her parallel is Our Lady of Regla, whose feast is kept on September 7, the feast of the Presentation of Mary.

Oyá is associated with high winds, death, and cemeteries. She can give protection from dying. Her symbol is the horsetail, and her colors are white and burgundy. Oyá's Catholic parallel is Our Lady of Candelaria (February 2).[4]

Among the slaves, however, were many committed practitioners and even priests of the Yoruba religions; as a consequence, their religious beliefs did not die out. In order to survive, the African religions took on an appearance of conformity to Catholic belief and practice. On the surface, devotees were venerating Catholic saints, but in reality they were using the images of the saints as representations of their native gods. Raúl Canizares, a priest of Santería, describes the result not as syncretism but rather *dissimulation,* a term he uses to emphasize that the practitioners often deliberately hid their beliefs and practices behind "masks"—especially behind the veneration of saints.[3]

We should not, however, overstress the aspect of dissimulation. It is possible that apparent similarities in belief and approach between the Yoruba religion and Roman Catholicism permitted syncretism. Both systems believed in a single High God, in supernatural beings who mediate between God and human beings, and in the existence of spirits of the dead. Both systems trusted in the power of ritual and made frequent use of ritual elements. Moreover, it was also easy to adapt the Catholic calendar of saints' days to the worship of native African deities.

Although the new religions of the Yoruba tradition do believe in a single High God, they differ from Catholicism in that the Yoruba God (as in many African religions) is in essence a neutral energy that does not show personal interest in individual human affairs. Human beings must approach the High God and can gain power only by contacting invisible supernatural beings, called **orishas.** (In Santería, they are often called **ochas;** in Voodoo, they are called **loa** or *lwa;* and in Candomblé they are called *orixas.*)

The orishas are sometimes called gods. They are appropriately likened to the gods of the Greeks and the Romans because the orishas have individual humanlike characteristics. They may be gentle, capricious, playful, or wise, and they like particular foods and colors. They are in charge of certain aspects of nature (for example, oceans, plants, lightning), and they know specialized crafts (such as metalworking). In order to make the orishas strong, to keep them happy, and to extract favors from them, human beings have to keep them fed—and the orishas are not vegetarian. When the orishas are interested in human contact, they may temporarily "mount" a believer, who goes into trance and magically "becomes" the god, often displaying his or her personal characteristics. While there are hundreds of these gods in the Yoruba religion of Africa, only about twenty to twenty-five are prominent in the Caribbean religions of the Yoruba tradition, and about a dozen are particularly popular. We should also note the difference between orishas and Catholic saints. Although both orishas and saints are prayed to in order to receive assistance with the problems of life, it is clear that orishas are considered divine, whereas saints in traditional Catholic piety are not.

An individual is initiated under the protection of one of the orishas, who becomes the person's guardian deity. Initiations are performed by priests (a male priest is called a **santero** and a female priest is a **santera**). Above them are the high priests (in Santería called *babalawos*). Only men may become high priests, although some are questioning this tradition. A woman in New York, Patri Daifa, claims to have been initiated as a high priest in Santería.

Services involve prayer, drumming, dance, offering of foods, and the descent of orishas. The sacrifice of animals—mainly chickens, doves, and goats—is a part of some rituals. Although Santería's sacrificial practice is opposed by many groups, its legality has been upheld by the United States Supreme Court (1993). In deference to the controversy, some Santería practitioners have begun using alternative offerings (such as drink and food) as substitutes for animals.

In Brazil, Candomblé has been recognized as an official religion, with its headquarters in Bahía, in northeastern Brazil. And because of widespread emigration from the Caribbean, Santería and Voodoo are becoming known in some large cities of the United States, such as Miami, New York, and Los Angeles. Voodoo has long been a part of the history of New Orleans, and several Voodoo museums exist in Louisiana. In addition to these three religions, related movements have developed in Jamaica (Obeayisne) and in Trinidad (the cult of Shangó).

THEOSOPHY

We turn now from movements rooted in indigenous religions to movements that draw upon the traditions of Hinduism and Buddhism. The first new religious movement of this type that we will consider is **Theosophy.** The term *Theosophy* means "divine wisdom" in Greek. In general, the term refers to mystical movements of all types, but it also refers specifically to a movement, beginning in the nineteenth century, that attempts a synthesis of esoteric (hidden) religious knowledge. The movement of Theosophy is eclectic. It shows particularly strong interest in mystically oriented teachings from all sources—among them, Hindu Vedanta, the Jewish Kabbalah, and Gnosticism.

The principal founder of Theosophy was the Russian writer Madame Helena Blavatsky (1831–1891), who with several associates began the Theosophical Society in 1875. Two of her books, *Isis Unveiled* (1877) and *The Secret Doctrine* (1888), were among the first works to popularize among westerners significant elements from Indian thought, such as karma, reincarnation, yoga, and meditation.

Blavatsky learned of these topics from her reading and travel, but she also claimed that she was taught by "ascended masters"—spirits of highly evolved human beings who continue to exist in a realm beyond the earth

Madame Helena Blavatsky was assisted in her work by Colonel Henry Steel Olcott. Together they established the Theosophical Society in India.

and who guide human evolution. (The notion is reminiscent of the Buddhist notion of bodhisattvas.) After time spent in the United States, Blavatsky moved to southern India in 1878, where at Adyar, on the outskirts of Madras (Chennai), she established her world center of Theosophy. She was ably assisted by Colonel Henry Steel Olcott (1837–1907). Olcott was one of the earliest Westerners to formally adopt Buddhism, which he did in 1880. He wrote a *Buddhist Catechism* and worked in Sri Lanka to revive and purify Buddhism there. Olcott stayed on in India, while Blavatsky guided European Theosophy from her center in London. After Blavatsky's death in 1891, her work was continued by Annie Besant (1847–1933) and Charles Leadbeater (1864–1934).

Jiddu Krishnamurti, the son of a Hindu Brahmin, was hailed as a new leader by early Theosophists. Later he abandoned Theosophy to teach that each person must find wisdom independently, free of any teacher or system.

Theosophists have a wide range of interests but generally share a similar view of reality. One premise, similar to Vedantist thought, is that all reality is basically spiritual in nature—that visible matter is "condensed spirit." Theosophists hold that the spiritual nature of reality can be experienced and that training (including meditation and trance states) can make possible and can deepen that experience. Sometimes Theosophists say that there are several increasingly spiritual levels of the human being (such as the *astral body*) and spiritual aspects of all physical realities (such as *auras*) that can be seen at times. Theosophists are interested in exploring what they believe are the little-known powers that lie hidden both in the nonhuman world and in human beings, such as levitation and clairvoyance.

Blavatsky had prophesied that a "world teacher" would arise to lead the world to a new stage of evolution. Leadbeater and Besant identified this person as a young man, Jiddu Krishnamurti (1895–1986), whom they discovered in Madras. At first Krishnamurti accepted the role imposed on him by the Theosophical Society and was trained to take over as its leader. However, he eventually abandoned that role and began to teach that each person must be his or her own guru.

Despite his disavowals of spiritual leadership, Krishnamurti attracted a large following of disciples. He created a center on a hilltop in Ojai, California, north of Los Angeles, where he wrote and taught for many years. The Krishnamurti Foundation there today runs a retreat center and continues his teachings through videos, books, and seminars.

Theosophy has undergone a series of splits. There has long been a rift between American groups and the international society that has its headquarters in India. Consequently, there are several branches of Theosophy. The type of Theosophy that has been centered in India is naturally closer to Hindu and Buddhist sources and interests. In contrast, Western Theosophy has a greater interest in European and American thinkers and in scientific experimentation into claims of telepathy, clairvoyance, and similar special powers.

One influential branch of Theosophy is **Anthroposophy** ("human wisdom"). It was begun by Rudolf Steiner (1861–1925), a thinker who was born and trained in central Europe. Steiner began as a Theosophist but broke away in 1909 and founded Anthroposophy in 1913. Influenced by the thought of German writer Johann Wolfgang von Goethe, English naturalist Charles Darwin, and German philosopher Friedrich Nietzsche, Steiner developed his own theories of spiritual evolution. Desiring to focus on practical means to achieve human wholeness and spirituality, he began the first Waldorf school for the training of young people. Its curriculum taught not only traditional academic matters but also agriculture, art, and interpretive dance, called **eurhythmy.** Waldorf schools around the world still promote Steiner's interest in the complete development of the individual. Among Steiner's many books are *Philosophy of Spiritual Activity, The Course of My Life,* and *The New Art of Education.*[6]

A contemporary offshoot of Theosophy is the **Church Universal and Triumphant,** now led by Elizabeth Clare Prophet (b. 1940). Followers believe that the Church gains assistance from the ascended masters, the spirits of great people who help human beings from a realm beyond the earth. The Church Universal and Triumphant blends elements from Catholic Christianity with Asian beliefs. For example, it teaches reincarnation and includes Jesus and his mother Mary among the ascended masters. It also encourages use of the Bible, the rosary, and devotion to saints. Lectures by Prophet regularly appear on television.

Theosophy has had much greater influence than its small numbers might attest. Blavatsky's books have influenced other movements, such as New Thought, the Unity Church, and Christian Science. Blavatsky's openness to phenomena of many types has led to reputable investigations by others (such as American psychologist and philosopher William James) into automatic writing (writing done in trance states), hypnotism, and the paranormal. Modern Western interest in Hinduism and the whole New Age movement (see chapter 12) can be traced back, at least to some extent, to the influence of Blavatsky and Theosophy.

SCIENTOLOGY

Like Theosophy, **Scientology** has roots in Indian spirituality. Scientology as a religion was founded in 1954 by L. Ron Hubbard (1911–1986), who had initially made his name as an author of science-fiction books. Beginning as a human-potential movement in the early 1950s, Scientology evolved quickly into a religion that is now called the Church of Scientology.

Hubbard created a system that he thought would help people clarify their understanding of the human process of knowing. He created a hybrid name for this system, from *scientia* (Latin: "knowledge") and *logos* (Greek: "reason," "understanding"). Scientologists think that if we can come to understand the human process of perceiving and reacting to the world, we will be able to see reality more clearly and respond to the world more rationally.

The underlying belief system of Scientology has parallels with many religions, but particularly with Gnosticism and some schools of Hinduism. The Church believes that there is a spiritual purpose to life, and it holds that the core of the human being is a soul or spiritual reality, which it calls the **thetan.** According to Scientology, the thetan is in something of a state of imprisonment in the material world, which is called **MEST**—an acronym for matter, energy, space, and time. (MEST recalls the notion of samsara, found in both Hinduism and Buddhism.) The thetan, the immortal spiritual being that is the core of each human being, longs for liberation.

Although belief in rebirth was at first a minor teaching of Scientology, it soon began to assert itself. People undergoing Scientology training spoke repeatedly of their need to overcome difficulties that had harmed them in previous lives and whose injurious results continued on into their present lives. This notion is clearly similar to Indian teachings about karma and reincarnation. As mentioned earlier, another similarity with Hindu and Buddhist worldviews is the notion that the goal of each individual human being is some type of psychological liberation that can be brought about by insight. Although Scientologists do not use the terms *moksha, nirvana,* or *enlightenment,* those ideas are strongly suggested.

Scientology presents a grand scheme of stages toward which the individual can aspire, each representing a step upward toward increased understanding and liberation. The steps are shown on an illustrated chart called the Bridge to Total Freedom—or simply, the **Bridge.** Scientology offers techniques and books (such as Hubbard's text *Dianetics*) to lead the individual upward. The person at the beginning of the Bridge is called a **"pre-clear,"** and the person who has reached a state of mental liberation (called **clear**) is known as an **operating thetan** (or *OT*).

Individuals may proceed along the path of mental liberation by themselves, using the books provided by Scientology. Individuals are encouraged, however, to undertake the path of mental liberation with the help of another person, a spiritual counselor called an **auditor.** The auditor guides the less-experienced person by means of exercises, called *processes,* which make use of a series of questions and mental images. The processes help the pre-clear to learn new ways of mental focusing. Together the auditor and pre-clear work to find blockages to the individual's growth. (These blockages, caused by earlier painful experiences, are called **engrams.**) Sometimes the auditor makes use of an **e-meter,** an electronic machine that reads the galvanic skin response of the pre-clear. The responses of the e-meter help detect blockages that can then be resolved. Fees are charged for the auditing sessions and for advancing through the stages of the processes, although service to the organization is sometimes accepted as a substitute for payment. Processing can also be done for groups.

> Scientology has accomplished the goal of religion expressed in all man's written history, the freeing of the soul by wisdom.
>
> —L. Ron Hubbard[7]

Scientologists insist that their religion can be practiced along with other religions and that it does not displace them. Scientology centers, in fact, do not look like churches or temples; they are usually office buildings located in urban areas. Nonetheless, the amount of time followers must devote to Scientology makes it difficult for them to practice another religion simultaneously.

Scientologists meet on Sundays for a service that includes a reading from Hubbard's writings (or watching a videotape of one of his speeches), a sermon by a minister on some point of Scientology, a sharing of viewpoints, announcements, and a closing prayer written by Hubbard. Ministers conduct naming ceremonies, weddings, and funerals. Scientologists keep some religious festivals (such as Christmas) that appear in their surrounding society. They also keep March 13 as a festival in honor of Hubbard's birthday.

Scientology has gained publicity because of such celebrities as John Travolta, Kirstie Alley, and Tom Cruise, who have embraced this religion. The movie *Battlefield Earth,* in which John Travolta had a leading role, was based on a book by Hubbard.

FALUN GONG

We now move to new religious movements closely related to traditional Chinese religions. One of the youngest new religious movements was founded by Li Hongzhi (b. 1951), who was born in China but currently lives in the United States. As a young man he began to practice and then teach **Qigong** ("energy force"). Qigong (pronounced chee'-gong) is a system of exercises based on Chinese martial arts that are thought to bring about increased health and strength. The movement called **Falun Gong** grew out of Li's interests in Qigong and in meditative practices; and although it was not publicly initiated in China until 1992, it has begun to grow into a worldwide movement. It is reminiscent of several strands of Chinese religious practice that we have already studied, such as Buddhist meditation, Taoist physical exercise, and Confucian self-cultivation.

The name *Falun Gong* literally means "law-wheel energy." (We might recall that the eight-spoked wheel is a Buddhist symbol and note that *law* is a synonym for Buddhist teaching.) The **falun** is believed to be an invisible spiritual wheel located in the lower abdomen that can be activated by a master. The falun, once it has begun to turn in one direction, is believed to draw energy from the universe. Then, when the wheel turns in the opposite direction, it sends that energy out in purified form through the body of the practitioner, bringing benefits to the practitioner and to others.

Followers practice five series of physical exercises, done while standing and sitting. The exercises are closely related to Taoist exercises and exercises associated with Chinese Buddhist monasticism, and the names of the exercises borrow from Taoist and Buddhist terminology. (Readers interested in knowing the names and details of these exercises can check websites for Falun Gong or Falun Dafa, another name for the movement.) People who

Followers of Falun Gong
practice meditative
exercises.

perform the Falun Gong exercises believe that they gain not only health and strength but also paranormal powers, such as physical invulnerability and the power to see and hear things at a great distance.

The practice of Falun Gong is currently banned in China (though not in Hong Kong). Some see behind this prohibition a fear of repeating history, as Chinese history offers several examples of religious groups that have destabilized governments. In response to the ban on their religion, Falun Gong followers have attempted to bring attention to their religious position through a variety of public demonstrations. Many of these demonstrators in China have been jailed.

It is hard to gauge the number of Falun Gong followers. Leaders of the movement claim that there are as many as thirty million practitioners in China and in Chinese-immigrant communities throughout the world. Critics, however, argue that the numbers are far lower.

CAO DAI

Cao Dai (pronounced *kao'-dai*), another strongly Chinese religious movement, is one of the world's most unusual religions. It blends elements of Taoism, Confucianism, Buddhism, and Chinese belief in spirits with Christian monotheism; it has a pope and an organizational structure that is reminiscent of Catholicism; and it venerates among its many saints the English statesman Winston Churchill, the Chinese leader Sun Yat-sen, and the French novelist Victor Hugo.

The name *Cao Dai* is a title for God. Literally, it means "high palace" and is used as a title of respect. According to followers of the religion, God revealed himself, beginning in 1921, to Ngo Van Chieu (1878–1926?), the government prefect of a rural Vietnamese island. This revelation occurred while Chieu was practicing spiritism (a ritualistic calling on spirits). After asking God for the ability to worship him in some visible form, Chieu repeatedly saw in the air the image of a large eye. Chieu realized that this was God's way of presenting an appropriate visual symbol to represent himself. (This symbol is very common in European Catholic churches, particularly in France. The eye is often enclosed in a triangle, a symbol of the Trinity. The same symbol is also used by the Masons, a fraternal organization; through their influence it found its way onto the back of the United States dollar bill.)

In 1924 Chieu went to Saigon, where followers who also practiced spiritism gathered around him. Some of his followers repeatedly contacted what they believed to be the spirits of their parents and ancestors. Increasingly, one spirit continued to manifest itself. That spirit revealed itself as the Supreme Being. Chieu and the others, convinced that they were all the recipients of some new divine revelation, joined forces and developed an organizational structure. In 1928 Chieu's followers announced the new religion.

A primary teaching of Cao Dai is that all religions are based on revelations of God but that earlier revelations have suffered from human misunderstanding. Cao Dai belief holds that all the great religious founders and teachers have been inspired by God and that God's revelation, which has gotten progressively clearer, has occurred in three great phases, or **alliances.**

The first period of revelation, called the First Alliance, came in the distant past, when mythic figures (such as an early incarnation of Laozi and a legendary early Buddha called Dipankara) brought divine revelation to the world. The Second Alliance occurred in that thousand-year period of religious ferment that gave birth to Laozi, Confucius, Siddhartha Gautama, Jesus, and Muhammad. The Third Alliance began in the nineteenth century, with the work of Victor Hugo, Sun Yat-sen, and the Vietnamese scholar Trang Trinh Nguyen Binh Khiem, all of whom pursued the ideals of justice and human liberation. The Third Alliance continued in the revelations to Ngo Van Chieu and his followers, to whom God seemed to be speaking in the clearest way possible. In Cao Dai belief, however, revelation has not ended. Cao Dai followers believe that the divine realm continues to contact human beings through revelations both from God and from heavenly spirits.

Cao Dai tenets include belief in God the Father (Cao Dai), a celestial Universal Mother, heavenly spirits, and souls of the living and the dead. Buddhist influence is apparent in a belief in karma, reincarnation, and a state of liberation called nirvana. Buddhist influence is also evident in much Cao Dai practice. For example, Cao Dai promotes the avoidance of alcohol and drugs, of luxury, and of lies and hurtful speech. It also prohibits the killing of living beings, which is expressed in the Cao Dai practice of a vegetarian ideal: regular believers are expected to abstain from eating meat for ten days a month, while higher spiritual authorities are expected to maintain a completely vegetarian diet. The influence of Confucianism is also

Believers offer incense before the all-seeing Eye in the Tay Ninh cathedral of Cao Dai.

apparent in many Cao Dai virtues: self-cultivation, family responsibility, social harmony, and attention to duty. The deliberate blend of religions is symbolized by the four colors of robes used at major services: yellow for Buddhism (the original color of monks' robes, symbolizing renunciation), red for Confucianism (the color represents yang), and blue for Taoism (the color represents yin). White is used by the pope and by legislators.

Adherents of Cao Dai may follow a communal path of practice by attending services at Cao Dai churches (services are held four times a day, every six hours, beginning at dawn), or they may pray at individual home altars. Special services are held during a new moon and a full moon. Believers of Cao Dai may also follow an individual path of self-perfection, which involves meditation and breathing exercises.

Cao Dai is governed by a hierarchical structure reminiscent of Catholicism: it is led by a pope and cardinals, and its headquarters, like the Vatican, are called the Holy See (the word comes from the Latin *sedes*, "seat"). The center of the religion, along with its large cathedral, is located in southern Vietnam in the town of Tay Ninh, just outside Ho Chi Minh City (Saigon). A center of the Cao Dai religion outside Vietnam is in Riverside, California, near Los Angeles, where a twin of the Tay Ninh cathedral is being built. A new temple has just been completed in Sydney, Australia. There are about five million followers worldwide, although most live in Vietnam or abroad in Vietnamese-immigrant communities.

RASTAFARIANISM

Rastafarianism, a religion strongly influenced by Christianity, arose in Jamaica in the 1930s. The history of the island—held by the Spanish until 1655 and then by the British until 1962—is a history of antagonism toward colonial power. Anticolonial feeling expressed itself in the development of a distinctly local culture and a deliberately antiestablishment form of Jamaican English; it also prompted the formation of communities of runaway slaves (and their descendants) who left urban society to lead communal lives in Jamaica's mountains. Ironically, Protestant revivalism and Bible reading, derived from British Christianity, contributed to the anticolonial feelings. Out of this milieu Rastafarianism emerged.

The most important early figure of Rastafarianism was Marcus Garvey (1887–1947). Garvey was born in Jamaica and in 1914 organized there the Universal Negro Improvement Association (UNIA), which taught a pioneering form of black pride. After a brief stay in the United States, Garvey returned to Jamaica in the early 1920s to preach in Kingston, Jamaica's capital.

Garvey taught that people of African descent were in a state of psychological and political servitude in Jamaica and that they and others like them everywhere should take pride in their African origins, rid themselves of their oppression, and unite in a world federation. He longed for the day when African culture would be taught in schools. To illustrate his ideas he wrote several plays, of which one was especially influential; it was called *The Coronation of the King and Queen of Africa.*

According to the accounts of followers, Garvey taught them to look to Africa for the crowning of a native king who would be their redeemer. In a fateful twist of history, in 1930 a nobleman named **Ras Tafari** (1891–1975) was crowned emperor of Ethiopia. (The name *Ras* is a title akin to *duke*, and Tafari was his family name.) The coronation ceremony in Addis Ababa was a major event, attended by diplomats from many countries and widely covered in newsreels. Ras Tafari took a new name when he became ruler of Ethiopia: Emperor Haile Selassie ("Holy Trinity").

There had already been a widespread belief in Jamaica that Ethiopia was a great example of an ancient black African kingdom that had remained

> Princes shall come out of Egypt; Ethiopia shall soon stretch out her hands unto God.
>
> —Psalm 68:31[8]

Emperor Haile Selassie arrives in Kingston, Jamaica, in 1966, and waves to crowds as he leaves his plane.

independent. Complementing this esteem was the belief of Ethiopians, accepted by many Jamaicans, that their emperor was descended from the biblical King Solomon and the Queen of Sheba. In addition, some Jamaicans began to believe that Haile Selassie was a new appearance of Jesus—and that he was therefore divine (Haile Selassie, a devout Coptic Christian, did not share these last beliefs).

Hope began to build in Jamaica that Haile Selassie would send ships to return black Jamaicans to Africa. This hope grew stronger after 1938, when Haile Selassie founded the Ethiopian World Federation and granted it five hundred acres of land in Ethiopia, intended for any people of African descent who wished to resettle there. The great symbolic importance of Haile Selassie was obvious when the emperor came to visit Jamaica in 1966: he had trouble leaving his plane because of the enormous crowds that came to greet him.

> Dry up your tears and come to meet Ras Tafari.
>
> —Rastafarian hymn[9]

Haile Selassie died in 1975, yet Rastafarians believe that he is still alive in his spiritual body. Prayed to under the name *Ras Tafari,* he remains a symbol of liberation. His importance for many Jamaicans both explains the name of the Rastafarians and makes understandable their focus on him as a center of their religious belief.

Rastafarianism is not a single, organized church but is rather a diffuse movement that continues to produce new branches. Among its many offshoots are the Rastafarian Movement Association, the Ethiopian National Congress, and a more recent branch called the Twelve Tribes of Israel. Despite differences among the various groups, several beliefs and practices have emerged that are shared by most Rastafarians. The first shared belief

is that there is one God, who is referred to by the biblical name *Jah* (the name is related to *Yahweh* and *Jehovah*). Another common belief is that Haile Selassie, called King of Kings and Lion of Judah, was (and is) divine. Thirdly, all Rastafarians believe that the Bible not only is the word of God but that it also has hidden meanings that are important for people of African descent. These passages can particularly be found in the Psalms and the prophetic books of Daniel and Revelation, which speak of a messiah and a "golden age" in the future. Lastly, Rastafarians hold that people of African descent—like the Israelites who were held in captivity for fifty years in Babylon—must seek liberation from any society that oppresses them.

Some Rastafarians have made connections with Ethiopian Christianity, as in this baptism at an Ethiopian Orthodox church in Kingston, Jamaica.

Rastafarianism at first was sharply racial, condemning white society (called Babylon) and seeking emancipation from it. These sharp edges, however, have been softened over recent decades as Rastafarians have sought to change society by entering government in Jamaica and elsewhere; moreover, many whites have converted to Rastafarianism. Increasingly, Rastafarians have begun to focus more on the ideals of human unity and on harmony with the environment.

Representative practices have grown up over time, although their origins are debated. One of these is the sacramental use of *ganja* (marijuana).

Bob Marley spread the teachings of Rastafarianism through his songs. He is pictured here at a concert in Massachusetts in 1978.

The practice may have come from its use by immigrants from India to the Caribbean. Rastafarians call ganja the "holy herb," and they point to several passages in the Christian Bible that they say refer to it. One favorite passage is taken from the story of creation: "And God said, 'Let the earth bring forth grass, the herb yielding seed'" (Gen. 1:11, King James Version). Another describes a future "golden age," when a river flows from the New Jerusalem. On each side of the river God has planted trees with medicinal leaves, for "the leaves of the tree were for the healing of nations" (Rev. 22:2, King James Version).

Another Rastafarian practice involves allowing one's hair to grow into long coils, called **dreadlocks.** (In Jamaican English, *dread* has often been used as an adjective to mean "strict," "upright," "righteous.") Although this custom probably began as a way of showing rejection of repressive social norms, it also has been explained as a following of scripture. The Torah prohibits males from cutting their beards and the hair on the side of the head (see Lev. 19:27), and it prescribes a special vow that keeps a male from drinking wine and cutting any hair of the head whatsoever (Num. 6:5). Biblical examples of people subject to this vow were Samson (Judg. 13:5), known for his bodily strength, and John the Baptist (Lk. 1:15), known for his strength of character.

Rastafarians, partially influenced by the dietary laws of the Hebrew scriptures, usually avoid pork and shellfish (Lev. 11:7–12). They prefer food with no preservatives, additives, pesticides, or herbicides. For health reasons, many Rastafarians are vegetarian—such as Ziggy Marley, Bob Marley's son, who once gave a television demonstration of his recipe for "Rasta Pasta."

Rastafarians have adopted the symbolic use of four colors: black, to represent people of African origin; green, to represent the hills of Jamaica and hope for the future; red, to represent the blood that was shed by martyrs for the cause; and gold, to represent Ethiopia, a focus of African pride. This color scheme can often be seen in hats, shirts, and flags.

Elements of Rastafarianism have entered mainstream culture, particularly through music. Following African practice, Rastafarians from the beginning used drumming for religious purposes, but it was the development of reggae music and songs after 1960 that particularly spread Rasta ideas and vocabulary. Jimmy Cliff, Bob Marley, and Bob's son Ziggy Marley are perhaps the best-known reggae musicians. (Bob Marley's house, since his death in 1981, has become a shrine.) The influence of this music has created a "reggae culture" (for example, in the world of surfing) that is far wider than Rastafarianism itself. Rastafarianism and its influence have spread throughout the Caribbean and to England, Canada, and the United States.

BAHA'I

We end our examination of specific new religious movements with a look at a movement descended from Islam. The origins of the **Baha'i** faith, another monotheistic religion, can be traced to the Shiite Islam of Persia (Iran). We might recall that Shiite Islam sees divine authority as residing in the line of Imams, the hereditary successors of Ali, who was the son-in-law of Muhammad. Many Shiite Muslims believe that the last Imam did not die, but lives in another realm beyond the earth, and that he will return. Many also expect that a messianic figure (sometimes identified with Jesus) will appear on earth in the future.

This Shiite sense of expectation was the context for a nineteenth-century religious movement in Persia. It grew up around a man named Siyyid Ali Muhammad (1819–1850), who declared in 1844 that he was the long-awaited Mahdi—the last Imam, returned to earth. He took a religious name, **Bab,** meaning "gate" or "door," and preached that there would soon arrive another divinely sent messenger who would be of even greater stature and would bring full revelation from Allah. That figure, he prophesied, would begin a golden age of unity and peace. Because of conflict with orthodox Muslims, the Bab was thrown into prison and executed in 1850.

One of the Bab's followers and a leader of the Babist movement was a young Persian aristocrat, Husayn Ali (1817–1892), who later became known as **Baha'u'llah** ("glory of Allah"). After the death of the Bab, Baha'u'llah was himself nearly killed by government authorities. Instead of being executed, however, he was jailed in Tehran, in the notorious "Black Pit"—an underground reservoir used as a prison. There he experienced several months of divine revelations. After release, he was banished from Iran and began a life of exile, wandering in many places, including Baghdad and cities in Turkey, Egypt, and Palestine. He continued to be the focus of the Babist movement, and in 1863 he at last declared that he was indeed the messianic figure whom the Bab had prophesied. He lived the last years of his life in Acre, near Haifa, in what is today the west coast of Israel.

Baha'u'llah wrote innumerable letters to his followers and public letters to world leaders, such as Pope Pius IX and Queen Victoria, outlining his practical ideas for a future of human harmony. In his books, such as the *Kitab-i-Iqan* ("book of certainty") and the *Kitab-i-Aqdas* ("book of holiness") he proposed setting up a world government. His ethical teachings are summarized in a short work called *The Hidden Words*.

After the death of Baha'u'llah in 1892, his message was carried to Europe and North America by his son, Abdul Baha (1844–1921). His grandson, Shoghi Effendi (1897–1957), continued to lead the religion and translated its scriptures into English.

The term *Baha'i*, which means "follower of Baha'u'llah," was widely used during the lifetime of Baha'u'llah. Muslims consider the Baha'i faith to be a heretical sect. Orthodox Muslims call Muhammad the "seal of the prophets," meaning that Muhammad was not only the greatest of the prophets but also the last. They therefore do not accept that Baha'u'llah was a prophet, and followers of the Baha'i faith in Iran—of whom about 350,000 still remain—have been severely persecuted. The Baha'i movement, however, is now a separate religion, fully independent of Islam, and has followers all around the world.

The Baha'i faith is among the most universalistic of religions. While it retains the monotheism of its origins, the religion defines God and other religious realities in broad terms that are appealing to a wide range of people. A major expression of Baha'i universalism is that Baha'is see all religions as partially true, but also as separate elements of a great mosaic of divine revelation that is still being shaped by God. Baha'is argue that all religious founders have offered some revelation from God but that earlier revelations have been tempered by the cultures and times in which they appeared. For Baha'is, revelation is necessarily progressive, because human beings continue to evolve in understanding. Baha'is believe that the revelations of Baha'u'llah are the most advanced ever given by God but that they continue those of earlier prophets, including Abraham, Moses, Zarathustra (Zoroaster), Krishna, the Buddha, Jesus, Muhammad, and the Bab.

Baha'is teach that all religions, in some fundamental sense, are one, and Baha'is therefore look forward to the day when divisions between religions will disappear. Although the writings of Baha'u'llah are considered scriptural, Baha'is also read selections from the scriptures of many world religions at their services. Baha'is not only strive for harmony among people of different religious faiths, they also try to overcome the differences between religious and scientific endeavors, which often seem to be at odds with each other.

Baha'i belief about the afterlife is reminiscent of other monotheistic religions, yet it is deliberately left somewhat undefined—a fact that gives Baha'i wide appeal. Baha'is believe that each individual has an immortal soul and that after death the soul can go on developing in realms beyond the earth. They also speak of places of reward and punishment in an afterlife. When Bahai's speak of "heaven" and "hell," however, they explain that these are metaphors for closeness to or distance from God.

Rather than focusing on an afterlife, Baha'is emphasize improving human life in this world. Baha'is seek complete equality between men and women, an end to poverty, and education for all. They work to end prejudice, and to accomplish this they not only allow intermarriage but even encourage it.

Baha'is have a strongly international focus. They want to see the establishment of an auxiliary world language—to augment rather than replace regional languages—for use in international communication. On a very practical level, Baha'is are active supporters of the United Nations and other organizations that, in their opinion, foster world harmony. Their ultimate hope is that a single world government will supersede independent nations and thus make war impossible. And although Baha'is do not become politicians themselves, they work in many other practical ways to achieve their goals.

World unity is the goal towards which a harassed humanity is striving. Nation building has come to an end. The anarchy inherent in state sovereignty is moving towards a climax. A world, growing to maturity, must abandon this fetish, recognize the oneness and wholeness of human relationships, and establish once for all the machinery that can best incarnate this fundamental principle of its life.

—Shoghi Effendi[10]

All Baha'i houses of prayer have nine sides, since for Baha'is the number nine is symbolic of completion and perfection. Pictured here is the house of prayer in New Delhi, India.

One unusual aspect of the Baha'i faith is its religious calendar, created by the Bab. It is made up of nineteen months, each nineteen days long (with four extra days added before the final month). The last month of the year is a period of fasting, reminiscent of Ramadan in Islam, when no food or drink may be consumed during the daytime. This period of purification lasts from March 2 through March 20; the new year begins on March 21. The first day of each Baha'i month is a time of meeting, prayer, and celebration.

Baha'is are not allowed to drink alcohol, and they are discouraged from smoking. In conjunction with a belief in gender equality, Baha'i does not allow polygamy, but it does allow divorce.

Baha'i has no priesthood; it is governed by assemblies that operate on the local, national, and international level. Followers often meet in each other's homes. Each continent, however, has one large templelike house of prayer, open to all, and more are planned. (The exotic, filigreed North American house of prayer is in Wilmette, Illinois, in the suburbs of Chicago. It has fine gardens and ponds. The Baha'i house of prayer in New Delhi, a totally unique building, is shaped like a water lily.) All houses of prayer have nine sides, because for Baha'is the number nine, being the highest single-digit number, symbolizes completeness and perfection. The Baha'i world headquarters and its governing body, the Universal House of Justice, are in Haifa, Israel. There are about six million Baha'is worldwide.

NEW RELIGIOUS MOVEMENTS: A SPECIAL ROLE

In reflecting on the new religious movements that we have studied, questions naturally come to mind. What traits make these movements attractive to people? What do they say about where religion is moving in the twenty-first century?

One notable trait of these new religious movements is that they are still relatively small and their members usually meet in small groups. As such, there is a strong sense of intimacy among members, giving them a feeling that they have a function, that everyone "counts." Members can also feel part of a group with a unique identity and purpose.

A second notable trait is the role that women play in several of the new religious movements—a role which many mainstream religions have blocked. Theosophy was co-founded by Madame Helena Blavatsky, a self-confident, well-traveled woman who was a writer as well as an organizer, and it was continued by Annie Besant, also a writer and organizer. An offshoot of Theosophy, the Church Universal and Triumphant is currently run by a woman, Elizabeth Clare Prophet. Moreover, women are the main practitioners of Wicca, and through it they worship the divine that is manifested as the female and mother. In the Yoruba-based religions, female deities play a major role, and worship of them is a significant part of the ceremonial life. Women play an important role, too, in the organizations of several other new religious movements.

A third trait is the importance of an active devotional life. We especially find an emphasis on the mystical element—the sense of union with something greater than oneself. This mystical element is often assisted by music and dance that lead to trance states, or by meditations on a divine spirit that everyone shares. The mystical orientation is strong in Wicca, in the Yoruba-based religions, in Theosophy, and in Rastafarianism, and it is a significant part of Baha'i and Cao Dai.

Lastly, many of the religions present clear programs for self-development, which often involve the body as well as the mind. In Cao Dai, self-cultivation is a major goal, and virtues are clearly described. Anthroposophy has worked out a system of self-development that is meant to complete the entire human person—physical, intellectual, and artistic. Followers of Falun Gong use exercises in meditation and bodily motion to increase inner harmony and strength. And Wicca encourages participants to imagine and work for practical goals that will enrich their lives.

The new religious movements fulfill human needs that may be unmet in the older mainstream religions. They also tell us about larger trends in the future of world religions. They are, consequently, a bridge to our discussion, in the final chapter, of the modern religious search.

The be-ringed finger of a Tarot reader points to the Wheel of Fortune card. The card can symbolize the coming of major change in one's life.

PERSONAL EXPERIENCE: CELEBRATING THE GODDESS

"Do you want to talk about your future?" a young woman asked me from the roots of a large banyan tree. I hadn't seen her sitting there at a small table at the base of the tree. It was about two weeks before Christmas, and I was walking quickly through one of the few leafy places left in Waikiki, looking for some last-minute presents at the nearby booths that sold coral jewelry, sarongs, aloha shirts, and carvings. "Would you like me to do a reading for you?"

I sat down, and she quoted me a price for my reading. She also told me her name—Diana—and then asked me my name and the date and time of my birth. She laid down her bright Tarot cards—first in intersecting lines, then a straight line on the side—and told me what she saw. She interpreted the colorful images on the cards: a tower with a bolt of lightning, a knight on horseback, an angel with two chalices, a hermit, two lovers, and a wheel of fortune.[11]

"Now you might like to ask some questions," she said. As I asked specific questions about my work and my future, she turned over one additional card for each question and gave me her interpretation of the cards. I liked her careful choice of words and her feeling for the symbolic nature of the images on the cards. She clearly believed in what she was doing.

At last we had gone through all my questions and all her cards. "Now I have a question myself," she said. "Would you like to come to a Yuletide celebration here in Waikiki next week?" I answered that I would and asked if there was anything I could bring. "Oh, just some food," she replied, "but wear red or green for the celebration."

A week later I was taking my shoes off (as we do in Hawai`i) outside the door of a ground-floor apartment in a small building from the 1930s. Somehow the low-rise building had survived in the middle of bustling, high-rise Waikiki. I'd brought sushi, wine, and a piece of mistletoe that I'd seen for sale at the grocery store. I noticed that of about twenty pairs of shoes only a few were men's.

Lady Diana welcomed me. (She had told me that this was her name as a high priestess of Wicca. Her given name was Lorraine.) She wore a floor-length gold dress with long sleeves. She held a child in her arms. Diana introduced me to her friends Isis, Aurora, Bridget, and at least a dozen others. Most of them wore elaborate necklaces and dangling earrings. A few even wore tiaras. The men, except for one named Thor, had less exotic names but all wore red shirts.

I looked around. A five-pointed star, made of Christmas lights, hung on the wall near the Christmas tree. A low square altar, covered in gold cloth, stood in the middle of the room, and on it were a statue of a woman with a deer and another of a horned Pan figure, a small cauldron, tall candles, and what looked like a fancy letter opener. A smaller round table next to the larger altar was covered with about twenty vigil candles.

About two dozen silver goblets stood on a side table, and I added my bottle of wine to the other bottles, some already open. People were eating and talking. Diana handed me a goblet of wine. "Circulate," she said.

After a half-hour of socializing, Diana asked us to stand in a circle around the altars. The women began a slow chant, which they repeated in a hypnotic way: "We all come from the Goddess/and to her we shall return/Like drops of rain/flow into the ocean." Carrying her child, Diana went to each wall of the room, praying to the spirits of the four directions. She then circled the room to enclose the group. We sat while Bridget and Isis enacted a short playlet about the myth of Demeter and Persephone, Greek goddesses who went into the darkness of the underworld.

When the two women had finished, Diana spoke. "We are celebrating the winter solstice and unite ourselves with this cosmic turning of time. The Christmas tree, the candles, and the greenery represent the return of life and light. Like the sun, we also will grow in strength as the year progresses."

She passed around a large goblet of wine, and each person put into it a bit of bread, as an offering to the Goddess. Diana put it on the altar. Each person lit a candle on the smaller altar and talked about hopes for the coming year. Then everyone joined hands and moved in a slow circular dance around the altars. "Peace on earth, good will to all," Diana sang during the dance. At last Diana stopped the dance and asked everyone to sit again in a circle on the floor.

Diana now went to each of the four sides of the room to address the spirits of the four directions. She spoke finally to the Goddess, ended the ceremony, and officially "opened the circle." She gave each of us a small cloth bag, telling us to write down our wishes for the coming year, to put the paper inside the bag, and to place the bag on our home altar. Then, just before we left, Diana said a blessing: "May the circle be open but unbroken. May the peace of the Goddess be forever in your heart. Merry meet, and merry part, till we merry meet again."

Isis, Bridget, and I left together. In the dim light just outside, my attention was devoutly focused on my feet: I was afraid that I might trip. I looked down carefully at each crooked, mossy stone of the uneven pathway, which was lined with ferns. When at last we reached the street, Bridget said, "Look!" She pointed up. Isis and I looked upward, but I saw only streetlights, bright shop signs, and the lighted upper floors of a condominium building. Then I saw what had caught her eye. Overwhelmed by all the lights below, but still visible in the sky, shone a crescent moon.

RELIGION BEYOND THE CLASSROOM

Religious centers for a wide variety of alternative religious movements can be found in cities across the United States. Check the yellow pages of the telephone book (look under "Churches"), and contact college departments of anthropology, history, and religion. The Internet is also a rich resource for learning more about new religious movements and locating places of religious practice both in cities and in rural areas. We should note, however, that a few new religious movements can be very aggressive in seeking new members; they often ask for names, addresses, and phone numbers of all visitors and callers. Consequently, it is a good idea to be cautious. Do not fill out guest cards or questionnaires or give out your address or telephone number unless you are sure that you want to be contacted again by a particular group. A good way to get around this difficulty is to say that you'll be in touch later if you're interested in learning more.

FOR FULLER UNDERSTANDING

1. Do research on the art, music, altar design, or ritual clothing of a Yoruba-based religion. Using books, recordings, or the internet, find examples, and report on what you find.
2. Search for Wicca websites on the Internet. What websites did you find, and where are they based? What are some of the names of the people who have posted the Wiccan sites? What types of information and merchandise do they offer?
3. In your area, look for a center of Theosophy or of one of its offshoots (Anthroposophy, Krishnamurti Foundation). Attend a meeting or contact the center for information.
4. Do research on the Waldorf schools. What is the philosophy behind them? How did they develop? Where are they located? If there is one in your area, visit it and learn about its curriculum. Report on your findings.
5. If there is a Vietnamese American community in your region, find out if Cao Dai is practiced there. Describe what you find.
6. Collect the lyrics of eight or ten reggae songs. Analyze them for their ideas and language, and list recurrent images. Try to find a few parallels in the Bible for the images, ideas, and language of the songs.
7. Create an imaginary religion dedicated to Bob Marley and based on reggae. What would be the sacred texts, the commandments, the images, the places of pilgrimage, the foods, the clothing, the holy days?
8. With friends, attend a Baha'i service or meeting. Write a report that gives details about the participants, the meeting place, the texts that were read, and the announcements that were made.

RELATED READINGS

Barrett, Leonard E., Sr. *The Rastafarians*. Boston: Beacon, 1997. A presentation of Rastafarianism that concentrates on its historical development.

Canizares, Raúl. *Cuban Santería*. Rochester, VT: Destiny Books, 1999. An account of the history, practice, and structure of Santería by a santero (priest).

Chevannes, Barry. *Rastafari: Roots and Ideology*. Syracuse, NY: Syracuse University Press, 1994. An academic but readable study of Rastafarianism, with excellent quotations from interviews, newspaper accounts, hymns, and prayers.

González-Wippler, Migene. *Santería: The Religion*. St. Paul, MN: Llewellyn, 1999. A thorough treatment of Santería by an initiate, with a focus on physical elements—herbs, drums, and music; objects used for divining; and food offerings.

Harvey, Graham, and Charlotte Hardman, eds. *Paganism Today*. London: Thorsons/HarperCollins, 1996. A collection of essays on Contemporary Paganism that gives a good overview of its history, branches, and practices.

Hubbard, L. Ron. *Scientology: The Fundamentals of Thought*. Los Angeles, CA: Bridge, 1997. A presentation of the principles of Scientology, taken from Hubbard's writings and speeches.

Hurbon, Laennec. *Voodoo: Search for the Spirit*. New York: Discoveries/Harry N. Abrams, 1995. A summary of Haitian Voodoo history and practice, with many excellent color photographs of altars, paintings, ritual objects, and ceremonies.

Martello, Leo. *Witchcraft: The Old Religion*. New York: Citadel, 1991. A view of Wicca by a practitioner who both discusses modern Wicca and presents the traditions of older Sicilian practice.

Métraux, Alfred. *Voodoo in Haiti*. New York: Schocken, 1972. A classic study that is valuable for its details about the pantheon of gods, possession, music, dance, and ritual.

Starhawk (Miriam Simos). *The Spiral Dance: A Rebirth of the Ancient Religion of the Great Goddess*. 20th anniversary ed. San Francisco: HarperSanFrancisco, 1999. One of the most important books that first brought public attention to Wicca; contains invocations, rituals, and exercises in self-affirmation.

Steiner, Rudolf. *Theosophy*. Hudson, NY: Anthroposophic Press, 1997. A discussion of the spiritual levels of human nature by an early Theosophist who later went on to develop Anthroposophy, a related school of thought.

KEY TERMS

Alliance: In Cao Dai, one of three periods of special divine revelation.

Anthroposophy (*an-thro-pah'-so-fee*): "Human wisdom" (Greek); a movement that grew out of Theosophy and emphasizes education and other practical means for spiritual development.

auditor: In Scientology, a counselor who through a series of questions works to guide a person to greater self-understanding.

Bab (*bahb*): "Door," "gate"; a prophet who was the forerunner of Baha'u'llah, the founder of Baha'i.

Baha'i (*ba-hai'* or *ba-ha'-ee*): A modern monotheistic religion that grew out of Islam and emphasizes unity and equality of individuals, cultures, and religions; a follower of the Baha'i religion.

Baha'u'llah (*ba-ha'-oo-lah'*): "Glory of Allah" (Arabic); the founder of Baha'i.

bard: A first-level initiate in Druidism; also, a follower of a path in Druidism.

Bridge: In Scientology, a diagram of the stages toward personal liberation.

Candomblé: The syncretic religion of Brazil that blends elements of Roman Catholicism and African religions.

Cao Dai (*kao'-dai*): "High palace"; a syncretic religion that began in Vietnam and that blends Confucianism, Taoism, Buddhism, and Catholic Christianity.

Church Universal and Triumphant: A religion that unites elements from Theosophy and Christianity; also referred to as CUT.

clear: In Scientology, the state of mental liberation; also, the person who has achieved mental liberation.

Contemporary Paganism: A general name for several movements that attempt to reestablish a pre-Christian European nature religion; also called Neo-Paganism.

dreadlocks: The long coiled hair worn by some Rastafarians.

Druid (*droo'-id*): "Oak-tree wisdom"; Celtic priest of two thousand years ago; a follower of the modern re-creation of Druidism.

e-meter: In Scientology, an electronic machine that reads galvanic skin response; sometimes used to assist the auditing process.

engram: In Scientology, an experience of earlier suffering (even from a past life) that keeps a person from relating healthily to the present.

equinox: "Equal night" (Latin); the two days of the year, in the spring and autumn, when the hours of daylight and nighttime are equal.

Esbat (*es'-baht*): In Wicca, the time of the full moon, often marked by a meeting or ceremony.

eurhythmy (*yoo-rith'-mee*): "Good rhythm" (Greek); a type of interpretive dance utilized in Anthroposophy as a technique for spiritual growth.

falun (*fah'-loon*): "Law wheel" (Chinese); an invisible spiritual wheel, believed by followers of Falun Gong to spin in the abdominal region, distilling and spreading energy from the universe.

Falun Gong: "Law-wheel energy" (Chinese); a modern Chinese religion that uses meditation and physical exercises.

loa (*lwah*): A deity in Voodoo; also spelled *lwa*.

MEST: In Scientology, an acronym for matter, energy, space, and time; the world of time and space, the world in which spirits must live.

ocha (*oh'-shah*): In Santería, any deity.

operating thetan: In Scientology, a fully liberated person; also referred to as OT.

orisha (*oh-ree'-shah*): A general name for a deity in the Yoruba-tradition religions.

Oshún (*oh-shoon'*): A female deity in Santería who is associated with love, fertility, and marriage.

ovate: A second-level initiate in Druidism; also, a follower of a path of Druidism.

pre-clear: In Scientology, a person who is not yet spiritually liberated and who is just beginning to undergo the auditing process.

Qigong (*chee'-gong*): "Energy force" (Chinese); a type of martial art that is thought to increase health and strength.

Ras Tafari (*rahs tah-fah'-ree*): The original name of the Emperor Haile Selassie, often used by Rastafarians to emphasize his religious significance.

Rastafarianism: A religion that began in Jamaica in the 1920s to emphasize African pride; it considers Haile Selassie (Ras Tafari) to be divine.

Rede (*reed*): Advice, counsel—a term used in Wicca to describe its maxim that an act is allowable if it does no harm: "An [if] it harm none, do what you will."

Sabbat (*sah-baht'*): One of eight seasonal turning points marked by Wiccans and Druids.

Samhain (*sa'-win*): "Summer's-end"; in Wicca, the end of the old year and the beginning of the new (around Oct. 31).

santera (*san-tay'-rah*): a priestess of Santería.

Santería (*sahn-te-ree'-ah*): "Saint-thing" or "saint-way" (Spanish); a Yoruba-based religion that developed in Cuba.

santero (*sahn-tay'-roh*): A priest of Santería.

Scientology: "Knowledge-study" (Latin and Greek); a modern religion that promotes a process of focusing thought and clarifying life goals.

Shangó (Changó) (*shahn-goh'*): In Santería, a popular god associated with lightning, thunder, and powerful storms.

solstice: "Sun-stands" (Latin); the two days of the year, at midwinter and midsummer, when the season begins to reverse itself.

Theosophy (*thee-ah'-soh-fee*): "Divine wisdom" (Greek); an eclectic movement, particularly influenced by Hinduism, that focuses on the mystical elements of all religions.

thetan (*thay'-tun*): In Scientology, the human soul.

Voodoo (Voudun): A religion that blends elements from French Catholicism and African religions.

Wicca (*wik'-kah*): A Contemporary Pagan movement that emphasizes feminine expressions of the divine.

CHAPTER 12

The Modern Search

 FIRST ENCOUNTER

It's the middle of April. You're scanning the newspaper's long list of the upcoming week's events in honor of Earth Day—April 22. The local university will be showing a series of films on the great mountain ranges of the world; a nearby high school plans to hold something called "energy workshops"; and the city has scheduled an Earth Week fair and an exhibition at City Hall of art objects made from recycled materials. At one church, there will be an "interreligious Earth Day service with dance processional." You also see a notice for a sunset service at a park, "in honor of the Goddess." Articles in the newspaper talk about recycling programs at area hotels and offices, the improving water quality of a local river, and the celebration of Earth Day in Europe. Even the comic strips take up the theme. One shows a smiling globe of the world topped by a lighted birthday candle.

Also listed are many volunteer events throughout the upcoming week. Various civic organizations have adopted environmental projects such as clearing a stream and cleaning litter from several roads.

If you want to help in the stream-clearing project, the newspaper advises, bring gloves and waterproof boots.

You have already agreed to join some neighbors on Saturday to plant flowering trees at a park near your house. When you arrive with your shovel just before ten in the morning, you see a much larger group than you had anticipated. The mayor is there, although you don't recognize her readily in her baseball cap, blue jeans, and work shirt. About ten ribboned shovels have been laid out for dignitaries. The Channel 4 News van is parked on the street, and a man with a heavy video camera is getting ready to do some taping for the evening news. The young trees, wrapped in burlap, have been carefully laid out in the spots where they are to be planted.

Before the planting begins, you listen to a speech from the head of the department of parks. "Parks are the lungs of a city; their trees help us all breathe," he says, before thanking everyone for volunteering to help. The president of the Nature Circle, a longtime civic organization, speaks of some of the world's great parks. And, of course, the mayor says a few words. The program director then divides the volunteers into small teams.

As you begin working, you think about Earth Day, which began only in 1970. What does all this interest in nature mean? Will Earth Day survive? Will it someday be seen as the holy day of a new religion? Is this part of an emerging religion?

MODERN INFLUENCES ON THE FUTURE OF RELIGION

It is obvious that religions in the modern world face both challenge and inevitable change. Numerous social and technological developments are responsible for bringing about change. Women are demanding roles in arenas traditionally dominated by males—including institutional religions. Scientific advances in such areas as reproduction, genetics, and organ transplantation pose ethical questions that the people in earlier times never had to answer. Many Western cities are homes to religions, such as Hinduism and Islam, that not too long ago were considered exotic and foreign. Finally, television and travel expose human beings worldwide to new cultures and their religions.

Change is happening so quickly that we must wonder about the future of religion. What if we could return to earth a thousand years from now? Would the religions that we know now have changed a great deal? What religions would even still exist? Would there be new great religions?

We cannot know exactly how the religious landscape will look in another millennium, but we can make a guess based on the influences at work today—influences that are pulling religions in different directions. As we've seen throughout this book, religions in general tend to be conservative and often change more slowly than their surrounding societies. But, indeed, they do change. They change as a result of forces both from within themselves and from their surrounding cultures.

In this chapter we will first look at a few of the modern developments that are shaping our future and the future of religions. We will consider the recurrent theme of change in religion. And we will look at two alternatives to organized religion. The first is the environmental movement and its almost religious view of nature. The second is what has come to be called eclectic spirituality, a tapping into various sources of inspiration, often through art and music, which are frequently associated with spirituality.

The New World Order

A century ago, the majority of human beings lived an agricultural life on farms and in villages, and many countries were ruled by monarchs. Over a relatively short amount of time, however, most kings and queens either disappeared or became largely symbolic; democracy became a common (though not fully realized) ideal; and large numbers of people moved to cities.

The political and economic landscape has changed dramatically over the past twenty years. After decades of dividing the world symbolically into communist and capitalist halves, the Berlin Wall came down in 1989. After many of its republics declared their independence, the Soviet Union dissolved in 1991 and abandoned communism. And mainland China, although it remains a communist nation, now includes highly capitalistic Hong Kong (returned in 1997) and tolerates, even encourages, free enterprise. International companies are becoming significant entities—sometimes with more real power than nations.

At one time, people traveled abroad in order to experience different cultures and different foods. Now, a person can buy a Big Mac at a McDonald's in Italy or a doughnut and coffee at a Dunkin' Donuts in Japan. And people who live in large cities have their pick of national cuisines—Chinese, Indian, Greek, Moroccan, Vietnamese, Japanese, and Thai, to name just the most common. But it is easy to go more deeply, too, into the lives of *people* of different cultures. Supporting the people who run these businesses are entire structures that include community centers, places of worship, and even television stations that broadcast in a multitude of languages. Once, foreign countries were genuinely foreign and far away. Now, through the use of satellites, news events in distant countries can be broadcast instantaneously across the world. And reruns of *Baywatch*, which now can be seen as far away as Bhutan, will be shown somewhere on the globe, one feels sure, until the world ends.

We cannot help but wonder how this cultural unification will affect religion. So far, most of the world's religions have remained fairly separate traditions—even those that have spread to different countries and cultures. But globalism may make it impossible for separate religions to remain separate.

Modern capitalism will also challenge religion, primarily by exposing relatively broad segments of populations to its promotion of a fairly positive attitude toward money—that is, its promotion of financial success as a means to attaining personal satisfaction. In the past, many religions preached the values of poverty, simplicity, and detachment—values that at one time were consistent with life as experienced by the vast majority. Now, many religions are

Old world boundaries are disappearing through the spread of technology. Here, a woman in rural Bangladesh uses a cellular telephone.

influenced by capitalist ideals, which esteem individual and group betterment; but it is a betterment that can be measured in material terms and can be paid for with money. As Robert Ellwood, a noted scholar of religions, has commented, the "idea that poverty could be a state of blessedness in itself, a favorite of preachers as recently as a century ago, is now hopelessly discredited.... Even the most conservative pulpiteers nowadays exhort their poor to get ahead, but to do it by nonviolent means."[1] We know that money can be used just as selfishly in the modern world as it was in the past. But money is not always used for selfish and useless reasons—take, for example, scholarships, contributions to disaster-relief projects, endowments to the arts. The modern culture of money-based betterment will increasingly challenge religions to produce what material cultures value. It will challenge the religious idealization of poverty and will question religions carefully about how much they contribute to measurable human betterment.[2]

Globalism will also challenge any incomplete visions of reality offered by traditional religions. Finally, urbanism will, challenge traditional religions to confront the tribulations of large-scale city life and to take advantage of urban opportunities, such as a wide choice of educational and career opportunities.

Multiculturalism and Interfaith Dialogue

The new world order makes crosscultural contact practically unavoidable as television, radio, film, travel, books, and the internet all work to narrow the gulfs that once separated people, nations, and even religions. Aside from crosscultural contact, there is a good amount of religious interchange, some of it unintentional. Consider, for example, how language—always quick to reflect new influences—picks up trendy words and concepts, including those of a religious nature. Today's international English includes the words *nirvana* (the name of a former rock band), *karma, samsara* and *zen* (the names of perfumes), and *Dharma* (the name of a principal character in the television sitcom *Dharma and Greg,* now in reruns). We find a similar appropriation of some religious symbols: the Christian cross is now an international fashion item, often worn with little regard for its historical associations; and the symbol for yin and yang is a logo for at least one company (as well as a feature of the South Korean flag).

It will be very difficult in the future for any religion to belong to a single culture or to be unaware of the teachings and practices of other religions. With awareness often comes adaptation, a phenomenon we have already seen with current religions. Certain forms of Pure Land Buddhism outside Japan, for example, have adopted the use of hymns and the Christian tradition of Sunday school. In Western forms of Zen and Tibetan Buddhism, married laypersons sometimes take leadership roles that have traditionally been performed by monks. African and Native American forms of Christianity now deliberately make use of native art, music, and dance. Roman Catholicism, which only a generation ago celebrated its rituals in Latin with uniform prayers and music, is today often as much a reflection of its specific community or church group as it is of Rome. Some Christian monasteries and other religious groups have adopted Zen meditation. Moreover, entirely new religions may frequently blend elements from several religions. We see this, for example, in religions such as the Unification Church, which began in Korea and blends Christianity and Confucianism, and in new Shinto religious offshoots, some of which blend elements of Shinto, Buddhism, and Christianity.

Another response to the growing awareness of cultural multiplicity can be seen in the increasingly frequent meetings held by representatives of different religions. The fact that these interreligious meetings are now being held is really a hopeful, new direction. (It was not typical in the past.) Although religions have too often battled each other or even promoted war, they all preach human harmony and offer visions of peace. They have much to gain from and share with each other as they investigate their religious similarities and differences. One natural focus of discussion concerns basic rules of living—all religions seem to value honesty and display a concern for the disadvantaged. Another possible discussion focus concerns mystical experience, which is described similarly in quite different religions. A third focus for discussion is the changing role of women in religion. And a fourth focus will increasingly be the practical problems of the world—poverty, overpopulation, destruction of natural resources—and what religions can do jointly to help.

One of the earliest examples of modern religious dialogue was the first World Parliament of Religions, held in Chicago in 1893. Swami Vivekananda, a disciple of Ramakrishna, brought the inclusivist Hindu approach to the attention of the world through his insistence at that conference that all religions value holiness and love. In 1990, a world conference was held in Moscow that brought together government leaders, scientists, and religious figures to work toward saving the environment. And in 1993, Chicago hosted a second World Parliament of Religions, with simultaneous meetings of religious leaders at many places around the world. At the tenth annual Convocation for Peace, held in Rome in 1996, Yasumi Hirose, a Japanese representative of Omoto, used the language of several religions to speak of his hope. "Unless we awake to the love and compassion of the God who created the heavens and earth, and realize that all creatures are filled with Divine Spirit and live by the grace of Amida Buddha, it will be impossible to change history to bring about a new century of co-existence. By rethinking the significance of human life and returning to the sources of religion, it is my deep hope that all the world's religions can work and pray together to realize a . . . future where peaceful co-existence between the races and nations of this earth is possible."[3]

Members of many religions met in the year 2000 at the United Nations for the World Peace Summit. Here representatives of Buddhism and Hinduism pledge mutual help in resolving political conflicts peacefully.

A major interreligious conference was sponsored by the United Nations and met in August, 2000, in New York City. It appealed for a new commitment to spiritual values and for religious freedom everywhere. Because religious leaders have often been criticized for not doing enough to calm violence between different religious groups, at the end of the conference the thousand envoys signed a Commitment to Global Peace, in which they pledged to help "manage and resolve" religious conflicts nonviolently. There is ongoing dialogue as well in less spotlighted circles, such as the Ecumenical Institute at St. John's Abbey in Minnesota, where scholars of different faiths spend months in conversation, study, and reflection. These dialogues may well chart a new path for religion in the future.

Women's Rights Movements

Some of the most significant movements of the past hundred years have involved efforts to liberate women from oppression and inequality. Just as the nineteenth century is seen as the century in which slavery was abolished worldwide, the present century may well be seen by future generations as the century in which women achieved full equality and political freedom.

In many societies, women have been restricted by tradition in multiple ways. They have been kept from acquiring an education, owning land, having professional careers, traveling, marrying and divorcing as they wish, voting, and holding office. But education and women's political movements—along with scientific advances that produced contraceptives and minimized the complications of pregnancy and childbirth—have slowly changed attitudes toward women's roles and rights. As a result, women are now indispensable in the workplaces of many cultures; they are earning their own incomes and making

Rabbi Leeza Taylor uses a ritual pointer to read from the Torah.

use of their new economic power. This new independence has led women closer to equality in government, business, and the arts.

Despite the controversy (even turmoil) engendered by women's movements, a few religious groups have permitted women to hold leadership roles. This has been especially true of smaller, more charismatic groups, such as some of the New Religions derived from Shinto and those Christian churches (such as the Christian Science Church and the Foursquare Gospel Church) whose founders were female. Christian churches in the Lutheran and in the Episcopal and Anglican traditions now ordain women priests and bishops (although this has caused great opposition, and some congregations have broken away in order to maintain their older practices).

Resistance to allowing women in key roles is, however, still strong. In Christianity, the Catholic and Orthodox Churches so far have staved off pressures to ordain women or otherwise allow them full participation in decision making. In Judaism, females have been ordained in the Reform and Conservative branches. The Orthodox, however, still will not accept the notion of a female rabbi. Buddhism is seeing stirrings in its communities of nuns, who traditionally have played only a small role in the religion. Today, Buddhist nuns are still only one tenth the number of all Buddhist monks, and they clearly do not have the same influence; but some nuns—Western women among them—want to have an equal voice.

Women's gains have been broader in areas that can be addressed without changing a religion's basic power structure. Thus we find new translations of sacred literature and prayer forms that attempt to be more gender-neutral. For example, words such as *Ruler, Creator,* and *Parent* are used in place of the exclusively male terms *Lord* and *Father* in some translations of the Bible. (A controversial feminist exhibit at the Jewish Museum in New York included an artwork that showed all "patriarchal" passages of the Bible marked for deletion.) Unity Church congregations address God as *Father-Mother*—a term used as early as 1875 by Mary Baker Eddy (see chapter 9), the founder of Christian Science, in her explanation of the Lord's Prayer.

There is also heightened interest in religions that envision the divine as being female or that value its feminine aspect. This explains the renewed attention paid to early nature religions that worshiped a major female deity (such as Astarte) or in which women have had an important role. As discussed in chapter 11, Wicca worships "the Goddess" in nature and in all women. In Judaism and Christianity, research into the contributions of women is common and even encouraged. Bible studies now talk of the great matriarchs, as well as the patriarchs, of Hebrew history. In Christianity, there is growing interest in medieval female mystics such as Hildegard of Bingen, Margery Kempe, and Mechtilde of Magdeburg. Likewise, Hinduism is being appreciated not only for its female divinities but also for the many female gurus it has produced; Shinto and shamanistic religions are being studied for the important roles women have played; and Taoism is receiving attention for its female imagery.

Much of this new insight still remains academic and theoretical. Whether male-dominated religions will be able to stand firm against the momentum of women's movements is anyone's guess. But many observers assume that women's liberation efforts, at least in industrialized countries, will eventually succeed.

Reassessment of Human Sexuality

Scientific developments, as well as the economic and ideological developments that we have already discussed in this chapter have all broadened our understanding of human sexuality to include more than procreation as its purpose. At the same time, through its development of artificial insemination and in vitro fertilization, science has expanded the possibilities for reproduction. The result of these developments is that reproduction has become a more intentional event. Medicine, clean water, and public sanitation have led to an explosion of the world population. This fact, combined with our new understanding of sexuality, has forced the rethinking of the purpose of marriage. Psychology has contributed an understanding of sexuality as being essential to the makeup of human beings. Biology has demonstrated the human connection with the animal world and revealed the great variety of animal sexual expression. Anthropology has made people aware of the variety in attitudes toward sex among different cultures and across historical periods.

As a result of these advances and findings, many people now grant that sex has key functions in human existence beyond the creation of children. Among these other important functions are intimacy, pleasure, self-expression, and even self-understanding. The acknowledgment of these functions has led many to question traditional sexual ethics and to rethink the appropriateness of sexual prohibitions in religious traditions.

Religions and their branches that stress morality have tended to react to sexual liberation movements by defending, often staunchly, the primacy of procreation as the purpose for sex, and marriage as its proper context. Typically, more conservative branches argue that procreation is the only justification for sex, while more liberal branches recognize other purposes as being equally valid and even go so far as to condemn only sexual acts that cause harm.

The ongoing discussion of human sexuality has raised numerous questions about the relationship between sex and religion and about the history of religious teachings on sex. Looking across the spectrum of the world's religions, we find great variety in the attitudes toward sex. Some religions see sex as having a sacred aspect. Other religions seem almost preoccupied with controlling sexual expression. At certain times and in some religions, any sexual expression has been held inferior in virtue to virginity and celibacy. In some quarters, male sexual expression is viewed quite differently from female sexual expression; often, female sexuality is repressed. Unfortunately, it is far easier to document the variety in attitudes than it is to explain where the attitudes came from and why they have been maintained.

The ongoing clash between traditional views of sexuality—views often codified in religions—and the modern outlook on sexuality probably will not be resolved any time soon. What we are likely to see, however, is greater tolerance for beliefs and practices that are somewhat contradictory—as is evident in teachings about the indissolubility of marriage as compared to the actual toleration of divorce or annulment. The arena of birth control is particularly fertile ground for debate. Although forbidding the practice of birth control acknowledges the primacy of the procreative purpose of sex, it also risks pushing people and even world populations beyond the point where they can satisfy physical and educational needs.

Another area of controversy exists regarding same-gender sexual expression and relationships. Some religions hold that all homosexuality runs counter to divine or natural laws. Some religions and denominations accept homosexuality as an orientation that occurs naturally in some people, but say that acting out that orientation in sexual behavior is wrong; still others value

A rabbi witnesses a contemporary commitment ceremony. It takes place under a *huppah,* a traditional canopy that symbolizes divine protection.

love, compassion, individuality, and privacy more than any abstract judgment of sexual acts, and thus accept gay men and lesbians as full members. Of course, for heterosexual men and women, with full membership come the rights to a religious marriage and ordination; few religions, however, have yet to extend the same benefits to gays and lesbians. Nonetheless, as the contradictions in a partial acceptance of gay members become more obvious and even painful, religions are beginning to reconsider past practice. Several governments have now legalized same-gender marriage, including Holland, Denmark, and Belgium. Same-gender commitment ceremonies are celebrated in increasing numbers of religious congregations—examples are to be found among Jewish congregations, Unitarians, Quakers, the Metropolitan Community Church, the Unity Church, Episcopalians, and Lutherans. The Episcopal Church in the United States in 2003 consecrated as bishop a man who is in a gay relationship; but this has caused conflict with other branches of the Church of England, particularly in Africa.

While debate over what constitutes legitimate sexual expression will continue, there is no denying the impact the sexual revolution has had on religion. Until recent times, religions were able to avoid complex debates on sexual matters because their teachings on sexual morality were regarded as obvious and "natural." Now, however, it is difficult for religious leaders to gather officially without discussing the matter of sex and having it reported later as front-page news. Even the Dalai Lama faces press-conference questions about Buddhist views on sex. Traditions that emphasize conservative positions will be most challenged by the changing views on sexuality.

Science and Technology

One of the engines that powers to some degree all of the movements we are analyzing has been science. Modern science made great early progress in the sixteenth and seventeenth centuries, with the work of Copernicus (1473–1543), Galileo (1564–1642), Kepler (1571–1630), Newton (1642–1727), and others. At first, the developments were theoretical, without much practical application. While theoretical science continued to advance, applied science in the eighteenth and nineteenth centuries led to many practical benefits, including the invention of machinery that could do the work that human beings had formerly done by hand. Scientists investigated the mysteries of lightning and electricity; inventors made engines powered by steam and coal; researchers made advances in understanding and preventing diseases; engineers designed train tracks that linked large cities to each other; and the telephone and electric light became commonplace. In the next century came the airplane, radio, television, and computers. Over these same centuries, scientific theory advanced, resulting in the theory of evolution, molecular theory, the theory of relativity, and theories regarding astronomy and quantum physics. These accomplishments have transformed both our physical world and our view of the universe.

Some religions have tried to reject or even ignore the contributions of science, arguing that science displaces God, questions religious belief, and undermines morality. Scientists, however, argue that science gives us a valuable view of the universe that should be appreciated. It represents, they say, the collective work of thousands of people over many centuries. If we think about how long it took for human beings to draw a map of the whole earth (accomplished by Gerardus Mercator in 1538), we can admire the efforts of science to give us an even grander "map"—a general view of reality.

The current scientific view of reality can be summarized quickly. Scientific theory and research state that the universe emerged in a great explosion approximately ten to fifteen billion years ago. (What came before the explosion is not and possibly cannot be known by science.) In fact, the universe is still expanding from that explosion—although scientists debate whether the universe will contract or continue to expand indefinitely. As the universe cooled, galaxies formed; there are at least a hundred billion galaxies, each containing about a hundred billion stars. Our planet, earth, is about six billion years old, belongs to a galaxy we call the Milky Way, and travels around a sun whose energy will be exhausted in another six billion years. All physical things are made of smaller units, called molecules, which in turn consist of even smaller units, called atoms, electrons, neutrons, and other particles; and, ultimately, the physical world can be seen as various forms

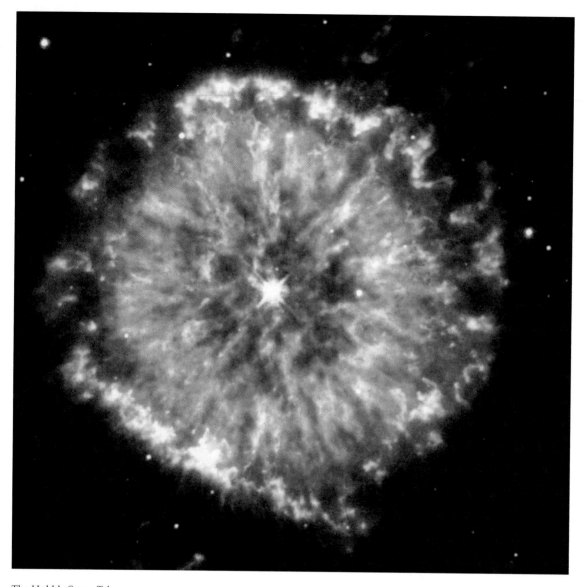

The Hubble Space Telescope photographed the stars near the center of the Milky Way Galaxy. The telescope's findings challenge not only some traditional religious formulations but also some commonly accepted scientific hypotheses. Science, like religions, is ever-changing.

of energy. Phenomena such as lightning and earthquakes have natural causes. Carbon-based life forms—possibly assisted by lightning, volcanic eruptions, and matter from comets—began to emerge on earth in one-celled form several billion years ago and, growing more complex, evolved in many directions on land and sea, finally producing the plants and animals we know today. The human being, which first appeared on earth about one or two million years ago, is part of the same evolutionary process but is the most complex life form known so far.

Although some scientific positions, such as those concerning evolution and molecular structure, are still called theories, they have enough proof underpinning them that they will almost certainly not be supplanted. The current general scientific vision of reality thus seems fairly firm; and although intriguing discoveries will certainly be made over the next centuries, the basic vision will probably not be totally overturned.

Just as science has advanced our understanding of reality, so it has replaced earlier worldviews. For example, we now see the earth not as a flat surface but as a sphere, in orbit around the sun; we understand most sickness to be caused by germs; and we know that earthquakes are generally caused by the movement of tectonic plates. Just as surely as electricity, television, and basic literacy are penetrating to the far corners of the world, so also will the scientific model of reality. Prescientific religions may continue to exist in the remotest cultures, but major religions will have to accommodate the scientific view of reality. It is the anvil on which all religions will be hammered and tested.

Science and technology have broadened our knowledge and enriched our lives. In addition, they have given people new choices. Some of these choices pose ethical questions, at least in some cultures and religious traditions; and having choices can force people to examine their most basic philosophical positions.

The following areas of possibility raise ethical questions in some of the religious traditions that we have considered in this text. In one or another tradition, the possibilities may pose great religious challenges; in another tradition, the same possibilities may be unremarkable. The multiplicity of responses to the following issues stems from several sources. One source is the variety of values that are attached to human beings, animals, and the environment. Another source is the variety to be found in religious conceptions of cosmic, karmic, or divine order.

Fertility assistance Medical science has made conception or a viable pregnancy possible for some women who in earlier times could not have conceived or carried a pregnancy to term. Fertility drugs and in vitro fertilization are two techniques that have made conception possible. But multiple births among women who have taken fertility drugs are common; women sometimes carry as many as seven or eight babies in the same pregnancy, knowing that some of them may die. Is the survival of one or a few babies worth the potential loss of the others? In addition, because of the high costs associated with fertility medicines, the procedures are primarily available to wealthier individuals. Should the enhanced possibility of bearing children be available only to the wealthy?

Birth control The number of contraception options for women and men is growing all the time; a pill for males will be available in the future. In some religious traditions the number of children born is viewed as originating in divine will. Is it moral then to use any means to limit the number of one's children? In other religious traditions, human ingenuity is seen as part of the divine will or cosmic order. Members of these traditions may worry that our world population may soon exceed the earth's ability to provide food, water, and shelter. In addition, bearing too many children, especially if the births are too close together, can seriously undermine the health of a mother. Is it moral then not to do what we can to prevent overpopulation of the earth and promote women's health?

Ethical termination of pregnancy Abortion is not a new practice, although its easy availability in many parts of the world is a recent development. But abortion raises moral questions. At what point in its development is an embryo or a fetus to be considered a human being and thus accorded basic human rights? Is there a moral difference between early abortion and late-term abortion? Are ethical considerations different in the case of a pregnancy resulting from rape or incest? Is a mother's right to life greater than that of an embryo or fetus? Several techniques now exist for examining an embryo or fetus for gender and for genetic abnormalities. Should the resultant knowledge be seen as justification for terminating a pregnancy?

Ethical termination of adult life Capital punishment has long been debated. Today the debate extends to using medical intervention to end a terminally ill person's life; such action has already been legalized, under strict guidelines, in Holland. The term "mercy killing" is indicative of the growing social acceptance of euthanasia (Greek: "good death"). Does social acceptance make such a procedure ethical? Do individuals have the right to end their own lives? Do they have the right to end the lives of others, such as spouses, relatives, or friends? What might be reasonable circumstances for euthanasia? Is there a right to "death with dignity"? If there is, what kind of legal requirements should accompany the right? Should a doctor be permitted to speed the death of a dying patient? Should the life of a person who is comatose or brain-dead be sustained as long as mechanically possible?

Organ transplantation Human body parts that have failed can sometimes be replaced by organs from another human being. Among the organs that are commonly transplanted are hearts, kidneys, livers, and corneas. Do we have an obligation to donate our body parts for transplantation? Should organs from executed criminals be used for transplantation? Is it ethical for people to sell parts of their body before or after their death?

Cloning Mice, sheep, and other animals have been replicated by cloning. Scientists hope to apply the technology someday to cloning human body parts to use as replacements for defective body parts. Some scientists wish to clone entire human beings. What moral considerations should guide decisions about human cloning?

Genetic manipulation Scientists are hopeful that research on the human genetic code will result in heightened intelligence, extended life spans, and new treatments for disease. Related research in plants is aimed at developing disease-resistant strains to feed our ever-expanding population. But experiments will inevitably produce unexpected, perhaps potentially dangerous, results. New forms of viral and bacterial life could be produced that might be disastrous to current life forms. What kinds of controls are needed in terms of the experiments that are allowed and the places where the experiments are performed? Should, for example, human embryonic tissue, a product of miscarriages and terminated pregnancies, be used in genetic and related research? Are human beings "playing God," or could a cosmic plan, if there is one, include an ability to modify the human species or to create new animal species?

Species rights Most laws derive from an assumption that human beings have basic rights. But some thinkers assert that animals, trees, and other elements of nature have rights of their own. Some argue, for example, that all animals and sentient beings have the right to not suffer from human infliction of unnecessary pain. This argument has raised questions about the legitimacy of using animals for food, clothing, sport, or scientific experimentation. Other thinkers (especially those in the movement called Deep Ecology) assert that forests, jungles, wildernesses, and oceans also have rights—to exist and to be protected from exploitation. From this they argue that control of population growth, of resource exploitation, and of pollution, such as acid rain, is a moral duty not only for the health of human beings but for the welfare of animals, plants, and other aspects of nature as well.

The founders of the major religious traditions never had to address these issues specifically. That does not mean, however, that their followers today should not concern themselves with these issues. At the same time, some would argue that these issues should be decided not in churches and temples by religious authorities but rather in secular courts by representatives of civilian governments. Deciding who should determine what is ethical and how ethics should be expressed in law are themselves important issues for this century.

The scientific approach to reality generally has helped—at least potentially—to make the earth a more interesting and pleasant place for human beings to inhabit than it was in past centuries. Granted, applied science has done a great deal to alter the landscape for the worse. Applied science has damaged nonindustrial cultures and polluted the environment. But science has also done much to help. It has reduced infant mortality, extended human life spans, and made human life generally more secure. This has been done especially by advances in medicine and sanitation. Today, life spans in industrialized countries are double what they were two hundred years ago. People now routinely expect to live to be 80 or more. Scientists are working on life extension, and it may become common for people to live to 100, 110, or even 120 years old. (We know that this is at least possible, because Jeanne Calment, a Frenchwoman who died in 1997, lived to be 122.) And scientists will attempt to extend human life even further. When this happens, death and the afterlife will seem increasingly distant, and the earth will seem more like our permanent home. The resultant feeling of security that has grown up in industrialized countries may have helped human beings within them to place a new value on the earth and on earthly life. It has helped to foster an approach to living that is not traditionally religious but rather secular.

Secularism

The word *secular* is often used as the opposite of *sacred*. As mentioned in earlier chapters, *secularism* refers to the modern tendency to separate religion (which deals with the sacred) from everyday life (the secular). In earlier centuries, as we have seen throughout much of this book, religion and everyday life were quite commonly intertwined. Today, they remain intertwined primarily in societies in which a single religion is the state religion or the predominant religion.

The impetus to separate religion from public life found its greatest support in Europe. Primarily because of the horrific religious wars of the sixteenth and seventeenth centuries, influential thinkers there began to envision a type of nation in which there would be no state religion and individuals would be free to practice their religions as they chose. This model was drawn on in the creation of the new United States and was detailed in the Bill of Rights, which was appended to the Constitution. Because the model is based on a general separation of church and state, it has led to a secular type of government.[9]

Furthermore, the model of no established religion has encouraged a secular style of life. After all, if people are free to practice any religion, they are equally free to practice no religion at all. *Secularism* thus has come to refer to a way of looking at life in which human values and rules for living are taken from experience in *this world*, not from divine revelation, from a world beyond this one, or from religious authorities or religious traditions.

Secularism seems to be gaining ground as science finds ways to extend human life and make it more secure. Consequently, for many people traditional religious worldviews have lessened in influence. Religions of the future will continue to be challenged by the secular vision, particularly when they have to work within secular political entities. To survive on a large scale, they will have to add to and give greater meaning to the modern secular world. This may not be impossible, however. After all, science seeks to describe reality, but religions seek to describe and create meaning. As the philosopher K. N. Upadyaya explains, "Religion is not antagonistic to science. . . . The antagonism comes only through a misunderstanding. It has to be understood that science deals with the physical. Religion, on the other hand, deals with something that is beyond the physical. But the methodology of the two is—or should be—exactly the same: observation, experimentation, and verification."[10] We might note, too, the many contemporary scientists, such as physicists Paul Davies (b. 1946) and Fritjof Capra (b. 1939), who have shown considerable interest in religion.

Agnosticism is a concept often associated with a secular worldview. The English biologist T. H. Huxley (1825–1895), who coined the term, was of the opinion that the existence of God could be neither proven nor disproven from a scientific point of view. He argued that agnosticism—a middle ground between theism and atheism—was the most reasonable theoretical position to hold. It is a view that is commonly held today by scientifically minded people, because it accommodates the study and teaching of science without reference to God or gods. Some people have found that everyday life can be carried on, too, without reference to God or gods. Both practical agnosticism and scientific-theoretical agnosticism may begin to replace traditional theistic religious belief and practice. This tendency may also generate attempts to redefine the conceptions of God; it may inspire a turn toward the nontheistic religions (such as Jainism or Theravada Buddhism); and it may promote the development of nontheistic expressions of values and beliefs.

Some would say that Marxist communism, which began in nineteenth-century Europe but took root elsewhere, is an example of a nontheistic religion. Although it is explicitly atheistic, communism in some forms took on many of religion's attributes. The tomb of Lenin in Moscow was for a long time a site of pilgrimage, with long lines of people. The writings of Marx and Lenin have been treated with an almost scripturelike reverence, and Mao's "little red book" of sayings took on a near-magical quality in China during his lifetime—hospital patients could even be seen clutching it on their way to the operating room. Although communism has weakened considerably (it has been called "the God that failed"), the factors that first produced it have not disappeared. It failed not because of its atheism but because of its lack of economic realism.

Communism, even where it has now been abandoned as an official ideology, succeeded in creating a fairly secular milieu. In Russia and many parts of eastern Europe, new generations of people have been raised without religion. Schools in the communist era often spoke of religion as an outdated method for providing solutions to life's problems—as outdated as horse-drawn carriages and whale-oil lamps. (There are exceptions in postcommunist eastern Europe, of course, such as Poland, but in Poland religion has been inextricably linked with nationalist aspirations.) The same antireligious stance has also been true of China, particularly since the Communist Revolution of 1949. The resultant secularism among the Chinese may have a significant influence on the world, as China, with its population of more than a billion, gains power in the international arena.

Some people welcome secularism—possibly with the same relief felt by many in the early confederation of the United States—because they want life to be carried on without religiously inspired rancor. Machines, such as computers, cars, and telephones, are secular in that they do not ask the religion of the person who operates them. In secular cultures, some wish human beings could be similarly accommodating.

Science offers explanations of reality that once came only from religion. Secular governments often promote values that were once primarily espoused by religion. And secular governments run hospitals, schools, and welfare programs, which at one time were under the exclusive control of religion. What then does this leave for religion? Will current religions move in the direction

Religions, Sacred Texts, and Violence

Religions almost universally preach peace. But they also face questions about the use of violence. Are there situations in which violence is justified? May violence be used for self-defense—to protect one's body, family, or property? Should violence be used to destroy a tyrant? May violence be used to bring justice to society? May violence be used in the conversion of nonbelievers? Unfortunately, religions do not speak with one voice on these matters, and even within the same religion we find contradictory advice. Adding to the difficulty, many sacred texts contain descriptions of justified warfare and killing. Sometimes such texts are meant as metaphors for the fight against evil, but they can too often be used to justify violence. We will look at a few examples.

Most religions accept that violence is justified if it is needed for the protection of oneself or one's family—a position that many people hold as reasonable. There are exceptions, though. Jainism and early Buddhist teachings reject using violence for any purpose whatsoever. The *Dhammapada*, an early Buddhist document, says this: "All beings tremble before violence. All fear death. All love life. See yourself in others. Then whom can you hurt? What harm can you do? He who seeks happiness by hurting those who seek happiness will never find happiness. For your brother is like you. He wants to be happy. Never harm him. . . ."[4] Nonetheless, in later Buddhism, particularly in China and Japan, Buddhist teachings about detachment and transience were sometimes employed to idealize the skillful soldier and the warrior-monk. And Buddhist sculpture shows many figures holding symbolic swords and other weapons.

Hinduism values nonviolence highly, as we see in Gandhi's teachings about non-harm (ahimsa). But we also know that the Bhagavad Gita, perhaps the most influential book in Hinduism, endorses fighting to overcome serious injustice. In the popular epic the *Ramayana,* Rama and his brother Lakshman engage in warfare in order to rescue Rama's wife Sita. And some of the Hindu deities, such as Durga and Kali, are known for their love of blood. Animal sacrifice is still used in their worship, and human sacrifice has not been unknown.

The Tao Te Ching says that the person of the Tao hates weapons (ch. 31). "Whenever you advise a ruler in the way of Tao, counsel him not to use force to conquer the universe," for "thorn bushes spring up wherever the army has passed."[5] It says that the person of the Tao hates weapons. But then the text adds that "he uses them only when he has no choice."[6] This opens a very wide door for fighting, as anyone who has seen a Chinese martial arts film can attest.

We see a fairly militant approach in some religions, possibly as a result of the tribal nature of their original societies. Perhaps because biblical Judaism grew up in a land without strong natural borders, it viewed Yahweh as "Lord of hosts" (Is. 6:3)—a commander of angelic armies that could protect his people. Psalm 135 makes clear this notion of Yahweh as a national protector: "He struck down all the first-born in Egypt, both man and beast. . . . He struck down mighty nations and slew great kings" (Ps. 135:8, 10).[7]

Psalm 18 also sees him as a personal protector: "Thou settest my foot on my enemies' necks" (Ps. 18:40). Psalm 137 is even more graphic about

of secularism? Will religions survive as pockets of belief and practice in a basically secular environment?[11] Could completely secular "religions" emerge? Or will religious instincts be expressed in increasingly nontraditional forms?

Environmental Challenges

Four centuries ago, the total human population was about 500 million. Now, the world's population is more than 6 billion. This growing population has migrated to cities to find jobs, and cities with a million people—once extremely rare—are now sprouting like mushrooms. Megacities—such as Mexico City, treatment of the enemy: "Happy is he who will seize your children and dash them against the rock" (v. 9). Since God "sets the time for war and the time for peace" (Eccl. 3:8), warfare seems at times to be approved and even commanded by God. The books of Joshua and Judges, for example, offer much justified warfare (Jos. 8:1–29). Yet we should also recognize that the Hebrew Bible balances this harshness with a vision of a God of compassion, concerned for the good of the lowly and poor (I Sam. 2:8).

Christianity began with strongly nonviolent principles, evident in the Sermon on the Mount (Mt. 5–7). We know that Jesus refused to lead an armed revolt against the Romans. Early Christianity continued this pacifism, and Christians at first did not become soldiers. Yet change came quickly, both in society and in sacred texts. The book of Revelation—one of the last biblical books written—portrays Jesus on a white horse, dressed in a robe that is covered with the blood of battle. Out of his mouth comes a sword; he rules with an iron rod; and he tramples on sinners like a harvester crushing grapes under his feet (Rev. 19:13–15). (This passage inspired the rhyming words of the Battle Hymn of the Republic: "the Lord," who holds "a terrible swift sword," tramples out "the vintage where the grapes of wrath are stored.") After Constantine became emperor, there was no longer any prohibition on Christians becoming soldiers—perhaps because Constantine was a soldier himself. A century later, Augustine elaborated principles that justified warfare. He also approved of using political force to compel "heretics" (nonmainstream Christians) to conform to orthodoxy.

By the time of the Crusades, the cult of the Christian soldier was complete, and it had military patrons such as St. George, St. Barbara, and St. Michael, who are often portrayed holding swords. (St. George is the patron saint of England, and his red cross is in its flag.)

We find a similar mixture of responses in Islam. The name of the religion itself is related to the Arabic word for peace, and Muhammad worked tirelessly for harmony among the many tribes of Arabia. Yet Muhammad thought that violence was sometimes justified, and he led his followers into battle. As the Qur'an records, God commanded him, "Prophet, rouse the faithful to arms" (8:65).[8] Muhammad spoke of a final day of divine reward and punishment, just as Zoroastrianism, Judaism, and Christianity also teach, and he described vivid punishments prepared by God for sinners: "Garments of fire have been prepared for the unbelievers. . . . They shall be lashed with rods of iron" (22:19). Yet the Qur'an equally counsels fairness and patience, such as in this passage: "If you punish, let your punishment be commensurate with the wrong that has been done you. But it shall be best for you to endure your wrongs with patience" (16:126).

What we see in the scriptures of many religions are words of peace and compassion, side-by-side with warnings of violence and punishment. Unfortunately, most texts offer possibilities for individual believers to choose passages that give authority to their cruelty and anger. Only scriptures (like those of the Jains) that allow no harm whatsoever can avoid being used to justify the use of violence.

São Paulo, Shanghai, Tokyo, New York, and Cairo—are becoming more common, even though most of them find it difficult to cope with their unchecked growth. Some cities have become bleak, inhospitable urban environments.

At the same time, the natural environment is being ravaged to provide resources for the increasing world population. The rainforests of Malaysia, Thailand, Indonesia, and Brazil are disappearing to provide wood and farmland, and the habitat of many animals, including all great apes in the wild, is being threatened. Nuclear energy is used to make electricity, but no one knows where to safely store the spent fuel. Pesticides are used for growing and storing many foods, despite their related health dangers.

The great religions of the past grew up in a quite different world and did not have to deal with the moral issues raised by population growth, urban life, corporate business policies, nuclear waste, and environmental pollution. Faced with these entirely new problems, old religions must try to discover within themselves the wisdom to handle these challenges. They will have to fundamentally rethink morality. Doing so will not be easy or straightforward, as we will see in a moment.

THE RECURRING CHALLENGE OF CHANGE

If our textbook pilgrimage of world religions has revealed a common denominator among religions, it is this: All religions that survive must ultimately adapt to changing circumstances, whether they acknowledge the adaptations or not. If there is a second common denominator, it is probably the fact that adaptation is seldom achieved without confusion, struggle, and pain. Indeed, we might argue that struggle, debate, "swings of the pendulum," the breaking off of splinter groups, and even the founding of new religious movements are all part of the process by which religion seeks to remain relevant in a changing world.

A good case study of a religion's processes of adaptation is found in the recent history of Roman Catholicism. Catholicism, because it has adherents in so many parts of the world, is always being challenged somewhere by changing circumstances. At the beginning of the twentieth century, Catholicism was challenged by new "scientific" understanding, particularly Darwinism and modern biblical criticism. Its response was initially a set of proclamations against the evils of modernism and secularism, movements that might bring the gradual elimination of the need for religious explanations.

To some extent, Catholicism's warnings against these new movements seemed vindicated by the instabilities of World War I and, shortly thereafter, of worldwide economic depression. Nonetheless, in some ways Catholicism was already adapting to the changing world order, particularly in the evolution of new Catholic social doctrine that was spelled out in several papal encyclicals. The horrors of World War II provided new opportunities for the expression of religious faith, but the same war ultimately fostered crosscultural contact, female emancipation, secularization, and—through the use of atomic fission—the power of science.

The aftermath of the war only increased the pace of change, and the movement of "tectonic plates" eventually produced a Catholic earthquake in the person of Pope John XXIII. This elderly, mild-mannered pope stated his desire to open the church to the modern world, and he initiated meetings of the world's Catholic bishops that were intended to help Catholicism remain relevant. By the end of the Second Vatican Council in 1965, Roman Catholicism had a different face, a face marked by an emphasis on human rights, a new tolerance for the secular world, an acceptance of separation between church and state, and an openness to diversity. This was the face of an old religion taking major steps to adapt itself to the modern world.

The view from the moon . . . gave new meaning to the word "religion." The English word for religion came from the Latin word *religare*. It means to connect. Religion is about how we are all connected to each other and to every creature and to the earth. Religion is about including, about every part belonging to the whole. "Religion" is the old word and "ecology" is the new word. The view from the moon shows that religion and ecology share the same meaning of connectedness.

—James Parks Morton, Dean Emeritus of the Cathedral of Saint John the Divine in New York, speaking of the 1969 photo of the earth taken from the moon[12]

This NASA photo of Earth has sometimes been called a religious icon that makes viewers realize the beauty of the earth and the interrelatedness of all its parts. ◀

But the case study does not end with the liberalization initiated by John XXIII. As history would have predicted, the pendulum swung back, particularly at the urging of Pope John Paul II, the first pope from a communist country. Perhaps the most telling mark of the swing away from change was the new pope's open embrace of the cult of the Virgin Mary, a cult that had been deemphasized by the Catholicism that emerged from Vatican II. Pope John Paul II insisted that only males could be priests and bishops. He also appointed bishops who reflected his own conservative beliefs; he reasserted the primacy of Rome; and he condemned the thought of some liberal Catholic theologians. Nonetheless, he also furthered his church's defense of human social rights, condemned the excesses of capitalism, and fought capital punishment. And, while reasserting the traditional Catholic opposition to divorce, the tribunals of his bishops oversaw overwhelming growth in the number of Church-granted marriage annulments.

The phenomena in this small case study are by no means unique to Roman Catholicism (although we must grant that it is a more monolithic religion than most). We review them here simply to illustrate the tensions and vacillations that surface when the traditions of a powerful religion are confronted by new developments that are incompatible with some of the old ways. Ultimately, as we saw in preceding chapters, religions must adapt and change. Often they initially fight the forces of change and in the process possibly become even more conservative, but such conservatism can be a stage of adaptive development that eventually grows into new forms of religious belief and practice.

The inevitability of conservative reaction to the onslaught of change is one way to understand a phenomenon that is sometimes called fundamentalism. Fundamentalist movements—occurring in many parts of the world—are often fueled by calls for a "return to the values of our founders" and to an earlier, more traditional vision.

The term *fundamentalism* was first used in the early twentieth century to describe certain conservative Christian movements. These movements sought to counter doubts about traditional beliefs by asserting what they held to be the "fundamentals" of Christian faith. Among the traditional beliefs being reasserted were several that had been called into question by science: beliefs in the physical resurrection of Jesus, in the virgin birth, and in the inerrancy of the Bible. In contrast to that limited usage of the word *fundamentalism*, the term is now used more broadly (perhaps too broadly) to refer in general to conservative movements in virtually all religions, most notably Hinduism, Islam, Judaism, and Christianity.

Fundamentalist movements reflect an effort to simplify a religion. They emphasize what followers see as the basics, the essential elements, of a religion. The personal rewards of fundamentalism are multiple: a sense of bettering society, of uniting with like-minded people, and of repairing a religion to make it useful once again as a clear guide to what is right and wrong. Although fundamentalist movements are motivated by many reasons, they represent primarily a response to the threat of change.

The best-known example of late-twentieth-century fundamentalism is possibly the Islamic Revolution in Iran, initiated by the late Ayatollah

Khomeini (see chapter 10); but Islamic fundamentalist movements are also occurring in many other countries, such as Egypt, Turkey, Pakistan, Indonesia, Malaysia, and Algeria. We see fundamentalism active in other religions as well—in Christianity, especially in the United States and Africa; in Hinduism in India; and in Judaism, particularly in Israel. In some of these countries, fundamentalist movements also serve to help assert ethnic or national identity. However, it may be increasingly difficult for fundamentalist religious movements to avoid being influenced by the pervasive secular environment that is spreading throughout the modern world.

The image of a swinging pendulum is a recurrent metaphor in this chapter. We return to it one last time, as we imagine the pendulum swinging away from fundamentalism toward another phenomenon, which may well be at the other end of the arc: a kind of neopantheism expressed through a semideification of nature. Just as the Ayatollah Khomeini and Pope John Paul II articulated the aspirations of monotheistic fundamentalist movements, so thinkers such as Julian Huxley (1887–1975), Aldous Huxley (1894–1963), Rachel Carson (1907–1964), and E. F. Schumacher (1911–1977) first articulated the "doctrines" of the "nature movement." Major religions, perhaps less anxious over the nature movement than over other forces of change, are now taking note of these doctrines. Older religions that focused on nature (such as native religions, Shinto, and early Taoism) are being looked at with new respect. The potential of this movement for growth and for assimilation by existing religions suggests that it is a possible new scaffolding for the cathedral of humankind's future religious expressions.

NATURISM: A NEW RELIGIOUS PHENOMENON?

For a long time, human beings have been searching for ways to relate to the natural world. On the one hand, nature is obviously beautiful and awe inspiring, and human beings are clearly dependent on "Mother Nature" for food, water, and air. On the other hand, anyone who has been lost on a hike or adrift in a boat understands that the natural world can be very unmotherly, dangerous, and uncaring. Nature can be too cold or too hot, too wet or too dry; it endangers us with disease, insects, and wild animals; it can hurt as well as help. Survival in nature can be precarious.

Out of necessity, human beings have tried to control the power of nature and its effects on their lives. Much has been done with tools and the elements of nature itself. We have learned to make fire, raise food, use medicines, and take other such practical measures. Developments in water purification, sewers, and sanitation were an immense step upward. So were vaccination and the discovery of antibiotics. The forms of control have now become so frequent and sophisticated that we don't even notice them. (For example, when was the last time you thought about the presence of glass windows, window screens, or streetlights?)

Unfortunately, complete physical control of every natural element is impossible. Therefore religions and philosophies have also been employed

Julia Hill lived in this ancient redwood for more than a year to protect it from being cut and to protest all old-growth logging.

to minimize the psychological impact of natural events. In particular, Taoism, Buddhism, and Hindu yoga teach ways to accept or work with the natural elements and their unexpected changes. Their premise is that if we cannot change the outside world, we can at least change our responses to it.

In their drive to overcome the injurious power of nature, however, some religions have virtually denied that human beings are a part of nature. They have viewed the earth as merely a way station on the road to a more permanent life after death and human beings as primarily spirits, temporarily imprisoned in their bodies. Some religions have architecturally separated their believers from nature in buildings that resemble bank vaults. Those religions that see nature as dangerous have too often paid little attention to its beauty.

Technology and commerce have also exhibited a limited vision of nature, treating it merely as a resource to be exploited. Nature has been valued not for its forests but for its lumber; not for its sand and soil but for its concrete; not for its rivers and waterfalls but for its energy potential in the form of dams and hydroelectric power.

Now, however, human beings are at a new place in the history of their relationship with nature. Because human life for a good number of people is less subject to discomforts and diseases, nature seems less fearsome than was the nature that once needed to be placated through ritual. The more recent exploitation of the environment is seen as inappropriate. People are beginning to recognize that exploitation must give way to protection. This new attitude respects nature for itself and refuses to view it simply as something that helps or hurts human beings. It sees the natural world not only as a pool of resources but also as a source of wonder. This approach has led thinkers to reexamine religious views of nature and has generated new interest in all those religions that esteem it. Native religions are appreciated for their reverence for the rights of trees, birds, and animals to continue in their own particular modes of existence. Taoism is looked to for its sensitivity to the mystery of the universe and for its influence on the Chinese artistic rendering of nature. This approach also looks to those forms of Mahayana Buddhism that see nature as "the body of the Buddha."

In Europe, a contemplative interest in nature is not entirely new. Its origins can be traced back many centuries to the nature mysticism of some medieval Cistercian monks and Franciscan friars beginning with Saint Francis of Assisi. It gained strength in those thinkers and artistic creations that are now recognized as part of the European Renaissance. An interest in nature is evident in the writings of Petrarch (1304–1374), in the poetry of Chaucer (c. 1340–1400), in Italian and English madrigals, and in many Renaissance paintings. Nature played a major role in the Romantic movement of the eighteenth and nineteenth centuries, which held that nature is the major manifestation of the sublime. Nature was thus of great importance in many artistic endeavors of Romanticism—in English and French painting, in German music, and in English garden design.

The growing exposure in Europe to Chinese ceramics in the eighteenth century and to Japanese art in the late nineteenth century may have added to the growing appreciation of nature. Chinese painting on ceramics (which we significantly call chinaware) frequently portrayed trees, birds, and nature scenes; and Japanese scrolls and woodblock prints, which revolutionized European painting, often showed the power and color of mountains and ocean.

In the late nineteenth and early twentieth centuries, the movement toward nature was strikingly evident in the painting of the Impressionists, among whom Claude Monet (1840–1926) was a significant example. Monet not only painted occasional scenes of nature in the countryside, but he left Paris to create a country home with a garden featuring a large water lily pond, which he painted regularly for the last forty-three years of his life. The garden he created at Giverny is virtually a place of pilgrimage today; his paintings of nature hang in many major museums; and reproductions of his paintings of water lilies have made his work well known and loved throughout the world.

The great open spaces of North America also inspired a feeling for the spirituality of nature—as depicted in the works of European and American painters of the nineteenth century. Travelers who visited the western part of North America wrote of its extravagant beauty. One of these was Scottish-born naturalist John Muir (1838–1914), author of *The Mountains of California* (1894) and *Our National Parks* (1901). Largely because of his efforts, Yosemite was made a national park, and his work helped to protect and develop the growing national park system; Muir demanded that beautiful regions important to the whole nation be protected.

Today, signs of this new approach to the natural world—an approach that is both practical and spiritual—are evident everywhere. Earth Day was established only a few decades ago, but has already become an important festival of nature. Television is crowded with wonderfully photographed programs on animals and insects, forests and lakes, coral reefs, fish, and oceans—films that have become an art form in their own right. Specialty stores now sell items that express the theme of nature—from semiprecious stones and interesting mineral formations to posters of dolphins and whales, to recorded music that incorporates the sounds of waves and rain. A whole new type of environmentally sensitive travel is becoming popular; *ecotourism* takes people to places like the Amazon and the Galápagos Islands. Zoos, which used to be little more than prisons for animals, are undergoing a revolution in design; they now try to provide a familiar, comfortable, and spacious environment for their animals. Legal protections are being created for endangered species. Art and music (discussed in more detail later in this chapter) have actually pointed the way, through over a century of works that have been strongly inspired by the natural world.

This entire movement, which we might call Naturism, is influencing our lives in important ways in the industrialized world. It is actually a network

Claude Monet's paintings provide a new way to contemplate nature. His garden near Paris, shown here in a photograph, has become a contemporary pilgrimage site.

of related interests, including groups that work for the protection of forests and jungles and endangered species. It has worked to set up sanctuaries for whales and dolphins. It has produced ardent animal rights groups, which oppose the use of fur, the killing of animals for sport, unnecessary animal testing, and the inhumane breeding and slaughter of animals for food. It has generated efforts to recycle and to minimize pesticide use. It inspires those groups that are seeking to reduce energy consumption and to use forms of energy that do not endanger human and animal life. Naturism encourages energy efficiency in architecture and car design. It expresses itself, as well, in efforts that encourage a healthy diet, regular exercise, vitamin supplements, and non-Western forms of medical treatment. As examples of its organizational expression, there are numerous groups dedicated to bettering the earth: Greenpeace, the Sierra Club, the Audubon Society, the Nature Conservancy, and People for the Ethical Treatment of Animals.

What I have called Naturism has interesting parallels with traditional religions. For example, it has a strongly prophetic aspect because of its moral rules. Like many religions, it dictates what a person should or should not eat, wear, and do. (Some bumper stickers illustrate this: "Fur looks good on animals," and "Think globally, act locally.") Naturism also has a mystical aspect in its emphasis on the fundamental unity of human beings and the universe. In fact, it offers as its supreme experience the sense of oneness with animals and the rest of nature.

So far, this movement is deficient in the sacramental, ritualistic element that usually characterizes religions—although this aspect has great potential

Ansel Adams devoted his life to photographing Yosemite. In his photograph *Moon and Half Dome* (1960) he suggests the unity of opposites—large and small, light and dark, the changing and the changeless.

for development in the next centuries. Events like Earth Day and summer solstice festivals may be a beginning of such rituals, and the religion of Wicca attempts to re-create pre-Christian nature rituals. We might see the evolution of nature-based ritual for the major seasons: Earth Day already marks spring; summer solstice rites mark summer; and autumn is marked by Thanksgiving or similar end-of-harvest ceremonial meals and rituals.

Like religion, Naturism also has its "sacred places." Destinations of eco-pilgrimage include Yosemite, the Rocky Mountains, wildlife preserves in eastern Africa and Costa Rica, Mount Everest, the whale sanctuary at Maui, Glacier Bay and Denali National Park in Alaska, and many others. (The word *sanctuary*, used in reference to animal preserves, is religiously significant.) Naturism is also developing its role models, many of whom, interestingly, are women: Dian Fossey (1932–1985), Jane Goodall (b. 1934), Rachel Carson (1907–1964),

Brigitte Bardot (b. 1934) and Rue McClanahan (b. 1935). There is a growing body of environmentalist "scripture"—for example, *Walden* by Henry David Thoreau (1817–1862) and *Animal Liberation* by Peter Singer (b. 1946). And sacred iconography extends from the nature photographs of Yosemite by Ansel Adams (1902–1984) to popular paintings of whales and porpoises by Christian Lassen (b. 1956), Robert Wyland (b. 1956), and others.

ECLECTIC SPIRITUALITY

It is quite common now to hear people say that they are not particularly interested in any one religion but that they are interested in spirituality. It is not always clear what they mean by *spirituality,* but the fact that people use this word to describe their religious stance does reveal an important contemporary phenomenon. Individuals now assemble elements of different belief systems to create their own spiritual system.

As has occurred with Naturism, "eclectic spirituality" has become associated with a particular set of attitudes and practices. Highly valued are practices that promote inner peace and a feeling of harmony between oneself and the outer world. The key belief of those who embrace eclectic spirituality is the interrelatedness of all elements in the universe. That belief is often expressed in an attitude of respect and reverence for all people and creatures. The respect and reverence are often cultivated through contemplative acts that dissolve separateness and promote ways of seeing beyond the superficial to the essential relatedness, even oneness, of all beings.

Traditional religions often engender spirituality, and eclectic spirituality is marked by borrowings from traditional religions. These borrowings range from meditative practices inspired by Buddhism to dancing inspired by Sufism. But there are other means to attain spirituality, and many find it outside traditional religion. We have all had the experience, for example, of going to a movie theater, sitting down in the darkness, and gradually being drawn into a film that does far more than merely entertain. At a certain point, we recognize that the film is evoking in us a response that is somehow fundamental to the human experience and at the same time transcendent—an experience of the "spiritual." Often we sense that others in the audience are sharing in that experience. At the end of such films, there is silence, a silence that may prevail even in the lobby as people leave the theater. Musical concerts can also induce a similar experience.

Psychologists such as Jung (1875–1961; see chapter 1) and Abraham Maslow (1908–1970) have written extensively of the necessary spiritual development of the human being. Maslow became preoccupied with it, first describing what he called "peak experiences," which are rare and transient, and then describing what he called "plateau experiences," which are contemplative experiences in everyday life that may be frequent and long-lasting. Maslow's most famous books were *Toward a Psychology of Being* and *Religions, Values, and Peak Experiences.* These works focus on contemplative experiences of many types, which Maslow identified through numerous interviews. He belonged

Religion and Movies

From their earliest days, movies have explored religious themes and the questions of spirituality—from the silent film *Intolerance* and films based on the Bible to more recent movies such as the *Matrix* series. Less overtly religious films also have explored moral and spiritual topics. Frank Capra (1897–1991), in his film *Lost Horizon* (based on a novel by the same title by James Hilton [1900–1954]), contrasted the utopian world of Shangri-la, hidden in the Himalayas, with the superficiality of the modern industrial world. The message of the movie is given by the "high lama," the founder of Shangri-la, whose very last words are "Be kind." In another film by the same director, *It's a Wonderful Life* (which regularly appears on television at Christmastime), a man discovers the value of his life only when he is on the brink of suicide. At that moment he sees all the good he has done, and he receives the affectionate care of his neighbors.

Some films bring a kind of enlightenment through their revelation of the value of everyday life. In the film version of the play *Our Town*, by Thornton Wilder (1897–1975), a girl goes back in time to her sixteenth birthday and sees her family in a new light. *Peggy Sue Got Married* does the same thing, when a woman is transported back to her high school days. *Late Spring* and other films by the Japanese director Yasujiro Ozu (1903–1963) reveal the beauty of the everyday through careful attention to the details of human life. They typically show a family at a turning point in its life, such as when a daughter gets married and must move away. Akira Kurosawa (1910–1999), in his *Ikiru (To Live)*, depicts a man's reflections upon discovering he is dying of cancer. The man, up to now an undistinguished city bureaucrat, fights to create a city park for children as the one major gift of his life, and in that struggle he becomes a spiritual hero. *American Beauty*, Sam Mendes's 1999 movie, explores similar issues, asking questions about finding meaning in life.

Science-fiction films about space travel also show interesting parallels with mythic religious stories of visitations by angels and deities or human ascensions to heavenly realms. Sometimes these films touch on the semireligious struggle between the forces of good and evil—take, for example, the *Star Wars* series. Many times (as in the film *E.T.*), they suggest that human beings need to learn lessons that can only be taught by representatives from other worlds.

to the school that has been called Humanistic Psychology. Another related school was Logotherapy, begun by Viktor Frankl (1905–1997).

An increased interest in spirituality may also have influenced the changing attitude toward the home. People increasingly think of their home as their "sanctuary." They want to include elements in their apartment or house that will promote tranquility in everyday life. (This may be part of the reason for the popularity of home makeover programs on television!) It is intriguing to see the resemblances to religious design that are appearing in some homes. There may be a small home altar, a meditation area, or a garden room for reflection. Plants and gardens are taking on a new importance, reminding us of their significance in several Asian religious traditions. Fountains are popular for both interior and exterior, and come in all sizes and shapes. They recall the uses of water in so many religions, such as Shinto, Hinduism, Christianity, and Islam. Sometimes larger houses even have "cathedral" ceilings. The home—as well as the church and temple—is now being conceived of as a sacred space.

The notion of spirituality, within but also increasingly apart from religion, permeates modern culture. Almost any big-city record store has a "spiritual music" section. There you may find the compositions of Arvo Pärt (b. 1935) alongside New Age music, recordings of birdsong and ocean

Physical exercise can also be a form of exercise for the spirit.

waves, and recordings of monastic chants from the Catholic and Tibetan religious traditions.

Because eclectic spirituality is difficult to define, we will try now to understand it through examples. We will look particularly at three aspects frequently thought of as characterizing modern spirituality: the sense of interrelatedness, an attitude of respect and reverence, and a contemplative approach to experiencing reality.

Interrelatedness

As we saw in earlier chapters, many religions have pointed to a relatedness among all beings, expressed perhaps most strongly in Buddhist and Hindu thought but also in the mystical teachings of many other religions. Interest in interrelatedness resurfaced as a cultural phenomenon in the 1980s, when a book on contemporary physics—which ordinarily would have had a readership of at most a few thousand—became a best-seller. Its title, *The Tao of Physics,* was a clear signal of the willingness of its author, Fritjof Capra, to leap across the traditional boundaries between religion and science. Its exploration of the subatomic world helped many readers understand that the relationality we can observe in the visible world mirrors what occurs in the very building blocks of the universe. This same interest in interrelatedness helps account for the popularity of such abstruse topics as chaos theory,

Religion and Pop Culture

Popular culture often presents religious themes. Comic strips and animated cartoon films, for example, look uncomplicated but sometimes have a depth that belies their appearance. (Pablo Picasso ([1881–1973] and other artists have highly valued comics for their economy of line—a great deal can be said with minimal drawing.) Some comic strips indict society in a prophetic way (such as *Doonesbury* or *Dilbert*); other comic strips often are explicitly religious (such as *Peanuts, Family Circus,* and *B.C.*). In many of Disney's animated films (*Dumbo, Bambi, Cinderella, Little Mermaid, Lion King, Tarzan, Dinosaur, Finding Nemo*), a host of loving animals have been created with such personality and charm that their portrayal as conscious, feeling beings on a par with human beings may have contributed to the growing animal liberation movement.

The creation of Superman and other heroic comic-book figures may be a popular form of biblical messianism. Like the messianic agent given authority by the Ancient of Days in the seventh chapter of the Book of Daniel, Superman comes to earth from another world to bring justice and truth. Biblical influence may have inspired the semibiblical "Krypton names" of Superman and of his father: Kal-El and Jor-El. (We might recall that *El* means "God" in Hebrew and occurs in names such as *Israel, Samuel,* and *Michael.*) Superman and other similar heroes help reinforce the human desire for justice and compassion.

The cult of Elvis Presley ("Presleyanity"), while perhaps not what one would call "spiritual," has multiple religious parallels: the death of Elvis at an early age, his later "apparitions" to the faithful, the supposed healing power of his photos, the common image of him dressed in white, the commemoration of his birth and death, the pilgrimage to Graceland and other sites where Elvis lived and worked, and the marketing of his gospel music. Followings centered on other musicians—Jim Morrison, John Lennon, Bob Marley, and the Grateful Dead—show similar religious parallels. These followings suggest that the religious urge remains, though its forms of expression change.

cosmology, and the meteorological relations between ocean temperature and distant weather patterns; it also explains the popularity of such books as *The Whole Shebang* by Timothy Ferris (b. 1914) and *A Brief History of Time* by Stephen Hawking (b. 1942).

Popular interest in interrelatedness is also evident in the reinterpretation of some artworks, particularly the paintings of Georgia O'Keeffe (1887–1986). O'Keeffe's paintings of flowers and animal bones and close-to-the-earth architectural forms have always been regarded as technically excellent. Her paintings have become so popular that one was reproduced on a commemorative U.S. postage stamp. Their recent popularity, however, may hinge more on their expression of interrelatedness and interchangeableness: because many of her paintings depict objects at very close range, the viewer may be unable at first glance to tell if the painting represents a flower, a part of human or animal anatomy, an adobe church, a hillside, or even a seashell. This ambiguity is surprising because, in fact, O'Keeffe's work is often closer to realism than abstraction. However, even that distinction is broken down by O'Keeffe's highlighting of the abstract within the specific. Overall, her paintings express interrelatedness on several levels; they invite the viewer to contemplate patterns and underlying similarities. Some reproductions of O'Keeffe's paintings have become almost icons of spirituality.

Abstraction has been used repeatedly to suggest both the state of interrelatedness and the human experience of oneness. Georgia O'Keeffe's nonrepresentational works frequently use curves of color with this intent, as in *Music:*

By showing ordinary objects at very close range, Georgia O'Keeffe's works, such as this painting of purple flowers, help us to see everyday realities in a new way.

Pink and Blue, Blue, and the *Series 1* paintings.[13] Mark Rothko (1903–1970), one of the greatest painters of pure spiritual experience, achieved a similar effect by superimposing squares of subtle color, which seem to float luminously above their backgrounds. Jackson Pollock (1912–1956) created spontaneous but very complicated worlds of relationship in color by spattering paint on canvases that he had placed on the ground. Viewing these artists' works can give the viewer a feeling of being either out in space, surrounded by stars and blackness, or within an atom, amid the active particles and surrounding emptiness.

Reverence and Respect

As we've already discussed, nature came to be seen during the late twentieth century not as something to use, exploit, and abuse, but rather as a part of ourselves that must be nurtured for the well-being of all. Beyond this

The large paintings of Mark Rothko have been called windows into eternity. They have the luminosity of stained glass but the mystery of the Zen circle.

reconceptualization of nature, best expressed in environmental movements, is a turn to nature as revelation—nature as an expression of the spirit that permeates all reality, nature as a phenomenon to be revered. This attitude is perhaps best expressed in the art of photography.

In an article that compares the qualities of some creative photographers with the virtues of the Taoist sage as espoused in the Zhuangzi, writers Philippe Gross and S. I. Shapiro describe Taoistic ideals, often using both the words of the Zhuangzi and of modern photographers themselves, placed side by side. The authors conclude that the vision of the Taoist sage and of many great photographers is the same: "Both the Sage and the taoistic photographer have the capacity for seeing with unconstricted awareness and are therefore capable of seeing the miraculous in the ordinary."[14] According-ing to Gross and Shapiro, the virtues shared by the Taoist sage and the contemplative photographer include freedom from the sense of self, receptivity, spontaneity, acceptance, and nonattachment—attributes that promote a general attitude of respect and reverence.

Contemplative photography reached a peak of sorts in the nature photography of Ansel Adams (mentioned earlier). His black-and-white photographs of Yosemite National Park, whose mountains and waterfalls recall the subject matter of traditional Chinese landscape painting, evoke a feeling of respect for the power and the beauty of nature. Another devotee of nature, Eliot Porter (1901–1990), photographed in brilliant color to let nature speak fully of its beauty. He became well known for his photographs of trees turning yellow in autumn, of reflections in ponds, and of river canyons. These photographs often elicit the same reverence in the viewer as a Taoist sage might have experienced in contemplating a waterfall or a distant mountain.

Photography has been particularly effective in recording the most minute details of the human face and of human life, once again inviting insight, respect, and reverence. Photography of the American Civil War by Matthew Brady (c. 1823–1896) includes portraits of people in terrible circumstances. Not long after, Edward Curtis (1868–1952) sensitively documented the vanishing indigenous life of Native Americans. Dorothea Lange (1895–1965) and Walker Evans (1903–1975) produced moving studies of people during the Great Depression. More recent masters have been Edward Steichen (1879–1973) and Diane Arbus (1923–1971). Steichen's published anthology of photographs, called *The Family of Man*, includes studies of the spiritual expressed in human faces and actions from around the world. Arbus drew our respectful attention to marginalized people in our urban societies.

The ability to evoke an attitude of respect and reverence is by no means limited to the art of photography. The details of ordinary human life can be treated with reverence in painting as well. Vincent van Gogh (1853–1890) did this repeatedly in his works—from his earlier portrayal of peasants, in *The Potato Eaters*, to his later paintings of the neighborhood postman, of sunflowers arranged in a vase, and of a neighborhood cafe at night. The same attitude of respectful attention can even be found in cartoons (consider the role of Lisa in the popular *Simpsons*). In fact, this attitude can be expressed by any art form or technique that promotes contemplation—the method for revealing spirituality to which we now turn.

> I'm not responsible for my photographs. Photography is not documentary, but intuition, a poetic experience. It's drowning yourself, dissolving yourself. . . . First you must lose your self. Then it happens.
>
> —Henri Cartier-Bresson, photographer[15]

Contemplative Practices

Although eclectic spirituality emphasizes the interrelatedness of all creation, it does not maintain that each person is automatically able to see interrelatedness. However, one can develop an ability to see interrelatedness, as well as an attitude of respect and reverence, by preparation. This is done through a variety of contemplative practices.

As we saw in the earliest chapters of this book, native forms of religious practice have often made use of techniques that result in trance states, in which ordinary reality is viewed in a transformed way. In later chapters we reviewed the forms of mysticism that exist in many of the world's religions and we touched upon the different contemplative activities—such as meditation, Sufi dancing, tea ceremony, and hatha yoga—that have to some extent supplanted the cultivation of trance states. The fact is that anyone—even the person who does not practice a traditional religion—is free to try any of the following contemplative practices that have been developed.

Traditional religions can provide a number of the practices that attract people who are charting their own eclectic spiritual path. Most religions make use of songs, chants, and other forms of music—some of them elaborate. Mahayana and Vajrayana Buddhism use complex chant, often accompanied by bells, drums, gongs, trumpets, conch shells, and cymbals. Christianity has produced a great amount of chant and other choral music. Shinto uses chants and gagaku (the solemn instrumental music derived from ancient Chinese court music). Much religious music is intended to help listeners experience a connectedness with the sacred. Until recently, there were few opportunities to experience religious music without attending a religious service. Today, however, through recordings, people can listen to this music and use it as part of their own contemplative practice at home or even in a car, while commuting or traveling.

Along with traditional religious music, some forms of secular music are also used for contemplative purposes. Today, a common form of contemplative practice is to listen to these types of music in a meditative way. During the late nineteenth century and early twentieth century, the Impressionist schools (particularly in France) developed not only a style of painting but also of music. What is notable about Impressionist music is that it aims not so much to satisfy classical requirements of form but to convey a sensual impression, through music, of a primarily nonmusical experience, such as the coming of dawn or the feeling of standing in a forest.

Much Western contemplative music today is a direct descendant of that earlier evocative music. One example of Impressionist music is *Prelude to the Afternoon of a Faun* by Claude Debussy (1862–1918). In his tone poem *La Mer* (*The Sea*), Debussy uses music to describe a sunrise and a storm on the ocean. His *Nocturnes* for orchestra include a meditation on clouds (*Nuages*), and his *Clair de Lune* creates the feeling of a quiet, moonlit night. Another French composer, Maurice Ravel (1875–1937), even used a wind machine to evoke nature in the full version of his *Daphnis and Chloe*. And both Ravel and Debussy created music for piano that suggests the relaxing play of fountains. A third composer in this contemplative line was the Englishman Frederick Delius (1862–1934), whose works are generally short impressions of seasonal moods. Among the finest are *On Hearing the First Cuckoo in Spring, Summer on the River,* and *The Walk to the Paradise Garden.* The English composer Ralph Vaughan Williams (1872–1958), who studied with Ravel, suggests with a solo violin the flight of a bird in *The Lark Ascending*—a delicate work that, when experienced in a quiet environment, has helped many a listener experience a connectedness with the sacred (the composition is also often used as a subject for modern ballet). His *Fantasia on Greensleeves* and *Fantasia on a Theme of Thomas Tallis* are equally contemplative. The moods created by these composers are today frequently echoed in what has come

What is the future of religion? Is it dusk or dawn?

to be called New Age music, some of which is performed on synthesizers. Trance-inducing music, often used for all-night raves, may also be seen as a new form of spiritual music.

In addition, the spread of modern orchestral instruments in Asia and the use of the synthesizer have made it possible for Asian composers to create complicated crosscultural works that offer new windows through which listeners can experience that which is within and beyond. The contemporary Japanese composers Toshiro Mayazumi (b. 1928) and Toru Takemitsu (b. 1930), for example, are often cited for their efforts to transport listeners through transcultural music.

Whether eclectic spirituality will expand into a fully developed religion is impossible to say. It is easier to predict that world growth will result in more crowded spaces, more noise, greater competition, and increased stress. Under such circumstances, the need for contemplation can only grow.

 ## PERSONAL EXPERIENCE: A NEW RELIGION

Recently I met with a few close friends for lunch. We had hardly sat down when the conversation turned to the world situation. They put me on the defensive—as if all the problems of the world were my fault.

"Why do religions seem to be the cause of so much fighting?" Kathy asked.

I hung my head. Oh no, not again. Why do they think I have answers to their impossible questions?

"Well, maybe it's not fair to say that they are the *cause*," Peggy said. Kind as always, she was trying to rescue me.

"All right," Kathy said. "But they are certainly involved somehow in all the violence. They seem to be more the problem than the solution. Why can't they be more helpful? They should teach people how to get along better together, don't you think?"

"Well, they do help," I said, defensively. "Look at all the hospitals and welfare projects sponsored by religions."

"You're right—partially," said John. "But somehow all that helpfulness and those good intentions don't seem to be enough."

"And look at all their schools." Peggy was adding to the list.

"Spreading ignorance, that's what they're doing," Kathy said. "And their ways of seeing the world are at least one or two thousand years old. Would you follow the medical beliefs of a thousand years ago? You'd have some doctor hammering a hole in your head to get the headache out."

"But what about all the beautiful buildings and art?" I asked. "Doesn't that count for something?"

"It's true. Religions have created stunning buildings and art," Kathy answered. "But you have to weigh that against the anger that religions seem to justify—and the destruction they've caused. They supposedly preach love, but isn't it mostly love just for insiders? They teach you to live apart from 'outsiders,' or convert them, or persecute them, or even kill them. Do any religions really teach loving *everybody?*"

John cut in. "Maybe the problem is the misuse of the word *love*. Religions shouldn't teach love. Better if religions would just teach tolerance. You can't make everyone eat the same food or speak the same language. Nature obviously loves variety. If religions just taught acceptance of differences, that would be enough."

"Forget trying to reform the religions," Kathy said. "It's impossible. They do more harm than good, and they're leading us to catastrophe. They should all be banned."

"Oh, who's going to ban them?" I asked. I reached out to pick up a whole wheat roll from the breadbasket.

"No, you can't get rid of religions," Peggy said. "Most people seem to be basically religious. But religions have an interest in staying separate from each other. What they really need is to learn from each other. I think that people in each religion should intermarry with people in other religions."

"Well," I said optimistically, "maybe some of the violence against outsiders will fade away, since people seem to be traveling a lot and intermarrying more often these days. And peaceful new religions might emerge. I know that you don't believe it, but our historical period could be the beginning of a whole new religious age." The conversation paused for a moment, as my friends digested that. "Just look at how many spiritual friends you have," I added. Everybody laughed. That gave me time to divide my whole wheat roll and pop a bite in my mouth.

"I think we should invent a completely new religion that is more gentle than the old ones," Kathy added. "I'll be the leader. You can be the followers." More laughter.

"I suppose you'll ask us to celebrate your birthday as the supreme holy day," John said. "And will you ask us to send you a part of our income each year, too?"

"Your suggestions are excellent," Kathy answered. "I could never have thought of them myself. Clearly you are acting as effective followers already. And I do look good in a crown. I would also enjoy being carried on a golden palanquin, covered in white silk." She paused to allow us to visualize the scene. "It could be sheer panoply."

Peggy stayed serious. "Maybe what we really have to do is figure out a way to make the religions that we already have much more gentle," she said. "What do you think about that?" She turned to me. "Is it hopeless? Or is it possible?"

Everyone looked at me for the answer. I had thought often about this matter and was ready to give just a few of my ideas. I swallowed the bread I had been chewing, took a sip of water, and cleared my throat.

At just that moment the menus arrived.

RELIGION BEYOND THE CLASSROOM

The national park movement is an expression of a growing sensitivity to nature. It shows an awareness of the connection between nature and the spiritual experience. In the continental United States, there are parks of special importance: Yosemite, Yellowstone, the Grand Tetons, the Grand Canyon, and Bryce Canyon. In Alaska, there are Denali National Park and Glacier Bay. In Hawai`i, there are Volcano National Park on the island of Hawai`i and the Na Pali Coast on Kauai. In the Canadian Rockies, Banff and Lake Louise are two sites worth visiting. In Central America and South America, the system of national parks is less developed but is under way, particularly in Costa Rica, Belize, Venezuela, and Brazil. In Africa, there are major wildlife refuges in Kenya, Tanzania, and South Africa.

FOR FULLER UNDERSTANDING

1. Islam and Buddhism are spreading in North America. How do you think each religion will be changed by contact with the widespread behavior and values of the surrounding culture?

2. How do you see feminism changing traditional religions over the next hundred years?

3. Design a ritual that expresses human relationships with nature. What music might accompany it? Where would it occur? How frequently would it be celebrated?

4. With a partner, write both sides of a debate on the assertion "Religions have in human history done more harm than good and therefore should be banned."

5. Design a home altar that expresses and celebrates the season. Take photos and share them with your class. Explain what elements you have included and their purpose.

6. Study the life and paintings of Georgia O'Keeffe. Describe the images she uses. What does she

seem to be expressing in the way she treats these images?

7. Study the life and photographs of Ansel Adams. List the places that he seemed to love to photograph. What makes his photographs distinctive? What similarities with Taoist ideals do you see in his photographs?

8. Study the life and paintings of Mark Rothko. How might his origins have affected his subject matter? Describe the difference between his early, middle, and late styles. What do the paintings of his mature style seem to be expressing?

9. It is commonly said that religion is a "crutch" to help an individual deal with pain, overcome loneliness, or create meaning in life. Is this a fair assessment? What examples would you give for and against such an argument?

10. Read one of the books listed in the bibliography. Write a review in which you show how the book expanded your understanding of basic teachings, ideas, or practices covered in this entire textbook. Conclude your review by explaining ways in which the book may be relevant in today's world.

11. What are your predictions for the state of the world's religions in 2050? In 2100? Offer support for your predictions.

RELATED READINGS

Azara, Nancy. *Spirit Taking Form: Making a Spiritual Practice of Making Art*. York Beach, ME: Red Wheel/Weiser, 2002. An encouragement to inner growth through the creation of art.

Byock, Ira. *Dying Well: Peace and Possibilities at the End of Life*. New York: Riverhead/Penguin Putnam, 1997. A book for both patients and caregivers about the spiritual possibilities of dying, written by a compassionate specialist in hospice care.

Cooper, Andrew. *Playing in the Zone: Exploring the Spiritual Dimensions of Sports*. Boston: Shambhala, 1998. An invitation to reflect on the meaning of why people engage in sports and on their spiritual possibilities.

deWaal, Esther. *Lost in Wonder: The Spiritual Art of Attentiveness*. Collegeville, MN: Liturgical Press, 2003. A practical guide for finding the spiritual in everyday life.

Gamwell, Lynn. *Exploring the Invisible: Art, Science, and the Spiritual*. Princeton, NJ: Princeton University Press, 2002. A well-illustrated discussion of how the images and worldview of science have contributed to the development of modern art.

Huxley, Aldous. *The Human Situation*. New York: HarperCollins, 1980. A brilliant book, based on lectures that Huxley delivered in 1962 in California, that was among the earliest books to point to the spirituality of nature and to call for environmental responsibility.

Murphy, Michael. *Golf in the Kingdom*. New York: Penguin, 1997. A humorous consideration—with the help of a fictional golf expert—of human striving, various philosophies, and life itself.

Seay, Chris, and Greg Garrett. *The Gospel Reloaded: Exploring Spirituality and Faith in* The Matrix. Colorado Springs, CO: Piñon Press, 2003. A knowledgeable discussion of religious symbolism and meaning in the film *The Matrix*.

Sutherland, Audrey. *Paddling My Own Canoe*. Honolulu: University of Hawai`i Press, 1978. On the surface, a lyrical description of paddling along the shore of Moloka`i; underneath, a charming classic by a legendary canoer and kayaker that presents a spirituality akin to Zen.

Notes

Chapter 1

1. The original painting is part of the permanent collection of the Boston Museum of Fine Arts.
2. William James, *The Varieties of Religious Experience* (New York: Collier, 1961), p. 377.
3. Rudolf Otto, *The Idea of the Holy* (New York: Oxford University Press, 1963), p. 62.
4. Some have criticized Otto's notion of the *mysterium tremendum,* arguing that his theorizing was overinfluenced by Protestant Christianity, in which he was raised.
5. Carl Jung, *Memories, Dreams, Reflections* (London: Collins, 1972), p. 222.
6. *Webster's New World Dictionary,* 2d ed. (New York: William Collins, 1972). Other Latin roots are also possible.
7. *Cassell's New Latin Dictionary* (New York: Funk & Wagnalls, 1960).
8. Similar lists can be found, for example, in William Alston, "Religion," in *The Encyclopedia of Philosophy,* vol. 7 (New York: Macmillan, 1972), pp. 141–42; and Ninan Smart, *The Religious Experience,* 4th ed. (New York: Macmillan, 1991), pp. 6–10.
9. Julian Huxley, *Religion Without Revelation* (New York: Mentor, c. 1957), p. 33.
10. "Between Mountain and Plain," *Time,* 20 October 1952, p. 33.
11. Alston, "Religion," 143–44.
12. Catholics touch the left shoulder first; Orthodox Christians touch the right shoulder first.
13. Kusan Sunim, *The Way of Korean Zen* (New York: Weatherhill, 1985), p. 168.
14. New Oxford Annotated Bible (New York: Oxford University Press, 1991).
15. Good News Bible (New York: American Bible Society, 1976). This version is a paraphrase.
16. For example, the Srimaladevisimhananda Sutra speaks of the enlightenment of a female lay ruler.
17. Martin Luther King, Jr., *Strength to Love* (New York: Harper & Row, 1963), p. 3.
18. See Daniel Pals, *Seven Theories of Religion* (New York: Oxford University Press, 1996).

Chapter 2

1. Nancy Parezo, "The Southwest," in *The Native Americans,* ed. Colin Taylor (New York: Salamander, 1991), p. 58.
2. Geoffrey Parrinder, *Religion in Africa* (New York: Praeger, 1969), pp. 18, 21.
3. Foreword to Peter Knudtson and David Suzuki, *Wisdom of the Elders* (Toronto: Stoddart, 1993), p. xxiv.
4. Gladys Reichard, *Navaho Religion* (Princeton: Bollingen, 1963), p. 286.

5. Florence Drake, *Civilization* (Norman: University of Oklahoma Press, 1936), quoted in John Collier, *Indians of the Americas* (New York: New American Library, 1947), p. 107.

6. Frank Willet, *African Art* (London: Thames and Hudson, 1993), p. 35.

7. One entire room at the Gauguin Museum in Tahiti illustrates Gauguin's interest in discovering a "primary religion." It also shows the religious origin of much imagery in his paintings. A significant collection of Gauguin's paintings and carvings can be seen at the Musée d'Orsay in Paris.

8. Sword, Finger, One Star, and Tyon, recorded by J. R. Walker, in "Oglala Metaphysics," in *Teachings from the American Earth: Indian Religion and Philosophy*, ed. Dennis Tedlock and Barbara Tedlock (New York: Liveright, 1992), p. 206.

9. See Parrinder, *Religion in Africa*, pp. 47–59 for more detail.

10. Åke Hultkrantz, *Native Religions of North America* (San Francisco: Harper, 1987), p. 20, cited in *Ways of Being Religious*, ed. Gary Kessler (Mountain View, CA: Mayfield, 2000), p. 71.

11. Quoted in T. C. McLuhan, ed., *Touch the Earth* (New York: Promontory Press, 1971), p. 42.

12. McLuhan, *Touch the Earth*, p. 56.

13. Knudtson and Suzuki, *Wisdom of the Elders*, p. xxv.

14. Colin Turnbull, *The Forest People* (New York: Simon & Schuster, 1968), p. 14.

15. Knudtson and Suzuki, *Wisdom of the Elders*, p. 29.

16. Knudtson and Suzuki, *Wisdom of the Elders*, p. 27.

17. Parrinder, *Religion in Africa*, p. 43.

18. Ibid., p. 32.

19. Joseph Campbell, *The Power of Myth* (New York: Doubleday, 1988), p. 6.

20. Parrinder, *Religion in Africa*, pp. 80–81.

21. Sam Gill, *Native American Religions* (Belmont, CA: Wadsworth, 1982), p. 98.

22. Ibid.

23. Collier, *Indians of the Americas*, p. 105.

24. Parrinder, *Religion in Africa*, p. 81.

25. For details, see William Sturtevant, "The Southeast," in Taylor, *The Native Americans*, pp. 17–21.

26. From Florence Drake, *Civilization*, quoted in Collier, *Indians of the Americas*, p. 107.

27. See John Mbiti, *Introduction to African Religion* (London: Heinemann, 1986), pp. 143–44.

28. Isabella Abbott, *La`au Hawai`i: Traditional Hawaiian Uses of Plants* (Honolulu: Bishop Museum Press, 1992), p. 37.

29. Ibid, p. 18. Four days were sacred to Ku, three to Kanaloa, two to Kane, and one day at the end of the month to Lono.

30. This is not unprecedented. In Samoa, universal claims were made for the god Tangaroa, possibly as early as 800 C.E. See John Charlot, *Chanting the Universe* (Hong Kong: Emphasis, 1983), p. 144.

31. John Charlot remarks that the first public Hawaiian temple service since 1819 was carried out by Samuel H. Lono on October 11, 1980. See ibid, p. 148.

32. Joan Halifax, *Shaman: The Wounded Healer* (London: Thames and Hudson, 1994), p. 5.

33. Isaac Tens, recorded by Marius Barbeau, in *Medicine Men of the North Pacific Coast*, Bulletin 152 (Ottawa: National Museum of Man of the National Museum of Canada, 1958), found in Tedlock and Tedlock, *Teachings from the American Earth*, pp. 3–4.

34. Ibid.

35. Quoted in Knudtson and Suzuki, *Wisdom of the Elders*, p. 70.

36. For a detailed study of the religious use of peyote by Native Americans, see Omer C. Stewart, *Peyote Religion: A History* (Norman: University of Oklahoma Press, 1987).

37. John Fire/Lame Deer and Richard Erdoes, *Lame Deer: Seeker of Visions* (New York: Simon and Schuster, 1972), p. 220.

38. Mbiti, *Introduction to African Religion*, p. 165.

39. Ibid., p. 166.

40. These are the commonly used names; nomenclature is in a process of change for some Northwest tribes.

41. Pat Kramer, *Totem Poles* (Vancouver: Altitude, 1995), pp. 48–49.

42. Richard W. Hill, Sr., "The Symbolism of Feathers," in *Creation's Journey* (Washington, DC: Smithsonian Institution Press, 1994), p. 88.

Chapter 3

1. Arthur Basham, *The Wonder That Was India* (New York: Grove, 1959), p. 16. Chapter 2 of Basham's book contains a detailed description of the Harappa culture.

2. Ibid., p. 23.

3. Also spelled *Rig Veda*. For representative prayers, see William T. deBary, ed., *Sources of Indian Tradition*, vol. 1 (New York: Columbia University Press, 1958), pp. 7–16.

4. Rig Veda 10:129, quoted in Basham, *The Wonder That Was India*, p. 16.

5. The same tendency toward philosophy existed in Greece at the time and a few centuries later in the Roman Empire.

6. The philosopher Shankara offered another interpretation—"to wear away completely."

7. These six notions are not fixed concepts in the Upanishads. They are more like centers around which speculation revolves, and there may be differences in how they are described, even within the same Upanishad. The notion of Brahman, for example, sometimes varies from that of a divine reality quite beyond the world to that of a spiritual reality that exists within the world.

8. Chandogya Upanishad 6:13, in *The Upanishads*, trans. Juan Mascaró (New York: Penguin, 1979), p. 118.

9. Shvetasvatara Upanishad, end of part 3, *The Upanishads*, pp. 90–91; emphasis added.

10. Ibid., part 4, p. 91.

11. Ibid.

12. See, for example, ibid., p. 92.

13. Ibid.

14. Brihadaranyaka Upanishad 2:4, *The Upanishads*, p. 132.

15. *The Song of God: Bhagavad-Gita*, trans. Swami Prabhavananda and Christopher Isherwood (New York: Mentor, 1972), chap. 5, p. 57.

16. Ibid., chap. 1, p. 34.

17. Ibid., chap. 18, p. 127.

18. Ibid., chap. 2, p. 38.

19. Rig Veda 10:90, as quoted in deBary, *Sources of Indian Tradition*, vol. 1, p. 14.

20. See Chapter 2 of the Bhagavad Gita.

21. Sometimes the term *caste* is reserved for what I call here subcastes—the hundreds of occupation-based social divisions (*jati*).

22. I follow the common practice of using the word *brahmin* (priest)—rather than the Sanskrit term *brahman*—to avoid confusion with the term *Brahman* (spiritual essence of the world) with a capital *B*.

23. See, for example, the description of Gandhi's "fast unto death" for untouchables in Louis Fischer, *Gandhi* (New York: New American Library, 1954), pp. 116–19.

24. The six orthodox schools of Hindu philosophy all developed as systems of personal liberation but disagreed about the views and methods that would bring liberation. The six schools are Nyaya, Vaisheshika, Sankhya, Yoga, Mimamsa, and Vedanta. (The terms Yoga and Vedanta, when used to denote schools of philosophy, have a precise and different meaning than when the main terms are used more generally.) Nyaya ("analysis") valued the insight that comes from clarity, reason, and logic. Vaisheshika ("individual characteristics") taught what it considered to be the correct way of understanding reality—seeing reality as essentially being made up of atoms. Sankhya ("count") was originally an atheistic philosophy that considered the universe to be made of two essential principles—soul and matter. Yoga ("union," "spiritual discipline") emphasized meditation and physical disciplines. Mimamsa ("investigation") defended the authority of the Vedas as a guide to salvation. Vedanta developed several subschools but tended to see a unifying principle—Brahman—at work behind the changing phenomena of everyday life; the individual can find salvation by attaining union with this principle.

25. Shankara's conception of Brahman is debated. For him, Brahman may have been a positive spiritual reality, or it may have been closer to the notion of emptiness found in Buddhism.

26. Shankara (attrib.), *Shankara's Crest-Jewel of Discrimination* (New York: Mentor, 1970), p. 72.

27. *The Song of God: Bhagavad-Gita*, chap. 2, p. 40.

28. Ibid., chap. 18, p. 128.

29. Although these sutras are attributed to an ancient grammarian named Patanjali, who lived before the common era, they may have been written later, from about 200 C.E.

30. Basham, *The Wonder That Was India*, p. 326.

31. Heinrich Zimmer, *Myths and Symbols in Indian Art and Civilization* (Princeton: Princeton University Press, 1972), p. 153.

32. Basavaraja, quoted in *Sources of Indian Tradition*, vol. 1, p. 352. Basavaraja was a twelfth-century Indian government official who founded a religious order devoted to Shiva.

33. *The Gospel of Ramakrishna*, quoted in deBary, *Sources of Indian Tradition*, vol. 2, p. 86.

34. *The Upanishads*, trans. Swami Prabhavananda and Frederick Manchester (New York: Mentor, 1970), pp. 70–71.

35. The term *darshan* also extends to viewing images of deities in order to experience the divine presence that they mediate.

36. See Ainslie T. Embree, ed., *The Hindu Tradition* (New York: Vintage, 1972), p. 279.

37. Fischer, *Gandhi*, p. 11.

38. Quoted in Fischer, *Gandhi*, p. 18.

39. Gandhi compromised his position on nonviolence somewhat during World War I, when he urged Indians to join the war effort on the side of the British. Later, he said that this position had been a mistake.

Chapter 4

1. Arthur Basham put it nicely: "Much doubt now exists as to the real doctrines of the historical Buddha, as distinct from those of Buddhism." *The Wonder That Was India* (New York: Grove, 1959), p. 256.

2. The tree may have been a form of banyan, which today is called the *Ficus religiosa* ("religious fig") because of its supposed connection with the Buddha.

3. As quoted in William T. deBary, ed., *Sources of Indian Tradition* (New York: Columbia University Press, 1958), vol. 1, p. 110.

4. Some scholars think that the Reclining Buddha images may also depict the Buddha sleeping, sometimes with his cousin Ananda looking on protectively.

5. Sometimes the term *Sangha* is used more widely to include devout laypersons.

6. See David Kalupahana, *Buddhist Philosophy: A Historical Analysis* (Honolulu: University Press of Hawaii, 1976), pp. 38–41.

7. *Buddhist Suttas,* trans. T. W. Rhys Davids (New York: Dover, 1969), p. 148.

8. *The Dhammapada: The Sayings of the Buddha,* trans. Thomas Byrom (New York: Vintage, 1976), chap. 15, p. 76.

9. From the *Sammanaphala Suttanta,* in E. A. Burtt, *The Teachings of the Compassionate Buddha* (New York: New American Library, 1955), p. 104.

10. Sometimes the order is reversed, and the SUTRA is designated as the first basket, with the Vinaya listed second.

11. The commonly accepted view about the introduction of form into Buddhist imagery has been questioned. See Stanley Abe, "Inside the Wonder House: Buddhist Art and the West, " in *Curators of the Buddha: The Study of Buddhism under Colonialism,* ed. Donald S. Lopez, Jr. (Chicago: University of Chicago Press, 1995), pp. 63–106.

12. Hirakawa Akira, *A History of Indian Buddhism* (Honolulu: University of Hawaii Press, 1990), p. 258.

13. For details about the origins of Mahayana, see John Koller, *The Indian Way* (New York: Macmillan, 1983), p. 163.

14. For information about Buddhist schools of philosophy, see John Koller, "The Nature of Reality, " in *Oriental Philosophies* (New York: Scribner's, 1970), pp. 146–79.

15. Kenneth Ch'en, *Buddhism in China* (Princeton, NJ: Princeton University Press, 1972), p. 385.

16. For more information see Richard Robinson and Willard Johnson, *The Buddhist Religion,* 4th ed. (Belmont, CA: Wadsworth, 1997), pp. 181ff.

17. Robert Buswell, *Tracing Back the Radiance: Chinul's Korean Way of Zen* (Honolulu: University of Hawaii Press, 1991), p. 5. See the introduction for a description of Korea's early Buddhist contacts with China and central Asia.

18. For a traveler's description of the monastery complex in the seventeenth century, see Li Chi, *The Travel Diaries of Hsü Hsia-k'o* (Hong Kong: The Chinese University of Hong Kong, 1974), pp. 29–42.

19. The meditation guidebook *Shikantaza: An Introduction to Zazen* (Kyoto: Kyoto Zen Center, 1990) contains instructions for zazen and a good selection of passages by Zen masters on the practice and effects of zazen.

20. See the story of Rinzai, who received a beating from his master Obaku as a koan-like response to his simple-minded questioning, in D. T. Suzuki, *Studies in Zen* (New York: Delta, 1955), pp. 68–70. Suzuki gives many examples of koan, with commentary. The actual use of the koan in Japanese monasteries over the last three centuries has become more formalized. Instead of working through a koan, a person in training (who hopes to take over his father's temple) now often refers to books for the appropriate answers.

21. For connections between Christianity and the tea ceremony see Heinrich Dumoulin, *A History of Zen Buddhism* (Boston: Beacon, 1963), pp. 214–24.

Chapter 5

1. Mahapurana 4:16; cited in William T. deBary, ed., *Sources of Indian Tradition*, vol. 1. (New York: Columbia University Press, 1958), p. 76.

2. Acaranga Sutra 1.6, 5, cited in deBary, *Sources of Indian Tradition*, vol. 1, p. 65.

3. See John Koller, *The Indian Way* (New York: Macmillan, 1982), pp. 114–15.

4. Selection from the Mul Mantra, cited in M. A. Macauliffe, *The Sikh Religion* (Oxford: Oxford University Press, 1901), vol. 1, p. 195.

5. From Asa Ki Var, Mahala I. Cited in Macauliffe, *The Sikh Religion,* vol. 1, p. 221.

Chapter 6

1. *Tao Te Ching,* trans. Gia-fu Feng and Jane English (New York: Random House, 1972), chap. 1. This translation is used unless stated otherwise.

2. *Lao Tzu: Tao Te Ching,* trans. Robert Henricks (New York: Ballantine, 1989), p. 72.

3. *Tao Te Ching,* chap. 3.

4. *The Wisdom of Laotse,* trans. Lin Yutang (New York: Modern Library, 1948), p. 76.

5. *Chuang Tzu: Basic Writings,* trans. Burton Watson (New York: Columbia University Press, 1964), p. 113 (sec. 18).

6. Ibid.

7. Ibid., p. 36 (sec. 2).

8. Cited in *The Way and Its Power,* trans. Arthur Waley (New York: Grove, 1958), p. 181.

9. Wing-Tsit Chan, "Man and Nature in the Chinese Garden" in Henry Inn and Shao Chang Lee, eds., *Chinese Houses and Gardens* (Honolulu: Fong Inn's Limited, 1940), pp. 35–36.

10. Ibid., p. 33.

11. *The Doctrine of the Mean* 20:18; in *Confucius: Confucian Analects, The Great Learning, and The Doctrine of the Mean,* trans. James Legge (New York: Dover, 1971), p. 413. (Legge's translation of the Four Books—the major Confucian books, which include the sayings of Confucius and Mencius—is used unless otherwise noted.) In the original translation, the word *right* is italicized and the word *way* is not. I have changed this to make my point clearer.

12. Ibid., 12:4.

13. *Analects* 5:25, 4.

14. Ibid., 2:4, 1–6.

15. R. D. Baird and Alfred Bloom, *Indian and Far Eastern Religious Traditions* (New York: Harper & Row, 1972), p. 169.

16. George Kates, *The Years that Were Fat* (Cambridge, MA: MIT Press, 1976), pp. 28–29.

17. See *The Doctrine of the Mean* 22:8 for a different order.

18. *Analects* 12:1, 1.

19. See *Analects* 12:1, 2 and *The Doctrine of the Mean* 13:3.

20. *The Doctrine of the Mean* 20:18; adapted.

21. *Analects* 4:16; trans. Arthur Waley (New York: Vintage, c. 1938), p. 105.

22. Ibid. 4:24.

23. *The Great Learning,* "Text of Confucius" verse 6.

24. *The Doctrine of the Mean* 1:1–2; adapted.

25. Ibid. 1:5.

26. *Mencius* 4:2, 12, trans. James Legge (New York: Dover, 1970); adapted.

27. See Chapters 18–20 of the *Tao Te Ching.*

28. See Chapter 80 of the *Tao Te Ching.*

29. *Mencius* 4:1, 9.2.

30. Ibid., 6:1.6.7.

31. Given in an introductory chapter of ibid., p. 81.

32. Cited in William T. deBary, ed., *Sources of Chinese Tradition* (New York: Columbia University Press, 1960), vol. 1, pp. 45–46.

33. Ibid., vol. 1, p. 436.

34. Since this visit, the Confucian Temple has been renovated.

Chapter 7

1. This myth begins the Kojiki ("chronicle of ancient events"); see *Translation of Ko-ji-ki,* trans. Basil Hall Chamberlain, 2d ed. (Kobe: J. L. Thompson, 1932), pp. 17–23. The etymology of *kami* is debated.

2. Ibid., pp. 21–22. The same story, with many variants, appears at the beginning of another ancient work, the Nihongi.

3. Ibid., pp. 50–51.

4. Also called Shrine Shinto. For details, see H. Byron Earhart, *Religions of Japan* (New York: Harper & Row, 1984), pp. 43–45 and 93–100.

5. Sometimes a distinction is made between the spirits of nature and the spirits of the deceased. It is debated whether a belief in one type of spirit was the origin of a belief in the other. See, for example, Carmen Blacker, *The Catalpa Bow* (London: Allen & Unwin, 1975), pp. 45–46.

6. For a translation, see *Nihongi,* trans. W. G. Aston (London: Allen & Unwin, 1956).

7. Such imagery was apparently much more common before Western influence—and its sense of decorum—entered Japan in the nineteenth century.

8. The sense that death is polluting and dangerous explains the regular rebuilding of some Shinto shrines and the destruction of the clothing and personal effects of a deceased person.

9. The torii is used as a gateway, but it can be placed anywhere to indicate the presence of kami.

10. See H. Byron Earhart, *Japanese Religion: Unity and Diversity,* 2d ed. (Encino, CA: Dickenson, 1974), p. 21.

11. Later, on a return journey to the temple, I discovered a Shinto shrine on a path just above the temple—another sign of the intermingling of Shinto and Buddhism. Dedicated to fertility and childbirth, Jishu Jinja is a place for worship of the protective kami that guards the temple.

12. Keiichi Nakayama, *Tenrikyo Kyoten Kowa* (Tenri: Tenrikyo, 1951), p. 3; cited in Harry Thomsen, *The New Religions of Japan* (Rutland, VT: Tuttle, 1963), p. 34.

13. A translation of Miki's poetic work, *Mikagura Uta*, can be found in Thomsen, *The New Religions of Japan*, pp. 41–48.

Chapter 8

1. This theory is called the Documentary Hypothesis. For details, see Stephen Harris, *Understanding the Bible*, 3d ed. (London: Mayfield, 1992), pp. 53–59.

2. The Greek translation of the Hebrew Bible is commonly called the Septuagint. For details about the Septuagint translation, see Henry Jackson Flanders, Robert Wilson Crapps, and David Anthony Smith, *People of the Covenant*, 4th ed. (New York: Oxford University Press, 1996), p. 21.

3. Translation from *Tanakh—The Holy Scriptures* (Philadelphia: The Jewish Publication Society, 1985).

4. Emphasis added.

5. The New Oxford Annotated Bible (New York: Oxford University Press, 1991).

6. The translation by the Jewish Publication Society (1985) simply gives the Hebrew phrase "Ehyeh-Asher-Ehyeh"; it adds a footnote, saying that the exact meaning of the Hebrew is uncertain but that a common translation is "I am who I am" (p. 88).

7. The words *Yahweh* and *Adonai* (also spelled *Adonay*) were ultimately blended to create the name *Jehovah*, used in English Bibles.

8. It is possible that the Book of Deuteronomy constitutes the first volume of a history about the Hebrews' entry into Canaan, which is continued in the Books of Joshua and Judges.

9. Exodus 20:2–17, from *Tanakh—the Holy Scriptures.*

10. The most famous is at Dura-Europos, in southern Syria.

11. Although today we might recoil at the thought of animal sacrifice, we must realize that it was common throughout the world of the time, even in India and China. It fulfilled several functions. Worshipers often thought the ritual of sharing a sacred meal would unite them with their deity. Punishment that might have fallen on human beings was thought to

be transferred to the sacrificial animal. It was also a sign that the deity was in charge of all life.

12. The New Oxford Annotated Bible.

13. There are two long passages in Aramaic: Daniel 2:4–7:28 and Ezra 4:8–6:18. Short Aramaic passages also appear in Genesis (31:47) and Jeremiah (10:11).

14. Many other religious books were popular but were not finally accepted as canonical by Jews in Israel. A few additional books, however, were accepted as canonical by Jews living in Egypt, such as Sirach, the Wisdom of Solomon, and Maccabees. (Later, they were also accepted as canonical by Catholic and Eastern Orthodox Christians.)

15. The name *Sadducee* may derive from the name *Zadok* (or *Sadoc*), a priest at the time of King David.

16. The name *Pharisee* may derive from a Hebrew word meaning "separate"—referring to a ritual purity associated with the careful practice of religious laws.

17. It is possible that the dualistic worldview of the Essenes was influenced by the Persian religion of Zoroastrianism and that their semimonastic lifestyle was influenced by monastic ideals that had come from India to Egypt.

18. Union Prayerbook (New York, 1959), part 1, pp. 166–67.

19. A passage from the *Zohar*, quoted in *The Wisdom of the Kabbalah*, ed. Dagobert Runes (New York: Citadel, 1967), p. 172.

20. Quoted in Gershom Scholem, *On the Kabbalah and Its Symbolism* (New York: Schocken, 1969), p. 103.

21. The beginning of the movie *Yentl* illustrates the value put on the mystical interpretation of the Book of Genesis.

22. Martin Buber, the great Jewish writer, collected and published two volumes of Hasidic sayings. Many tales of the Baal Shem Tov appear in the first volume, *Tales of the Hasidim: Early Masters* (orig. pub. 1947; New York: Schocken, 1973).

23. Louis Newman, *Hasidic Anthology* (New York: Schocken, 1975), p. 148.

24. Ibid., p. 149.

25. Bella Chagall, *Burning Lights* (New York: Schocken, 1972). This book contains thirty-six drawings by Marc Chagall.

26. Anne Frank, *Diary of a Young Girl* (New York: Pocket Books, 1959), p. 222.

27. Ibid., pp. 192–93.

28. Ibid., p. 233.

29. The origin of the Sabbath is uncertain. It may have been inspired by Babylonian culture, or perhaps

it was unique to the Hebrews. It is logical, however, to divide a lunar month into four seven-day periods.
30. The literal truth of this story is doubtful. We might note that the names of Esther and Mordecai are suspiciously close to the names of the Babylonian divinities Ishtar and Marduk. As such, the festival may derive from a Babylonian fertility festival.
31. The fact that Passover occurs in the first month of the Jewish lunar calendar may be an indication that it was once the Jewish New Year.
32. It is also possible that pigs and shellfish were considered "imperfect" animals. Perfect land animals (such as sheep and goats) chewed a cud and had divided hooves; perfect sea animals had scales. All others were considered "less perfect."
33. Leo Trepp, *Judaism: Development and Life* (Belmont, CA: Dickenson Publishing, 1966), p. 75.
34. Ibid.
35. From *I and Thou*, quoted in *The Writings of Martin Buber*, ed. Will Herberg (Cleveland: Meridian/World, 1961), p. 46.

Chapter 9

1. Jerusalem Bible (Garden City, NY: Doubleday, 1966).
2. American Bible Society translation, in *Good News Bible* (Nashville: Nelson, 1986).
3. Ibid.
4. Jerusalem Bible translation.
5. Ibid.
6. See James Charlesworth, *Jesus and the Dead Sea Scrolls* (New York: Doubleday, 1992).
7. King James Version (Cambridge: Cambridge University Press, n.d.).
8. Acts 9:4, Revised Standard Version (RSV) (New York: New American Library, 1974).
9. RSV translation.
10. Jerusalem Bible translation.
11. RSV translation.
12. For more information on Christian Gnosticism, see Elaine Pagels's *The Gnostic Gospels* (New York: Random House, 1979) and *Adam, Eve, and the Serpent* (New York: Vintage, 1989).
13. Jerusalem Bible translation.
14. Earlier lists, such as the Muratorian Canon, differ from the present-day canonical list of New Testament books. The list, as we now have it, is mentioned in the *Festal Letter* of Athanasius of Alexandria, circulated in 367 C.E., and is the same list of books translated by Jerome into Latin. For further details, see

Dennis Duling and Norman Perrin, *The New Testament* 3d ed. (New York: Harcourt Brace, 1994), p. 134.
15. Jerusalem Bible translation.
16. *The Confessions of St. Augustine*, trans. Rex Warner (New York: New American Library, 1963), pp. 182–83.
17. Jerusalem Bible translation.
18. See David Knowles, *Christian Monasticism* (New York: McGraw-Hill, 1972), which emphasizes the development of Benedictine monasticism.
19. *St. Benedict's Rule for Monasteries* (Collegeville, MN: Liturgical Press, 1948), chap. 1, pp. 2–3.
20. See Christopher Brooke, *Monasteries of the World* (New York: Crescent, 1982), for excellent maps, diagrams, and photographs.
21. Nikos Kazantzakis, author of *Zorba the Greek* and *Saint Francis*, lived for a time on Mount Athos and considered becoming a monk.
22. *The Disciplinary Decrees of the General Councils*, trans. H. J. Schroeder (St. Louis: B. Herder, 1937), p. 19; quoted in Colman Barry, ed., *Readings in Church History*, vol. 1 (Westminster, MD: Newman Press, 1960), p. 85.
23. Nicholas Gage, *Eleni* (New York: Ballantine Books, 1983), pp. 122–23.
24. For the mysticism of Gregory of Nyssa, see *From Glory to Glory: Texts from Gregory of Nyssa's Mystical Writings* (New York: Scribners, 1961), particularly the introduction by Jean Daniélou. For Augustine's mysticism, see *The Essential Augustine* (New York: Mentor, 1964), pp. 127 and 148.
25. Origen, prologue to the "Commentary on the Song of Songs," in *Origen*, trans. Rowan Greer (New York: Paulist Press, 1979), p. 217.
26. From Sermon 6, in *Meister Eckhart*, trans. Raymond Blakney (New York: Harper, 1941), p. 131.
27. Julian of Norwich, *Revelations of Divine Love*, trans. Clifton Wolters (New York: Penguin, 1982), Chap. 59, p. 167.
28. Pamphlet, *Prayer of Saint Francis*, (Columbus, OH: Christopher House, 1996), p. 4, adapted.
29. See Erik Erikson, *Young Man Luther: A Study in Psychoanalysis and History* (New York: Norton, 1962).
30. King James Version.
31. A similar development occurred in the Buddhist Pure Land movement. In Japan, Shinran concluded that only trust in Amida Buddha's grace was enough for the devotee.
32. A. J. Raboteau, "African-American Religions," in *World Religions* (NY: Simon and Schuster Macmillan, 1998), p. 18.

33. Bennetta Jules–Rosette, "African Religions," ibid., pp. 7–10.

34. The term *Mass* comes from the dismissal at the conclusion of this ceremony, when the priest said in Latin, *Ite missa est* ("Go, it is the dismissal").

35. Albert Schweitzer's classic study *J. S. Bach* (orig. pub. 1905 Neptune, NJ: Paganiniana, 1980) emphasizes the religious character of all of Bach's work.

36. Thomas Keating, interview with Kate Olson, in *Trinity News*, vol. 42 (1995), 4, pp. 8–11, cited at www.thecentering.org/therapy.html.

37. Ibid.

Chapter 10

1. Also spelled *Mohammed*, although this spelling is now considered less accurate than *Muhammad*. We might also note that there is some disagreement about the details of Muhammad's life, particularly those regarding his early years.

2. John Esposito, *Islam: The Straight Path*, 3d ed. (New York: Oxford University Press, 1998), p. 3.

3. Also spelled *Kaaba*, *Ka'bah*, and *Kaba*.

4. For further details see Thomas Lippman, *Understanding Islam* (New York: New American Library, 1982), pp. 34–38.

5. Also commonly spelled *Khadija*.

6. It is possible that Khadijah was younger than this, given the fact that she gave birth to at least six children.

7. 96:1–19 passim; from *The Koran*, trans. N. J. Dawood (London: Penguin, 1993), p. 429. This translation is used unless otherwise noted.

8. Lippman, *Understanding Islam*, p. 44. Guides in Jerusalem sometimes point to marks in stone, which they say are footprints left by Muhammad. The account of Muhammad's journey may have influenced Dante's vision of paradise in the *Divine Comedy*.

9. 49:10.

10. In Islamic belief, punishment in hell is not necessarily eternal for all.

11. 2:163; from *Holy Qur'an*, trans. M. H. Shakir (Milton Keynes, England: Mihrab Publishers, 1986).

12. In Islam, a "messenger" is a prophet with a special call from God.

13. Some Shiite Muslims combine these into three periods of prayer.

14. Another translation is, "Allah is greater (than anything else)."

15. 2:144.

16. Although only Muslims may make the pilgrimage to Mecca, many films document the practice. See, for example, the classic film *Mecca: The Forbidden City*, by Iranfilms.

17. 2:158 (Shakir translation).

18. Muslims were originally permitted to drink wine, but later revelations to Muhammad prohibited it. There is, however, some variation in the keeping of this regulation. Countries that have experienced strong European influence (such as several in northern Africa—Morocco, Algeria, Tunisia) often produce wine, and countries that depend heavily on tourism usually allow the serving of alcohol in tourist hotels.

19. Female circumcision is sometimes said to be based on a hadith (a remembrance of Muhammad's early followers); see Annemarie Schimmel, *Islam: An Introduction* (Albany: State University of New York Press, 1992), p. 55.

20. 4:34.

21. An exception is made in some cases, such as the tombs of rulers and publicly recognized holy persons.

22. Although the early versions did not contain vowels or diacritical marks, later versions do; consequently, some differences exist between versions.

23. 1:1–5.

24. Esposito, *Islam: The Straight Path*, p. 6.

25. There is some disagreement over this matter among Sunni and Shiite Muslims.

26. Also called the Battle of Poitiers.

27. *The Economist*, May 31, 2003, p. 37.

28. 50:16. See also John Williams, ed., *Islam* (New York: Washington Square, 1963), pp. 122–58.

29. 3:29 (Shakir translation). See A. J. Arberry, *Sufism* (New York: Harper, 1970), pp. 17–22.

30. 2:115.

31. Arberry, *Sufism*, p. 28.

32. Ibid., p. 228.

33. Afkham Darbandi and Dick Davis, introduction to *The Conference of the Birds*, by Farid Ud-Din Attar (Hammondsworth, England: Penguin, 1984), p. 10.

34. Quoted in F. C. Happold, *Mysticism* (Baltimore: Penguin, 1963), p. 229.

35. Esposito, *Islam: The Straight Path*, pp. 105–106.

36. For representative samples of the writings of theologians, see the chapter "Kalam" in Williams, *Islam*, pp. 159–96.

37. Williams, *Islam*, pp. 138–41. Williams claims that al-Arabi influenced the Spanish mystics and poets John of the Cross and Ramón Lull and possibly Benedict de Spinoza, a Dutch philosopher.

38. Islamic influence on Christian architecture is almost certainly demonstrated by the use of these alternating lines of color, such as in the cathedrals of Siena, Pisa, and Florence.

39. See 2:25, 3:136, and 10:9.

40. See 2:25.

41. http://news.bbc.co.uk/2/hi/middle_east/1571144.stm.

42. Jon Basil Utley, http://www.mises.org/fullstory.asp?control=1313 I am grateful to this article for several points in this paragraph.

43. Lawrence Mamiya, "Malcolm X" in *World Religions* (New York: Simon and Schuster Macmillan, 1998), p. 19.

Chapter 11

1. See Leo Martello, *Witchcraft: The Old Religion* (New York: Citadel Press, 1991), chap. 5.

2. For further information, see Philip Shallcrass, "Druidry Today," in *Paganism Today* (London: Thorsons/HarperCollins, 1995), pp. 65–80.

3. See Raúl Canizares, *Cuban Santería* (Rochester, VT: Destiny Books), pp. 38–48.

4. For greater detail, see Migene González-Wippler, *Santería: The Religion* (St. Paul, MN: Llewellyn Publications, 1999), chap. 5.

5. *Theosophy* (Hudson, NY: Anthroposophic Press, 1989), p. 164.

6. "Rudolf Steiner," in *The Encyclopedia of Philosophy,* vol. 8 (New York: Macmillan, 1967), pp. 13–14.

7. *The Church of Scientology: An Introduction to Church Services* (n.p.: L. Ron Hubbard Library, 1999), p. 32.

8. King James Version.

9. Quoted in Leonard Barrett, Sr., *The Rastafarians* (Boston: Beacon, 1997), p. 123.

10. *The Baha'is* (Oakham, UK: Baha'i Publishing Trust of the United Kingdom, 1994), p. 54.

11. For good sample illustrations and interpretations, see Leo Martello, *Reading the Tarot* (New York: Avery Publishing, 1990).

Chapter 12

1. Robert Ellwood, *The History and Future of Faith* (New York: Crossroad, 1988), p. 137.

2. Ibid., p. 141.

3. "Which Humanism for the Third Millennium?" *Aizen* 16 (July–August 1997): 3.

4. *Dhammapada,* ch. 10. *Dhammapada,* tr. Thomas Byrom (New York: Vintage, 1976), p. 49. The translation presents the material divided into stanzas.

5. *Tao Te Ching,* Ch. 30, tr. Feng and English (New York: Vintage, 1972).

6. Ibid., Ch. 31.

7. All biblical quotations here are taken from the New English Bible.

8. Dawood translation is used for the passages from the Qur'an. *The Koran* (London: Penguin, 1993).

9. Government in the United States, however, is not fully secular. We might note, for example, the use of prayer and chaplains in legislative houses, the mention of God in the Declaration of Independence, the use of the word *God* in court and on currency, and tax benefits given to churches and church property. See Ronald Thiemann, *Religion in Public Life* (Washington: Georgetown University Press, 1996), in which the author argues against the complete separation of church and state.

10. *Honolulu Advertiser,* 26 July 1997, sec. B, p. 3, adapted.

11. For a good discussion of secularism in the modern world and its relation to religion, see Ellwood, *The History and Future of Faith,* chap. 5, pp. 96–117. Ellwood sees religions surviving in the future within a secular milieu but existing rather separately from it.

12. "Speech of the Very Rev. James Parks Morton at the Esperanto Conference, 1996, July 22, Prague," *Aizen* 16 (July–August 1997): 6.

13. See Maurice Tuchman, ed., *The Spiritual in Art: Abstract Painting 1890–1985* (New York: Abbeville Press, 1986) for many examples.

14. Philippe Gross and S. I. Shapiro, "Characteristics of the Taoist Sage in the *Chuang-tzu* and the Creative Photographer," *Journal of Transpersonal Psychology* 28:2 (1996), p. 181.

15. *Modern Photography,* October, 1988, p. 94; quoted in ibid., p. 177.

Note: Boxes on the Pueblo and Dogon (in chapter 2) have drawn on many sources, among which I especially recommend: Alph Secakuku, *Following the Sun and Moon: Hopi Kachina Tradition* (Flagstaff: Northland, 1995); Frank Waters, *Book of the Hopi* (New York: Penguin, 1977); Ronald McCoy, *Summoning the Gods* (Flagstaff: Museum of Northern Arizona, 1992); Tom Bahti, *Southwestern Indian Ceremonials* (Las Vegas, NV: KC Publications, 1992); John Collier and Ira Moskowitz, *Rites and Ceremonies of the Indians of the Southwest,* rev. ed. (New York: Barnes & Noble, 1993); Frank Willet, *African Art* (London: Thames and Hudson, 1993); www.dogon-lobi.ch; whc.unesco.org/exhibits/afr_rev/africa-o.htm; www.uiowa.edu/~africart/toc/people/Dogon.html; www.crystalinks.com/dogon.html; wpni01.auroraquanta.com/pv/dogon.

Credits

Index